PHILANTHROPY

from Aristotle to Zuckerberg

PAUL VALLELY

BLOOMSBURY CONTINUUM
LONDON • OXFORD • NEW YORK • NEW DELHI • SYDNEY

BLOOMSBURY CONTINUUM
Bloomsbury Publishing Plc
50 Bedford Square, London, WC1B 3DP, UK

BLOOMSBURY, BLOOMSBURY CONTINUUM and the Diana logo are trademarks
of Bloomsbury Publishing Plc

First published in Great Britain 2020
Copyright © Paul Vallely, 2020

Published with the kind support of the Pears Foundation

Paul Vallely has asserted his right under the Copyright, Designs and Patents Act, 1988,
to be identified as Author of this work

The source notes for this book can be found at www.philanthropyatoz.com

A catalogue record for this book is available from the British Library

Library of Congress Cataloguing-in-Publication data has been applied for

ISBN: HB: 978-1-4729-2012-6; eBook: 978-1-4729-2013-3; ePDF: 978-1-4729-2014-0

2 4 6 8 10 9 7 5 3 1

Typeset by Deanta Global Publishing Services, Chennai, India
Printed and bound in Great Britain by CPI Group (UK) Ltd, Croydon CR0 4YY

FSC
www.fsc.org

MIX
Paper from
responsible sources
FSC® C020471

To find out more about our authors and books visit www.bloomsbury.com
and sign up for our newsletters

For Thomas

sapere aude

Praise for this book

'Timely and fascinating'

Peter Hennessy, Attlee Professor of Contemporary British History, Queen Mary University of London

'This is the definitive book on philanthropy – its history, contradictions and future. Exploring its Jewish, Christian and classical roots, showing how it was transformed by the Black Death, examining the changing role of the state and the dangers of philanthrocapitalism, among other key issues, *Philanthropy – from Aristotle to Zuckerberg* is a deep and probing study of a highly complex practice that is an increasingly powerful force in our world.'

John Gray, Emeritus Professor of European Thought, LSE

'Deeply researched and wonderfully written, this book is much more than a sweeping, erudite history. It is a fascinating exploration of why people give – and a powerful call for philanthropy to do a better job of melding empathy with effectiveness.'

David Callahan, Editor of *Inside Philanthropy* and author of *The Givers: Wealth, Power and Philanthropy in a New Gilded Age*

'A magisterial treatment of the history of Western philanthropy. Paul Vallely has produced the best single volume on the ideas that have shaped philanthropy, the institutional arrangements that have structured it, and the outsized personalities that have marked it. Vallely's book immerses you in the history of philanthropy with an eye toward informing you about its present-day practices, potential, and problems. Stuffed with astonishing stories and illuminating interviews, this book will be a lasting resource for scholars, philanthropic and NGO leaders, and individual donors.'

Rob Reich, Professor of Political Science, Stanford University and author of *Just Giving: Why Philanthropy is Failing Democracy and How It Can Do Better*

'Paul Vallely has done all those involved in philanthropy a service with this comprehensive and panoramic overview of the field.'

Beth Breeze, Director of the Centre for Philanthropy, University of Kent

'There are good books and there are important books. Good books lay out the lie of the land. Important books change it. This book does both. Beautifully written, passionately argued and crammed full of fascinating detail, Paul Vallely insists that giving needs to restore its spiritual dimension whereby the giver respects the one who receives – something we have lost sight of with modern philanthro-capitalism's drive for greater efficiency.'

Giles Fraser, priest and philosopher

Contents

Introduction

Nobody is ever impoverished through the giving of charity.
MAIMONIDES

One autumnal morning in 1968 an obscure middle-aged American walked off the street into the Galton Laboratory, the centre of the pioneering work on human genetics at University College London. The stranger had no credentials, held no academic position and had no appointment. He demanded to see the professor of bio-statistics. When the head of the laboratory appeared, the stranger simply declared in a rather condescending high-pitched voice: 'My name is George Price. Here's my equation. What do you have to say about this?' Ninety minutes later he left, having been given an honorary fellowship and the keys to his own office. It appeared that the unknown American had discovered the scientific explanation for altruism.

George Price was a maverick. Born in New York in 1922 and brilliant at school, he had gone on to Harvard and then the University of Chicago to study chemistry. There during the 1940s he had been recruited to a team of scientists racing to develop the atomic bomb – the so-called Manhattan Project. But Price could not settle. He moved from job to job, working in cancer research and then in the newly emerging computer industry in the 1960s. At IBM he claimed he had come up with the concept of computer-aided design before leaving disgruntled, saying his idea had been stolen by his bosses. By his mid-forties he had become disillusioned at his failure to be accorded sufficient appreciation in every field he entered. So great was his thirst for recognition that at one point he was communicating with four separate Nobel laureates in four separate fields of research – trying to convince each of them he had achieved some major breakthrough that would make his name. 'There was something in George that was really frantically searching for greatness,' says Price's biographer, Oren Harman.[1] In every field Price felt he was being denied the acclaim his brilliance warranted. He decided to leave New York for London in November 1967.

But George Price did not simply leave behind an unfulfilled career. He also left his wife, Julia, whom he had married in 1947, and two young daughters. Julia was a scientist too – they had met on the Manhattan Project – but she was also a devout Roman Catholic. Her husband's scathing views on religion had put too much of a strain on the marriage and eight years later they had divorced. Now in London and living off the insurance payment from a botched thyroid operation, Price spent a year reading eclectically and thinking in the city's libraries. Perhaps unsurprisingly, one of the topics which came to preoccupy the scientist who had abandoned his wife and children was the 'problem' of explaining why humans lived in families. What was fatherhood for, scientifically speaking, he wondered. His musings led him on to the wider question of how altruism had evolved.

Altruism had been a problem to scientists since the writings of Darwin. The great stumbling block to his theory of evolution, Darwin reflected, was the existence of ants and bees. How could such co-operative insects exist in a world where competition drove natural selection and only the fittest survive? Worker ants are not only co-operative, they are also sterile, and so have zero fitness in terms of the survival of the fittest. They ought to be extinct, yet there they are in every generation sacrificing their own reproductive ambitions to serve the fertile queen and her drones. Natural selection ought to be intrinsically stacked against altruistic individuals surviving long enough to pass on their altruism. It was theoretically impossible that altruism could have evolved. And yet it had.

More than that, altruism is actually common throughout the animal world, from the lowest to the highest orders. In cellular slime moulds, when individual amoebae run out of food, some cells sacrifice themselves and form a multicellular body which produces fruit to ensure the survival of the others. Vampire bats regurgitate blood to give to other bats who failed to feed that night. And when predators approach a vervet monkey it will give out an alarm call to warn fellow monkeys of the approaching danger, even though doing so draws attention to itself, increasing the first monkey's chance of being attacked. All this threatened to undermine Darwin's theory of evolution.

The problem was solved by a young biologist who signed his research paper 'W. D. Hamilton'. In 1964 he suggested that altruism could have evolved within family groups. An individual altruist might be at a disadvantage, but collectively individuals who shared the genes associated with altruism could influence one another's behaviour in a way which gave their group an advantage over the selfish individuals around them. Bill Hamilton's idea of kin selection also explained why a parent would sacrifice their own life in defence of their offspring. The evolution of altruism was no longer paradoxical. Individual altruism was, in fact, genetically selfish, an idea which Richard Dawkins later popularized in *The Selfish Gene*. It was this paper of Hamilton's which George Price came across late one night in London's Senate House Library.

Price was shocked. He was seized with the conviction that Hamilton must be wrong. He had to be. If he was not, then Price had violated his evolutionary destiny by selfishly pursuing a career when he ought to have been supporting the children he had abandoned. He set out to disprove Hamilton's thesis. Surely, he argued, if altruism could be passed through kinship groups, so could morally undesirable qualities such as cruelty or spite? But Price's exhaustive work on Hamilton's hypothesis only proved to him that Hamilton was correct. In the process he derived the Price Equation, which offered a mathematical proof of the relationship between character traits and the genetic linkages within family and wider kinship groups. It suggested that the more genetically remote two organisms are from each other, the less likely they are to show altruism towards each other. Altruism is not selfless and moral, but rather selfish and genetic. We can take no credit for it.

Yet though George Price was proud of his science he was horrified by the implications of what he had done. Something flipped in Price's brain. The science was clear. But some instinct told him it was not right. There was a conflict between his heart and his head, something which, as we will see, is a recurrent theme in the history of philanthropy. Price's response to this was characteristically extreme. He underwent an intense religious conversion. The man who had been an outspoken atheist and ultra-rationalist all his life suddenly converted to evangelical Christianity. He spent days obsessively reading the

Bible, searching for hidden codes. Bill Hamilton, who had by now become a close friend, thought he had gone 'completely crazy'.[2] Price continued to work on his science, developing revolutionary ideas about evolution and game theory, but also told Hamilton he had 'sort of "encountered" Jesus', who had told him, 'Give to everyone who asks of you.'[3]

Increasingly depressed by the implications of his equation, Price began to indulge in acts of random kindness to complete strangers. He invited the homeless to live in his house. Sometimes there were so many that there was no room for him and he would sleep at the Galton Laboratory. When the alcoholics he had invited home stole his belongings, he became depressed. His vicar advised him against being too literal in his interpretation of the words of the Bible, but Price carried on – even giving away his only pair of shoes and the big aluminium cross he had taken to wearing round his neck. Giving became a compulsion, even an addiction. Obsessed with the idea of selflessness, Price next moved into a squat where eventually he took his own life. At his funeral on a cold winter's day in 1975 the only mourners were a handful of homeless people and two of the great evolutionary biologists of the age, John Maynard Smith and Bill Hamilton. Afterwards Hamilton declared that George Price had been 'perhaps the most brilliant thinker he had ever met'.[4] It was as if Price had set out to become the living refutation of his own equation. By adopting an altruism which was all-consuming, George Price had perhaps done, in the end, what he had so conspicuously failed to do for his own children – giving away everything, even his own life. Perhaps he demonstrated that there is a moral dimension to giving which no amount of genetic determinism can quell within the human spirit.

Philanthropy is not the same thing as altruism. But there are significant overlaps between the two. Those who give like to think that their motives are altruistic. They hope or assume that others will take the same view. But what this book shows is that philanthropy is something far more complex, which interweaves all manner of motivations and intentions, personal and social, political and economic.

Certainly a thread of ethical altruism is woven through the past two thousand years of philanthropy, from the first-century scriptural declaration of Jesus Christ that 'it is more blessed to give than to receive'[5] to the stern twentieth-century injunction of Martin Luther

King: 'Every man must decide whether he will walk in the creative light of altruism or the darkness of destructive selfishness. This is the judgement. Life's persistent and most urgent question is "What are you doing for others?"'[6]

The term altruism was coined by the French philosopher Auguste Comte in the nineteenth century. He defined it as unselfish action for the welfare of others, contrasted with egoism, which is regard for one's own interest.[7] In fact, both altruism and egoism are at work in philanthropy. Nor does the individual philanthropist need to make a choice between acting altruistically and egoistically in order to act in the public good. That is particularly so today since philanthropy is defined by contemporary thinkers in terms of 'private initiatives for the public good', 'voluntary action for the public good' or 'the private giving of time or valuables . . . for public purposes'.[8] What this book will suggest is that the history of giving shows that these contemporary conceptions of philanthropy are impoverished and in need of enrichment.

CAN THE RICH SAVE THE WORLD?

Modern philanthropy is impoverished? The numbers seem to fly in the face of such an assertion. The mega-donations of modern philanthropists have brought a huge expansion in philanthropy today. The intergovernmental economic organization, the Organization for Economic Co-operation and Development (OCED) in Paris, wrote in 2018 that 'private philanthropy is reshaping the development landscape like never before'.[9] The same year Harvard University established a new Global Philanthropy Report, which shows that nearly three-quarters of the world's 260,000 philanthropy foundations have been established, in 38 countries, in just the last 25 years.[10] Between them they control more than $1.5 trillion, of which more than $150 billion is being given out in grants each year. And that figure does not include the gifts of rich individuals whose charitable activity is below $1 million a year. The most generous nation is the United States, whose population donates around 2 per cent of its national income every year.[11] The Bill & Melinda Gates Foundation alone has a bigger budget than 70 per cent of the world's nations'.[12] The second most generous nation is the United Kingdom, where philanthropic giving hovers around 0.7 per cent of GDP. This may seem small by comparison with UK

government welfare spending of nearly 30 per cent. But the significance
of this philanthropic giving lies less in the quantity than in the qualities
it reflects in British public life. In 2019 the British Parliament set up
an All-Party Group on Philanthropy and Social Investment to deepen
lawmakers' understanding of this burgeoning field by bringing together
politicians, donors, social investors and philanthropy experts to
develop policy to improve and increase the amount of giving and social
investment in the UK.

The good done by philanthropy in the modern world is now on
an epic scale. The wealth, drive and business acumen of tech titans
like the Microsoft founder Bill Gates have brought huge benefits for
humankind, of which the Gates Foundation is the exemplar with its
championing of a more creative capitalism. Its enthusiasts christened
it 'Philanthrocapitalism', and declared that through it 'the Rich Can
Save the World' by applying business methods to social problems
which until now have eluded solutions by the public, private and
charitable sectors.[13] Philanthrocapitalism is data-driven and metrics-
obsessed – like the businesses to which it brought an extraordinary
accumulation of wealth. And it brings hitherto unthought-of sums
to philanthropy and uses its wealth and political influence to leverage
even larger sums.

The Gates Foundation now spends more annually on global health
than does the government of Germany. When the Foundation made
its first big grant for malaria research, it nearly doubled the amount
of money spent on the disease worldwide. It did the same with polio.
Thanks to Bill and Melinda Gates, 2.5 billion children have been
vaccinated against the disease and cases of polio have been cut by 99.9
per cent. Polio has been virtually eradicated. Philanthropy has made
good the failures of both the pharmaceutical industry and governments
across the world. The Gates Foundation has expanded beyond disease
control to maternal and child healthcare, hygiene, family planning,
gender equality, nutrition, agriculture, financial services, clean water and
sanitation. In 2005 the leader of the next generation of digital giants,
Mark Zuckerberg, announced that he and his wife Priscilla Chan were
pledging 99 per cent of their shares in Facebook – then worth around
$45 billion – with the intention of 'preventing, curing or managing'
all the world's greatest diseases.[14] The ambition of philanthropy today
apparently knows no bounds.

THE ANTHROPOLOGY OF GIFT-GIVING

Underlying all this is a deep social psychology of what happens when we give a gift. The pioneering anthropologist Marcel Mauss offers some intriguing insights from his studies of gift-giving among pre-capitalist Pacific Islands societies and Native Americans. In his seminal 1923 essay, *The Gift: Forms and Functions of Exchange in Archaic Societies*, he suggests that gift-giving is a universal phenomenon which manifests itself in many different forms. In all societies, gifts of any kind are signs of status. Giving them constitutes an assertion of superiority, and receiving them is an acknowledgement of inferiority or subservience – unless 'the receiver then makes a gift of equal value in return.'[15] 'When a gift cannot be reciprocated, moral credit accrues to the donor but the recipient suffers a wound,' suggests Jonathan Benthall, the former Director of the Royal Anthropological Institute.[16]

The continuous exchange of gifts between individuals creates social order and stability. Mauss cites, by way of example, a traditional Native American ceremony known as a potlatch. These were commonly held to mark important occasions such as births, deaths, adoptions and weddings. At a potlatch there would be feasting and dancing. But, most importantly, the host would lavish gifts on his guests, the quantity and quality of those gifts varying according to the status of the individual recipients. Hierarchical relations within and between clans, villages and nations were reinforced through the distribution of physical gifts, along with rights to hunt, fish or gather berries on part of the host's land. The status of individuals and families within these indigenous societies was demonstrated not by the amount of wealth they held but by the amount they showed themselves able to give away. If a 'person of consequence' had suffered a bodily injury or an indignity, he could 'cover his shame' by a potlatch, which would prevent any other member of the tribe making reference to the incident in the future.[17]

Potlatches did not just involve gifts. The host would often also destroy precious things at a potlatch to demonstrate his power and wealth. Through this destruction the gods and spirits would accept the share of wealth and happiness offered to them, as with burnt offerings in other pre-modern societies. 'Mauss saw all gifts as metaphorically entailing sacrifice: when I make a gift, I give a part of myself,' writes

Benthall.[18] The potlatches of North-Western America often featured the host putting slaves to death, burning his precious oil, setting his house on fire, and destroying highly prized shields of beaten copper which were considered more valuable even than slaves.[19] The idea so offended Western sensibilities that in 1884 the Canadian government made potlatching illegal as part of its assimilation agenda.

Judaism, and then Christianity and Islam, according to Mauss, instilled the idea that almsgiving should replace these sacrificial offerings to God. This came at the point in history when the theology of these three Abrahamic faiths taught the elite to see the poor as fellow human beings. The rich were required to give to the poor in emulation of the way that a generous God had given to them. Alms-giving, Mauss suggests, is 'ancient gift morality' raised to become 'a principle of justice'. The rich were obliged to be generous and share what they have with the needy, as 'the gods and spirits consent that the portion reserved for them, and destroyed in useless sacrifice, should go to the poor and the children'.[20]

From the outset there were different views about who should best be the objects of this fellow feeling. Aristotle thought philanthropy should be directed towards family and neighbours. Confucius two centuries later in China drew concentric circles of compassion around the individual, which suggested each individual should love their father most warmly, and then their family, then others in lesser degree according to their distance from the centre, but with particular care of 'widows, orphans, childless men, and those who were disabled by disease'.[21] In ancient societies there was a clear understanding that gratitude must follow generosity, and this is shown in the English legends of the eighth-century BC Celtic king, Leir of Britain, whose story Shakespeare adapted in *King Lear*. One moral of *King Lear* is that the duty of the father to his offspring should be reciprocated by children who are not unnatural.[22]

Intriguingly, though the old gift morality generally gave way to this new conception of giving, traces of the potlatch survived throughout history. In 1621 King James I of England (and VI of Scotland) spent £3,300 on a Twelfth Night 'ante-supper', which was made purposely not to be eaten but ostentatiously thrown away as a conspicuous sign of his wealth. It was reported that 100 cooks spent 12 days preparing 1,600 dishes at a cost equivalent to the annual income of a wealthy English landowner. The king's favourite, the notoriously extravagant

Earl of Carlisle, encouraged the monarch in this reckless display with the flamboyant aphorism: 'Spend and God will send.'[23] The English nobility were horrified rather than impressed. Such behaviour has continued throughout history. The phrase 'conspicuous consumption' was coined[24] in 1899 at the height of the so-called Golden Age of Philanthropy. 'Robber baron' philanthropists of the Carnegie/ Vanderbilt/Rockefeller era would hold banquets of huge extravagance, attracting so many members of the public to gather outside their Fifth Avenue mansions to gawp that the police had to be called to keep order. When their ideas for exorbitant indulgence were exhausted, they dreamt up the 'poverty social' – to which wealthy guests came dressed in rags, were seated on old buckets, and were served beer in rusty tin cans.[25] When such degenerate and morally bankrupt pleasures no longer proved satisfying, the robber barons turned to philanthropy. It is much the same today. Contemporary philanthropists, because of their giving, gain access to what the economist Fred Hirsch called 'positional goods' – objects which gain their desirability from being limited in number – such as boxes at the Royal Opera House or flats overlooking Central Park.[26] 'Philanthropy is in part a positional good,' acknowledges Britain's leading philanthropy researcher, Beth Breeze, director of the Centre for Philanthropy at the University of Kent. 'For some donors its value lies in the fact that other people cannot afford to buy their way on to charity boards or get access to tickets for prestigious fundraising events.'[27] That becomes more true when the gap between the rich and the poor widens – as it is doing in much of our world today – because while more material goods can always be manufactured, positional goods by definition can only be redistributed.

The insights of Marcel Mauss raise a different set of questions about philanthropy. If George Price shows us that philanthropy and altruism are not the same thing, Mauss suggests that we should also consider the relationship between philanthropy and power. This book shows how that has taken different forms through the ages: from philanthropy as an expression of citizenship in Ancient Greece and Rome, of artistic prestige in Renaissance Europe, of personal wealth for those Indian maharajas who gave away their own weight in gold, of reputation laundering for robber-baron philanthropists like Andrew Carnegie, and of power for today's hyper-rich digital tech titans who are now determined to revolutionize philanthropy. Marcel Mauss prompts us to ask whether much of this extraordinary efflorescence constitutes a true gift or whether it is merely an investment in status or political power. The answer will emerge in these pages if we keep in mind Mauss's central insight that gift-giving can be both an expression of self-interest and also a concern for others. For much philanthropy does both at the same time.

THE DONOR, THE RECIPIENT AND WIDER SOCIETY

Story after story in this book reveals that there is far more at work in philanthropy than mere altruism. At their best they show that it is still possible to fulfil the criteria set by Marcel Mauss that the noblest form of philanthropy aligns the interests of those who give, those who receive and the interests of wider society. This book considers philanthropy from each of those three perspectives.

The interests of those who give begin with the question: Why do the rich give? The personality and life experiences of the donors are almost always the starting point. Personal or family tragedies trigger giving. So does gratitude to a hospital, school or university. Those who come from immigrant backgrounds often talk about wanting to give something back to the society which had given refuge to their family.[28] Philanthropy can be learned; it is passed down in families, peer groups, business networks and religious communities. It can spring from religious commitment or a sense of civic duty. 'Giving liberates the soul of the giver,' wrote Maya Angelou.[29] But there is also a source of personal satisfaction that comes from directly meeting the needs of others. Those who consider themselves to be 'strategic philanthropists' often speak dismissively of those they call 'warm glow givers'. But research on the human brain using magnetic resonance imaging has recently shown that this warm glow is a very real phenomenon – voluntary giving increases activity in the parts of the brain associated with reward, which burst into life under the influence of addictive stimulants such as cocaine.[30] Charity, these scientists have shown, can get you high. By contrast the American psychologist Paul K. Piff has done some interesting work with the non-philanthropic rich, which suggests that philanthropists are unusual since wealth generally increases meanness.

Many philanthropists themselves acknowledge psychological benefits – feeling good about giving, or growing with the challenge of learning about a new activity. In the past it was common for individuals, having created a substantial fortune, to change gear at some point and switch from money-making to activities which generate a greater sense of meaning in their lives. Some have a desire for acknowledgement, prestige or honour. But more are said to desire the approval of their family and peers – 'my children will feel proud' – than look for plaudits from wider society, according to Theresa Lloyd who conducted interviews with 100 wealthy donors in the UK for her book *Why the Rich Give.*[31] A significant number, however, take active steps to avoid publicity or recognition. Almost all her interviewees reported more than one reason for each donation: a cause they believed in, a sense of wanting to make a difference, or the satisfaction they gained from building relationships with other donors, charity staff and the beneficiaries themselves. Philanthropy can even be said to assuage 'a desire for immortality': donating a wing in a hospital, gallery or museum was 'a way of leaving "footprints on the sand of time"', in the words of one donor.[32] But it can also arise out of a sense of identification with or empathy for the plight of others – something which is far from restricted to the wealthy. During the 1984 miners' strike, when political supporters in the south of England were sending food parcels north, in one of the distribution centres where the striking miners gathered to collect their bags of food, they first conducted a collection amongst themselves for the victims of the Ethiopian famine.

The interests of donors are varied but fairly clear. But those of the recipients of philanthropy can be more difficult to discern. On the surface these all too often seem self-evident. But as this book shows, the history of philanthropy is also littered with projects and programmes which fail. Sometimes these arise out of an inadequate analysis of the roots of the issue the philanthropist sets out to address. But all too often, even in the case of major givers such as Bill Gates and Mark Zuckerberg – or perhaps even more so in the case of such mega-donors – the problem lies in the over-confidence of philanthropists that the qualities which brought them such extraordinary success in business can simply be transferred to more complex social situations. Problems often look different from the top down than they do when viewed from the grassroots. Assisting people to find their own solutions may often be more effective than narrowly targeted data-driven business strategies which allow the interests of those who give to overshadow the interests of those on the receiving end.

Bringing the interest of wider society into the equation, as Mauss suggests, complicates things further. In part this is because the social and political mores of each era change. Early discourse on philanthropy was dominated by talk of virtue. But by the time the French political scientist Alexis de Tocqueville visited America in the early nineteenth century that had changed. De Tocqueville was impressed by the number of civic organizations and associations which stood between the individual and the state in the young United States. Philanthropy played, and continues to play, a bigger part in American life than in any other country in the world. But what struck the French thinker was that these groups did not see themselves as vehicles to promote virtue but rather as mechanisms through which the self-interest of individuals could be harnessed to work for the wider interests of society. This 'civil society' was a positive development for civilization, de Tocqueville argued, because self-interest was in much greater supply than virtue.[33]

Such a shift was not confined to the United States. Nor is the development which sees philanthropy as not just about gift-giving but also about investment. As we will discover in the coming pages, there is not much which is new in philanthropy. Inviting donors to put money into a project that both benefits society and returns a modest investment was the formula which undergirded the religiously motivated pawnshops – the *monti di pietà* – of fourteenth- and fifteenth-century England and Italy.* It was also the foundation of Octavia Hill's nineteenth-century 5 per cent philanthropy to build housing for the poor in Victorian Britain.† Today it is embodied in Muhammad Yunus's Grameen Bank, which serves the poor of Bangladesh, or in Ronald Cohen's social impact investment bonds, or in the Catholic social investment funds encouraged by Pope Francis.‡

---

* See pages 153–7 below.
† See page 284 below.
‡ See pages 465, 717 and 718 below.

JUST WHO DO PHILANTHROPISTS THINK THEY ARE?

The word 'philanthropy' was not used in English until 1623, according to the *Oxford English Dictionary*, which records it as meaning a 'disposition or active effort to promote the active happiness and well-being of one's fellow men'.[34] But the history of philanthropy since then is not simply a history of giving. It is the history of relationships between social classes, of religious and nationalist identity, of charity and welfare, of wealth and taxation, of government and the private sector, and much else. Similarly, the definitions of philanthropy have changed and developed, encompassing campaigning for the abolition of slavery, prison and housing reform, and the political emancipation of the working class and of women. Our current common-sense usage of 'a rich person giving a lot of money' is too limited. And today philanthropy has been widened to include voluntary activity, campaigning, corporate social responsibility, shop-floor giving, sponsored fundraising, charitable telethons and the new phenomenon of crowdfunding.

But when it comes to the relationship between philanthropy and wider society something is also aroused which is the opposite of empathy. Philanthropy can provoke suspicion and even hostility. Scepticism at the motives of those who give has long been part of the history of philanthropy. The idea that hand-outs to the poor can make things worse rather than better has been around since medieval times when Church leaders and theologians began to make distinctions between the deserving and undeserving poor, and draw up hierarchies of the relative worthiness of those in receipt of charity. Those who gave less generously often derided the more generous as foolish. Aspersions began to be cast upon the motivation of donors for other reasons. At the Reformation, fired up by theological indignation and political opportunism, Protestants began erroneously to suggest that the great almsgiving of the Middle Ages was motivated only by a venal desire by donors to get to heaven more swiftly.

After the Enlightenment, when philanthropy was characterized more by the activism of penal reformers like John Howard or abolitionists like William Wilberforce, their opponents attacked their high-mindedness as a lack of realism about how the real world worked. During what was called the Golden Age of English Philanthropy in the early Victorian era, individual charities blossomed to address the wide range of issues being thrown up in the wake of the Industrial Revolution – from child labour and slum housing to the rescuing of 'fallen women' and 'truss societies' – a response to the fact that a fifth of the male population then suffered from hernias in the ports and manufacturing districts. But these Victorian 'do-gooders' were ridiculed by critics ranging from the novelists George Eliot and Charles Dickens to the august editorial writers of *The Times* newspaper.[35] The historian Hugh Cunningham has complied an extraordinary catalogue of disdain and vituperation expressed by editors of *The Times* during the nineteenth century against the philanthropy of the age, which it variously described as 'puffing', 'pseudo', 'sham', 'false' and 'unscrupulous'. The twenty-first-century adjectival equivalents include 'ruthless', 'tax-dodging', 'sinister', 'status-seeking' and 'self-righteous', according to the more contemporary research by Beth Breeze.[36] Wealth and power remain an uneasy combination.

The root of the antagonism towards philanthropy in many quarters today appears to lie in the fact that in rich economies, such as the UK and the US, governments grant tax relief on charitable donations to encourage giving. The result is that if a non-taxpayer wants to donate £100, that is what they must pay out. But if the standard rate of income tax is 25 per cent, the government pays £25 of a £100 donation by an ordinary taxpayer; so the donor pays just £75. Where higher incomes are taxed at 40 per cent, the government pays £40 and the richer person pays only £60 of a £100 donation. A public mythology has arisen in response to this differential rate of tax relief which insists that philanthropy is therefore some kind of tax dodge. In fact, despite the enhanced tax relief, the philanthropist is still out of pocket. Beth Breeze is bemused by this. If the chap-next-door donates £100 to a foreign disaster appeal his act generally finds approval. 'But once a few zeros are added onto the size of a donation, there's a clear shift from "well done mate" to "what's your game?"', she laments.[37] This cynicism about the motivations of donors – more widespread in Britain and the rest of Europe than in America – is revealing. It almost certainly tells us less about what the public thinks about giving than it does about what many think about rich people. Attitudes to philanthropy can be a lightning conductor for feelings about something more deep-rooted in a world where inequality is constantly on the increase.

There is somewhat more to it than that. If a philanthropist makes a massive donation to his favourite opera house and a significant proportion of the donation comes from ordinary taxpayers, that raises issues of democratic process. A majority of taxpayers might prefer that their tax money be spent on something more popular with the general public than opera. An elite art form is being subsidised from the public purse, and those taxes are not being spent on something which might have had more general appeal. This has repeatedly led to friction, as this book will show. If a philanthropist or a philanthropic foundation is going to enjoy this kind of influence over how taxpayers' money is spent, many argue that society should have some greater say in the kind of causes a rich donor should be allowed to choose. We shall consider the idea of such reform, though historically, governments have been ambivalent about this.

The state generally approves of philanthropy, particularly when it funds causes of public benefit, because it relieves the state of the need to spend government funds in those areas. In addition, a succession of British governments, of all parties, have attempted over the past three decades to hijack the voluntary sector to turn charities into subcontractors funded and controlled by the state. Politicians feel most comfortable when philanthropy adheres to strictly 'charitable' purposes. But in the modern world, as the examples of philanthropists such as Bill Gates and Mark Zuckerberg have shown, philanthropy is increasingly entering into the realm of policy-making – and even party politics. Towards the end of the book we will explore the tensions between philanthropy and democracy more fully. Politicians can be hostile when philanthropy supports charities which challenge their policies. Conversely, we will examine examples of how the personal convictions of individual mega-rich donors can distort the wider public interest. As the resources available to super-rich philanthropists grow ever larger, this debate will only grow more acute. These are only the start of the paradoxes of philanthropy.

ENGLISH PHILANTHROPY AND BEYOND

When I began the five years of research for this book my intention was to write about English philanthropy and that remains its central thread. But it swiftly became evident that a narrow national focus made no sense. The order of this book is chronological. But each chapter deals with a particular theme: philanthropy and society, religion, the state, democracy, and celebrity, concluding with reflections on philanthropy and contemporary capitalism. After each chapter is a free-standing interview which seeks to illuminate how that history and those themes assert their influence on society today. All that makes it abundantly clear that English philanthropy cannot be considered in isolation.

Gift-giving goes back at least to ancient Mesopotamia, a thousand years before the Greeks coined the adjective *philanthropon* to describe someone who is gentle and kind towards others. The philosophical roots of philanthropy lay in Ancient Greece, and took a profound switch in direction because of the evolving theology of the Jewish people, a change which was subsequently developed by both Christians and Muslims. It injected into philanthropy the idea that both those who gave and those who received were bound together in a relationship which was in some ways reciprocal. But that was destroyed by the devastating impact of the Black Death, which killed between a third and half of the entire population of Europe – and also brought a tectonic shift in the attitudes of the rich to the poor across the whole of the Latin-speaking world.

After the Renaissance and Reformation, the Catholic and Protestant countries of Europe influenced one another, as this book shows, far more than previous histories of philanthropy have supposed. In Catholic and Protestant states alike the rise of the merchant class shifted control of philanthropy from churchmen to lay people. All across the continent the state began to involve itself through poor laws in the charity which had once been the exclusive province of the Church. The impact of the European Enlightenments was continental rather than national – and although the Victorian era, with its extraordinary range of charitable activities, marked a high point of a distinctively English style of philanthropy, it was soon jostled by external influences. Socialism arrived from continental Europe as much as it was nurtured in native English soil.

But the biggest development in the history of philanthropy, in the century which followed, came from a Scotsman, Andrew Carnegie, whose vast fortunes were amassed on the other side of the Atlantic, where he became the richest man in the world and established a new model for philanthropy. Carnegie was not only the biggest philanthropist of his era: his philosophy of 'he who dies rich, dies disgraced' also inspired generations of philanthropists who followed. It directly influenced the establishment of the Bill & Melinda Gates Foundation. He continues to be cited regularly by a host of today's philanthropists. The idea of 'a new way of doing philanthropy' occurs repeatedly throughout history; yet the revolutions in philanthropy supposedly ushered in by today's philanthrocapitalist titans such as Bill Gates and Mark Zuckerberg owe much to the philosophy developed by Carnegie.

So English philanthropy cannot any longer be regarded as something discrete and distinct. At the turn of the twentieth and twenty-first centuries, philanthropy has gone global in both its influences and in its paradigms. This book attempts to chronicle the long journey from the ancient Greeks to the modern geeks – and to critique it. For something has been lost along the way.

Throughout this book footnotes appear at the bottom of the relevant page but the extensive source notes – which are indicated by small superscript numbers in the text – can be found with weblinks at www.philanthropyatoz.com

Chapter 1

Two Visions of Philanthropy

The word 'philanthropy' first appears in the fifth century BC in the ancient Greek tragedy *Prometheus Bound*. The Greek *philanthrôpía* is a compound of two roots – *phílos*, which means something beloved, cherished and important, and *ánthrôpos*, a human being. Common usage today takes philanthropy to mean the donation by a rich person of a large amount of money to a good cause. But the term has encompassed a far richer variety of meanings over the centuries, tying it into personal relationships, social hierarchies, the politics of cities, the spread of religions, the shaping of laws and the governance of states. Yet it is no coincidence that the word first appears in what survives of the dramatic retelling by Aeschylus of the foundational myth of Prometheus, the benevolent god who dared to share divine fire with mere mortals and incurred the wrath of Zeus for his impertinence. The fire, which the Olympian Gods wanted to reserve for their private use, was brought from the heavens to a dark and despondent earth. Human control of warmth and light brought about a transformation. The gods accuse Prometheus of being a 'human-lover', intending the term in an unfavourable sense, because he confers on human beings benefits that belong only to the gods.[1] For his philanthropy Prometheus was punished by Zeus, who had him chained to a rock and condemned to never-ending torture – by day an eagle would eat away his liver, which the Greeks believed to be the seat of human emotions. Overnight it would grow back again, ready for the torture to begin again the next morning. Philanthropy was, from the outset, a risky business.

Philanthropy from early on encompassed two radically different interpretations. For the Greeks, and then the Romans, it was about the relationship of the individual to society, and it was bound up with notions of status, honour and approval. For the Jews, and later the Muslims, it was about the relationship of the individual to God – a relationship mediated through a sense of community with fellow believers. Out of a synthesis of these two visions emerged the Christian conception of philanthropy which was to shape ideas of charity and giving for a thousand years of Christendom. This was then tempered by the Reformation and subsequently the Enlightenment, in ways which we shall see were both helpful and unhelpful, enriching and impoverishing.

The concept of gift-giving as a public rather than a private act is older, however, even than the word. Over a thousand years before Aeschylus, the great Babylonian epic poem *The Epic of Gilgamesh* celebrated generosity and self-sacrifice while relishing the misfortune of misanthropic kings. It reflected the cultural consensus of its time. From as early as the third millennium BC the kings of Babylon had fixed codes of law which decreed special punishments for the strong who abused the weak. Justice and clemency were already then hallmarks of nobility. In Egypt, around 1,500 BC, from the beginning of the New Kingdom, sacred funerary texts were already in use in Thebes which were to form part of *The Book of the Dead*. They made it clear that a successful passage to the afterlife depended on a lifetime's record of benevolent acts towards the suffering. The Egyptian deities would only grant immortality to those who could swear that they had never denied food to the starving, drink to the thirsty, or clothing to the ragged. The first charitable foundations were probably temples caring for the sick in ancient Egypt. In Sri Lanka, in the fourth century BC, hospitals were established by King Pandukabhaya, as they were by King Ashoka in India a hundred years later.

But the Greek myth of Prometheus is an apt starting place. The divine spark which he gifted was a vivid metaphor for bringing enlightenment to humankind. Prometheus, whose name means 'forethought', is depicted by Aeschylus as teaching men the arts of civilization, including agriculture, writing, mathematics, science and medicine. Because Prometheus, in bringing fire to humanity, engaged in an act of rebellion against the authority of the gods, *philanthrôpía* to the Greeks became associated with the power play of politics and their great innovation of democracy. The early laws of Athens were described as 'philanthropic and democratic', the two notions entwined to suggest that it was philanthropy which made humankind capable of self-government.

THE GREEKS — *PHILANTHRÔPÍA* AND HONOUR

To the first philosophers in ancient Greece, in the third century BC, philanthropy and education were also inextricably linked. Socrates, the father of classical thought, is quoted by his pupil Plato in his dialogue *The Euthyphro* (c. 400 BC) as using *philanthrôpía* to describe 'the friendship for humankind'[2] which motivates him to educate others. 'My love of man makes me talk to everyone whom I meet quite freely and unreservedly, and without payment.'[3] This is the first recorded use of philanthropy as a noun. In the Socratic dialogue the adjectival form of *philánthrôpos* also appears twice, each time describing a god's attempt to moderate the aggressive human attitude which, if uncontrolled, inexorably leads men to commit injustice. Euthyphro, an arrogant and insensitive member of the Athenian elite, is about to prosecute his own father for the manslaughter of a slave. The dialogue takes place as Euthyphro is on his way into court. Where Euthyphro is motivated by self-righteousness, Socrates is motivated by friendship, *philia*, for humanity, *ánthrôpos*. His 'pouring out' of his thoughts, freely and without charge to his listeners, was described by Socrates as his public-spirited *philanthrôpía*.

Again the double-edge of philanthropy is evident; the same *philanthrôpía* will later prove to be the death of Socrates when his fellow Athenians accuse his free thinking — the gift communicated to mortals by the maverick god Prometheus — of corrupting the youth of the city. The link between philanthropy and education is there again when one of Plato's followers compiled a dictionary of 184 philosophical terms which came to be known as *The Definitions*. It described *philanthrôpía* as 'a habit of moral conduct that easily leads to a friendship with man', which sprang from the process of moral education.[4] Philanthropy became, for the Greeks, an educational ideal, whose goal was *arête* — the fullest development of body, mind and spirit, and the essence of liberal education.

Philanthropy soon extended from the love of learning into wider areas. From the outset the arts were seen as an area which should benefit from *philanthrôpía*. In the fourth and fifth centuries BC, rich citizens, acting as individuals and in groups, paid for the staging of the major Greek dramatic festivals which became the first great collective expressions of Western art. Rich men, and women, built theatres, commissioned scripts from the writers who became the founding fathers of world theatre – Aeschylus, Sophocles, Euripides and Aristophanes – and paid for the actors, costumes, masks and other equipment needed to shape the lessons in civility and citizenship which were the bedrock of Greek religion, culture and social polity.

Yet for the Greeks there was still another dimension to philanthropy. Xenophon, another student of Socrates, in his biography of Cyrus the Great, the *Cyropaedia* (c. 370 BC), lauds the first emperor of Persia, then the biggest empire the world had ever seen, as 'the Ideal Ruler and the best form of Government'. He singles out the king's 'supremely philanthropic soul' as capturing the essence of his entire character. Among Cyrus's philanthropic practices Xenophon cites love of learning; thoughtful and lavish gift-giving; his donation of prizes at horse races and gymnastic and choral competitions; his match-making; his serving guests the same food he himself eats; his gifts of food to servants; and his care for those who are ill. All these were marks of philanthropy. Xenophon suggests Cyrus is motivated by a fondness for humans that involves feelings of pity, sympathy, affection and care. Cyrus even prefigures Christ's simile that a king is like a shepherd, because both must know how to benefit their flocks in order to draw benefits in return.

But Xenophon notes a new development – the mixed motives which are to characterize the entire history of philanthropy. His gift-giving does not simply demonstrate Cyrus's love of his fellow beings, it also wins him honour and also minimizes the threat of others plotting against him. *Philanthrôpía* is married with *philotîmia*, a love of being honoured, praised, approved of and appreciated. Cyrus wants others to feel the fondness for him that he feels for his fellows. Because these practices were 'so thoughtful and so unique' to the king, Xenophon observes, his gifts rendered his followers more loyal to him than they were even to their own families.[5] The king's love of honour and love of humanity are intertwined in ways difficult to disentangle – and stand in contrast to Socrates's distinct lack of concern for his own reputation among his fellow citizens. Cyrus's altruism and political pragmatism are, Xenophon suggests, a far cry from Plato's Philosopher King, who is motivated out of a pure passion for conceptualizing the perfect state in conformity with the idea of the Good. The *philanthrôpía* of Cyrus has become highly political.[6]

The Greeks coined a special word for this; it was not *philanthrôpía* but what classical scholars have come to call euergetism,[7] from the Greek word *euergetes*, meaning 'benefactor'. ('Benefactor' is an English word with a Latin root, which is appropriate because the Romans came to adopt the same concept.) Euergetism was more than munificence: it was munificence which was rewarded with honours, a fact that was consciously or unconsciously assumed by the donor.[8] Love of humanity, *philanthrôpía*, was bound up with love of honour, *philotîmia*.

A sense of exchange was implicit. There was more to this than altruism. As the anthropologist Marcel Mauss has noted,[*] public gifts were a sign of status and a confirmation of social hierarchy, for they implied the recognition of superiority and the acknowledgement of inferiority or subservience.

At the heyday of Athenian democracy, in the fourth century BC, a system known as liturgy, *leitourgia*, was used to persuade members of the wealthy elite each individually to finance a specific public initiative – from funding a chorus for a play or sending a sports team to a tournament to extremely expensive projects like building a temple or arming the most powerful warship of the day, the trireme. Prominent citizens sought to outdo one another in the extravagance of their gifts, to show the superiority of their own civic virtue. Those who refused to pay risked ostracism by their peers and the opprobrium of the ordinary people. But eventually the rapid increase in military expenditure during the Peloponnesian War began to undermine the liturgy system. Aristophanes in 405 BC has one of the characters in his comedy *The Frogs* remark: 'You can no longer find a rich man to be *trierarch* [major donor]: each puts on rags and goes about whining "I am needy!"' From that point on, in Athens, as in other Greek city states, the term *philanthrôpía* took on a new dimension. Originally it had referred to the relationship of the gods to humans. Next it came to be applied to rulers who were generous to their subjects. Now it was extended to the wealthy more generally. From the third century BC onwards, all across

---

Greece, a system of patronage became established which was to endure through to Roman times. The wealthy personally financed the creation of city walls, armouries, amphitheatres, racetracks, granaries, fountains, gymnasia, schools, libraries and other municipal amenities.

THE ROMANS, ARISTOTLE, AND THE PHILANTHROPY OF PATRONAGE

Patronage was a system which was to reach its high point under the Romans, who saw the advantages of philanthropy as a political investment. Gaius Maecenas, one of the counsellors to the first Emperor of Rome, Augustus Caesar, supported several of the great poets of the day, including Virgil and Horace. His intent was that they would glorify this new Augustan age and guide public opinion through the delicate political transition from the Republic to Imperial Rome. One of the greatest patrons of the arts in the Roman era was Maecenas, a figure so celebrated that a form of his name has passed into French, *mecene*, as the word for donor or sponsor. Another of the lieutenants of Augustus, the great general Agrippa, tried to buy the favour of the people of Rome in less elevated ways – distributing salt and olive oil to the masses, paying barbers to give free haircuts to the plebeians, erecting statues in the public baths, building aqueducts and repairing public buildings. One of his greatest public relations triumphs was to clean out Rome's great sewers – and he celebrated the end of the feat by travelling in a small boat through the main drain, the Cloaca Maxima, and out into the River Tiber.[9] Agrippa was the force behind the great boast that the Emperor Augustus had 'found the city of brick but left it of marble'. Public edifices in Rome often bore the inscription *D. S. P. F.* (*De Sua Pecunia Fecit*, 'Done with His Own Money') along with the name of the benefactor. In return his fellow citizens put up a statue to him, which is why tearing down statues became a great symbolic gesture in any revolt or sedition.

Roman culture valued gifts. They were the glue which bound together families, marriages and social hierarchies. Roman society was obsessed with maintaining social distinctions and there was a steep social pyramid of power, privilege and prestige. Gift-giving created the bonds between the different levels. The Emperor alone had the right to make certain gifts, such as the inauguration of gladiatorial games. On special occasions emperors gave *donatives*, gifts of gold, to high-ranking civil servants and soldiers, including their entire Praetorian Guard. They routinely handed out regular gifts, *sportulae*, to officials and individuals they favoured. Throughout society those with wealth and influence emulated the practice. A wealthy aristocrat might support a large number of clients. These were expected to show deference to their patron, often calling upon him each morning to offer a ritual greeting, *salutatio*, which might be accompanied by a request for help or favours. In return patrons expected their clients to assist them in their private and public life and vote as they were instructed in public assemblies. The system trickled down the social scale. Clients could make requests to their patron on behalf of their own clients. Pliny the Younger, according to his letters, sent 15 such requests to the Emperor Trajan. The system was not reciprocal; a client could not return a favour to his patron – that would have been impertinent. Instead he showed his gratitude through loyalty and deference – and by echoing the imperial patronage on a small scale. Pliny gave his home town a public library, bequeathed large sums for the construction and upkeep of public baths, and paid for an annual sumptuous banquet for the townsfolk. In return the town placed an inscription on the baths eulogizing Pliny's career and benefactions. For the Romans, as for the Greeks, there was a clear understanding that a donor would receive appropriate recognition for his gifts. Philanthropy was about civic responsibility rather than personal generosity. The trick, according to Pliny, was to be able to win the affections of your social inferiors without irritating your betters.

In both Greece and Rome philanthropy was not an intuitive practice; it was something which required considered reflection. This is clear throughout the writings of the philosophers of antiquity. Perhaps the greatest of them, Aristotle, a century after Socrates, devoted an entire chapter of his *Nicomachean Ethics* to the virtue of *eleutheriotês*, variously translated as generosity or liberality (*liberalitas* to the Romans). For Aristotle generosity should not be motivated by compassion or pity for those in need; rather its point was to develop the good character of the donor. 'Generosity resides not in how much one gives, but in the moral character of the giver,' he wrote, and developed two corollaries which have remained germane throughout the history of philanthropy. 'There is therefore nothing to prevent the man who gives less from being the more generous man' – a thought continued by Christ in his parable of the woman who gives away a penny when that is all she has.[10] Aristotle also adds a psychological insight: 'It is not easy for the generous man to be rich, for his skills lie not in taking or keeping but in giving away.' He 'does not value wealth for its own sake, but as a means to giving'.[11] Generous people are also often easy to cheat, and can be persuaded to give to flatterers and fraudsters, he observes. Even so, that is a lesser fault than meanness. Proportion is key to Aristotle's philosophical outlook. Gifts should be in proportion to the resources of the donor but also to the needs of the beneficiary, he adds. The Stoics similarly focused on motivation in gift-giving, but they held that a gift which binds the social order is superior to a spontaneous act of charity.

The Romans, too, gave much thought to the regulation of philanthropy. The philosophers Cicero and Seneca both composed manuals on the proper giving and receiving of gifts. The great lawyer and orator Cicero, who introduced the Romans to the chief schools of Greek philosophy, used the Latin term *humanitas* to convey the concept of *philanthrôpía*. For Cicero, *humanitas* was not a formal doctrine but a style of thought; a man who practised *humanitas* was confident of his worth, courteous to others, decent in his social conduct, and active in his political role.[12] Writing in the century before Christ, Cicero argued in *On Duties* that there were two kinds of donors – the prodigal, who paid for feasts and games to flaunt his wealth and win popularity, and the authentically generous, who ransomed captives and paid off others' debts. Seneca, who was tutor to the Emperor Nero, articulated the notion, centuries before Marcel Mauss, that the purpose of philanthropic donations by the elite was to generate gratitude among plebeians which would bond the vertical ranks of Roman society. It was important, therefore, Seneca wrote in *On Benefits* around AD 60, that benefactors should select beneficiaries carefully and choose those who would be best at publicly acknowledging the act of generosity. Gifts had to be chosen wisely to maximize public gratitude.

To summarize, philanthropy had many aspects in the Graeco-Roman world. It was about the fullest possible education of the mind, body and spirit of citizens. It was about politics and public-spiritedness. It was about honour, prestige, fame, status and reputation. It was about developing the good character of the donor. It was about maintaining the social order. But there was one key thing it was not about, in stark contrast to the history of philanthropy which was to follow. It was not about the recipients. It was not about kindness or a duty of common humanity. It was about the rich rather than the poor.

THE PLACE OF THE POOR IN GRAECO-ROMAN PHILANTHROPY

The Greeks had made some distinction between the respectable working poor, *penētes*, and destitute beggars, *ptōchoi*. The latter 'depend on others for everything', according to Evelyne Patlagean,[13] whereas the *penes* is a person whose efforts at work 'were not enough to provide him with a satisfactory and secure living'. Aristophanes, in his play *Plutus*, has a character named Poverty say: 'The beggar . . . never possesses anything. The poor man lives thriftily and attentive to his work; he has not got too much, but he does not lack what he really needs.'[14] But in ancient Greece the poor were never singled out as the object of *eleutheriotês*. The poor received gifts only indirectly, as part of the civic community.[15] And both *penētes* and *ptōchoi* stood in contradistinction to the rich, *ploūsioi*.

The Roman vision of society was even more binary. A whole range of socio-economic grades were collapsed into two classes: patrician and plebeian. Even relatively prosperous artisans, craftsmen, shopkeepers were all in Latin lumped together as 'the poor', *pauperes*. Poverty was more about a lack of power than a lack of material assets. And while the Roman elite tended to idolize the rural poverty of those who worked the land, it reserved an aristocratic contempt for the urban poor. The poor of the city were often seen as dishonest, idle, seditious and complicit in their own hardship. As C. R. Whittaker notes, the Romans used terms like *inopes* (resourceless), *egentes* (needy), *pauperes* (poor), *humiles* (lowly) and *abiecti* (outcast), fairly indiscriminately and frequently combined them with abusive terms for the mob such as *vulgus, turba, multitudo*, or simply *plebs*.[16] In Rome the urban poor were regarded as a threat to social harmony and stability. Cicero speaks of *sordem urbis et faecem*, 'the poverty-stricken scum of the city', conveying the combination of fear and disgust with which the patricians regarded the plebeians.

Philanthropy was unthinkable toward such creatures. The fourth-century AD philosopher Themistius, who wrote much on *philanthrôpía*, asserted that virtue belonged only to the leisured class. He observed that it was nothing but 'ridiculous . . . to attest to love of mankind in a weaver or a carpenter who has a mean dwelling, and scarcely leaves his house through weariness and lack of leisure'.[17] Instead, the disdainful Roman elite assumed that the base appetites of these lower creatures could only be satisfied by *panem et circenses*, bread and circuses – a phrase coined at the end of the first century AD by the satirical poet Juvenal, lamenting what he saw as the lack of a sense of civic duty among the plebs.

Yet contempt for the poor was not universal in antiquity. The Epicureans accepted the poor and illiterate into their schools and clubs. The Cynics did so too, since they thought poverty a virtue. But it was the Stoics who most developed a sense that the virtuous man had a moral duty to be generous to the poor. Even this, however, was not concern rooted in a high sense of altruism for those most in need. Plato, for example, said we feel compassion not for those who are most in need but rather for those who are most like us: 'The true object of pity is not the man who is hungry or in some similar needy case, but the man who has sobriety of soul or some other virtue, or a share in such virtue, and misfortune to boot.'[18] And Aristotle repeatedly suggests – in *The Rhetoric*, *The Poetics* and his *Nicomachean Ethics* – that fellow feeling is rooted only in pity and terror: we pity others when they suffer, and we fear the same might happen to ourselves. Still, Cicero extensively advocated giving surpluses to the needy and helping the poor. And the most prominent of the Stoics, Seneca, goes further. He says we should help the needy, not out of pity but because it was a rational extension of our nature:

It is indeed worthy of great praise, when man treats man with kindness! Shall we advise stretching forth the hand to the shipwrecked sailor, or pointing out the way to the wanderer, or sharing a crust with the starving? Yes. . . Nature produced us related to one another . . . She engendered in us mutual affection, and made us prone to friendships. She established fairness and justice. According to her ruling, it is more wretched to commit than to suffer injury. Through her orders, let our hands be ready for all that needs to be helped.[19]

Seneca is venturing here beyond the usual parameters of euergetism and *philanthrôpía*. Perhaps the great Stoic was drawing on the influence of his father, Seneca the Elder, who famously wrote that 'among those laws

that are unwritten, and yet set in stone . . . are the obligations on all to
give alms to a beggar and throw earth on a corpse'.[20]

A different approach to giving to beggars is clear in the teaching
of one of the other great Stoics of the Imperial era, Gaius Musonius
Rufus, who also declared: 'how much more commendable than living
a life of luxury, it is to help many people'.[21] He introduced the idea
of justice, saying that 'for man, evil consists in injustice and cruelty
and indifference to a neighbour's trouble, while virtue is brotherly love
and goodness and justice and beneficence and concern for the welfare
of one's neighbour'.[22] Musonious, some scholars suggest, was closer to
a Cynic in some aspects of his teaching. A story is told of him that
he ordered a thousand sesterces – a large sum – be given to a beggar
who claimed to be a philosopher. On being told that the man was a
con man, Musonius said the rogue should be given the money anyway.
Since money is a primary source of all evils, the best place for it was in
the hands of a man who was already a rascal.

But giving to the poor, even among these more enlightened classical
thinkers, was incidental not institutionalized. However great the role
of euergetism in the Graeco-Roman world, there was no place for the
poor in its aesthetic of society. Bread and circuses were provided to the
poor, not as an act of kindness, but rather to maintain peace on the city
streets. Acts of generosity, where they did occur, were – as Aristotle,
Cicero and Seneca all emphasized – important only for the light they
cast on the motives of the giver in a culture which saw generosity as the
essence of the noble person's virtues.[23] The intense feeling – preached
by Jews, Christians and Muslims – that outright neglect of the poor was
ugly, and that charity was not only prudent but also beautiful, is absent
from the ancient world. The emergence of the poor as a separate object
of concern was connected with the rise of Christianity in the Roman
world. It is not until the third century AD that the Greek word for pity,
eleêmosunê, is used in non-Christian Greek writing to mean alms or a
gift to the poor.[24]

There is a revealing postscript to all this. Around AD 360, Julian the
Apostate – the Roman Emperor who tried to overturn Constantine's
establishment of Christianity as the official religion of the Roman
Empire – wrote a letter to one of his pagan high priests in Asia Minor.
In it he ordered that large quantities of corn and wine should be
distributed to the inhabitants of Galatia. A fifth of it, Julian specified,

should be given to the poor, and the rest to strangers and beggars. He then explained his motives:

> For it is disgraceful that, when no Jew ever has to beg, and the impious Galilaeans [Christians] support not only their own poor but ours as well, all men see that our people lack aid from us. Teach those of the Hellenic faith [pagans] to contribute public service of this sort.[25]

Julian may have wanted to junk Christianity and turn Rome back to Hellenistic polytheism, but he wisely understood where Christianity had the edge over Graeco-Roman religions. Its care for the poor and needy was attractive to ordinary people. Julian wanted to turn pagan temples into equivalents of Christian charitable institutions. It was a measure of how thoroughly Christianity had unsettled the Roman worldview. But Julian's last-gasp throw failed. Within decades Greek and Roman euergetism was dead – and was replaced with a system of almsgiving organized by the Christian Church. But Christianity had inherited that idea from another culture altogether.

THE JEWS – GIVING IN IMITATION OF GOD

Long before Socrates was born, a significant development had taken place among a people who lived, 40 days' journey away, a thousand miles to the south-east of Athens. Towards the end of the Iron Age, ten centuries before Christ, in a land that is now Israel, one of the local groups of Canaanite religions underwent a gradual shift from worshipping many gods to believing only in one. They traced this insight back to Abraham, a man who had been called by this one God to travel from the East to the land of Canaan, an undistinguished terrain which was then little more than a buffer zone between Egypt and the great powers to the East. God promised to make it Abraham's own, and that of his descendants, so the story was told. From that, Abraham became the father of the three great Abrahamic faiths – Judaism, Christianity and Islam. Whether Abraham was an historical or a mythical figure is unclear, but what is certain is that, in the millennium before the heyday of classical Greece, an important shift took place elsewhere – from worshipping many gods to just one God. Monotheism was to have a profound impact upon the history of philanthropy.

The descendants of Abraham were initially a religious and ethnic group rather than part of an organized state. Archaeologists suggest that they became differentiated from the Canaanites around them through cultural practices which included a prohibition on intermarriage and a sense of religious distinctiveness. Their story was that they were taken into slavery in Egypt, and were then led to freedom by Moses, and after 40 years of wandering in the desert they arrived in the Promised Land. The narrative of the Exodus became the foundation of the Jewish faith and left it with a unique legacy.

Judaism saw this one God as the epitome of generosity. Not only had he given the Israelites the Promised Land but he had rescued them from slavery beforehand. They arrived in Israel, and were sheltered there by God, with the specific status of refugees: 'for the land is mine; for you are strangers and sojourners with me'.[26] Israel from the outset defined itself as a foundling nation and developed a self-understanding of itself as 'an orphan, a slave, whom the Lord rescued from Egypt'.[27] Its people felt themselves called to a special duty to imitate God by, in their own turn, rescuing and protecting the weak. 'Love the stranger therefore', said one of the first books of the Hebrew Bible, 'for you were strangers in the land of Egypt.'[28] The stranger, the widow, and the orphan are singled out as being deserving of charity. And the poor are particularly identified as favoured by God.[29] Yahweh is spoken of as the God of the Poor, a phrase never applied to any Greek or Roman god. A radical democratization took place when, in the Book of Genesis, the image of God was transferred from the sacred king found in many Mesopotamian societies to Adam and Eve and thereby to every human being. It is in this worldview that the foundation for Jewish charity lies. In giving alms to the needy, the donor imitates God. That means giving more than food or money; the donor is required also to share his or her compassion and empathy. This is far beyond the understanding in the Graeco-Roman world of the few thinkers, such as the Stoics or Musonius, who expressed sympathetic feelings towards the poor.

Yet the God of the Torah, the Hebrew Bible, is more than the epitome of generosity. He is a God of justice and righteous judgement who warns:

You shall not wrong or oppress the stranger, for you were strangers in the land of Egypt. You shall not abuse any widow or orphan. If you do abuse them, when they cry out to me, I will surely heed their cry; my wrath will burn, and I will kill you with the sword, and your wives shall become widows and your children orphans.[30]

So among the ancient Israelites, those who help the poor are promised divine reward – and those who do not will incur a divine reckoning.

There is another major difference from Graeco-Roman philanthropy here. It is essential to the Jewish understanding that men and women are social creatures, so that the relationship between God and Israel is a relationship with a whole people. In the very first book of the Torah, God says: 'It is not good that man should be alone.'[31] The Hebrew Bible is the history of a people, in its social relations. The Covenant that God made was with Israel, not with individual Israelites. Where Graeco-Roman philanthropy was about society, Jewish philanthropy is about community. Social harmony is an essential, which is why the Jewish word for peace, *shalom*, goes beyond an absence of conflict and encompasses health, well-being, prosperity, harmony and justice. Judaism sets out to create a community in which the fortunate and the less fortunate can live in harmony together.

PHILANTHROPY AND THE JUST SOCIETY

An awareness of justice, the anthropologist Marcel Mauss has suggested, is what transforms gift-giving into a concern for the poor. When a society comes upon this realization, he writes, 'the gods and the spirits accept that the share of wealth and happiness that has been offered to them, and had been hitherto destroyed in useless sacrifices, should serve the poor and children'. This, he observes, 'is the moral history of the Semites'.[32] The ancient practice of making an offering to God by burning a gift as a sacrifice was a common practice among the early Israelites. In the Book of Leviticus, Moses sacrifices a ram upon an altar: 'It was a burnt offering with a pleasing aroma, a food offering for the Lord, as the Lord commanded Moses.'[33] So it is significant that the word which the Torah came to use for giving to the poor and needy was *tzedakah* – a word that was also used to talk of righteousness, fairness or justice. Moshe Weinfeld, sometime Professor of Bible at the Hebrew University of Jerusalem, has shown that *tzedakah* carries the meaning of charity in many places in the Bible, especially the Prophets, Psalms and Wisdom Books.[34]

In Judaism, giving to the poor is therefore not viewed as an act of generosity or charity but rather as one of justice. If God is the creator of the world then everything in the material world belongs to God: 'The earth is the Lord's and all that it holds, the world and all its inhabitants.'[35] So gifts to the poor constitute their due from heaven. To provide alms is a requirement and a duty, a *mitzvah*; it is merely giving to the poor that which is rightly due to them. It is not a matter of charity but of economic and social justice. For the Greeks and Romans, *philanthrôpía* was always a voluntary activity among the elite; by contrast, *tzedakah* is a religious obligation which falls, proportionally, on both the rich and those with smaller incomes. It is the duty of individuals but, just as importantly, it is the collective responsibility of the people as a community. This has a number of implications. If the poor are to be assisted they must also be viewed with compassion, and certainly never oppressed. Almsgiving is not just an entitlement for the recipient, it is also a duty for the giver. It must be done with joy and without resentment or rebuke to the beggar. The donor benefits from the gift as much as the recipient, indeed perhaps more; the poor receive material assistance, but the donor receives the merit of sharing in the work of the Almighty. Philanthropy becomes rooted in Jewish DNA; conversely, misanthropy, meanness and even indifference becomes an implicit rejection of God.

So much here was different from the Graeco-Roman worldview. Jewish culture singularly conceived of charity as religious obligation. It was characterized, in Derek Penslar's words, 'by exceeding compassion, generosity of spirit and communal solidarity'.[36] It manifested a respect for the dignity of the poor person. And it did not merely concern itself with addressing the symptoms of poverty but tried to address its causes. It did this by creating mechanisms to thwart institutional pauperization and foster the economic independence of the poor. Judaism understood that poor people often had to borrow when they were struck by illness, crop failure or other disaster. In anticipation of this its religious laws demanded not only that the poor should be allowed to glean the fields after harvest each year but that farmers should leave the crops in the corners of their fields – at least one-sixtieth of the harvest – to enable the poor to gather enough to survive.[37] Fields were to be left fallow every seven years and the poor were to be allowed to gather whatever grew wild there.[38] The private ownership of property was clearly sanctioned,[39] but the owner was a trustee who must use his possessions for the general good as well as personal satisfaction.

But the books of Moses went far further. In a basic agricultural community land was the basis of all economic relationships. Land was capital. To deprive someone of their land was to rob them of their status within the community and break faith with the Covenant under which God had delivered the people of Israel from slavery in Egypt. So the Mosaic injunctions insisted land could only be sold for a fixed price and not according to supply and demand.[40] An Israelite who sold his land might eventually be forced to sell himself into slavery, but his servitude had to end after seven years.[41] When a slave was freed he had to be given an endowment to help him set up on his own.[42] All debts were to be cancelled every seven years.[43] It was sinful to refuse to lend to a poor man simply because the sabbatical year was near when all debts must be wiped away.[44] A tax was to be paid every three years to relieve the destitute.[45] It was forbidden to take interest on any loan to a fellow Israelite.[46] And if a pledge, such as a man's cloak or millstone, was taken, it had to be returned when needed.[47] Loans must be given in a way which respects the dignity and integrity of both borrower and lender. In total these measures represented a mechanism for restoring any social imbalance which threatened to disenfranchise members of the community by robbing them of the basic element of their membership of the people of God. Poverty was not simply a lack of food and clothing. It had become a spiritual and psychological dispossession, as shown by the fact that 'the poor' is rendered variously in Hebrew in 36 biblical passages as 'those who lack', in 31 as 'those who are dispossessed', in 57 as 'those who are frail', in 61 as 'those in need' and in 80 as 'those who are oppressed'.[48] Deuteronomy even goes so far as to assert: 'There need be no poor people among you, for in the land that the Lord your God is giving you to possess as your inheritance, he will richly bless you.'[49]

That said, the poor were expected to work for their living: they had to glean from the fields, not simply receive a handout; they had to sell themselves as bondsmen to the rich to pay their debts. The law seeks to fulfil the needs of the poor person, not to bestow riches upon them. But a mechanism was established which placed limits on their enslavement. It ensured justice for the poor, rather than leaving them to the mercy of the charitable impulses of the rich, and ensured that they could never become trapped in a permanent cycle of deprivation. It placed social justice and cohesion above the ability to maximize profit.

Historians are divided on the extent to which these religious injunctions were carried out in practice. These first laws laid down in the Book of Exodus and in the Holiness Code of Leviticus and Deuteronomy are thought to have been written during the first centuries of settlement. Archaeological evidence suggests that in the early centuries they were put into in effect. The ruins at Tirzah seem to bear this out. There, according to Roland de Vaux:

> The houses of the tenth century BC are all of the same size and arrangement. Each represents the dwelling of a family which lived in the same way as its neighbours. The contrast is striking when we pass to the eighth-century houses on the same site. The rich houses are bigger and better built and in a different quarter from that where the poor houses are huddled together. Between these two centuries a social revolution had taken place.[50]

Certainly it is clear that later in the history of ancient Israel many of these Mosaic injunctions were honoured more in the breach than the observance. As the economy urbanized under the rule of Israelite kings in the ninth century BC, a small group of aristocrats and plutocratic landowners began to enrich themselves even as the rest of the population were impoverished. In the eighth and seventh centuries BC a succession of prophets warned that God would surely bring his judgement upon the rich.[51] Early in the fifth century BC groups of Israelites were complaining to the Jewish leader Nehemiah about their own rich relatives. One group complained that they had been forced to pledge their children to obtain cereals. Others had had to pledge fields, vineyards and houses. Others had been forced into bankruptcy and slavery by steep debt repayments.[52] The writers of the Psalms echoed this in lamentations which self-identified with the poor and destitute.[53] In the Second Temple period, some 500 years before the birth of Christ, the notion of 'the pious poor and the wicked rich' was articulated in some apocryphal writings.[54]

Yet however faulty the application of these commandments, in practice the principles towered – both symbolically and aspirationally – over the nation of Israel and its teachers. As the economy of the Near

East changed, and an agrarian society became an urban one dominated by crafts and commerce, new forms of assistance came to the fore. Rabbis recast *tzedakah* into monetary terms. Synagogues created spaces in which alms could be deposited discreetly, with donors leaving gifts in one room and beneficiaries collecting them from another to remove any potential shame from the transaction. In addition to private voluntary charity, public funds were set up. Mark Cohen sets out how public means of collecting gifts for the poor, distributing food and clothing, and providing shelter, were articulated in the various codes of law compiled from the Jewish oral traditions of the first and second centuries AD.[55] The contemporary equivalents of food banks and soup kitchens were developed. The *tamhui* was a daily distribution of food for the wayfarer. The *quppa*, or literally 'basket', was a weekly dole of bread or cash for the local poor. Of the 613 commandments in the Torah, the Jerusalem Talmud says, there is no greater *mitzvah* in Judaism than giving to others.

Rabbis, teachers and Jewish thinkers began to reflect philosophically on the nature of their religious giving. They asked questions such as: How should the poor be defined? How should we discriminate between the deserving and the undeserving poor? How should individuals and the community apportion their giving between family, needy neighbours and poor strangers? There was almost universal agreement that poverty is always a misfortune; Judaism, unlike some forms of Christianity and Sufi Islam, does not embrace the idea of voluntary poverty as a form of piety. But giving to the poor, and to poor fellow Jews in particular, was universally regarded as a virtuous constituent part of membership of the people of Israel.

Then, sometime around the second century AD, the notion of redemptive almsgiving – the idea that God wipes away your sins if you give to the poor – enters into Jewish thinking. The scholar Roman Garrison details the texts in The Book of Wisdom, the Prophets and Psalms that make God's blessing dependent on kindness to the poor,[56] and also cites Rabbis Ishmael, Akiba, Eleazar and Meir as proponents of the doctrine.[57] This is significant in the history of philanthropy for it shows that redemptive almsgiving was not some medieval Catholic corruption, as Protestant reformers were to claim after the Reformation – leading to the development of a skewed relationship between donor and recipient in Anglo-Saxon philanthropy thereafter,

as we shall see in later chapters. We will look at further developments in
Jewish thinking on philanthropy during the Middle Ages in Chapter 3.
But before that we must consider how Jewish philanthropy impacted
on two other religious communities, the Muslims and, in Chapter 2, on
the followers of a humble Galilean carpenter who declared that he had
not come to abolish Jewish law but to fulfil it.[58]

ISLAM – PHILANTHROPY AS SOCIAL SOLIDARITY

Sometime around the year 570 a boy was born into a family of desert
merchants in Mecca on the Arabian peninsula. Muhammad's father
died six months before he was born. When he was aged six his mother
died too, leaving him an orphan. The boy passed into the care of his
grandfather, but only two years later the old man also died. So, at the age
of eight, Muhammad became the responsibility of his uncle, Abu Talib,
the head of the Hashim clan. But in sixth-century Arabia, according
to the Islamic historian William Montgomery Watt, weaker members
of the tribe were not accorded priority: 'Muhammad's guardians saw
that he did not starve to death, but it was hard for them to do more
for him, especially as the fortunes of the clan of Hashim seem to have
been declining at that time.'[59] Given the deprivation which the Prophet
Muhammad knew in his own childhood, it is perhaps unsurprising
that the care of widows and orphans should be so prominent in the
revelation of Islam that Muslims believe God gave to him later in life.
'Do not treat the orphan harshly, do not rebuff the beggar'[60] is one of
the Qur'an's constant exhortations.

Muhammad was born into a pre-Islamic Arab culture which valued
generosity and hospitality as part of a code of desert chivalry. Surplus
wealth was not traded, spent or given away in pursuit of power,
according to the historian Michael Bonner.[61] When a man made a gift
to someone, a relationship – as patron, client or ally – was established
or consolidated. But Islam goes further. It puts the poor and needy at
the heart of its economic universe; Muslims, both rich and poor, are
expected to feed the hungry, free captives and debtors, and give shelter
to the orphan and the widow. It is a duty of Muslims to make sure that
no one goes hungry in their community.

Philanthropy is a central tenet of Islam. Compulsory almsgiving,
known as *zakat*, is one of the five defining articles of the religion

along with the declaration of faith; prayer; fasting throughout the holy
month of Ramadan; and the once-in-a-lifetime pilgrimage to Mecca.
Repeatedly in the Qur'an, prayer and almsgiving are linked; *zakat*
is mentioned as mandatory on 32 occasions, and on 27 of these it is
linked to prayer. Islam is thus a religion that requires its adherents to
believe and act in equal parts. Four of the five pillars can be fulfilled
by the act of one individual, but the fifth, *zakat*, is possible only as
part of a community. So much so, that the first wars conducted in
the name of Islam, shortly after the Prophet's death, were not against
unbelievers but against tribes who refuse to pay *zakat*. Philanthropy
was seen as essential to the identity of the Islamic community from the
outset. As Muslim conquest spread Islam across the Middle East, North
Africa and Central Asia, a theological economy was established which
placed the poor at its heart. There was more to this than theory, noted
the English lexicographer E. W. Lane who was a long-term resident in
Cairo during the nineteenth century: 'Benevolence and charity to the
poor are virtues which the Egyptians possess to an eminent degree, and
which are instilled into their hearts by religion.'[62]

The Arabic root of *zakat* offers an interesting insight into Islamic
almsgiving. *Zakat* is due annually on any assets that grow in value. It
was traditionally calculated on five sources of wealth: herds of animals,
agricultural crops, gold and silver, mines, and merchandise. But as
Muslims moved from agricultural trade into urbanized economies it
became computed as a percentage, 2.5 per cent being the traditional
figure. The word *zakat* carries associations of both purification and
growth. The idea is that giving away part of your income cleanses the
remainder, so that the owner can enjoy it with divine blessing. The
giver's heart is purified as well as his remaining wealth.

The other meaning of *zakat*, growth, offers the suggestion that
the benefactor's generosity will be multiplied many times over by
God in the afterlife:[63] those who give alms will find the sum doubled
by Allah 'and theirs will be a rich reward'.[64] By contrast those who
do not pay, the Qur'an says, are condemned to hideous sufferings
on the Day of Judgement. *Zakat* is obligatory; it is therefore not a
gesture of altruism but submission to a divine commandment. It is,
in the words of Amy Singer, 'first and foremost a sign of belief in and
obedience to God, and not an expression of beneficence toward other
people'.[65] *Zakat* has been, in the words of Natalie Zemon Davis, 'an

essential marker of Islam over the centuries'.[66] So much so that many
Muslims who do not practise their faith throughout the year, or fast
during Ramadan, nonetheless make some kind of charitable donation
during that holy month. But Islam also has a category of voluntary
charity known as *sadaqa*, which Singer reckons historically surpasses
zakat in volume and frequency of payments. We shall return to this
in Chapter 3.

Philanthropy is part of the glue which holds Muslims and the Islamic
community together. Muslims are linked to each other through their
obligations to God. So an act of *zakat* or *sadaqa* strengthens the bonds
of gratitude and subservience which reinforce Muslim identity and
deepen the sense of the solidarity of the global Muslim community,
the *umma*. Where gift-giving was about society for the Greeks and
Romans, for the Muslims, as with the Jews, it is about community.
Integral to Islam is the impact it has on human obligations and
entitlements. Social justice is at the heart of Islamic philanthropy. The
Qur'an claims that the poor have a right, *haqq*, to share in society's
prosperity.[67] The word *haqq* conveys the sense that this right is not
merely a justifiable claim by the poor; it is also a duty on the rich. So
both the donor and the recipient have a responsibility here. Moreover,
the Qur'an and the *hadith* (the authoritative collections which record
the sayings of the Prophet) specifically insist that wealth must be
circulated among the community: 'God has laid the obligation of
alms on their possessions, to be taken from the rich among them and
returned to the poor.'[68] Surplus wealth must be kept moving to create
a virtuous circle: alms pass down the social ladder from rich to poor,
and as the poor get richer they in turn give alms in a repeated cycle
of exchange. Michael Bonner goes so far as to assert: 'The Qur'an
provides a blueprint for a new order in society, in which the poor will
be treated more fairly than before.'[69]

But this blueprint does not concern itself only with actions.
Intentions are as important as acts in Islam. The Qur'an makes clear that
God distinguishes between those who merely go through the motions
and those who act with sincerity. Without the right intention, *niyya*,
no benefit will accrue to the giver from his or her philanthropy. By
contrast, if the intention is authentic, the size of the gift is immaterial:
a small amount of food taken to a poor or sick neighbour, a coin
dropped into the hand of a beggar, assisting a man with his beast or

his baggage, removing stones or thorns from someone's path – the smallest act counts as charity so long as it is performed with the right intent. Even food from a sacrificed animal should be shared with the poor, a practice continued by many Muslims today. One *hadith* quotes the Prophet as saying that even half a date or a kind word may guard against hellfire.[70]

In different times and different cultures *zakat* and *sadaqa* have taken many different forms. Charity is commonly exercised on Fridays, the day of communal Muslim prayer – so much so that, in all places and eras, beggars would gather at the entrances to mosques anticipating the generosity of the observant. Holy days in the Muslim calendar are punctuated by charitable giving. So are rites of passage, such as birth, circumcision, marriage and death. Seven days after the birth of a child, an animal might be slaughtered and its meat shared with the poor in a sacrifice known as *aquiqa*. The newborn baby's head might be shaved and the hair weighed, and then the same weight in gold or silver be distributed among the needy. In Afghanistan the safe delivery of a child might be celebrated by cooking *halwa* at the shrine of a saint and then sharing the sweet with the beggars there. The English lexicographer E. W. Lane noted how, in Cairo in the nineteenth century, children went begging from door to door during one of the four holy months, Muharr. They pleaded for 'A couple of grains of wheat! A couple of grains of rice!' and at every house would be given a small coin. Lane also records how the funeral procession of a rich man 'is sometimes preceded by three or four or more camels, bearing bread and water to give to the poor at the tomb . . . A buffalo, to be sacrificed at the tomb, where its flesh is distributed to the poor, sometimes closes the procession.'[71] The custom was called the Expiation, *el-kaffárah*, and was supposed to wipe away some of the minor sins of the deceased on the Day of Judgement – 'but not great sins'. This is a clear example of how Islam too embraced the notion of redemptive almsgiving.

In some eras *zakat* was specifically tied to the status of the giver in a very public manner. In sixteenth-century Istanbul some Ottoman sultans would distribute *zakat* ceremonially to their ministers, army officers, scholars and other clients, as well as to the poor – but each would receive a different amount of money or kind of food according to their social rank. The grander folk would eat first and in private rooms, whereas the poor would eat in communal refectories.[72] In the early twentieth century the Aga Khan, Sir Sultan Mahomed Shah, was weighed in jubilee years of his reign against gold, diamonds and platinum contributed by members of the Ismaili community from around the world. Photographs of his Diamond Jubilee show him sitting in an armchair on a huge set of scales watching cases of diamonds being placed on the opposite balance. The fortune collected each time was donated to support an array of social and cultural services organized within the community itself for needy people around the world. Today the philosophic traditions of the Ismaili community take a more modern form; the present Aga Khan discontinued the weighing ceremony and instead set up the Aga Khan Development Network, a private fund supporting health, culture, rural and economic development through a broad variety of international programmes 'to realize the social conscience of Islam through institutional action'.[73]. Practices varied according to the historical period, the geographical location, and other factors such as class, gender, education and the environment. Doctrinal differences emerged between Sunni and Shia Muslims, but philanthropy was integral to both Muslim traditions. As the centuries passed, theologians and jurists elaborated rules for the finer points of Islamic practice. Among their rulings was one that charity was an acceptable compensation for other Islamic failings, such as not completing some part of the ritual surrounding the pilgrimage to Mecca, or as a legitimate substitute for fasting at Ramadan for those who are ill or pregnant. The significance of philanthropy was not merely sustained by such developments; it grew in importance. In the words of Muhammad, recorded in one hadith,[74] 'We prophets leave no heirs; we leave only alms behind us.'

As with Judaism – and Christianity – much personal philanthropy in Islam goes unrecorded. Muslims particularly favour direct or person-to-person charity over institutional giving. An anthropologist in Morocco recounts one family discreetly 'adopting' a neighbouring widow and her children as the recipients for their *zakat*. A baker named Abu Illya noticed, after the death of his neighbour, that the widow next door, Lalla Fatiha, was struggling to get by. Her children's clothes grew shabbier. She did not buy them books for school. But the crunch came when she could not afford to buy a sheep to sacrifice during the holy month in which Muslims celebrate the pilgrimage to Mecca. The baker delivered a small sheep to her door. After that, each week he left a sack of flour outside her door on his way home from the bakery. When her children's school fees were due, an envelope was delivered to the door containing money. The baker's sister began tutoring the widow's daughter in maths and the baker's son helped her other children with English. When her daughter became ill, the local pharmacist told the widow that her bills were being paid by Abu Illya. Occasionally Lalla Fatiha would protest at the baker's generosity, only to be told: 'This is only temporary. When your son finishes [school] he can be responsible for you. But if he doesn't get an education now how can he support you?' The baker told the anthropologist: 'This isn't charity. This is *zakat*. Our honour is to offer it and her honour is to use it. All is provided by God, not by us. This time we have sufficient for our needs; later it may be Lalla Fatiha's turn to provide for us when her children are educated and work as doctors and engineers . . . Lala Fatiha helps us be better Muslims . . . Isn't this the way Islam is to be lived?'[75]

But charitable institutions also became important. Islam is responsible for the invention of the *waqf*, a trust which can be endowed by individuals or families as a perpetual charitable foundation. These *waqfs* were used to fund the establishment of mosques, hospitals, schools and other public services. The building of mosques has been a principal form of Islamic philanthropy from soon after the Prophet's death. So has the building of hospitals – a word which was used in its early days to mean a hostel for pilgrims and travellers, rather than in its modern meaning as a place for the treatment of disease. Muslims used the word *caravanserai* for this kind of accommodation for wayfarers. Less than a century after Muhammad, the Caliph Umar is reported to have said: 'Establish inns in your lands, so that whenever a Muslim passes by, you will put him up for a day or night and take out of his animals; if he is sick, providing with hospitals for two days and two nights; and if he has used up all of his provisions, and is unable to continue, supply him with whatever he needs to reach his home town.'[76] The hospital was one of the first examples of inter-faith co-operation. Around AD 700 the Christian community in Damascus aided the local Islamic community in the construction of a hospital, probably the first prominent Islamic hospital. By the twelfth century a hospital was an essential feature of any large Islamic town and these appear to have been far superior to their Christian equivalents at the time, as they included separate areas for men and women, wards for different ailments, and even the creation of psychiatric units.[77]

CHILDREN OF ABRAHAM

The overlap between the Jewish and Muslim faiths is more than merely practical; the theological worldview of Islam has much in common with that of Judaism. Like the Hebrew Bible, the Qur'an stresses that all wealth comes from God and ultimately belongs to God. God is the epitome of generosity. *Karim*, which means 'the generous one', is one of Islam's 99 names for God. Generosity therefore consists in emulating God, using what has been given by God. The Arabic word *sadaqa* derives from the same Aramaic linguistic root as the Hebrew *tzedakah*, and both embrace notions of right, privilege, grant and gift. In Arabic additionally, *sadaqa* has connotations of 'being sincere', 'speaking the truth' and 'fulfilling one's promise'; these echo the Jewish associations of *tzedakah* with righteousness, fairness and justice. The two faiths hold in common a basic set of assumptions about wealth and poverty which, as will become clear in the next chapter, are also shared by Christianity, the third religion that traces its origins back Abraham. Many of the questions the three faiths first raised more than a thousand years ago are questions we are still asking today: What should we give, how and to whom? How should we prioritize? What is the healthiest relationship between donor and recipient? Abrahamic attitudes to the relationship between the rich and the poor went on to shape the history of philanthropy over the next millennium and longer. As we shall see, even in our increasingly secularized age, they continue to shape our thinking now in the twenty-first century.

Interview: Jonathan Sacks on Jewish philanthropy

Jonathan Sacks is an Orthodox rabbi, a theologian and philosopher. In addition to serving as the Chief Rabbi of Britain and the Commonwealth for more than two decades, Lord Sacks is a distinguished academic who has written widely on the ethical dimensions of modern politics and economics. He won the Templeton Prize in 2016 for his work affirming life's spiritual dimension.

What has been the distinctively Jewish contribution to philanthropy?

The Hebrew word *tzedakah* is untranslatable because it means both charity and justice. Those two words repel one another in English because if I give you £100 because I owe you £100, that's justice. But if I give you £100 because I think you need £100, that's charity. It's either one or the other, but not both. Whereas in Hebrew, *tzedakah* means both justice and charity. There's no word for just charity in Hebrew. Giving is something you have to do; it's not something you want to do. Somebody who is entirely dependent on charity must still be given enough so that he or she can, in turn, give to charity.

That's a very interesting idea. During the miners' strike in Britain in the 1980s I saw miners gathered in a Yorkshire pit village to receive food parcels which had been sent from other parts of the country. As they got together, the first thing they did was to have a collection for Ethiopia, which was undergoing a terrible famine.

That's beautiful. To receive and not to give is considered humiliating in Judaism. Jewish law is as much concerned with the psychology of philanthropy as with the material benefits of it. Philanthropy must be exercised so as not to make the giver arrogant, or the recipient feel ashamed.

There's a clear concept in the Bible on the alleviation of poverty. It's part of the basic structure of Mosaic Law. In an agricultural economy, we leave the corner of the field for the poor. You see this in the Book of Ruth where she and her mother-in-law come back after their men have

died and they're penniless. Ruth goes to gather corn from the corner of
the field. In Judaism, nobody should be left in abject poverty, especially
the widow and the orphan who had no families to look after them. At
festivals you're expected to include in your celebrations anyone who
doesn't have a family of their own, the orphan, the widow, the stranger
in your gates and so on. It became a communal responsibility. It's not
a fully egalitarian society, but it's a society where everyone has equal
access to dignity. That has a fundamental economic dimension.

**That is in contrast to the rest of the ancient world. To the Greeks
and the Romans philanthropy was about honour and status. Why
was Judaism so different?**

It's because – and we often miss a sense of how revolutionary this
was – in the opening chapter of the Hebrew Bible it is made clear that
every human being is created in the image and likeness of God. That's
an incendiary remark in a culture where only the Pharaoh was seen as
a god: Ramses means child of the sun god. Only emperors and other
rulers were thought to be made in the image of God. Then Judaism
suddenly comes along and says 'Everyone is in the image of God.' That
is revolutionary and it ultimately leads to a profoundly anti-hierarchical
understanding of society.

Since no economic distribution is ever perfect – market economics
is very good at creating wealth, not very good at distributing it – there
has to be a moral bond between the people who have more than they
need and the people who have less than they need. This is a very anti-
hierarchical thing which is the opposite of an honour society. Honour is
all about your positioning in the hierarchy.

**The anthropologist Marcel Mauss says that there came a point
in history where people stopped offering sacrifices to God, burnt
offerings and so forth, and instead made their offerings to God in
the form of gifts to the poor. How did that come about in Judaism?**

In the year 70, under the Emperor Titus, the Romans destroyed the Second
Temple. That meant no more priests, no more temple, no more sacrifices.
Now, sacrifices occupy pretty much a large part of the Book of Leviticus
which is the central book of the five Mosaic Books. It's book number three,
and Hebrew prose style always gets the climax in the middle, not at the
end. So you have to ask how in the year 70 this whole structure – on which
Judaism had been predicated for at least 1,000 years – comes to an end.

In fact, Judaism didn't miss a beat. It found three major substitutes for sacrifice. Number one, in the spiritual sense, was prayer. Number two was charity. And number three was hospitality – when you invited the stranger into your house he or she had a meal at your table, and in Hebrew the words for 'altar' and 'table' are very similar. The Rabbis said that when the altar was destroyed, the table became the altar. So you had these very radical substitutions.

This was around the time when society was shifting from life in the countryside to the town?

Yes. A lot was happening at roughly the same time. After about 1,500 years Jewish society shifted from a more agrarian focus to become more urban. The whole charity/philanthropy system moved from crops to money. It was a period of intense change. Christianity emerged from it. People were highly religious and spiritual, keenly aware that a certain era was ending and a new one was beginning.

So it was partly economic as well as spiritual?

The two were bound together. When you have highly destabilizing times that involve a lot of poverty, then the need for charity becomes more prominent. In the case of Jews, however, it remained exceptionally prominent for another reason as well, which was the sheer geographic insecurity of being Jewish. You never knew when a community would have to leave and travel elsewhere. If it did, it would try to travel to where there was already at least some small Jewish community. That meant that the established community had to establish provisions for an influx of a lot of immigrants.

One of the distinctive developments in the history of philanthropy comes with the medieval rabbi Maimonides. He came up with the idea that there should be a particular hierarchy of giving*.

Maimonides was the greatest Jewish thinker in the Middle Ages. He was also the most original legal codifier. He took a lot of inchoate material and gave it structure. Regarding the idea of a hierarchy of giving, very little of what he says is completely original to him. He's quoting Talmudic sources, early rabbinic sources. But he put it in a

---

* see pages 94–97 below

ladder with eight ranks. Nobody had thought of doing that before. This hierarchy is essentially psychological because when you're nearing the top, you're getting to a point where the recipient doesn't know who gave to him – and the giver doesn't know who received what he gave. So there can be no arrogance on the one hand, or shame on the other. Then, finally, at the top of the ladder, you get to this extraordinary idea that the greatest charity of all is to make somebody not need further charity because you give them a job or help them to start a business.

Is that part of the consciousness of Jewish thinking today?

Absolutely central. Even if people didn't know about Maimonides's eight stages, his ideas have been internalized by everyone. Philanthropic giving – both financial and through voluntary contributions – is an integral element of our community and one that has been recognized by those outside our community as well.

When you look over the history of philanthropy it is striking how disproportionately generous the Jewish community seems to be. A survey in Britain in 2019 showed that 93 per cent of British Jews gave to charity compared with 57 per cent of the rest of the population. And religious Jews give more than secular Jews.* A very large percentage of those who have signed the billionaires' Giving Pledge, launched by Bill and Melinda Gates, are Jewish.

It's a long-standing phenomenon. It goes back many, many centuries. It comes partly from need. Jews had no one else to turn to. Jewish communities were oriented around helping your fellow Jews – and, then, to the extent that you were integrated into the wider society,

---

* In the *Sunday Times* Giving List in 2014 more than 12 per cent of the most charitable givers were Jewish, though Jews constitute less than half of one per cent of the UK population according to the last census. In the United States more than half of the first millionaires to sign the Giving Pledge were Jewish, according to the *Chronicle of Philanthropy*, with more than three-quarters of their donations going to non-Jewish causes. Sources: David Graham and Jonathan Boyd, *Charitable Giving among Britain's Jews*, Institute for Jewish Policy Research, 2019. Simon Rocker, 'Over 90 per cent of UK Jews give to charity, with Orthodox and over-60s most generous, report finds', *Jewish Chronicle*, 22 March 2019. Jacob Berkman, 'Jews take 5 of top 6 spots in annual list of top US givers', *Jerusalem Post*, 9 February 2011.

helping that society as well. But it is partly theological, because it grows from an understanding that we are blessed, that what we achieve is not purely by our own resources. God has entrusted us with our wealth and He expects us to do good with it. That is what makes us so thrilled when we meet someone like Melinda Gates, for instance, who has a very similar approach to giving.

So how do Jews strike a balance between giving to fellow Jews and their giving to the wider community?

It comes really from the letter that Jeremiah the Prophet sent 26 centuries ago to the Jews exiled in Babylon. In it he says, 'Seek the peace and welfare of the city to which God has sent you because in its peace and prosperity, you will find peace and prosperity.' He lays down this line: when Jews are in a minority in some other country, they have to make a contribution to its welfare. That's determined Jewish existence in the diaspora ever since. For 26 centuries this tiny community has always tried to give back.

Is there a rule of thumb on what proportion of giving you give to fellow Jews and how much to good causes in wider society?

No. In general, I think everyone understands one has to give to both.

What's the place of philanthropy in wider society? A century ago people thought the welfare state would replace philanthropy. We've come to realize that's not the case. Not just because the state can't pay for everything, especially at times of austerity. But also because, even if all the equipment in a hospital is paid for by the state, the government won't pay for clowns to go to the children's ward. How do you see the balance between the state, the community and the individual here?

I've always found that philanthropy is constitutive of the third space called civil society, the bit that isn't the economy and isn't the state. Philanthropy, by and large, establishes an I/thou relationship, a personal relationship. Government must, of its essence, be impartial, be impersonal.

Ever since the 1840s there has been an enormous proliferation of charities both in the United States and in Britain. Some are big, some small, but there is an enormous amount being done in society that is not being done on a market basis, and it is not being done by the government. The end result is strong civil society. And strong civil societies stay free societies.

In America, this tended to be led by religion. In Britain, it tended to be led by the Royal Family, who lent their name to a lot of charities. But Germany and France did not have that kind of civil society. They never valued this thing that was not the market and wasn't the state. Rousseau, Hegel and Marx had no time for it. To them everything that matters is to be done by government. But Britain and America had a tradition that said: 'No. There are certain things that matter very much indeed and they are not done by government. They are done by human interaction, largely at the local level.'

You can see why that would be the case in the United States. The original settlers went out in search of freedom. But why has it arisen in Britain, which has a rigid and hierarchical history? Is there something peculiarly Anglo-Saxon about it?

I think the British tended to want limited government. That emerged out of the 'Glorious Revolution' of 1688. Milton and Locke, both have this sense of limited government. I think deep down it's one of the better heritages of Puritanism. Puritans tend to read the Old Testament much more closely than anyone else. Catholics take their authority from the Church. Lutherans take their authority mainly from the Pauline Letters. But the Puritans recognized that if you look at Deuteronomy you will see the extraordinary phenomenon of a king without legislative powers. It didn't exist anywhere else. Everything about the king in the Hebrew Bible is limiting the power of the king. In Deuteronomy 17 it says: 'Let him not have many wives, many horses, or how much money. Let him not hold himself above his brothers.' He's the only person commanded to be humble in all of the Bible. This is limited constitutional monarchy.

This is saying politics is not the most important thing there is. The most important thing is loving your neighbour and helping the stranger. Community is more important, in that sense, than society, because community is society with a human face.

In Greece and Rome, the highest achievement was to serve the state. In the Hebrew Bible, nobody serves the state. That's why I find our current liberal democracy much more acceptable than the democracy of Athens, because in liberal democracy the state serves the individual, not the other way around.

So it comes out of monotheism – the idea that there is only one God that you serve?

It comes out of saying that God is not embodied in the king or the ruler. God is embodied in every one of us. And when every one of us opens ourselves up to another one of us, something of the divine presence is revealed. That is incredibly important. Robert Reich coined the phrase 'the secession of the successful'.* That's what's happening now in the States today. If you're wealthy, and if you want to, you can easily go off and spend your time with other very wealthy people. The essence of philanthropy, by contrast, is that people who've been very successful get involved, in hospitals, in schools, or working with inner-city children from abusive families. That's a very important thing that philanthropy does for the philanthropist. It gets them to honour their responsibility to society, which paying taxes, so that government can do it for you, does not do.

One of the big splits that's opened up in all the Western democracies is between the very rich and the very poor, and I do not see anything in contemporary society telling the very rich what their responsibilities are to the very poor – and they're not just to write a cheque.

That's why locating it in a religious value system makes a big difference. It's much more effective if you're accountable to God in the context of community. Research has shown that being part of a religious community encourages you to get more involved in social action.

It's very striking, even in secular Britain, how many individuals who do become philanthropists are motivated by religious faith. You hear so little about that because the British media is, by and large, not religious and indeed is embarrassed by religion.

That's a very standard factor in all the philanthropists I know. They are mainly driven by the idea of collective responsibility and human dignity. I don't think we're suffering any diminution of altruism. I think it's hard-wired into our achievements.

---

* Robert B. Reich is an American economist who served in the administrations of Presidents Gerald Ford, Jimmy Carter and Bill Clinton. He taught political economy at Harvard University. Robert B. Reich, 'Secession of the Successful', *New York Times* magazine, 20 January 1991. Not to be confused with Rob Reich, the philosopher, in Chapter 16.

Chapter 2

The Foundations of Western Philanthropy

Jesus was a Jew, so it is unsurprising that Christian attitudes to philanthropy owe much to the worldview established by the Jewish tradition over the millennium before Christ's birth. St Paul, who set the philosophical framework for Christianity, was also a Jew but he was, in addition, a Roman citizen who wrote in the Greek which was the lingua franca of the Eastern Mediterranean throughout the Hellenistic, Roman and Byzantine era. That was the world in which the early Christians grew from their first beginnings as a small sect. So it is unsurprising that elements of the Graeco-Roman philanthropic worldview were also amalgamated into Christian notions of almsgiving. The resulting approach to charity has dominated the history of philanthropy over the past 2,000 years, and in many ways continues to do so.

When the itinerant mystical preacher Jesus of Galilee first appeared on the scene, he was anxious to stress his essential continuity with the Judaic tradition in which he had been formed. He announced: 'Do not think that I have come to abolish the Law or the Prophets; I have not come to abolish them but to fulfil them.'[1] He told a story about a rich man, whom tradition came to name Dives, who neglected a poor man, Lazarus, who had lived for years outside his house. When Dives dies and is being punished in hell for his negligence, the rich man asks Abraham to send a messenger to Dives's brothers – to warn them not to make the same mistake. Jesus has Abraham reply: 'They have Moses and the Prophets; let them hear them.'[2] The heritage of Judaism will suffice, the preacher from Galilee insists.

Many of Jesus's themes hark back repeatedly to those of his forebears. 'Blessed are the poor,' he says repeatedly.[3] 'Give to everyone who begs

from you and do not refuse anyone who wants to borrow from you.'⁴
He announced the start of his ministry in the synagogue of his home
town, Nazareth, by reading from the scroll of the prophet Isaiah:

> The spirit of the Lord is upon me,
> for he has anointed me
> to bring the good news to the poor.
> he has sent me to proclaim liberty to captives,
> sight to the blind
> to let the oppressed go free,
> to proclaim a year of favour from the Lord.

> And he rolled up the scroll and gave it back to the attendant and sat
> down. And the eyes of all in the synagogue were fixed on him. And
> he began to say to them: 'Today this Scripture has been fulfilled in
> your hearing.'⁵

The Feeding of the Five Thousand reveals Jesus inherits the
understanding that those in need require practical as well as spiritual
assistance.⁶ His Parable of the Talents⁷ embraces the notion that wealth
brings with it the duty to use it for the benefit of others. Property is to
be held in stewardship for the good of all. It is not for the unrestrained
consumption of the owner. The rich are rebuked by Jesus, as they
were by the Hebrew prophets, not only for exploitation or malice
but for blindness to the needs of others.⁸ Hypocrisy is attacked.
Interestingly, Jesus's particular target were the Pharisees, a group of
religious radicals who in the century before Christ set out to employ
a meticulous application of the purity laws, extending to everyone
provisions which previously applied only to the priestly caste. Jesus
accused them of ignoring social justice while focusing fastidiously on
unimportant detail: 'Woe to you, Scribes and Pharisees, hypocrites!
For you tithe mint and dill and cumin, and have neglected the
weightier matters of the law: justice and mercy and faithfulness.'⁹ He
made such accusations repeatedly: 'Beware of the Scribes, who . . .
have the best seats in the synagogues and . . . who devour the houses
of widows.'¹⁰

Jesus goes further, explicitly articulating much of what was implicit
in Jewish philanthropic principles. He declares that he is bringing the

good news of which Isaiah spoke. In response to an enquiry from John the Baptist, Jesus specifies to whom his good news is brought: 'Go and tell John what you have seen and heard: the blind receive their sight, the lame walk, lepers are cleansed and the deaf hear, the dead are raised up and the poor have good news preached to them.'[11] The poor are the only social class singled out here as recipients of that good news, a notion which would have made no sense to the Greeks or the Romans. Jesus furthermore makes overt the Jewish tradition that those who give to the poor give to God: 'Truly, I say to you, as you did it to one of the least of these my brothers, you did it to me.'[12]

But Jesus also goes further than Jewish law requires. In his parable of the Good Samaritan, he suggests that philanthropic obligation extends beyond one's kinship or faith to those outside it.[13] Giving must transcend ethnocentric notions of racial superiority, caste privilege or self-interest. Jesus is also clear about his priorities when it comes to a clash between the letter and the spirit of the law. 'The Sabbath was made for man, not man for the Sabbath,' he replies when he is reprimanded for curing illness on the Jewish holy day. 'The Son of Man is lord of the Sabbath.'[14] And he repeatedly violates laws of ritual purity by associating with tax collectors, prostitutes, lepers, a haemorrhaging woman and others. There is a more fundamental truth. His disregard for Jewish ritual purity becomes unconcealed when he says: 'A man is not defiled by what enters his mouth, but by what comes out of it.'[15]

JESUS THE JEW — AND THE JESUS OF THE GOSPELS

At times Jesus offers counsels of perfection. He tells one rich young man (who claims to already keep all the commandments of the Jewish law) that 'if you would be perfect', he should sell everything he possesses and give the money to the poor which will provide him with 'treasure in heaven'. Jesus then tells the young man to 'come, follow me.'[16] The theologian Rudolf Bultmann has suggested that this passage is distinctively un-Jewish and tells us something significant about the historical Jesus. Other scholars have likened Jesus's attitude here to that of the contemporary Roman Stoic, Seneca, and even to that of the Greek Cynic Diogenes, who lived 400 years before the time of Christ.[17] The New Testament scholar Runar M. Thorsteinsson in a recent study, *Jesus as Philosopher: The Moral Sage in the Synoptic Gospels*, suggests that in the account of the life of Christ in the Gospels of Mark,

Matthew and Luke it is possible to see Graeco-Roman philosophical influences alongside the more obvious Jewish legacy.[18] The authors of those synoptic Gospels, he persuasively demonstrates, consciously drew on the ethics of classical virtue in their portrayals of Jesus.

The evangelist Mark is particularly interesting. He portrays Jesus, in some aspects, as a latter-day Socrates, 'the wise man *par excellence* who was the master of argumentation and debate'. Both men are teachers of ethics. Neither wrote down what they taught; our knowledge of them is filtered through others. Both match their deeds to their words. The Jesus of Mark's Gospel is ascetic: 'take nothing for the journey except a staff – no bread, no bag, no money'.[19] That comes close to what Diogenes wrote in a letter to his pupil, Crates: 'I hope that you brought all your property to the assembly, delivered over to your fatherland, and, standing in the midst of the people, cried out "Crates, son of Crates, sets Crates free". The family of Jesus want to restrain him from his roving ministry because they think he must be mad';[20] this also echoes Socrates who, in the *Phaedrus*, says a philosopher is inevitably 'rebuked by the vulgar, who consider him mad and do not know that he is inspired'.[21] The way Jesus debates with Jewish scholars – and clearly avoids the logical traps they lay for him – is reminiscent of the portrayal of Socrates in Plato's dialogues. The charges against Jesus, and the process of his trial, recall the charges against Socrates and the predetermined outcome of his trial too. Both represent 'the ideal innocent philosopher', says Thorsteinsson, who concludes that 'much like Jesus, Socrates made himself useful to others by dying voluntarily'.[22]

But, again, there are points of departure. The Gospel of Luke, and the Epistle of James, juxtapose Jesus's particular concern for the poor with a strong disapproval of the rich. In Luke, Jesus turns upside down traditional Graeco-Roman notions of reciprocity and patronage. He instructs a leading Pharisee: 'When you give a dinner or a banquet, do not invite your friends or your brothers or your relatives or rich neighbours, lest they also invite you in return and you be repaid. But when you give a feast, invite the poor, the crippled, the lame, the blind, and you will be blessed, because they cannot repay you. For you will be repaid at the resurrection of the just.'[23] Similarly, in the Gospel of Mark, though Jesus is an ascetic whose worldview is well aligned with the philosophical approach of the Stoics, he has a major point of divergence from them. Where, for the Stoics, material possessions are a matter of indifference, Jesus cares about what happens to them;

he wants the personal wealth of the rich shared with the poor. Here Jesus is an intriguing amalgam of the Graeco-Roman and the Judaic. Runar Thorsteinsson sees other points of hybridity. Mark's Jesus does not precisely fit the standard classical descriptions of the philosophical sage. Although he is presented as a person of great mental strength and authority, who knows no fear and acts like the ideal philosopher, he is also a man of great emotions. By turns he is angry, feels grief, is distressed and fearful. What Mark – and Matthew and Luke – are doing in the writing of the Gospels is drawing on Graeco-Roman traditions in addition to the mainstream influence of the Jewish tradition. Their aim, Thorsteinsson concludes, 'was to show that Jesus was not only on a par with the great philosophers, he was superior to them'.[24]

ST PAUL – JEWISH SENSIBILITY AND HELLENISTIC THINKING

The man the Church came to call St Paul made a revolutionary contribution, not just to Christianity, but to the history of the world. He was a clever philosophical thinker and a man of deep religious convictions who may well have been a Pharisee before his conversion on the road to Damascus. His sudden conviction that Jesus was not just the Son of God but God himself[25] had an inevitable corollary: if there was only one God, he could not be reserved for a particular people but must be for all peoples. Christianity could not be a reformed sect of Judaism but must be a religion for everyone, for Gentiles as well as Jews. It was the first real basis for a world religion.

But that extraordinary development set a false trail in the history of philanthropy. The received view – certainly in the Western circles which have dominated the writing of the history of the subject – is that philanthropy, like religion, at this point shifted focus from the particular to the universal. This is very neat, but it is wrong. Runar Thorsteinsson has shown, in his comparative study of Roman Stoicism and Roman Christianity,[26] that there were significant continuities between Hellenistic and Christian attitudes to philanthropy. He undoubtedly goes too far in his assertion that Stoicism was a universal philosophical creed whereas early Christianity was unashamedly sectarian in its focus. Intellectually, there may have been a universalism about Stoic theory, but in practice its application was limited by the prejudices of an aristocratic Roman elite which did not include plebeians and slaves in its fullest computations of what it meant to be human. And Paul – with his intuition that Christ must be for all people – planted the seeds of a revolution, though it only glacially came to embrace the implications of the Pauline insight that 'There is neither Jew nor Gentile, slave nor free, nor is there male and female, for you are all one in Christ Jesus.'[27] Many would wryly observe that institutional Christianity has still not fully come to terms with the depth of Paul's understanding.

The Epistles of St Paul are the earliest Christian writings, composed only 20 years after the death of Jesus, several decades before the Gospels were compiled. His approach is deeply embedded in the Judaic vision of a community which looks after the vulnerable as God looked after the Jewish people when they themselves were vulnerable. Paul famously summarizes Christ's teaching in the words 'faith, hope and love' and declares 'the greatest of these is love'.[28] This enables a radical social ethic which requires all Christian believers to become untiring philanthropists. Paul's letters are filled with injunctions to be generous to the poor and with warnings against greed[29] (though he also admonishes that 'anyone unwilling to work should not eat').[30] Among the first Christians, the obligation of love was demonstrated in acts of mercy and justice: the poor were fed, the sick were cared for, the dead were buried, prisoners were visited, captives were ransomed, and hospitality was extended to visiting missionaries and strangers.[31]

From early in the life of the Church, the holy day of the week was switched from the Jewish Sabbath to the day on which Jesus was believed to have been resurrected, Sunday.[32] The collection of money for the purposes of the Church on a Sunday began from very early in that period, according to the Dominican scholar Richard Finn,[33] who adds: 'In early Christian practice it was central to your Christian identity that you give to the poor'. According to the oldest extant Christian catechism, the first-century Didache, which is thought to have been written by the second generation of Christians, alms were given on two days of the week in a way which became an added marker of distinct Christian identity. The funds raised were spent on widows and orphans, people in prison, the sick and those who acted as ministers to the Christian faithful. In addition to this organized giving, there was an expectation that Christians would also give to beggars on the streets or who called at their homes.

Yet for all the universality of the Apostle Paul's theology, in practice the early Christians focused their concern for the poor primarily within their own community, as Judaism had done. The reason was as much practical as philosophical. Most of the early Christians were from the lower strata of the social hierarchy. The urban communities to which Paul wrote were predominantly what the Romans would have called plebeians – artisans, labourers, immigrants and slaves. Many of them, both in Roman Palestine and outside of it, would have lived near subsistence level. There was thus a significant overlap between 'the poor' and the Christian community. Charity began at home because that was often where it was most needed.

In the decades immediately following the Resurrection there were so few moderately wealthy members of Christian house churches that Paul felt it worth referring to them by name – Phoebe,[34] Gaius,[35] Philemon[36] and others who acted as funders for Christian communities. These comparatively wealthy Christians had to shake off the Roman system of patronage and become protectors to their poorer neighbours. Paul commanded them to be humble and not haughty, and put their hope in God rather than material wealth.[37] Attitudes to slavery must similarly be revised, Paul said. He tells one rich man, Philemon, that he is sending back to him a fugitive slave named Onesimus who has now converted to Christianity. But he tells Philemon to welcome Onesimus home not as a slave 'but . . . as a beloved brother . . . receive him as myself'.[38] (Onesimus, tradition has it, eventually became a bishop.) The apostle also stressed the need for a wider solidarity within the community, asking wealthier Christians all around the Mediterranean to send funds to the impoverished Christian mother community in Jerusalem. Such daughter communities, Paul said, had a duty to share their material wealth with those who had shared spiritual riches with them.[39] It was not just the rich, but all believers, who had the responsibility to contribute to the wider Christian community, which was 'one body in Christ' in which 'individually we are members one of another', Paul wrote in his Letter to the Romans.[40] Every member of the community had some gift to contribute which would make them a benefactor and a patron in their own way, regardless of their standing in Roman society. Members of the community were equal in God's sight.

The early assemblies of Christians mentioned in the continuation of Luke's Gospel known as the Acts of the Apostles, had a distinct philanthropic characteristic. 'All who believed were together and had all things in common,' Luke records. 'They would sell their possessions and goods and distribute the proceeds to all, as any had need.'[41] The community ate common meals and held their funds in a shared treasury, the common chest. As a result, Luke wrote, 'there was not a needy person among them, for as many as owned lands or houses sold them and brought the proceeds of what was sold. They laid it at the apostles' feet, and it was distributed to each as any had need.'[42]

Historians have argued over whether such passages describe a real or an idealized Christian community, but since the early Christians were seized with the conviction that the world would end with the return of Jesus within a generation,[43] it seems perfectly plausible that the normal human emotional attachment to material goods would have been strikingly lessened. The realization, as the years passed, that this prediction could not be taken literally probably brought with it the overthrow of this primitive communism, though Thomas Aquinas later argued that its abandonment had been brought about by human sin.[44] But what is clear, to quote Helen Rhee's study of wealth and poverty in early Christianity, is that salvation for early Christians was 'a corporate phenomenon in that it occurred within a community context and necessarily entailed social responsibility' as well as personal virtues.[45]

All this prompted a revolution in attitudes to the poor. In Jewish tradition the obligation to give to those in need was rooted in acting generously in emulation of God. But Christ had gone further by insisting that those who gave alms to the hungry, the thirsty, the naked, the stranger and those in prison were giving them to God himself: 'Truly I tell you, just as you did it to one of the least of these who are members of my family, you did it to me.'[46] The poor were not just made more visible; their status was transformed. The Romans had viewed them as a part of the social structure to be exploited and placated. The Jews had seen the poor as unfortunate fellows in need of assistance. Now Christians saw them as reflections of God's incarnation.

A seminal study by Evelyne Patlagean noted the contrasting language with which the Graeco-Romans and Judaeo-Christians spoke of the poor: the former convey a strong sense of the poor as placed within the hierarchy of the civic order, whereas the latter, using more scriptural language, speak of poor people in terms of their need.[47] More radically, now in the Christian era, in the words of Richard Finn, 'the poor become your friends'. From very early in the Christian era the idea that the poor person represented Christ was key. 'Moreover, building on verses in Luke's Gospel, they could pray for you to get you into heaven,' Finn adds. Judaism had not placed great emphasis on the afterlife or on eternal rewards and punishments. Fulfilling the law was an end in itself. But Christianity now saw charity not just as necessary to promote harmony and stabilize the social hierarchy. It also influences the afterlife. The poor were transformed from passive recipients to active agents who offered the possibility of spiritual growth to the rich. No figure was more transformed than that of the beggar. By recasting the beggar as a friend of Christ, giving to beggars was redefined as an honourable charitable practice.

This new parity between giver and receiver turned almsgiving back into a form of what Marcel Mauss had called gift-exchange. Rich donors traded material goods for the spiritual goods offered by the poor recipients, who, in turn, interceded with God on their benefactors' behalf. Passive recipients were transmuted, to quote Finn, into 'agents of redemption'.[48] This is an early manifestation of the theology of redemptive almsgiving – the idea that giving can expunge sin. This idea was to prove of immense significance in the history of philanthropy after the Reformation, shaping philanthropic practices for centuries, for good and ill. But for now what was key was that it created a two-way relationship between philanthropic donor and recipient. As with the Apostle Paul's insistence upon remodelling the relationship between the master Philemon and the slave Onesimus, so the language of friendship, family and fellowship was mapped onto the relationship between donor and recipient. The classical virtues of *philanthrôpía* and euergetism were being reshaped. The theory and practice of charity in Christian antiquity did more than shape the emergence of a distinctively Christian identity: they also transformed the social understanding of the poor.

THE ARRIVAL OF RICH CHRISTIANS

Attitudes to giving developed as the Christian community grew from a small 'Jesus movement' into a significant social force.[49] Over the second and third centuries the Christian Church saw significant growth, both inside Palestine and outside it. Its spread was uneven but significant in the urban centres of the Greek-speaking world in Syria, Egypt, Asia Minor and Greece, and among the Latin speakers of Italy and North Africa. Increasing numbers of the upper classes converted, especially in Alexandria and Rome. As members of the top decile of Roman society became Christians, old-style Hellenist pagans became increasingly unsettled by the phenomenon. The second-century Greek critic Celsus scornfully proclaimed that Christianity attracted only the uneducated, slaves, outcasts and women[50] – an assertion which may have been broadly true in the first decades of the Jesus movement but was no longer the case. By this time the Christian community was fairly representative of the make-up of society in the Roman Empire – with the vast majority in the lower social strata, a rising number from their wealthier artisan and merchant classes, and a growing minority from the aristocratic elite.[51] Among the converts were a number of high-status women. All this forced the Church Fathers to begin to address the issue of how rich and poor could live together while embracing the philosophy of Christ and Paul. Their solution was to cast wealth as something positive because it enabled giving.

One of the earliest texts to address this was a book which, in the early years of Christianity, was accorded a status alongside the Gospels. *The Shepherd of Hermas* was written sometime around AD 150. It records the series of visions, commandments and parables given by angels to Hermas, a Christian living in Rome in the first part of the second century.[52] The writer shows concern for both the poor and the rich. He lists the good works everyone must do to be saved: 'to minister to widows, to look after orphans and the destitute, to be hospitable'.[53] He allows that wealth has a value and purpose within the Christian community. It binds the rich and poor in a symbiotic relationship for which Hermas invokes the image of a barren elm tree around which is entwined a fruitful vine: only by working similarly together can the rich and poor support one another and build the common good. But the generosity of the rich does not simply benefit the overall interests of the Church community; it helps the rich towards salvation. Jesus had declared that it was easier for a camel to go through the eye of a needle than for a rich man to enter the kingdom of heaven.[54] This was because the distraction of riches makes the wealthy deficient in the things of God. The rich are prey to a spiritual complacency which can lead to a neglect of their social responsibilities. By contrast, the poor have in plenty the qualities which the wealthy lack. The rich can supply the material needs of the poor, but the poor can pray more effectively on behalf of the rich – for God more readily hears the intercessions of a poor man or woman. Only in this way, Hermas says, the rich man may enter the kingdom of heaven:

> The rich man has much wealth, but he is poor as touching the Lord, being busied about his riches, and his intercession and confession towards the Lord is very small . . . But when the rich man rests upon the poor, and gives him what he needs, he believes that what he does to the poor man can find a reward with God, because the poor man is rich in intercession and confession, and his intercession has great power with God . . .'[55]

Hospitality is what will earn the rich person a place 'with the Angels'.[56] Hermas also conjures a vision of a cosmic tower, which represents the Church. The rich are integral to the construction of the tower, but they are round stones who must first be transformed into square stones – and this must happen by 'cutting away' their wealth. It is not money and property that are evil but 'lack of sharing'. Riches therefore must not be eliminated entirely; some must be left 'so that they might be able to do some good with that which was left to them, and they will live to God'.[57] Those who swiftly seek out the hungry, and do good work with their wealth, may enter the kingdom of heaven. Hermas tells the wealthy, instead of buying land, to use 'unrighteous Mammon' to 'purchase afflicted souls'. They should do this by looking after widows and orphans: 'For this reason did the Master made you rich . . .'[58] Fasting, he suggests, is of little use unless the money saved is given to the poor.[59] Almsgiving, according to Hermas, is already a key element in Christian identity.

ALMSGIVING AND CHRISTIAN IDENTITY

The extent to which this approach quickly became embedded in Christian tradition is clear from the words of Clement of Alexandria, one of the first Christian apologists, writing at the end of the second century, not long after Hermas. Although he was perhaps the Christian theologian most influenced by Greek philosophy, Clement nonetheless embraced, like Hermas, the Jewish notion of 'the pious poor and the wicked rich'. Speaking to the affluent and educated Christian elite of Egypt, Clement lauds the spiritual superiority of the poor and sees wealth as an obstacle to salvation for the rich. Again he wants the rich to give generously to the poor, who will, in turn, intercede with God on behalf of their benefactors. Almsgiving is thus, for the rich, in Helen Rhee's reading of Clement, 'a necessary part of the care of self, which is an indispensable part of the journey of salvation, the path to perfection'.[60]

Clement's key work on giving is a sermon entitled *Quis dives salvatur* (*Who is the Rich Man that is Saved?*), which begins by describing the corrupting effects of money and Jesus's conversation with the rich young man in Mark's Gospel.[61] Clement spiritualizes the incident and concludes that wealth itself is not wrong, so long as it is used charitably. To be saved the rich man must use his riches to alleviate the suffering of his poor neighbour. But Clement, perhaps influenced by Aristotle, wants to pursue a philanthropic middle way. Faced with the insistence of second-century puritans such as the Encratites, who insisted Christians should renounce all their wealth – along with wine, meat and sexual intercourse – Clement advocates a more sustained approach to almsgiving. Wealth should not be given away all at once; instead, giving should be steady and gradual. Even so, giving, for Clement, is perhaps the most important expression of love; together with faith it is the essential path to salvation.

The attitude of the Christian Church to possessions and riches was necessarily ambivalent. On the one hand, Christ had been fairly unequivocal that material possessions were a distraction from what was truly spiritually important. On the other hand, the Christian community relied upon its shared treasure to sustain itself, especially after it became clear to the early Christians that the world was *not* about to end. By AD 250 the Church in Rome was said to be as many as 50,000 strong and 'the largest association in the city'[62] and, according to the historian Eusebius, was supporting as many as 1,500 widows and poor people.[63] The Church in Antioch at this point supported 3,000 widows and virgins, together with an unspecified number of the sick and poor, according to the early Church Father, John Chrysostom.[64]

The great step change came with Constantine, the emperor who legalized Christianity, paving the way for it to become the official religion of the Roman Empire. It was the start of the institutionalization of Christian charity. After the Council of Nicaea, which Constantine called in 325, Christianity attracted increasing numbers of wealthy Roman converts. It also brought with it new categories of worthy recipients of charity. The celebrated story of St Nicholas of Myra, the historical template for Santa Claus, points to this development. He is said to have tossed bags of gold, rather than mere pennies, through the window (not down the chimney) of a needy family. But they were not destitute. Rather they were aristocrats who had fallen on hard times. The recipients of St Nicholas's largesse were not three starving girls but the virgin daughters of an impoverished nobleman who was on the point of sending the girls out, not to beg, but to become prostitutes. Protecting chastity, by saving women from prostitution, or giving nubile girls the money for dowries, was to become a familiar practice in Christian charity in the centuries which followed. The story of St Nicholas was deemed to have a number of morals. By tossing the gold through the window, the saint demonstrated the special merit of giving to those who do not ask, of giving secretly to avoid shaming the victim, and giving anonymously to avoid public praise.[65] All of these were to become debating points in the history of philanthropy more generally.

Perhaps the most significant of the changes which occurred under Constantine was the strengthening of the role of the bishop in the Christian Church. The Emperor took the old imperial model of benefaction and turned it into an institutionalized Christian system of almsgiving. It was a counter-cultural innovation which broke the classical link between giving and patronage. After the Council of Nicaea the Emperor gave the Church responsibility to care for the poor. He agreed that bishops – a position which had evolved from that of the presbyter who chaired the council of elders in early Christian communities – should take responsibility for running hospitals (pilgrim hostels) in every cathedral city of the Empire. That was only the beginning. Before long the bishops were also organizing hostels for the destitute and sick, poorhouses, orphanages and leper colonies all across the Roman world. Some were financed by bishops themselves, others by wealthy individuals at a bishop's behest. Bishops became the civic patrons of the poor.

The Dominican Richard Finn in his magisterial study, *Almsgiving in the Later Roman Empire: Christian Promotion and Practice (313–450)*, describes the fundraising innovations established by the episcopacy to assist the poor – Sunday collections, special collections, alms-boxes and a system of tithes which he suggests developed initially as a way of putting peer pressure on Christians to shame rich members of the community into giving. Eloquence was essential to the bishop in raising funds for distribution to the poor. The bishop then distributed the alms in the form of food, cash, clothes or goods in kind, often using deacons to manage the delivery. Alms were distributed to a hierarchy of beneficiaries, in this order of priority: widows, orphans, consecrated virgins without other means, aged and sick Christian beggars who could not work, the destitute and then the non-Christian poor. Needy Christians not in good standing with the Church had probably a better claim than non-Christians. Priorities differed from one Christian community to another. In some, captives or the shipwrecked had particular claim; others gave special care to the suddenly impoverished. How far any particular church's funds would stretch was another determining factor.[66]

Almsgiving became fundamental to a bishop's authority and inadequate provision exposed him to criticism. One third-century text contains a graphic description of a bishop sunk up to his knees in a river of fire, being stoned with rocks by four evil angels. His offence was that he 'had not compassion on widows and orphans'.[67] But the episcopal embrace of the poor went further than the distribution of alms. A bishop would invite the poor to his table to eat with him at Easter time, echoing the earlier practice among first-century Christians of the *agape* meal – a communal feast which preceded the Eucharist – a custom that had been abandoned during the second and third centuries. There was, says Finn, 'a huge difference between being fed at the door and invited to sit down with someone'. So it progressed. In 511 a Church synod, the First Council of Orleans, named bishops as 'fathers of the poor' and instructed them to devote a quarter of their revenues to the needy.

The great exemplar of this new style of bishop was Basil of Caesarea, a fourth-century ascetic who had a major influence on the history of philanthropy in both theoretical and practical terms. Basil shared the view of previous Christian thinkers that since God was the great philanthropist, Christians should imitate God's *philanthrôpía* both in feeling pity and compassion, and in sharing generously. But to the previous notions he introduced a new idea – that the rich have a duty towards the poor which is rooted in a sense of justice. The rich are subject to a divine 'trial by wealth' which will reveal whether at heart they are just or unjust. God allows the rich man to prosper, Basil said, 'to see if, when his soul had at length attained satiety, it might then awaken to liberality and to kindness'.[68] His ideas, together with the practical experience of a great famine in Caesarea in 368 – 'the worst ever recorded' according to one contemporary[69] – did not just lead to advances in thinking on philanthropy: they also created what is thought to be the world's first hospital in the modern sense of the word.

The cruel famine, which was a defining event in the life of the man who came to be called St Basil the Great, was prompted by an intense drought. He describes it movingly in a sermon he gave that year, which has been given the title *On the Rich*.[70] The distress was widespread and made worse by speculators hoarding grain in the hope of selling at inflated prices. Basil's words to the rich of Caesarea were excoriating. He attacked 'you who dress walls, but will not clothe a man; who spruce up horses, and overlook an unfashionable brother; who leave grain to rot, but will not feed the starving; who bury your money and despise the oppressed.'[71] Basil suggests that God tests the rich and poor in different ways; the trial of the poor is through the scarcity of the goods of life, but that of the rich is through their plenitude of possessions, and what they choose to do with them. The poor can find it difficult to preserve their souls from despair in hard times. For the rich the temptation is that prosperity brings arrogance, insolence and hubris. Then Basil addresses the rich man:

> To what lengths will you not go for gold? Your grain becomes gold for you, your wine solidifies into gold, your wool is transformed into gold; every exchange, every thought produces gold for you. Gold itself brings forth even more gold, multiplying itself through loans at interest. There is no satisfying the craving; no limit to the desire is to be found.[72]

The rich of Caesarea, Basil suggests, have let their greed obscure their vision of those in need. To open their eyes he tells the harrowing story of a father forced by hunger to sell one of his children into slavery, and of the debate he has with his wife over which child to sell, only to find that when he steels himself to take one of his children to the slave market, the rich buyer haggles over the price, increasing the grief and the tragedy for the wretched father. 'Tears do not move you,' Basil chides the rich, 'groans do not soften your heart, but you remain adamant and unbending. In everything you see gold.'[73] Wealth brings the greedy a kind of insanity, Basil says. He berates the wealthy for punching beggars and sympathizes with mendicants for having to tread a tightrope between appearing too well dressed to need alms, as a result of clothes they had been given, or so ill clad in 'rotting rags' as to excite only disgust. (This gap between theology and practice was not restricted to Basil's time and place. A generation later, in Constantinople, St John Chrysostom spoke of beggars who approached and accosted people at home and in the streets. Some were successful in obtaining alms, others were given a raft of excuses which Chrysostom records: the beggars were too young and healthy, they were work-shy or runaway slaves, and some of them were alleged to have deliberately blinded their children to increase their value as beggars.) Basil preferred to give beggars the benefit of the doubt, arguing that those living on the streets of Caesarea were vulnerable to illness and at risk of early death. The intensity and vehemence with which he reprimands the rich recalls the rigour of the language of the Hebrew prophets:

> Did you not come forth naked from the womb, and will you not return naked to the earth? Where then did you obtain your belongings? If you say that you acquired them by chance, then you deny God, since you neither recognize your Creator, nor are you grateful to the One who gave these things to you. But if you acknowledge that they were given to you by God, then tell me, for what purpose did you receive them?[74]

But Basil was in search of more than spiritual remedies. He demanded practical change:

> The treasuries of injustice well deserve to be torn down. With your own hands, raze these misbegotten structures. Destroy the granaries from which no one has ever gone away satisfied. Demolish every storehouse of greed, pull down the roofs, tear away the walls, expose the mouldering grain to the sunlight, lead forth from prison the fettered wealth, vanquish the gloomy vaults of Mammon.[75]

Basil set an example by spending his own personal inheritance on famine relief. The rich were shamed into action. They opened their granaries and Basil and his deacons supervised the distribution of grain and other foods to the hungry. The bishop 'set before them basins of soup and such meat as was found preserved among us', his friend Gregory of Nazianzus recounted at Basil's funeral. 'Then, imitating the ministry of Christ, who, girded with a towel, did not disdain to wash the disciples' feet . . . he attended to the bodies and souls of those who needed it, combining personal respect with the supply of their necessity, and so giving them a double relief.'[76]

But Basil's practical action went further than that. After the famine he used the resources at his disposal – as well as soliciting extra funds from the city's wealthy citizens – to create a ground-breaking philanthropic foundation: a complex of buildings just outside the city which included a church, a warehouse for the storage and distribution of goods to the poor, a hostel for travellers, a school, a poorhouse for the destitute, a leprosarium and a clinic where monks, nuns and lay physicians provided free healthcare to the sick. The monks and nuns lived in monastic houses from which they practised their vocations through prayer, and manual and mental labour. It became known as the Basiliad and was in effect both Christianity's first authoritative monastic institution and the world's first hospital for the general sick. Roman *valetudinaria* restricted themselves to treating ill or wounded slaves and soldiers for the military or the wealthiest slave-owners. And temples dedicated to Asclepius, the Graeco-Roman god of healing, required donations and sacrifices from sufferers and rarely employed professional physicians, and certainly would not care for the terminally ill. The Basiliad was something new.

After Basil's death in 379, Christian hospitals on the model of the Basiliad sprang up across the Roman Empire and were to be found in most cities within a century. The modern hospital is thus, in its origin and conception, a distinctively Christian philanthropic institution. At Basil's funeral Gregory of Nazianzus declared 'a noble thing is philanthropy', and described the Basiliad as a 'new city' and compared it to the Colossus, the Pyramids, the walls of Babylon and other contemporary Wonders of the World. In this 'storehouse of piety', he said, Basil demonstrated his 'care for the sick, and the relief of their wounds, and the imitation of Christ, by cleansing leprosy, not by a word, but in deed'.[77]

Behind it all was a new departure in philanthropic thinking. Basil insisted that giving was not merely a matter of honour, status, civic duty, emulation of the deity or worship, but of justice. All property belongs to all men, he argued. The rich, in effect, seize the fruits of the world which are 'meant for the common use of all'. A rich man may argue: Whom am I wronging so long as I keep what is my own? But Basil admonishes in reply: 'The bread you are holding back is for the hungry; the cloak you keep locked in your chest belongs to the naked; the shoe that is rotting in your storehouse belongs to the barefoot; the silver you keep buried in the earth is for the needy . . . thus you do a great injustice to all those whom you could succour.'[78] Indeed, Basil considers the unjust retention of what one possesses to be a form of theft, arguing that the rich 'seize common goods before others have the opportunity, then claim them as their own by right of pre-emption. For if we all took only what was necessary to satisfy our own needs, giving the rest to those who lack, no one would be rich, no one would be poor, and no one would be in need.'[79] Each person's right to the use of their own possessions is secondary to the right of all men to a fair share of the earth's goods. 'Wealth left idle is of no use to anyone, but put to use and exchanged it becomes fruitful and beneficial for the public.'[80]

PHILANTHROPISTS AS LOVERS OF THE POOR

In the fourth century, as the Christianization of the Roman Empire took hold, organized charity for the poor became the principal vehicle for philanthropy. The twin inheritances of Basil the Great – the episcopacy and the monastery – took their place at the heart of this centralized almsgiving. Something of a power struggle began between them.

Monasticism had grown from the practice of solitary celibate Christian hermits in the deserts of third-century Egypt beginning to come together for Sunday worship. (The word was derived from the Greek *monachos*, which meant 'living alone'.) But it was Basil's system of monastic rule which became the model for the spread of monasteries across the eastern Roman Empire. Ascetic but not so severe as the regimes of the Desert Fathers, it was based around a life of prayer, liturgy and work. The self-dispossession of the early monks attracted Christians to give alms to the monasteries for distribution to the destitute. Some monastic leaders resisted this, arguing that, in Richard Finn's words, 'a monk should be making enough by his own labour to support himself and have something left to give away rather than being eager to accept money himself'.[81] But the regulation and distribution of alms through the monasteries became an established fixture of Christian philanthropic practice.

All this was occurring at the time when the figure of the bishop was becoming the focus of both social cohesion and social control within the Christian community. The clergy were thus also seen as the worthy recipients of almsgiving since their financial probity had to be relied on for the appropriate distribution to the poor. Christians gave freely, though, to judge from contemporary sermons, not as freely as their preachers instructed. Lay people were encouraged to give, at set times and in particular places, through the bishop and his deacons. But they were also to give directly to the poor. Formal systems of tithes were not established until the fifth or sixth century; it was only by the medieval period that they became a sort of ecclesiastical tax. Competition between episcopal and monastic systems inevitably led to conflict as almsgiving came to be seen as an effective tool for self-promotion and the consolidation of power for bishops who were not so ascetically minded as Basil.[82]

The problem only grew as increasing numbers of the very rich and very poor entered Church communities across the Empire after the fourth century. It was among these wealthier Christians that practices began to emerge which were to set philanthropic models for the centuries to come. The affluent would offer alms in the form of *agape* meals for the poor, and when they arrived at shrines after a pilgrimage, and on their deathbeds. Bishops became simultaneously leaders of the Christian community and members of the aristocratic elite. Their actions could be confused, confusing or designed to appeal to multiple constituencies. Some early Christian bishops became, according to Giuliana Gemelli, locked in vicious power struggles with old pagan elites for control of crumbling Roman imperial cities. Portraying themselves as 'lovers of the poor' became as much of a political tactic as a theological imperative.

These new Church politicians revised doctrine on alms, wealth and poverty to win the support of particular sections of the expanding Christian community. 'Fidelity to Jesus's more selfless teachings was sacrificed,' Gemelli writes, 'as bishops toned down earlier rebukes of the wealthy, courted rich donors with preferred places in new congregations, and increasingly described almsgiving as a means by which the ordinary faithful could atone for their personal sins under reinforced Church discipline.'[83] The tactic worked in temporal political terms. Where buildings in Rome had once been erected through civic high-mindedness and had borne the name of the man who had paid for them, alongside the inscription *D. S. P. F.* (*De Sua Pecunia Fecit*, 'Done with His Own Money'), now funerary inscriptions proclaimed dead donors to be *amatores pauperum*, lovers of the poor. This appropriation of a title first associated with bishops indicates the extent to which the centrality of almsgiving had gained purchase upon the imagination of Christians. It was around this time that donors' names, in Rome, began to be recited during the central Christian Eucharistic celebration, the Mass.

Ambrose of Milan was not one of these political revisionists. He was, however, a consummate politician whose approach set the model of relations between Church and State which was to dominate Europe throughout the Middle Ages and set the template for philanthropy for over a millennium. Born into an aristocratic Roman senatorial family around 340, Ambrose had been the highly popular governor of the Roman province of Liguria for just two years when, in 374, he went to restore order at the assembly to elect the city's next bishop, which was riven in two factions. As he was addressing the crowd, a cry went up 'Ambrose for Bishop'. It was taken up by the room and he found himself unexpectedly elected by acclamation. His transition from unbaptized layman to bishop took just eight days and showed how intertwined were the Roman imperial and clerical elites. Ambrose further united the Graeco-Roman and Christian traditions of philanthropy in one of the first great works of Christian ethics, *De officiis ministrorum*. Written in 386, it was closely modelled on the *De officiis* of Cicero, the great Roman work of moral philosophy from the first century before Christ. Ambrose synthesized Cicero's Stoic principles on how to live a moral life with the qualities of humility, charity and self-denial which Christianity had inherited from Judaism. His aim was to establish new models of behaviour for a Christianized aristocracy in Milan.

On almsgiving Ambrose adopted much of the key teaching of Basil the Great, though he went further and spoke with greater ferocity. Cicero had suggested that *liberalitas*, the virtue of giving freely, could well be exercised towards close relatives who were in need. But Ambrose recast the Roman notion of *liberalitas* in Christian terms, insisting that the destitute, widows and orphans, must take priority over close relatives, unless the need of the relatives was even greater. The extent to which this is a departure from the classical practice is clear from the care Ambrose takes to counter hostile comment by family members who consider themselves cheated of the money which is given to the poor. Cicero had suggested that fasting was essential to moral development, but, again, Ambrose goes further than the Stoic attack on gluttony; he maintained that fasting did no good unless the money which was saved from not eating was distributed to the poor.

Like Basil, Ambrose made reference to Jesus's parable of Dives and Lazarus, but Ambrose criticized the rich citizens of Milan for being even worse than Dives, who had at least allowed the poor man Lazarus to gather up what dropped from his table. The rich classes of Milan, the second city of the Roman Empire, profited from an institutional violence, Ambrose suggests, which extracted wealth from its political victims – so that the goblets of the rich 'dripped with blood from the executed'.[84] The rich, in Ambrose's startling turn of phrase, were draining the lifeblood of the poor. Christianity was slowly giving the poor a new level of visibility.

Perhaps most significantly for the history of philanthropy, Ambrose gave still greater prominence to the notion that almsgiving could be redemptive. God, he said, has given wealth to some that they may gain eternal life by employing it to atone for their sins: 'so that you may redeem your sins for the price of compassion'.[85] The greatest theologian of the early Church, St Augustine of Hippo, whom Ambrose baptized, took up this theme. One in five of his 500 sermons includes some call to give alms. For Augustine the need to expiate daily sins required almsgiving as regular as 'the waterwheel continually turning to irrigate the fields'.[86] Ambrose, who dominated the cultural and political life of his age, was, in Augustine's view, the model bishop. He established, in the words of the early Church historian Peter Brown, 'the medieval concept of a Christian emperor as a dutiful son of the Church, "serving under orders from Christ" and so subject to the advice and strictures of his bishop'.[87] It was a paradigm which was to endure until the Reformation.

IS ALMSGIVING REDEMPTIVE?

There is an important footnote to add before we can turn our attention to how philanthropy was institutionalized for a thousand years during the Middle Ages. It concerns the issue of redemptive almsgiving, which was to bedevil relations between Catholics and Protestants after the Reformation and skew the way most mainstream histories of philanthropy have been written. And it was to divert the development of philanthropy down a path which had some strengths but significant weaknesses.

Christians saw philanthropy as an imitation of Christ. The Christian must be generous because God is generous. Almsgiving also had the useful social function of moderating the gap between the rich and the poor in early Christian communities; it was a method of redistribution which bonded Christians together. But from the outset there was another attitude towards giving. It was that giving to the poor would

earn the giver forgiveness for his sins. Theologians came to call that
redemptive almsgiving. From the fourth century onwards, according
to Peter Brown's *The Ransom of the Soul: Afterlife and Wealth in Early
Western Christianity*, the balance shifted. Almsgiving became 'less a
gesture of solidarity' and more 'a purely expiatory action that involved
little or no bonding with the poor themselves'.[88] At the Reformation,
Protestant reformers were to take issue with this. They argued that it
was only Christ's sacrificial death which atoned for all human sins and
that it was believing in this which brought salvation. Good works, like
giving to the poor, might show that someone was saved, but were not
the cause of their salvation. Redemptive almsgiving, the Reformation
said, was a corrupt doctrine of the Catholic medieval Church.

On the face of it, and certainly to the Protestant reformers, there
appears a contradiction here. In Mark's Gospel, Jesus had ridiculed the
idea that a rich man could enter heaven.[89] In the Gospel of Luke, Jesus
does not just say 'Blessed are the poor' but adds, 'Woe to you who
are rich, for you have received your consolation. Woe to you who are
full now, for you will be hungry.'[90] Yet the early Christian Church was
perfectly at home with both the idea that the death of Jesus made full
atonement for all the sins of humanity and the idea that almsgiving
could expunge sins. Roman Garrison, in his study *Redemptive
Almsgiving in Early Christianity*, suggests that this is because the New
Testament provides a foundation for both these interpretations. The
unique atonement is made explicit in the letters of Paul and Hebrews,
yet redemptive almsgiving is implicit in the teachings of Jesus as when
he said 'Give alms . . . and see, everything will be clean for you.'[91]

As we have seen, redemptive almsgiving was part of Christianity's
inheritance from Judaism. It was there in those parts of the Prophets
and Psalms that make God's blessing dependent on giving succour
to the poor, and it was spelled out categorically in rabbinic Judaism,
certainly after the destruction of the Temple by the Romans.[92] But there
is more to early Christianity's unequivocal embrace of the doctrine.
The Apostolic Fathers had boldly advocated redemptive almsgiving.
The earliest Christian catechism, the Didache, speaks of almsgiving
as 'atonement for one's sins'.[93] Another early text, the Second Epistle
of Clement, insists 'almsgiving is therefore good as repentance from
sin; fasting is better than prayer, but almsgiving better than both'.[94] *The
Shepherd of Hermas* tells the wealthy, instead of buying land, to 'purchase
afflicted souls' by looking after widows and orphans. It was Cyprian of

Carthage, a convert to Christianity around 246, who developed what became the strongest theological argument for redemptive almsgiving. Jesus's death and almsgiving did not compete with one other. Rather both are expressions of God's abundant grace and it is only by God's grace that almsgiving can be meritorious. For Cyprian almsgiving is a lifelong penance[95] and 'riches offered the remedy for the very harm they caused'.[96] Cyprian's *On Works and Almsgiving* became a foundational text in the Western Church during the centuries that followed.

But perhaps the staunchest advocate of redemptive almsgiving is John Chrysostom who, a century after Cyprian, clearly sees material possessions as a potential route to redemption. Addressing the wealthy he says: 'He has made you rich, that you may assist the needy, *then you may have release of your own sins*, by liberality to others. He has given you money, not that you may shut it up for your own destruction, but that you may pour it forth for your salvation.'[97] Philanthropy is indeed, for him, essential to salvation: 'It is impossible, though we performed ten thousand other good deeds, to enter the portals of the kingdom without almsgiving.'[98] And he acknowledges that, while baptism provides the initial cleansing from sin, almsgiving is the foremost means of 'wiping off the filthiness' of sin.[99] In addition to all this, the great churchman Ambrose, as noted above, also upholds the idea that the rich can have their sins forgiven if they give generously to the poor.

The fact is that the doctrine of redemptive almsgiving was taken up by early Christianity and stood unchallenged for centuries within the Church as a key motive for philanthropy. Contrary to what was suggested after the Reformation, redemptive almsgiving was not some corruption of medieval Catholicism. It was there from the outset among the early Christians and a long line of Church Fathers. The early Church happily reconciled the doctrine that Christ died for our sins and the notion that almsgiving could bring us to salvation. Philanthropy and penance were deeply intertwined. But past and present scholarship on Christian almsgiving, says Richard Finn, has been hampered by prejudiced Protestants determined to see redemptive almsgiving as a Catholic debasement of the pure doctrine of charity set forth by the early Christians.[100] It is what John Lawson calls 'a good example of the neo-Reformation attack upon the ancient Church'.[101] This piece of denominational propaganda was to have damaging consequences for the direction of English philanthropy for centuries.

Interview: Jonathan Ruffer on Christianity and giving

Jonathan Ruffer was one of London's wealthiest financiers – until he gave away £320 million and shot to the top of the 2019 Sunday Times *Giving List. (He was fourth in the 2020 list). He made his fortune running the investment company Ruffer LLP, managing £20 billion of assets in 2019. A Christian, born in 1951 in the north-east of England, in 2012 he bought Auckland Castle (the private dwelling of the Bishop of Durham) in Bishop Auckland, along with its dozen seventeenth-century paintings by the Spanish artist Francisco de Zurbarán, and then donated it all to the region.*

The castle, with its art, has become the centre of his massive £160 million regeneration project designed to rejuvenate a region hard-hit by the closure of traditional industries such as mining. The project includes three art galleries, a new faith museum, and a spectacular historical drama employing hundreds of local people and a thousand volunteers. He is now adding other visitor attractions designed to bring in half a million visitors to the depressed area each year. He divides his week between his London investment firm and his Auckland project.

Tell me how you first got into philanthropy? Was it something that came late in life or was it there from the outset?

It was an 'ought to do' rather than just a natural part of my personality. At the tail end of university in Cambridge I met a chap who was very influential on my early Christian life. He ran the Mayflower Family Centre in the East End of London. That gave me a taste for worlds that I had never previously considered. That was my training ground.

Were you giving money or volunteering?

I'm extraordinarily impractical. It was money and management. I was a trustee. I did the funding.

What was the first significant amount of money that you gave?

That was to buy a small house for a church worker in the village where I lived. I had no idea I was going to end up earning a lot of money. I never saw the wealth coming. I've always been uninterested in money. So I didn't think giving it away was a hardship; it didn't need a huge moral victory over myself to do it. If you're a successful fund manager, then the rewards that you get from that are out of all proportion. I don't really regard the income as mine. I just see it as something that I need to pass on.

The accretion of wealth is an externality, and it hasn't got to do with who I am. When money comes the question is: 'What do you with it?' I'm frightened of money because I can see it corrodes people. That's what happens with money if you keep it. It can make you arrogant. It can make you nervous. It can make you feel inadequate. Any number of things, but they're all negatives. My response is: if that's the case, get rid of it. Get rid of it.

In 2010 you went on a retreat to St Beuno's – the Jesuit spirituality centre in North Wales. When you came back you decided that you needed to begin working with the poor. Did you have some moment of epiphany?

It was a silent retreat, but you're expected to talk to your spiritual director for 45 minutes in the morning. Then there was Eucharist in the afternoon. On the first evening they announced that two members of the community were ill. Father Joseph, who had a heart attack and had been taken off to hospital, and Maria in the kitchens, who had had a funny turn and had also been taken off to hospital.

On the following night, we had a long report on how Father Joseph was getting on, and nothing at all on Maria. I said to the spiritual director the next day, 'What happened with Maria?' He had no idea really. She just worked in the kitchen. It was like she didn't matter very much. I remember being in the chapel and really angry, saying 'Lord, who will fight for a little person?'

That's a dangerous question to ask. Because there's only one answer.

Yes. That was the moment that I knew I was done for.

So what did you conclude from that?

I equated it with giving up this business. I thought I was being called to work in community centres and that kind of thing. And I really liked the idea of giving up the alpha male parts of my life. I had a vivid sense of calling to do this.

Yet here you are, in the City still . . .

When I first came back from Beuno's I said to my successor: 'Will you take over in two years' time?' I had the idea that I'd do something like the Auckland Project one day a week and then after two years give up the world of finance and go full-time there. I'm in a really good place now psychologically and spiritually, which I could never have been if I hadn't made the decision to give this up full-time. I'm here three days a week and in Auckland the other two and at the weekend. I live a piston-rod existence; this is where I earn it, and that's where I spend it. That's how it works.

Do they feel like compartments of your life or do they feel integrated?

They're integrated. They're just absolutely integrated.

So having decided to work with the poor, how did you end up buying a 900-year-old crenelated castle filled with exquisite Spanish baroque art?

At that point I only knew that I was going to come back to the North-east, but I didn't know what I was going to do. It was like Abraham, being called on a journey, but without being vouchsafed a destination. I collected art, particularly baroque art, and that's how I heard that the Zurbaráns had come up for sale.

The paintings were being sold by the Church of England when it was strapped for cash. I remember that seemed a terrible shame because the paintings – of *Jacob and his Twelve Sons* **– had been bought by a seventeenth-century bishop out of sympathy for the plight of the Jews in England. The fear was this amazing set of paintings would now go to a foreign buyer.**

The price was £15 million. I decided to sell everything I'd put into the charity I'd set up in 1992 and buy them. Amazingly when I sold up, the total came to just £10,000 over the £15 million. That seemed a bit of God! And there was something else. These were baroque paintings and the word 'baroque' was originally an insulting word. It's a Portuguese word that means deformed. A deformed pearl, instead of being completely round, has had the grit in the wrong place in the oyster so it forms a stream of iridescence which is useless in terms of jewellery.

What struck me is that if you read Christ's words – about the merchant who finds a pearl of great price and sells all he has to buy it – you think of Christ giving his all for humanity. And yet that humanity was not perfect but was deformed. It's our helplessness that attracted him. The pearl of great price for Christ was not a pearl that was bigger and grander and more perfect, it was a deformed pearl and he still gave all that he had for it. And I thought to myself, 'This is a following after Christ.' That's what I'm doing; I'm giving all that I've got to go to a community that is wounded.

The deformed pearl is the wounded poor.

Yes.

You've said that many people nowadays underestimate the symbolic power of art. Certainly some critics today say that philanthropists should give their money to soup kitchens rather than buy high art. They argue that the government should allow donors to claim more tax relief on donations that go to the poor.

The whole principle of charity falls apart if one charity starts to be officially defined as better than another. If the state takes over prioritizing and directing, it distorts the charitable impulse.

What is charity, then?

That's a good question. There's a problem once you start having either the government or the legislature taking a view on it. At one point the definition of charity was very widely drawn on the basis of the word 'need'. Then one of the charitable acts redefined 'need' as 'poverty'. What we're trying to do in Bishop Auckland is to marry these different philanthropic impulses: the symbolic power of art and the need of the community for regeneration. They're not divisible. It's a bit like me meeting you when you're down and out and being absolutely prepared to feed you but not to give you a coat. A person is a whole person. The creation of a visitor attraction at Bishop Auckland was about how you change people.

Change people – in what way?

Take the night show that we started. It's called Kynren – which derives from the Anglo-Saxon for kin or community. It's like the opening ceremony of the Olympics but it's the history of England through the eyes of the North-east. The lighting, the music, the fireworks, the horses, everything is sensational. The stage is seven and a half acres. The stadium has 8,000 people. Rising out of the lake in front of you is a full-size Viking ship with fire coming out of it. As the ship comes up, you suddenly realize standing on the ship are four Vikings. So the first thing you see is their swords coming out and then there they are, dripping as they come out of the water. The effect is astonishing. But the key thing is that it's a thousand volunteers who do it. There are no professional actors; they, and the people who run the lighting and all the rest, they're all volunteers. The effect on the town has been absolutely astonishing. Because here are people doing something which is one of TripAdvisor's five must-sees in the UK.

It's the first fruit of what we're trying to do. At the end of it the audience are blubbing, the actors are, and it brings something of elemental power to a place that hasn't got it. So Kynren is open. The castle and the Zurbaráns have undergone a three-year refurbishment and have just been opened to the public. There's a Miner's Art Gallery which is very powerful and moving. There's a seventeenth-century walled garden and Auckland Tower, a great big thing. The Faith Museum will be the last thing to open in 2022. There's a research centre where we've been working with Durham University and its archaeology, history, theology and geothermal departments, and I'd like to draw them more into Bishop Auckland.

So all this has provided hundreds of jobs but also a boost in self-esteem for the volunteers . . .

Yes. The regenerative team that we've got there are so impressive. It's a mighty, mighty work going on in some of the most inaccessible, the darkest, the most needy places in County Durham.

As a boy you grew up nearby but in North Yorkshire, which is relatively more affluent. But you've chosen to spend the money you made in London further north. Did you see a North-South

dimension to that – a transfer of wealth from the rich part of the country to one of the poorest?

Absolutely. I'm not at all a proselytizer but I was brought up in the North-east, moved to London, did well, and to me, it seems I'm simply acting as a conduit to bring the money back to the North-east. I'm amazed that not everybody would do that. County Durham is very good at exporting great people. But do they come back and bring back the fruit of their success elsewhere? They don't. There's one guy locally who is selling his grouse moor for £25 million. You wouldn't think that you'd need much imagination or goodwill to think that – if one of the very few world-class things that happens in County Durham is making you a barrel full of money – to think, 'Let's leave a bit of it behind.' But very few do.

You once said: 'It's no good a poor man telling a rich man to change his behaviour. Only a rich man can tell a rich man to change his behaviour.' Is that what you are doing?

I got rich because I see the world differently than other people do. It just happens that the way I see the world is the way that the world is and so I read future events with a certainty which to me doesn't require great insight. I just see it.

You were one of the few City financiers who predicted the credit crunch.

It seemed obvious. It's like you saying to me, 'Look, I'm going to Moscow in February', and me saying, 'Well, take a warm coat. It'll be jolly cold.' And you come back and say, 'Amazing. You were right about that one.'

What a lot of people don't seem to realize is that it's very liberating to give money away. It's a wonderfully releasing thing. Giving money away is like life as a colour film after black and white. I once asked a great Northern wealth creator why so few people followed his example of beneficence. He said: 'because they don't realize how much fun it is'. And it is. It has so many uplifting qualities.

Chapter 3

Medieval Charity

Every morning, just before 10 o'clock, thirteen elderly men, each clad in a black gown embroidered with a silver Cross of Jerusalem, make their way slowly across the cloistered quadrangle of the Hospital of St Cross just outside the ancient city of Winchester. Removing their flat Tudor bonnets, they enter the hospital's Norman church. Its rounded arches, zigzag mouldings and foliate capitals reveal that it dates from not long after the foundation of the hospital sometime between 1132 and 1136. St Cross is said to be the oldest continually operating charity in England. It is not a hospital in the modern sense; its name originates from the ancient use of the word for a place of hospitality. Its story embodies a vision of philanthropy which shaped English and European attitudes to giving for over a thousand years.

Henry of Blois, a grandson of William the Conqueror, was less than 30 when in 1129 he was appointed Bishop of Winchester. Soon after, tradition has it, he was walking in the meadows by the River Itchen. There he saw in the distance a young peasant girl, with a baby on her arm, and carrying a pail upon her head. He was seized with the conviction that this was the Virgin Mary bearing the Christ child and wearing a crown. As he approached her, the young woman begged for help, saying that she and her people were starving because of the civil war which had laid waste to the land. Henry had played his part in this. The two rival armies belonged to Henry's brother (who in 1135 would become King Stephen) and his cousin (the Empress Matilda, wife of the Holy Roman Emperor Henry V). The power struggle between them inflicted upon England a period known as The Anarchy, which lasted almost two decades – described by the Peterborough Chronicle as 'nineteen long winters, when Christ and his saints slept'.[1] The new bishop – described by another contemporary chronicler, Henry of Huntingdon, as 'a new kind of monster . . . part monk and part knight'[2] – had first supported Stephen, then switched sides to Matilda, and then back again to his brother. Perhaps the warrior-bishop felt the need to repent. Perhaps he saw in the young girl's request an opportunity to consolidate his political power. Either way, he decided to found a hospital in the place where he had had his vision of the Virgin. His foundation made provision for a group of thirteen poor men to be supported inside his new Hospital of St Cross.

The almshouse was to be a home, in Henry's words, for men who were 'feeble and so reduced in strength that they can scarcely, or not at all, support themselves without other aid'. These men were to be provided with 'necessary clothing' by the Prior of the Hospital. They were to be given 'beds fit for their infirmities' and 'a daily good loaf of wheaten bread of the weight of five measures' along with 'three dishes at dinner, and one for supper'. The generous sum of three pence a day was set aside for feeding each man. They were also to have 'drink of good stuff in sufficient quantity'.[3] That sufficient quantity was defined by the authorities as three quarts of strong beer a day. So they 'must have been a merry crew', in the view of the Hospital's historian, Peter Hopewell. In return for their shelter, clothing, food and drink, the thirteen men – numbered in emulation of Christ and his Apostles – were to be required only to attend Matins each morning, where they were to 'pour out prayers to the Almighty for the souls of Henry of Blois, his predecessors, and the kings of England'.[4] If any of the brethren recovered and became strong enough to fend for themselves, they were 'dismissed with honour' from the hospital to make room for a poorer replacement. The cohort of the thirteen Brothers of St Cross has been maintained without a break to this day.

But there was more to Henry's philanthropy than just a chantry to offer perpetual prayers to atone for his sins. He also made provision for the feeding of the local poor. Victuals were provided on a daily basis for one hundred men at the hospital gates. In the words of the founder: 'Modest persons, of the most indigent that can be found, shall be received at the hour of dinner, to whom a course of bread of the

same weight shall be given, and two messes of flesh or fish, as shall seem
meet, according to the convenience of the day, in the cup of the same
measure.' Since the local water was considered unfit for drinking, they
too were to be allowed three quarts of ale, though they had to make do
with small beer rather than the strong variety served to the Brothers.
Their meal was to be cooked by 'the hundred-menne-cooke' served from
'the hundred-menne-pot' using 'the hundred-menne-ladel'. To aid the
distribution of this daily charity a special Hundred-Menne-Halle was
built close by the hospital gate. The portions of food given out were
generous and the hundred men were allowed to take away with them
what they did not consume at table in the hall. The leftovers were such
that, Hopewell estimates, around six to seven per cent of local people –
a sizeable proportion of Winchester's population – were in receipt of
the hospital's philanthropy.[5]

There was a third dimension to the hospital's mission. Situated as it
was on the pilgrim route from Glastonbury to Canterbury, it provided
hospitality to travellers. Pilgrims could call and request the wayfarers'
dole – a loaf of bread and a quart of ale or wine. The tradition has
been maintained unbroken for almost a thousand years, although
now travellers who request the dole are given a small porcelain cup
of ale and a token square of bread. The bread was produced in the
hospital's bakery until the 1970s, but it has since been replaced with
sliced white.

Here, within the hospital's medieval limestone walls, has been
preserved the key elements of a millennium of Christian philanthropic
vision. There is more to this than redemptive almsgiving, although Henry
de Blois clearly hoped that his almsgiving would assist his salvation in
the afterlife. The material poverty of the wider community is addressed.
So are the needs of travellers. In addition, there is a clear understanding
that philanthropy is a communal activity. The construction of the
church and its associated buildings made a massive impact on the local
economy, with over a hundred stonemasons and carpenters employed
there for decades. The nursery rhyme 'See-Saw Marjorie Daw' is said to
have its origins in the recruiting policy of Henry de Blois, whose name
was Anglicized in Hampshire as Messer de Blaw, which then became
Marjorie Daw. Johnny was an Everyman name for craftsmen working
on the Hospital of St Cross. The episcopal 'new master' offered a hugely
attractive wage – a penny a day – although the craftsmen were required

to work no more swiftly than in lesser paid jobs. Hopewell suggests the original version of the rhyme was:

See Saw, Messer de Blaw
Johnny shall have a new master.
He shall get a penny a day
Yet shan't have to work any faster.

The church inside St Cross was the size of a small cathedral. It became a powerful institution in the ecclesiastical landscape. In 1187 Pope Clement III granted powers of sanctuary to St Cross, designating it as a place which could 'receive clerkes or laymen fleeing from the secular power. . . without contradiction from anyone'. At a time when the relationship between Church and State was such that an individual could claim sanctuary for only 40 days in a church before having to surrender to the king's law or quit the kingdom, Pope Clement was in effect placing St Cross above both the spiritual and temporal laws of the land. A fugitive could effectively remain in the hospital forever.[6] Almsgiving had acquired a political dimension. The Hospital of St Cross was thus rooted in its local society – spiritually, philanthropically, economically and also politically. It was the epitome of a unified holistic medieval view of Church, State and society which was to have a profound impact on the development of English philanthropy.

THE PARISH AND ITS TITHES

The phrase the Middle Ages was coined by modern scholars studying the Italian Renaissance. It was a disparaging term for the long period between the era of classical Greece and Rome and the artistic and cultural rejuvenation of fourteenth-century Europe. It was seen as a period of cultural backwardness which could be passed over. Such a dismissive attitude fostered the assumption that during these 'dark ages' nothing much had changed. This could not be further from the truth. There were significant developments in philanthropy over this millennium which were rooted in the religious, economic and political developments of the medieval period.

During the early centuries between the end of the Roman Empire in 476 and the year 1000, commerce went into decline and with it the monetary economy. Self-sufficiency and forms of bartering became the norm. A feudal society began to emerge in which powerful nobles divided their lands into manors. Those living on the land paid rent by their labour, working as serfs and villeins* on the acreage of the lord of their manor as well as working on their own small plots or strips of land. But feudalism was a tripartite system in which the clergy occupied a key place alongside the nobility and the peasantry. It was through the Church that the philanthropic impulses of medieval society were expressed.

The local parish was the main vehicle for the collection and distribution of alms to the poor and needy. In Rome the Christian community was divided into 40 parishes before the end of the third century, and there is evidence of a parochial system in Alexandria and Asia Minor around the same time. A century after that, Pope Gelasius had introduced the system of tithes – by which one-tenth of all goods and produce were to be donated to the bishop to fund church maintenance, pay the clergy, and provide relief for the poor. But in Britain, where churches were built by individual Saxon lords on their manorial demesnes, the parish system came into being more slowly. One of the first references to tithes in England comes from the Venerable Bede, who was writing in and around 734. Bede lamented the fact that towns and hamlets in remote places paid their tithes and yet were without a resident minister, suggesting that the parish system was then only in rudimentary form.[7] The payment of tithe was encouraged by the Council of Cealchythe in 785, which was attended by the kings of Kent, Mercia, Wessex and Northumbria, and endorsed by the Witenagemot, the assembly of nobles.[8] From that time tithes were frequently mentioned in Saxon laws. King Alfred (ruled 871–899) declared that tithe should be paid on all 'moving and growing things'. But it was the law-code of Æthelstan (925–939) which reveals how tithes evolved into a detailed and complex system. His laws, together with those of Edmund (939–946) and Edgar (959–975), listed a vast variety of dues which, as well as *tēo đung* (tithe), included *cyricsceat* (church-scot), *sāwlsceat* (soul-scot), *weaxgescot* (wax-scot), *lēohtgesceot* (light-scot), *sulhœlmessan* (plough-alms) and *Rōmfeoh* (Peter's Penny).

---

* A serf was tied to a piece of land and obliged to work it for his lord. A villein was a serf in his relationship to his lord, but a freeman in relation to others.

The Canons of Edgar, drawn up under the reforming Archbishop of Canterbury, Dunstan – who was, until Thomas Becket in the twelfth century, the favourite saint of the English people – stipulated that every religious fast should be accompanied by almsgiving. Dunstan directed that priests must preach on alms every Sunday. They were to explain that plough-alms should be paid 15 days after Easter. A tithe of young colts, calves, kids, piglets and lambs was due at Pentecost. A 'fruits of the earth' tithe was required at All Saints on 1 November. Peter's Penny – a one penny tax on every house with a fireplace – was to be paid to the Pope in Rome on the feast of St Peter. Church-scot (most likely a tithe on harvested grain) fell due in the autumn at Martinmas. Priests were to distribute alms 'as to please God, and dispose the people to almsgiving', singing psalms as they distributed the alms and bidding the poor to pray for all people.[9] So important was all this that it appeared in the Canons directly after the instruction that 'no Christian eat blood of any kind' – and before the injunction governing the behaviour of priests. (They should avoid drunkenness, oaths, consorting with women, unbecoming occupations 'as ale-scop or glee man' – a reciter or composer of oral poetry. Nor should a priest be a hunter, hawker or dicer.) Plough-alms was a penny for each ploughland owned.[10] Soul-scot was a payment for burial 'at the open grave'.[11] Light-scot, a half-pennyworth of wax, was a donation to provide candles for a church, to be paid at Christmas, Candlemas in February, and Easter.[12] Wax-scot appears to have been something similar.[13]

Tithes soon ceased to be philanthropic and became a form of ecclesiastical levy. Saxon Canons began to list penalties for non-payment of tithes. Under Æthelstan tithes became compulsory. Failure to pay Peter's Penny incurred a fine twelve times the original scot.[14] Repeated refusal could bring excommunication, under Edmund's Laws, and confiscation of all assets, under Edgar's Canons, with half going to the king and the other half to the bishop.[15] Although the prelates and lawmakers continued to talk about tithes as almsgiving – the laws of King Æthelred 'the Unready' (973–1016) insisted 'God's dues are to be willingly paid'[16] – to the ordinary people tithes were regarded as a form of charitable taxation. But most acts of charity remained outside tithes. In the early centuries of the medieval period, money did not enter much into the business of charity, according to the historian John Bossy. In this age of subsistence and barter, 'all the corporal works of mercy – feeding the hungry, clothing the naked, extending hospitality to strangers, visiting the sick and those in prison, and burying the dead – could perfectly well be carried out without any money changing hands'.[17]

What shattered the order of this neat Anglo-Saxon world was the invasion of England by William the Conqueror in 1066. The Norman invaders brought with them very different ideas about how society, and the Church, should be run. Throughout Europe apocalyptic fears gripped Christendom as the millennial year 1000 approached, leading to a surge in the building of churches, cathedrals, monasteries and abbeys amid fears that the world might be about to end. In Normandy aristocrats deployed their philanthropy to compete with one another to see who could build the grandest religious houses. They brought the practice with them to England. During the 50 years after the Norman Conquest most of the major church buildings in the country were rebuilt and many new ones were begun. The new Norman overlords whom King William installed across England imposed their own preferences not just on the construction of buildings but also on the appointment of bishops and priests. As Edward L. Cutts noted in his comprehensive study, *Parish Priests and their People in the Middle Ages in England*, 'just as in the early Saxon period every thane thought it incumbent upon him to build a parish church on his estate, so now it became almost a fashion for every great noble to found a monastery'.[18] Most significantly, many of these new Norman *seigneurs*, instead of exercising the traditional Saxon *advowson* – the right to nominate the priest to his manorial church – passed that to the new monasteries. This gave the new monasteries control over all the lands designated to provide a living for the parish. Nearly half the parishes of England were now stripped of the best part of their endowments in order to found and enrich the monasteries.[19] In many cases the monasteries kept this income themselves and appointed a low-paid vicar or curate to minister to parishioners.[20] This inevitably reduced the amount available for distribution in alms to the poor. It constituted a significant shift in philanthropic power.

THE RISE OF THE MONASTERIES

During late antiquity Christianity had spread through the cities of the Roman Empire as a predominantly urban phenomenon. Its bishops were still based in church communities in the cities of the late Roman world. But monasticism was an impulse of withdrawal from the world, so its great centres were often located in remote and even isolated places. Christianity now became implanted in the rural world and the monastery competed with the parish to be the chief vehicle of philanthropy. To the alarm of the more ambitious bishops, monasteries were particularly successful in attracting alms from the Catholic community, which previously the bishop would have controlled and distributed to the poor. As Edward Cutts put it:

> The religious fervour of the monks, who abandoned the world and practised self-denial as a means to spiritual perfection and closer communion with God, naturally excited awed admiration; the picturesque surroundings of their profession, the frock and hood, the shaven head and mortified countenance, the hard life of the cloister and the manifold services in the Church, impressed the imagination; and consequently the popularity of the monks threw the secular clergy into the shade. The great churches of the monasteries rivalled the cathedrals in magnitude and splendour; the great abbots – relieved by the Pope from the jurisdiction of their bishops, exercising themselves jurisdiction over their own estates, summoned to parliament, wealthy and learned – were the rivals of the bishops; and the 'lord monks' held a higher rank in public estimation than the parish rectors.[21]

Monks, a good number having jettisoned their own wealth, were, certainly in the early years, seen as trustworthy conduits for handling donations, and may even have attracted donations which would otherwise have gone directly to the poor.[22] The sixth-century Rule of St Benedict directed monks to perform good works, to give their old clothing to the indigent, to wash the feet of paupers on Holy Thursday, and to make distributions to the poor as part of monastic observances for the dead. Chapter 53 of the Rule set out the monastic obligation to hospitality. Guests were to be treated as if they were Christ himself. But by the ninth century, Benedictines had begun to distinguish between rich and poor guests; there were hospices for the wealthy and separate *hospitalia pauperum* for the destitute and needy.

But monasteries also became great centres of learning, which added to their ethos of nobility. Younger sons of aristocratic families often found a monastic career more attractive than a life without land or inheritance. There men studied Greek and Latin – 'ever taking delight in learning, teaching, and writing', in the words of Bede – copying and preserving manuscripts which would give the world access to the great works of antiquity and scholasticism. At a time when barbarian invasions were terrorizing the continent of Europe, the monasteries of the British Isles offered a safe haven for learning.

The plan for the ideal early medieval monastery drawn up for the Abbey at St Gall in Switzerland in the eighth century, during the reign of Pepin the Short, is the only surviving major architectural drawing from the period between the decline of Rome and the thirteenth century. It includes not just a great church with monastic houses, and a complex of supporting buildings, but also an infirmary and a hospital to offer rest and respite to the needy, travellers and pilgrims.

Gradually, the root word of hospital was extended by the writers and interpreters of medieval canon law to include concern for the relief of the poor in general. The phrase the canonists used to describe the responsibilities of parish clergy for poor relief was *tenere hospitalitatem* – 'keeping hospitality' – and almsgiving to the poor was soon subsumed into that notion.[23] The central importance of this was enshrined in the code of laws published after the Second Lateran Council in 1152, which formed the basis of Catholic canon law until 1917. The section dedicated to 'Hospitality and the role of the Bishop' makes clear that no priest found to be lacking in hospitality could be consecrated a bishop.[24] In England alone some 220 hospitals were founded in the twelfth century and 310 more in the thirteenth century.[25] As the population grew within Europe, so did the emphasis on the need to provide philanthropically for the poor, the sick and the needy. By the middle of the thirteenth century, hospitals were being built all across Western Europe with designs taken from the descriptions of pilgrims and crusaders who returned from the East with tales of the vast and impressive hospitals there – where Islamic hospitals included separate areas for men and women, wards for different ailments, and even units for the mentally ill.[26]

By the early thirteenth century, bishops in Germany were doing more than merely adding hostels to monasteries. Instead they were constructing far larger separate hospitals with more specialist medical facilities to deal with the plague and leprosy.[27] This was a legacy of the

Council of Clermont in 1130, which forbade monks to practise medicine for fear it might undermine their spiritual calling.[28] However, though the running of hospitals was taken out of the control of monasteries, the new hospitals were still staffed mainly by monks and nuns. Their duties, indeed, were constantly expanding. They were still charged with hospitality for pilgrims and travellers. They still cared for the sick and the poor. But to those responsibilities were now added the care of orphans and foundlings, which involved finding wet nurses, foster parents, arranging adoptions, and providing training in useful trades or domestic service for the children who remained in the care of the hospital. Some of the new hospitals specialized in looking after people with leprosy. Some were pest houses to confine those with highly infectious diseases such as tuberculosis, cholera, smallpox or typhus. Others were convalescent hospitals. In Italy plague houses, known as *lazaretti*, were used to fumigate visiting sailors or confine troublesome beggars.[29] The Florentine hospital of Santa Maria Nova from the 1320s onwards declared its aim to be to assist 'the sick poor' rather than 'the sick and the poor', and as a result has been called the first proper hospital in Christendom.[30]

In England the Dissolution of the Monasteries prosecuted by Henry VIII in the mid-sixteenth century effectively ended monastic charitable hospitality for more than three centuries. Although the medieval monastic hospitals had limited capacity in terms of medical treatment, they nonetheless offered a place of shelter for the old and the needy. Their closure constituted what the medical historian Roy Porter calls 'rapacious asset-stripping carried out in the name of religious reform', which brought about 'a major setback' in healthcare for the poor.[31] It was not only England which was so affected. Monastic hospitality continued in countries that remained Catholic at the time of the Reformation – a practice which was ended in Germany only when religious property was confiscated under the 1648 Treaty of Westphalia, to the benefit of Protestant princes and the detriment of the poor, sick and refugees. Monastic hospitals continued to offer some provision for the sick poor in France up until the French Revolution in 1789, out of which the modern secular medical hospital grew.[32] The change, while bringing medical benefits, was to have a damaging effect upon the development of modern philanthropy for, with the advent of Protestant theological attitudes towards the poor, something of the spiritual and sacramental character of philanthropic hospitality was lost.[33]

MEDIEVAL ISLAMIC PHILANTHROPIC INSTITUTIONS

Philanthropy was institutionalized in the Jewish and Muslim communities over this period in a similar way. In the Islamic community, scholars suggest, most giving was direct, from individual to individual. There is little evidence in the documentary record but artefacts and travellers' tales reveal the importance of direct charity all across medieval Islam as it spread into Spain, southern France and Italy in the early Middle Ages. The Samanid culture of the ninth-century Persian Empire, which stretched from modern Iran to Uzbekistan, has left plentiful proof in the proverbs which were set into bowls used for serving and eating food. Messages such as 'generosity is the guardian of honour and property' testify to the Samanid belief that it was shameful to eat alone. The homes of the wealthy were always open to guests and wayfarers. But giving went beyond hospitality to those who might reciprocate. Another Samanid motto declared: 'Generosity is not just giving money from excess, but rather sharing with the poor.'[34] After a visit to Mecca in the fourteenth century, the Moroccan traveller Ibn Battuta recorded how poor members of the community would gather at the communal ovens to be given a share of the bread:

> The citizens are . . . of consummate generosity, liberal to the poor and to those who have renounced the world, and kindly toward strangers . . . When anyone has his bread baked and takes it away to his house, the destitute follow him . . . and he gives each one of them whatever he assigned to them, sending none away disappointed. Even if he has but a single loaf, he gives away a third or a half of it, conceding it cheerfully and without grudgingness.[35]

When the sixteenth-century French scholar Guillaume Postel, who worked for the French ambassador at the court of the Ottoman Sultan, travelled throughout the Middle East to collect manuscripts, he found charitable giving everywhere:

> You find poor people who have nothing to give but who understand that offering help to people consists not only of food and drink, but of all kinds of needs: some spend a lifetime repairing bad roads by bringing stones, wood, filling holes and improving their surfaces;

others arrange the course of streams and water sources . . . Rich
people in Anatolia . . . who see travellers coming down the roads
invite them to eat drink and sleep in their homes, for the sake of their
souls, and take nothing for it from anyone; neither rich nor poor pays
anything, and the next day one thanks them heartily, invoking God's
blessing on them in recompense. And these kind of people are most
respected among Muslims because they send their charity to Paradise
ahead of them.[36]

Such philanthropy, which falls under the Islamic category of *sadaqa*
(voluntary giving), has mostly gone unrecorded by historians. It is
charity given discreetly and anonymously.

But large amounts of evidence is available for the charitable
foundations, both large and small, which Muslims characterize as
waqfs. Often the legal document which is the basis of the charitable
endowment articulates the desire of the founder to come closer to God.
Sometimes an abridged version was carved in stone on the front of the
building erected through the benefaction. It preserved the name of the
founder and asked grateful users to pray for the founder's soul. The
waqf loomed as large in Islamic philanthropy as the monastery and
hospital did in Christianity.

Under a *waqf* a donor set aside funds which would be earmarked
in perpetuity for a charitable purpose to do some good to the general
community. It might be something as small as a fountain to provide
water to passers-by. Or it might be as large as a mosque attached to
a business which provided it with income. Or a *waqf* might even be
a more modest gift – a rug for the mosque, a holy text for an Islamic
college, or a stipend for an orphan student. Or a room might be rented
out to provide a weekly income for a holy man to recite prayers for
the soul of the deceased at his tomb.[37] At the other end of the scale
is the celebrated Grand Bazaar in Istanbul. It was created by a *waqf*
to finance the mosque which Sultan Mehmed the Conqueror installed
inside the great Byzantine church of Aya Sofya in the fifteenth century.
In between were a vast range of mosques, schools, colleges, bridges,
kitchens, hospitals and caravanserais – roadside hostels where caravans
and travellers could rest overnight. Drinking fountains also began to
appear in great numbers all across the Islamic world from the ninth
century onwards.[38] Among the more famous *waqfs* are the early

ninth-century pool at Darb Zubayda on the pilgrimage route from Baghdad to Mecca; the thirteenth-century hospital at Divrigi in Eastern Anatolia; the colleges that ring the Dome of the Rock in Jerusalem; and the sixteenth-century Süleymaniye mosque complex in Istanbul, with its schools, hospice and baths. The world-famous seventeenth-century Taj Mahal in Agra was a *waqf*. So was the nineteenth-century mosque-school-kitchen compound established in Kavala by Muhammad Ali Pasha, the founder of modern Egypt.[39] In the Mamluk and Ottoman empires, scholars and religious institutions, and their students, were sustained in large part by such endowments.[40]

From about the tenth century these *waqfs* replaced *zakat* – the compulsory annual charitable tithe on the wealth of every Muslim – as the main vehicle for Islamic philanthropy, according to the historian of Islam, Marshall Hodgson.[41] Such foundations were proclamations of prestige and power as well as pious commitments to fulfil the injunctions of the Qur'an on almsgiving. They even came to be used as a kind of tax dodge, since an endowment would preserve family capital intact in a *waqf* from which family members, or individuals, might benefit – without the fortune being divided upon the death of the owner as Islamic law requires. It had the additional benefit of creating a safe haven for family wealth lest it be confiscated by the Sultan when an individual fell out of favour.

The collection of *zakat* was similarly codified. Although the Qur'an lays down requirements about the payment of *zakat*, it offers little in the way of practical instruction for its payment and distribution. Islamic scholars, over the centuries, laid down a series of regulations about the payment which came, in effect, to be a kind of tax. The prominent jurist and philosopher Abu Hamid Muhammad al-Ghazali, who died in 1111, wrote a point-by-point guide to giving *zakat*, called *The Mysteries of Almsgiving*. It touched on a wide range of philanthropic themes – personal ambition, anonymous versus public giving, public and private shame, cultural conventions, economic concerns and spiritual sincerity. It dealt with both *zakat*, which was obligatory, and *sadaqa*, which was voluntary. 'One act of *sadaqa* shuts seventy gates of evil,' al-Ghazali wrote. Other thinkers and politicians made their own contributions. Before the coronation of the great sultan Saladin, scourge of the Crusaders, in 1174, the people of Egypt had paid their *zakat* directly to the needy and deserving. But, just as Æthelstan had done in Saxon England when he made tithes compulsory, Saladin transformed the charitable payment into a formal government tax, opening an Office of Zakat.[42] Later jurists added more regulations and precedents. The sixteenth-century mufti of Istanbul, Ebu-s-Su'ud Efendi – who harmonized secular Ottoman law with Islamic sharia – ruled that the Sultan too had an obligation to pay *zakat*, a custom which reached its most colourful apogee in India. There, in the sixteenth and seventeenth centuries, the Muslim Mughal Empire rulers of the subcontinent – then the greatest economic power in the world – established the tradition of weighing sultans and princes on their solar and lunar birthdays against sacks of coins, silk, perfume, copper, iron, butter, starch, salt, grains, rice and other commodities, which were then distributed to the deserving.[43] It was even declared that citizens could count contributions to the Ottoman Navy as *zakat*, so long as the monies were not used for purposes contrary to Islamic law.[44]

FROM 'POVERTY OF STATUS' TO 'POVERTY OF POSSESSIONS' AMONG MEDIEVAL JEWS

Judaism, too, codified its laws of charity in the medieval period. The richest evidence for this was found in a hoard of forgotten manuscript fragments discovered by two nineteenth-century Scottish scholar-adventurers, Agnes and Margaret Smith. They were unearthed in the *geniza* – a hidden chamber for sacred papers awaiting permanent disposal – in the Bin Ezra synagogue in Fustat, old Cairo. The store consisted of 300,000 letters and other documents which had been lodged in the Cairo Geniza over a 200-year period between 1000 and 1250. They are, according to the leading historian of Jews in the Islamic world, Mark R. Cohen, 'the richest body of material for the history of poverty and charity in the Jewish world of the Middle Ages'.[45] They tell the story of how one prominent medieval Jewish community dealt with the constant presence of poverty in its midst.

Four of the letters chosen for comment by Cohen are particularly revealing. One begins:

> I am dispatching this letter to the most illustrious elders, may God preserve them, to inform them that the bearer of this [letter] is a man who was healthy, working strenuously in order to 'conceal' (*li-yastura*) himself and his family, when Fate betrayed him and he became weak

(*daif al-hayil*), such that anyone looking at him needs no explanation about his condition. Whoever assists him with something with which he can maintain his way of life shall be deemed to have made an offering [to God]. He is ashamed (*mustahi*), for this has never been his habit. Whoever does him a good turn shall be deemed to have done so for the sake of God, and the Creator will magnify his reward.[46]

The main purpose of the letter is to invite the writer's relatives in Qalyub, a town near Fustat, to attend a family celebration at a forthcoming holiday time. But the writer has entrusted delivery of the letter to someone consumed by a crisis of poverty. The writer devotes a preface of eight lines to telling the unhappy tale of the bearer of the letter. He then pleads that his relatives in Qalyub should help the unfortunate man.

A second Geniza letter, conveying a similar message, also stresses that the needy letter bearer, one Solomon b Benjamin, is 'a good and deserving man (*hagun*), crowned with humility, a modest person, from a good family (*mi-benei avot*) of noteworthy householders whose table was always set and whose houses were always wide-open'. However, the man and his family 'fell from their wealth',[47] became poor, and 'were forced to turn in their need to others'. A third letter, penned by the great Hebrew poet Judah ha-Levi, who passed through Egypt in 1140–1 on his way from his home in Spain to the Holy Land, commends the deliverer of the letter for charitable assistance; he too 'had been well off and now is the opposite'. Moreover, 'he suffers from poor health and eyesight, and is far from family and homeland'. The fourth letter tells the story of a formerly rich man who had fallen on hard times after being attacked by brigands on the road between Damascus and Jerusalem; he too arrives at the synagogue in Egypt carrying a letter beseeching charity from the Jewish community.

A significant shift is being recorded here. In the time of the Romans, and the early Christians, and in the early feudal Middle Ages, the word 'poor' was used to mean those without political power. It meant poverty of status rather than lack of possessions. According to the great historian of medieval poverty, Bronislaw Geremek, who viewed a thousand years of European history from the perspective of ordinary people, until the early Middle Ages the great contrast was between *pauper* (poor) and *potens* (power).[48] But these Jewish texts from the eleventh century show something very different. In the Geniza fragments 'poor' is used in its modern economic sense – lacking material possessions or money. The change reflects a shift from an economy of agricultural self-sufficiency and bartering to one which was urban, commercial and monetary. That shift brought with it new economic growth. But it also enlarged the ranks of the poor. In the Geniza texts, says Cohen, the 'weak' are those lacking the physical or emotional capability to work and who need charitable assistance, rather than those who are dependent upon the politically powerful.

So, two types of poverty are being discerned here. There is the structural poverty of people who live in permanent destitution because of ill-health, disability or old age – and therefore cannot work – all those in vulnerable states such as widows and orphans. But there is also what social historians have called the 'conjunctural poverty' of people who earn just enough through their labours to support their family. Such folk can become 'poor' by a downturn in trade or a glut in the market. This was a significant shift. The Geniza papers provide some of the earliest documentary evidence of this change. Attitudes to the destitute versus the working poor, to those in structural and conjunctural poverty, were to become a theme throughout the history of philanthropy, overlapping with notions of the deserving and undeserving poor.

MAIMONIDES AND THE HIERARCHY OF GIVING

Among the treasure trove of letters found in the Cairo Geniza's forgotten store are several from the greatest of the medieval Jewish legalist scholars and philosophers, Rabbi Moshe ben Maimon, whom history has come to know as Maimonides and some of his followers call Rambam. This great Sephardic thinker was born in Córdoba, Spain, in 1135 but lived in Egypt for most of his life, dying in Fustat in 1204. His Geniza autograph letters contain information about both his personal and public life and his views on the role of charity. Maimonides offered his fellow Jews three reasons to give. The first was that 'charity is an identifying mark for a righteous person, a descendant of Abraham, our patriarch'.[49] To explain his views he quotes Genesis.[50] Furthermore, Maimonides continues, 'the throne of Israel will not be established, nor will the true faith stand, except through charity' – in support of

which he cites the Prophet Isaiah.[51] His second reason for giving is that
it will make others compassionate toward the giver: 'Everyone who is
merciful evokes mercy from others,' he says, quoting Deuteronomy.[52]
Here Maimonides adds that 'a person will never become impoverished
from giving charity'. Nor will harm or damage ever be caused. This is
because, he adds, quoting Isaiah, 'the deed of charity is peace'.[53] His
third reason, for which he also cites the same prophet, is that charity
'will bring the redemption of Israel'.[54]

Maimonides here restricts his focus to within the Jewish community,
writing:

> . . . the entire Jewish people and all those who attach themselves to
> them are as brothers, as Deuteronomy [14:1] states: 'You are children
> unto God your Lord.' And if a brother will not show mercy to a
> brother, who will show mercy to them? To whom do the poor of
> Israel lift up their eyes? To the Gentiles who hate them and pursue
> them? Behold their eyes are pointed to their brethren alone.

His distrust of those outside the Jewish community is clear:

> Whenever a person is cruel and does not show mercy, his lineage is
> suspect, for cruelty is found only among the Gentiles, as Jeremiah
> [3:42] states: 'They are cruel and will not show mercy.'

Any Jew 'who turns his eyes away from [giving] charity' is labelled by
Maimonides as 'rebellious'.

But the contribution of Maimonides goes beyond its impact upon
philanthropy within Judaism. There is a universality to his emphasis
that *tzedakah*, the Jewish word for charity and almsgiving, is also the
Hebrew word for both righteousness or justice. For any religious person,
this suggests, establishing a right relationship with God inescapably
involves creating a just relationship with one's fellow men and women.

The great contribution of Maimonides to the history of philanthropy,
however, is his hierarchy of Eight Levels of Giving. This became
known as Rambam's Ladder, for it offers guidance to climbing the
rungs from the lowest level of giving to the one of which Maimonides
approves most highly. In these Maimonides deals with a range of the
issues which philanthropy raises in every time and place: reluctance,

proportion, solicitation, shame, boundaries, corruption, anonymity and responsibility:[55]

- At the bottom of the Eight Levels are gifts which are given without good grace, reluctantly or grudgingly. 'Whenever a person gives charity to a poor person with an unpleasant countenance and with his face buried in the earth, he loses and destroys his merit even if he gives him 1,000 gold pieces.'[56] For 'it is forbidden to scold a poor person or to raise one's voice against him'.[57]
- The second rung consists of giving less than is appropriate but with 'a pleasant countenance and with happiness, commiserating with him about his troubles'.[58]
- The third rung is giving directly to the poor upon being asked.[59]
- The fourth rung is giving before the poor person asks.[60]
- The fifth rung is when 'the poor person knows from whom he took, but the donor does not know to whom he gave'. Maimonides here gives the example of 'the great Sages who would bundle coins in a sheet and hang them over their shoulders and the poor would come and take them [without being seen by the donor] so that they would not be embarrassed'.[61]
- The sixth rung is reached when the donor knows the identity of the recipient, but the poor person does not know who made the donation from which he or she profits. Maimonides cites here 'the great Sages who would go in secret and throw money into the doorways of the poor'.[62] This was a particularly useful mechanism, he said, in situations where those in charge of official distributions to the poor might be untrustworthy (*see the next rung*), for 'a person should not give to a charity fund unless he knows that the person managing it is faithful, wise, and capable of administering it in a proper manner'.[63]
- The seventh rung is when a gift could be made through a mechanism which meant that both giver and recipient are unknown to each other. Communal funds, administered by responsible people, were within this category. Maimonides writes that this type of giving was exemplified by the 'secret chamber' which existed in synagogues. Donors left gifts

discreetly in the room and then the needy collected the offerings unseen by their benefactors. Maimonides wrote: 'The righteous would make donations there in secret and poor people of distinguished lineage would derive their livelihood from it in secret.' The virtue of this level of giving was that the recipient was immune from any shame in the transaction and the donor could have no ulterior motive. It was thus, Maimonides wrote, 'an observance of the *mitzvah* [commandment] for its sake alone'.[64]

- At the top of Maimonides' Eight Levels of Giving is charity which allows the recipient to become self-sufficient. 'The highest level beyond which there is none,' he writes, 'is a person who supports a Jew who has fallen into poverty' by 'entering into partnership with him, or finding him work, so that his hand will be fortified so that he will not have to ask others'.[65]

Maimonides confines charity to within the circle of the Jewish community. This is probably because, as Derek Penslar notes, medieval Jews lived in tightly knit communities:

> Prosperous Jews were unable to translate their wealth into landed property, and so retained large amounts of liquid capital, much of which went to tax payments and poor care for the community. Lacking the characteristics of the Gentile nobility, wealthy Jews lived cheek by jowl with their poorer brethren. The Gentile authorities demanded this elite care for the Jewish poor, and, due to both compulsion and a sense of obligation, the Jewish elite fulfilled this demand.[66]

The need for the Jews to care for their own poor was reinforced by the fact that in Europe they were excluded from the two main philanthropic vehicles – the Church and the associations of craftsmen and merchants known as guilds. Just how hostile the environment was to Jews, Penslar notes, is illustrated by the fact that one of the most prominent philanthropic activities within the Jewish community in this period was the ransoming of Jews taken captive in wars and acts of brigandage. Gradually over the centuries, however, Jewish philanthropy began to develop along the lines set by the models of philanthropy established within the culture of Christendom.

THE TWELFTH-CENTURY RENAISSANCE — A NEW
ECONOMY AND A NEW THEOLOGY

In the second half of the tenth century the climate grew warmer and milder in Europe and the population began to grow rapidly. A number of changes were triggered, and reinforced, by this development. More land was cleared to feed the rising population. Early medieval agriculture had concentrated on the light soils of the lower hillsides, but now the more fertile soils of the valley bottoms were brought under cultivation. Heftier ploughs were invented to cope with the heavier soils. Waste and marginal lands were reclaimed. New crops such as beans and oats were introduced with patterns of crop rotation which reduced the amount of land left fallow. This agricultural revolution meant that, by the end of the eleventh century, Europe could feed itself with less labour, leaving more people free to do other work. Alongside this more intensive method of farming, the wool and linen industries grew. A drift to the cities began and places which were once merely centres of ecclesiastical administration became centres of artisan manufacture and trade, and learning.[67]

Trade grew at first locally, then regionally, and finally internationally, with merchants taking Europe's raw materials and manufactured goods along the Silk Road to the Far East, bringing back exotic spices and textiles in exchange. The agricultural revolution was supplemented by a commercial one. The formation of merchant companies, the creation of instruments of credit, bills of exchange, double-entry bookkeeping, partnership contracts and the basics of deposit banking, laid the foundations for the growth of entrepreneurial capitalism. The new merchant class evolved into a major engine of social and economic change, and became more literate. The result was what the medieval historian Maureen Miller has called a period of 'cultural efflorescence' in which 'the stolid round vaults of the Romanesque gave way to the soaring pinnacles of great Gothic architecture'.[68] Primitive feudalism was embellished by the notion of courtly love. And where once had been a culture of general illiteracy there now developed the first universities in which thinkers once again began to grapple with the fundamental problems of metaphysics which had been neglected since the days of antiquity. This twelfth-century Renaissance marked the start of what historians call the High Middle Ages. It was to lay the foundations for the literary and artistic revitalization of Europe in the Renaissance of the fifteenth century and the scientific and philosophical revolution of the eighteenth-century Enlightenment. But more immediately it had a major impact on the development of philanthropy.

The stable and prosperous economy of the twelfth century saw most of the poorer people, peasant farmers, rooted to their land and living in small villages. Mass unemployment was unknown and the destitute were comparatively few in number, their misfortunes arising from personal catastrophes such as crippling accidents, long illness or the feebleness of extreme old age. Life expectancy in England in that era was little more than 30 years[69] – which is why widows and orphans loom so large in the concerns of the philosophers and theologians who worked through this new philanthropy in schools that developed into the first universities at Bologna in 1088, Oxford in 1096 and Paris in 1200. Increased contact with the Islamic world in Spain and Sicily, and through the Crusades, allowed these European thinkers new access to the great works of the ancient classics, most notably those of Aristotle, whose works had been preserved in Arabic translations. Attitudes to both giving and to the poor were significantly developed in these centres of intellectual activity.

The task for the theologians and philosophers of this period was how to reconcile the radical simplicity of Christ and his message with a social and political economy which was changing rapidly all around them. The key tension at this time was a conflict between private property and communal rights. How could private ownership of property be reconciled with God's gift of the earth to all in common? Could charity balance resources between rich and poor? They worked towards an answer using Aristotle's notion of the ideal mean – through which the balance and harmony of justice is to be achieved. A great debate ensued between successive generations of medieval theologians who wrestled with many of the issues immediately recognizable to a student of philanthropy today. That debate, as it developed through the twelfth and thirteenth centuries, is set out in two masterful studies by the eminent medievalist Brian Tierney.[70] These seminal works have had a profound impact on medieval historians, but they have been generally neglected by historians of philanthropy, who have produced a distorted vision of modern philanthropy as a result. Until now.

RECONCILING MEDIEVAL CONTRADICTIONS –
GRATIAN'S *DECRETUM*

The ideological foundation of organized Christian charity was in a
thoroughly chaotic state at the beginning of the twelfth century. In his two
magisterial works on medieval charity Brian Tierney reviews more than a
thousand years of diverse accumulated material. First come the opinions of
revered Church Fathers such as Clement, Basil, Ambrose and Augustine.
Then came the decrees and judgements of local and general Church
councils. Next a case history of ecclesiastical and civil law developed.
Finally came the decrees and decretals of a succession of popes, who had
recommended that between a quarter and a third of Church income
should be devoted to the relief of poverty. But all this had never been
adequately codified and writings on it were full of internal contradictions.

The man who sought to rectify that was a monk from Bologna
named Gratian who, around 1140, created a great systematization
of the Christian inheritance which became known as the *Decretum*.
Gratian's method was to state a problem, then cite all the authorities he
considered relevant, sometimes offering a solution which he felt brought
the discordant texts into agreement. The *Decretum*, which became the
standard Catholic reference text for centuries, was so immediately
influential that more than a hundred different commentaries and glosses
were written on it by other theologians before the end of the twelfth
century. One of the earliest of these, by Peter Lombard in 1150, was
so weighty that the thirteenth-century English scholastic Roger Bacon
grumbled 'it takes a horse to carry it'.[71]

The starting point of the twelfth-century theologians was the teaching
of the Church Fathers which, as we have seen in the previous chapter,
had been fairly uncompromising from the first to the fourth century.
Clement had embraced the notion of 'the pious poor and the wicked
rich'. Basil had berated the rich and insisted that the relationship between
them and the poor must be rooted in a sense of justice. Ambrose had
declared that giving to the needy should take precedence over giving
to our relatives. Augustine had insisted that we needed to atone for
our constant sinning through almsgiving as regular as 'the waterwheel
continually turning to irrigate the fields'.[*] Gratian's response to this

---

[*] See pages 63 to 70 above.

tricky subject was often to collect the various views of the Fathers without any attempt to reconcile them. That task was undertaken, over the next century, by commentators known as Decretists, who offered varying conclusions. They were clearly influenced by the changing social and economic circumstances of their times, though almost all, like Gratian, took it for granted that charity in some form was necessary for the remission of sins.

The Decretists, Tierney observes, elaborated 'a whole legal philosophy which related the claims of the poor to a coherent theory of natural law and property'.[72] That philosophy dealt with the moral and legal status of the poor, the appropriate attitudes of the donor and recipient, and the administration of poor relief by Church bodies. The starting point of these twelfth-century philosophers and theologians was the assertion that the poor had certain rights to the property of the rich, especially in times of urgent need. This notion, they believed, was implicit in natural law. Certain principles of justice and fairness were imprinted upon human minds by God. All property is common property in times of necessity.[73] The poor had the right to use, though not to own, the property of others. Moreover, they had a claim on the surplus wealth of the community.[74]

In the early years most thinkers held to a fairly stark view of the relationship between the wealthy and the poor. Riches were a great danger to piety, said the Parisian theologian Petrus Comestor in the 1170s.[75] Preaching in 1189, Alan of Lille asked, 'Where does Christ live?' and replied, 'Only among the paupers of Christ, of whom he said, "Blessed are the poor in spirit".'[76] His contemporary Robert of Flamborough, in a small book of instruction for priests to use in the confessional, the *Liber poenitentialis*, declared, 'whoever does not receive guests in his home, as God has ordained, nor give alms, if he makes no amends by bread and water for an equivalent period, let him do penance'. In the confessional almsgiving was seen as the most efficacious remedy for sin.[77]

The rich were under an unceasing obligation to help the poor. Pope Innocent III (1198–1216) derived much of his teaching direct from Gratian. He asserted: 'Fasting is good but alms are better ... for through fasting, one's own flesh is weakened, but through alms that of another is renewed ... It is better to pray with works than with words.'[78] Peter of Poitiers likened those who relieved the poor to Mary Magdalene when she anointed Christ's feet.[79] Peter of Blois, Archdeacon of London, called the poor man 'the Vicar of Christ', a title which later came to be used exclusively for the Pope. Joannes Teutonicus around 1216, in perhaps the most influential commentary of the thirteenth century, taught that any rich man could be compelled by legal process to give alms to the poor. An act of public denunciation and excommunication could be performed by a pauper against the rich man, though whether this was ever done in practice is unclear.[80] Peter the Chanter, who died in 1197, even maintained that secular rulers should force the rich to discharge their charitable duties to relieve the poor.[81]

The mood of the times was clear, and there was more to it than theological theory. This was the era in which movements of evangelical poverty swept through the Church. One such was the Humiliati, a group of Lombard noblemen, former prisoners of war, who assumed a penitential garb of grey and gave themselves up to a life of self-mortification and almsgiving. In 1134 they entered a monastery at Milan, where their wives formed a parallel convent. The Humiliati movement at its highest point had 94 monasteries. Not long after, around 1173, another ascetic group, the Poor Men of Lyons – who became the Waldensians, often seen as the forerunners of the Reformation – gave away their goods and property and preached a life of apostolic poverty. The idea of renunciation was to continue in Christian philanthropy long after this era.

Then in the thirteenth century a new religious grouping evolved, the friars. These men dedicated themselves to the religious life – but lived it out in the community rather than hidden away in monasteries. The friars gave ferocious sermons, often on the Dives and Lazarus parable, which took the side of the Virtuous Poor against the Evil Rich. Among the friars the Dominicans and Franciscans were most prominent in taking this view. In one vivid extended metaphor the Dominican, Peregrine of Opole, compared contemporary society to the Red Sea, in which the big fish – tempted by the Devil into selfish greed – devoured the little fish who represented the poor. Peregrine saw the sea as literally red, a symbol of the blood of the victims. Around the same time another Dominican, the Englishman John Bromyard, used Aesop's fable of the country mouse and the town mouse to contrast the rural poor with an urban elite who had acquired their wealth by methods which brought 'troubled conscience and danger to their souls'.[82]

But others were less robust in their condemnations. Instead they followed the approach of Clement of Alexandria, who in the second century had interpreted Christ's command that the rich young man should sell all as purely metaphorical. In *The Romance of the Rose*, written around 1280, the great medieval French poet Jean de Meun wrote: 'When God commands the good man to sell all he has and give it to the poor and follow him [Mark 10:21], he does not therefore want him to serve him in beggary. . . He means rather that he should . . . follow him with good works.'[83] Without wealth how were you to help the needy? (Margaret Thatcher asked the same question in her retelling of the parable of the Good Samaritan seven hundred years later.) Giordano of Pisa in 1304 went even further, suggesting that riches could lead to heaven: 'Many saints . . . were very rich. They climbed up on this tower, or this mountain, and they were nearer to God. The more they had . . . the higher they were, and the nearer to Heaven, grateful to God for it, and thanking him for it and loving him the more for it.'[84] And indeed, statistical analysis confirms that the majority of medieval saints were indeed of noble or upper-class origin.[85]

What accounts for this stark contrast in approach? The answer lies in the economics of the day. The changing commercial climate created by the activities of the moneyed mercantile elite nurtured the idea that riches were, perhaps, not so bad after all. But it did more. Some began to argue that poverty might perhaps be bad, spiritually, because it could distract the poor from attending to the proper worship of God. Jean de Meun, personifying poverty as female, suggested it could cause sin, 'for she torments and gnaws at soul and body, not just for an hour but as long as they dwell together, and brings them not only to condemnation but also to larceny and perjury and many other difficulties'.[86] That idea found backing from medieval philosophy's most distinguished thinker, Thomas Aquinas. In the 1260s he wrote that poverty could be useful when 'it removes the anxiety that is occasioned by riches', but it could also be harmful by leading the impoverished into 'worse occupations'. In such circumstances, poverty 'is simply an evil'.[87] Poverty could also give rise to the sins of jealousy, covetousness, envy and 'the refusal to accept one's condition'.[88] The pauper who refused to accept his condition with humility was scathingly referred to as the *pauper superbus*.

Other Decretists tried to follow a middle way between the two polarized positions that on the one hand all riches were evil, and on the other hand all poverty was bad. Large sums of money might tempt the weak into wickedness, they argued, quoting Ambrose. Moreover, riches could also act as an incentive to philanthropic virtue. These advocates of a Middle Way also cited Augustine's neutral attitude to riches. Wealth, Augustine had said, like other earthly things, could assist man on his pilgrimage through life, but it was not to be desired for its own sake. One prominent twelfth-century thinker who took this view was Bernard of Clairvaux, the great monastic reformer who established the Cistercian order. In his *De consideratione*, around 1150, he wrote to one of his disciples who had become Pope Eugene III, that gold and silver 'in themselves, as regards man's spiritual welfare . . . are neither good nor bad, yet the use of them is good, the abuse is bad; anxiety about them is worse; the greed of gain still more disgraceful.'[89]

The rediscovery of the works of Aristotle, which had been preserved by Islamic scholars and came to medieval Europe in the thirteenth century, helped the canonists of the High Middle Ages towards a reconciliation of these varying and diverse positions. One of Aristotle's central doctrines was of the desirability of the mean, or midway point, on any given spectrum of temperaments or values. He argued that moral virtue was to be found halfway between competing emotions such as anger and apathy, courage and cowardice, or extravagance and meanness. At one end of every scale was excess and at the other deficiency; virtue, like happiness, was to be found somewhere between the two extremes. Thomas Aquinas imported this notion into Christian philanthropic thinking, asserting in the 1260s in his *Summa Theologica*, that 'it is evident that moral virtue observes the mean'.[90] Jean de Meun put it more colloquially: 'The soul can be just as thoroughly ruined by excessive poverty as by excessive wealth; both wound with equal severity.'[91] Wealth and beggary are two extremes. Virtue lies at the mean, halfway between them.[92]

THE RIGHTS OF THE POOR AND
THE DUTY OF THE RICH

But how is the mean to be found? The canonists decided that owning riches and property was not wrong in itself; what was sinful was the accumulation of *excess* riches. Gratian in the *Decretum* quotes the fourth-century Church Father Ambrose as insisting that a rich man is not free to dispose of his goods as he pleases but has a duty to employ his superfluous goods to help others. Gratian suggests no one 'is as unjust and avaricious as the man who holds the food of many people which is of no use to him'.[93] Aquinas, writing a century later, echoes this, again quoting Ambrose: 'Feed him that dies of hunger: if thou hast not fed him, thou hast slain him.'[94] Aquinas accepts Ambrose's claim that we are guilty of murder when we neglect to aid the poor and instead spend money on anything other than necessities. The Angelic Doctor expands the point:

> The temporal goods, which God grants us, are ours as to ownership, but as to the use of them, they belong not us alone but also to such others as we are able to succour, out of what we have, over and above our needs. Hence, Basil says: . . . It is the hungry man's bread that you withhold, the naked man's cloak that you have stored away, the shoe of the barefoot that you have left to rot, the money of the needy that you have buried underground: and so you injure as many as you might help.[95]

Aquinas goes further. In cases of extreme need, the poor, therefore, have the right to steal from the rich.[96] Private property is justified as the most orderly way for each person to meet his or her needs, but in cases of urgent and manifest need it is morally acceptable to steal.[97] Such are the rights of the poor.

As to the duties of the rich, Aquinas codified seven primary Christian obligations: *vestio* (to clothe), *poto* (to give water), *cibo* (to feed), *redimo* (to redeem from prison), *tego* (to shelter), *colligo* (to nurse) and *condo* (to bury). These became the basis for the medieval doctrine of the Seven Corporal Works of Mercy. To fulfil them, Aquinas says, we must be open-handed and free with the goods we possess. Generosity is not shown by the *amount* we give but by the *proportion*. This means that the poor too, in their turn, are expected to give alms.[98] To be virtuous we should consume only what is necessary and give the surplus to those who will benefit from it most.[99] What we 'need', says Aquinas, will vary with the position we hold in society, along with the number and nature of our dependents.[100] The key consideration is that we have a healthy attitude towards our wealth, using it justly. What we must avoid is an unhealthy attachment to material possessions. We should not allow them to take the place of God as our ultimate object of love and devotion.[101] An immoderate desire for possessions ultimately makes us deeply restless, for it is an appetite that can never be sated. By the same logic, almsgiving that is motivated by a desire for public acclamation rather than love is not only without merit, it is positively sinful.[102] Acts of caring for the poor must grow from 'heartfelt sympathy for another's distress'.[103] There must be no expectation of reciprocity.[104] Aquinas believed that, in this way, surplus wealth would be continually distributed through society. This was very close to the Muslim view of the circulation of wealth through trading.*

All this resonates with later debates in philanthropy which also wrestled with questions about the relationship between charity and justice. Another thirteenth-century decretist, Johannes Teutonicus, had an interesting thought on that. He suggested that those who gave from their surplus engaged in an act of justice. But those who denied themselves something, to find the money for almsgiving, were performing an act of mercy, which he implied was superior. Aquinas went further. For him charity grows out of justice.[105] Charity can go beyond justice, but it can never replace it. An employer, for example, could never consider the payment of fair wages as almsgiving, for they are due as a matter of justice.[106] Other canonists added further refinements. Guido de Baysio, chancellor of the University of Bologna in the first decade of the fourteenth century, insisted that alms given from stolen goods were illegitimate, as were those given by usurers, corrupt government officials, lawyers who charged extortionate fees, and doctors who cheated the sick out of their money. Alms given by such individuals would do their souls no good. This is a subject which would be given particular currency in the nineteenth and twentieth centuries with the activities of the 'robber philanthropists' such as John D. Rockefeller, Andrew Carnegie and J. P. Morgan.†

SHOULD THE RICH DISCRIMINATE IN THEIR GIVING?

A second key development in the history of philanthropy occurred in this period. Canonists in the second half of the twelfth century became

---

* See the interview with Naser Haghamed, pages 118–9 below.

† See pages 337–364 below.

very exercised by the question of whether or not it was legitimate to discriminate when giving. Two distinct approaches were adopted. The first suggested that alms must be given to everyone who asks. The second insisted that it is necessary to discriminate between deserving and less deserving recipients. This is significant for two reasons. The first is that a number of writers have argued in various histories of philanthropy that religious charity, as opposed to that motivated by secular impulses, has an indiscriminate character. The evidence of the debates among the canonists of the High Middle Ages clearly demonstrates that this is wrong. But it is also important because the disputes between the great medieval thinkers laid the groundwork for the distinction between the deserving and the undeserving poor which was to become a major theme in the history of philanthropy.

Gratian, as ever, had it both ways. He presented views from both sides of the argument. He advanced the case for indiscriminate giving thus: 'In hospitality there is no regard for persons, but we ought to welcome indifferently all for whom our resources suffice.' In support he cited the opinion of John Chrysostom, who had responded with indignation to those quizzing a beggar about his circumstances before offering help. 'Let us put a stop to this ridiculous, diabolical, peremptory prying,' the fourth-century Church Father had exploded. 'If someone genuinely asks for food, do not put him to any examination.'[107] For Chrysostom the generosity of the giver was more important than the merits of the recipient. One thousand years later Guido de Baysio, in his great commentary on Gratian, agreed and added that where a donor gave alms to aggrandize himself, rather than out of genuine love, the act was in fact sinful.[108]

But Gratian also cites Church Fathers who take the opposite view and who favour distinguishing between more and less worthy beggars. He cites Ambrose as saying that Christians should have first claim to the generosity of the Church, along with those who cannot work because of age, sickness or other misfortune – and he quotes Ambrose's view that special consideration should be given to the impoverished who are too ashamed to beg publicly. Gratian goes further, citing Augustine's insistence that no alms should be given to practitioners of 'vile professions' such as actors, prostitutes and gladiators. And twice in the *Decretum* he quotes an apparently more extreme view of Augustine that charity can sometimes promote bad behaviour: 'It is more useful to take bread away from a hungry man than to break bread for him if, being sure of his food, he neglected righteousness.' These words of Augustine have been regularly cited over the centuries by those who advocate a system of poor relief which seeks to punish recipients or 'correct' their behaviour.

To reconcile these opposing positions Gratian makes a fine distinction between *hospitalitas*, hospitality, and *liberalitas*, generosity. Hospitality requires the giving of alms gratuitously, without discriminating between persons. But generosity allows the giver to discriminate between friends and strangers, the honest and dishonest, and the humble and the arrogant. Gratian concludes, 'we give first to the just, then to sinners'.[109] Gratian's distinction between *hospitalitas* and *liberalitas* foreshadowed the modern distinction between charity and welfare.[110]

It was from this point on that the tradition became established within philanthropy that it was acceptable to discriminate in giving. Early Decretists such as Peter Lombard had been perplexed as to whether it was legitimate to give to family and friends before needy strangers.[111] Now, only a century later, a clear consensus emerged among canonists that this was perfectly permissible. Later writers, including Aquinas and the fourteenth-century Dominican and Franciscan preachers, insisted that discrimination in almsgiving was not just permissible but proper. Economic and social forces added impetus to this tradition, as severe inflation set in during the late twelfth and early thirteenth centuries. This deprived monks of real income. So did the arrival of the Dominicans and Franciscans. Their new followers among the gentry diverted their charitable donations from the old monastic orders towards the new friars. Shortage of funds in traditional monasteries forced the almoners in Benedictine monasteries to begin discriminating over who would receive their alms. They also cut the handout of food at abbey gates, from once a day to just two or three times a week. It was the 'naked poor' who suffered most.[112]

But how should priorities in almsgiving be fixed? The canonists warned against donors being swayed by physical revulsion at the smell and sight of the poor. Some quoted Seneca's remark that the wise man 'will not avert his countenance or a sympathy from anyone because he has a withered leg, or is emaciated and in rags, and is old and leans upon a staff'. The noted early thirteenth-century preacher, Jaques de Vitry, echoed that sentiment. He said of contemporary hospital patients:

'One must have the courage of a martyr to overcome one's repugnance at the unbearable filth and stench of the patients.' Indeed, by the late fifteenth century, one Sienese Dominican was declaring that the more repulsive the beggar, the greater the charity shown by the almsgiver[113] – a teaching which Bronislaw Geremek suggests encouraged beggars to flaunt their physical degradation with 'ostentatious displays of their infirmity to confer legitimacy on their begging'.[114] The paintings of Hieronymus Bosch show numerous examples of this. Setting aside physical revulsion, two factors governed the thinking here. The first was what to do when resources were limited. The second went much further by asking whether it was, in some circumstances, desirable or even morally imperative to *refuse* to give.

Many canonists took as their starting point the 'ladder of perfection' drawn up by Ambrose in the fourth century. The thirteenth-century Spanish Dominican Raymond of Penyafort, now the patron saint of lawyers, compiled the *Decretals* of Pope Gregory IX – which were for 700 years to form the basis of Catholic canon law. In them he argued that charity should be indiscriminate when 'you have enough for all', but that when resources were limited Ambrose's priorities should be brought into play.[115] This 'ladder of perfection' required a man to love first God, then his parents, then his children, then those of his own household – and, only finally, strangers.[116] These strangers were accorded their own order of priority, starting with faithful fellow Christians, then the old, the sick, and those who fell blamelessly from wealth into poverty – a group labelled from the thirteenth century as the *pauperes verecundi* or shamefaced poor.[117] These were distressed gentlefolk – merchants or even nobility and others who had fallen temporarily or permanently from their station in life because of a commercial or political disaster. Reduced status was from this point to become one of the most important medieval meanings of poverty. Poverty had begun to be accompanied by shame.[118]

The canonist who perhaps had the most influence upon his contemporaries was Rufinus; he developed a 'charity begins at home' approach. His commentary on the *Decretum*, known as the *Summa Decretorum*, was completed at Bologna in the years 1157 to 1159. From Ambrose's 'ladder of perfection' Rufinus refined a *caritas ordinata* – an 'ordered discrimination'.[119] This declared that four criteria should govern philanthropy: the character of the person seeking alms; the resources of the donor; the reason charity was required; and the amount requested. The first criterion was whether the beggar was *honestus* or *inhonestus*. If resources were sufficient, all those who appeared to be *honesti* should be helped. If funds were limited, the rules of Ambrose should be applied – but beggars known to be dishonest and capable of working should receive nothing.[120] In England a similar compromise was set out by the Anglo-Norman school of canonists in a *Summa* probably written at Oxford about 1186, which made a primary distinction between the 'known poor' and strangers. Among the 'known poor' deserving cases were to be preferred to the less deserving.

Yet everywhere there was still a readiness to err on the side of charity. Where it was not possible to distinguish the worthy from the unworthy, Guido de Baysio argued, an almsgiver ought not to withhold small sums for fear his generosity was being abused.[121] In case of doubt, Joannes Teutonicus declared, 'it is better to do too much than to do nothing at all'.[122] All strangers were to be given food, unless they were claiming to be a priest – a caveat which appears and reappears constantly in the writings of the medieval canonists for whom the question of clerical impersonation seems to be a particular obsession. Again, any man who was capable of working with his hands was not to be given anything but was to be told to go to work.[123]

Others took an even harder line. Jean de Meun decreed that begging was legitimate only among those without work due to sickness, old age, educational activities, or economic conditions. The Catalan Franciscan, Francesc Eiximenis, argued that it was not desirable for cities to support beggars – even the handicapped could find honourable work, he said; the list of less deserving candidates for charity in medieval Barcelona was unbendingly deemed to include slaves, serfs, Jews, Muslims, prostitutes, pimps, bastards, blind and deaf beggars, and foreigners.[124] And everywhere, tough-minded canonists agreed, almost universally, only common foodstuffs, and not rich delicacies, should be given to the poor. This was not out of moral superiority but as Simon de Bisignano, a teacher of canon law in Bologna in 1170, said, quoting Galen, luxurious foods were bad for the poor just as coarse foods were bad for the rich.[125]

Another issue which features prominently throughout the history of philanthropy emerges in this period. Should donors aim simply to alleviate hardship or should they attempt to correct or discipline those with undesirable lifestyles and morals? That question was addressed by Huguccio, the greatest of the twelfth-century canonists from the Bologna school whose Summa – the most extensive and authoritative commentary on the *Decretum* of the age – came to be accepted throughout the Middle Ages as the standard exposition of the problem. If funds permit, the great canon lawyer said, strangers should receive assistance without investigation (unless they claimed to be priests). Non-strangers should receive aid unless they would be morally harmed by charity. Into this category of 'those who would have their morals harmed by charity' fell able-bodied people capable of working but choosing to be idle. But there was now deemed to be nothing wrong in helping people in 'vile professions' – prostitutes, jesters and so forth[126] – so long as the alms did not aid them in 'the exercise of their evil arts'. Huguccio's stance was approved by Pope Gregory IX and accepted into the *Glossa Ordinaria* of Johannes Teutonicus, which became such a standard scholastic textbook throughout the Middle Ages that it was regularly bound together with Gratian's *Decretum*.[127] This authoritative ruling, that some recipients were more deserving than others, laid the groundwork for the distinction between the deserving and the undeserving poor which was to become a major characteristic of the history of philanthropy in Europe and the United States.

RICH AND POOR ENCOMPASSED IN
A COMMUNITY OF LOVE

By the end of the High Middle Ages, then, a distinct worldview had emerged on the relationship between the rich and the poor. A whole philosophy of philanthropy was taking shape. It was rooted in the precepts of early Christianity but shaped by the institutions of feudal society and it had a significantly different outlook to those of the Greeks, Romans, Jews and Muslims who had gone before. It took for granted the starting point of the First Letter of Clement to the Christians of first-century Jerusalem: 'The use of all things that are in the world ought to be common to all men but through sin one man claimed this as his own, and another that, and so division was made amongst men.' But it added, citing Plato, 'just as the air cannot be divided, nor the splendour of the sun, so the other things of the world which were given to be held in common by all ought not to be divided'.[128] The rich therefore have an obligation to pass on their superfluous wealth to the poor; and the poor have a duty to give thanks by praying to God for the salvation of the wealthy.

This medieval worldview accepted automatically that the things of the spirit were more important than the physical or material. It embraced without challenge the statement of Augustine of Hippo that 'the things of which we have charge do not belong to us, but to the poor'.[129] Its teaching bristled with grave injunctions like: 'Whatever you have beyond what suffices for your needs belongs to others'; 'A man who keeps to himself more than he needs is guilty of theft'; 'If you do not feed the poor, you kill them'.[130] They took these injunctions literally, chiefly because, as Brian Tierney suggests, the men and women who lived under feudalism saw their economy as a zero-sum game with only a given amount of food and other goods available. 'A man who acquired more than was due to him was therefore necessarily depriving someone else of his fair share,' Tierney writes. 'He was literally guilty of theft.'[131]

But there was more to this than the limited productivity of a feudal economy. Undergirding it all was the belief that every human being is created in the image of God,[132] and that all were united in that creation 'so we, being many, are one body in Christ, and everyone members of another', as St Paul put it. The medieval theologians, citing Augustine, called this the Doctrine of the Mystical Body.* It meant that charity must be more than mere altruism. Giving alms, Aquinas declared, was 'a deed whereby something is given to the needy, out of compassion and for God's sake'.[133] Love of one's neighbour is imperative but it is secondary to the love of God and the instincts implanted in us by natural law.[134] Charity was not divisible from justice. But neither could be separated from the cosmic unity of the entire world. This had both institutional and philosophical implications.

In our modern world we invariably think of the Church and State as separate institutions with their own distinct spheres of activity. That was not how medieval men and women saw it. Life had a twofold destiny – that of the body and that of the spirit – and they were ineluctably bound together. Kings and bishops were united by that

---

* See interview with Rowan Williams, pages 194–5.

single vision. Body and spirit worked together and, certainly in the early Middle Ages, if there was one which took the lead it was the spiritual rather than the temporal. There was only one Church in the Middle Ages and everyone was a member, apart from a small minority of Jews and heretics – and even they had to obey the laws the Church made and pay the taxes it levied. The Church had its own courts which robustly enforced its laws. It was an international society – the only international society – with an effective international bureaucracy. The State acquiesced or enthusiastically joined in, ceding jurisdiction over many spheres of life which would today be regarded as the concern of only the secular power. As F. W. Maitland, widely regarded as the father of English legal history, put it: 'The medieval church was a state . . . We could frame no acceptable definition of a state which would not comprehend the church.'[135]

But for the history of philanthropy it is the philosophical implications of this which are most significant. If all are 'one body in Christ', then giving involves not simply the donation of money or material goods, but a relationship between donor and recipient which is spiritual, reciprocal, communal and inclusive. The spiritual dimension means that giving is not simply the donation of money or material goods but also the manifestation by the rich of the love for the poor demanded by Christ. Aquinas quoted St Paul: 'If I bestow all my goods to feed the poor but have not love, it profits me nothing.'[136] Francis of Assisi went further; to help the poor is not just a duty, it should be a desire. The medieval view was reciprocal in its acknowledgement that philanthropy required something of both the giver and the receiver, and that it placed both responsibilities and rights on each side. Medieval charity embodied a mutuality which was both social and spiritual.[137] (So much so that Brian Pullan has suggested that *philanimy*, friendship for the soul, might be a better word than philanthropy here.)[138] It was communal in its implicit understanding that philanthropy is about relationship – and is a key part of what binds a community or even a society together. A distinguishing feature of Catholic acts of mercy was that they could require action, not by the individual, but by the community. It was inclusive in that it allocated important roles to rich and poor alike; the rich had a duty to assist the poor materially, while the poor – whose prayers had special intercessory value – had the obligation to pray for the salvation of the rich. No one could be excluded from the circle of concern.[139] Philanthropy, in later centuries, lost key aspects of this holistic vision, as subsequent chapters of this book will demonstrate. Restoring it must be part of a new direction for philanthropy, as the last chapter will show.

This is not to suggest that the world needs to revive twelfth- and thirteenth-century Catholic scholastic philanthropy. Aquinas and his fellow theologians and philosophers were men of their time. In modern terms they were deeply conservative. In accordance with the peculiar sensibility of the medieval period, Aquinas thought that women were 'misbegotten males';[140] Jews were 'wicked';[141] heretics could be executed, on the grounds of love;[142] maiming and execution were morally acceptable punishments;[143] and serfdom and slavery were ethically justified.[144] The medieval canonists took social hierarchy for granted and found a rationale for it. God had intentionally placed the rich and the poor in their respective positions, Aquinas believed, to encourage them to cultivate different virtues – generosity on the part of the rich and patience for the poor.[145] Structural poverty was simply accepted as an inevitable part of the order of things. Indeed, to Aquinas one of the evils of the gap between rich and poor was that it threatened equilibrium of the spiritual and social unity of Christendom. So the teaching of the Decretists about the philanthropic imperative had no egalitarian implications. They pressed only for the wealthy to give out of their 'superfluities' or a sense of sacrifice. They thought different standards of living were appropriate to people with different stations in the hierarchy – which is why they were so exercised about helping the 'shamefaced' poor, those well-born folk who needed to be restored to their proper station. The canonists wanted to restrain greed rather than promote a radical redistribution of wealth; they saw philanthropy as a way to foster personal conversion by the rich. Aquinas was well aware of the misery of poverty – he knew there were poor people who could not afford even one meal a day – but he did not see that the solution to entrenched poverty might require change in economic, social and political structures in the way we now understand.[146] Justice is, for Aquinas, a virtue of individuals, not institutions or social orders.[147]

To modern eyes the medieval canonists seem myopically focused on maintaining the feudal system by making it more just and kinder, rather than reforming or replacing it. They were naively treating the symptoms rather than the disease itself. Yet despite their paternalistic attitude to the poor, the Decretists made a number of important advances. They focused as much on the position of the beneficiary as on the ethics of the benefactor.[148] Aquinas questioned the traditional Christian idea that the soul and the body were separate, like a driver in a car, with the body being less important. He had a sophisticated notion, which he took from Aristotle, that the soul was not a separate thing but somehow the 'form' that the body took. The complexity of that need not detain us here, but it meant, as Stephen J. Pope has observed, that Aquinas 'sees that in particular cases corporal alms are more valuable . . . than spiritual alms', and that 'a hungry person should be given food rather than taught philosophy'. Aquinas, with his emphasis on 'the psycho-physical unity of the human person', was perhaps the first Christian philosopher to take the corporeal character of human existence seriously.[149]

The feudal view of property ownership that medieval philosophers endorsed, which required serfs and villeins to work without payment for the Church and the lord of the manor, was exploitative and oppressive, but did secure the peasants some rights – to housing, common grazing and sharing in the produce of the village hayfield. The serf was 'bound to the soil' but also had a right to that soil which afforded the poor a certain minimum of security and stability which, in later centuries, working people were to lose entirely.[150]

The teaching of Aquinas and his fellows offers a number of important lessons of which modern philanthropy needs to be reminded. When they said that almsgiving was an act of love, they were not articulating some sentimental impulse; they were insisting – using the word 'love' in its broadest Christian perspective – that almsgiving is essentially an act of justice. As Brian Tierney puts it: 'The neighbour might be personally repugnant – the poor often are – but he [is] nonetheless entitled to affectionate respect and help in need for the sake of Christ.'[151] This reduced excessive humiliation on the part of the recipient. Charity was designed to promote not just personal salvation but also social harmony, concludes the medieval and early modern historian, Miri Rubin.[152] The ethic of charity criss-crossed medieval society in a network of expectations and obligations which brought social cohesion, peace and order. Medieval theologians universally subscribed to the sentiment enshrined in a famous phrase of the fourteenth-century Italian canon lawyer Joannes Andreae: '*Paupertas non est de genere malorum* – poverty is not a kind of crime'[153] – an understanding which got lost in the later

history of philanthropy – and remains so in today's society. This was a
world in which 'in case of doubt it is better to do too much than do
nothing at all'[154] – the opposite often applies today. The intrinsic human
dignity of the poor was to be respected: 'the poor man is an honourable
person'[155] – an insight which has been lost by many nowadays.

The medieval canonists understood that charity could be abused
but they did not assume, as nineteenth-century reformers came to do,
that abuse was routine and embedded in human nature. Instead the
thirteenth-century canonists regarded such offences as abnormalities.[156]
There will be from time to time periodic abuses, Aquinas concedes, but
these should not be used as excuses for radically restricting almsgiving
or for abandoning the practice altogether.[157] The medievals, concludes
Tierney, 'no more thought of punishing a man for being afflicted with
poverty than we think of punishing a man for being afflicted with
tuberculosis'.[158] The phrase 'poverty is not a kind of crime' echoes,
Tierney adds, 'like a challenge thrown down in advance to all subsequent
centuries of punitive and deterrent poor law'. Where resources were
limited, the canonists established an order of priorities, but even the
most hard-line medievalists said that alms should be given to all in
need, apart from the wilfully idle. Poverty was not to be assumed to
be a moral defect on the part of the poor, as it came to be seen in later
centuries.

But this was the theory. How did it work in practice? And how did it
stand up to the seismic social, economic and political changes of what
has been called 'the calamitous fourteenth century'?[159]

Interview: Naser Haghamed on Islamic charity

Naser Haghamed was a child refugee who fled Eritrea at the age of 13 and lived in four different countries before arriving in Britain and settling in Birmingham, where he is now Chief Executive Officer of the world's biggest Muslim relief and development agency. Islamic Relief Worldwide has a staff of 2,500 and had a budget of £128 million in 2018. It works in 50 countries serving communities in need – regardless of race, political affiliation, gender or belief. Founded in 1984 it became, two decades ago, the first Muslim non-governmental organization to receive British government funding. It now has partnerships with all the major UK aid agencies, six Western governments, multiple UN agencies, and is a member of the Disasters Emergency Committee in the UK. The organization combines contemporary Western thinking – aligning its programmes to the UN Sustainable Development Goals – with the tenets of the Islamic faith.

How do the traditions of Islamic giving work in practice today?

The teaching of the Prophet Muhammad, peace be upon Him, has been passed from generation to generation. Giving in Islam is there at every aspect of our life. *Zakat* is one of the five pillars of Islam. There are two kinds of *zakat*: *zakat al-fitr* is the cost of a meal which is given to a poor person at the end of the fasting in Ramadan. If you are unable to fast on a daily basis you need to give to feed a poor person on a daily basis. *Zakat al-mal*, which is one of the five pillars of Islam, requires that, once a year, you pay 2.5 per cent of your eligible wealth to the poor and needy. *Zakat al-mal* is mandatory. In addition there is a voluntary payment, which we call *sadaqa*. That is not a fixed amount; for most people it is a larger amount than *zakat*. Giving to the poor is considered as purifying your wealth in Islam.

The Prophet's teachings are that even when you die, what counts after your death is the benefit you leave to society. That can be money, or knowledge, or any sort of giving. Giving – to the poor, the needy or the stranger – is there at every turn in our life. The Prophet said that a person is not a true believer if he goes to bed with a full stomach and his neighbour is hungry. What neighbour, doesn't matter. Black or white. Muslim or non-Muslim. You can't go to sleep with a full stomach while your neighbour is hungry.

How is it paid?

People can pay their *zakat* or *sadaqa* in a variety of ways, and they can do so directly to beneficiaries or through third parties. It is common nowadays that at the mosque, before the Friday prayer, people will go around with buckets asking for money, which is usually general *sadaqa* although it can be for particular situations or causes. Usually it's for the running of the mosque, but during Ramadan they allow other charities to come and collect in the mosque. *Zakat* is calculated once a year, usually at Ramadan, because the reward to the giver is considered higher during Ramadan. Muslim charities such as Islamic Relief are significant third-party conduits of *zakat* and *sadaqa*, and therefore big recipients of both donations.

The spiritual reward?

Yes. Every Ramadan all Muslims look at their wealth. To calculate it, you deduct any debts that you have, then you add up anything you have that's not being traded – money, savings, gold, jewellery, any other expensive items . . .

Like your car or your house?

No. Anything that you're using is not zakatable. *Zakat* is wealth you hold which is stored or invested. Because the idea is that your wealth should be employed in trading to boost the economy for the community.

So *zakat* is a disincentive to hoarding?

Yes. The Prophet said, 'Don't let your money be eaten by *zakat*.' It promotes the circulation of wealth in the economy. If I keep my wealth to myself, I have to pay *zakat* on it to the poor. But if the money is trading then I don't because I'm creating jobs. That is better for the entire community. Islam does not encourage begging, but also it does not encourage rich people to sit on their wealth. That is why, in Islam, interest is *haram* – forbidden.

If you have money in the bank which earns interest . . .

You must give it as a charitable donation, because that money does not belong to you. You should give it to poor people.

What percentage of the income of Islamic Relief Worldwide comes from *zakat*, and what percentage from *sadaqa*?

In most Muslim charities, 30 to 40 per cent of the income is *zakat*, the rest is *sadaqa*. Globally, *zakat* raises about $600 billion each year. The percentage of 2.5 per cent has been there since the time of the Prophet. It is not in the Qur'an but it is in the *hadith*, the teachings of the Prophet recorded by others. The importance of giving has been passed down through the generations. With each generation we try to teach our children to be generous in giving. When the bucket is being passed around the mosque for *sadaqa* we usually give our money to our children so they put it in the bucket.

Zakat is so deep in Muslim culture that even Muslims who don't practise, who don't pray, who don't fast in Ramadan, still give *zakat*. They will say, 'OK, I'm sinful in that I'm not praying or I'm not fasting, but I still have a duty towards the poor.' That obligation seems to stick with everybody.

When you pay *zakat* how do you decide whether to give it to an institution like Islamic Relief or to the widow next door who is in difficult circumstances?

Every individual makes their own assessment. But the basic teaching is that you start with those closer to you. You don't go and feed someone far away when your neighbour is hungry. You give directly to needy individuals and also through local charities. Some say *zakat* should be spent in your country of residence, and not abroad. But most say that, because people here have access to social security and other benefits, the need is greater abroad. In addition many Muslims have relatives who live in other countries who need financial support. So we send money to them. But people also send to the very poorest, people they do not know, but who they know can be reached through charities like Islamic Relief. Most people give in a mix of all these ways.

Effective altruists say that it is better to spend £10,000 curing blindness in 10,000 people in a poor country than to give that £10,000 to one child to have a sophisticated treatment for leukaemia? How would Islamic tradition approach that kind of problem?

In Islam there are basic requirements that people have the right to ask for – shelter, food and water. Water has a special place in Islam. In the Qur'an it says: 'We made everything living from water.' No water, no life. So drilling wells and other water and sanitation projects are a huge priority. Another priority is looking after orphans.

Because the Prophet Muhammad was an orphan?

Yes. He said: 'The sponsor of an orphan will be closer to me in paradise.' So the orphan has a very important place in Islam. People come to us and say: 'I want to sponsor an orphan. Find me an orphan in any country.' So those are the priorities: food, shelter, water, and the care of orphans. Anything else that is very expensive, like the treatment of leukaemia, would not be so high a priority. Being effective to the maximum number of people is important.

Is there, in Islam, a difference between what we might call small-scale charity and large-scale philanthropy?

We have what's called a *waqf*, which is like an endowment. Philanthropists who can afford huge one-off lump-sum payments are encouraged to put money into endowments because that's continuous charity and the Prophet said that, after you die, the only thing that will benefit you is continuous charity. Through a *waqf*, big givers build schools, hospitals or other big projects.

We have a couple of properties now in the UK donated by philanthropists who wanted to make a *waqf*. We rent them out and use the income for charitable purposes. But we've also become a bit more sophisticated, to try to maximize giving. For those who cannot afford a big lump sum we offer them a share in a *waqf* at around £1,500 a share.

Do contemporary Muslims tend to prioritize giving to other Muslims first or do they just give to anybody in need?

When it comes to *Zakat-al-mal*, there are some schools of thought that say: 'It should go only to Muslims' – and it should go directly to the beneficiary, not through an intermediate institution like a hospital or charity. In my view that is a very limited understanding of *zakat*. The other view is that you give it to anyone who needs it. But the Qur'an gives priority to eight categories: the poor, the needy, the administrators of *zakat*, new converts to Islam, those in bondage or slavery, those in debt, in the cause of God, and to impoverished travellers. 'Poor' means those who have only enough food to last the day. The 'needy' are those who have even less, i.e. the extremely poor. The cause of God means those defending Islam or promoting Islamic values which is spiritual jihad. Those like Islamic Relief who administer *zakat* are one of the eight categories and therefore are entitled to take up to an eighth of the *zakat* for the costs of the charity, which is 12.5 per cent.

Does that ever get controversial with the money for spiritual jihad going to causes which could be seen as terrorism?

That is not the mainstream interpretation. Spiritual jihad is not the fighting of wars. It is a spiritual struggle to do the right thing in accordance with Islamic values. The controversy comes with institutions, like banks, who fear that because you are a Muslim charity, there's a chance that some of your money might be funnelled to terrorist groups. There can be problems for humanitarian organizations like Islamic Relief with the international banks who are preoccupied with what they call de-risking; they have become nervous about processing payments to environments deemed high risk for money laundering or the financing of terrorism. They are afraid that they will be accused by the US government of being involved with illegal financing, as some of them have previously been fined for infringements such as dealing with rogue states and involvement in money laundering, financing arms deals and the drugs trade.

Does that cause problems for humanitarian operations on the ground?

In some areas where we're working – Syria, Iraq, Afghanistan, South Sudan, Palestine – we can have problems transferring money across. Banks can sometimes block or delay payments to these regions, or charge higher fees, or close accounts. Our money sometimes disappears in the financial system, then it reappears months later. Usually, we get it back, but we've heard of cases where money vanished in the system for up to nine months. But we're still the largest international NGO working in Gaza and also in Yemen. We continue to work.

Islamic Relief does a lot of work in co-operation with other charities – religious ones like Christian Aid and Cafod or secular ones like Oxfam or Save the Children. How does that fit with Islamic theology?

It fits perfectly. When the Prophet says, 'A true believer does not go to bed with a full stomach when his neighbour is hungry', our scholars interpret neighbour non-religiously. You help anyone, full stop. So if you are going to help anybody, you can collaborate with anyone – Muslims, Christians, Jews, anybody who is trying to alleviate poverty and suffering. There is no limitation.

We co-operate with other agencies. If the Catholic agency Cafod has better organization on the ground in one place we work through them. Where we have better grassroots partners, like in the Middle East, they work through us. It works very well. Islamic Relief worked with Catholic Relief Services, and World Vision, in Central Africa, where we brought together Muslims and Christians who were in conflict, supported by USAID funding. All three organizations, using scriptural teachings from Islam and Christianity, brought the community together. In the modern world, faith is all too often seen as the source of a problem, but it can be the source of the solution.

Social justice is an important part of Islamic tradition. So we use our religion to campaign for justice for the marginalized. Last year we drew together Islamic teachings about women, and the rights of women, to present the case for gender justice and counter the cultural misappropriation of scripture to justify discrimination and violence against women. One of the sources of poverty is inequality and injustice. The most affected people in inequality are women and children. So we consulted Muslim scholars and developed the first Islamic Gender Justice Declaration, which is building momentum and support.

Did you get a backlash from traditionalists on that?

Surprisingly not, because we consulted very conservative Muslim scholars as well as liberal ones – so our campaign for the rights of women proceeded from an Islamic perspective. We did the same thing with climate change. Some people would say: 'What does climate change have to do with religion?' So we point to the relevant verses in the Qur'an. Chapter 7 verse 31 says: 'Eat, drink and don't overconsume.' Climate change is about over-consumption and that is killing the planet. In Chapter 10 verse 14 it says that God has appointed men and women as 'custodians of this earth'. If you are a custodian and you're supposed to be looking after something, you look after it very well. You don't damage it.

Who does Islamic Relief answer to? To whom are you accountable?

First and foremost we are accountable to God. This is a responsibility that we have been given and we have to fulfil it. We are also accountable to both our donors and beneficiaries. Accountability to the donor is obvious because they can say: 'We gave you this money, what did you do with it?' If you want money from them again you have to have a good answer. But we are also accountable to our beneficiaries as well, and that's more difficult. We exist fundamentally to serve them, and we use their photos and their stories to bring in money, so we should be accountable to them. More importantly, Islamic principles require that we must consider the dignity of the beneficiary. They have been unfortunate to be recipients of aid, but it doesn't mean I'm better than them so I should not mistreat them. Human dignity is big in Islam.

Do you have systems and mechanisms to protect the dignity of the recipients, or is it just a question of attitude?

When we started it was all about attitude, and the way we recruited people and taught them the principles of Islam. But that is not enough. We have developed systems and mechanisms that are industry standard and we comply with them. We are the only Muslim organization so far to be accredited by the Core Humanitarian Standard which focuses on the beneficiary. To that we've added the scrutiny of governance by using Accountability Now, a German-based system which focuses on governance and the quality of managers, as well as our own Islamic Relief Quality management system (IRQMS), which is based on the Picasso IT platform. And we feed all that into our own mechanisms and tools in a system called Ihsan – which is Arabic for excellence – based on the best practice available out there. So we have a complaints mechanism, a whistle-blower mechanism, and other policies and systems. Obviously, the most important thing is to prevent anything going wrong in the first place, but in case it does, we should be able to easily detect it and manage it and learn from it.

Does Islamic charity have anything particular to teach secular philanthropy?

The whole basis of Islamic social finance is different to secular finance. When we do microfinance projects, and give loans to the very poor, we don't charge interest. If you give a very poor person money to alleviate their poverty but charge them 10 or 15 or 20 per cent interest, you're just making them poorer. We don't do it that way. We only charge a very small admin fee and yet we've got a very high percentage of the capital we lend being repaid – between 95 per cent and 98 per cent – so that we can then lend it out again to more people.

But if you give money without charging interest isn't there a lack of discipline to enforce people to repay it?

No, we don't find that. We work with groups rather than individuals, and a sense of community pride and accountability in tight-knit communities influences repayment rates strongly. Together we identify the beneficiaries, we do the needs assessment, we train them, we put a monitoring mechanism together. Then the community enforces its own discipline through peer-pressure. The others say to the person who has borrowed: 'Listen, if you don't pay it back, there will be no money to go, one by one, to the rest of the group.' It works.

Five or ten years ago people were asking: 'Why do we need Muslim or Christian charities? What value do they add?' But now the UN bodies and other institutions have recognized that faith-based organizations and faith actors are so often the ones that are trusted and respected by their communities. They are often the organizations through which the alleviation of poverty and social justice can be delivered most effectively.

Chapter 4

How the Black Death Changed Everything

The request came from no less a person than the Queen of France. But John Peckham was adamant in his refusal. At the centre of their disagreement was a medieval parson named Peter Blaunc. It was 1284 and Peckham, appointed Archbishop of Canterbury five years earlier, had been travelling along the foot of the great ridge of chalk hills on the Pilgrims Way in Kent. Passing through the village of Wrotham, he was alarmed to discover that its parish priest was absent. He encountered the same problem in the parish of Lyminge some 40 miles away also in Kent. In both places he found 'the cure of souls neglected' and 'the poor parishioners afflicted with hunger through lack of a good provider'.[1] The absentee priest, Peckham discovered, was in both cases the same man, Peter Blaunc. In both places Blaunc was drawing the tithes provided by the local parishioners for their priest – but was serving in neither. Peckham wrote a caustic letter to the truant cleric, commanding him at once to dispense alms to the value of five pounds in each of his parishes. He summoned him to a meeting to discuss the future administration of his churches. Blaunc, it turned out, was working as clerk to the Queen of France. But when she wrote to the archbishop asking that Blaunc be made available to her on important business, Peckham replied, undaunted, that he could not accede to her request, 'at least until he shall provide in some fashion for the souls committed to his care'.[2]

At various points in the Middle Ages the Church was bedevilled by the problem of priests who took money from their parishes but were never there to say Mass, provide for the pastoral needs of the people, or distribute alms to the poor. The abuse was known as pluralism. In a few cases there was a good reason for their absence. John Wycliffe, one of the first translators of the Bible into English, lived much of his life in Oxford but drew his income from two distant parishes, in Lincolnshire and Somerset, and rarely set foot in either of them.[3] Peckham was tolerant of priests who had gone abroad to somewhere like the great University of Paris to study for a time. But soon after being consecrated as Archbishop of Canterbury in January 1279, he embarked upon a mission to stamp out the pluralism, along with a variety of other malpractices, which afflicted the Church in his day.

Peckham was a staunch advocate of the care of the poor. Although theologically conservative – he was a Platonist who disputed the Aristotelian thinking of Thomas Aquinas – he had no less a sense of a Christian's duty towards the needy. And as one of the great administrators of the Church, as well as an academic theologian, he had considerable impact on ensuring that the high teachings of the medieval scholars on wealth and poverty were actually put into practice. Philanthropy, in the archbishop's eyes, was not a form of optional generosity but a Christian duty.

Even in all his pomp as Archbishop of Canterbury, Peckham never forgot his Christian formation as a Franciscan friar, one of the orders of religious clerics who did not sequester themselves away in cloisters but lived and worked among the poor. Even as archbishop he preferred to be known by the title of Friar John. When he returned, in his grand archiepiscopal robes, to the Benedictine convent at Lewes in Sussex in which he had been educated, he processed round the town in great pomp 'arrayed in his pontificals' and sang the Mass at the high altar and ended the festival with a great feast for the poor. But rather than eating there himself, Peckham, according to the archives of the Priory of Lewes, 'put off his splendid attire, and in his grey coat, rope-girdle, bare of foot, he entered the refectory, and partook, with his usual moderation, of the simple fare of the delighted monks'.[4]

For all his personal humility, and initial reluctance to take on the post at Canterbury, Peckham was unafraid to do battle with the powerful. His first act on arrival in England as archbishop was to call a church council at Reading in 1279. It set out a programme for ecclesiastical reform but also decreed that a copy of the Magna Carta should be hung in every cathedral and collegiate church, a move which did not go down very well with King Edward I. Royalists swiftly labelled Peckham as 'not a true-hearted Englishman'.[5] But it was the vested interests inside the

Church who took greatest exception to him – for they were the prime targets of his reforming zeal. Peckham determined to root out clerical absenteeism, pluralism and the growing laxity in England's monasteries, and rectify the lack of education among the clergy. He railed against the priests of his day with what he called their hard hearts of iron and feet of clay revealed in their love of 'carnal luxury'.[6] The main instrument of his reform was a detailed schedule of visitations – inspections of various dioceses of his province – many conducted by himself in person. These visitations were pursued with an unprecedented vigour. Peckham persisted in them even when, in 1280, they brought him into conflict with the king after he compelled Antony Bek, the king's secretary, and later Bishop of Durham, to surrender five benefices. So rigorous was Peckham's campaign that, after two years, the suffragens of Canterbury drew up 21 articles complaining of his visitations and the way in which he and his officials conducted them.

But Peckham was unbending. Under his influence a provincial council in 1281 decreed that philanthropy was to be provided according to the resources of each church, 'so that at least extreme necessity among poor parishioners is relieved'.[7] In 1284, when famine haunted the English landscape, the archbishop wrote to his senior clerics instructing them that the laws of poor relief were to be strictly enforced in every parish. He proclaimed: 'you are to compel, by your letters, all rectors and vicars of our jurisdiction to provide for their subjects according to the adequacy of their resources in this time of pernicious famine, as the laws of the gospel, and the canon laws subordinate to them, plainly laid down'.[8] And in 1287 Peckham promulgated a set of eight articles, to be read out regularly in church 'so that they remained in the memory of the ministers', reminding them that they should 'provide for the bodily necessities of the poor and needy' as well as for the spiritual care of their parishioners.[9]

Nor were the monasteries immune from Peckham's scrutiny. His *Register*, which detailed the systematic and searching nature of his visitations, contains instructions and injunctions of such a number and such intensity that one group of monks mutinied against him. These individuals, whom Peckham branded as 'certain sons of Belial', were eventually outvoted by their fellow monks – and the articles they had drawn up in defiance of the archbishop were publicly burned by Peckham.[10]

Even the aristocracy was not safe from Peckham's vigilant gaze. In 1281 he rebuked Bogo de Clare, the third son of the Earl of Gloucester, who like many prominent courtiers lived off a number of benefices he had been granted by the monarch without, it seems, ever even having been ordained a priest. His lack of clerical status was no excuse in Peckham's eyes, who fired a broadside at him: 'We complain that on visiting certain of your churches, or rather, churches held in your name, that you did not perform the duties of a rector but rather acted as ravisher (*raptor*) because, while gathering the goods of the poor, you minister little or nothing to them.'

Neither were senior clerics exempt. In 1281 the archbishop refused to confirm the election of Richard de la More as Bishop of Winchester after finding that he drew the income from two benefices without permission. The bishop-elect appealed to Rome, where he won the support of a number of cardinals, but Peckham prevailed and Pope Martin IV quashed the election. Two years later Peckham did something similar at Rochester forcing a bishop, John Kirkby, to resign. He removed several benefices from the Dean of Wolverhampton, Tedisio de Camilla, who was later made Bishop of Turin. And when he found that the Bishop of Coventry was not living in his diocese, Peckham ordered the absentee to return 'in order that you, who are not adequate to minister spiritual things, may at least provide temporal goods for the poor.'[11]

DID MEDIEVAL PHILANTHROPY WORK IN PRACTICE?

The priority for the poor, which Thomas Aquinas and his fellow theologians had set out, was embodied in the work of John Peckham. Yet there has been much disagreement among modern historians – their views largely coloured by their pro- or anti-Catholic prejudices – on the extent to which the theory was put into practice. The life of John Peckham gives a clear indication that the words of the scholastic philosophers of the High Middle Ages were made flesh. At the start of the twentieth-century, Cardinal Francis Aidan Gasquet, a prominent Benedictine historian, lauded Peckham as 'the celebrated Archbishop of Canterbury',[12] and wrote of how a 'constant claim' on parish priests was 'the relief of the poor, strangers and wayfarers'.[13] This responsibility, Gasquet declared, quoting the great thirteenth- and fourteenth-century canonist William Lyndwood, was 'well understood and practised in

England, where the churches, to meet those calls, were better endowed than they were abroad'.[14] There can be no doubt, Gasquet insisted in 1906, that 'this claim was fully accepted and carried out'.[15] But this view was attacked two decades later by the sulphurous controversialist scholar G. G. Coulton. A fierce anti-Catholic polemicist, Coulton asserted in the 1930s that theory and practice diverged dramatically in the Middle Ages. Everyone knew, he agreed, that the poor were legally entitled to a third or at least a quarter of all tithes, but they were routinely cheated of their due by wicked medieval clerics and perversely ingenious canon lawyers.

Gasquet and Coulton were perhaps as bad as one another, though biased in opposite directions. Gasquet knew much of the medieval source material intimately. But his scholarship, according to the pre-eminent twentieth-century scholar of this period, Brian Tierney, was 'handicapped by an apparent congenital blindness to all the less edifying aspects of medieval Catholicism and by a somewhat cavalier attitude to the conventions of historical documentation'.[16] Gasquet was, says the prominent contemporary Catholic historian, Eamon Duffy, 'both a bad workman and not entirely scrupulous about what he said'.[17] But the Protestant Coulton was equally partial in the other direction. Where Gasquet cites instances of rich vicars with incomes ample enough to assist the poor, Coulton lists many more who were too poor to support themselves, let alone help the poor in their parishes. Both men press-ganged the facts in support of their propaganda. Both were highly selective in their use of evidence; the Catholic cardinal cited a mere half a dozen examples, and though the Protestant polemicist offered more than 200, both examined a mere fraction of the 8,000 parishes in medieval England. As Tierney puts it, 'Coulton concentrated on abuses practically to the exclusion of all else; thus he presented a picture as remote from reality as Gasquet's sunlit landscape of medieval Merry England'.[18] But Coulton's view was the one which became the received wisdom in the twentieth century. The idea that the theory of the obligation of the rich towards the poor was not much followed in practice became the orthodoxy among historians of philanthropy.

Yet mainstream historians of the medieval period have now changed their view. 'The collective distribution of alms remained a widespread custom throughout the Middle Ages,' wrote the Polish historian

Bronislaw Geremek in his magisterial survey, *Poverty: A History*, towards
the end of the twentieth century.[19] This shift owes much to the work of
Brian Tierney, who assembled, in his authoritative study *Medieval Poor
Law*, a wealth of detail which suggests that the teaching of theologians
like Aquinas were indeed consistently put into practice throughout
the Middle Ages.[20] That happened all across the social spectrum, from
monarchs and high-ranking prelates to humble parsons and their
ordinary parishioners.

Throughout the High Middle Ages a succession of bishops
emphasized and re-emphasized the responsibility of the Christian
community to take care of the poor and needy. The provincial Council
of Oxford summoned by Archbishop Stephen Langton in 1222 decreed
that prelates must choose, as their almoners – distributors of alms –
honourable clerks who would be hospitable.[21] Richard Wych, Bishop
of Chichester from 1244 to 1253, instructed parish priests 'to pay
attention to hospitality'. In parishes run by monasteries there should be
a vicar appointed to watch over the safety of souls 'until then we wish
to be assigned a portion of the revenues out of which . . . the vicars may
be able to show themselves hospitable to the poor'.[22] In 1250 Bishop
Grosseteste of Lincoln, considered by many to be the greatest bishop of
the century, declared that the duty of a parish priest lay 'not only in the
administration of sacraments and the saying of canonical hours, and
the celebration of masses . . . It consists in the feeding of the hungry, in
giving drink to the thirsty, including the naked, in receiving guests in
visitation of the sick and prisoners, especially of one's own parishioners,
to whom the temporal goods of the churches belong'.[23]

These were not the words of an academic lawyer but rather of a great
administrator who, for two decades, ruled over the largest diocese in
England with considerable vigour. He was so especially active in the
visitation of his churches that, Tierney concludes, 'it is hard to believe
that any comfortably endowed parish priest in Grosseteste's diocese was
allowed to forget his canonical obligation to relieve the poor'.[24] His
opposition to the appointment of foreigners to benefices in England
was rooted in the fact that they 'could not even take up residence to
minister to the wants of the poor and to receive travellers'.[25]

After Pope Alexander IV wrote a letter to the English bishops
reminding them of their obligations to the poor in 1261, John Gervais,
Bishop of Winchester, decreed that not less than one-tenth of parish

tithes were to be spent on the needy.[26] Around the same time Bishop
Bronescombe of Exeter required his archdeacons to make strict enquiry
as to whether parish priests were using their revenues for the purposes
specified in canon law or wasting them on luxuries. Those found
wanting were to be prosecuted.[27] The chain of instruction came from
higher still. The bishops themselves were quizzed by Robert Winchelsey
when, as Archbishop of Canterbury, he set out to visit the dioceses of
his province in the 1290s; each one was grilled as to 'whether he was
hospitable, merciful, and gave alms, and whether he had an honourable
cleric as almoner'. On one occasion Winchelsey rebuked an abbot
so sternly that the monk suffered a fatal heart attack. Such was the
commitment of these senior clerics to the cause of the poor that in
1307 Bishop Swinfield of Hereford even refused to hand over a benefice
to King Edward I until provision was made for the poor within the
parish – an act of some courage since Edward was one of the most
formidable of medieval English monarchs.[28]

Those who have been swayed by post-Reformation propaganda
against the medieval Church were determined to put a negative gloss on
its persistent championing of the poor. The eminent Victorian scholar
Sir William Ashley insisted that the fact that thirteenth-century bishops
consistently repeated their injunctions on behalf of the poor must surely
indicate that the previous laws were not being obeyed.[29] Tierney and
later historians have assembled a formidable body of evidence, from
which I quote in the paragraphs that follow, which shows that Ashley
was wrong.

The chronicler Matthew Parris, who died in 1259, averred that the
provision of poor relief in ordinary parishes was indeed common practice
in thirteenth-century England. He wrote that 'a custom has heretofore
prevailed and been observed in England that the rectors of parochial
churches have always been remarkable for hospitality and have made
a practice of supplying food to their parishioners who were in want'.[30]
The claim was reiterated on many occasions throughout the thirteenth
century. In 1222 the provincial Council of Oxford summoned by
Archbishop Stephen Langton decreed the minimum stipend for English
vicars should be five marks[31] a year – around only half the pay of a
skilled craftsman – and yet even on this income a vicar was expected to
provide hospitality to the poor, sick and elderly. A parson would collect
more from his parishioners in tithes but the expectation was that he

would provide for the needy from that. The portrait of a good priest painted by Chaucer a century later in the Prologue to the *Canterbury Tales* suggests that this model persisted. Still, in 1390, Chaucer sees the ideal priest as a good man of religion, poor of income but rich in holy thought and work, a learned man who preached Christ's gospel truly and cared physically as well as spiritually for his parishioners:

> Full loath was he to threaten for his tithes,
> But rather would he give, without doubt,
> Unto his poor parishioners about,
> Of his offering and also of his substance.[32]

'A better priest,' Chaucer concludes, 'I trow, there nowhere is.'

Yet Ashley chooses to assume that Chaucer's parson was an exception, asserting that it is 'improbable that the ordinary parochial clergy distributed in alms any large part of their income'.[33] Tierney attributes this prejudice on Ashley's part to early nineteenth-century attitudes which assumed, as did the 1834 Poor Law Act, that 'if a man was destitute he was probably an idle lout who deserved punishment'. The only way to force such people to work was through 'the most bitter humiliations and hardships'. To such Victorians, Tierney observes caustically, 'there seemed a kind of outrageous perversity in the naïve medieval view that the kindest way of dealing with a hungry man was to feed him'.[34] So Ashley's writing is sprinkled with casual accusations that medieval philanthropy was 'haphazard', 'indiscriminate', 'reckless', 'demoralising' and 'pauperising'.[35] Such judgements, Tierney concludes, were the result of anachronistically viewing the Middle Ages through the assumptions of the world after the Industrial Revolution. We will consider in Chapter 8 how such suppositions changed the attitude of the rich towards philanthropy.

There is another piece of evidence which suggests that poor relief was indeed commonplace in practice in the High Middle Ages. This was an era in which parishioners were ready to bring all kinds of accusations and charges against their priests – and yet there is hardly ever a complaint about a priest refusing to give alms. A visitation of 90 parishes in the diocese of Exeter in 1342 uncovered only one complaint of inadequate almsgiving. Rather, parishioners protesting to their bishop about absentee priests, or priests who held more than one benefice, often included in their grounds for complaint the fact that priestly truancy resulted in the diminution of public philanthropy.[36] In the thirteenth century almsgiving was not seen as a form of generosity which went beyond the call of duty; rather, Tierney concludes, it was seen as 'the barest minimum that could be exacted even from those in other ways unworthy of their office'.[37] Perhaps Abbot Gasquet was nearer to the truth than his critics suggest when he wrote that the obligation of the better-off towards the poor 'was fully accepted and carried out' in the High Middle Ages – 'not because all priests were burning with zeal and Christian charity', as Tierney put it,[38] but because a parish priest who refused to give alms would have found himself the subject of strong complaints at the next episcopal visitation.

In any case, the parish was not the only vehicle of medieval philanthropy. The thirteenth century saw extensive growth in almshouses and endowed hospitals. The charitable activities of craft guilds, as we shall see below, became a prominent social force in this period. Monasteries continued to hand out substantial doles of food and other alms to the needy. Bishops often sent commissioners on visitations to monasteries, as well as parishes, to check that the monastic obligation of care for the traveller, the sick and the poor was being fulfilled. Such scrutiny was needed in a few cases; there were complaints, for example, towards the end of the thirteenth century that the great Abbey of Saint-Denis near Paris was spending a miserly three per cent of its large income on assistance to the poor.[39] But, generally speaking, the visitation records of the High Middle Ages do not suggest that abbeys and monasteries were parsimonious in this regard. Complaints about ungenerous provision for the poor were rare. The most detailed of all the episcopal registers which survive from the thirteenth century – that of Archbishop Odo of Rouen – provides clear evidence of abundant monastic charity.[40] The same was true of England where, even on the eve of the Reformation, the monks were still providing a substantial contribution to the relief of destitution.[41] Critics of the medieval Church often point to the survey of monastic income and expenditure, the *Valor Ecclesiasticus*, which was made in 1535 on the orders of Henry VIII just ahead of the Dissolution of the Monasteries. This also suggested monks were giving only about three per cent of their total income to the poor. But it turns out that what was being recorded was merely the donations on which they were allowed to claim exemptions for tax – the sums which legal requests *obliged* them to give to the poor. All other donations by the rich to the monasteries were not recorded in this survey.[42] There were similar problems with the review of the account rolls of individual abbeys conducted by R. H. Snape in 1926. Tierney, writing half a century later, concludes that – while it is true that monastic charity was likely to be more indiscriminate and less effective than alms distributed at parish level – it is very difficult to extract reliable information about medieval philanthropy from monastic accounts. This was because the accounts largely failed to record the most common form of monastic almsgiving – the distribution of food. The elaborate care with which this distribution was regulated suggests the amounts involved must have been substantial.[43] In hospitals, too, food for the poor was a high priority; food was the principal medicine of the medieval world. 'The essential fact about [the Middle Ages] remains the enormous quantity of alms which continued to be distributed and ease with which the poor could obtain aid,' Bronislaw Geremek insists.[44] The medieval charitable movement 'formed a vast jumble of institutions of varied size, resources, personnel, and governance', according to James Brodman's 2009 authoritative survey of organized charity in the Middle Ages.[45] 'I am inclined to think,' Tierney concludes, 'that, taken all in all, the poor were better looked after in England in the thirteenth century than in any subsequent century until the present one.'[46]

So if philanthropy worked passably well in the High Middle Ages, what went wrong in the later medieval period? Two factors were responsible for what was to become a major shift in the culture of giving. The first was the development by the Church of the doctrine of Purgatory. The second was the arrival of the Black Death.

THE IMPACT OF THE DOCTRINE OF
PURGATORY ON GIVING

Purgatory is not mentioned anywhere in the Bible. The idea that a place existed in the afterlife – somewhere between Heaven and Hell, where sinners are purged of their offences before being admitted to the presence of God – began to emerge in the Christian imagination in the early Middle Ages. But it took 500 years to develop to the point where it was to have a major influence on the development of philanthropy.

The first thinker to articulate the notion fully was Pope Gregory the Great in his *Dialogues*[47] written around the year 593. He took as his starting point a statement of Christ that a particularly grave sin would not be forgiven 'either in this world, or in the world to come',[48] and concluded that it must be possible for sins to be forgiven after the sinner had died. To that he married a passage from St Paul in which the apostle talks of how some will be saved 'as through fire'.[49]

The germ of the medieval vision of Hell, Purgatory and Heaven is found in the final book of the *Dialogues* in which Pope Gregory talks about what happens after death – and sets out various visions of those who have come back from beyond the grave.[50] The dead find themselves in a place where fires of purgation burn away the venial sins of those who have otherwise led a good life. One such is a deacon named Paschasius, 'a man of a wonderful holy life, a marvellous giver of alms, a lover of the poor'.[51] After his death Paschasius was found standing in the waters at the public baths by a bishop who, struck with fear at the sight of the dead man, asked him why he was there. Paschasius answered that, while he lived, he had committed a sin in that very place and was condemned to haunt it. The bishop promised to pray for the dead man and, after he had done so, the ghost of Paschasius was never seen in the baths again. Gregory concludes that Paschasius had been removed from Purgatory by the prayer of another person, which showed that, despite the dead man's life of plentiful almsgiving, after death he 'could work nothing at all for himself' in terms of earning his salvation.[52]

Pope Gregory also told the story of a monk named Justus, who on his deathbed was found to be in possession of three gold crowns in violation of his vow of poverty and, as a punishment, was buried with the money without a Mass being said for the repose of his soul. When one was eventually celebrated, 30 days later, that very night the ghost of Justus appeared to a brother monk to announce, 'Hitherto have I been in bad case, but now I am well; for this day have I received the communion.' It was apparent, Gregory wrote, 'that the dead monk was by the holy sacrifice [of the Mass] delivered from his pains.'[53]

The *Dialogues* was one of the most popular books in the Middle Ages. From then on, in the words of the church historian John Bossy, the doctrine of Purgatory crept up on Western Christendom.[54] Through folklore, and the work of theologians, an entire legend was embroidered. Purgatory was an annexe of Hell, with the same fires reflecting the same torments upon dead souls – but with the blessed relief that they knew their state was temporary and eventually they would see the face of God. There was great debate about the physical and geographical location of the place. Some medieval writers insisted that the story of Paschasius suggested that souls were punished in the places on earth where they committed the sins which must be expiated.

The notion arose that the severity of the soul's punishment must be directly proportional to the severity of the sinner's offence. Between the eighth and eleventh centuries various precursors of Purgatory were proposed,[55] but it was only with the great cultural and intellectual Renaissance of the twelfth century that the concept of Purgatory took on full theological shape. It was formed, according to Jacques Le Goff, by a group of scholastic thinkers around 1170. That was when the French theologian Petrus Comestor turned the adjective 'purgatorial' into a noun, *purgatorium*.[56] The development took place in a society in which a growing middle class of merchants and bankers felt the need to atone for their lives of usury, avarice, material excess and spiritual disregard. The idea of Purgatory was then defined with increasing precision at the Council of Lyon 1274, and then that of Florence in 1439 and Trent in 1545.

Church dogma specified neither the location of Purgatory nor the penalties to which souls there were subjected. But while the Church Fathers preoccupied themselves with theological concerns – about sin, penance, satisfaction, temporal punishment and the legitimacy of praying for the dead – the ordinary people concerned themselves with gruesome and vivid imaginings about the nature of the purgation. A few thinkers, such as Dante in his great exposition of Purgatory in *The Divine Comedy*, written shortly after 1300, focus on it as a place of hope and renewal. But in almost all the English literature on Purgatory 'it is portrayed as a torture house, a dungeon of ice or fire, or a kind of infernal concentration camp where the guards and torturers are gleeful demons, let loose to do whatever they fancy to the suffering souls', to quote Eamon Duffy. Tortures included inmates having their hearts and bowels torn out and raked with sharp irons, or being nailed up in barrels full of poisonous snakes. Individuals trapped in this horrible fire, Duffy writes, quoting a vision recorded in 1422, 'had so grete paynes that for drede I might not describe them'.[57] Such visions were not confined to the uneducated. Thomas More in his *Supplication of Souls* of 1529 described Purgatory as a place for 'abydyng and enduryng the grevouse paynys and hote clensyng fyre that freteh and burneth oute the rustye and filthy spottes of oure synne'.[58]

While they were alive ordinary believers could shorten their time in Purgatory through prayer, fasting and, above all, almsgiving. All these were penances handed out to those who came to confess their sins to their priest. The practice of confession was made compulsory by Pope Innocent III at the fourth Lateran Council, which in 1215 established the rule that every Christian must confess to a priest at least once a year. At confession, almsgiving was seen as the most efficacious remedy for sin.[59] 'Alms extinguish sins,' said Bartholomew of Exeter, about the same time; the act of giving harnesses the prayers of the poor on the donor's behalf – and God listens more attentively to the prayers of the poor than to those of the rich.[60] Out of this idea developed a notion that a set dispensation, known as an indulgence, could be given which would reduce the amount of time which had to be spent in Purgatory. An indulgence assumed that the sinner was repentant and had confessed their sins; it then deducted a set number of days from the time to be spent in purgatorial fire after death. An indulgence could be attached to a particular religious practice – a pilgrimage to a holy place, a particular set of prayers, or a novena, but also to participation in a crusade or even socially useful activities like the building or upkeep of a church or bridge.[61] From 1300 onwards popes ruled that this merit was transferable.[62] Indulgences could thus be used by the living to release the dead from penance, or part of it. Pope Leo X decreed that there was no difference between the living and the dead in respect of qualification for indulgences.[63]

Before very long praying for the dead became a major preoccupation among medieval Christians. Churches increasingly focused on catering for those who had died. In the words of Eamon Duffy, 'architecture, glass and wall painting, carving and music, not to mention the services of educated clergy and musically talented boys, were all directed . . . to the service of the dead'.[64] The philanthropy of the period became so focused upon this that the urban historian Clive Burgess has described late medieval parish churches as 'ante-rooms of Purgatory'.[65] A significant proportion of almsgiving funds was diverted from the relief of poverty and given over to helping speed the passage of relatives' souls through Purgatory and on towards Heaven.[66] Prayers for the dead, and indulgences secured on their behalf, were used to transfer grace accumulated from good deeds on earth to those who had passed over to the other side. The phenomenon grew rapidly through the fourteenth and into the fifteenth century. In Norwich between 1370 and 1439 around a quarter of those rich enough to leave a will left provision for Masses to be said on their behalf; that figure almost doubled between 1490 and 1517.[67] In his wide-ranging study *The Stripping of the Altars*[68] Eamon Duffy collected wills from all over England which suggested that some late medieval people were so deeply affected by the new terrifying visions of the torments of Purgatory that they directed that Masses should be said on their behalf, and alms distributed in their name, 'as soon as I am dead without any tarrying'.[69]

The doctrine of Purgatory gave new impetus to the idea of redemptive almsgiving. Medieval theologians built on the old belief that alms had the power to wipe away sins. They did this in two ways. Almsgiving had a direct impact upon the soul of the giver, said William of Auxerre.[70] But the prayers of those who received the alms, in addition, transferred to rich donors the grace which accrued to the prayers of the poor. This would 'make all things clean' said Odo of Châteauroux, echoing the words of Christ in Luke's gospel: 'Give alms . . . and see, everything will be clean for you.'[71] Earlier in the Middle Ages doubts had been expressed about the idea of redemptive almsgiving; in the eighth century, Pope Zacharias had written to the English specifically forbidding that alms should be thought to commute penance – 'those who think that God can be bribed thus, make their alms useless to them, and add to their guilt,' the Pope wrote.[72] Such an approach was folly, he said, for it would simply encourage people to sin, safe in the knowledge that they could wipe away the guilt by almsgiving: 'if a man may thus buy his punishment and get others to repent for him, a rich man would be sure of salvation, and only the poor be in danger'. But by late medieval times such reservations had largely been set aside.

The philanthropic giving of alms and the saving of souls were now inextricably linked. In 1301 Mary of Bassingbourn gave an endowment to an Augustinian priory to fund four 'canons regular' to pray for her soul and the souls of her family. But she also left funds for an almshouse to give a home to seven poor and infirm men – and for food handouts to a thousand poor people three times a year.[73] These chapels dedicated to praying for the soul of the benefactor were known as chantries and became increasingly popular throughout the later Middle Ages. When Henry VII died in 1509 he established a chapel in Westminster Abbey and funded three additional monks, who were to be called the king's chantry monks, to say Masses in an attempt to reduce the time his soul must spend in the fires of Purgatory. His endowment specified:

> On every anniversary, the greatest bell of the monastery was to be rung for an hour, and the bells rung as at the most solemn anniversaries. A hundred wax tapers, each 12 lbs. in weight and 9 feet long, were to be set upon and about the herse, and there continually to burn during all the time of the service of the *Placebo*, the *Dirge*, with lessons, lauds, and mass of *Requiem*, and all the orations, observances, and ceremonies belonging thereto. Also 24 new torches were to be held about the herse all the time of the service. Twenty pounds [30 marks] were to be given in alms, viz. 25 marks among the blind, lame, impotent, and most needy people, 2d. to each man and woman, and 1d. to each child so far as it will go; and 5 marks to be given to the 13 bedesmen* and 3 bedeswomen provided in the said monastery (of whom one was to be a priest, and all under the government of a monk), 12d. to each. A weekly obit was to be held, at which the bells were to be rung; and alms given to the 13 bedesmen and 2 bedeswomen and 124 others, 1d. to each.[74]

Such provision was at the grandest end of the social scale. Founding a private chantry was beyond the means of all but the wealthy. Yet among ordinary people the practice of paying for Masses for the souls of the departed became hugely popular.

There was another significant development. In Matthew's Gospel Jesus had used a monetary metaphor in talking about punishment when he warned against pious individuals who want to make sacrifices to God without having dealt justly with their fellow humans. He warned: 'You will be thrown into prison. Truly I tell you, you will never get out until you have paid the last penny.'[75] The image resonated with the merchants and bankers who were increasingly dominating thirteenth- and

---

* A bedesman, from the Middle English for 'a man of prayer', was commonly a pensioner or almsman whose duty it was to pray for his benefactor.

fourteenth-century society, encouraging the development of what Robert Durling calls an 'accountancy of punishments'.[76] The period spent in Purgatory began to be counted in days. Indulgences were reckoned by the number of days expunged: as time exists on earth so it must exist in the place of purgation, where 'time is restored for time', as Dante put it.[77]

All this had a strong appeal among the mercantile cities of northern Italy, 'where the arts of accounting were both the glory and the pitfall of prosperous burghers'.[78] For many the afterlife became subject to what another French medievalist, Jacques Chiffoleau, called the 'mathematics of salvation', as the wealthy tried to reckon the time they would have to spend in Purgatory, and then work out how much they needed to give to pious causes to minimize their suffering in the afterlife.[79]

Critics of medieval Catholicism seized upon what sounded like a crude bargain with God. Medieval views on poor relief, polemicists later complained, were merely theoretical constructs designed to enable the wealthy to enter Heaven. Gifts to the Church by the rich, and their alms to the poor, were said to be merely motivated by spiritual self-interest. 'Philanthropy directed toward social reform was singularly absent from the late medieval world, both in theory and in practice,' concluded Joel T. Rosenthal,[80] anachronistically judging medieval conduct by the expectations of a later epoch – but vividly illustrating why the selling of indulgences in the early sixteenth century provoked the total rejection of the doctrine of Purgatory as part of the Protestant Reformation. The Reformers rebelled against those corrupt sellers of indulgences, 'who say that as soon as the money clinks into the money chest, the soul flies out of purgatory', as Martin Luther famously put it.[81]

The truth was more nuanced. If the relationship between giver and receiver was sometimes cast in symbiotic terms – alms in exchange for prayers – the great medieval thinkers rejected such a crass reciprocity. To illustrate the danger of such simplistic thinking the Cistercian prior Caesarius of Heisterbach included in his *Dialogus miraclorum* (Dialogue on Miracles), written around 1223, the admonitory story of a wealthy man from Bavaria who, sometime after his death, appeared to his wife complaining about his eternal punishment. Bewildered, she reminded him of the large amounts he had given in alms during his life. But these were worthless to his soul, he told her, because they had been given not out of charity but out of vainglory. Such subtlety was lost on most ordinary folk.

Stephen of Bourbon, a thirteenth-century Dominican preacher, recalled a sermon he had heard by Odo of Châteauroux warning his listeners not to make the mistake made by a certain man who heard his parish priest say that the Lord had promised to reward almsgivers 'one hundredfold'.[82] The man decided with his wife to give their cow to the priest in order to reap the promised rewards. As time passed the man grew increasingly irritated that the divine reward had not materialized. The priest, he decided, had lied. So the man set out one night to exact his revenge by murdering his promise-breaking parson. But on the way to commit the terrible deed, in the dark he discovered a stash of gold and realized that the priest's promise had been fulfilled.[83]

By contrast most medieval theologians insisted that alms were not simply a method of purchasing salvation on the cheap, but rather a means for transforming the very character of the sinner.[84] Intentions mattered and the redemptive power of alms, in the words of Spencer E. Young, derived from the act, rather than the fact, of giving them.[85] The motives of ordinary people were more mixed, says the Reformation historian J. J. Scarisbrick: 'Folk were giving because they wanted to do good for themselves and their families in the next world and good for their neighbours and perhaps their own reputations in this.'[86] Prayers for the dead were a way of extending the fellowship and obligation of the living to their relatives who had passed to the next world. Intercession for the dead, says Eamon Duffy, was 'less like fire insurance than the extension of the obligations of friendship and family and neighbourhood into the dark world of the dead . . . Prayers for the dead were the measure and last proof of our love for them.'[87] Purgatory gave society a new lease on eternal life, in the form of a second chance at salvation, says Jacques Le Goff.[88] But the emergence of Purgatory was not the main cause of the seismic shift which took place in the attitudes of the rich towards the poor. For that we must look elsewhere.

HOW THE BLACK DEATH CORRUPTED RELATIONS BETWEEN RICH AND POOR

In 1343 a Mongol army led by the fearsome Tatar king Khan Djanibeg besieged the trading colony which Genoese merchants had set up at

Caffa in the Crimea. The siege lasted almost three years and it only ended when, in the words of one Italian merchant, Gabriele de Mussis, the 'hordes of Tatars' were struck by a disease characterized by 'swellings in the armpit or groin caused by coagulating humours, followed by a putrid fever.' Thousands upon thousands died every day. The Tatar king ordered that the stinking cadavers of his dead troops should be catapulted into the city 'in the hope that the intolerable stench would kill everyone inside'.[89] It is said to be the first recorded use of biological warfare in world history.[90] Large numbers inside the city perished but a few Italian merchants escaped in an armed ship in the hope of returning to Genoa. They did not make it. They landed at Messina in Sicily. They had thereby brought the Black Death to Europe. In 1348 a great plague swept across the entire continent. Just under half the entire population was wiped out in a matter of months.[91] It was the Black Death and its economic aftermath – rather than doctrinal developments such as Purgatory – which did the most to change irrevocably the attitude of the rich towards the poor. It was to send philanthropy in an entirely new direction.

With the Black Death people of the fourteenth century felt that the Last Judgement had arrived. The plague spread swiftly from place to place, all across Europe, following no obvious pattern. Everywhere it killed with devastating suddenness, usually within a few days. People began to believe, in the words of Agnolo di Tura, a tax collector from Sienna who lost his wife and five children, 'This is the end of the world.'[92] When the plague reached England in the port of Bristol nine out of ten inhabitants died.[93] It hit capriciously; some places were hardly touched whereas elsewhere whole villages and hamlets ceased to exist, their entire populations wiped out.[94] King Edward III saw his subjects reduced, in less than 18 months, from some four million to perhaps two and a half million souls.[95] It was a human disaster of almost unimaginable proportions.

The medieval mind quickly attributed meaning to the pestilence. Writing in the mid-1360s, John of Reading suggested that the plague was a punishment from God for the 'greed, scorn and malice' of the nation. To placate the divine anger strange practices of contrition emerged. Barefoot penitents travelled from town to town, arriving in procession, two abreast, chanting and publicly whipping themselves with three-tailed knotted scourges until their backs were covered in blood.⁹⁶ In places where there were no priests left to perform the last rites some plague victims attempted to bury themselves alive in holy ground. The end of time seemed near.

If it was not the end of the world it was certainly the end of life as the feudal system had known it – and that was to change the relationship between the rich and the poor irrevocably. The great improvements in the medieval economy charted in the last chapter – the agricultural revolution which had created surpluses of food and wool for trading, the rise of the merchant classes, the growth of towns and the monetization of the economy – all these were accelerated by what Brian Tierney calls 'the fortuitous calamity of the Black Death'.⁹⁷ With almost half the population dead, there was an acute shortage of labour, and many of the serfs who had been tied to the land in feudal society quit their manorial homes and went in search of landlords who were prepared to hire them at higher wages. 'In a society accustomed to very slow changes in conditions of life, the market value of labour had been doubled at a stroke,' G. M. Trevelyan wrote.⁹⁸ A new class of landless migrants, with no firm roots and no fixed prospects, emerged. They were 'masterless men', to borrow A. L. Beier's striking designation.⁹⁹

Feudalism became untenable as the manorial system began to break up. The nobility did their best to resist the changing economic climate. In 1349 Edward III issued the Ordinance of Labourers, which tried to outlaw this new mobility and higher wages. Feudal nobles attempted to enforce the Ordinance, instructing local justices to track down absconding villeins and 'drag them back to servitude' and 'to exact the ancient dues' from those who remained on the land. But some labourers simply migrated to distant estates where they were employed by other landlords with 'no questions asked'. Others fled to the woods and became Robin Hood-style bandits; it was in this historical period that the legend of the man who robbed the rich and gave to the poor has its roots, Trevelyan suggests.

It seemed to the feudal nobility that the world had turned topsy-turvy. The lower orders were getting out of hand and all-important social distinctions were becoming blurred.¹⁰⁰ But there was no holding back the tide of change. As Trevelyan concludes: 'No statute could make two loaves or two labourers where there was only one. No Act of Parliament could repeal the Black Death or abolish the spirit of the age.'¹⁰¹ Towards the end of the century there were feudal rebellions in Italy and France and, perhaps most famously, in England – the great Peasants' Revolt of 1381. All this was to bring about a significant shift in the attitude of the rich towards the poor which was to alter permanently the course of philanthropy.

THE DEATH OF FEUDALISM AND THE RISE
OF THE BEGGAR

Some of those who quit their feudal homes in search of better wages found a better standard of living. But many did not. As the feudal system collapsed, the old, the sick and the disabled – who had been afforded some limited protection by their old lords of the manor – found themselves destitute and sometimes homeless. The dwindling population throughout Europe created unemployment blackspots despite the wider labour shortage.[102] The jobless set out on the open road in search of a better life. 'There was never a time when so many men had such strong incentives to wander away from the towns and villages to try to better their condition,' writes Brian Tierney, 'and the roads became filled with vagrants looking for work or loot or lured by promises of fabulously high wages in the depopulated parts of the country.'[103] Those who could not find work resorted to begging, and some sought alms in preference to work. Beggars were constantly on the move, their movements guided, Bronislaw Geremek suggests, by a calendar they had memorized of the days on which alms were distributed in various places, mainly from monasteries. 'The dates are often fixed and known in advance, and beggars often travelled long distances to be at the right monastery on the appointed day,' he writes. 'This wandering from monastery to monastery made up the substance of their lives.'[104]

Three other factors swelled the ranks of these wandering mendicants. Despite the plague, the Flemish woollen industry flourished. With a steady demand for wool, and a lack of peasants to plough and sow, English landlords enclosed more arable land for the grazing of sheep. This sometimes led to the eviction of whole village populations, a phenomenon which Tierney suggests was more widespread and occurred much earlier than economic historians have generally supposed. The problem was compounded when a stream of poor peasants arrived in the growing urban areas seeking employment, where their eagerness to work brought wages down, forcing townsfolk to join the ranks of beggars and those dependent on charity. Earnings were also forced down by the primitive industrialization beginning in towns, which meant that craftspeople, masters and journeymen lost control of their skills, tools, materials and production processes and became wage labourers under the direction of merchant entrepreneurs.[105]

But the other significant factor contributing to the growth of vagrancy was the arrival of waves of soldiers discharged from the army. The Hundred Years War (1337–1453) had been running long before the Black Death. After each major campaign thousands of soldiers were discharged. Many went back to their farms. But others, who found that prospect too dull, would swell the bands of vagabonds – half-beggars, half-bandits, as Tierney describes them – beginning to infest the countryside. This increase in the number of wandering beggars, 'some of them reckless marauders, trained in the use of arms, and not likely to shrink from shedding blood,' he says, 'made the whole problem of vagrancy seem increasingly formidable. The homeless wanderer became the object of fear and suspicion as well as pity.'[106] The sight of such 'sturdy beggars' at a time of acute labour shortage was deemed not just an affront to the old feudal aristocracy but also a threat. The wording of the 1349 Ordinance of Labourers made that clear:

> And since many sturdy beggars . . . are refusing to work, and are spending their time instead in idleness and depravity, and sometimes in robberies and other crimes; let no one presume, on pain of imprisonment, to give anything by way of charity of alms to those who are perfectly able to work, or to support them in their idleness, so that they will be forced to work for a living.[107]

From this point onwards the problem of relieving poverty – which had been essentially a matter of philanthropy – became inextricably intertwined with the problem of suppressing vagrancy. The old distinction between a beggar and a vagrant became blurred. In the Early and High Middle Ages almsgiving had been seen only as a way to help the unfortunate. Now it also became a vehicle to punish bad behaviour or incentivize socially useful conduct. The fear of beggars – combined with a greater psychological association between poverty and plague – led to an increasing victimization of the poor. Philanthropy had started what proved to be a tectonic shift.

The old idea that the poor were the representatives of Christ on earth gave way to a distinction between the poor of Christ and the poor of the Devil.[108] The Church Fathers and the scholastic philosophers of the High Middle Ages, such as Thomas Aquinas, had made distinctions between different groups of the poor so that, where resources were limited, there was an order of priority for dispensing philanthropy. Some categories of the poor, as we have seen, were regarded as more deserving of alms than others. But now systems began to be devised to put this thinking into practice.

In the thirteenth century special metal tokens had been issued to those entitled to charity which also prevented them from collecting alms twice. Tokens were first mentioned around 1240 by Richard Fishacre, a Dominican from Oxford, in what was the first practical measure to impose stricter control over the poor.[109] Now cities such as Venice, Genoa and Milan introduced licensing systems which officially recognized legitimate brotherhoods of beggars. Those who were indisputably blind or lame were given official permission to beg. They were issued with a Brotherhood of Beggars badge so that citizens could give them alms confident that the recipients were genuinely needy. In the fourteenth century a municipal ordinance at Nuremberg restricted begging to those who had been issued with a metal token to prove that they were locals; beggars from outside were allowed to remain in the city for a maximum of only three days.[110]

But it was not just about identifying the local needy. Practices were beginning to emerge to enforce the distinction between the deserving and the undeserving poor. In the mid-1300s the Breton canon lawyer, Henri de Bohic, a councillor to King Philip VI of France, whose views held sway in medieval France for more than 200 years, distinguished between those in extreme want, who were always to be helped, and others who were not – such as the 'ribald folk' who played dice all day and who were to be refused any alms at all.[111] Later thinkers, such as Geiler von Kayserberg, a fifteenth-century Catholic humanist preacher from Strasbourg – best known for his shockingly frank condemnations of sexual immorality and the greed of lawyers – went further, declaring that giving alms to the wrong sort of pauper was bad for both the recipient and donor.[112] In the past poverty had never been regarded by church canonists as a crime and no one was excluded from receiving assistance on the grounds of past wickedness or folly. After the Black Death the new fear of the poor was to change that. Poor relief was no longer a method of charity. Philanthropy became a method of control.

THE CHURCH LOOSENS ITS GRIP ON PHILANTHROPY

There was also a key shift in the method of delivering philanthropy at this juncture. Throughout the Middle Ages giving had been dominated almost entirely by the Church. But from this point onward lay people and their associations began increasingly to involve themselves in charitable activity. Economic growth, in the twelfth and thirteenth centuries, created centres of trade and manufacture which became an alternative focus of social and political power to the old feudal structures. The class of benefactors was expanded to include the elite merchants of the towns. But the towns did not just create a class of urban rich; there was also a new urban poor who existed unprotected by the old clerical and feudal safety nets. Fears of contagion carried by the wandering poor after the Black Death only added to the civic authorities' sense of urgency that they needed to take control of poor relief. Philanthropy increasingly became a concern of lay organizations and public institutions. Many of those canonized during this period were made saints because of their charitable work, including founding a hospital or working in one. And among these charitable saints a significant number were laypeople.[113]

In the years after the Black Death benefactions by the rich grew significantly, in three ways: in gifts to mark significant moments in their lives; through new bodies known as confraternities and guilds; but also in the legacies they left in their wills to pious foundations. Marvin Becker records that in Florence in the second half of the fourteenth century giving grew 'astronomically'.[114] Such a shift was not confined to one city or country. Towns and cities across the continent gradually began to exercise oversight of hospitals and founded new institutions to meet new needs – from orphanages and foundling homes to sanitariums and pawnshops. Each was financed by collections among well-to-do citizens to meet the needs of their less fortunate fellows. The idea of centralized aid for the poor, based in financial institutions and run by the municipality, began to take hold everywhere with a particular concern for the activities of vagrants and beggars.

During the fourteenth century, as towns and cities grew in size, wealth and importance, responsibility for care of the destitute and hungry, orphans and old folk, disabled and infirm, the dying and the dead, was assumed by civic authorities all across Europe. Responsibility for poverty was becoming secularized. Hospitals, orphanages and centres from which poor relief was distributed all grew increasingly dependent upon funding from public authorities and upon associations of pious merchants and artisan laymen for their administration.[115] There had been some involvement of lay people in charitable institutions in previous centuries. What was different at the start of the fourteenth century was the scale on which this secularization of giving took root.

Faced with the challenges posed by this new growing urban poverty, and fired by pious ardour, medieval laymen and women began to involve themselves more, both individually and collectively, in *opere pie* – holy works. These sought to promote the physical and spiritual betterment of their cities.[116] One of the most celebrated masterpieces of Renaissance painting embodies this new urban ideal. In 1423 Felice di Michele Brancacci, a Florentine silk merchant, his fortune boosted by the decline of the wool trade, commissioned the artist Masolino da Panicale and his apprentice, the 21-year-old Masaccio, to paint a series of frescoes depicting the life of St Peter in his family chapel. Art historians celebrate them as representing a radical break from the medieval tradition of symbolic art. Masaccio, left to work alone by his master, introduced the innovation of perspective and a vivid new naturalistic style. But the frescoes also embodied a philanthropic innovation. They showed alms being distributed by the saint and his fellows dressed in the garb of fifteenth-century Italian merchants. Philanthropy had become the province of lay people rather than being run by the clergy.

What is depicted in the frescoes of the Brancacci Chapel is a radically new sense of the ideal Christian community and a new departure in Christian philanthropy as lay people rather than churchmen took the lead. The Apostles were ordinary men performing simple acts of charity in city streets and in countryside identical to that of contemporary Tuscany. The motives of this new secular elite were mixed. They acted, in the words of Cosimo de' Medici (1389–1464), for 'the glory of God, the honour of the city, and the commemoration of myself'.[117] Powerful patricians struggled for control of influential charities as a means of enhancing their reputation and manipulating the institutions' resources for the benefit of their own family, and as a way to provide for poor relations and enable them to conceal their decline.

The changes which were pioneered in Florence spread within half a century to Venice and across Europe, particularly in southern Germany. As the Belgian historian Paul Bonenfant suggests, these late-medieval precedents laid the groundwork for the many governments which decided to regulate aid to the poor after the Reformation.[118] Some of these early initiatives were ambitious in their scale. In 1355 the will of a wealthy townsman of Lübeck gave instructions for the distribution of alms to 19,000 poor people at a time when the entire population of the town was less than 24,000. In England, too, the medieval civil authorities intervened in poor relief. After the draconian attempts to control beggars in the 1349 Ordinance of Labourers, a more benign statute was issued in 1388. It provided for the relief of 'impotent' paupers who were genuinely unable to earn a living (though it forbade them to wander as vagrants, insisting that they remain where they were when the statute was issued or return to the place of their birth). As the century turned, and the economy continued to grow, so did the numbers of the poor. In Cologne in 1403 the Hospital of the Holy Spirit fed 1,400 beggars each week; by 1475 the same hospital was supporting almost 5,000 a week.[119] 'The act of charity,' in the words of Bronislaw Geremek, 'became almost a mass phenomenon.'[120] In 1458 the city of Antwerp set up a Chamber of the Poor. In 1475 the tax list of Augsburg listed beggars as a professional group. In Saxony and the Low Countries from the 1520s to the 1560s there were a raft of attempts to reorganize poor relief.[121]

All this philanthropy was in the hands of lay people, yet their motivations, albeit reinforced by concerns for social order, were still seen as religious. Even in the early sixteenth century the city government of Ypres, a pioneer of poor relief, justified its schemes by saying that:

The canon laws do determine that alms should be given to feeble and weak persons, to such as are broken with sickness or forgone in years and to them that through impotency be not able to get their living: and seeing also that the same laws reckon those whole and strong persons that take alms as thieves and robbers.[122]

Two new institutions became the vehicle for this new secularization of poverty. The first were the medieval associations of craftsmen and others which were known as guilds and fraternities. The second was a new style of body which brought philanthropy together with something that was a cross between a credit union, a pawnbroker and a bank – the *mons pietatis* (fund of compassion or charity). The idea was pioneered in England but developed into an influential phenomenon in Italy as the *monte di pietà*.

GUILDS AND CONFRATERNITIES

The medieval guild, or gild, was a singular development in the history of philanthropy. Guilds began as groupings of merchants, craftsmen and artisans which were set up to regulate the conduct of particular trades. But by the eleventh century they had become one of the key institutions of medieval social, economic and religious life. Representing every occupation from apothecaries to wheelwrights, they were the vehicle through which each occupation's techniques and trade secrets – known as 'mysteries'* – were passed on from one generation to the next. They set standards for the quality of products – thus candles could be made of varying qualities of tallow, animal fat, or at the highest end beeswax, as used in church or by the moneyed classes and aristocracy. Guilds also oversaw the training of practitioners as they graduated from lengthy apprenticeships to become journeymen and finally master craftsmen. But guilds soon transitioned into protecting their members from competition by outsiders. Guilds thus became a cross between standards bodies, trade unions, masonic lodges, monopoly cartels and associations for mutual aid and comfort. Their spokesmen were gradually transformed into the mayors, aldermen and burghers of towns and cities all across Europe. In a Christian society whose holistic vision of life blurred the boundaries between the temporal and the spiritual, the guild also developed a distinct philanthropic dimension.

As guilds grew in prestige and power, feasts were held in the guildhalls to raise funds. Members made gifts and bequests of property to the guilds, the greatest of which became powerful and wealthy corporations. Most had their own chaplains and some their own chapels. One of the guild's

---

* Hence the term 'mystery plays' for the religious dramas regularly produced by the medieval guilds and fraternities.

key responsibilities was to ensure that members had proper funerals conducted with great solemnity. Priests were salaried to say Masses for the repose of the souls of departed members and their families. Ordinary folk could not afford to endow chantries as the wealthy did – to offer prayers to lessen their sufferings in the afterlife. But guilds became, in effect, the chantries of the ordinary person. This connected guilds inseparably with the doctrine of Purgatory, the sacrificial efficacy of the Mass and the veneration of saints – all of which was to cause them problems with the Protestant activists in the sixteenth century.

Guild funds were used philanthropically to soften the hardships of medieval life. Edward Cutts, in *Parish Priests and their People in the Middle Ages in England*, characterizes these as sickness, old age, poverty, wrongful imprisonment, or 'losses by fire, water, or shipwreck'.[123] Many of these payments were restricted to the guild's own members. But guilds, some more than others, also focused on enterprises for the benefit of the whole community – founding hospitals, almshouses and grammar schools; building and repairing bridges and highways, and making liberal gifts to the poor especially 'on great occasions of public need'.[124] Guilds were also the first lay sponsors of the arts. In addition to funding paintings and sculptures for medieval churches, each guild was required – in return for their trading licences – to perform one in a cycle of mystery plays, dramatizing appropriate Bible stories from Creation to the Last Judgement. These were performed on carts through the streets during key religious festivals. All in all philanthropic giving was a key feature of the guilds.

FROM FLAGELLATION TO PHILANTHROPY

Philanthropy was important too in another major medieval institution. Confraternities were associations which centred their activities not around one commercial trade but around a particular religious devotion. Confusingly, some of these called themselves guilds. St George's Gild at Norwich was founded in 1385 to hold an annual equestrian procession through the city on the saint's feast day. The Corpus Christi Gild in York organized a great annual celebration in honour of the Eucharist. These bodies were of significant social importance. In 1415 the York Gild staged a procession through streets of the city involving 96 craft guilds in 54 biblical dramatizations with actors drawn from a roll of 14,850 members.

Many confraternities grew out of the groups which had formed during the great flagellant movement that had sprung up across Europe after the Black Death. After the plague receded, these groups did not disband but rather transformed themselves into hundreds of lay religious fraternities. Many of these, as Brian Pullan put it, 'turned in effect from flagellation to philanthropy'. Crucially they remained strictly under lay management; priests were their chaplains, not their masters.[125] Many of them took their models of activity from the mendicant friars whose urban missions of the thirteenth century emphasized praise-singing, penitential flagellation, processions, funerary and requiem services, but also mutual support, egalitarian brotherhood and charity exercised towards confraternity members and the poor.

Confraternities ranged in size from a few dozen members to hundreds. They were active in almost every urban area and often in the countryside too. Towns sometimes had as many confraternities as guilds. In total, all across Europe, millions of medieval men and women exercised their Christian faith, with varying degrees of piety or zeal, through these fellowship groups which complemented and sometimes even eclipsed the local parish. It was the confraternity, rather than the parish, which organized the funerals of their departed members, with the entire membership following the cortege in a long procession. Some were motivated purely by religious piety but others saw the fraternities as ladders to social status, political influence, economic advantage, mutual insurance, or simply a sense of shared community.[126] Even the humblest had a communal cup from which to drink one another's health and prosperity at their convivial gatherings.[127] But they also took on extensive social responsibilities, running hospitals and hostels, almshouses and orphanages, and providing alms and dowries to the needy and the sick.

In both confraternities and guilds, philanthropy and self-interest and the communal good were deeply entangled. A good deal of confraternity energies and finances were directed into liturgical and ceremonial celebrations to honour their patron saints and those of their town or city. The needs of the poor, some critics complained, could sometimes take second place to the demands of the beauty of holiness. Yet other confraternities, as the thirteenth century progressed, did the opposite, prioritizing their poor-relief activities over ceremony.[128] Certain large confraternities acted as civic almoners, distributing food and money on behalf of town governments.[129] As James Brodman's *Charity and Religion in Medieval Europe* details, there is plenty of evidence that confraternities provided a good deal of practical help for the poor in the century before the Reformation.[130]

Between them the guilds and confraternities did much to shape the philanthropy of medieval life. By the fifteenth century virtually every market town had a number of guilds and fraternities. Each had its own coffers, however modest, funded by the annual subscriptions of its members, and perhaps a little jointly held stock – even if this was just a few cows or sheep fed on the common pasture. The profit from the animals swelled the common fund used to help members in straitened circumstances and also to give alms to the local poor. Their lavish annual banquets were, according to Bronislaw Geremek, responsible for alms distributions on a huge scale.[131]

A NEW PHILANTHROPIC INSTITUTION – THE *MONTE DI PIETÀ*

The final innovation which the Middle Ages contributed to the development of philanthropy was an institution which proved to be a cross between charitable giving and an early version of a pawnbroker and a mutual bank. It originated with the notion of what medieval churchmen called a *mons pietatis* (compassion fund), but it was secularized, becoming immensely influential in fourteenth- and fifteenth-century Italy where it became a mainstream alternative to the excessive rates of interest demanded by conventional moneylenders. The *monte di pietà* (plural *monti di pietà*) was an exercise in philanthropy in that it relied on the collection of voluntary donations made as acts of charity by wealthy individuals, guilds and other corporate bodies. These were paid into a fund which was then available for needy citizens who would apply to the fund for a loan, pledging an item of value as a surety. But these *monti di pietà* extended Christian charity beyond simple almsgiving by enabling those who were poor but not destitute to obtain cash loans on easy terms. The institutions spread with the growth of the mercantile economy as the vicissitudes of trade tipped unsuccessful merchants and unlucky gentlefolk into genteel poverty.

These new institutions strove to put into practice Christ's teaching – "lend, expecting nothing in return" (Luke 6:35) – which medieval theologians articulated as *mutuum date nihil inde sperantes* – 'lend, make mine thine, and expect to gain nothing from the loan'.[132] But money in the Middle Ages was hard to come by since Christians were forbidden from charging interest on loans – a practice denounced as usury. The Church drew this teaching from the philosophers of the ancient world, from Plato and Aristotle to Cato and Seneca, who had all condemned the charging of interest. The Fathers of the early Church had declared that it was contrary to mercy and humanity to demand interest from a poor and needy man. Canon law throughout the Middle Ages, from Gratian onwards, prohibited the practice. The result was that the lending of money in medieval society largely became the monopoly of wealthy Jews, whose religion outlawed the charging of interest to fellow Jews but not to those outside their faith.[133]

Since the laws and traditions of Christendom excluded members of the Jewish community from other kinds of trade or industry, many turned to moneylending – a practice to which the secular Christian authorities, perceiving the need for economic liquidity, were happy to turn a blind eye. In fourteenth- and fifteenth-century Italy, Jewish moneylenders typically charged interest rates of between 25 and 30 per cent, or even as much as 60 per cent in Milan at the turn of the century. But if Christians perceived Jewish moneylending as a necessary evil, it was also a goad to medieval anti-Judaism. Pope Sixtus IV, who was otherwise friendly to the Jews,[134] insisted that because they were willing to lend to people of dissolute inclination, who ruined themselves through drink or gambling or worse, Jews helped to create poverty rather than alleviate it. By contrast officials at the *monti di pietà*, who charged only 5 per cent interest, were required to vet borrowers by asking what they intended to do with their loan – though in reality many borrowers from the *monti* simply lied, perjuring themselves with false oaths when quizzed.

Like some other medieval lenders the *monti di pietà* required the borrower to pledge a valuable item as surety to get the loan. The pawnbroking element was first introduced when the Bishop of London, Michael Northburgh, on his death from the plague in 1361, left 1,000 marks of silver for the establishment of a fund in old St Paul's Cathedral that would lend money on pawned objects, without interest, for a year – at the end of which the loan was to be repaid or the pledge sold. But the expense of running the fund was drawn from the initial legacy, so eventually the capital was consumed and the bank closed. The idea did not catch on in northern Europe where pawnbroking provoked mixed reactions. Some argued that it fostered self-reliance and kept the poor from beggary, whereas others believed pawnbroking promoted improvidence and chronic indebtedness; the pawnshop, it was famously said, sat next door to the public house and over the way from the gaol. After the Reformation pawnshops were dismissed as popish, continental and bureaucratic.[135] But before that they were seen as generators of honesty and good citizenship and as a public service rather than a dodgy business.

The first recorded *monte di pietà* was founded in Perugia in 1462. Two hundred more followed by the end of the sixteenth century.[136] Their spread was significantly the work of mendicant friars who, following the example of Francis of Assisi, were stout advocates of the cause of the poor. They encouraged the establishment of a *monte* in every town they evangelized. These Observant Franciscans were, says Brian Pullan, 'eloquent moralists who combined economic realism with the determination to identify with the poor and take their part against oppressors, usurers included'.[137] Again there was sometimes a distinctly anti-Judaic undertone to their mission. One, Marco di Matteo Strozzi, left a set of memoirs that outlined his goal to rid Florence of Jewish moneylenders and to replace them with Christian pawnshops which would allow the poor to acquire cheap credit.[138] To acquire capital for their *monti* the Franciscan friars declared Palm Sunday as a day on which alms should be donated to its fund.

In practice, however, the very poor and destitute were not much assisted by these new funds. The truly impoverished had nothing suitable to pledge. The *monti* catered for those whom the Dominican Annio da Viterbo in the 1490s described as the *pauperes pinguiores* or 'plumper poor', who took small loans to tide them over during crises caused by sickness or stoppages. They had possessions to pawn – and would work hard not to forfeit them.[139] Some *monti* deliberately set out to find, in a discreet and tactful manner, the newly impoverished, who had not been born in poverty and were ill-equipped to extract themselves from it by means of labour or trade – and who were ashamed to reveal their poverty.[140]

Borrowers were typically offered loans representing two-thirds of the value of their pawned goods. The records of the *monti* reflect the delicacy of their social plight. The funds' administrators preferred to accept pawns of gold rings, silver plate or other precious metals rather than soft goods. Fine robes and linen required more care – with regular shaking and beating to get rid of moths and mouse droppings. Such pledges could easily deteriorate and would almost certainly have to be destroyed as infectious items if plague broke out. But, says Pullan, 'genteel pledgers often preferred to pawn linen, normally folded away in drawers, rather than pop the family silver whose shameful absence was far more difficult to conceal'.[141]

Yet though the *monti di pietà* made loans available at considerably less than the market rate, they did not put the Jewish banks out of business. The two types of lender appealed to different sectors of the market. Many proud people preferred a discreet transaction with a Jewish banker even if they had to pay five or ten times the rate for a 5 per cent *monte* loan. Moreover, the lending of really large sums was often beyond the resources of a *monte*.

The *monte di pietà* did more than provide another vehicle for medieval philanthropy. It played a part in the transition from the mercantilist economy of the Middle Ages to a capitalist one. It prompted a modification in the rigid views of scholastic theologians towards the idea of interest on loans. The cost of running the *monti* softened the Church's condemnations of usury and prepared the way for a generalization of the principle that moderate interest might justly be charged.[142]

Earlier denunciations of usury were based on the idea that it was wrong to charge interest on loans which were needed to sustain life. That idea survived into the early sixteenth century in the works of one of the major theologians of the Thomist school, the Dominican Tommaso De Vio, known as Cajetanus, a staunch champion of the poor. But from the fourteenth century it became increasingly common to borrow capital for trading purposes and investment. By 1515 Pope Leo X had accepted the case for *monti di pietà* to charge moderate interest, arguing that 'one who enjoys the benefit should also shoulder the burden'. Indeed, he went so far as to invert the logic of Cajetanus, instead suggesting that the larger the sum borrowed, the more the beneficiary ought to pay. In a papal bull he ruled that an institution like a *monte* could not be called usurious.[143]

Not everyone agreed. Some continued to argue that the *monti di pietà* promoted carelessness in contracting debt, destroyed the work ethic, and contradicted the principle of free competition. Such views found fewer supporters as time went on. It became the received wisdom that the *monti* not only saved individuals from financial ruin when temporary disaster struck, they but also extended affordable credit to the working poor. Indeed, they eventually became a convenient source of capital to the city's elites. In Florence or Bologna they even became a central treasury to hold the funds of the major charities of the city.[144] The *monti* also introduced the idea that an institution could be owned by the poor themselves. And as these common chests, administered by lay people rather than clerics, became more established, they strengthened the hand of local authorities seeking to resist the control of the early modern centralizing state.

THE ARRIVAL OF THE SHAMEFACED POOR

The gradual arrival of the new merchant middle class on the philanthropic scene throughout this period added a new dimension to the charitable relationship between the rich and poor. Fluctuations in the new mercantilist and monetary economy meant members of the growing merchant and artisan class could fall suddenly into poverty. Such folk did not fit the traditional description of the 'poor of Christ', but a belief developed that individuals and families who lost fortunes were especially deserving of pity. These were the 'shamefaced poor', known as the *vergognosi* in Italy. There, from the mid-thirteenth century, specialist almsgiving confraternities were established just to cater for such respectable folk in distress but who were too embarrassed to ask for help. Philanthropy thus became a device to protect the social hierarchy by preventing distressed gentlefolk and poor relations from slipping down the social ladder or bringing their class into disrepute.

England's oldest extant charity, the Hospital of St Cross in Winchester,* originally founded to assist the poorest, reflected this development. From 1445 its thirteen black-gowned poor Brothers

---

* See page 79 above.

were accompanied to Matins each morning by a similar number of old men in red gowns and caps. They were members of what was called the Almshouse of Noble Poverty. It had been founded that year by another Bishop of Winchester, Cardinal Henry Beaufort, who extended the hospital's cloister with handsome sets of chambers on the model of an Oxford college. Its Brothers, in their claret livery and silver cardinal's badge, were to be gentlefolk who had fallen on hard times, including the cardinal's own relatives and retainers as he approached retirement from public life. And so it came to pass. At the height of his career Beaufort was the richest prelate in the land, so wealthy that he financed Henry V's campaign at Agincourt in 1415. But he was on the wrong side in the Wars of the Roses, and when the Yorkist King Edward IV came to the throne Beaufort lost many of the manors and lands on which he relied to fund the extended almshouse.

The shamefaced poor included not just decayed gentlefolk, failed merchants or the widows of lawyers and physicians but also craftsmen and shopkeepers who had scruples about begging. Brian Pullan offers a graphic account from 1409 of a Florentine of whom it was said 'only a couple of days ago he was one of the richest merchants in the Oltrarno'. He was found with no wine and bread in his house, and with a family of several grown-up daughters for whom he had not a penny to give in dowry. Special concern was aroused for the chastity of young women plunged into poverty. Almsgivers began to dispense lump sums in the form of dowries for such young women. In 1400 repentant usurers were urged to give to widows or to maids who had no dowry, rather than to men. Bequests to dowry funds became increasingly common in the late fourteenth century. By the fifteenth century, in one city, they accounted for around 11 per cent of all pious gifts made through wills.[145]

THE PHILANTHROPIC LEGACY OF THE MIDDLE AGES

To sum up, ever since the Renaissance a stereotype has emerged which portrays the Middle Ages as a time of backwardness and obscurantism. As we have shown in this chapter, this image of a thousand years of medieval Christendom as some kind of Dark Age is in many ways false. Those centuries were, as the wide-ranging medieval historian Bronislaw Geremek observed, characterized by a high degree of coherence and continuity, with periods of significant enlightenment and learning, and a consistent generosity in that era's approach to philanthropy.

Over the last half-century historians of the period have come to understand that. But this insight has not penetrated through to historians of philanthropy, who have until now continued to repeat the calumny that medieval charity was at best inefficient and haphazard and at worst failed to put into practice its high-minded theology. Its system of poor relief has even been labelled as positively pernicious in its effects.[146] As we have seen, the actual evidence shows that philanthropic giving was extensive. A range of institutions offered alms or assistance in a variety of ways. Churches set up tables in the porches and naves from which food and money were distributed to those in need. Monasteries cared for the sick within their hospitals and sanatoriums and, on a regular calendar, handed out doles of food and cash from their gates. Wealthy individuals financed foundations with the multiple motive of saving their souls, adding to the prestige of their families, and giving succour to the poor. Guilds and confraternities likewise, though they watched out for the interests of their members, also made widespread contributions to public projects and the relief of the poor. Individual members of society, down to the working poor themselves, routinely gave food and small change to the destitute. None of this was centrally organized or co-ordinated, but it was far from haphazard.

A greater measure of control and coordination did enter in, however, as independent territories, city states and urban centres began to take an interest in the business of poor relief. But it was economic and political factors which brought this about. The rise of the merchant class created a new class of benefactors and new vehicles for philanthropy. The Black Death accelerated the decline of feudalism, liberating many in the labouring classes but also increasing the numbers of beggars. A desire for social control brought politics as well as philanthropy into the business of charity. All this brought about a significant alteration in the attitudes of the rich towards the poor, and particularly the destitute, which was to mark a seismic shift in the attitude of donors towards those who were the objects of their generosity. It was in the late Middle Ages, in the thirteenth and fourteenth centuries, that the foundations were laid for the highly discriminatory systems of poor relief which were to follow in the early modern era.

The seeds of another important shift were planted in the medieval era. The Middle Ages had begun with philanthropy being largely vested in bishops and monasteries and administered by ecclesiastical institutions. By the thirteenth and fourteenth centuries, however, lay men and women – as individuals and through their associations, and through civic, municipal and state institutions – became increasingly involved in the business of philanthropy. There was a transfer of influence, power and management from the clergy to the laity. This was not secular in the modern sense of the term. What occurred was a kind of laicization, not secularization.[147] As Nicholas Terpstra has pointed out, 'for medieval, Renaissance, and early modern society, our modern distinctions between "sacred" and "secular" were largely meaningless'.[148] Most charitable establishments and institutions retained an avowedly religious purpose, albeit blended with civic and social concerns.[149]

What the evidence therefore shows is that much of what was claimed to be innovation by Protestants after the Reformation was already present in some way in Catholic Europe before that. Poor relief became a tool to transform the dependent into industrious artisans, good housewives, obedient servants. Jobs could be created, if necessary artificially, by financing road or bridge building or other public works. The state began to play a role, with prosperous citizens being pressured by appeals for the good of the Commonwealth as much as out of Christian charity. By the fifteenth century, Geremek indicates, systems like this had been put into practice in many European cities.[150] Medieval poor relief was widespread and effective, and the developments so often associated with Protestantism were present in Catholic Christendom for a century or two before Martin Luther affixed his note to the door of Wittenberg Cathedral.[151]

But something vital was lost after the Reformation and the Enlightenment reshaped European thinking. Almsgiving, for all the later Protestant parodies, was not regarded as deriving its value solely from the spiritual benefits conferred on the almsgiver. Undoubtedly there was, according to Catholic theology, benefit to the soul of the giver, yet there was clear consideration given to the spiritual and bodily needs of others. But there was a more holistic dimension to the medieval vision of philanthropy. Care for the poor was central to the medieval understanding of what it meant to be Catholic. At its heart was, in the words of Richard Finn, 'the notion that the relationship between the rich and poor involved mutual respect, as brothers and sisters in Christ, and was embedded in a complex network of social, religious, economic and political linkages'. Today philanthropists, politicians and policy-wonks are much concerned about 'social inclusion'; medieval thinkers had no such concerns because at the heart of their theology and practical polity was a unified vision of society from which, by definition, none were excluded. The notion of 'social exclusion', Finn suggests, only makes sense from the perspective of our own 'impoverished contemporary view of society, from which so many are alienated or marginalised'. By contrast, though medieval beggars might be ignored or disparaged, the poor generally were seen to perform a crucial religious function. The widow and the orphan were the altar on which the material was transformed into the spiritual. Medieval philanthropy was rooted in a sense of relationship.

This was lost, laments John Bossy in his magisterial study, *Christianity in the West, 1400–1700*, with the profound shift of thinking prompted by the Reformation, when Christianity ceased to be conceived as a community of believers and instead became understood in terms of rival confessions of belief. This, Bossy argues persuasively, was a wholly negative development. It led to a diminished religious universe, in which Christianity no longer performed the social miracle of ritualized reconciliation. Instead it emphasized a distinction between the godly learned elite and the mass of ordinary believers whose views and behaviour needed to be regulated by printed catechisms. Christianity was reduced to what could be taught and learned.[152] Belonging came to be replaced by belief. A society which once had embraced the poor now set itself on the road towards excluding them. Of course, the medieval worldview exhibited serious shortcomings; its fatalism placed the poor in a social and economic position which was entirely unacceptable to modern notions of equality. But with the withering of the medieval vision something has been lost – in the relationship between giver and receiver – which modern philanthropy would do well to recover.

Interview: John Studzinski on art, religion and philanthropy

John Studzinski is an investment banker who has advised governments, pension funds, corporations, sovereign wealth funds and rich individuals through leading financial firms on Wall Street and the City of London. He divides his time between London and New York. His philanthropy ranges widely across the arts, human trafficking, modern slavery and homelessness. A devout Roman Catholic, he works as a volunteer at The Passage, a shelter for the homeless attached to Westminster Cathedral. His professional and philanthropic activities have seen him awarded the CBE, numerous philanthropy awards, and twice made a papal knight. He is an art collector. He was named Banker of the Year in 2007 and Catholic of the Year in 2017.

Your philanthropy is very catholic – in all senses of the word. It embraces the arts, the homeless, human rights and religious causes. Do you see a link between these? Or do they just reflect different aspects of your personality and interests?

Today a lot of philanthropists are like architects. They have very clear views about the very precise architecture of their philanthropy. Architects want to get everything fine-tuned: the plumbing, the electricity, the lighting and everything else. But I think a philanthropist should be more like a gardener planting a seed. You don't know how long it's going to take to grow, and what the plant's going to look like. As the plant evolves, you might prune it, you might fertilize it, it might have different reactions to different types of climate.

So philanthropy is like planting a tree. You won't sit under that tree, but you have faith that somebody will one day sit under it.

When I commissioned the composer James MacMillan to write a Stabat Mater – a thirteenth-century text reflecting one of the most deeply spiritual moments in the New Testament, when Mary is watching her son Jesus dying on the cross – I gave MacMillan the text and said: 'I'll say nothing else. You're a channel for the divine.' He replied: 'I'm not sure about that.' But I told him: 'Human beings don't determine whether they channel the divine. The divine chooses who are its instruments and vehicles.'

You were demonstrating faith in him, you mean? Certainly the terrible pain of a mother watching her son die is agonizingly vivid in that piece of music.

It's very powerful. It's very compelling. And there's no question that you are listening to one of the great moments in the history of Western civilization. The face of Christ is about human dignity.

And that's a central concern in your philanthropy.

Yes. It underlies the work of the Sisters of Charity at The Passage, the shelter we founded in the early '80s with Cardinal Basil Hume at Westminster Cathedral for care of the homeless on the streets of London. It's there in the work I have done for human rights victims around the world, bringing Human Rights Watch to Europe. It's there in Arise, which I now chair and which is the largest group in the world to combat human trafficking and modern slavery; it has 1.5 million religious sisters in 90 countries teaching young children how not to be trafficked, even though these young people want to improve their lives through migration. It underlies the Genesis Foundation which is about giving someone their first break in the arts. All of it is about acknowledging someone's dignity. It's a bit like giving a homeless person a job. It helps them redefine their role in society.

That's the highest level of charity according to the medieval Jewish sage, Maimonides – giving someone a job.

I agree. Philanthropy should be win, win, win. When Basil Hume's seventieth birthday came up, I wanted to give him a present. I knew a young composer called Roxanna Panufnik was just starting her career and had become a Catholic in her early twenties. There hadn't been a Mass commissioned in over 50 years for Westminster Cathedral. I just thought: 'You can give the Cardinal a present. You can give the cathedral a new Mass. And you can help a young artist by giving them a high-profile commission.' Win, win, win. That was the origin of the Genesis Foundation. Twenty years later we've had over 5,000 people who've had Genesis Director training at the Young Vic, Old Vic or Royal

Court. There's a network of them. The first was Rufus Norris, who's now running the National Theatre.

Can you have that same win-win between your career as a banker and your work as a philanthropist? Or do they reflect different spheres in your life?

Ah, God and Mammon! I often get people saying, 'I don't understand. You've got this career on Wall Street for over 30 years where you work at Morgan Stanley, HSBC, Blackstone, and now PIMCO, all these financial firms, tough capitalist vehicles. How do you reconcile that with your faith – with commissioning religious music and everything else?'

Do they assume that you are assuaging your guilt with good works? That's what medieval Catholics were accused of, after the Reformation. Protestant reformers claimed that Catholics only gave alms to get time off Purgatory.

The idea that philanthropy is a kind of penance? That's ridiculous. I regard philanthropy, like banking, as about asset allocation. God has given you what I call all the Ts: time, talent, treasure, trust, ties (by which I mean networking) and technology. I'm an asset manager in my day job, and in my philanthropy, I'm allocating a certain amount of my wealth – not just money but all those Ts – to give to society. When someone says to me capitalism conflicts with philanthropy, or conflicts with Christianity, I say: 'No. If you give someone a job, you give them their dignity.' You give them a role in society. You give them a sense of identity and a sense of being. In the Gospel in the Parable of the Talents [in which a Master gives his servants varying amounts of money in coins called 'talents'], God gets cross with someone who's given one talent and buries it in the ground to keep it safe. He's much happier with someone who's given one talent and uses it to produce three or five more. From him to whom much has been given, much is expected.

I've been given a lot. My parents were immigrants but the thing they gave me was a rich education and a great faith. From a young age, I had the role model of working in a homeless shelter, dishing out soup.

That's what your whole family did?

Yes. The human element is a very important part of the business of giving. In my day job I spend a lot of time with very wealthy people.

Sometimes one of them will say: 'I'd like to get my children more involved in philanthropy and I'm going to give them money to give away.' And I always say: 'Well, find out what their passions are first and have them start by giving their time or talent before they actually give their treasure. It's easy to give out money, but to actually sit down in a homeless shelter for four hours, that's more difficult . . .

You give away a certain percentage of your income. How do you decide how much to give away? How do you decide what to give it to? Do you have a notion in advance that you're going to spend this much on music and that much on human rights?

No. It's a bit like going shopping and saying, 'I only want to spend £100', but finding there are two or three really interesting things, so I end up spending £300. In meetings the trustees sit and look at me and say: 'You shouldn't be spending that much money. We've committed to this, this and this over the next three years.' I say: 'Yes, but this is a really good opportunity and I want to do it.' Sometimes even to the point that I'll say: 'Fine, I'll sell a painting in order to do that.'

So you're responding to stimuli. Or in religious language you're open to the signals God is sending to you.

Yes, I believe in the power of the Holy Spirit. I recently commissioned James MacMillan's latest symphony, which was premiered at the Edinburgh Festival. It's on the theme of the Holy Spirit and called *Le Grand Inconnu* (The Great Unknown). That was really to try to give people a better sense of what the Holy Spirit is.

How does that fit with your policy of mentoring young artists and developing new talent? MacMillan is well established. He is one of Britain's most distinguished composers.

We've done five commissions with James MacMillan. One of the other things I've learned in philanthropy is to partner with people. Whether it's James MacMillan or Harry Christophers or Stephen Daldry or the Sisters of Charity, it's best to partner with individuals rather than institutions. Institutions are interested in taking your money to solve their problems, their short-term needs and their strategies. But if you want to make change based on your passion or your conviction, then you have to find partners. Good philanthropy is about good partnerships. If you have certain rich collaborations, rich partnerships, you develop them.

You have to have a certain degree of engagement in all of your projects. Cheque-book philanthropy, passive philanthropy, doesn't have any type of nurturing benefits to the donor. You get much more out of something if you don't just use your treasure but if you use your time or your talent or try to nurture your talent or other aspects of yourself.

That's interesting. Because it's much more in line with medieval attitudes to philanthropy than to the dominant style of philanthrocapitalism today, which is more about solving some social problem through a project-orientated approach. Your vision is more holistic and involves a relationship between the one who gives and the one who receives.

I see philanthropy as a nurturing of the soul, something that helps you better understand yourself. God has given everybody a purpose, and you might not know your purpose in this life. But you go through life and you find that your talents and God's will converge on what you're going to contribute in this life. In project-oriented philanthropy the human element sometimes gets overlooked. I think the human element is the most important element in giving.

That is why, I suppose, you also give your time, through volunteering, as well as giving money. What impact does hands-on volunteering have on you?

It changes every year depending on my travel schedule, but I've always volunteered at The Passage since I became involved thirty years ago. I used to work in the kitchen, but lately what I do is I volunteer on Sunday evenings as the receptionist in the men's shelter, Passage House. I get to spend time with the men, and talk to them about their problems. Homeless shelters are not just about food. They're not just about a clean bed and proper health care advice. They are about listening, in a non-judgmental way, about respecting someone's homelessness and their dignity.

But what do you get out of it?

It allows me to better understand the types of support mechanisms professionals really need in a homeless shelter.

Forgive me, but you're avoiding the question, by talking about better understanding and better support. What impact does it have on *you* emotionally, psychologically, spiritually?

The other night I was walking in New York City, walking home to my apartment. The homelessness problem is getting really bad there, as in London and elsewhere. There was a man on Fifth Avenue, sitting there with his cat in a little box and everything very well organized around him. But it was bitterly cold. So I asked him, 'Why don't you go to the Times Square shelter?' He said, 'I was mugged in the Times Square shelter last week.' So I named another shelter and said, 'Why don't you go there?' And he said, 'Well, I don't have enough money.' So I gave him some money and said: 'Take this. I don't want you sleeping here tonight.' He looked at me. He had a great sense of dignity, great spirit. He was more worried about his cat than himself. But it was clear that, though he took the money, he was going to sleep there on the street. It was very cold. But he wouldn't go to the shelter.

When I go to The Passage I feel like I'm embracing people. The fundamental spiritual element of life is that we're all the same. We're all the same. When you're working there in the shelter, you're embracing the fact that we're all human beings and we all have to give and to take. It's like holding a mirror up to yourself and you realize, 'I could be homeless, and if I was homeless how would I react to this situation? How would I cope?' So whether it's a human rights victim, a survivor of trafficking, someone in the night shelter, a homeless person, real philanthropy, to my mind, is about mutual respect. That's why I can't stand project-orientated social impact investing. Because people don't want to be someone's project.

That's why the man I met on the street was so moving, because that was his environment. He wanted me to respect the fact that he was coping perfectly on Fifth Avenue in the cold damp night with his cat – and then part of me tried to 'improve' him by making him a project. By talking to me as a person he quickly pulled me back to reality and said, 'Hey, mate, this is the way it is. I'm coping, I'll be fine.' That's when I said, 'OK.' No one wants to be someone's project. Philanthropy should be about partnership. It's about two people locking arms.

So how do you respond when people say: 'The problem of homelessness, human trafficking, modern slavery, is so grave, how can you waste money on the arts? Why not give all your money to the homeless?'

Because there is more than one dimension to the human condition. I'm realistic about the fact that there's an infinite number of problems in the world that relate to poverty, hunger, homelessness. You can nurture the soul through the visual arts, through music, as much as you can by dealing with the harsher issues in society like poverty. The arts are part of the richness of life and you want the richness of life for the homeless person as much as you do for yourself.

There are many aspects of the soul, and you can't separate them. That's what the homeless man on Fifth Avenue was teaching me. I was projecting my life onto him. But he had his own life, with his belongings and his cat. He had no bitterness. He was like someone out of *Pilgrim's Progress*. He taught me that the other person can be just as happy, or happier than you are, about certain things. In the end, it's about human dignity.

Chapter 5

The Great Myth of the Reformation

The Reformation is a turning point in the history of philanthropy. That, at any rate, has been the received wisdom among historians of philanthropy throughout the twentieth century. It is still unquestioningly accepted in much writing on the subject today. The argument goes that the charity of the medieval Catholic Church was haphazard, ineffective and that it increased – and entrenched – poverty rather than reducing it. All this purportedly changed with the arrival of a Protestant theology which insisted that Christians were saved not by their own good works but by the grace of God alone. Almsgiving could therefore not bring spiritual benefits to the donor. Acts of charity, under this new worldview, were outward signs that an individual was already saved by God. They were not the cause of that salvation, merely an external mark of an individual's righteousness.

The implication of this was that Christian philanthropy should not be about accumulating brownie points in heaven – or alleviating the sufferings of dead friends and relatives in Purgatory. It should focus rather on the needs of the poor and of wider society. Charity is about the living rather than the dead. The new Protestantism was said to enable philanthropy to become more rational and systematic. In towns and cities run by religious reformers new systems sprang up. Indiscriminate Catholic giving was replaced by a Protestant discrimination between the deserving and the undeserving poor. There was now a common chest for poor relief, administered by lay people not clergy, with well-conceived policies legislated and enforced by governments and councils. It all sprang from the new Protestant theology.

All this is wrong. It is true that there were fundamental shifts in philanthropic thinking at this time. But, as the last chapter has shown, they were linked with long-running economic, social and political changes rather than a sudden religious one. The Black Death, the decline of feudalism, the rise of the merchant class, urbanization, the monetization of the economy – all these were at the root of changes which later came to be dubbed as 'secularization'. It was chiefly the rapid growth in numbers of the poor which changed social attitudes towards them. Moreover modern scholarship, with the distinguished medieval historian Brian Tierney in its vanguard, showed as long ago as 1959 that medieval Catholic charity, far from being casual and haphazard, was widespread and effective. Nor was it undiscriminating. Tierney charted how medieval Catholic thinkers had long distinguished between different categories of the poor. They did not use the terms 'deserving' and 'undeserving' poor, but they nonetheless suggested that different philanthropic approaches to different groups were appropriate. For good or ill, that was not a Protestant innovation.

A decade later another pioneering historian, the sixteenth-century specialist Natalie Zemon Davis, argued in a seminal article entitled 'Poor relief, humanism, and heresy: The case of Lyon'[1] that in practice differences between Catholic and Protestant welfare arrangements were cosmetic. Around the same time another early modern specialist, Brian Pullan, published a ground-breaking study of poor relief, *Rich and Poor in Renaissance Venice: The Social Institutions of a Catholic State, to 1620.*[2] It provided detailed evidence that overturned the long historiographical tradition which dismissed Catholic relief schemes as undiscriminating, unsystematic and unsuccessful. What he showed about Italy was shown to be true of Europe in general in later research by others.[3]

Over the next 30 years Pullan published a series of authoritative studies which revealed that the post-Reformation view of poor relief in Western Europe in the fourteenth and fifteenth centuries was a caricature.[4] Many of the changes later attributed to the Reformation had been anticipated by earlier generations; they were, Pullan demonstrated, 'changes in degree rather than in kind; quantitative changes, rather than changes in principle; changes stimulated by graver economic needs, rather than by radical alterations in intellectual attitudes'.[5] Catholics largely shared Protestant reactions to the increased numbers of poor people, beggars and vagrants, and – frightened by plague, crime and a sense of crisis – put in place very similar laws to seek to control them.[6] Systems to offer the poor loans as well as, or instead of, charity were common to both denominations.[7] In Catholic and Protestant towns and cities alike the measures put in place were merely a more thorough re-enactment of those which had first been attempted well before Martin Luther was even born.[8] Research by historians over the last five decades has proved Tierney, Davis and Pullan right.[9] So how did the notion come about that it was Protestantism which caused a permanent shift in Western philanthropy? And why has it stuck?

PROTESTANT PROPAGANDISTS

The original sixteenth-century reformers themselves were enthusiasts for the idea. In previous centuries reformers had attacked corruption and the abuse of power within the Church after medieval popes became powerful temporal rulers, as well as spiritual leaders, and got entangled in the politics of the continent. Abuses such as the sale of indulgences by a clerical hierarchy anxious to fund grandiose churches, and to subsidize a sometimes decadent clerical lifestyle, had attracted reproach from outraged critics throughout the medieval era. Perhaps the best known of these was William Langland, whose long epic poem *The Vision of William Concerning Piers the Plowman* was the second most famous work of medieval literature after Chaucer's *Canterbury Tales*. *Piers Plowman* appeared in its earliest version around 1362. It was a caustic protest against clerical and state abuses of the fourteenth century – and an appeal by Langland for the creation of an ideal society. Its author may well have been inspired by his contemporary, the reformer John Wycliffe, who translated the Bible from Latin into Middle English and protested against the wealth, luxury and worldliness of the clergy. *Piers Plowman* had a deep impact upon its time and became a rallying cry for change during the Peasants' Revolt of 1381 and was later invoked by English propagandists at the Reformation.

But fourteenth-century reformers such as Langland and Wycliffe called for the internal reform of the Church. What made the Reformation different was that Martin Luther saw the root of the problem as theological rather than merely the venal behaviour of flawed clergymen corrupted by power. He thought that the Church's very doctrine on redemption and grace had been warped by a Catholic hierarchy which had allowed

God's free gift of grace to become perverted by the sale of indulgences. To Luther, salvation was a personal matter between God and man. The traditional idea that the Church was needed to mediate between man and God was at best unnecessary and at worst corrupting, he believed. The sale of indulgences showed that. Faith must henceforth take priority over charity.[10] This was to turn Luther's initial call for reform into a rupture which split the Church and the whole of Western Christendom.

Other reformers followed Luther's lead. 'The Papists are incessantly urging a concern for the dead; and by their importunate declamations cause it to be preferred to all the duties of charity,' wrote John Calvin in Geneva.[11] In Zurich that other great Swiss reformer Ulrich Zwingli took a very selective view of Catholic theology, lampooning its view of almsgiving as a method of notching up merit points in heaven, and ignoring its subtler and richer dimension that charitable giving imitates and obeys God – and transforms the character of the giver. Zwingli accused Catholicism of encouraging a class of professional beggars – because alms were deemed valid if they were given in good faith, irrespective of the merits of the recipient.

Protestant horror at this is clear from the following question-and-answer record of the interrogation of a beggar in 1558 in the city of Augsburg – the place in which the doctrinal basis for the Lutheran schism had been codified three decades earlier. Augsburg, in this period, was acrimoniously divided between a Protestant majority and a sizeable Catholic minority, many of whom lived just across the river in the village of Oberhausen – home to a Catholic fraternity known as the Corpus Christi brotherhood, which was to become pivotal during the Counter-Reformation.[12]

The tensions between the two communities, connected by the Wertach Bridge, also known as Beggars' Bridge,[13] are clear from this transcript of the interrogation of the beggar, who lived in Catholic Oberhausen and had been caught soliciting alms in largely Protestant Augsburg:

Thursday, the 25th of February 1558, Simon Schweyer, beggar boy from Lindau testified without torture as follows:

How long has the boy been begging here and how often has he been put out of the city? He has been around here with his mother for seven winters or so, and his mother sent him into the city to beg. He has been put out six or seven times.

Is it true that he has been locked in the Fool's House* at least fifteen times, and that he has taken an oath to stay out no less than five times? He has never been in the Fool's House, but his brother Michael, who is two years older, was in it about three times. Michael does not come here to beg anymore, and is in Oberhausen with their mother and father.

Where is he staying here in Augsburg, or who is giving him shelter? He has very seldom spent the night in the city, and when he has, he stays in a bathhouse on Lech Lane behind the bakers. He does not know the bather's name.

It is known that his father and mother are staying in Oberhausen, and that what he and his mother have earned begging, they squander out there. With whom are they lodging? They are lodging with a young man named Schneidt in Oberhausen, whom they give 6 kreuzer a week for rent. His father drinks about a measure of wine (about one litre) per month.

What do they have to pay for their lodging, and what do they have for income besides begging? In summer, his father sometimes makes hackles† and sells them, and he also repairs pots. Otherwise they have no trade other than begging.

Is it true that his mother claims to have epilepsy whenever someone does not want to give her anything or threatens her under questioning? She also sometimes pretends to have an attack and falls down on the street, but is only faking to move the people to have more sympathy for her so they will give her something. His mother is ill and does not trick people with it.

They eat and drink the best in Oberhausen, and support not only themselves by begging here but also their landlords. No, they do not do that.

His father also goes begging; what illness or infirmity does he claim to have? His father does not beg, but he has a bad back.

What other beggars are there in Oberhausen who support themselves only from begging, and make enough from it to feed themselves? There

---

* A low cage next to the Council House where a delinquent, very often a drunkard, would be subject to ridicule while awaiting to appear before officials.
† Combs for flax.

are a lot of beggars outside the city, but he does not know them, and does not know what they have to support themselves or how.

Where are these beggars staying? He does not know the names of the peasants they stay with.

He and his father and mother also beg on Wertach Bridge; how long have they been doing it? They have never sat on the bridge or begged on it, rather they have sought alms here and there. The boy requests mercy.

Punishment recorded: Simon Schweyer, a boy of sixteen years, was put out of the city seven times for begging, and each time he was strictly forbidden to return, but in spite of this he came back in. Therefore he was disciplined in the irons and earnestly warned not to be found here again or he would face public corporal punishment.[14]

The questions, it might be thought, reveal a good deal more than do the answers. The fear that the Catholics of Oberhausen were infesting Protestant Augsburg with the overflow of their beggars is clear; but so too is the draconian nature of the system of deterrence and punishment. Zwingli, in Zurich, went further, insisting that all pre-Reformation almsgiving was inherently flawed because it was never performed for the proper reasons: to honour God and for the good of one's neighbour. Rather the motivation was, he sweepingly asserted, always self-serving and guided by false values – 'out of the fear of the devil and of hell, or of God as a tyrant, or in order to purchase time or eternity'.[15]

Others were more wilful in their propaganda. *Piers Plowman*, which two centuries earlier had circulated in manuscript form, was first published as a book in 1550 by a Protestant pamphleteer and printer named Robert Crowley.[16] By deleting parts of the original to downplay its Catholic characteristics, and adding a preface and marginal notes, Crowley converted the poem into a powerful Protestant screed against the Roman Catholic hierarchy and monasticism. He emphasized its clarion call for a reforming monarch who would purge corruption from the religious orders. This turned the fourteenth-century poem into a piece of sixteenth-century anti-papist propaganda and harnessed its vision to the rhetoric of reformers demanding ecclesiastical, social and political change.

So successful was Crowley in this enterprise that lines from the poem actually found their way into the Preamble of Elizabeth I's *Statute of*

Charitable Uses of 1601, setting a definition of public philanthropy that was to endure for centuries – and which still, in many ways, holds sway today. In Langland's fourteenth-century allegorical poem the figure of Truth sends a letter to wealthy merchants advising them, if they would save their souls, to buy and sell boldly, and put their profits to good philanthropic use. They were told to repair hospitals to help the unfortunate, mend bad roads, rebuild broken-down bridges, provide maidens with dowries so they could marry or become nuns, send boys to school or apprentice them to a craft, and assist religious orders by increasing their endowments.[17]

Two centuries later Langland's list was transferred to the Preamble, becoming the first statutory definition of charitable purposes. It was a clear sign of the particular philanthropic activities which the Tudor government believed were of general benefit to society. These were the areas in which the state wanted to encourage private contributions. British parliamentary documents[18] declare that this list then became the foundation of the modern definition of charitable purposes, being repealed from English law only in 1960. In the intervening centuries English case law, when considering whether or not a particular purpose is charitable in law, has tended to look for an analogous precedent in the list first encoded by the medieval poet and then promoted as a piece of religious propaganda.

NEW SYSTEMS OF POOR RELIEF

Certainly Protestant cities all across Europe put new systems of civic poor relief in place. But the same also happened in Catholic towns. The progress of new poor laws across the continent began in northern and eastern Germany during the early 1520s, but Catholic areas in eastern France and northern Italy were doing the same thing by the middle of the same decade – and it was not until the 1530s that the trend travelled north to Scandinavia and crossed the Channel to England.[19]

More significantly, the new schemes were often merely improved versions of systems which were in place as much as seventy years before the Reformation began. Italian cities had anticipated the attempts by German post-Reformation cities to pool resources in a common chest.[20] They had made distinctions between the deserving and undeserving poor. Even in Germany many of the most important changes pre-date the Reformation. In Strasbourg as early as 1498 a cathedral preacher, Johannes Geiler von Kayersberg, had been arguing that civil authority should be responsible for the poor and provide them with work, education and relief.[21] In many areas the civic authorities built on the work of the Catholic confraternities; already in 1521 in Venice a well-articulated social welfare system was being created in which 125 confraternities acted as civic almoners, distributing food and money on behalf of local government. Similar processes were at work in other northern Italian cities as key components in the creation of these more organized civic systems.[22]

Demographics and economics ushered in such changes, not theology. Indeed, the role of the laity was more prominent in some Catholic towns and cities than it was in reformed communities. By contrast, in Geneva and in other Calvinist communities, ardent reformers insisted that poor relief be 'consecrated' by declaring that local hospital commissioners should be regarded as deacons of the Church.[23] Moreover, a sociologist might find it hard to detect practical difference in the consequences of the Catholic assertion that almsgiving could be redemptive and Calvin's theological suggestion that the Chosen, those predestined by God to be saved, should forward their wealth to Heaven like advance baggage by way of the poor.[24]

The same was true in England in the era when the Protestantization of the Reformation accelerated, during the reign of the boy king Edward VI. Even in that period, many of those making philanthropic donations in their wills began with Protestant preambles but nevertheless left money for deeds of charity for which the benefactor expressed the pious Catholic hope that the gift would be 'meritorious for the health of my soul'.[25] Reformation theology did not, to borrow the famous phrase of Queen Elizabeth I, 'make windows into men's souls'. It was the same on the Continent. A study of Last Wills and Testaments in eighteenth-century Amsterdam reveals that Protestants as much as Catholics often left charitable bequests which contained a request commending their soul to God's mercy; in 1781 a woman named Johanna van Mekeren left 30,000 guilders to the Reformed Charity, which recognized the gift with the very Catholic-sounding assurance that her work of mercy would be 'rewarded with eternal salvation'. The idea that philanthropy would reap rewards in the afterlife was lodged deep in the psyche of Protestants and Catholics alike.

THE ROLE OF HUMANISM

Insofar as there was a philosophical underpinning to this common approach it may well have been rooted in another intellectual development than Lutheran theology. The Renaissance saw the birth of a new Christian humanism, within the Catholic tradition, featuring such celebrated figures as Erasmus, Baldassare Castiglione and Thomas More. Rooted in the study of the texts of classical Greece and Rome, many of which had been recently rediscovered, humanism focused on issues of philosophy, ethics and politics without reference to the dualism of medieval thinking that had framed its views about secular concerns with constant reference to spiritual ones. As a way of looking at the world, humanism was more empirical and aimed at an understanding of what was inalienable to the human being. It was an important inspiration behind the civic reforms of the period.

The most influential Catholic humanist tract on the subject of public philanthropy was written in 1526 in Bruges by the Spanish humanist Juan Luis Vives. Bruges, like other European cities, was in those days beset by problems of urban poverty, overcrowding, vagrancy and crime. Vives, though a Catholic, begins his work *De Subventione Pauperum* (On the Support of the Poor) by quoting Cicero rather than Christ. He then argues that the state has a duty to provide some level of financial relief for the poor. Vives adds that it has a responsibility to offer education to clever boys, apprenticeships to the rest, and dowries to girls. He also makes a more formal discrimination between 'deserving' and 'undeserving' poor. He suggests restrictions on private almsgiving. And he recommends that public philanthropy be used to influence or coerce the behaviour of the poor, and even to compel them to work. This fuses elements from various thirteenth- and fourteenth-century practices from across Europe into a single integrated system. Vives's radical humanism inspired and directed many of the innovations of early modern poor relief.

The city of Bruges did not implement his suggestions until 1557, but Vives's proposals influenced social relief legislation elsewhere across Europe during the 1530s. It can persuasively be argued that the so-called secularization of philanthropy in this era had as much to do with humanism as Protestantism.[26] So too was the idea that poor relief could be used to change the behaviour of the poor – and the insight that giving should place the service of the living above the service of the dead.

THE MORAL CHARACTER OF THE POOR

One change which emerged at this time, again in both Catholic and Protestant societies, was the idea that charity could be used to 'raise moral standards' among the poor. Previous historians of philanthropy have attributed this change to Protestant theology. Calvinism, after all, saw work and wealth as signs of divine favour. The Protestant work ethic was for years seen as one of the major motors of the growth of capitalism.[27] Certainly the rhetoric of reformers concerned itself with reclaiming souls through the raising of moral standards. Calvinist deacons set out to make the poor work – cleaning streets or repairing bridges and fortifications – in return for their alms. One popular Protestant technique was to conduct censuses of the poor, enquiring into their habits; these provided pretexts which gave the authorities the ability to give or withhold relief in such ways that they felt would create a more godly society.

Yet, as Brian Pullan notes, in Protestant areas of Saxony and the Low Countries there were also, from the 1520s to the 1560s, many attempts to reorganize poor relief without such a corrective or punitive spirit.[28] And though Thomas Max Safley suggests that Catholic and Protestants had different attitudes toward begging – with Catholics being more ambiguous and lenient[29] – both civic and popular opinion in Catholic towns and cities was similarly inclined to want to control or eliminate certain categories of beggars.

Some Catholic theologians, including Emperor Charles V's chaplain, the Spanish Dominican Domingo de Soto, continued to teach that all persons, regardless of circumstance, should be allowed to beg in accordance with the dictates of the Church Fathers. But the magistrates of Catholic Venice, for example, threatened to mutilate the noses of mendicants, or send them to row in the galleys, if they were caught repeatedly begging in the streets of the city.[30] And the Parlement of Paris, in Catholic France in 1576, ordered that all beggars who remained in the capital for more than twenty-four hours were to be hanged or strangled without trial.[31]

'The Catholic and Protestant community showed an almost equally strong tendency to transform the wandering penniless stranger into the fearful and repulsive figure of the vagrant,' writes Pullan. He was now 'a threat to public order, a presumptive criminal, a masterless man untouched by the family's control, a breaker of children's limbs to increase their profitable pathos, a burden on rates and stocks of food, or one who defied inclusion in a stable hierarchy and tidy confinement within administrative boundaries.'[32] In practice, Safley reports, there were no major differences between Catholic and Protestant philanthropy in the treatment of the poor. Rather it was common to both that relief was placed in the hands of political authorities, with begging prohibited by law, financial resources centralized, and assistance awarded according to individual circumstances.[33]

The Jewish community took a similar approach. It also shifted giving from an individual to a communal activity. A statute issued by the elders of the Jews of Avignon in 1558 requested their fellow Jews to give poor individuals only small amounts of aid and instead instituted a certificate system for the receipt of communal alms. The Jewish authorities in Kraków in 1595 outlawed begging door to door.[34] The engine of all these changes was not religion but fear of the stranger generated by famine, disease, war and demographic shifts. That is what engendered concerns around law and order and brought about a revision of charitable priorities.

THE LOSS OF THE MONASTERIES

But all these insights rest on comparatively recent scholarship. The history of philanthropy, in English at any rate, has until now been dominated by accounts which largely took the assertions of the Protestant reformers at face value. From the outset many have found this politically expedient. When Henry VIII determined upon seizing the wealth of the English monasteries to fund his military campaigns, his Chancellor, Thomas Cromwell, sent official 'visitations' to nearly 900 religious establishments. Unsurprisingly, these partisan investigators found those monasteries, priories, convents and friaries to be corrupt, superstitiously filled with relics of dubious provenance, and a 'slander of God'.[35] Their assets were therefore deemed eligible for seizure.

In truth, there were probably then too many religious houses in a period when religious vocations were declining;[36] Cardinal Wolsey had earlier, with the blessing of Pope Clement VII, closed twenty-eight houses where the number of monks or nuns had dwindled to single figures.[37] And monasteries were undoubtedly wealthy, owning about one-third of all the land in England and Wales.[38] The smaller monasteries were sometimes in a parlous financial state, but the big ones grew increasingly rich with the rise of the wool trade. What percentage of their income the monks gave to the poor is unclear. 'The abbeys in the north parts gave great alms to poor men,' testified Robert Aske in 1537, adding that 'much of the relief of the Commons was by succour of abbeys'.[39] His testimony was supported by other contemporaries who complained after the Reformation that the poor previously fed by monasteries and hospitals were now starving in the streets. The new secular landowners who had seized the monastic lands did not pay 'one halpenyworth of alms . . . unto the peple of those parishes'.[40] But in the 1920s a Russian scholar, Alexander Savine, undertook a detailed analysis of the *Valor Ecclesiasticus* – the valuation of the property of the 200 richest English religious houses which was recorded for Henry VIII. Savine concluded that a mere 3 per cent of the monks' income went to the poor. 'Taken at their face value these figures would suggest that the monastic charity was of little consequence,' writes the Tudor historian John Pound, 'but it must be remembered that the *Valor Ecclesiasticus* . . . was only concerned with the amount of obligatory charity [which arose as a result of the bequests left to the monasteries] and made no allowance whatsoever for the generosity of the monks and nuns in other ways.[41] The primary philanthropy – the direct distribution of food, clothing and money – was unrecorded in the *Valor Ecclesiasticus.*

Dom David Knowles, probably the most comprehensive of the historians of the English Monasteries, estimates that the proportion of monastic giving to charity was closer to 10 per cent;[42] given the extensive wealth of the monasteries, this was a substantial amount. Another specialist historian of the period, A. L. Beier, concludes that 'the figures do not suggest that monastic charity was insignificant'. Indeed, he calculates it to have been worth double the amounts raised through poor-relief taxation in the Tudor and Jacobean eras.[43]

Monasteries did not just distribute a great deal of relief to the poor in the form of cash, food and clothing.[44] They offered the only schooling for clever boys whose parents could not afford an education – and monasteries proved to be a 'highly successful educator'.[45] Monks and nuns were often experienced healers with a deep knowledge of medicinal herbs who provided the only medical help available to ordinary people during an epidemic or plague, with many of the larger abbeys, convents and monasteries containing purpose-built hospitals.[46]

These institutions offered the only hospitality available to ordinary pilgrims and travellers.[47] 'Whatever their other shortcomings,' writes John Pound, 'the monks seem to have maintained this tradition well. There is no evidence of any general falling of standards in the early 16th century'.[48] For all these reasons monasteries were often popular with local people – so popular that in the north of England a rebellion, the Pilgrimage of Grace, broke out in 1536 in protest against their suppression.[49] Elsewhere layfolk wrote bold letters to the king begging for their local monastery to be spared.[50]

But there was a key group with a vested interest in promoting change – the class of Protestant gentry who profited from the seizure of the property of these religious foundations. They lent influential support to the notion that English monasticism was thoroughly corrupt and in decline – a view embraced by historians for centuries. It is embodied in the work of A. G. Dickens, whose *The English Reformation*[51] was once the standard work on the subject. Dickens was convinced that Protestantism was an idea whose time had come, and that medieval Catholicism was degenerate and unpopular.[52]

More modern scholars such as J. J. Scarisbrick, Christopher Haigh and Eamon Duffy take a different view and their critique is now accepted as the orthodox understanding.[53] Scarisbrick insists that the evidence shows that Dickens and his predecessors were wrong. 'On the whole, English men and women did not want the Reformation and most of them were slow to accept it when it came,' he writes.[54] Duffy goes further: the Reformation in England was 'not an event waiting to happen' nor 'an idea whose time had come', but rather it was fiercely resisted by ordinary people. 'Late medieval Catholicism was neither decadent nor decayed but was a strong and vigorous tradition and the Reformation represented the violent rupture of a popular and theologically respectable religious system,' Duffy writes.[55] Change was not implemented from the grassroots but was imposed from above by statute, proclamation and royal commission, and enforced by a gentry class enriched by the closure of religious houses so that, Haigh writes, 'by the end of the century, prolonged clerical efforts had succeeded in creating "a Protestant nation, but not a nation of Protestants"'.[56] The early modern historian Ian Archer concludes that this most recent research reveals 'we have underestimated the damage done by the dissolutions, both because the scale of the alms distributed through monasteries and fraternities has been underestimated, and because the fraternities provided an institutional framework within which informal support could be offered'.[57]

The Dissolution of the Monasteries – in which over 800 religious houses were closed in just four years, 1536 to 1541 – destroyed much of the infrastructure of English public philanthropy. The Protestant reformers, initially, had nothing to put in its place. Eventually, as we shall see in the next chapter, the state felt forced to intervene in an unprecedented way. In the meantime, Protestant preachers and pamphleteers tried to cover their embarrassment at their initial lack of an alternative by railing generally against Catholic charity and against the general public for not spontaneously creating any alternative to it.

In 1542 the Protestant polemicist Henry Brinkelow lashed out against the citizens of London for being blinded by popish superstitions and preoccupation with prayers for the dead while neglecting their Christian obligation to relieve those in desperate want. He attacked 'merchants who left £6 to £12 a year for superstitious masses for the dead while scattering only a few pennies on the Sabbath for the care of the derelict'.[58] Conscious of the accusation that they had destroyed the infrastructure of public philanthropy, Protestants worked particularly hard at disparaging the reputation of the monasteries. Another prominent preacher, Thomas Becon, chaplain to the radical reformer Archbishop Thomas Cranmer, lambasted the 'rich [Catholic] worldlings' of the past who had built 'great monasteries for the bellied hypocrites, great colleges, chantries, and free chapels for soul-carriers and purgatory-rakers', but who declined to build 'so much as a cottage to harbour the silly poor man'.[59] The Protestant conception of charity, by contrast, Becon insisted, was pure rather than venal in its motivation.

SPIN AND STATISTICS

Others sought to assert the superiority of Protestant charity over Catholic charity by using statistics. A massive compilation of the good works of London's merchants was made in 1598 by John Stowe. *The Survey of London* catalogued, in parish after parish, ward after ward, the philanthropic acts of the mercantilist elite, creating a eulogy to Protestant generosity. A controversial Puritan preacher Andrew Willet made use of Stowe's figures in 1614 for more overtly polemicist purposes, compiling *A catalogue of such charitable workes as have been done in the times of the Gospell within the space of 60 yeares, under the happie raignes of King Edward, Queene Elizabeth, King James, our Gratious Soveraigne.* Protestant charity, it insists, is superior to Catholic charity in both quality and quantity; in quality because 'theirs were done in the pride of the heart, in opinion of merit to purchase remission of sinnes', whereas the gifts of Protestants were only intended to serve as 'testimonies of our faith'; and in quantity because, he confidently asserts, six decades of Protestant charity exceeded the sums raised 'in the like time in popery',[60] and had created more schools and almshouses 'than in the whole of the Middle Ages'.[61]

Willet's propagandist approach is clear. Moreover, many of his statistics were mere guesses since he admits that he had 'no auditors account in hand' and confesses that 'sometimes I doe but rove at the summe'. Revealingly his 'golden catalogue' omits any mention of charitable bequests in the reign of the Catholic Queen Mary. But for all the unreliability of his figures, Willet's claims were soon fully absorbed into the body of Protestant propaganda. The great poet and preacher John Donne unquestioningly repeated the assertions of Willet's dodgy dossier when, as the Dean of St Paul's Cathedral, he proclaimed from its pulpit that 'there have been in this kingdome, since the blessed reformation of religion, more publick charitable works perform'd, more hospitals and colleges erected, and endowed in threescore, than in some hundreds of years of superstition before'.[62]

But the vehemence and frequency of the reformers' denunciations of 'the Romish brags' of Catholic philanthropy[63] – together with their acute sensitivity to the criticisms of the 'carping popelings'[64] – suggests an implicit acknowledgement that the Dissolution of the Monasteries had increased hardship among the sixteenth-century poor. Willet's Cambridge mentor Laurence Chaderton admitted as much in a sermon of 1578, saying that:

> . . . the papistes alwayes cast in our teeth the great and famous hospitalitie of their nobility and cleargie, the buylding of Abbies, Monasteries, and Nunneries, Cathedrall Churches, colledges, with many other outward works which in deede are such as do stoppe our mouthes and put us Protestants to silence.[65]

The Catholic criticism clearly stung. Henry VIII had promised that the wealth of the monasteries would be used to help the poor.[66] But two-thirds of all the monastic land was sold to families whom Henry considered loyal and much of the money which accrued to the king was squandered in vanity wars against France.[67] Similarly, when Lutheran Denmark abolished its Catholic foundations, their wealth was transferred mainly to the Crown, the nobility and the aspiring gentry. Again it was not spent on the poor.[68] And when reformers in an iconoclastic mood insisted, in Zwinglian Zurich, that only the poor were in the true image of Christ, they undoubtedly reduced spending on images of saints and lavish decorations for churches but, again, there is no evidence that the savings went to the poor.[69]

The early reformers' hopes that the monastic resources would be redirected towards social welfare were shattered – and left them vulnerable to Catholic charges that members of the new Protestant gentry had simply lined their own pockets from the spoliation of the Church.[70] The gentry responded by declaring that the swarms of beggars on the streets of London, and elsewhere – which, as we have seen, were in reality the product of economic and demographic change – were rather evidence of the corruption of the Catholic Church which had squandered its charitable resources on the debased appetites of idle monks and clergy.[71] What is beyond dispute, however, is that the Dissolution of the Monasteries created a gentry class opposed to any return to Catholicism and powerfully committed to the embrace of Protestant views on philanthropy.

WHY THE MYTH HAS PERSISTED

The conduit by which the myth of a new Protestant form of poor relief entered modern histories of philanthropy was through the work of German scholars in the nineteenth century, led by the anti-Catholic polemicist Albert Emminghaus. In his 1870 work *Poor Relief and the Poor Law in European States*[72] the economist and journalist argued that Protestantism was in a de facto superior position to Catholicism in meeting the needs of the poor. The medieval emphasis on almsgiving as atonement for sin (and a way of winning a reward in the next world) meant Catholics ignored the real needs of the beggar, Emminghaus argued, and as a result 'the number of poor greatly increased'.[73] The focus of Catholicism was on individual action and on its priesthood controlling the behaviour of the population; Protestantism, by contrast, created a more scientific form of state intervention designed to promote more vigorously the welfare of the poor themselves, and hence to further the good of society.

His thesis received a swift and sharp rebuke from another German, the great medieval scholar Franz Ehrle, who was also a Jesuit cardinal. Ehrle replied with a substantial list of scriptural and patristic texts which countered Emminghaus by showing there was plenty of ecclesial authority for the idea that public philanthropy should be given with discrimination and only in cases of genuine need.[74] He also set out detailed analyses of the poor-relief systems of Nuremberg (1522) and Ypres (1525), arguing that their social reforms were rooted in pre-Reformation precedents. Ehrle had the best of the verbal duel, according to modern scholars.[75] Even at the time scholars criticized 'the unsupported generalizations of Emminghaus'.[76] But the Protestant economist's partisan position better suited the temper of the times when Protestants were trying to identify their religious and social traditions with the growing industrial state of Bismarck's Germany.[77]

His standpoint was espoused, as we saw in the previous chapter, by Sir William Ashley in his influential *Introduction to English Economic History and Theory*.[78] Ashley's approach was influenced by the pioneering German school of economic history and he absorbed many of its Protestant assumptions. This is clear from the internal contradictions in his work.* Many of his conclusions seem ideologically rather than evidentially based: he calls monasteries 'centres of pauperization',[79] insisting of monastic charity that 'the reckless distribution of doles cannot have failed to exercise a pauperising influence'.[80] 'Cannot fail' seems a tenuous basis for a historian's judgement. He is also unable to understand the medieval worldview with its mystical insistence that the poor had an important cosmic role to play through their prayers and humility. Instead, the Victorian historian judges the poor by the prejudices of his own era which assumed that a man who was not in work was idle and in need of correction. Ashley made deceptive oversimplifications[81] which subsequent writers accepted uncritically.

---

* See pages 131–2 above.

Among them was Benjamin Kirkman Gray, a Protestant socialist who wrote the first modern history of English philanthropy on which almost all twentieth-century historians of philanthropy have drawn. His *A History of English Philanthropy from the Dissolution of the Monasteries to the Taking of the First Census* is cited in all the substantial histories of philanthropy, including the massive studies of W. K. Jordan and David Owen.[82] Kirkman Gray, who had been brought up as a Congregationalist but became a Unitarian, takes his line uncritically from Emminghaus. 'Catholic charity is closely connected with the doctrine of *poenitentia* – the act of repentance, recompense or contrition,' he writes. 'This meant that 'the effect of almsgiving on the soul of the donor was theoretically more important than its effect on the body of the recipient'. The Protestant revolution therefore brought a major shift in philanthropy. It is impossible to write about pre-Reformation philanthropy without considering the subject of the donor's motive, Gray argues. But it is 'quite easy to do so for the post Reformation period when, although this motive was still operative, it was ceasing to be explicit'.

Sidney and Beatrice Webb, two other socialists, embraced this same approach in their *English Poor Law History* of 1927.[83] The Webbs acknowledged the counter-argument of Ehrle – which is more than Gray did, as he did not even mention the German Catholic medievalist. 'The diligent student can pick out all down the centuries, from the more statesmanlike Catholic writers, isolated sentences pointing to the duty of practical wisdom and almsgiving,' the Webbs wrote. 'But the overwhelming tendency of regarding alms as an act of piety, like fasting and prayer, principally from the standpoint of the state of mind of the giver', led to the 'dismissing all considerations with regard to the character of the recipient'.[84] This was disingenuous, for Ehrle had done far more than collect 'isolated sentences' from the Church Fathers: he had produced a comprehensive catalogue which made clear that Catholic thinkers had, for centuries, considered the impact of alms upon the recipients. But by now the idea that the Reformation brought a revolution in philanthropy – making it secular, centralized and focused on the poor recipient rather than the wealthy giver – had become firmly entrenched. Sociologists of religion, such as Max Weber in 1905 and Ernst Troeltsch in 1931, repeated it, with Troeltsch branding Catholic philanthropy as mere 'charity', while Protestant philanthropy was credited with the formulation of a more far-reaching scientific 'social policy'.[85] Even more anachronistically, he accused the Catholic Church of having no desire to eliminate poverty, because of its anxiety to preserve opportunities for the rich to be charitable.[86]

This new received wisdom was consolidated by the two major histories of philanthropy published in the second half of the twentieth century. Wilbur K. Jordan's *Philanthropy in England, 1480–1660: A Study of the Changing Pattern of English Social Aspirations*[87] became an influential work in the history of the subject. Published in 1959 out of Harvard University, where Jordan was Professor of History, it was unequivocal in labelling the schism between Catholicism and Protestantism as the key factor in the development of modern philanthropy. Based on a detailed analysis of almost 35,000 charitable gifts and bequests recorded in wills in ten English counties, Jordan declared that in the decade from 1480 to 1490 around two-thirds of all charitable donations in England were for religious purposes – and then suggested that, by contrast, throughout the whole of the Elizabethan era fewer than 7 per cent of donations were religious. This, he proclaimed, was an explosion of charitable giving for secular purposes by the merchant class. He then declared that the Reformation was responsible for what he called 'one of the few great cultural revolutions in western history: the momentous shift from man's primary religious preoccupations to the secular concerns that have moulded the thought and institutions of the past three centuries'.[88] Jordan's data and methods have since been widely challenged by historians, but their criticisms have so far made little impact on students of philanthropy.

Jordan's approach is problematic in several ways. There is much charity which never gets into wills. Jordan's focus on testamentary bequests ignores the charity of living donors, giving at church, personal giving of money, food and clothing, or giving by subscription (a phenomenon of increasing significance towards the end of the period he covers). The latest evidence is that the parish rates raised far more money for poor relief than Jordan thought.[89] He also does not take into account the inflation in the period, which was considerable – the value of money was almost quartered between 1480 and 1600. This means that charitable giving, which Jordan says fell in the run-up to the Reformation and then increased dramatically thereafter, was actually largely steady. It may even have declined after the Reformation,[90] and it certainly did not offset the destructive impact on poor relief inflicted by the Dissolution of the Monasteries.[91]

But perhaps the most devastating assault on Jordan was levelled early on by the pre-eminent Tudor historian of the twentieth century, G. R. Elton, who regarded the Harvard scholar as hopelessly naive. In two reviews of Jordan's work Elton was comprehensive in his demolition. Jordan ignores inflation. He fails to see that a few very rich givers skew his figures. He neglects the giving of rural gentry where 'there is more daily giving and frequent casual relief between landlord and tenant and labourer than there can be in a town'. He is naive in his acceptance of the pious thoughts expressed in last testaments. Elton concludes that Jordan 'is too ready to make a doctrinaire division between mediaeval and post-Reformation times' and he makes 'over-large claims and over-dramatic juxtapositions' which 'hide some weakness in the argument'.[92] When Jordan published a second volume, containing the evidence he claimed supported his first, Elton was even more withering in his conclusion that Jordan had utterly failed to substantiate his claim that there was, after the Reformation, a marked increase in the proportion of the nation's wealth devoted to charity. Jordan was, Elton concluded, 'documenting his convictions rather than proving his case'.[93]

It is extraordinary that, after such a comprehensive annihilation, writers on philanthropy continued for another half-century to accept Jordan's analysis at face value. The next major book on the subject, *English Philanthropy, 1660 to 1960*, published in 1965 by another Harvard historian, David Owen, accepted without question the idea that Protestantism created a new kind of philanthropy. England, Owen concluded, had given birth to a new national tradition in which a 'Protestant social ethic' was combined with 'a new sense of national consciousness'.[94] And that notion has persisted in philanthropic studies even up to the publication in 2015 of Rhodri Davies's otherwise impressive volume *Public Good by Private Means: How Philanthropy Shapes Britain*.[95]

Why did these caveats not filter through to students of philanthropy? Probably because the lie was too useful. It suited the ideological or religious presumptions of writers in various eras. What you see depends on where you stand. To Emminghaus and his Protestant contemporaries the calumny was evidence of the superiority of the religious culture which undergirded the new Prussian state that was defining itself by culture wars with Catholicism. To socialists such as Kirkman Gray and the Webbs the supposed transition from a Catholic to a Protestant vision of charity was part of the journey from feudalism to capitalism that would inevitably lead to some form of socialist economy in which philanthropy would be unnecessary. To Jordan and Owen, each supported in their research by the Ford and Russell Sage Foundations[96] – both then bulwarks of White Anglo-Saxon Protestantism – the idea of a distinctively Protestant form of charity was foundational to the ideas of 'efficient philanthropy' promoted by the robber baron capitalists of the early twentieth century.[97] The Protestant faith of these men, as we shall see in Chapter 9, was instrumental in their establishment of philanthropic foundations dedicated to mimicking the business strategies with which they had made their vast fortunes. Efficient philanthropy, they decided, was the way to offset the worst excesses of the unregulated free market.

THE TRUTH ABOUT POST-REFORMATION PHILANTHROPY

The reality was rather different, as this book has shown. Medieval almsgiving was not conceived of primarily as a gift which brought spiritual benefit to the donor. It was a manifestation of Christian love, involving a two-way relationship – and even an act of social justice. This notion was lost by campaigners angered by medieval abuses over the sale of indulgences. Their subsequent reforms replaced something profound and spiritual with something transactional and material; the baby was thrown out with the bathwater. Historians such as the great Victorian Sir William Ashley began to judge the Middle Ages anachronistically, by the standards of their own age. In Ashley's time that meant seeing poverty as some kind of moral failing. In the eras which followed, the philanthropy of a thousand years of medieval Christendom has been variously accused – by similar ahistorical standards – of failing to agitate for equality, democracy, free enterprise or the systemic abolition of poverty. Marxist critiques even insist that the real purpose of medieval philanthropy was to make the poor docile and dependent to further the economic interests of the elite. Such perspectives lose sight of something in the medieval worldview whose loss has made the subsequent development of philanthropy significantly the poorer. Yet for all that, few would disagree that as the Middle Ages gave way to the early modern era changes were afoot which were to spur the state to intervene massively in the business of philanthropic giving.

Interview: Rowan Williams on Christian philanthropy

Rowan Williams has had a distinguished career as an academic at the universities of Cambridge and Oxford, where he was Lady Margaret Professor of Divinity for six years before becoming an Anglican bishop and then the 104th Archbishop of Canterbury. He is a poet and philosopher as well as one of the most profound theologians of his time. A scholar of the Church Fathers and a historian of Christian spirituality, he is now Professor of Contemporary Christian Thought at the University of Cambridge where he is Master of Magdalene College. Lord Williams is Chair of the Trustees of the international development charity Christian Aid.

What is distinctive about Christian charity by comparison with philanthropy generally?

One place to start is to ask who it is you're serving. And in some sense you're serving Christ – you see the image of God in the needy person. That goes back to St Francis embracing the leper, honouring what's there. While I don't think Christian philanthropy has always lived up to that, if you're asking for a distinctive thread, that might be it.

That sounds very different from the idea that Christians who give to charity are just trying to buy their way into Heaven. Yet that was how the first thousand years of Catholic charity was lampooned by many Protestants after the Reformation. Is that just a caricature?

I think so. It's also underrating the sheer ordinariness of charity in the Middle Ages. Almsgiving was just something you did. It was one of the many acts that were built into things. It's true that institutions like the monasteries or almshouses in the Middle Ages were endowed by people who wanted to save their souls, but as John Bossy argued years ago in his book on late medieval and modern Catholicism,* those institutions

---

* John Bossy, *Christianity in the West 1400 to 1700*, Oxford, 1985.

kept a lid on violence and competition and acquisitiveness. Charity was a way of levelling the playing field. It was much bigger than just doing good to the poor. A lot of historians make a sharp distinction between pre- and post-Reformation, but I don't think it's quite as marked as that.

Many rich folk left money in their wills for a chantry where prayers could be said for their souls, but they also left funds for an almshouse, for the feeding of a thousand poor people, and so on.
That's right. It's not an either/or.

In recent decades there have been big shifts in understanding among mainstream historians of what happened at the Reformation. But histories of philanthropy don't reflect that. Instead they rely on the old parody of 'Catholic charity bad, Protestant philanthropy good'. The new insights haven't filtered through at all.
No. And of course, the opposite – 'Catholic good, Protestant bad' in some historiographies – is equally wide of the mark. At the beginning of the English Reformation you have a figure like William Tyndale who is basically concerned that the charitable system of the Middle Ages ends up enriching church institutions, not poor people. So he wants to see fewer chantry chapels and more soup kitchens or schools. What happens, unfortunately, as the English Reformation proceeds, is that a great deal of very imaginative charitable and educational thinking is sat on by greedy aristocrats who are interested in land grabs and are not interested in transferring the monastic lands and resources to the public purse.

Many of the reforms which did come about, all across sixteenth-century Europe, happened equally in Catholic and Protestant states. They were driven much more by population shifts, changing economics and the emergence of capitalism.
Yes. And perhaps a different sense of civic involvement too. Schools became a new focus for charity as part of a big investment in literacy, because it was important for people not just to hear but to read the Scriptures. But that also connected with the idea that you're increasingly needing a rather more flexible workforce. You're not just an agrarian society, you need people who can read and do the accounts. I think

that's part of it, as well as a deep commitment to reading Scripture or reading the Prayer Book.

So, in general, do you see any distinction between a Catholic and a Protestant style of philanthropy – or is that not meaningful at all?

I find it very hard to pull them apart, to be honest. I suspect though that, as time goes on, something distinctive comes through with the fact that Catholic philanthropy has tended to invest a bit more in what you might call the No Hope environments: Father Damien and the leper colony on Molokai,* Mother Teresa, and others who demonstrate a very, very powerful sense of the worthwhileness of being alongside people for whom there's nothing to be done. And there's a touch, by the nineteenth century, in a lot of Protestant mentality, of utilitarianism. Given the choice, it says, do you really want to go and spend your time ministering to the doomed or do you want to invest in people who've got a future?

And that's where, in the nineteenth century, the idea of the moral reform of the poor becomes big in philanthropy. The idea that it's the poor that need to change ...

Not the rich. That's right.

There was a mutuality in the medieval notion of philanthropy. It was a relationship between the rich and the poor – and how they related to the wider community, and related to God. But that got lost with the arrival of the Protestant work ethic. And it remains lost for many of today's philanthrocapitalists.

Well, I have a lot of questions about the Protestant work ethic. But what is lost is the sense that you find ritualized in the Middle Ages, that the poor, the leper, the outcast, are actually to be venerated, and not just patronised. You can't imagine, by the late eighteenth century,

----

* Father Damien (1840–89) was a Catholic priest and missionary who ran a leper colony in Hawaii for 15 years, where he died from the disease he caught from the people to whom he ministered. He was made a saint in 2009 after being described as a 'martyr of charity'. Mother Teresa was a Catholic nun who founded the Missionaries of Charity, an order which worked among the poor in India and worldwide. She won the Nobel Peace Prize in 1979 and was made a saint in 2016.

even a Wilberforce bowing to the ground before the slave who is to be emancipated. But that's the medieval picture. And I do think that that vanishes. Some of the things which in the Middle Ages were still rituals very directly performed by the monarch – like the washing of feet on Maundy Thursday – get delegated or redefined or shuffled sideways so the monarch doesn't actually have to be in the presence of the poor. That's what shifts.

The philanthrocapitalist, as you say, is pretty systematically kept at arms' length from the experience of poverty. One of the things we've tried to do with Christian Aid recently is develop programmes that will actually take major donors to the projects that they're supporting and ask them to spend a week or two, just mucking in and finding out what happens. Several of them have said that it's been a really life-changing thing for them – because to be there, doing the washing up, involves a kind of give-and-take about what's working, what isn't working, and strategic questions and ideas are exchanged. Those that have come back from these experiences have all said that what mattered most was just the face-to-face physical presence.

Part of the philanthrocapitalist model is to say: 'These are the techniques I used to make all my money, so they must work in philanthropy too.' But what you are saying is that, instead, the philanthrocapitalist needs to go and listen.

Yes. That's been something that's come through very strongly in this particular programme with Christian Aid which has been running for about ten years now. The principle seems to us to be a very important one. People should have a chance of seeing in the flesh what they were making possible. And they should have a chance of being touched, enlarged and challenged by it directly. It's that reciprocal thing that the object of your charity becomes a subject in their own right. To me, that's one modern way of recasting St Francis and the leper. Through it we see that the Other is somebody with dignity, agency, freedom and ultimately is representing Christ here.

Even if you're not a Christian, what you are after is creating agency not dependency. For that to happen, you have to have that kind of attention to what's actually being asked for – and to attend to people's own account of where they are and who they are.

That's really important. It's what later in this book I call Reciprocal Philanthropy – in contrast to the Effective Altruism and Strategic Philanthropy which currently dominates.

Absolutely. The Effective Altruism movement is really worrying.

What worries you about it?

A number of things. But one thing, certainly, is the absolute depersonalization of the relationship between the one who gives and the one who receives. Effective Altruism recommends that you should go off to be a banker and make a lot of money then give it all away. It sounds neat but it has a complete disjuncture between means and ends. It says go and make your money, in a fundamentally unjust and unbalanced market, and then just dump it, rather than yourself changing or growing as a person, learning or flourishing.

That leads to the second big worry in my mind. What exactly are you doing all this for? And what kind of humanity are you creating when you say: 'Oh, there's a problem. I'll throw money at it and solve it.'

It's reductive?

Yes. Then you get the 'very moral high ground' argument that an evening at the theatre, or buying an ice cream, becomes a profoundly immoral thing. But the kind of humanity that enjoys going to the theatre, and enjoys ice cream, is the kind of humanity I want to spread around rather than just saying: 'You've got a problem, I'm going to solve it for you.' There is a hatchet-faced side to all that. And it ends up saying, 'I do not have to change, I do not have to learn or receive.'

There are a few concepts in medieval and Reformation theology which are key influences on the development of philanthropy. Tell me about the medieval notion of the Mystical Body of Christ, which shaped attitudes to charity for a millennium and more.

The image of the Mystical Body is, first of all, the idea that every part of the body, when it's functioning well, enables the whole body to function well. The whole body does not function well if its parts are not functioning well. That means if a part is malfunctioning, is frustrated, diseased, damaged or whatever, then everybody suffers. That's the basic model. That means every part of the body has something which it actively contributes. Therefore, when you address questions about philanthropy, you're addressing not the solving of a problem, but the releasing of a gift.

So, when I give, I'm not solving a problem. I'm setting you free – to give and to act too. I need you to do that because, just as your good depends on me, my good depends on you. It's that sense of the organic interconnection of everybody's well-being, and the implication of that, which is that everybody has something to give.

It's all there in 2 Corinthians, Chapters 8 and 9, where Paul exhorts some of his congregations to dig into their pockets because, he says: 'You're actually going to produce a positive spirit of thanksgiving and love in somebody else.' Who knows when you're going to need that positive spirit in your turn? If you've got a superfluity you can share, then share it because it will come back to you. It's self-interested in a way, but it's also assuming that the whole pattern is the flow of giving and receiving.

What about the idea of redemptive almsgiving – the idea that acts of charity can earn you salvation? All through the Middle Ages, and thereafter, people to and fro on that, unable to make up their mind on whether or not it's a good or a bad thing. How did that play through the Reformation? And where do we end up with it today?

Good question. Almsgiving, right back to the early days of Christianity, is regarded as an absolutely fundamental visible sign of Christian discipleship. You want to know what Christian-like life looks like? Watch people giving. The awkwardness comes in, I suppose, when you say: 'Oh, well, I've failed in this respect, so I'm in debt. Maybe I can clear the debt by paying off to the poor.' That's actually a form of philanthrocapitalism in another setting. Let's clear the debts, let's rebalance in a way that's to my advantage. So it becomes instrumental . . .

. . . rather than an outward sign of something inner.

That's right. Again it keeps the 'object' of your charity at arm's length.

The third dilemma that we've inherited from the first centuries of Christianity is the question of whether you should discriminate in giving? Is there a hierarchy of giving? Should you give to your

family more than others? Should you give only to the most needy? Out of all that comes the idea that you can distinguish between the 'deserving' and the 'undeserving' poor.

At the moment we're in the middle of a major structural reorganization at Christian Aid, which is causing endless headaches in just this way. If we've got a project with drug rehabilitation in Columbia, and a project with women's economic rights in Malawi, and we can't fund both of them, how do we prioritize?

Effective Altruists would say you must devise a matrix to measure which saves most lives.

I think it's extremely difficult to have any kind of rule about this. This is my worry about the effective altruism argument: faced with a choice, I can give £200 to dig a well in Africa to provide water for a whole village and say to the fundraisers for my local hospice: 'Sorry, I'm giving my money to Africa where it will save more lives.' The trouble is, if everybody gives £200 to the well in Africa, what happens to the hospice? You might say, 'A hospice in a middle-class, middle-England area, will score very low on a global scale of need or suffering.' But the suffering there is not unreal. To dismiss it as a 'comfortable privileged suffering' is to suggest that a middle-class parent losing a child is somehow less serious than the same thing happening to a poor parent in Africa.

Someone may say: 'Stop wasting your money on privileged forms of suffering. Start giving it where it's needed.' But, again, I'd respond: 'What kind of humanity does that finally lead us to?' We have to remember St Francis and the leper and the principle which tells you to value the suffering of the other.

So, in some ways it's actually a good thing that charitable giving is so chaotic. I'm not saying that, in the great scheme of things, it all evens out. But it's quite important that some people do act on their immediate affinities and networks and natural sympathies, and I don't think they should be made to feel bad about that. I wouldn't want to say that could ever be anything but a personal choice.

At Christian Aid, we're very conscious that some of our projects don't have the same emotional appeal as Save the Children's, but I can't think of anybody in Christian Aid who would not want Save the Children to be there. We just hope that we're able to speak to a slightly different mindset which says, 'Well, somebody's got to do the strategic long-term work. Somebody has got to secure the water supply as well as sending the medicine for the victim of malaria.' We're all involved in these calculations one way or another. But there is an ecology of charity and we have to recognize that there are going to be different impulses, connections, bells rung in your emotions. That's all right, I think.

A recent philosopher of philanthropy, Rob Reich, a political scientist from Stanford University, has suggested that governments should vary the tax relief on charitable gifts to encourage philanthropists to give to soup kitchens rather than donkey sanctuaries. Is it the job of the state to do that?

I hope not. That would create an instant hard hierarchy of need. And while, of course, there are hierarchies of need, we need to discover them for ourselves. I think that's giving the state a dangerously high level of discretion. I quite see that, say, a massively well-resourced independent school which has charitable status poses a bit of a problem. But I think the danger is greater if you start having political debates about the acceptable limits of charity.

This is eggshell territory, isn't it? But when it comes to letting the state determine what is an acceptable use of my resources, I suddenly get a bit conservative. The more the state takes on a role of moral scrutiny, the more I worry. The state is there to secure justice and law, equality before the law, and defence. That's the business of the state. If the state then sets out to make us better people by lots of direct intervention, I think the state needs reining in. I remember in church debates people saying: 'Well, the state should make the Church do the right thing.' I just want to say 'Whoa' when people are ambitious for the state to push in that way. It's an immense act of blind faith in the state – and the history of the last hundred years ought to tell us that a hyper-activist state with lots of moral convictions is pretty bad for everybody.

So where does that leave us on the question of whether it is right for people to discriminate between the so-called 'deserving' and 'undeserving' poor? It is nascent in the Middle Ages but it gets big in the Elizabethan Poor Law and even bigger in Victorian philanthropy. And it's still around today.

It certainly is. Yes, it's there a bit in the Middle Ages but, on the whole, it becomes an issue when you've got what some people call 'an underclass' emerging – not just the poor but what are seen as disruptive elements of it. So then charity is derailed by concerns about public security. Hence, all these Elizabethan enactments about vagabondage. The upheavals of the Tudor period had put a lot of people on the roads, and the Elizabethan Poor Law has a great deal to do with protecting settled communities against sturdy rogues. They're a threat to public order.

So the 'undeserving poor' start out probably as a problem for public order. But increasingly, this is moralized. Then the 'undeserving poor' are the feckless, the sexually immoral, the people who don't work, or won't work – and who aren't grateful.

You see that in the Victorian idea of the moral reform of the poor. But you still see it today in television programmes like *Benefits Street.**

Absolutely, yes. We are hungry for stories about the 'undeserving poor' because it lets us off the hook. It says: 'Phew. They're not really victims after all, so I can relax.'

So we don't have to give them any money and we don't have to feel bad about it.

That's right. We don't have to worry about 'them'. The problem is that this leaves the definition entirely on my side. You don't listen to people's own account of themselves. One of the things I found quite moving in Dickens is how good he is with the 'undeserving poor'. In *Bleak House*, and some of the other great novels, you can see Dickens recognizing the 'undeserving poor' and letting their voices come through. You see his own deep scepticism about some kinds of organized charity. I would give him a lot of credit for just letting that voice through, the people who, when they're visited by the domineering charitable woman or man, will basically say, 'Bugger off.' Most readers of Dickens, I think,

---

* A popular fly-on-the-wall documentary series on Channel 4 in 2014 which depicted the lives of welfare claimants, showing them involved in petty crime and lacking motivation to find a job. It was criticized as 'poverty porn'.

raise a cheer at that. But the idea that some people are 'undeserving' goes very deep. And it persists.

Yet to look at the other side of the argument, Maimonides says that the highest level of giving is to lift people out of the situation where they need charity at all. You give them work which gets them out of a dependent frame of mind. That's a way of dealing with the 'undeserving poor' which is positive.

I think so. It's back to this question of dependence. Often the 'deserving poor' are the people who you recognize as reaching a certain standard of acceptable effort and who are appropriately grateful. You're creating a client, a reliable client. The hard work is building up a relationship which undermines dependency by allowing people some liberty of self-definition. It's a hard call sometimes, but I'm with Maimonides all the way. But that means understanding why somebody can't or won't work. Why some people get stuck in cycles of self-destructive behaviour – whether through addiction, or unplanned pregnancy, or whatever. Why do they get stuck in that? Finding that out is the proper business of philanthropy.

Chapter 6

The Business of the State

His name was Nicholas Blunt. Or Nicolas Blount. Or Nicholas Genings. Or Genynges. Or perhaps Jennings. He was an epileptic. Or a madman. Or a shipwrecked sailor. Or an unemployed hatter. Or a retainer discharged by a member of the gentry who had fallen on hard times. Perhaps he was all of these, or just some, or perhaps none. At any rate he was undoubtedly the most famous beggar in Elizabethan England. It was said about him that he collected nearly 14 shillings in one day's begging – at a time when a labouring man would count himself fortunate to earn a mere half a shilling for a day's work in the fields. The stories told about Blunt reveal a significant shift in the attitudes of philanthropic givers towards the recipients of their benevolence.

Blunt came to public notoriety because on All Hallows Day in 1566 he knocked on the door of the lodgings in Whitefriars of a man who happened to be a magistrate visiting London from the country. The Justice of the Peace, Thomas Harman, later wrote an account of the encounter. Blunt appeared, naked from the waist upwards, in ragged clothes, his face smeared in mud and fresh blood, asking for alms. The unsuspecting beggar had had the misfortune to knock on the door of a man who had become so suspicious of beggars in his home county of Kent that he had written a book about them entitled *A Caveat or Warening for Common Cursetors Vulgarely Called Vagabones*.[1] By chance Harman was in London to supervise the printing of its first edition. He questioned the beggar, who told him he had been suffering from the 'falling sickness' – epilepsy or palsy – for eight years. But Harman became suspicious when the beggar was offered a clean cloth and water to make himself clean, but refused them saying that washing would merely reopen his wounds. He had been discharged from the Bethlehem mental hospital near Bishopsgate (known colloquially as Bedlam) just two weeks earlier, he claimed. The magistrate commissioned two boys to follow the beggar, and they watched him all day. They observed him, from time to time, refreshing the blood on his face from a bladder, and putting new mud on his clothes. While they were doing that, Harman checked with the governor of Bedlam, who declared that no one matching Blunt's description had been discharged from the madhouse a fortnight before. Meanwhile one of the two boys eventually followed Blunt south of the river, to Newington, and to his home. The other boy fetched his master – who happened to be Harman's printer – who summoned a constable to apprehend the impostor. The beggar was stripped naked by the policeman and found to be fit and well – and in possession of the proceeds of his day of importuning, the handsome sum of 13s. 3½d.[2]

But this was not the end of the story. Blunt gave the policeman the slip and, under cover of darkness, escaped 'naked as ever he was born' across the fields. Realizing that his cover as an epileptic was blown, Blunt then arrayed himself in the clothing of a mariner and went about begging, claiming he was a sailor whose ship and cargo had been lost at sea. Then, by another extraordinary coincidence, Harmon's printer, walking out on New Year's Day 1567, came across Blunt again. The fraudster was now well dressed in 'a fair black frieze coat, a new pair of white hose, a fine felt hat on his head, [and] a shirt of Flanders work esteemed to be worth 16 shillings'. He told the printer: 'My name is Nicolas Genings, and I came from Leicester to seek work, and I am a hat maker by my occupation, and all my money is spent; and if I could get money to pay for my lodging this night, I would seek work tomorrow amongst the hatters.'[3]

But the printer, recognizing him as the counterfeit epileptic, had Blunt arrested for a second time. A search of Blunt's home in Newington showed it to be 'a pretty house', 'well stuffed' with comfortable belongings. The fraudster was taken to Bridewell prison and then stood upon the pillory in Cheapside, alternately in both his handsome attire and his beggar's rags, before being tied to the back of a cart and whipped through the city to the door of his home and back again to the prison. After he was eventually released his portrait was retained in the prison as 'a monument' to his nefarious criminal record so that he might be identified in future.[4]

Blunt was unfortunate in having encountered Harman, for the magistrate had created a taxonomy of what he claimed were the 24 classes and categories of rogues, vagabonds and fraudsters in Elizabethan society.[5] At the top of the pecking order was the so-called Upright Man, the leader among a group of beggars, the strongest and most skilled of the professional thieves, some of whom had the outward look of respectability.[6] At one point Harman lists Blunt as an upright man. But elsewhere he calls him a Counterfeit Crank – a fake epileptic who wore rags and carried white soap so that he could foam at the mouth.[7] He was also a Whipjack or Freshwater Mariner, a con man who elicited public sympathy by pretending to be a shipwrecked sailor.[8]

These were just three of the many classes in Harman's collection of vagabonds. A Sturdy Rogue was a thief as well as a beggar.[9] A Wild Rogue was born of rogue parents and was therefore 'more subtle and more given by nature to all kind of knavery'.[10] A Hooker or Angler was a beggar who, by day, visited houses to beg alms, but returned by night with a long crooked iron stick to reach through windows to steal clothes and linen.[11] A Palliard, or Clapperdudgeon, was a beggar who rubbed herbs like sperewort or ratsbane into his legs to raise great blisters, provoking pity and transforming himself from a sturdy beggar into a deserving one.[12] A Frater was a cheat who pretended to be a proctor and used a false licence to collect alms for hospitals.[13] A Bristler cheated the gullible with loaded dice.[14] A Prigger pretended to be a gentleman's servant, who stole horses and took them 'at least threescore miles off' to sell.[15] An Abraham man was named after the main ward in Bedlam and pretended madness, following people around until they gave him money to go away.[16] A Dummer pretended to be unable to speak and carried a licence certifying his dumbness. Most dummers, Harman bizarrely reckoned, came from Wales. Female vagrants were known as Morts. A Demander for Glimmer was someone, usually a woman, with a bogus licence claiming that she had been made destitute by a fire at her home in a far-off county. A Doxy was a loose beggarwoman who would sleep with any rogue in exchange for their keep. A Bawdy Basket was a pedlar woman who carried 'baskets of laces, pins, needles and silk girdles of all colours' but who stole washing left to dry on hedges, and was also a prostitute who plied a trade in 'lewed lothsome lechery'.[17]

The sheer breadth of this classification marks a significant change in social attitudes to the poor. The distinction between the deserving and the undeserving poor had been a thread in the writings of some of the medieval canon lawyers, but it hardened significantly into social policy in Tudor England. The poor, once looked upon with sympathy or pity, now became objects of suspicion. Philanthropy began to look at the world through a new and harsher lens.

THE BEGGAR IN TUDOR PROPAGANDA

Thomas Harman, as a magistrate, was a key official in the local government in Kent where he was charged with enforcing the new laws against vagrancy enacted by Henry VIII and Elizabeth I. These enshrined this major shift in the attitude of the philanthropic classes towards the poor. Harman's taxonomy is shot through with heavy moralizing and a political analysis which typify the thinking of the Tudor establishment. His language is heavily Protestant with its emphasis on punishing 'sin and wickedness', and turning wrongdoers to 'labour for their living' would save their souls which 'Christ, the second Person in Trinity, hath so dearly bought with His most precious blood'. But his purpose is clearly political when he says that 'true labour and good life' would ensure 'the amendment of the commonwealth' to promote 'joy, relief and quietness of mind' throughout the realm.[18]

Harman was far from alone in his analysis or his moral indignation. In the 1530s the pamphleteer and social reformer William Marshall, an associate of Henry VIII's chancellor, Thomas Cromwell, wrote with horror about the 'divers diseases, contagions and infirmities' and the 'heinous deeds, detestable sins, crimes and offences' of the poor. The humanist Thomas Starkey wrote that the 'multitude of beggars here in our country showeth much poverty', which he felt was caused by 'much idleness and ill policy'.[19] In 1537 King Henry himself amended the statement in the Bishop's Book which decreed that the rich should succour the poor. The king excluded those who 'lived by the craft of begging slothfully'.[20]

Everyone in authority, from the monarch at the top to the lowliest parish priest, pilloried the idle and the vagabond whose existence was at complete odds with the hierarchical body politic that the authorities approved. A sizeable number of pamphlets and popular tracts were published purporting to expose the misdeeds of an underworld of beggars and vagabonds. Many of the tales they told were far-fetched, according to the historian A. L. Beier, but the readers of such tales were happy to believe them.[21] Beggars, along with witches, entered the popular imagination as the bogeymen of the era.

The beggar provoked compassion but was also simultaneously feared and despised – and it was the latter characteristics which began to dominate in Elizabethan times. That much is clear from the literature of the era. In *King Lear*, written in 1606, Shakespeare has the Duke of Kent list beggars along with the most insalubrious company when he describes the steward Oswald as 'a knave, beggar, coward, pandar, and the son and heir of a mongrel bitch'.[22] Shakespeare inevitably offers a more sophisticated and nuanced portrait of the beggar than many of his contemporaries. *King Lear* conveys a clear sense of the ambivalence which the beggar provoked in the contemporary mind. The Duke of Gloucester's son Edgar takes on a disguise in which he pretends to be 'Poor Tom', a deranged figure who speaks of:

> Bedlam beggars, who with roaring voices
> Strike in their numbed and mortified bare arms
> Pins, wooden pricks, nails, sprigs of rosemary . . .[23]

Part of the tragedy of *King Lear*, writes the literary scholar Gillian Woods, 'is not so much that there are fraudsters who pretend to be mad to secure charity, but that society has left little other option'.[24] The Tudor beggar embodied contradictory ideas about work: he was on the one hand unfortunate because he did not have work – yet on the other hand undeserving of sympathy because he would not look for it. Much of this mindset, developed in Tudor times, persists into our own age and continues to impact upon attitudes towards philanthropy.

The vagrant beggar also violated the religious worldview of the Tudor and Stuart eras. In Francis Merbury's play *The Marriage Between Wit and Wisdom*, written in the 1570s, a character named Idleness disguises himself at one point as a poor beggar. To the Tudors and Stuarts 'idle' meant more than inactive; it implied a moral failing. Work was integral to the Anglican vision of what it meant to be human. The Church of England's official *Homilie Against Idlenesse*[25] spells this out: 'It is the appointment and will of God, that everyman, during the time of this mortal and transitory life, should give himself to such honest and godly exercise and labour . . . Man (saith Job) is borne to labour.' To be idle, therefore, was to go against the will of God. As the Puritan preacher Thomas Adams put it: 'the Idle Man is the Devil's Cushion, whereupon he sits and takes his ease'.[26]

Idleness and beggary alike required chastisement: 'It is a point of justice to whip an idle beggar, but more excellent to prevent Idleness and beggary,' said the puritan Richard Vines in a sermon during the Cromwellian era.[27] Since to be idle was to 'hunt and runne' after sin, idleness did not lead to inactivity but to the wrong kind of activity.[28] Beggars and vagrants were feared for their ability to ferment sedition and rebellion and all manner of disorder, including witchcraft. Government, in an era in which popular rebellions were not uncommon, feared the disorder bred by idle vagrants, whose lifestyle was an implicit rebuke to anyone who worked and who might spread disruptive egalitarian ideas.[29] As we saw in Chapter 4, the aftermath of the Hundred Years War saw ex-soldiers swell the ranks of vagabond beggars, adding the threat of violence to the phenomenon. Now vagrants became associated with insurrection, as is clear from the writings of another of Thomas Cromwell's propagandists, Richard Morison. In *A Remedy for Sedition* in 1536 he wrote of 'the lack of honest crafts, and the abundance of idleness' which 'breed thieves, murderers and beggars' and all too easily would 'provoke . . . men to rebellion'.[30] The common fear of the authorities, writes A. L. Beier, was that 'the dispossessed were disorderly and criminal and, if left to their own devices, will overthrow those in power'.[31]

VAGRANTS AND THE THREAT OF INSURRECTION

All this explains why the most feared category in Harman's catalogue of rogues was the Ruffler – former soldiers or serving men who had chosen to become 'sturdy vagabonds who begged from the strong and robbed the weak'.[32] Such men had been trained in the use of arms, either as retainers of the great noble households or in the service of the king. In feudal times armies had been raised by levies of loyal tenants, but in the Tudor period things changed. Henry VII's determination to dilute the power of the English nobility led to many of them laying off their retainers, who were not easily absorbed into the local economy. These former servants did not accept the situation with good grace, as John Pound acidly put it in *Poverty and Vagrancy in Tudor England*.[33] Thomas

More wrote in his *Utopia*: 'in the mean season they that be thus destitute
of service either starve for hunger, or manfully play the thieves'.[34]
Starving for hunger was not the option most of them preferred. They
were not just trained in arms, they had become accustomed to the thrill
of danger and had tasted a higher standard of living than they could
expect back in civilian life as a labourer or an artisan.

With the death of feudalism a vicious circle set in. Governments
had conscripted vagabonds since the reign of Edward III (1327–77),
but now royal armies began to be drawn primarily from the poor and
criminal classes, who had no loyalty to the state as feudal armies had.[35]
The problem grew worse as the century progressed, with vagabonds
recruited into the army for individual campaigns and then, when those
campaigns were over, released back into civilian life. Unlike continental
states, England had no permanent standing army.[36] These demobilized
soldiers and sailors who flooded onto the labour market were, in Pound's
estimation, even more dangerous than the discharged retainers. Groups
of them roamed the countryside, sometimes, according to the Somerset
magistrate Edward Hext, as many as 400 in one shire, terrorizing whole
villages, or splitting into smaller groups for begging activities.[37] Those
who were arrested by local constables, and put in the stocks, were
rescued by the sheer weight of numbers of their fellows. So menacing
were some of these groups that local authorities and magistrates were
often afraid to oppose them, and the vagabonds were so well organized
that they often knew in advance of plans to move against them made at
local assize sessions and magistrates' assemblies.[38]

The accounts of Harman and his fellow magistrates may well have
been unrepresentative or sensationalist. But they powerfully illustrate
the changed attitude of the Tudor establishment towards the newly
mobile poor – which was to alter English attitudes to philanthropy
for ever. The distinction between the deserving and the undeserving
poor now calcified into a distinction between the settled and the
mobile poor. Harman fails to acknowledge any difference between
criminal vagrants and poor people on the road in search of work. He
has difficulty 'distinguishing the unemployed, the under-employed, the
multi-tasked or in-transit labouring poor from the incorrigibly idle or
"sturdy beggar"'.[39] And he is equally ambivalent about the travelling
salesmen he describes as Swadders and Pedlars. Such folk, he concedes,
'be not all evil' but are rather 'of an indifferent behaviour'.[40] Harman

makes no concession to the possibility that a hard-working respectable citizen could unexpectedly be turned vagrant by adverse circumstances.

Harman is also curiously anachronistic in his attitude to money. He is repeatedly outraged that these vagrants beg for cash or sell wares. The truly deserving, Harman suggests, would exist on the subsistence level and immediately eat any food they acquired. But throughout his book he accuses beggars of selling the food they are given to obtain ready money – a fact which Patricia Fumerton suggests shows that the vagrants 'are products of, and participants in, the new money market where . . . value is transferable'.[41] Pedlars were symptoms of the new economy since they sold cheap manufactured goods which depended upon the new industries of Elizabethan towns – pins, buttons, nails, gloves, combs, ribbons, lacework and stockings.[42] The Elizabethan vagabond in this way represented a small milestone in the development of early capitalism. It was a milestone too in the development of philanthropy. This new openness to the use of money was common to all categories of wanderer – the con man, the entrepreneur and the genuine beggar. For the latter it restored some sense of agency and control which had diminished with an end to medieval philanthropy's sense of participation in a theology of giving.

In any case, there was far more of a continuum between begging, work and petty crime than was previously supposed. Paupers often made ends meet by using all three methods in a single day if necessary.[43] Court records suggest that many of those prosecuted for vagrancy offences had legitimate trades, which they exercised when they could. A. L. Beier, who extensively researched the documentation around the arrests of more than 6,000 vagrants at the end of the sixteenth century, suggested that only a third of them were career criminals.[44] He reports the case of one Wiltshire man arrested in 1605 who was serially employed[45] as a weaver, a surgeon, a minstrel, a dyer and a bullard.* Vagrant crime tended to be opportunistic, with thefts of property, especially clothing, being commonplace,[46] and often reflecting desperation since those who resorted to theft faced the death penalty if they were caught stealing anything valued at more than one shilling. Even taking birds' eggs could, on occasions, result in the hapless culprit being hanged.[47]

---

* A man who looks after bulls.

Despite Harman's detailed descriptions of organized bands of vagabonds, most itinerants travelled alone, or in pairs – as is borne out by the complaint of the Somerset magistrate Edward Hext, who noted that, unlike 'that wicked sect of rogues the Egipsions', the rufflers and other stout rogues 'go by two and three in a company', making them harder for the authorities to monitor.[48] His remark about the Egipsions (Egyptians) is thought to be the first reference in English to gypsies, who probably first entered Britain a few decades earlier.[49]

THE EXPLOSION IN POVERTY

What is beyond doubt is that there was in this period a massive increase in the number of poor people, both those who remained at home and those who took to the road to make a living. Contemporary observers reported that between a quarter and a half of the population were poor.[50] This may not be much of an exaggeration. Taxation records suggest that a quarter to third of all English citizens lived in or near poverty in the 1520s.[51] A census taken in Sheffield almost a century later revealed that out of a total population of 2,000 people almost one-third, 725, were 'begging poor'.[52] At times of famine or epidemic the numbers of the poor might rise to half the populace.[53] In part this was because of an overall rise in population. During the reign of Elizabeth I it grew by 25 per cent – from three to four million people. 'The kingdom became then much more populous than in former times, and with it the poor also greatly increased,' wrote Sir Matthew Hale a century later.[54]

But the explosion in poverty was also a reflection of a new pauperization. The poor unquestionably got poorer between 1500 and 1650 due to a variety of factors.[55] A high birth rate and a falling death rate meant increased pressure on resources. The baby boom lasted almost two centuries. Inflation was rampant because the rise in population combined with the import of silver from the New World, and because Henry VIII debased the coinage, reducing the silver content of coins by more than two-thirds between 1543 and 1551.[56] The enclosure of arable land to create pasture for sheep, which brought landlords far greater profit, forced small tenant farmers off the land, and sometimes out of their homes, depopulating whole villages.[57] Bad harvests occurred every few years in the seven decades after the 1550s, which led to rocketing prices.[58] At the same time incomes fell because, with more people looking for work, landowners and employers could cut wages, most particularly those of unskilled labourers.[59] Wages were as much as halved in real terms.[60] Malnutrition was common and there was mass starvation in Cumbria, for example, between 1586 and 1588.[61] Outbreaks of plague, which occurred every five years or so, did the same – and also plunged families into penury when the breadwinner perished. It was a vicious circle and those already living on the margins were plunged into poverty. Many people had little alternative but to join the ranks of the itinerant vagabonds.[62]

Some of the philanthropic legacy of the Middle Ages endured. Elizabethan commentators still maintained considerable sympathy for those poor people they regarded as worthy recipients of charity. In *The Description of England* by the chronicler William Harrison, published in 1587 as part of *Holinshed's Chronicles*, the 'great store' of poor people are divided into three groups:[63]

Some are poor by impotency, as the fatherless child, the aged, blind, and lame, and the diseased person that is judged to be incurable . . .

The second are poor by casualty, as the wounded soldier, the decayed house-holder, and the sick person visited with grievous and painful diseases . . .

The third consisteth of thriftless poor, as the rioter that has consumed all, the vagabond that will abide nowhere but runneth up and down from place to place (as it were seeking work and finding none) and finally, the rogue and strumpet.[64]

The first two groups should be sustained by a weekly collection in every parish, to ensure that they remained at home. The third group, which Harrison estimated across the nation to number 'above 10,000 persons', should be corrected with 'sharp execution' and the 'whip of justice'.

The essence of Tudor philanthropy was summed up in these words of Harrison. The 'true poor' were to be assisted. The primary motive for doing so was religious, nominally at any rate, though a secondary motive is clear; charity will contain the deserving poor in their parishes to ensure that they 'shall not scatter abroad and, by begging here and there, annoy both town and country'. Significantly, the state was to intervene to facilitate public philanthropy, by requiring weekly collections through which the wealthy could help the needy. The 'thriftless poor', by contrast, though they consist of a wide variety of characters – the riotous consumer, the vagabond, the rogue and the strumpet – are united by the common factor that they 'run to and fro overall the realm'. So the wandering poor, whether deserving or undeserving, were seen as an annoyance to 'both town and country'. The mobility of the poor was undesirable for the stability and security of the state.

Despite the fine words about charity for the 'true poor', in the early years Tudor monarchs and politicians felt that poor relief could be left to the private philanthropy of wealthier members of society; even as late as 1495 and 1531 the main aim of Tudor parliaments was to prevent the poor from wandering.[65] The hungrier and more desperate poor people became, the more the state was to intervene.

HUMANISM AND A NEW POLITICS

A number of factors persuaded Tudor monarchs and their ministers that the management of the poor could no longer be left to private philanthropy. Three were particularly significant. The first was the growth in sheer numbers of poor people. The second was a new optimism about the abilities of government, which made politicians feel that a poor law could be successfully implemented by public authority, and done comprehensively.[66] The third was the shift in intellectual fashion brought about by humanism. As we saw in the previous chapter, humanists across Europe in the fourteenth century rediscovered the classic texts of the great Greek and Roman thinkers and through their study developed a new way of looking at the world. They abandoned the medieval insistence on seeing philosophy and politics as adjuncts of Christian theology. This meant that they rejected traditional assumptions and aimed instead at a more empirical analysis of perceived experience. As a result they developed a more human-centred vision. They drew on the Roman concept of *humanitas* as the development of human virtue to its fullest potential. This involved reflection on those qualities which were essential to being human, but it also meant being an active participant in life. Contemplation and action were complementary and must be kept in balance.

The implication of their stand on education, as A. L. Beier puts it, was that poverty was not inevitable. Through education or apprenticeship, the able poor could be taught the skills to support themselves. Delinquent children could be taken off the streets. Even prostitutes might be 'corrected' to lead honest lives.[67] If the appropriate institutions could be established, then poverty could not just be alleviated, it could perhaps be totally eradicated. According to the humanists, the first requirement must be Christian charity, as the medieval Fathers had outlined. But it must be rationally organized and focused on the recipients rather than on the salvation, or self-satisfaction, of the donors.[68] The aim of the charity should not be relief but reform, particularly moral reform. That meant condemning beggary and vagabondage, the humanists argued.[69]

Humanists, because of their insistence on a balance between contemplation and action, were actively interested in politics. In England Henry VIII surrounded himself with humanists as courtiers, tutors and propagandists. He chose a leading humanist, Sir Thomas More, to be his Chancellor. More, in his *Utopia* of 1516, took vagrancy as its starting point for an analysis of England's social ills. It was More, a Catholic, who was one of the first sixteenth-century writers to call for the prohibition of public begging as a disgrace to a Christian society.[70] Humanists such as Richard Morison and Thomas Starkey* figured prominently in the circle of Henry's later Chancellor, Thomas Cromwell, the man at the heart of the politics of centralization and control characterizing the governance and polity of Tudor England. Morison and Starkey were among those responsible for the first laws to curb vagrancy and relieve the needy.

The humanist critique of poverty, A. L. Beier suggests, 'was perhaps the single most important influence upon policymakers in early modern Europe', and humanist teachings became the received wisdom in schools and universities in Catholic and Protestant countries alike.[71] As a result, from about 1520 onwards many European cities and states set out to introduce a more systematic approach to poor relief based largely on the writings of Erasmus and Juan Luis Vives, the Dutch and Spanish humanists who both had close links to England.† Catholic towns such as Ypres, Lyon or Venice, as well as Protestant ones like Strasbourg or Geneva, followed the same pattern.[72] But nowhere was the humanist vision more comprehensively implemented than in Tudor England.

---

* See pages 203–5 above.

† See page 177 above.

FIRST ATTEMPTS AT A POOR LAW

Under the Tudors and the early Stuarts, from 1485 to 1649, English parliaments passed more than two dozen statutes dealing with the poor.[73] At the outset they did not much depart from the practice of monarchs of the late Middle Ages. Early Tudor laws were aimed essentially at social control. But, as the century progressed, they developed a greater concern for the 'true poor' – with the licensing of begging, the organization of parish poor relief, and finally a shift from philanthropic charity to an organized form of taxation. No such progression occurred in attitudes to the 'thriftless poor', however, and over the next century a variety of repressive measures, of varying degrees of severity, were put in place to discourage the incorrigibly idle.

Early Tudor laws followed very much in the tradition of fourteenth-century laws such as the 1349 Ordinance of Labourers, the 1351 Statute of Labourers and the 1388 Statute of Cambridge, which sought to fix wages at pre-Black Death levels, set minimum terms for contracts, and restrict the geographical movement of working people and their ability to change occupations. These laws differentiated between, on the one hand, the infirm, disabled and elderly poor and, on the other, sturdy beggars who were capable of work. The legislation of the first Tudor monarch, Henry VII, took much the same line. His 1495 Act Against Vagabonds and Beggars decreed that 'vagabonds, idle and suspected persons shall be set in the stocks for three days and three nights and have none other sustenance but bread and water and then shall be put out of Town'.[74] Anyone who gave alms to such idle persons was to be fined 12 shillings. Beggars who were genuinely unable to work were to be allowed to beg but only in the hundred (district) in which they had previously lived.[75]

But no distinction was made between idle vagrants and those on the move genuinely seeking work. Numbers of the latter swelled with the severe economic depression of the late 1520s, when thousands of people were thrown out of work in the clothing industry after diplomatic relations with the Low Countries were broken off.[76] Henry VIII responded to the crisis with his 1531 Act Concerning Punishment of Beggars and Vagabonds. Again, its main aim was to keep the poor from wandering. But it widened the net of those considered undesirables. The act defined a vagabond as 'any man or woman whole and mighty in body and able to labour, having no land, master, nor using any lawful merchandise, craft, or mystery whereby he might get his living'.[77]

The process of extending the definition of troublemakers continued throughout the Tudor period, with the government seeking to bring a great array of 'dangerous trades' under control. Among those required to carry licences or testimonials, because the authorities saw their wandering as a threat, were pedlars and tinkers, healers, soldiers and sailors, students and clerics – and wizards. All manner of entertainers also fell under suspicion, from fiddle-players to actors.[78] 'To the jaundiced Elizabethan eye, the casual labourer and the wandering rogue were virtually indistinguishable from the itinerant actor,' writes John-Christophe Agnew, 'so that few would have been entirely surprised when, in 1572, players themselves were placed under the force of the Vagabond Act.'[79] To the authorities anyone or anything which encouraged crowds of people to gather together might be the occasion for a riot.

Like its 1495 predecessor the 1531 act distinguished between the able-bodied itinerant and the impotent poor. But now, instead of merely being placed in the stocks, an idle rogue was to be 'tied to the end of a cart, naked and . . . beaten with whips . . .till his body be bloody'.[80] He was then to return to his native parish 'and there put himself to labour, like as a true man oweth to do', since idleness, the act insisted, was the 'mother and root of all vices'. But even the truly needy were more restricted; they were now to be allowed to beg only in an area to which they were assigned by Justices of the Peace, and licences were to be restricted to the disabled, sick and elderly. Beggars seeking alms outside their designated area were to be set in the stocks for two days and nights on bread and water. As the distinguished Tudor historian G. R. Elton, surveying the whole period, put it, 'from the reign of Richard II in the fourteenth century to 1531, little more was done than to punish vagrants and talk piously about the need for charity to the genuinely poor'.[81]

THE DISSOLUTION OF THE MONASTERIES

At the same time that the 1531 act was passed, Henry VIII was busy getting divorced from Catherine of Aragon (a process finalized in 1533). This was to have a significant impact upon poor people. In 1529 the king's attempts to persuade the Pope to agree to the annulment of his first marriage had been foundering. That same year was the first in which the anti-clerical Reformation Parliament sat. Thomas Cromwell joined Henry's Royal Council twelve months later. And in 1531 Henry VIII became 'head of the Church in England and Wales as far as the word of God allows'.[82] By 1536 the Dissolution of the Monasteries had begun and, despite the king's promise that the endowments of the religious houses would be 'used and converted to better uses', most of the money went directly into government funds and was squandered on foreign wars.

Some Protestants, such as Bishop Hugh Latimer, strove to save part of the proceeds for relieving and employing the poor, but without success. Had a quarter of the money from the sales of monastic lands been spent on poor relief, as was done in German Protestant states, it would have surpassed all the money raised through taxation for the poor over the next 150 years.[83] Instead, the old Catholic vehicles for delivering help to the poor were dismantled. The religious houses were suppressed and their poor relief vanished overnight; by 1540, monasteries would be dismantled at a rate of fifty a month.[84] All of the charities operated by the Catholic Church terminated during the 1530s, including sheltered housing, accommodation for travellers, and hospitals for the elderly and infirm, which had provided an average of one bed for every two parishes in the country. The lay fraternities and guilds withered – and with them went their welfare and educational services and the guild system of apprenticeships. Many of the stocks of land and animals which had earlier been given to the parishes to provide an income for poor relief were confiscated.[85]

The replacement of such institutions by lay secular equivalents, through the generous donations of prosperous individuals or by the intervention of the civic authorities, was painfully slow. While the huge increase in poverty and vagrancy cannot be said to have been 'caused' by the Dissolution of the Monasteries, as some Catholic apologists once suggested, it is clear that, in the words of A. L. Beier, 'to abolish institutions with the capability of relieving it was disastrous'.[86]

Yet in the early phases of the Tudor poor law the assumption of the king's ministers was that the philanthropy for the truly needy would be private; the state could restrict itself to measures of control and coercion against the thriftless poor. They continued to look to religion to supply the money to relieve the needy. As late as 1596, after two successive crop failures – with famine blighting the land, high food prices and acute suffering among the poor – the Privy Council, fearing food riots, instructed the Archbishops of Canterbury and York to compel parish clergy to preach on the theme of hospitality. They were told to advocate general fasting and almsgiving on Wednesdays; the food and money saved was to be given to those in need – regardless of the cause of their distress or the quality of their behaviour.[87] Well into the Reformation old medieval Catholic models of charity persisted.

But in other regards significant change was underway. A major shift in attitudes came in 1536 with a law entitled An Act for Punishment of Sturdy Vagabonds and Beggars.[88] The title of the law suggests that the motives of the lawmakers were still primarily concerned with the need to control the wandering poor. Indeed, that was a central focus but the law also contains something new. It was probably drafted by the pamphleteer William Marshall, a close ally of Thomas Cromwell and a member of the circle of humanists around Henry VIII. Marshall had recently translated into English the pioneering poor-law ordinances which the Catholic city of Ypres had drawn up between 1524 and 1529 and had sent to the highest tribunal in the Catholic world, the University of Paris, for approval. The town authorities of Ypres had laid down two principles which ran counter to the medieval ideas of philanthropy. The first was that it was the duty of towns, rather than merely their inhabitants, to look after the poor since almsgiving was not now sufficient for the needs of the day. The second was that civic authorities which took over poor relief from individual philanthropists were therefore justified in prohibiting begging and vagrancy. These innovations led to a great discussion among the Catholic theologians of the Sorbonne who, on the whole, approved of these reforming ideas.[89]

In 1535 Marshall drew up a comprehensive scheme for England rooted in a similar humanist philosophy. Marshall was one of the first policymakers to realize that vagrancy was increasing largely because there was not enough work to go around. This was a revolutionary insight. Marshall was years ahead of his time. His solution was to draw up a scheme to create jobs for the unemployed, repairing roads, renovating ports, dredging rivers and rebuilding towns or, in the words of his fellow humanist, the social reformer Thomas Starkey, 'some other magnifical work'.[90] The children of the poor were to be taught a trade and also set to work.

All this was to be financed by a comprehensive graduated income tax to be gathered every Sunday in parish churches where priests were each week to provide sermons praising charity and condemning sloth. The focus was to shift from the hundred to the parish as the base unit of public administration.[91] Casual almsgiving was condemned as harmful and was to be restricted. It was all to be coordinated nationally by a Central Council. Marshall's 1535 plan was to set the contours of future Tudor and Stuart poor laws.

Yet at that stage his scheme was too radical even for the Reformation Parliament. When the law was passed in 1536 it was diluted. The idea of public job creation was removed. So was the income tax. So was the Central Council. But the idea had been set in law that each parish was responsible for looking after the 'impotent poor' with a weekly collection to be organized by two churchwardens in every parish. Casual almsgiving was outlawed and those who ignored this order could be fined. All charity was to go through a 'common box' in every parish.[92] Most begging was banned, even by the aged and impotent, since they would receive cash payments from the parish. Those who could work, but would not, were treated savagely: for a first offence they were whipped and sent to their home parish to be set to work; for a second offence the upper part of the gristle of their right ear was to be cut off; for a third offence they could be indicted as felons and executed. Children under fourteen and over five who were caught begging could be put into service or forced into an apprenticeship.[93] The statute was widely ignored in towns and rural parishes far from London.[94] Local authorities were reluctant to enforce the act[95] and it lapsed soon after it was passed, according to Paul Slack.[96] But it defined the strategy for the future: work and harsh punishment for the idle poor; cash for the impotent poor; a ban on casual almsgiving; and public philanthropy to be administered by designated parish officers, who supervised weekly collections in each parish to which all being financially able were expected to contribute.

UNEXAMPLED SAVAGERY AND CIVIC PERSUASION

When Henry VIII died, in 1547, he was succeeded by his nine-year-old son, who became Edward VI. Those exercising power on behalf of the boy king were acutely aware that the reign of a minor was particularly vulnerable to political instability. Even more than usually, then, the politicians of the day wanted to clamp down upon the possibility of civil unrest. With vagrants continuing to loom in the minds of the powerful as a potential source of riot and insurrection, the authorities renewed measures to control the itinerant population.

The House of Commons, in the words of John Pound, 'proceeded to act with unexampled savagery'.[97] Even more draconian punishments for vagrancy were introduced in a statute passed in the first year of Edward's reign. Anyone who remained unemployed for three days or more was deemed a vagrant. If convicted by magistrates they were to be branded with a hot iron with a V on their chest and then handed over as a slave for two years to whomever had informed upon them. The slave master was obliged only to feed them on bread and water while the slave was to perform any task given to them. The law said that the master could sell the slave to someone else for his two-year servitude. Any slave who ran away more than once was to be executed,[98] though there is no evidence these severe laws were actually enforced.[99] 'The idea of turning Englishmen, even poor ones, into slaves was so unappealing that the act remained a dead letter until its appeal in 1550,' wrote one historian.[100]

And yet the double-tracked approach which William Marshall had pioneered in 1535 continued even in the fearful years of Edward VI. That was clear from the title of the legislation, An Act for the Punishment of Vagabonds and for the Relief of the Poor and Impotent Persons (1547).[101] Under it cottages were to be erected for the disabled. Leprous and bedridden vagrants were authorized to appoint persons to beg for them by proxy.[102] And an attempt was made to consolidate the practice of parish collections for poor relief every Sunday, with priests being told to exhort generosity. This law was reinforced by later measures in Edward's reign which first introduced an element of civic persuasion into charitable giving for the poor. The government ordered surveys in every parish so the needs of the poor could be precisely measured. The law then provided that when people were at church, and had heard 'God's holy word', two official parish collectors should 'gently ask and demand of every man and woman what they of their charity will be contented to give weekly toward the relief of the poor'.[103] Records were to be kept of the pledges and those who failed to pay were, in an echo of medieval canon law, to be reported to the bishop. There was even a proposal in 1552 that donations should be made compulsory. This approach of the young Protestant king was essentially continued by his Catholic half-sister when she succeeded him as Mary I. Her parliament, in its 1555 Act for the Relief of the Poor,[104] decreed that begging could be authorized where the poor were too numerous to be relieved by the parish collection. It also instructed richer parishes to assist poorer parishes in their neighbourhood.

Things were to change under her successor Elizabeth I. It was taken for granted in the time of Henry VIII and his predecessors that almsgiving was essentially voluntary. That presupposition had been tempered by an element of public persuasion under Edward and Mary; now under Elizabeth, persuasion was to turn to coercion and then compulsion. Philanthropy was to be supplemented by taxation.

PHILANTHROPY VERSUS TAXATION

One of Queen Elizabeth's most able ministers and her most powerful, Robert Cecil, Lord Burghley, grew increasingly concerned at the number of homeless and unemployed individuals within the realm. Such folk, he feared, could pose a serious threat to law and order. As a consequence, in 1563, An Act for the Relief of the Poor[105] was passed, which further strengthened the provisions of earlier Tudor parliaments. Almsgiving was still voluntary: the donations made at the weekly parish poor-relief collection were still regarded as a gift. There was no attempt to stipulate a specific sum of money, but the statute increased the pressure on citizens to give. The process of assessments was obligatory with the instruction that those who 'obstinately refuse to give weekly to the relief of the poor according to his or their abilities' – despite the exhortation of the bishop – could be bound over to the Justices of the Peace, who could fine those who refused ten shillings – and that fine could be collected under pain of imprisonment. Those who refused to act as parish collectors could be fined £10 and if they failed to produce quarterly accounts they could be imprisoned.

But moves against vagrants also intensified, particularly after a group of nobles from Northumberland and Westmorland led the Northern Rebellion, aimed at deposing the Protestant Elizabeth and replacing her in 1569 with the Catholic Mary, Queen of Scots. The crackdown on vagabonds which ensued was of such intensity that it has been called the Whipping Campaign[106] of 1569 to 1572. It created 'something like a state of war between the city authorities and the suburban vagrant,' according to A. L. Beier.[107] Local magistrates and justices were required to send the Privy Council the names of all apprehended vagabonds, 'to trace Popish agitators and spies'.[108] This link between vagrants and Catholic insurrection grew stronger after the abortive invasion by the Spanish Armada in 1588, when the authorities became convinced that vagabonds might be 'friars, priests, Jesuits, or Popish scholars' in disguise.[109] There is plenty of evidence that these vagrancy laws were now enforced: from 1569 to 1572 reports from 18 counties list details of more than 750 vagrants seized.[110] In the Middlesex sessions, between 1572 and 1575, some 44 vagabonds were sentenced to be branded, eight were set to service, and five sentenced to be hanged.[111]

A law passed in 1572 reflected the increasing sense of panic among politicians. It contained harsher measures against vagrants than anything passed since the slavery statute of 1547. First offenders were to be whipped and burned through the ear with a hot iron one inch in circumference; for a second offence they were to be condemned as felons; and persistent beggars were to be hanged without being allowed access to a priest. But again the law reflected the lack of confidence among the political establishment as to the best way of tackling the problem. The name of the 1572 statute – An Act for the Punishment of Vagabonds and for Relief of the Poor and Impotent[112] – revealed that ambiguity. Despite its severity on vagrants, it can, in the words of John Pound, 'properly be regarded as a watershed in the poor law history of the 16th century'.[113]

In many ways it merely reinforced the approach of the previous Tudor monarchs. From a weekly collection, known as the Poor Rate, help was given to the poor, old, sick, disabled, widows and orphans of the parish. Each received a sum of money and/or food every week. Those who were unable to collect it had it delivered to their homes. The children of the poor were given apprenticeships, boys until they were 24 years old and girls, up to the age of 21 or when they married. The statute continued the move away from casual almsgiving by households towards a more public approach to the problem of poverty. But, in other respects, it was more thorough than previous statutes. It finally recognized that contributions to poor relief needed to be compulsory and stipulated that weekly amounts must be given for their support. Surveys of the impotent and aged were ordered to be drawn up. Any leftover monies were to be used to set up Houses of Correction for rogues and vagabonds. As before, the residents of each parish were expected to administer the system; those named as the collectors and distributors of the funds were not to be paid for their public service, and they could not refuse to perform these duties.[114]

But what also made the 1572 act a watershed was that it was the first piece of Tudor legislation to acknowledge that there were some able-bodied men seeking work who were unable to find any. It made specific mention of seasonal harvest workers and servants whose masters had died or who had fallen on hard times and been forced to dismiss their staff. It was the first recognition by central government that there were some men who were genuinely unemployed through no fault of their own – an insight which was reinforced four years later in the 1576 Act for Setting of the Poor on Work, and for the Avoiding of Idleness,[115] which required every town, and house of correction, to lay in stocks of wool, hemp, flax and iron as the raw materials to set the able-bodied jobless to work.

THE TOWNS TAKE OVER FROM THE MONASTERIES

Interestingly, there was nothing in the 1576 act which had not already been tried before in the larger towns of England, particularly London and the centres of the lucrative wool trade, Ipswich and Norwich. For it was in such places that innovative methods of handling the growing numbers of poor people were developed. Tudor politicians acknowledged this by appointing the mayor of Norwich, John Aldrich, to the parliamentary committee which addressed the issue in 1572. Aldrich was a key figure behind the comprehensive and successful poor-relief scheme which had been pioneered in Norwich. Such towns were in the forefront of new approaches to public philanthropy because their populations grew alarmingly in this period. In the 1520s as many as 15 per cent of the population quit their native village in the countryside and moved to the towns. The urban population quadrupled between 1500 and 1700, with the most rapid growth occurring in London. In those two centuries the population of the capital rose from 50,000 to a staggering half a million inhabitants.[116] Of these a significant number were vagrants – around 10,000 a year, it has been estimated.[117]

So grave was the problem that, within just four years of the end of monastic healthcare after the Dissolution of the Monasteries, Henry VIII was forced to consent to the re-endowment of London's hospitals to cater for the different categories of pauper in the capital. St Bartholomew's was endowed in 1544 and St Thomas's in 1552 to serve the diseased and disabled. Christ's Hospital was to look after foundling children. And Bridewell, a former Royal Palace, was converted to a House of Correction for idle rogues who were put to work, making wire, caps and feather beds.[118] King Henry required that the citizens of London should pay for the maintenance of the hospitals. But the civic authorities were unable to raise enough revenue from voluntary contributions. So they replaced Sunday church almsgiving with a mandatory collection for the poor. It set a precedent which was followed by compulsory measures in Norwich in 1549[119] and in Cambridge, York, Colchester and Ipswich in the decade that followed.[120] By 1598 Philanthropy had given way to taxation.

But if poor relief was legislated from the top down, it was made real from the bottom up. Different towns tried different approaches. Some used poor-relief money to try to prevent future problems by binding poor children as apprentices, expelling pregnant strangers from town, or paying for housing elsewhere for local paupers. Other towns used it in direct relief, giving cash, bread, shirts and shoes, lodging or firewood. Still others laid in stocks of flax or wool which the poor could spin and provided spinning wheels and other tools for the able-bodied.[121] Some towns set public stores of grain for the poor to use in times of scarcity.[122] Others continued the medieval Catholic practice (which zealous reformers had condemned at the Reformation) of maintaining a herd of cows or flock of sheep to yield an annual revenue for poor relief: St Mary's in Shrewsbury, for example, was letting out ten cows and three sheep in 1554, producing an annual income of £1 1s. 8d. a year for the poor of the parish. Such parish herds and flocks continued well into the seventeenth century as a valuable adjunct to poor-relief collections. Some towns even collected corn from parishioners and used it to brew ale to sell to raise cash for poor-relief funds, until the practice was suppressed by the Puritans.[123] Although legislation was national, in many towns and rural areas parliamentary initiatives and Privy Council directives were often ignored or enforced only reluctantly. In the end local constables and magistrates were left to decide who was a vagrant and who was deserving of poor relief.[124]

Perhaps the most comprehensive poor-relief scheme was introduced in Norwich, then the largest and wealthiest city outside London. There a comprehensive census was compiled in 1570 after the aforementioned mayor, John Aldrich, complained that vagabonds were creating an intolerable problem for the city. The impetus for this may have been political. The census showed Norwich had only around 25 vagabonds a year,[125] but there was fear of a plot being laid in the city by malcontents. A year earlier the Northern Rebellion had sought to replace Elizabeth with Mary, Queen of Scots. And Norwich was seen as a potential hotbed of insurrection because, just two decades earlier, the revolt known as Kett's Rebellion had begun just ten miles south of the city. The poor of Norwich numbered 2,300 men, women and children, the survey showed. These individuals 'for the most part' claimed to have trades but in fact 'went daily abroad from door to door, counterfeiting a kind of work, but indeed did very little or none at all'.

The townsfolk, the authorities lamented, gave these beggars more than they needed – for having 'over-gorged' they threw away their leftover 'pottage, bread, meat, and drink' in the street. This over-generosity in almsgiving by wealthy Norwich citizens made begging more profitable than work. In a document known as the Norwich Orders for the Poor[126] the horrified civic leaders denounced the vagabonds who lived in 'church porches, cellars, doorways, barns and hay chambers, and other back corners'. These folk were unkempt, disease-ridden and verminous as well as constantly drunk and abusive – and hence, in John Pound's words, were 'thus a source of physical as well as moral contagion'.[127]

The Norwich solution was twofold – to assist the needy and punish the idle. To assist the needy, everybody in the city who was capable of contributing to poor relief was expected to do so, according to their means. City aldermen paid a shilling a week but most of the population paid two pence a week or less. Poor relief was not just distributed within each parish; rich parishes were instructed to provide for the poor of other parishes as well. The wealthy parish of St Peter Mancroft, for instance, donated to no fewer than six other parishes. Throughout the decade from 1570 to 1580, and intermittently afterwards, just 950 citizens provided support for those who were old or infirm – but also for around 380 pensioners, most of whom were individuals unable to work because of broken limbs; they were not, therefore, permanently on the dole but individuals able to return to work after they recovered. Similarly, building workers who were unemployed at the time of the census received alms varying between one penny and six pence a week.

Punishing the idle was just as carefully calculated. Norwich's poor-law system allowed it to ban begging in the city precincts entirely. Vagabonds caught begging were placed in the city's Bridewell prison, which had been purchased in 1565. Its resident bailiff, paid a salary of £30 a year, assisted by two wardens, ensured that 'vagabonds, idlers, loafers or drunkards' were set to work from 5 a.m. to 8 p.m. in the summer and from 7 a.m. to 6 p.m. in the winter, with half an hour allowed for a meal break and a quarter of an hour for prayer. Those who refused to work received no food. Women worked shorter hours than men. Children were taught the rudiments of reading and writing. The city was transformed by 'fear of the terror of the house of Bridewell', since vagrants preferred to find a normal job than be compelled to work in such a place. Norwich's poor-law system was by far the most successful attack on the problem of urban poverty carried out in contemporary England. It formed the model for national reforms, as we will see below.[128]

CIVIC PHILANTHROPY AND PRIVATE GIVING

Official poor-law collections and the emergence of civic philanthropy did not replace private giving. Leading families in the individual towns felt it their duty to set a good example on almsgiving. As the Tudor and Stuart historian Marjorie McIntosh points out, Elizabethan England had little hidden charity of the kind that is given quietly to avoid making recipients feel humiliated or donors feel self-satisfied.[129] Those who gave expected to be recognized and praised for their generosity. Often the name of the donor was incorporated into the institution, as in Lady Cecil's Bequest for Poor Tradesmen in Romford in Essex.[130] Those who founded almshouses often expected their occupants to wear a distinctive robe when they appeared in public, labelled with the name of the institution's founder.

Residents were also expected to pray for their beneficiaries, a feature which was just as strong in Protestant as in Catholic almshouses, despite the Reformation propaganda.[131] Nor did the Catholic tradition of charitable distributions at funerals die out under Protestantism; some 80 per cent of giving took the form of funeral doles, contrasted with just 10 per cent as endowments.[132] These so-called medieval habits of giving persisted until the time of Oliver Cromwell.

Many Protestant civic leaders were happy to ignore the purities of Reformation theology and instead resort to whatever seemed to work. The aldermen in the wealthy wool town of Hadleigh, near Ipswich, which had been an early centre of Protestantism in the middle years of the century, were happy to buy back the town's medieval guildhall in 1573. The building, which had housed the town's vigorous lay fraternities before the Reformation, who used it to distribute alms to the poor, once again became the base for the administration of poor relief, with firewood, bedding and clothing distributed as well as cash.[133] That said, Protestant theology did make an impact on poor-law practice; Calvinists were the driving force behind many of the schemes for assisting the poor in English towns and villages in the 1580s and 1590s,[134] and Protestant theological language prompted both a singularly harsh stance towards the undeserving – 'drunkards, bastard bearers, hedge-breakers and other rogues'[135] – and a particularly generous attitude to those it deemed genuinely deserving.[136]

There was another factor at work: Tudor political attitudes towards the body Commonwealth – a theory of society fashionable among the learned and powerful of the sixteenth century. It held that society was an organism whose interdependent parts work together as did the parts of the body, 'with the monarch . . . portrayed as the head or the heart, magistrates as the eyes, artisans as the hands and husbandmen as the feet'.[137] Shakespeare gives vivid expression to this in the fable of the belly in *Coriolanus* in which the other parts of the body rebel against the stomach, only to be told that it is the organ which vitally distributes nutrition to the rest:

> Because I am the store-house and the shop
> Of the whole body: but, if you do remember,
> I send it through the rivers of your blood,
> Even to the court, the heart, to the seat o' the brain;
> And, through the cranks and offices of man,
> The strongest nerves and small inferior veins
> From me receive that natural competency
> Whereby they live.[138]

Both aspects of Tudor policy towards the poor were embodied in the metaphor. For in a living body no part could be idle, because then the whole body would not function properly – hence idleness must be condemned. But since all parts of society are mutually interdependent the rich must not neglect the poor and needy. Poor relief was thus considered necessary on grounds of Christian mercy, political polity and practical expediency. The more the social fabric was threatened by the increasing poverty which was evident all around Elizabethan society, the greater was the need for both aspects to be reinforced by the state.

THE ELIZABETHAN POOR LAW

It was famine which forced the hand of the Elizabethan government into the final piece of legislation that consolidated the Tudor poor law. After two decades of good harvests things changed dramatically in the 1580s. Three years of bad harvests led to famine. There were reports of starvation in Cumbria. Food riots broke out in the West Country. The Privy Council sent out instructions to all magistrates early in 1587 ordering them to make detailed surveys of all the corn in the possession of every citizen. Households were allowed to store as much as they would need for their personal use, but any surplus had to be brought to market and sold at what was deemed a fair price.[139] Two years later, after an abortive military adventure in Portugal, large numbers of English soldiers returned home and were demobbed on the south coast. Their officers told them they could keep their arms and uniforms, assuming that they would sell them to make up for their low pay. Large numbers of these demobbed soldiers travelled up to London, where a gang of 500 of them threatened to loot Bartholomew Fair. In response the government declared martial law, brought in 2,000 city militiamen, and hanged a number of the former soldiers.[140]

Things got worse in the following decade, with four successive bad harvests from 1593 to 1597. The harvest in 1596 was disastrous; the price of wheat almost doubled,[141] and by 1597 corn prices were more than four times the average of preceding years.[142] Parts of England in 1596 were hit again by famine. Many parishes found they lacked the resources to maintain the local poor.[143] There were riots across the country from Somerset to Oxfordshire to Norfolk. In London 20 rioters were executed after civil unrest over the cost of bread. Hunger was the driving force behind the activities of the 400 rampaging vagabonds who pillaged the county of Somerset – of which the magistrate Edward Hext wrote to complain to the queen's chief minister, Lord Burghley, that same year.[144] To the Tudor authorities 1596 seemed a crisis year.

Parliament was convened in October 1597 and sat until February 1598. Its debates ranged over the crisis and its many causes and symptoms. Both vagabondage and poor relief featured prominently in the discussions and no fewer than 17 bills were put forward on the subject. The House of Commons set up a parliamentary committee to consider what should be done; its members included some of the great figures of the time – Sir Francis Bacon, Sir Thomas Cecil, Sir Edward Coke and Magistrate Hext. The titles of the 12 bills they considered give some idea of the many aspects of the subject they discussed. They included bills for 'erecting of Houses of Correction and punishment of rogues and sturdy beggars'; for the 'necessary habitation and relief of the poor, aged, lame, and blind in every parish'; for 'relief of hospitals, poor prisoners, and others impoverished by casual losses'; for 'the better relief of soldiers and Mariners'; for 'the better governing of hospitals and land given to the relief of the poor'; for 'extirpation of beggary'; 'against bastardy'; for 'setting the poorer to work' and erecting of 'working houses for the poor'.[145]

The result was two statutes in 1597 and 1598 which defined Elizabethan poor law – An Act for the Relief of the Poor[146] and An Act for the Punishment of Rogues, Vagabonds and Sturdy Beggars.[147] The first law decreed that all those with sufficient means were to be taxed to relieve the poor – and provide materials with which the poor could be set to work and their children given apprenticeships. The money was to be raised based on an official assessment of the value of the property which each person owned, including land, houses, tithes, coal mines and woods. It was to be collected in each of the nation's 15,000 parishes by the churchwardens and four Overseers of the Poor chosen by the local magistrates from 'substantial householders' of the parish. The overseers were required to meet monthly and produce annual accounts. They could be fined 20 shillings if they failed in these duties. They were given powers to seize goods of recalcitrant non-payers. Rich parishes were to aid poorer ones.[148]

The second law carefully defined vagabondage, ruling that all beggars were to be declared rogues except those who begged for victuals in their own parish and soldiers or sailors who were licensed to beg while journeying home. All the rest were to be arrested, whipped until bloody, and then sent by the most direct route to their home parish. If they dawdled on the way they were to be whipped again. When they got home they were to be set to work. Incorrigible rogues were to be put in a House of Correction or imprisoned, and if that did not succeed, they could be banished from the realm, sent permanently to the galleys, or executed as felons[149] – though the evidence is scant as to whether such penalties were enforced.[150] Together the two acts, which constituted the Elizabethan Poor Law, remained in force in all essentials for almost 250 years.[151] The 1601 law,[152] The Statute of Charitable Uses, which is widely described as the comprehensive statement of Elizabethan poor law – it has been called 'the foundation and text-book of English Poor Law'[153] – is largely a restatement of the 1597–8 acts with some small amendments.[154]

What was most significant for the history of philanthropy about the 1601 legislation was a secondary act that defined the law on charitable trusts. Elizabeth's ministers realized that religious exhortation, and firm government legislation, were not enough to encourage the philanthropic giving by the merchant and gentry classes which was necessary to complement the poor law. Donors also had to be assured that their money would be appropriately spent. The Statute of Charitable Uses 1601 was designed to create a procedure to investigate the misuse of charitable assets.

But it was the Preamble of the legislation which was to have the most significant effect. Using words drawn from the medieval poem *Piers Plowman*, the Preamble created what became the Elizabethan definition of charitable activities. According to a lawyer of the time, Francis Moore, it set out to suggest a list of activities which would simultaneously relieve poverty and also reduce the burden on local parishes imposed by the poor-relief legislation passed in the same year. This list of charitable activities which the state wished to encourage reveals something of the priorities of Elizabethan political, economic and social policy. That is why the building and maintenance of prisons – an important part of the poor-law scheme – was accounted charitable. So was the repair of bridges and harbours, and assisting the poor to pay their taxes for the raising and equipping of the queen's army. The law was intended to channel the philanthropy of the English gentry and merchant class to government-approved ends. Gifts would count as charity if they were given:

> For the relief of aged, impotent and poor people . . . For the maintenance of sick and maimed soldiers and mariners, [For] schools of learning, free schools and scholars in universities . . . For the repair of bridges, ports, havens, causeways, churches, seed banks and highways . . . For education and preferment of orphans . . . Towards relief, stock or maintenance of Houses of Correction . . . For marriages of poor maids . . . For [the] aid and help of young tradesmen, handicraftsmen and persons decayed . . . For relief and redemption of prisoners or captives . . . And for aid or ease of any poor inhabitants concerning payments of fifteens,* setting out of soldiers† and other taxes . . .[155]

The categories established in the Preamble of the Statute of Charitable Uses proclaimed what the first English historian of philanthropy, Benjamin Kirkman Gray, called 'a noble conception of what a society ought to be'.[156] Extraordinarily, this approved list of charitable activities even now remains the basis of English charity law. When judges are today asked to make a ruling on whether some new activity can be considered charitable, they turn to this 1601 list as the basis on which to search for analogies to apply to contemporary law.

THE LEGACY OF TUDOR PHILANTHROPY

The Elizabethan Poor Law marked a turning point in the history of philanthropy. It saw the intervention of the state in what had previously been an entirely private activity. It brought coercion and compulsion into what had once been voluntary. It created a very particular definition of charitable activity. And it fundamentally altered the relationship between the rich and the poor. All this came about through the confluence of demographic, social and economic change. Early forms of capitalism were emerging. Humanist thinking was creating a new politics.

---

* Fifteens were a Tudor property tax.
† A tax to raise and equip a royal army.

The new poor law emerged through a century of legal experiment in which Tudor politicians tried simultaneously to grapple with how to fulfil their moral duty towards the needy and destitute while at the same time reforming the idle and heading off the threat of civil insurrection. The wealthy began to harden their attitudes towards the poor, prompted by the sheer numbers of newly impoverished people, but also stimulated by a new humanist philosophy of the state and sharpened by the vehemence in Reformation religious rhetoric against the thriftless and idle. Attitudes to the poor became more hostile than they had been during the medieval period.

Despite the government's recognition that some poor people were unemployed through no fault of their own, the severity of the laws against beggars and vagrants, together with the new Puritan theology, created a sense that the poor need to reform themselves morally and change their habits. The poor began to be seen as suffering from some kind of moral failing, as is evident from an exchange in Ben Jonson's 1629 play *The New Inn*. In it the Nurse (an aristocrat in disguise) indignantly asks 'Is poverty a vice?', to which the undisguised aristocrat, Lord Beaufort, ripostes: 'Th'age counts it so'.[157] It was not just that age which counted it so. The idea that the poor were in some way to blame for their own poverty was to persist for the next four centuries, indeed some would say that we have not, in our own times, completely shaken it off.

The constant restatement and modification throughout the sixteenth century of the provisions of English statute law – oscillating between the generously enlightened and the savagely repressive – reveals how hard it was for successive governments to calibrate an effective response to the growth of poverty and the related problem of vagrancy. It was a process of trial and error which was more acutely manifested in England than elsewhere in Europe, where political leaders also struggled with how to produce a more systematic approach to poor relief in tune with the changing economy and the growth of more controlling centralized government.[158] In practice, attempts to discriminate between the 'truly poor' and the 'thriftless poor' broke down. Some of the able-bodied received relief and the genuinely needy were sometimes punished.[159] In England the problem was, in any case, perceived as more complex than merely relieving the vulnerable and controlling the vagrant. The Tudors' increasingly paternalistic centralization of the English state also aimed at stemming the flow of people from the countryside to the cities and sought to control the price of grain and regulate markets to ward off popular unrest and food riots. The poor law protected the English elite from unrest, in contrast to neighbouring France where the poor starved and rioted when food ran short.[160] The local tax for the poor was unique to England, says Paul Slack, and could not have been achieved in a state less used to central government than Tudor England.[161]

All this had massive implications for philanthropy. Society did not merely acknowledge that the poor had a right to relief in cases of extreme need or destitution; by the end of the sixteenth century people accepted that it was the duty of the state to provide it. Poor relief became an entitlement under the Elizabethan statutes, as a matter of practical politics as much as moral imperative. The state now had the responsibility to relieve the indigent and provide work for the able-bodied. So long-standing was this legacy that in the early nineteenth century William Cobbett was able to proclaim that 'the poor man in England is as secure from beggary as the king upon his throne, because when he makes known his distress to the parish offices, they bestow upon him, not alms, but his legal dues'.[162] It also became clear that English people were willing to pay taxes to support their needy neighbours – or were at least prepared to do so without revolt.

In early Tudor times the political establishment hoped that charitable giving would still supply the majority of the needs of the poor, but they acknowledged the necessity for the state to intervene where that failed. As time went by the balance between voluntary charity and compulsory taxation shifted. Much later that progression was to lead towards the development of a welfare state. But it was under Elizabeth I that the state first arrogated to itself the role of an organizer of philanthropy. It was to leave public-spirited individuals with no alternative but to seek another conduit for their philanthropic impulses.

Interview: David Sainsbury on philanthropy, business and government

David Sainsbury inherited a fortune at the age of just 26, as an heir to the Sainsbury supermarket empire in which he played a prominent role for four decades, ending as chairman. After being made Lord Sainsbury for his services to philanthropy, he was, for eight years, a member of the Labour government as Minister for Science and Innovation. He has been said to be the single most generous individual philanthropist in the UK for the past five decades. The first Briton to have donated £1 billion to charity, he topped the Sunday Times *Giving List in 2020.*

Many of today's big philanthropists have made huge fortunes and then, later in life, turned their attention to giving them away. Your background is very different. You inherited your wealth at an early age but you also inherited a family tradition of philanthropy. How has that governed your approach to giving?

I very much inherited the tradition from my parents that if you had money, you should use it well. Part of that was giving some of it to charity and I think that was very much my initial inspiration. In due course, I made the discovery that I could use the money to help with issues I thought were important socially and economically.

At the age of 26 you set up a charitable foundation. Why did you call it the Gatsby Trust?

When I inherited my Sainsbury's shares, I went along to our solicitor to discuss what to do with them and she said that people usually set up a charitable trust and call it after a favourite house, place or book. My favourite book at that time was *The Great Gatsby*.

That book is set in the 'Gilded Age' of extravagant wealth in 1920s America – a very strange world . . .

It was a very strange world but the book is not about wild partying as most people think. It is about people being empowered by dreams and hope for the future. I thought that that was quite a good name for a charitable trust.

Over the past half century you have donated £1 billion to an eclectic range of causes – plant science; neuroscience research; mental health; agriculture in Africa; scientific and engineering education; the Institute for Government which is a think tank aimed at improving the dysfunctional elements in government; and the arts. How did you choose the causes you have supported over the years?

They are all areas which I think are important and where I think there is a major opportunity to change things for the better. At university I met a fellow student called Roger Freedman. He was a scientist in my year at King's College, Cambridge, and we started talking about the major discoveries being made in genetics. I became fascinated. It had never occurred to me, up to that point, that science was remotely interesting or challenging. I was reading History but he inspired me to switch to science, which King's – amazingly liberal-minded – let me do even though I had no 'A' levels or 'O' levels in science. I switched to Psychology, which in those days ranged from physiology to behavioural studies of rats, to visual illusions, psychiatry, to how do neural networks process information – what we now call neuroscience. As part of the course I was also taken to Fulbourn, the Cambridge mental hospital, which was a very grim place in those days. As a result I became very interested in genetics, neuroscience and mental health.

And all of that fed, later, into your philanthropy?

Yes. When it later became clear that you could genetically modify plants I became convinced that they could produce a new agricultural revolution across the world which would have a huge impact on food security and a beneficial impact on the environment. It turned out that we had in the UK some brilliant young researchers in that area who, if nothing happened in England, would probably go off to America to do research. The research councils weren't putting any money into this area as they judged it was high-risk. I was able to say, 'Let's do it, because this is really important', and we did it.

The same with mental health?

Yes. With modern drugs, it became clear that you could allow many people in mental hospitals to live again in the community because you could ameliorate their behaviour with drugs. The real question was: 'Which of those people could go back into the community, and what support services did they need? And which other people would never be able to come out of a mental hospital?' So Gatsby set up a project to look at how to make these decisions, and which services would be needed in the community – because no one had given any thought to such issues. That was the beginning of the Gatsby Centre for Mental Health.

What about the arts?

My parents built up an extraordinary art collection over their lives, buying works by Francis Bacon, Giacometti and Henry Moore in the days when they were unknown. The house I was brought up in London was full of these amazing pictures and sculptures and Henry Moore was my godfather, so I always felt I was a custodian of the collection. So when Sainsbury's became a public company, and I could do so, I provided the money to build a museum to house the collection. My wife, Susie, is a great lover of the theatre, and as a result we have also supported a number of theatre projects such as the rebuilding of the Royal Shakespeare Company's theatre at Stratford-upon-Avon.

Basically, your philanthropy has been driven by personal interests really.

Yes. They're all areas that I'm interested in and think you can make the system work better. I think you can only really make philanthropy work if you're prepared to give the time and effort to finding out what the problems are – and how you can change things. And you will only do that well if you think the areas are socially important ones.

You wrote your first cheque for a specific charitable cause at the age of 26. What was it for?

It was to the Liverpool School of Tropical Medicine. I read in the newspapers that one of the world's leading schools in tropical medicine was in Liverpool – because in Victorian times it had been the great port for trade with West Africa. I just wrote them a cheque for £50. A couple of years later they contacted me and I discovered that they were great proponents of the idea that the way to deal with health problems in the Third World was not to build a big hospital in the capital city. It was to put your resources into primary healthcare – with field workers who could go out and get the very basic things right in the field. I thought this was a really exciting idea. I gave them money – not, in the greater scheme of things, huge sums of money. But they were among the people who then persuaded the World Health Organization to give a priority to primary healthcare. So I like to think I played a tiny part in achieving what was clearly a major improvement in health policy in the developing world.

That is one of the distinctive functions of philanthropy – to fund something innovative, to try and change people's view of an issue, and then hand it over to government or an inter-governmental body. Did that then become a conscious paradigm for your philanthropy?

Yes. Governments find it very difficult to be innovative and take risks; but this is something charities can do, and I think one of the roles that philanthropy can play in a society is to do the research on social issues which needs to be done.

There have been three distinct threads to your public life – business, politics and philanthropy. You have had a long career in the family supermarket business. You were a government minister for eight years. And your giving adds up to making you the biggest philanthropist in Britain. Have these been compartments in your life or have you been aware of cross-fertilizations between them?

There has clearly been a lot of cross-fertilization. The fact that I had funded a number of scientific research projects and knowledge transfer projects before I went into government was a great help to me when I became a minister.* Also, when I came out of government I set up the Institute for Government to improve the efficiency and effectiveness of government as a direct result of what I had seen whilst I was a minister.

What have you learned about the respective roles of business, politics and philanthropy? What do each of those do best? And what are they least well-equipped for?

Government is not good at innovation. If you're in government, you say, 'Look, I've got this idea for a very innovative way of doing things.' The

---

* As Science Minister, Lord Sainsbury oversaw the doubling of the science budget, the hiring of large numbers of physics teachers, and the creation of a Higher Education Innovation Fund which successfully increased the transfer of knowledge from universities to British industry.

first thing the officials say in response is: 'Prove to us that this is a good use of public money.' But the point about innovation is you cannot prove that it will be successful because no one has tried it yet. Philanthropy and business are much better at innovation and risk-taking.

Give me an example of something that you've done, which you could do as a philanthropist but you couldn't do in government.

When we set up the Sainsbury Laboratory in Norwich in 1990 to study disease resistance in plants it was clearly a high-risk project. We also funded it fully, so the young researchers could focus on fundamental high-risk projects rather than spending all their time trying to get grants for small safe projects. As a strategy this has been very successful, but it was not something the government could do.

Big gifts by philanthropists can influence, or even skew, public policy. Our system of tax relief means that if a philanthropist makes a big donation to some personal interest of theirs, the taxpayer makes a significant contribution to it too. How are philanthropists to be held accountable for what they do with their money – and with some of ours?

You can only spend a charitable donation in specified areas, and that seems a necessary accountability. If you want more accountability, you could change those criteria. But I would be against a more elaborate form of accountability – because, it seems to me, the big argument in favour of charitable giving is that charities can take risks and support unpopular causes, things which are not everyone's favourite subject. That allows them to innovate and take risks in a way that public bodies can't. More control of that by public committees would lose that value.

Over the years you have given over £25m to political parties – Labour, the Social Democrats, the Liberal Democrats, the Remain campaign and even the Scottish Conservatives. Are the impulses and thought processes which have governed your political donations the same as those which motivated your philanthropic donations – or are they rather different?

No. They are very much the same. A major theme in both cases is: how do you create a dynamic economy which provides good jobs for all and facilitates social mobility?

In 2013 you and your wife Susie signed the Giving Pledge which commits you to give away more than half of your wealth to philanthropy during your lifetime, or in your wills. What was your thinking in signing that?

I was asked by Bill Gates to sign. I have a great admiration and respect for Bill because he's prepared to really get to know the areas where he's putting money and learn a lot about it before settling on very clear goals for changing things. I think he does that immensely well. Bill Gates's campaign to get wealthy people to give more money through philanthropy is also one I admire. We said when we signed the Giving Pledge: 'We do not believe that spending any more money on ourselves or our family would add anything to our happiness. However, using it to support social progress we have found deeply fulfilling.' We were very happy to sign.

Will Gatsby spend all its funds before you retire?

It carries on for 10 years after my death. There will then be significant endowments to the major organizations I want to see carrying out their missions long term.

It won't carry on indefinitely like the Rockefeller or Carnegie foundations?

No. Again, I agree with Bill Gates on this. I once heard him say: 'Look, in the future, there'll be new problems and there will be new people to deal with them. I don't want someone in 25 years' time looking at some musty old document and saying, "What would Bill Gates want us to do if he was alive today?"' All my daughters have their own charitable trusts because they wanted to. I encouraged that. They all do different things. We haven't really involved them in Gatsby at all. That goes back to the philosophy which says, 'You should do things which you really care about. They will not necessarily be the same things as your parents cared about.' That's one of the few bits of philosophy I have about philanthropy.

Chapter 7

The Philanthropist as Activist

The first man in English history to be called a philanthropist was not someone who gave large sums of his own money to good causes. Instead John Howard, the pioneer of prison reform, gave his time. In doing so he personified the way in which the eighteenth century turned philanthropy in a new direction. This was the era of the philanthropist as activist. John Howard was born in 1726 and came into a sizeable inheritance at the age of 16 when his father, a wealthy upholsterer, died, bequeathing him their country estate at Cardington in Bedfordshire. Howard did not know what to do with his legacy. After a strict Calvinist schooling, his father had apprenticed him to a wholesale grocer so he could learn the ways of business, but Howard had not enjoyed it. At the age of 22 he set out on a Grand Tour of the continent of Europe, as was the practice of fashionable young men at the time. On his return he became seriously ill and was nursed in lodgings by his landlady Sarah. Her care was so attentive and affectionate that he married her, despite being 25 while she was 52.[1] But marriage, like business, was not to bring him contentment. Sadly, Sarah died just three years after they wed and in 1755 Howard set off again on his travels in the hope of easing his bereavement. It was on this second trip that he was to discover the vocation which was to dominate the rest of his life.

As his packet ship, the *Hanover*, made its way to Portugal, it was seized by French privateers who treated him with great cruelty. Howard was stripped of money and clothes and thrown into a filthy, stinking dungeon in the castle at Brest on France's north-west coast and languished there in terrible conditions for six days without food, apart from a joint of mutton thrown into the cell which he and his fellow prisoners tore to pieces and gnawed like dogs. After being transferred to two other prisons along the French coast he was eventually released in exchange for a French naval officer. Back in London he called immediately on the Commissioners of Sick and Wounded Seamen to seek help on behalf of his fellow captives who were being treated with such barbarity that 'many hundreds had perished'.[2] Howard had encountered a cause which he was to pursue with extraordinary zeal for more than three decades.

THE FIRST ENGLISH PHILANTHROPIST

John Howard's humanity, nurtured by his Christian faith, was evident from the start. Soon after he took over his father's country estate at Cardington, he had the tenants' hovels pulled down and rebuilt, giving each their own simple cottage with a neat white-fenced kitchen garden in which to grow vegetables and potatoes. He set up an elementary school for their children. And he provided stocks of materials to give work to the under-employed. He financed all this from his personal fortune, and the sale of the jewellery of his second wife Henrietta.[3] But he saw it as his duty, also, to take a care of his tenants' moral as well as their physical welfare. In return for his improvements they were required to attend a divine service – of any denomination[4] – and avoid ale houses and cockfighting. After Henrietta also died, Howard once more set off in 1770 for an extended tour of the Continent, visiting France, Italy, Germany and Holland. At the end of his trip he wrote from Rotterdam: 'Very desirous am I of returning with a right spirit, not only wiser, but better; with a cheerful humility – a more general love and benevolence to my fellow creatures – watchful of my thoughts, my words, my actions – resigned to the will of God, that I may walk with God, and lead a more useful and honourable life in this world.'[5] It was like a manifesto for what was to follow. His reputation grew such that in 1773 he was appointed High Sheriff of Bedfordshire, among whose duties was the supervision of the county prison. His predecessors had delegated this chore to an under-sheriff, but Howard was motivated to do the job himself. On visiting Bedford Gaol he was appalled to discover that the conditions were not much better than those he had personally experienced in France. This led him to visit other gaols in the neighbourhood – and then beyond. The insanitary state of the dungeons horrified him. Prisoners were chained by the neck, waist, hands and feet in heavy irons. Many were almost naked without shirts, shoes or stockings. They slept on the floor on dirty straw which was often so old it had turned to dust, unless they could afford to pay for a bed at 3s. 6d. a week. If those on the floor wanted fresh straw it cost them a penny a day. The walls were filthy and had not been whitewashed for years. Gaol fever killed prisoners regularly; so did hunger and cold. Boys as young as 13 were confined along with hardened felons.

By the summer of 1774 Howard had visited almost every county gaol in England and Wales, and many prisons in cities and towns as well. He took the evidence he had gathered to the House of Commons, who were persuaded to pass two penal reform acts. The first of these was to end the practice of 'discharge fees' – these, Howard had been shocked to learn, were the sums of money which prisoners had to find to pay off their gaolers. Those in charge of the prisons, Howard had discovered, were not paid a salary by the state but earned a living from money taken from those in their charge. This created a perverse incentive for prisoners not to be released – even after they had been acquitted by the court. Unless they could find the money – not easy for those locked up in gaol – they were, in Howard's words, 'dragged back to gaol and locked up again till they should pay'.[6] The first of the 1774 Gaol Acts required that gaol discharge fees be paid by the county;[7] the other required changes to improve conditions with measures for adequate clean water and sewage systems, better hygiene and an upgraded diet for prisoners.[8] Howard had copies of both acts printed at his own expense and sent to every prison in the country.

But Howard was not satisfied. Over the next year he visited many English gaols for a second time to check whether the new laws were being enforced – and found that many gaolers were ignoring them. He decided to visit prisons elsewhere for comparative purposes. In 1775 he travelled to Scotland, Ireland, France, Switzerland, Germany, Flanders and the Netherlands. When he got back he embarked upon a second complete survey of English gaols. He was almost constantly on the road, travelling on horseback, averaging more than 40 miles a day. In England and Wales he was accompanied by his groom, John Prole, who kept his own records in addition to those of his master. The pair stayed in modest inns, as Howard did when he travelled by himself. His reputation was such that he gained easy access to most gaols. Where, overseas, he met resistance, he persevered and always got access by some method. By 1777 he had undertaken some 350 visits to

around 230 different institutions and assembled a wealth of material
which he published in a massive 500-page volume entitled *The State of
the Prisons in England and Wales, with Preliminary Observations, and an
Account of some Foreign Prisons.*

The work had an immediate impact. Despite, or perhaps because
of, his plain and understated writing style, Howard's detailed accounts
of the inhumane conditions of the nation's prisons caused widespread
dismay. In addition to his reports the book contained tables of fees,
regulations and statistics about prisoners and executions. It included
the plans of prisons which he admired. The book was widely read, not
least because Howard fixed the price of the volume so low, to ensure
wide distribution, that he failed to recover his printing costs – using his
personal fortune to finance his obsessive mission. He also gave away
many copies to people of influence. In 1778 Howard was visited by
Jeremy Bentham, the founder of the philosophical movement which
became known as utilitarianism. Bentham later recorded Howard's
working method:

> He carries his plan with him in his head. He is set down at the door
> of a prison, makes enquiries under a certain number of heads which
> exhaust the subject, does his business and drives off again to another.
> His thoughts, his conversation, his writings are confined to this one
> subject.[9]

As a result of his approach, Howard was to be lauded, a century later,
as a father of social science. It certainly made him the father of modern
penal reform, for the basic principle on which he operated – that
prison should transform inmates into better citizens rather than merely
punishing them – has remained at the heart of prison reform.

But still John Howard had not completed his self-imposed task. Next,
he toured the ships used for the detention of convicts condemned to be
transported to Australia, a practice suspended because of the outbreak of
the American War of Independence three years earlier. In 1778 Howard
gave evidence to the House of Commons, declaring conditions in these
prison hulks to be dangerously grim. Then, using the money left to him
by his sister who had died the year before, he set out on another tour
of European prisons. This time he was in search of good examples he
could bring back to present to the English public and Parliament. He

visited the Netherlands, Flanders and France once more – where, thanks to Anglo-French enmity over the struggle for American independence, he was forced to disguise himself as a fashionable Parisian gentleman to escape arrest in Toulon.[10] The French authorities, 'who could not possibly persuade themselves that he did this in his private capacity', presumed he was an English spy.[11] Then he visited gaols in Germany, Bohemia, Austria, Switzerland and Italy. Sometimes he presented himself as a doctor to gain entry,[12] but by now his celebrity had become international and doors were opened at the mere mention of his name, and not just prisons.

In Vienna he was invited to dinner by the Queen of Hungary. At table with the British ambassador he spoke critically of the prisons of the Emperor of Austria. Upon being chided by the diplomat and warned that his words would be reported to the monarch, Howard replied: 'What! Should my tongue be tied from speaking truth by any king or emperor in the world? I repeat what I asserted, and maintain its veracity.' A deep silence ensued at the table.[13] Yet when word did eventually reach Emperor Joseph II, the result was an invitation to an imperial audience. On Howard's next visit to Vienna, on Christmas Day 1786, the celebrated philanthropist had a private meeting with the Emperor at which the Englishman spoke frankly about the deplorable abuses and conditions he had seen in prisons throughout the imperial dominions, resulting in some improvements being made.

John Howard's boldness was rooted in his strong faith. Personally puritanical, he compulsively sought out God's purpose for him – which his Calvinist doctrine convinced him the Almighty had predestined. Each day he rose at 3 a.m. to work. So disciplined was he in his use of time that, when engaged in a conversation, he sat with a watch on his knee so that he could end the exchange at the time he had allowed for it in advance. Always frugal in his habits and plain in his dress, he grew more so as his mission progressed, becoming a teetotaller and vegetarian. Staying in a Capuchin monastery in Prague in 1778, Howard was shocked at the self-indulgence of the monks. So much so that he upbraided the Capuchins and refused to join them at their table 'sumptuously furnished with all the delicacies the season could afford'. Their monastery, which ought to be a place of abstemiousness and prayer, he said, was instead 'a house of revelling and drunkenness'. Moreover, he added as a parting shot, as he left to stay in a hotel instead,

he was going later to Rome where he would make the Pope acquainted
with the impropriety of their conduct. Next morning several of the holy
friars turned up at his hotel to plead with him not to report them to the
pontiff. The nonconformist Englishman rather grandly responded that
he could make no promise but that if they pledged to mend their ways
'he might . . . be silent on what was past'.[14]

Howard was always high-minded in his campaigning, preoccupied
with the moral as well as the physical condition of those he found
incarcerated. In Rome, in a prison for boys and dissolute young men
attached to the Hospital of S. Michele, he found a Latin inscription
Parum est coercere improbos poena nisi probos efficias disciplina, which he
translated as 'For the correction and instruction of profligate youth: that
they, who, when idle were injurious, might when instructed be useful
to the state.' Howard declared that, in that simple phrase, 'the grand
purpose of all civil policy relative to criminals is expressed: it is of little
advantage to restrain the Bad by Punishment unless you render them
Good by Discipline.' Howard felt, said his friend Dr John Aikin, that
'he would almost have thought it worth his while to have gone to Rome
for this sentence alone'.[15] But in that city Howard was, indeed, invited
to meet Pope Pius VI, who waived the requirement of his visitor to kiss
the papal toe as was customary. An eyewitness recorded the encounter
between the English Dissenter and the Holy Father:

> It was a noble thing to see these two illustrious men – alike remarkable
> for their public virtues and their private sorrows – casting aside the
> traditional and religious antipathy which each conscientiously felt
> towards the creed of the other, and meeting together as men and as
> Christians on the common ground of human charity. At parting, the
> pious pontiff laid his hand upon the head of the distinguished heretic,
> saying good-humoredly, 'I know you Englishmen care nothing for
> these things, but the blessing of an old man can do you no harm.' A
> truly noble and catholic sentiment, which his visitor was too large-
> minded not to accept in a becoming spirit.[16]

There is no record of whether Howard reported to the Pope the
behaviour of the hard-drinking Capuchins of Prague.

Yet Howard consorted with the rich and powerful only when it suited
his purpose. Moving on to St Petersburg in 1781, the philanthropist

was summoned to appear before the Empress of Russia, Catherine the Great. Howard immediately declined the invitation and told the messenger from the imperial court 'with his usual frankness . . . that he had devoted himself to the task of visiting the dungeon of the captive and the abode of the wretched, not the palaces and courts of kings and empresses – and that the limited time which he had to stay in the capital would not allow of his calling upon her imperial majesty'.[17] Instead, after a tour of the Russian capital's gaols, and a meeting with the executioner who whipped people to death with a barbarous device known as a knout, Howard set out for Moscow, travelling by carriage over 500 miles in less than five days, 'never having his clothes off either by night or day'.[18] Even when stricken by fever, and so sick he could hardly hold up his head, he insisted on continuing his progress.

At the end of his journeys he had travelled a total of 42,033 miles. By now his reputation had become as prodigious as his travelling. Edmund Burke, in a speech at the Guildhall in Bristol before the general election of 1780, made mention of John Howard and then added:

> I cannot name this gentleman without remarking that his labours and writings have done much to open the eyes and hearts of mankind. He has visited all Europe – not to survey the sumptuousness of palaces, or the stateliness of temples; not to make accurate measurements of the remains of ancient grandeur, nor to form a scale of the curiosity of modern art; not to collect medals, or collate manuscripts – but to dive into the depths of dungeons, to plunge into the infection of hospitals; to survey the mansions of sorrow and pain; to take the gauge and measure of misery, depression and contempt, to remember the forgotten, to attend to the neglected, to visit the forsaken, and compare and collate the distresses of all men in all countries. His plan is original; and it is as full of genius as it is of humanity. It was a voyage of discovery, a circumnavigation of charity. Already the benefit of his labour is felt more or less in every country.[19]

Howard fiercely resisted the acclaim. His philanthropy was, throughout his life, guided by the biblical principle: 'When thou doest alms, let not thy left hand know what thy right hand doeth: that thine alms may be in secret.'[20] When 615 of his admirers subscribed together to erect a statue of him in 1786, he sent a message from Vienna to the

Gentleman's Magazine insisting that the project be abandoned. 'Have I not one friend in England that would put a stop to such a proceeding?' he wrote to the journal. Yet Howard was pleased to be able to record, in *An Account of the Principal Lazarettos in Europe*, the last work he ever published, an accolade of an altogether humbler kind:

> In all my visits to the gaols and prisons, in this, and other kingdoms I never received any insults either from keepers or prisoners, nor have I lost anything in any of them, except, that in one of our prisons, I once lost a large new handkerchief out of my pocket, which I did not miss for some time, but on a subsequent visit, about ten months after, it was immediately presented to me by a prisoner, as he said, he believed that I had dropped it when I was here last.[21]

The book in which that is recorded was the fruit of the final period his life. While in Europe in 1785 he had begun to become interested in measures to control the plague, an extension of his campaigning to eliminate gaol fever. Having witnessed many cases of malignant fever – and having, on several occasions, caught fevers from which he almost died – he became persuaded of the effectiveness of a contemporary remedy known as Dr James's Powders with which he had treated himself and others. Howard became convinced that they might cure the plague and determined to make the dangerous journey beyond the boundaries of Europe to test his theory. He had already visited quarantine units – *lazarettos* – in Marseilles, Genoa, Leghorn, Naples, Valetta, Zante, Corfu and Venice to discover how plague victims were treated and how cargoes from plague areas were fumigated or purged. He had even deliberately travelled on a ship with a foul cargo – and did not catch the plague, though he had to spend 40 days afterwards in quarantine in a lazaretto. It seemed he might be immune. Even when Howard was in the presence of those with the contagion, he did not catch it.

In Constantinople at the time of Howard's visit, a virulent plague was raging, yet he fearlessly visited hospitals and entered the dwellings of the dying and the dead. Called upon to treat the daughter of a prominent member of the Ottoman elite, though he had no medical training he applied the knowledge he had acquired on his travels and treated her successfully. Her father pressed upon Howard a princely purse in gratitude, but the philanthropist would take as reward only a

Among the Ancient Greeks philanthropy was seen primarily as a device to strengthen social relationships. Its purpose, said Aristotle (*above*), was to improve the moral character of the giver – but it must also consider the needs of the recipient.

The Romans saw philanthropy in part as a political investment to buy the favour of the people. Those who gave money – for temples, public baths, roads or aqueducts – often erected a stone with the inscription *de sua pecunia fecit* (DSPF) or Done with His Own Money. Here the Roman Emperor Trajan boasts of extending the Appian Way from Benevuto to Brindisium.

Judaism brought a revolution to philanthropy. God had a special love for the poor and therefore so should all believers. Giver and receiver were bound together with God and the entire community in a mutual relationship. Later the Jewish sage Maimonides (*right*) codified giving into a Ladder with eight stages of ascending merit. The highest is helping others towards self-sufficiency.

Ambrose of Milan in 386AD wrote the first great work on Christian philanthropy, synthesizing Roman Stoic principles with the Jewish vision of charity. He insisted that the rich should give priority to the destitute, widows and orphans – before close relatives.

Basil the Great in the 4th century insisted that giving is not merely a matter of honour, status, civic duty or imitation of God. It is a question of justice. He spent his own fortune on famine relief, created the model for the modern monastery and opened the world's first hospital for the general sick.

For a thousand years, from the 5th to the 15th century, giving was regulated throughout Europe by the Catholic Church. Charity was institutionalised in a system of tithes. Parishes distributed alms. Monasteries offered hospitality for travellers, nursed the sick, and cared for widows, orphans and the destitute. Church thinkers systematized rules on giving from which none were exempt. Kings, like Louis IX of France (*above*), in the 13th century still personally washed the feet of the poor. Feudal society trapped serfs and peasants in lives of economic hardship but religion created a spiritual bond between giver and receiver which has been lost in much philanthropy today.

During the Black Death (1347-51) pious sects whipped themselves in the streets, asking God to end the plague (*above, 1493 woodcut*). After the pandemic many of these flagellants turned to philanthropy. A tide of vagrant beggars swept the continent, provoking the rich to develop a much more hostile attitude to the poor. The new idea that the poor were in some way to blame for their own poverty was to shape philanthropy for the next four centuries. It still lingers today.

A hundred years before the Reformation, cities grew in size and wealth and control of philanthropy shifted from priests to lay people. In Florence, a rich silk merchant, Felice Brancacci, commissioned frescoes (*above*) in his family chapel showing 15th century Italian merchants with the apostles distributing alms.

The word philanthropy was imported into England from France from the philosophers of the 18th century Enlightenment. It denoted a social activist rather than a giver of money. The first man in England to be called a philanthropist was the prison reformer John Howard (*below*). Perhaps the best known of these 'agitator philanthropists' was William Wilberforce (*left*). In addition to his life-long campaign to abolish slavery, he also supported scores of other causes including vaccination, hospital and factory reform, and also fought to end bear-baiting.

BARONESS BURDETT-COUTTS

The great Victorian philanthropist, Angela Burdett-Coutts at first spent her huge banking inheritance on charities and projects tinged with moral reform and social control. Later, influenced by Charles Dickens (*above left*), she gave to those at the bottom of the heap: prostitutes and paupers, flower girls and chimney sweep boys. This 'Queen of the Poor' was so popular that she featured on cigarette cards (*above right*) and her funeral eulogy was given by King Edward VII.

Statement of JESUS CHRIST

Showing (1) how the family are at present obtaining a living ; and (2) in what manner applicant thinks they can be permanently benefited, etc.

Applicant stated that he lived almost entirely upon alms, principally obtained from women. He tramped about with a number of low fellows who sometimes did odd jobs, fishing and the like. They had been accused, he admitted, of stealing an ass's foal, and had the reputation of being infidels, and violators of law and order. When asked how the Society could benefit him, applicant asked for a little temporary relief while he was propagating his economic and moral views. He also asked to be introduced to the other applicants, but was told that this was against Charity Organisation Society rules.

The following should be the order of reporting information received relative to the Case from : (1) Relieving Officer ; (2) Previous Addresses; (3) Present and Former Employers; (4) References; (5) Clergy and District Visitors; (6) Children's Schoolmaster; (7) School Board Visitor and other Persons; (8) Inquiry Officer's Report.

Heads of Information Dated and Numbered as above.		Report.
Date.	No.	
July 3	1	Report.—The relieving officer said that he had no knowledge of applicant, except that he heard once of him from his (officer's) grandmother. The people living at applicant's previous addresses also knew nothing about him, except his name; one man had seen his picture, and another said he heard that he wrote a book about hell. Applicant's former employers were all dead, and modern employers " had no need of such hands " (referring no doubt to certain marks applicant had accidentally received, for the committee noticed that his hands were bleeding). The references were wholly unsatisfactory and inadequate.
,, 4	2	
,, 5	3	
,, 6	4	
,, 7	5	The Right Reverend Caiaphas and the Reverend Pharisees and the Church-workers and Scribes all said that applicant, though a powerful preacher, had a devilish spirit and radically unsound and dangerous views. He set class against class, discouraged thrift, spake with blasphemous familiarity of God, called the rich and the rulers names, etc. They begged the Society not to assist him in any way.
,, 18	8	Inquiry Officer thought, that though applicant looked a good fellow and strong, the heat of the weather had affected his brain. He talked a great deal about his Father and his mansions, but his father was said to be dead, and applicant could not tell where the mansions were, but told officer they were " within." He asked officer to give up Charity Organisation Society work and to follow him, but refused to guarantee any stipend. Applicant appeared to believe in a Social Revolution, which should make the last first and the first last, but officer refused to waste time upon him.
,, 28		Applicant appeared before the committee, and was rebuked for his utter want of thrift, industry, temperance, and for the bad company he kept. He was offered a set of carpenter's tools by a lady if he would return to carpentry, but the Society refused to do anything for him, except recommend him to go to the infirmary, lunatic department, or else to live a more business-like and practical life.

The Society for Organising Charitable Relief and Repressing Mendicity (later the Charity Organisation Society) was the most powerful Victorian philanthropic institution. It aimed at the moral reform of the poor – and a 'scientific philanthropy' to prevent cunning able-bodied paupers exploiting charities. Critics said its initials stood for 'Cringe Or Starve'. One submitted a mock application to the COS (*above*) on behalf of an itinerant preacher named Jesus Christ. He was refused assistance.

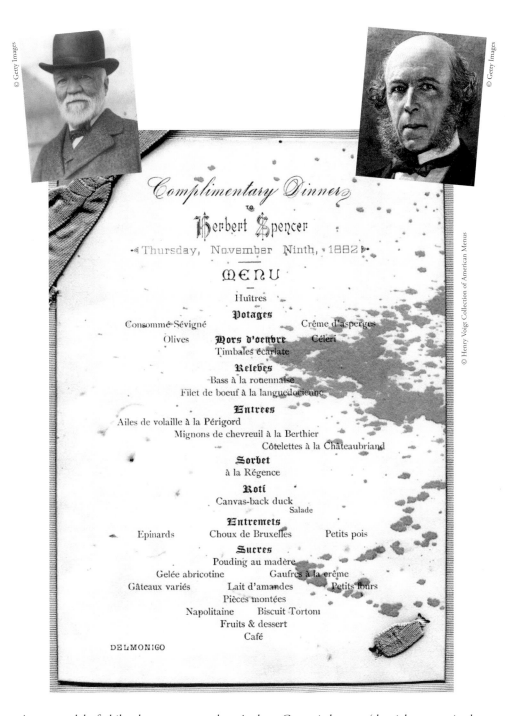

Complimentary Dinner
to
Herbert Spencer
◄ Thursday, November Ninth, 1882 ►
MENU

Huîtres

Potages

Consommé Sévigné   Crême d'asperges

Olives   **Hors d'oeuvre**   Céleri

Timbales écarlate

Relevés

Bass à la rouennaise

Filet de boeuf à la languedocienne

Entrees

Ailes de volaille à la Périgord

Mignons de chevreuil à la Berthier

Côtelettes à la Châteaubriand

Sorbet

à la Régence

Roti

Canvas-back duck

Salade

Entremets

Epinards   Choux de Bruxelles   Petits pois

Sucres

Pouding au madère

Gelée abricotine   Gaufres à la crême

Gâteaux variés   Lait d'amandes   Petits fours

Pièces montées

Napolitaine   Biscuit Tortoni

Fruits & dessert

Café

DELMONICO

A new model of philanthropy was set when Andrew Carnegie became 'the richest man in the world' in 1901. Carnegie (*above left*) followed the philosopher Herbert Spencer (*above right*) in applying Darwin's theory of evolution to human society. It was Spencer, not Darwin, who invented the phrase 'survival of the fittest'. The new super-rich took this to mean that bosses were superior to their workers – and better suited to decide how their philanthropy should be spent. When the inventor of this Social Darwinism visited New York, he was feted by Carnegie and his fellows with a lavish dinner at Delmonico's. The menu (*above*) survives, complete with rich gravy stains.

Andrew Carnegie was not only the biggest philanthropist of the Gilded Age of Philanthropy, he also invented the idea that 'he who dies rich, dies disgraced' – a philosophy that inspired generations of later mega-givers including Bill Gates. Carnegie's giving was on an unprecedented scale, building 3,000 libraries, parks, art galleries, museums and concert halls around the world. It inspired laudatory cartoons (*right*). But he attracted satirical attacks in equal measure like the one (*below*) which shows him dispensing ill-gotten largesse obtained by cutting the wages of his workers in the steel industry.

FORTY-MILLIONAIRE CARNEGIE IN HIS GREAT DOUBLE ROLE.
AS THE TI GHT-FISTED EMPLOYER HE REDUCES WAGES THAT HE MAY PLAY PHILANTHROPIST AND GIVE AWAY LIBRARIES, ETC.

sumptuous bunch of grapes from the family garden.[22] Throughout he insisted on scrupulous cleanliness, washing his hands constantly when treating the walls of his residences with fresh lime-wash and boiling water.[23] Howard became even more strict in his vegetarian diet, though he had already subsisted for years on no more than vegetables and water, with a little bread and green tea. (His only indulgence on his travels was a little brass tea kettle, teapot, and cups and saucers.) Once asked how he protected himself from infection, he replied, with temperance, cleanliness, and the goodness and mercy of God.[24]

Shielded only by those qualities John Howard now determined to leave England once again to venture into Russia, Turkey, Egypt and the shores of Barbary in pursuit of a cure for the plague. But this time he set off filled with foreboding that he might never return. In November 1789, having settled his affairs at home, he bade a solemn farewell to his friends and tenants. He clearly had some premonition of what might transpire from his work on the plague. In *An Account of the Principal Lazarettos in Europe* he had written:

I am not insensible of the dangers that must attend such a journey. Trusting, however, in the protection of that kind Providence which has hitherto preserved me, I calmly and cheerfully commit myself to the disposal of unerring wisdom. Should it please God to cut off my life in the prosecution of this design, let not my conduct be uncandidly imputed to rashness or enthusiasm, but to a serious deliberate conviction that I am pursuing the path of duty.

That sense of duty took him through the Netherlands, Germany, Poland and Russia to Kherson in what is now Ukraine where, on his final hospital visit, he contracted typhus fever (not plague) and died, aged 63, on 20 January 1790. He was buried on the shores of the Black Sea. His philanthropy had resigned him to his fate. In one of his last letters, to his friend Dr Price, he had written: 'my medical acquaintance give me but little hopes of escaping the plague in Turkey', in spite of which 'I labour to convey the torch of Philanthropy into these distant regions, as in God's hand no Instrument is weak.'[25] John Howard's death was announced in the *London Gazette*, a rare honour for a commoner. The statue he had so long avoided was commissioned by public subscription and, despite his being a Dissenter, became the first statue of a civilian to be admitted to St Paul's Cathedral. The inscription on the plinth of the statue erected near the entrance to the crypt reads: 'In every part of the civilised world, which he traversed to reduce the sum of human misery; from the Throne to the Dungeon his name was mentioned with respect, gratitude and admiration.'[26] More simply, the writing over his grave reads: 'Whoever thou art, thou standest at the tomb of thy friend.'[27] John Howard's extraordinary activism had changed the face of English philanthropy.

THE NEW PHILANTHROPY OF THE ENLIGHTENMENT

The model for John Howard's new approach to philanthropy had arrived in England from the Continent. In France, at the start of the eighteenth century, a new style of thinking marked the start of what came to be known as the Enlightenment. The word *philanthropie* first appeared in 1712 in an essay by a Catholic archbishop and theologian François Fénelon entitled *Dialogues of the Dead*. The essay, written in his role as tutor to the grandson of King Louis XIV, created an imagined three-way conversation between the philosopher Socrates, the misanthrope Timon of Athens and the politician Alcibiades. In it Fénelon makes a distinction between fake and true philanthropy. Fake philanthropy is the kind practised by Alcibiades. It is driven by a corrupt desire 'to please men, to dazzle them, and flatter them' and act as a 'baited hook' to catch a fish. By contrast the true philanthropy of Socrates is selfless, quiet, and seeks primarily to assist others.[28] As previous chapters have shown, there was nothing new in this contrast, but Fénelon's restatement was to prove extremely influential, not least because of his prominent position at the royal court. His Socrates argued that even if men are flawed, we have a responsibility to love them and do them good – and not expect anything in return.[29]

In parallel with this Catholic notion was an idea central to Freemasonry, which made its first appearance in France around the same time, though its members in the 1720s were mostly émigrés from the English, Irish and Scottish elites. Its foundational document was a 1737 discourse by the Scottish philosopher Andrew Michael Ramsay, a tutor to the exiled Bonnie Prince Charlie and a Christian universalist who held that all people would eventually be saved. He held the four essential Masonic qualities to be 'sound morals', secrecy, a taste for science and the fine arts, and philanthropy – by which he meant both mutual assistance between Masonic brothers but also a concern for the well-being of the whole human race.[30] Ramsay was keen to get endorsement for his discourse from the Catholic authorities, but they firmly rejected it – a development which was to give a distinctly anti-clerical or even anti-religious tone to the way philanthropy developed in France. There Enlightenment philosophers, schooled in rationalism and imbued with an optimistic view of human nature, increasingly promoted philanthropy as a secular alternative to Christian charity.[31]

At first philanthropy was embraced by secular and religious alike. Prominent rationalists, such as Diderot and D'Alembert, and the Jesuits of the time, all adopted the word *philanthropie* from Fénelon. One rationalist wrote that it was integral to the nature of man that he had an interest in the well-being of his fellows – since each man recognizes other men as being like him. The Jesuits came to the same conclusion; *bienfaisance* (beneficence) was the true religion and the main purpose of the Gospel, they wrote.[32] Beneficence, expanded Voltaire, in his *Philosophical Dictionary* in 1764, is due to all regardless of their faith or personal morals. The word *philanthrope* (philanthropist) was defined as 'he who by disposition and natural goodness is inclined to love all men' in the 1762 French Academy *Dictionary*, and as 'the friend of mankind' in the 1771 edition of the Jesuit dictionary, the *Trévoux*. Since man was by nature good, according to the philosophy of the Enlightenment, society was therefore perfectible. So the first and highest virtue must be a universal affection for humanity demonstrated in doing good to others.

By the eve of the French Revolution, the concept of *philanthropie* had developed from an abstract philosophical virtue and had become a doctrine of action among the reformist elites. In 1780 came the foundation of the *Société Philanthropique de Paris*, created by seven members of the French bourgeoisie – an industrialist, a banker, two doctors, a scientist, a philosopher and a public official – two of whom were prominent Freemasons. The model swiftly spread beyond the French capital. Philanthropic societies were soon founded in other French towns, in Brussels, in London and in the United States (where the Philadelphia Society for Alleviating the Miseries of Public Prisons was formed in 1786). The manifesto that the *Société* drew up in 1787, just two years before the outbreak of the French Revolution, declared that philanthropic activity was the prime duty of any citizen.[33]

In practice many of the immediate aims of these societies had much in common with those of over a thousand years of Christian charity: they targeted their assistance on octogenarians, families with large numbers of children, workers injured by industrial accidents and young blind people. Moreover, they spoke not just of supporting the Parisian poor but of restoring their dignity. But, in addition to traditional charitable almsgiving, the societies were keen to find innovative, more scientific, ways to practise their philanthropy. These included pensions for the disabled, schools for the blind, campaigns to abolish the slave trade and reform prisons, and the establishment of insurance and mutual benefit systems. The first social statistics in France were developed by philanthropic societies, which conducted field surveys and investigations to understand the roots of social ills.

The label of philanthropist was now attached to any inventor or innovator. One such was Piarron de Chamousset, a doctor who in the 1760s abolished the practice of hospital beds being shared by as many as five people. Another was the German educationalist Johann Bernhard Basedow,[34] a friend of Goethe, who created innovative teaching methods based on conversation and play, and developed them into a new style of school which he called a *philanthropinum*. In the 1770s a philanthropist became any public figure admired in liberal or progressive circles – Turgot, the tax reformer and early pioneer of economic liberalism; Antoine-Augustin Parmentier, the nutritionist and promoter of the virtues of the potato, who also set up the first mandatory smallpox vaccination campaign; and Benjamin Franklin, the first American ambassador to France, a polymath who invented bifocals and the lightning rod, among other things.[35]

In France philanthropy now took a distinctly anti-clerical turn. To the new rationalists 'love of mankind' neither required the intercession of God nor was to be channelled through Catholic institutions. Voltaire had been even more critical of the Church, insisting that philanthropists, however vainglorious and driven by venal personal motives, were more virtuous than prayerful hermits. Philanthropists, he said, improved society without expecting personal salvation in return. Many French philanthropists contrasted their new activity with the historical failure of Christian charity to eradicate poverty. In the years after the French Revolution, *philanthrope* became a synonym for *patriote* (patriot) – a supporter of the Revolution and the First French Republic, which was deeply hostile to Christianity.

But the secularizing influence of the French Enlightenment, in its harshest anti-religious form, was not an approach which travelled across the Channel to England. In Britain philanthropy was not contrasted with religion; indeed, religious motivations remained a key driver in the development of philanthropy, as the example of John Howard has shown. But the English adopted entirely the new French notion of the philanthropist as an activist rather than a mere donor.

WILLIAM WILBERFORCE AND THE PHILANTHROPIST AS 'A MAN OF FEELING'

The England into which this new philanthropic sensibility was imported was one where the relationship between rich and poor was still dominated by the model set by the Elizabethan Poor Law. Over the previous 100 years the state had continued to attempt to control the behaviour of the poor and restrict their movements. In 1662 the Act for the Better Relief of the Poor of this Kingdom – otherwise known as the Settlement Act[36] – was passed. It allowed a parish to attempt to reduce its bill for poor relief by deporting those requiring assistance. It allowed those deemed to be 'likely to be chargeable' on the parish poor rates to be returned to their place of origin, which was usually the place where they were born or grew up. This was referred to as their place of 'settlement' regardless of how long they had been away from it. A woman was deemed to share the place of settlement of the man she had married, and a child the place of settlement of his father. Only illegitimate children were granted settlement in the place where they were born – a fact unpalatable to some parish overseers, who would try to get rid of an unmarried pregnant woman before the child was born. Sometimes they transported her to another parish just before the birth. At other times they paid a man from another parish to marry her.

Further refinements to this practice were embodied in the Poor Relief Act of 1691,[37] when it was deemed that a boy who had been apprenticed – which could happen any time from the age of seven – would take the place of his apprenticeship as his place of settlement. It also declared that anyone who had been in continuous employment for at least a year would switch their place of settlement to their place of work.

Reluctant parishes tried to get round this by encouraging employers to give contracts of work for 364 days rather than a full year. Labourers who were reluctant to find themselves trapped in a disagreeable parish might, conversely, quit their job before the year was up.

The new philanthropy was in stark contrast to that. It wanted to drive change through the action of individuals rather than the state. And it wanted to replace the cold policy of the Poor Law with the zeal of personal mission. The philanthropist was now a 'man of feeling' in an age in which a 'cult of sensibility' held that moral truths could be uncovered by examining our emotional responses to experiences. The impact of this on philanthropy was summed up in the comment of Isaac Wood, one of the directors of the Shrewsbury House of Industry, a workhouse which placed great emphasis on the training of the young. In 1795 Wood wrote a proud account of its nursery, school room and manufactory, and also of the philanthropists he showed around. Visitors were not only interested, he recorded, they also became moved emotionally. 'I have seen the tear of benevolent sensibility trembling in the eye of [John] Howard, and several other exalted characters, as I have accompanied them through the working rooms . . . where they frequently stopped to indulge their generous emotions.'[38] Compassion in France, according to the French historian Katherine Ibbett, had been in the seventeenth century 'wrenched away from a private devotional context to become a masculine and public emotion',[39] but in England, by contrast, it had become gendered as female. That was to change. A fervour and zeal had returned to philanthropy. It had a double mission – to reform society and to reform the poor.

No one embodied this more than William Wilberforce. History has remembered him as the man who led the movement to abolish the slave trade, much as it remembers Howard with the single focus of a prison reformer. Certainly Wilberforce was tireless in his efforts which began in 1787 with the formation in London of the Society for Effecting the Abolition of the Slave Trade. Bills introduced by him in Parliament were defeated by vested interests in 1791, 1792, 1793, 1797, 1798, 1799, 1804 and 1805, but he persevered. When, in 1807, the slave trade was finally abolished in the British colonies, making it illegal to carry enslaved people in British ships, Wilberforce became a national hero. Next he moved to abolish not just the British slave trade but to outlaw it internationally, with Britain leading efforts to blockade the

THE PHILANTHROPIST AS ACTIVIST

slave ships of other nations. He finally saw slavery abolished throughout the British Empire with the 1833 Slavery Abolition Act – passed, providentially, just three days before he died. But there was more to Wilberforce than the fight against slavery. He incarnated the spirit of this new philanthropy in the wide range of his other interests, all of them focused upon the object of a total reform of English society.

As a boy Wilberforce had spent several years living with his Aunt Hannah, whose brother was the Christian philanthropist John Thornton, an international merchant who had inherited wealth from his father, a former director of the Bank of England. By the time of his death in 1790, Thornton had amassed the second largest fortune in all of Europe, despite having given away hundreds of thousands of pounds to charitable and evangelical activities throughout his lifetime. Thornton was known to give away half his annual income each year. Hannah was also friendly with a man Wilberforce always referred to as 'old Newton', the former slave trader John Newton, who became an evangelical minister and is now best known for having written the hymn 'Amazing Grace'.[40]

Yet despite this uncompromising family background William Wilberforce had drifted into a dissolute life as an undergraduate at Cambridge. As a young socialite in London he joined no fewer than five exclusive gentleman's clubs and got heavily into drinking and gambling. A dilettante interest in politics led him to stand for parliament, and Wilberforce, who had inherited a large fortune from his grandfather, spent £8,000 of it (around half a million pounds in today's money) campaigning to become MP for his native city of Hull in 1780. He continued his libertine lifestyle. But four years later he underwent an evangelical conversion – something which was deeply unfashionable in polite society at the time. He secretly sought advice from Newton about resigning as an MP and becoming a religious minister. Wilberforce had began to feel contempt for his wealth and the luxury in which he lived and bemoaned the 'shapeless idleness' of his past. But Newton told Wilberforce it was God's intention that he should remain in Parliament, telling him: 'It is hoped and believed that the Lord has raised you up for the good of his church and for the good of the nation.'[41]

On Sunday 28 October 1787 – not long after his conversion to Christianity – William Wilberforce wrote in his diary: 'God Almighty has placed before me two great objects, the suppression of the slave trade and the reformation of manners.'[42] To Wilberforce 'manners' did not mean etiquette but 'morals'. He considered British society in his time to be degenerate, inveighing against 'the torrent of profaneness that every day makes more rapid advances';[43] it could only be saved, in his view, by both a revival of individual Christian observance and a revitalization of the Church. In April 1797 Wilberforce published *A Practical View of the Prevailing Religious System of Professed Christians in the Higher and Middle Classes of This Country Contrasted With Real Christianity*. It was an exposition of New Testament teachings, illustrated by his own personal testimony. It called for his fellow citizens to abandon their token embrace of Christianity and, instead, be converted to a vibrant evangelical conviction. Only such a revival of 'real Christianity' could arrest the moral decline of the nation. The book was a bestseller by the standards of the day and was translated into several languages. His words were embodied in his deeds. Wilberforce made goodness fashionable.[44]

In addition to his tireless campaigning over slavery Wilberforce – dubbed 'the prime minister of philanthropy' – was active in support of 69 philanthropic causes for the welfare of society.[45] These included campaigns to secure smallpox vaccination; improve conditions in hospital care, fever institutions, infirmaries, and asylums; champion orphans, single mothers and juvenile delinquents; protect child textile factory workers and chimney sweeps; aid victims of shipwreck, French refugees and other foreigners in distress; ban duelling in England and suttee in India; limit capital punishment and the severe punishments meted out under the Game Laws; and eliminate bear-baiting and other forms of cruelty to animals. Wilberforce was not a force for change in all areas. His evangelical Christianity made him conservative in some areas of domestic policy where he thought the moral reform of the poor was needed; he spoke in favour of government moves to outlaw meetings of seditious British workers and suppress trade unions. He supported the suspension of *habeas corpus* and opposed an inquiry into the Peterloo Massacre in which troops launched a murderous onslaught against a political meeting in Manchester in 1819, killing eleven people.[46] William Cobbett, as a result, branded him a hypocrite.[47] Wilberforce also disapproved of women anti-slavery activists as 'unsuited to the female character as delineated in Scripture'. But overall he was active in the public relief of poverty, popular education and prison conditions. In addition to all that, annually he gave away at least a quarter of his income, donating thousands of pounds every year to clergymen to distribute in their parishes. He paid off others' debts, supported education, and in a year of food shortages his donations to charity actually exceeded his income. So personally charitable was William Wilberforce that his home was full of old and incompetent servants whom he could not bear to sack.[48]

REFORMING THE POOR

William Wilberforce was far from alone in the emotional intensity of his desire for reform. Other philanthropists also considered themselves to be men and women of feeling. But they too wore the heavy imprint of the century of poor law begun under the Elizabethans. The desire of these philanthropists for change focused less on society in general, and more on the need, as they saw it, for moral reform among the poor. The workhouse was by now the dominant institution of the poor law. But what had begun as a place to provide work for the able-bodied jobless had now largely become a punitive deterrent. In 1723 the Workhouse Test Act[49] compelled all those seeking poor relief to enter a workhouse. The act was designed to keep costs down in the local parishes by ensuring – at a time when the numbers of the poor continue to increase – that only the totally destitute would claim poor relief. The hope was that it would also increase the nation's productivity. A publication in 1725 which described the operation of over 100 workhouses, entitled *An Account of Several Workhouses for Employing and Maintaining the Poor*, expressed the hope that the workhouse would solve three problems at once. It would 'answer all the Ends of Charity to the Poor, in regard to their Souls and Bodies'. It would at the same time assist by 'increasing our Manufactures, as well as removing a heavy Burden from the Nation'.[50] And it would also introduce 'among the poor, habits of sobriety, obedience, and industry, which will . . . lay such a foundation for the future comfort of [the] poor as will make them useful to one another, and not a little beneficial to the public'.[51]

Parishes in large cities had banded together to form Corporations of the Poor specifically to build workhouses all across the country, from Bristol to Norwich, between 1696 and 1712. They were supported by a new kind of organization – Societies for the Reformation of

Manners which had been set up as part of a moral revolution after the Catholic King James II was replaced by the Protestants William and Mary in 1689. These societies aimed to suppress popular vices, lewd entertainment, masquerades, theatres, fairs, skittle grounds outside taverns, prostitution, pornography, homosexuality, keeping unlicensed ale houses, swearing and drunkenness – and failure to attend the Anglican church on Sundays. They brought more than a thousand prosecutions a year.[52] The result was 'a puritanical and militant philanthropy' directed particularly at the behaviour of the lower classes.[53] So much so that the Society for the Suppression of Vice was later renamed by Reverend Sydney Smith 'The Society for the Suppressing of the Vices of persons whose incomes do not exceed £500 per annum'. Smith wrote: 'A man of £10,000 a year may worry a fox much as he pleases [but] a poor labourer is carried before the magistrate for paying a sixpence to see an exhibition of courage between a dog and a bear'.[54]

The emphasis on moral reform increased in the 1720s and 1730s. The recently founded Society for the Promotion of Christian Knowledge, which had lobbied for the passing of the Workhouse Test Act, began running its own workhouses with the aim of instilling piety into the poor. The Society injected an element of both religious idealism and philanthropic ideology into the workhouse movement. Earlier enthusiasts for the system liked the workhouse because it reduced the drain on the public purse caused by poor relief; some also saw the workhouse essentially as a mechanism to control a dangerous vagabond class. But the SPCK viewed it through a theological lens, returning to the Elizabethan notion that poverty somehow reflected a moral failing on the part of the poor.

To these Christian campaigners 'anyone sinful enough to end in a workhouse had first to be inured to labour, then brought to God, and through religion given a criterion for [better] behaviour, and finally through workhouse discipline forced to adopt an habitual and virtuous way of living', writes Tim Hitchcock, an historian who has specialized in the relationship between eighteenth-century paupers and preachers.[55] 'At the heart of all the Society's activities was the belief that no-one could be both devout and lazy'. Hence to cure the poor of their idleness and cure them of their lack of piety was one and the same thing.[56] And making the poor more pious would also make them more industrious. Crucial to this, in the eyes of the SPCK reformers, was educating the children of the poor to 'inculcate in them moral attitudes and the teaching of the Protestant religion'. Schools figured prominently inside the workhouses.[57] The Society believed that the catechism, learned young, was the key to national reform.[58] The same philosophy lay behind the hundreds of charity schools which it founded across the nation.

PHILANTHROPY BY SUBSCRIPTION

Charity schools, like charity hospitals, boomed in the early eighteenth century. Support for both was fed by the new appetite for moral reform, as is shown by a sermon delivered in 1746 entitled *Hospitals and Infirmaries Considered as Schools of Christian Education for the Adult Poor: and as a Means Conducive Towards a National Reformation in the Common Peoples*. But what gave these schools particular impetus was a new method of financing. In the eighteenth century, as David Owen noted, 'charity became less a person-to-person affair . . . and more of a collective effort'.[59] The British economy at this point was being increasingly driven by a new device – the joint-stock company in which investors pooled their finances by becoming shareholders in a limited company. The same model was now transferred to philanthropy.

Charitable giving became increasingly financed by funds gathered from named subscribers. The subscription now usurped money left in wills as the prime engine of philanthropy. The significant philanthropists of the period thus came from middle-class backgrounds. *Noblesse oblige*, Owen wrote, had turned into *richesse oblige*. Donors now came overwhelmingly from trade and commerce rather than from great families.[60] These subscriptions, unlike the small donations to twenty-first-century charities, were for substantial amounts. Only the wealthy members of the new commercial classes, together with a handful of aristocrats, could afford the amounts which were fashionable. But in eighteenth-century society it was an important way of signalling social status for the *nouveau riche* to have their names seen on a subscription list or charity board in church.

Peer group pressure was increased still further by charity annual reports which not only listed the amount given by each subscriber that year but sometimes also gave the accumulated sum donated by each philanthropist. Sarah Flew cites a vivid example of this when one philanthropist, asked for money by his vicar, replied: 'Well, if you have a collection in Church I shall give probably a shilling, whereas, if you have a subscription list, of course I shall give a guinea'.[61] Thousands of schools, for hundreds of thousands of children for whom no other means of education existed, were financed by this method – 1,419 throughout England and 3,500 in Wales in 1729.[62] For eighteenth-century subscription philanthropists 'the charity school was their favourite form of benevolence,' wrote Mary Gwladys Jones in her study of the Charity School Movement.[63] Commentators at the time were in no doubt as to its importance. Writing in *The Spectator* in 1712, Richard Steele described free schools for the children of the poor as 'the greatest instances of public spirit the age had produced'.[64] His colleague Joseph Addison went further the following year, describing charity schools as 'the glory of the age we live in'.[65]

Hospitals were funded in a similar way. Subscription lists were often solicited at bi-annual church services followed by collections and dinners from which the subscription lists were compiled. Artists such as Hogarth and musicians like Handel were enlisted for fundraising events; Handel's *Messiah* received its first performance at a fundraiser for the Dublin Lying-in Hospital, which opened in 1745 having been funded by subscription following a model established in London. In the first half of the eighteenth century a succession of hospitals were built in the English capital –Westminster in 1719, St George's in 1733, the London in 1740, and the Middlesex in 1746 – but also outside the English capital with the Edinburgh Royal Infirmary built in 1729, followed by Bristol in 1734, Winchester in 1736, York in 1740, Exeter in 1741, Bath in 1742, Northampton in 1743 and many others.[66] The practice spread across the Atlantic: private subscription was used to found the Pennsylvania General Hospital in 1751. By 1755 some 21 hospitals had been established in the English provinces.[67] These new hospitals described themselves as 'voluntary', which made them independent of both State and Church. They were run by volunteers, and even physicians and surgeons who worked in them received no pay, being content with having the poor to practise upon'.[68] In 1687 the English College of Physicians had resolved in a unanimous vote 'that all members of the College, whether fellows, candidates, or licenciates, shou'd give their advice gratis to all their sick neighbouring poor, when desir'd, within the City of London, or seven miles round'.[69] These hospitals received no money directly from the state, though some Poor

Law Guardians who sent patients to them did make contributions. Eighteenth-century hospitals, argues Hugh Cunningham,[70] thereby laid the foundations of 'civil society'.

Not all hospitals dealt with medicine. Many institutions still took the name Hospital as a reference to hospitality. One such was the Magdalen Hospital for Penitent Prostitutes, which opened its doors in 1758 in a disreputable part of Whitechapel notorious for its brothels-cum-theatres and taverns, many of which had been forced out of the City of London by the civil authorities. It was a charitable home for the rehabilitation of 'poor, young, thoughtless Females, plunged into ruin by those temptations, to which their very youth and personal advantages expose them, no less than those passions implanted in our nature' – to quote from the original proposal for the charity written by its founder Robert Dingley, a London silk merchant. He lamented that such unfortunate females, 'abandoned by the Seducer, deserted by their friends, condemned by the world', now appeared to be the only group of the needy 'who are not yet cached the attention of public benevolence'.[71] The inmates, as they were called, had to be under 30 years of age and 'sincere in their desire to be reformed'. The women were trained in needlework and laundry work and had to attend religious services twice a day. When places were limited, preference was given to women who had been prostitutes for the least length of time or who were the youngest requesting admittance.

The cause swiftly attracted donors, not always, it seemed, for the right reasons. A letter written by Horace Walpole, son of the Prime Minister Robert Walpole, recounts how he took various friends – including a member of the royal family and several aristocrats – to visit the hospital as an amusing 'entertainment'. In the letter Walpole, clearly titillated, remarks on how handsome were several of the Magdalens and recounts, shamelessly, that two of the women 'swooned away with the confusion of being stared at' by him.[72] So popular was the charity, among wealthy donors, that in 1772 it was able to move to new premises on a six-acre site in St George's Fields. There its octagonal chapel became a fashionable place of worship for subscribers, whose interest was piqued by the fact that a choir of selected inmates sang during the services behind a screen to hide them mysteriously from the public gaze.

The mix of penitence and veiled sexuality was clearly a potent cocktail. The advertising campaign for the Magdalen Hospital for Penitent Prostitutes included case histories which purported to include details of the penitents' emotions and inner thoughts. The hospital's chaplain, Reverend William Dodd, was famous for his melodramatic and sensationalist sermons, wildly popular with fashionable Londoners. Perhaps the most bizarre was delivered at St Lawrence's Guildhall in the form of a monologue spoken by a fictional prostitute to induce donations from the congregation in what Sarah Lloyd has described as 'a piece of philanthropic ventriloquism'.[73] Dodd was later hanged for forgery, the last person in England to be executed for the offence.

BENEVOLENCE AND THE NATIONAL INTEREST

Mixed motives were not uncommon in other ways in eighteenth-century philanthropy. The first and perhaps finest expression of the new joint-stock model of secular charity was the Foundling Hospital established in London in 1739. The philanthropist behind it, Thomas Coram, had a double motive. He was horrified by the sight of abandoned babies, lying dead and dying in the streets of London. But, as a dedicated entrepreneur, the solution that he came up with was one which he thought would make the nation more productive.

Abandoned children had traditionally been cared for in the English capital at Christ's Hospital, the only institution to take in babies found in the street – foundlings – as well as orphan children. But by 1676 it was refusing to take children born out of wedlock. Captain Thomas Coram, who had spent his early years in the American colonies building ships, returned to England in 1704 at a time when economic migrants from the countryside were filling London with more impoverished folk than parish poor-relief funds could bear. Mothers who were unable to care for their newborn infants, either because of poverty or because the child was illegitimate, often abandoned their babies on doorsteps, outside churches and even on rubbish heaps. A thousand a year were so discarded.

Coram was spurred into action through humanitarian rather than religious motives. He undertook 17 years of dogged campaigning, persuading members of fashionable society – including seven duchesses, eight countesses and five baronesses – to add their names, and pledge considerable sums of money, to a petition to King George II. Nearly two decades later the monarch granted a royal charter permitting the foundation of a Foundling Hospital 'for the care and maintenance of exposed and deserted young children'.[74] It became London's most popular charity.

But though his motive as 'a man of feeling' was altruistic, Thomas Coram was enough of a mercantilist to insist that the children taken into the hospital were educated and then apprenticed. The boys, at the age of 14, were indentured for seven years to a variety of occupations. The girls, at 16, were found posts as domestic servants for a minimum of four years. David Owen sees Coram's inspiration in the comments of Joseph Addison, who had denounced the abandoning of babies by their 'cruel and unnatural parents' because 'it robs the Commonwealth of its full number of citizens'.[75] Coram's view was that abandoning babies to die was not just a moral outrage, but it also wasted labour that could be put to productive use for the national economy.

He was not alone in such thinking. The Quaker John Bellers in his 1714 essay *The Improvement of Physick* calculated that 'Every Able Industrious Labourer, that is capable to have Children, who so Untimely Dies, may be accounted Two Hundred Pound Loss to the Kingdom'. Bellers argued that it was in the interest of the rich 'to take care of the poor and their education'. If all 'the present idle hands of the poor of this nation' were put to work, he suggested, it would bring England 'as much treasure as the mines do Spain'. Jonas Hanway, a governor of the Foundling Hospital, wrote a text defending the institution in which he calculated that every life saved would, by the time the child reached the age of 50, represent a net gain to the national economy of £176 10s.[76]

This sort of political arithmetic allowed the very lives of the poor to be transformed into so much wealth which might be added to the general stock of the nation. Hanway went on to put his theory into practice by convening a group of merchants to found another organization with a dual purpose. The Marine Society took deserted boys from the streets and offered them a new life 'separated from their evil companions, cleansed from their rags and filthiness, softened into habits of subordination and obedience, [and] inured to gentle discipline'.[77] Once educated they were ready to become recruits to the Royal Navy or merchant fleet, solving with a single initiative the twin problems of destitute boys and naval recruitment. 'The hopeless youth rescu'd from misery and ruin [was] train'd to serve and to defend his country.'[78]

Hanway was also a proponent of the Enlightenment's more scientific approach to philanthropy. Appalled at the quality of care by parish nurses, he undertook a study of the poorhouse in St Luke's parish in Chelsea and discovered that, though it had taken in 53 children between 1750 and 1755, none had survived.[79] Between 1757 and 1763 he visited workhouses across London, collecting statistics about the mortality rate of young children. In another parish, St Clement Danes, Hanway described Nurse Hannah Poole, who ran a large nursing home for poor pregnant women, as 'an angel of death' for killing off so many of her young charges.[80] He pushed for legislation for all children abandoned in parishes in London to be registered and then cared for outside the polluted capital city where they had a better chance of survival. Hanway was something of a trend-setter. As well as the Foundling Hospital and the Marine Society he was involved in a wide range of popular philanthropic projects, including the Magdalen Hospital – and was apparently the first man in London to carry an umbrella.[81] The memorial to him in the north transept of Westminster Abbey records him as a Christian, a Merchant and a Citizen of the World.

Throughout the eighteenth century philanthropy, moral reform and the economy marched together.[82] 'Thus might Charity, Humanity, Patriotism and Economy be made to go hand-in-hand,' wrote Joseph Massie in 1758 in his *Plan for the Establishment of Charity-Houses for Exposed or Deserted Women and Girls, and for Penitent Prostitutes*.[83] Those who were not moved by compassion alone should remember, William Sharp preached in 1755, that if the poor were not helped, 'they will soon grow up to public nuisances, infect your families with their idle disorderly behaviour, fill your streets with vice and violence'. But, he added, 'take the same persons under your patronage, teach them what is right and hear how you will be repaid. They will be serviceable to you in many ways by themselves, and by their examples, Industry, Sobriety, Good Order and Good Manners will get ground among you. Your city will be stocked with honest laborious ingenious artisans, some of the most useful members of the community; wealth will increase.'[84]

Mixed motives also lay behind the great missionary endeavour of the late eighteenth century in which British philanthropists such as Wilberforce and many others sought to spread the message of Christianity to the 'heathen' overseas. Again philanthropic efforts to bring 'Christianity and civilization' to the foreign poor went hand in hand with the business of Britain building an empire. Historians have argued as to whether missionaries or the officers of imperial power were in the driving seat. But the alliance between spiritual and temporal power is undeniable. Both also gained potency by harnessing the optimism and confidence the Enlightenment had injected into the European worldview. The 1790s were a key decade in this, as Hugh Cunningham has noted, with the Baptist Missionary Society sending people to India in 1792, the London Missionary Society setting up in the South Pacific in 1796, and the Methodists and Anglicans in Africa by the end of that decade.[85]

The bond between Christianity and Empire was further strengthened by another campaign of William Wilberforce, who in 1793 successfully lobbied to force the British East India Company to pay for teachers and chaplains to further the 'religious improvement' of the Indian population. Many would argue that religious proselytization is something separate from philanthropy. But what is indisputable is that the same individuals who were behind the great philanthropic innovations of eighteenth-century England also drove the massive foreign missionary effort.

Both at home and abroad there was in evidence the same combination of evangelical piety, benign humanitarianism and an acute sense of Britain's economic and political interests. Both overseas and back home, eighteenth-century enthusiasts for change held to an optimistic vision of the improvability of society. The philanthropists of the day were well pleased with themselves. Their self-satisfaction was summed up by Hannah More, a philanthropist and philosopher who sought to embody the moral voice of the nation: 'The many striking acts of public bounty, and the various new and noble improvements in the shining virtue, justly entitled the present age to be called, by way of eminence, the Age of Benevolence.'[86]

THE BACKLASH AGAINST DO-GOODERY

Not everyone in the eighteenth century was of the same mind. There were many who accused these prominent philanthropists of self-aggrandizement or even hypocrisy. The elaborate social events and anniversary celebrations held for fundraising were particular targets. At such events it was common practice for the hapless individuals who were the 'objects' of the charity to be paraded around the room 'as the wealthy givers tucked into their turtle soup'.[87] The historian Sarah Lloyd catalogued all the charitable events in fashionable London in a single year, 1755, and found that the big metropolitan charities, together with a plethora of minor benevolent societies, courted London society with a deluge of invitations to dinners, exhibitions or concerts – paying, for example, half a guinea each to hear Handel's *Messiah* in the Foundling Hospital chapel.[88] Men could, in addition, support various hospitals and other good causes by dining in taverns and City Livery Halls in company with civic and ecclesiastical dignitaries, aristocrats and royal dukes. Women could attend charity services, ornamented with special music – in the chapels of hospitals, dispensaries, lying-in charities and religious societies. Again they could watch charity schoolchildren arrayed before them. By the mid-eighteenth century such events had settled into an annual pattern linked to the social calendar. Some charities moved their anniversary date to obtain a better position on that calendar. The cost of these extravaganzas was significant, with as much as a third of the profit from fundraising being spent on the event itself. Such 'society philanthropy' was easy prey for its critics, who asserted that the charity was more about the interests of the donors than those of the recipients.

Prominent philanthropists also left themselves open to accusations of hypocrisy from those who disagreed with them politically. As we have seen, the radical pamphleteer William Cobbett, and others, attacked William Wilberforce for campaigning for the abolition of slavery abroad while ignoring the terrible conditions in which British workers lived. 'Never have you done one single act, in favour of the labourers of this country,' Cobbett complained.[89] For all his concern about the downtrodden abroad, the domestic conservative Wilberforce opposed workers' rights in England, attacking trade unions as 'a general disease in our society'.[90] The essayist William Hazlitt criticized Wilberforce on similar grounds, as someone 'who preaches vital Christianity to untutored savages, and tolerates its worst abuses in civilised states'.[91]

Such criticisms, both moral and political, hit home. That much was clear from the impact they had upon popular culture. In France, Gustave Flaubert depicted philanthropists in his early novels as well-meaning but tedious members of the bourgeoisie 'whose philanthropic actions were full of silliness and vainglory'.[92] As early as 1838, in *Ivre et Mort* (*Drunk and Dead*) he sardonically describes a philanthropist as a 'man who loves others, like a naturalist loves museums of dead animals'. Elsewhere Flaubert mocked scientific philanthropy in the form of enthusiasm for the advent of railways or the cultivation of potatoes to feed the poor. In England a very different kind of writer, Charles Dickens, cast a satirical eye in *Bleak House* in 1852–3 over Mrs Jellyby's devotion to the cause of the missions overseas. She is portrayed as so preoccupied with her project for Borrioboola-Gha on the left bank of the Niger that she neglects the needs of her own children. The Whig politician and historian Thomas Macaulay in 1857 railed against 'all the philanthropic cant of Peace Societies, and Aboriginal Protection Societies, and Societies for the Reformation of Criminals', which he dismissed as 'effeminate mawkish philanthropy'.[93] George Eliot, in *Middlemarch*, published in 1871–2 but set in the 1830s, also puts philanthropy under the microscope. 'A philanthropist,' she has a journalist write, is someone 'who cannot bear one rogue to be hanged, but does not mind five honest tenants being half starved: a man who shrieks at corruption, and keeps his farms at rack rent . . . We all know the wag's definition of a philanthropist: a man whose charity increases directly as the square of the distance'.[94]

But her portrait of philanthropy is more wide-ranging. Two of the novel's characters are philanthropists. Mr Brooke is of the secular variety; for him philanthropy is 'mainly about punishments and that kind of thing', and it is merely a vehicle for gathering votes when he runs for Parliament on a Reform platform. But he lets his own tenants live in poverty and squalor and only addresses their conditions when the scandal is mercilessly exposed by the press. Mr Bulstrode is a philanthropist of the evangelical Christian kind, who uses philanthropy to cover up his shady past as a pawnbroker and cheat. Only the novel's heroine, Dorothea, comes out of it well, as Hugh Cunningham notes: 'she dutifully surrounds herself with "her particular little heap of books on political economy" as a guide to action, but quickly puts them aside to follow the dictates of her heart'.[95]

THE PHILOSOPHERS OF FREE-MARKET PHILANTHROPY

As the century progressed, philanthropy was exposed to criticism by conservative thinkers, from the right, and from radical thinkers and the forerunners of socialism on the left. Phrases such as 'misplaced benevolence', 'misguided and sanguine philanthropy' and 'misdirected philanthropy' began to appear by the late 1860s.[96] (The Charity Organisation Society, with its systematic and scientific philanthropy, was an attempt to address such criticisms, as the next chapter will show.) But the roots of the criticism went back further. In 1723, the same year that the Workhouse Test Act was passed, a damning essay on *Charity and Charity Schools* had been published by Bernard Mandeville, a physician and political philosopher. Mandeville was opposed to educating the poor, arguing that this would only increase their desire for material things and make them discontented with their station in society. In any case, education did not promote moral good; the highly educated but degenerate upper classes were proof of that, he asserted. But his critique went far deeper into the underlying philosophy of philanthropy.

Here, and in an earlier work *The Fable of the Bees*,[97] Mandeville set out the idea that it was human vices, rather than human virtues, which provided the driving force to make the economy work. The book sent a shudder of scandal throughout English society. Mandeville maintained that vicious greed could lead to invisible co-operation if properly channelled. Take the vice of pride: without it, he suggested, there would be no fashion industry, as individuals would have no motive to buy new and expensive clothes with which to try to impress their peers. Eradicating pride would leave hundreds of companies bankrupt, create widespread unemployment, risk the collapse of industry, and devastate both the economic security and military power of the British state. Without thieves, there would be no locksmiths. Without quarrels over property, there would be no lawyers. Private vices therefore produced public benefits. Philanthropy, in his view, was conducted only for the pleasure and self-congratulation of donors.

This went against the conventional wisdom of the time which was summarized by Thomas Secker, Archbishop of Canterbury, when he asserted: 'If we succeed, we have exquisite joy: if we fail, it is no inconsiderable comfort that we meant well'.[98] Such arguments, said Mandeville, were economic nonsense. 'Pride and Vanity have built more Hospitals than all the Virtues together,' he wrote.[99] Writing, as he did, at the height of the popularity of charity schools, Mandeville's views were highly unpopular. But they laid the intellectual basis for a later critique of the eighteenth-century style of philanthropy. Improvements in living conditions would come from the growth of industry, he believed; charity would only make people more lazy.

Mandeville's attack on philanthropy was underscored towards the end of the century by the new philosophical movement of Utilitarianism, which saw 'the greatest good of the greatest number' as the determining principle for creating a good society. Its founder, Jeremy Bentham, held that human beings were unrelentingly driven by narrow self-interest. His fellow Utilitarian, John Stuart Mill, by contrast, felt that sympathy for fellow human beings was a key characteristic of human nature. But both considered philanthropy an inadequate answer to the scale of the social problems faced by an industrializing Britain. Both saw the solution in an interaction between philanthropy and government. Bentham drew up a grand scheme for 'Pauper Management' made up of a national company controlling a chain of 250 huge workhouses.[100] They were to be financed by large numbers of small investors. His idea was that each workhouse would make a profit by housing 2,000 inmates who would be put to lucrative work. Mill wanted charities to be compelled to invest in state bonds and be subject to close supervision by the government.

Utilitarians sought to align philanthropy with the increasingly free-market ideology of the era. The *Westminster Review*, the Utilitarian journal which Bentham and Mill founded, commenting on the *Eighth Report of the Commissioners appointed by Parliament to enquire respecting Charities of 1823*, concluded: 'To convince the public, twenty or thirty years ago, of the goodness of a charity, it was sufficient to shew that the objects relieved were in a state of real distress . . . But now . . . all former reasonings on the subject of charity . . . are invalidated.'[101] It then went on to cite Reverend Thomas Malthus, whose infamous *Essay on the Principle of Population* of 1798 had attacked public poor relief.[102] In the view of the demographer, political economist and pessimist Malthus, it only encouraged marriage and fertility rates at a time when real wages in the economy were declining. Handouts to the poor therefore merely perpetuated unsustainable population growth – reinforcing Malthus's central thesis that the world will eventually run out of food to feed this ever-rising population. Conservative thinkers such as Edmund Burke opposed government assistance to the poor but were willing to permit private charitable donations to the needy;[103] Malthus went further by opposing both government relief and private charity. Philanthropy was now under philosophical attack.

That attack was ratcheted up in 1833 when the French political writer Alexis de Tocqueville visited England and was struck by the number of beggars he saw. The book he wrote as a result, *Memoir on Pauperism*, published in 1835, began by puzzling as to why this was. Travel in a poor country such as Portugal or Spain, he wrote, and you will see very few beggars. But in England, then the wealthiest country in Europe, 'you will discover with indescribable astonishment that one-sixth of the inhabitants of this flourishing kingdom live at the expense of public charity'.[104] Tocqueville was here referring to the fact that, since a particularly bad harvest in 1795, 'every poor and industrious' Englishman whose earnings fell below a given standard – determined by the price of bread and the size of his family – would receive a subsidy from the parish to bring his income up to subsistence level. It was called the 'Speenhamland system' and its result was that a considerable number of labourers became dependent upon the parish. Malthus had urged that this new extended poor law be abolished, but in 1832, the year before Tocqueville arrived, a Royal Commission had recommended reform rather than abolition.

The French thinker, who was able to observe several court sessions where judges determined whether poor people were entitled to alms, drew two conclusions from his visit – one on public and the other on private philanthropy. On public poor relief he concluded that 'any measure which establishes legal charity in a permanent basis, and gives it an administrative form, thereby creates an idle and lazy class, living at the expense of the . . . working class . . . [and] the more permanent and extended the right to relief is, the more it degrades'.[105] This is because the right to relief creates an unhelpful sense of what Gertrude Himmelfarb called 'entitlement' and what today we would call a dependency culture.[106] Public philanthropy, Tocqueville argues, should be applied in cases of 'the helplessness of infancy, the decrepitude of old age, sickness, [and] insanity' and temporarily at times of public calamities.[107] Anything else would 'pauperise' the able-bodied poor. Any permanent, regular system to provide for the needs of the able-bodied poor:

> will breed more miseries than it can cure, will deprave the population that it wants to help and comfort . . . will dry up the sources of savings, will stop the accumulation of capital, will retard the development of trade, will benumb human industry and activity, and will culminate by bringing about a violent revolution in the State, when the number of those who receive alms will have become as large as those who give it.[108]

Contrasted with this public evil was a private good: private philanthropy is better able to distinguish those who truly need from those who merely want, Tocqueville argued. It creates a moral tie between giver and receiver.[109] And because it is temporary and voluntary it can alleviate need without creating dependency. Private philanthropy could not provide all the answers, he admitted. Individual charity seems quite weak when faced with the problems thrown up by an industrializing society, but 'its very weakness is a guarantee against dangerous consequences. It alleviates many miseries and breeds none . . . Individual charity is a powerful agency that must not be despised, but it would be imprudent to rely on it. It is but a single means and cannot be the only one'.[110] Already, Tocqeville was beginning to glimpse, the scale of the poverty created as the downside of the Industrial Revolution was so great that private philanthropy could never meet the need.

So what is the answer? Tocqueville asks that question at the end of his *Memoir* – and promises to offer a solution in a second memoir. But by the time he died in 1859, his incomplete second manuscript on the subject offers no remedy, perhaps because he could never find one. Yet, despite that, his insistence that government assistance to the poor can sometimes do more harm than good is an assertion that has resonated through the centuries ever since.

There were clear differences between the views of Mandeville, Bentham, Mill, Malthus and Tocqueville. But between them they established a new agenda for philanthropy – one which sought a more complex relationship with the state and that set a new style of thinking about the interaction between those who gave and those who received. We shall look at the relationship between philanthropy and the free market in the next chapter.

SOCIALISM – A RADICAL ALTERNATIVE
TO PHILANTHROPY

But this new free-market framework for philanthropy was, from the outset, not to have it all its own way. An alternative, more radical, critique emerged towards the end of the eighteenth century. Those who attacked the Age of Benevolence were not simply critical of 'society philanthropy' or political hypocrisy. Many of the heralds of a free-market political economy also saw philanthropy as dangerously radical. It is not hard to see why. In 1795 the English Unitarian George Dyer, calling for more justice and less charity, wrote that 'every philanthropist should be a reformer'.[111] Removing 'the defects and excesses of governments,' he insisted, would be far better for the poor 'than the erecting of a thousand hospitals'. To Dyer and his ilk the very point of philanthropy was to deliver social justice. Conservatives began to see the word 'philanthropist' as a term of abuse. The radical political philosopher Tom Paine, a passionate enthusiast for the French Revolution, was attacked in 1797 by the ultra-Tory periodical, *The Anti-Jacobin Review*, with the epithet 'Tom Paine the Philanthropist'.[112] The nascent left owned the term so much that one of the earliest trade unions and mutual aid societies, founded in Newcastle in 1812, used the word in its title: The Philanthropic Society of House Carpenters and Joiners.[113] The first attempt to create an umbrella organization for all the trade unions in London in 1818 called itself the Philanthropic Hercules.[114]

At the same time radicals began to be sceptical about the kind of 'society philanthropy' practised by the elite. After a revolt by labourers in 1838, an official sent to investigate produced a report entitled *Riot in Kent – Report on the State of the Peasantry*. It revealed that the rioters took a very dim view of the philanthropy of their masters. 'Feelings toward the rich are not merely envious but vindictive,' it stated. The charities of the rich were seen as merely 'a miserable fraction of the wealth they have extorted' from the work of the labourers. Philanthropic largesse was received by the rioters 'with ingratitude and sullenness'.[115]

Their views prefigured those of Friedrich Engels, who scattered his *Condition of the Working Class in England* with barbs against 'pharisaic philanthropy' and capitalists who place themselves 'before the world as mighty benefactors of humanity' but in reality 'give back to the plundered victims the hundredth part of what belongs to them!'[116] He proclaimed himself to be 'filled with wrath and resentment against the class which boasts of philanthropy and self-sacrifice, while its one object is to fill its purse'.[117] In France the forerunners of socialism were equally critical. The utopian socialist Charles Fourier often wrote about how hypocritical leaders used 'the mask of philanthropy' to serve their own interests.[118] Marx suggested that philanthropists wanted to 'turn all men into bourgeois' by denying the antagonism which he insisted was integral to relations between the working class and their masters.[119] The anarchist Pierre-Joseph Proudhon declared in 1863 that philanthropy kept the poor passive and dependent on the structures of bourgeois society.[120]

Yet despite the uncompromising tone of socialist philosophers, in practice the relationship between socialists and philanthropists was more ambivalent. Their efforts at social transformation often overlapped. Many socialists had been active in philanthropic organizations before embracing socialism – and often continued with some kind of philanthropic activity. A few even made the journey the other way, from socialism to philanthropy.[121] John Trevor, a Baptist-turned-Unitarian who was a social and community activist in Manchester in the 1880s – where he eventually founded a Labour Church – believed that 'socialism of any worthy sort includes philanthropy, but also goes far nearer to the root of our evils than philanthropy alone can do'.[122]

Others vehemently disagreed. The Social Democratic Federation regularly denounced philanthropists for their 'patronising attitude' as well as the inadequacy of the solutions they offered. 'Philanthropists', railed a writer in Sunderland's socialist newspaper in 1894, purported to help poor people but actually treated them 'as things to be amused, educated, restricted, lectured [and] advised'. They gave the poor 'everything except fair play'. The working class would work out their own salvation, the writer continued, and did not require the 'canting sympathy and foolish patronage' of philanthropists.[123]

On the ground things were a good deal less polarized. Across the north of England socialists set up what they called Cinderella Clubs. Through these they fed and entertained working-class children – and offered them socialist 'truths' to counter what Chris Waters, in *British Socialists and the Politics of Popular Culture*, calls 'the value-laden didacticism that characterised the charity work of the established churches'.[124] The administrators of these clubs were conscious of a paradox at the heart of their work. The Cinderella Club in Rotherham in 1906 articulated this unease, writing: 'Our main work as socialists is to abolish the need for charity by establishing a system of justice for the workers, and making it the duty of the state to care for the sick and the needy'.[125] But meanwhile, in the absence of such a society, they regarded the work of the Cinderella Club as an important socialist activity.

The dangers of this approach were seen in the Manchester Cinderella club, where wealthy upper-class philanthropists, including aristocrats such as the Earl and Countess of Derby, made donations to the work of the club but in return let it be known that it might be a good idea to 'tone down or eradicate the expression of socialist sentiments at their gatherings' so as not to deter them from further donations.[126] There were similar debates among socialists in Bradford who argued endlessly about whether or not they should help support the work of the Bradford branch of the Guild of Help[127] – an organization set up by the city's worthies, and which later spread across the north of England, to foster the idea of civic responsibility and 'lend a hand' to individuals. One Labour councillor there, E. R. Hartley, insisted that the Guild was merely a dodge to keep the working class quiet, but one of the socialists active in the Guild riposted: 'In the good time coming the Guild's work will be unnecessary, but the time is not yet, and . . . I am not so optimistic as to suppose it will come in my day . . . meanwhile, what?'[128]

Socialists found it difficult to reconcile this conundrum. One who attempted, unsuccessfully, was Julie Dawson, editor of the women's column in Manchester's weekly socialist newspaper, *The Clarion*. In 1896 she attempted to discover what her readers thought about philanthropy. She suggested that the motives of philanthropists were often suspect but that some philanthropic attempts at redressing social grievances were legitimate, though only as an adjunct to socialist activity. Where philanthropy refused to acknowledge the need for social reform, it was to be condemned. After a lengthy discussion she asked her readers: 'Ought socialists [to] take part in any philanthropic work where they are absolutely prohibited from infusing any knowledge of socialism?' To her dismay her readers voted Yes by a small majority.[129]

Nor could socialists and philanthropists agree – even within their own camps – about the nature of philanthropy, and in particular whether or not it ought to promote 'self-improvement' among poor working people. Socialists routinely complained about moralistic philanthropists seeking to impose their own middle-class values on poor people.[130] But nor were they always happy when those they saw as do-gooders provided something closer to what the people actually wanted – such as excursions to the seaside: 'Better than all the whirligig holidays spent by the average north-country toiler at Blackpool . . . is a week spent with nature,' thundered *The Clarion* in 1895.[131] High-minded socialists condemned as patronizing the proposal in 1890 by William Booth, founder of the Salvation Army, for what he called 'Whitechapel-by-the-Sea', a seaside holiday camp which Chris Waters has called 'a veritable philanthropic Butlins'.[132] There, the teetotal evangelist General Booth hoped, workers would no longer be tempted by drink and sensational entertainment but would instead be subjected to endless amounts of rational recreation, and would be improved in a museum complete with 'a panorama and stuffed whale.'[133]

William Morris, the designer, poet and early socialist activist, sent out confusing messages. Towards the end of his life, in his 1896 essay *How I Became a Socialist*, published in the socialist paper *Justice*, he condemned the work of philanthropists in the most forthright terms.[134] Morris insisted that his 'consciousness of revolution stirring amidst our hateful modern society prevented me . . . from wasting time and energy in any of the numerous schemes by which the quasi-artistic of the middle classes hope to make art grow when it has no longer any root'.[135] Such philanthropic schemes were a diversion, he declared. Yet earlier in his life Morris had been happy to take part in such activities. Although he had always taken a low view of what he called the 'preaching type' of philanthropist, he held in greater esteem those hard-working and dedicated individuals who engaged with the great social problems of society.

One such was Charles Rowley, who was elected to Manchester City Council in 1875 on a manifesto of 'Baths and Washhouses, and Public-rooms for Ancoats', a slum area of the city. Rowley believed that the modern city was a city of strangers where rich and poor no longer met – except through what he called the 'sentimental philanthropy' doled out by Lady Bountilfuls.[136] As an alternative Rowley founded the Ancoats Brotherhood, in which 2,000 ordinary working people enrolled, paying a shilling a year. At its heart was a Hall of Sweetness and Light where he organized Sunday morning reading parties – rather severe gatherings, says Chris Waters, at which Samuel Rawson Gardiner's formidable ten-volume *A Student's History of England* was read aloud. There was a lending library, a bookstall, rambling and cycling clubs, and a series of Wednesday lectures on Civic Life and Civic Duties. Prominent socialists spoke at the gatherings, including William Morris, on several occasions. Run by the Ancoats Recreation Committee, its aim was 'to give the workers . . . some taste of the best that has been thought, said and done'.[137]

But the idea of radical philanthropy began to fade. Socialists left it behind as their vision became more exclusively political and tied to the notion that change had to come from the state. Radical philanthropy gave way to municipal socialism and then, as we shall see in Chapter 10, to the Welfare State. The ultra-conservative political theorist Herbert Spencer, who coined the phrase 'survival of the fittest', told Andrew Carnegie: 'The wave of opinion carrying us toward Socialism and utter subordination of the individual is becoming irresistible.' He also announced melodramatically that he was, therefore, giving up political writing.[138] Meanwhile, as we shall see in the next two chapters, philanthropy increasingly aligned itself with the dominant social and economic ideology of the time, unfettered laissez-faire capitalism. Philanthropy and radical activist politics went their separate ways.

Interview: Bob Geldof on philanthropic activism

Bob Geldof is perhaps the most prominent philanthropic activist in recent decades. When a devastating famine hit Ethiopia in 1984–5, he responded by persuading his fellow pop stars to raise funds for famine relief with two charity records – Do they Know it's Christmas in the United Kingdom and Feed the World in the United States. After that he organized Live Aid, with its two concerts, one in the UK and the other in the US, in July 1985. Together they raised more than £150 million for famine relief and economic development in Africa in what became a new democratization of philanthropy. His later Live 8 concert, in 2005, was broadcast simultaneously in the world's eight leading industrial nations. Knighted in 1986, he has throughout continued as lead singer of his band, the Boomtown Rats.

When the footage from that terrible famine in Ethiopia first appeared on our television screens in 1984, most people responded by sending off some money to one of the aid agencies. That wasn't enough for you. You had to do something more. What motivated you to want to do something different?

The reports on the screen were harrowing in the extreme. So the first imperative was to write a cheque and send it off to one of the large charities because people were dying – and dying live in your living room, in effect. So the normal human response is to put a pound in the Oxfam box. And that's charity – the most profound of human emotional responses. Without it, something inside will wither and die. But this great hunger was so extreme it demanded something more – something of the self. So what could I do? I write songs and I make records. So, me and my friend Midge Ure wrote a song and we made a record. Had the Boomtown Rats been selling millions of records then, the Rats would've done it on our own. But, to maximize the amount it raised, the purely pragmatic thing was to get the people who were making the big hits at the time to come along to do the record. And then the record became a phenomenon that was not anticipated. The response to it became almost a superseding news item.

The record was bigger than the famine?

For a moment it became that, at least in terms of a news story. What became the story was the charitable gush that emerged at a time when people otherwise were feeling very divided – with people quoting the prime minister, Margaret Thatcher, as saying 'there is no such thing as society', the coal miners were on strike and the times felt very fractured. And suddenly something different was happening. The DJ who was the first to play the record on the radio, Simon Bates, told his listeners, 'I am going to play this record three times an hour, I don't care what my producer says, and you are to buy this record whether you like it or you don't like it.' That was the first thing. Then there were queues outside record shops, which was abnormal. People were buying 40 copies and giving back 39; that became common. A butcher's shop in Plymouth had it in his window – with the turkey, goose and pork – Band Aid records. Fortnum and Mason rang me to ask: 'How does one sell a pop record?' Everyone was playing ball – all the big institutions, the record companies, the major retailers, the publishing world. Something was going on and everyone felt good about doing this thing.

I'd hoped it might raise £100,000, which I'd give to Save the Children, but the demand was so phenomenal that soon every record-pressing plant in Europe was only pressing this record. So eight million quid later John Kennedy, the Parlophone lawyer, told me, 'You've got to set up a trust to spend it.' So we did, Band Aid Trust. But now the media were saying, 'What. . . are you going to do with the £8 million? You've got to go to Africa to decide how to spend it. Otherwise the story dies. We've done the famine. We can't keep doing the famine.' I said: 'I've got a Rats tour coming up.' And then one of them said: 'You started it. Don't you feel responsible for it?'

So you went to Africa – and travelled right across sub-Saharan Africa, from Mali in the west to Ethiopia in the east.

Yes. The only thing I could think of doing was getting all of the aid agencies in each country in one room and saying: 'OK, there's £1 million here for Mali, or whatever. I don't know your world so you decide what to do with it. Set aside your rivalries and agree together. We will come back in two hours and if you have agreed on something, then that will be Band Aid here.'

But it was all a terrible strain. I remember you caught me crying once because it was all just too much. The horror I was being exposed to. Those pitiful people. The sounds of dying. The stink of the camps. Was I doing the right thing? Was I saying the right things? Meeting politicians and heads of state and ludicrous guards of honour and the occasional murderous scumbag. And constantly surrounded by media who were just desperate to get a 'Bob with black baby photo' and I hated that. And I got really confused about whether I was handling any of this right. But what I already understood at that point was that this wasn't enough. I was beginning to see that famine is nothing to do with hunger; famine is to do with economics. People with money don't die of hunger. It's so obvious. So that stayed with me.

But it didn't shape your next move. You were still carried along by the momentum of events.

Just before we left for Africa, Harry Belafonte rang me. Now Harry Belafonte is a dude: during the civil rights struggle he marched with Martin Luther King; he took Frank Sinatra to the South where Frank then refused to play to segregated audiences; Harry was blacklisted in the McCarthy era. The first black person to have a national TV show in the US. He took all these slave songs and put them in the top three of the American charts. And here he was – on the phone to me! He said to me: 'We are fucking ashamed of what you Brit kids did.' And I said to him: 'I'm Irish.' And he replied: 'Same fucking thing!' Then he said: 'I got Michael here.' And I heard: 'Hi Bob, it's Michael.' It was Michael fucking Jackson – on the phone to me! And he said: 'It's really great what you're doing. We want to do that over here. Will you come over?'

So when we got back from Africa, I went over to do US Aid for Africa. This was 28 January 1985. I walk in and there's Willie Nelson, Paul Simon, Bruce Springsteen, Bob Dylan, Smoky fucking Robinson, Ray fucking Charles, Stevie Wonder, Michael Jackson and Quincy Jones. The heroes of my life! And Quincy Jones goes: 'Everybody pay attention. Now we all know Bob Geldof.' (And I think: No, no, nobody in here knows Bob Geldof!) 'He's just come back from Africa and he wants to explain why we're doing this. Bob, go ahead.' Fucking Hell!!!!

You were overawed to be in this rock 'n' roll Hall of Fame?

Yes and No. I went around getting autographs and taking pictures. I'm a fan. They probably thought I was a terrible wanker. But then they all started asking for autographs from their heroes!! Dylan is quite a piss-taker. He went over to Stevie Wonder and said: 'Hey Stevie, I'm not sure how to sing my line – "We are the World"'. Stevie said: 'It's easy Bob', and he played it and sang it as a terrible Dylanesque drawl. 'Oh yeah,' said Dylan, 'I reckon I can do that.' Michael Jackson was pissing himself. I got a great photo of the three of them.

What did you say in your speech to them?

I spoke of what I'd just seen. I spoke to the possibility of alerting America in the same way that Band Aid had done in Europe and then I said: 'If this record works, guys, I may come back to you.' As I was speaking, the idea was forming in my mind that we could do the two records live the following Christmas. They could appear here, and we could do ours back at home, and we could link the two live, via satellites. That was the dawning inkling of what became Live Aid.

And did it work?

It was the biggest record ever sold in the world. So I began to sketch out the idea of performing the two songs live. During the next Rats tour, in the afternoons I made phone call after phone call: we organized Live Aid very rapidly. All the big acts wanted to be involved. Why wouldn't you be? It was going to be huge.

What made you bring Live Aid forward to July rather than Christmas as you had originally thought?

Because of the public momentum. News of how bad the famine was kept coming in. Then there was the availability of the stadiums. And the summer is the touring season when big stars, like Springsteen, were available. But above all it was the urgency of the need of the unfolding horror in Africa which was seared in my head from my first visit. Now it was bad not just in Ethiopia but all across the continent. And, in retrospect, I suppose I also could see that the politics was starting to work. If one person puts a pound in the Oxfam box, it's a profoundly human gesture; but if a million people put a pound in that box, that's political, because politics is only about numbers. But I wasn't thinking about politics at that time, I was just thinking about getting as much money as quickly as possible to stop as many people dying as possible.

Your most celebrated line at Live Aid has gone down as you telling the audience 'Give us the fucking money' – though you never actually said those words.

People asked me how much we were planning to raise and I said £10 million. In fact I knew we already had £10 million in the bank from sponsorship and ticket sales. So that would mean any penny over the £10 million would be seen as a victory. You have to be able to give people a victory. Their victory. So that others in the future would be encouraged. So it was about cash. That's why I went mad on the day and shouted at everyone to get the money in fast.

The flow of calls to pledge leapt three hundredfold after you swore.

But it was about a lot more than money. On the day people seemed connected in some way. We seemed to be all talking to each other in some shared unspoken understanding of what it is to be human. Of humanness. Which is the essential definition of the word philanthropy. I don't think it was anything to do with the bands – although, if you watch the tapes, you see that all the bands elevated themselves and were absolutely playing at their top level. They were all magnificent. And they still talk about it. All of them say: 'Fuck me, what a day!' But there was a sense of something beyond a rock 'n' roll concert. I only understood the romance of it when I walked out onto the stage with the Rats – the band I'm in – and this wave of emotional approbation washed over me – and I thought this to be may be the best day of my life. And I said so. But I thought then that that would be it.

But it wasn't.

Afterwards someone who'd seen me on the TV wrote to me and said: 'You look really afraid and tired.' I was. I was shitting myself. Suddenly I'm talking to Margaret Thatcher or whoever and I'm thinking, 'Fucking hell, I might be out of my depth here!' Anyway, this person who wrote said he'd been in the same boat, in a smaller way, and he wanted to send me something he'd found very useful. He sent me this quote from a 1950s book by a guy called W. H. Murray, which said once you're

definitely committed to something all sorts of things happen, all sorts
of events move in your favour – which you could never have foreseen.

Murray was a climber with the Scottish Himalayan Expedition in the
Fifties. He wrote:

> Until one is committed there is hesitancy, the chance to draw back,
> always ineffectiveness . . . The moment one definitely commits
> oneself, then Providence moves too. All sorts of things occur to help
> one that would otherwise never have occurred. A whole stream of
> events issues from the decision, raising in one's favour all manner of
> unforeseen incidents and meetings and material assistance, which
> no man would have believed would have come his way.[139]

And he ends with two lines from Goethe:

> Whatever you can do, or dream you can, begin it.
> Boldness has genius, power and magic in it!

**You're making it sound like you were just carried along by the
momentum or events. But when you were a teenager in Dublin
you worked for a charity for the homeless, the Simon community.
So in a sense you had been schooled in the voluntary impulse.**

It goes back further than that even, and it was deeply personal. I was
brought up in Catholic Ireland and went to a school where the teachers
were priests from a missionary order, the Holy Ghost Fathers. They
were always going on about their time in Africa. Looking back, I think I
must have absorbed something of the sense of wonder that these rural
Irish men had discovered when they went to Africa. We could always
trick them away from teaching Latin declensions by asking them about
their missionary life and suddenly they were back with the Yoruba in
Nigeria. They had come back with a heightened sense of different
spiritualities, which I could detect even if I didn't really understand it.

But what was more significant was the fact that my mum had died
when I was seven and my dad, who was a travelling salesman, was
away all week. I had two sisters – who were ten years and five years
older than me – but they were pretty much doing their own thing, and
largely ignored me because I was a pain in the arse. So I would go
home and do my own shopping, and light my own fire, and do my own

cooking. From being seven or eight I knew how to scramble eggs. And I remember boiling rice, with a couple of rashers of bacon sliced up in it, and an Oxo cube, for my evening meal. And I liked that. Retrospectively, several things happened: I was obliged by my circumstance to learn organization very quickly. I learned independence. And because you are pretty much in charge of yourself you don't really develop an idea of what authority is.

Not even at school?

The priests would accost me, but when the central poles of a child's world – their two parents – are simply not there to tell you what to do, you don't really understand where the parameters of behaviour are. You don't understand it because you've never been told. In a borderless world the teachers at school just don't have an authority that's recognizable to you. Or later, say, a policeman. That's why so many kids now who haven't got fathers at home haven't got a clue how to act with adults – so that when they rub up against the police they immediately give them lip or turn violent or whatever. For me school spiralled out of control. I got beaten all the time. But it was low-level. I was smart enough not to get kicked out, but just be a pain in the arse – which was fun-ish. I got noticed. But I didn't get any exams.

Was that in some way making up for the loss of the love and attention of your Mum, do you think?

I suppose so. It's a terrible cliché but losing your mum (and dad) probably generates the urge to say to everyone else: 'Look at me, look at me, look at me.' Like Bono says, 'It's not normal to want to play to 20,000 people a night and have them all telling you that they love you.' It's not normal and that's what this is: I lost my mum, Bono lost his mum, Paul McCartney lost his mum, John Lennon lost his mum, Sinead O'Connor lost her mum. The list goes on and on and on and on. Springsteen's dad just simply wasn't present. But the main thing is that when both your parents have gone there is no authority you will accept or even understand.

And that was fed by the books you were reading as a young kid.

I read all the time. Sometimes when I got in from school I couldn't be arsed to light the fire, so I would sit with the oven open and read. I didn't do any work but I read: Dickens, Steinbeck, Studs Terkel, then Bob Dylan turned me onto James Baldwin. I would sit with my feet in the gas oven and read – and listen to Radio Luxembourg. I didn't really think of this as freedom. It was just all that I knew and yet some part of you thinks: 'This is shit.' Because you see your friends going home to their families. Sometimes I would tag along to get fed, but really just to be with people. Looking back I think this generated a sense of injustice – a sense that 'This is not fair.' And that was underscored by what I was reading. I read Baldwin and the others and *Cry, the Beloved Country*, and I liked those books maybe because they were about situations of injustice.

So all this meshed. I was 13 then and after I learned about apartheid I heard the South African rugby team were coming to Ireland. I joined the Anti-Apartheid Movement and went out onto the streets and started giving out anti-apartheid leaflets to stop their visit to Dublin. This little scar here, on my forehead, is where I got whacked by a police baton during the anti-apartheid protest. The lesson I learned was that the world is not immutable, it can be changed, and you can give it a little heave on the way. It was all young people too. Dylan was singing his protest songs and I thought, yes, that's right, The Times They Actually Are A-Changing' Change was going on all around me. There was a rupture with the 50s and the American Dream. The hippies were rejecting that. Vietnam was accelerating it. Pop music was the rhetoric of change and the platform for change. And change was clearly not only inevitable but desirable.

But what made you decide to go down to volunteer to work with the homeless at the Simon Community?

After a few years I began to feel: what is the point of me going home after school? There is no one there and I'm fucking sick of the house being dark and freezing. So one day after school I took the bus and, instead of going south to come home, I went north into Dublin. I had heard of this crowd who helped with the homeless, the Simon Community, and I found their address down on the dockside. I sat there, I remember, at a table and watched these people come and go into the room. Very bare room, a bit of furniture, and a kettle, and these thin, whey-faced, pinched little girls – streetwalkers, hookers, junkies, I now know, but didn't then. This was what I'd been reading about in

Steinbeck. But this wasn't Oklahoma, it was my home town. I thought: I don't have to be Woody Guthrie, riding the rails, I just have to come downtown in Dublin. And here it is.

The first thing I had to do was collect food from the grocery shops as they were about to close and then we went to Smithfield market and built a fire and made soup. And the homeless people would gather round this huge fire for warmth. They were lost men and women. Their stories really interested me. No matter what I was not learning at school, it just couldn't compete with life. When we formed a band it always had intent and purpose. I found the name for the band in one of the books I was re-reading, Woody Guthrie's *Bound for Glory*. Woody was the great musical activist and rock 'n' roll was always for me a sort of musical activism. You can spot it from our first songs. I was working in an abattoir when I wrote the first Number One; 'Rat Trap' was written about those people in the Five Lamps [a rough part of Dublin], who were trapped and who have no chance whatsoever. All the songs were that sort of stuff. So I find it weird that people think that Band Aid came out of the blue. It was all in a line with the rest my life – learning independence, organization, questioning authority, challenging injustice, rock 'n' roll, and learning that change is possible in the world – and that you can help to make it happen.

So was all this philanthropic activism internally driven? Did you not feel answerable to anyone else – to the public who gave the money or the starving people in Africa?

I wasn't sleeping before Live Aid because there was so much going on. Paula [his then girlfriend] used to put towels under me at night because I would break out in cold sweats. In part, it was because of the possibility of personal failure – global personal public failure: that people would say, if it didn't work: 'Geldof – what a wanker!' But that was overwhelmed by the idea that I might let down the bands who had given up so much on my personal say-so: Eric Clapton had given up three nights in Las Vegas without me even asking; Queen, the Beach Boys, Led Zeppelin and Black Sabbath all re-formed for the Live Aid concert; McCartney nervous playing for the first time in six years; Bowie moved to tears by the scenes of hunger; Duran Duran flew to America because there was no room on the bill in London. People went to immense effort but never went on about it and never charged a penny. It was the same with Live 8. Stevie Wonder's crowd said: 'OK, Bob, Stevie's great. He'd love to do it. Who's paying for the musicians and covering all the expenses?' And I said: 'Stevie is.' They said: 'Look, Bob, there's 30 people.' And I said: 'Yes. Sorry, but that's how it is' – because I'd promised that every penny donated to Band Aid would go to Africa, with nothing deducted for expenses or administration. And that was the end of the conversation. Stevie paid and they all just arrived.

When Madonna did Live 8 it probably cost her $10 million: she had to give up recording, fly to LA, hire all those musicians and 30 dancers at her own expense, pay for their flights from LA and put them all up. Just to do 10 minutes – because you can't do Madonna with just an acoustic guitar. It had to be a great show. So she did it. No questions asked. No invoice received. So the second thing was fear of letting down the musicians and crews who had put their faith in me making it all work.

But most awful was my fear of letting down the people in Africa in whose name we were doing this in the first place. Think of the disaster if this failed. So of course I didn't sleep. I was constantly aware I was accountable to these three groups. To the punters, for leading them up the garden path to think we could achieve this. The bands, and the crews and everyone who made it happen. And most importantly the people in Africa if it was all a grotesque failure.

And, of course, it wasn't – though that still didn't stop the cynics who said this is all just about Bob trying to revive his flagging pop career.

Yeah, well, that didn't work, then! Actually, my career may have been on a dip but it was viable enough. The Rats had just come off a 40-date sell-out tour. It had sold out before I even thought of doing Band Aid. And it would have been a little extravagant to put on Live Aid just to get the Rats back in the singles charts!

The first man ever described as a philanthropist in England was John Howard, the penal reformer. Men like him and the anti-slavery campaigner William Wilberforce were not philanthropists in the modern sense of the world – they didn't give away large

sums of money – they were activist philanthropists. Do you see any parallels between that and what you have done?

Fuck off! To compare me with them is ridiculous. Wilberforce, in campaigning against slavery, was challenging the entire economic basis of his world. The economy of Britain and the United States was built on slavery at that time. In 20 years he overturned that so that the British Navy went from escorting slave ships to, almost overnight, imprisoning them. So, no, there is no comparison whatsoever.

One common factor was determination and a refusal to give up. Both Howard and Wilberforce devoted decades to their causes. And that's what you have done. You said you were just going to make the record. Then you were just going to do the concert. Then you were just going to do the Commission for Africa. Then you were lobbying the leaders of the world's top eight nations. And you are still active. You have demonstrated extraordinary longevity in your commitment.

Well, I didn't set out to. I only do it 'cos the damn thing keeps working. And one thing leads you to another and then the responsibility thing kicks in and next minute you're off on the next adventure which is actually not at all exciting but rather hours of tedium, learning, persuading, begging, endless fucking meetings and boredom. But it works. So things can be changed.

(For Bob Geldof's interview on philanthropy and political power, see page 536.)

Chapter 8

Victorian Virtues and Vices

Only women should be rent collectors. So believed Octavia Hill, a diminutive but indomitable English woman who embodied a new kind of philanthropy which became fashionable in the second half of the nineteenth century. Her notion of '5 per cent philanthropy' ushered in a raft of novel ideas which suggested that philanthropists inspired by enlightened self-interest could make a profit from their benevolence, though one she limited to that fixed percentage. She brought with it a sense that the poor were to be partners in the enterprise of their own improvement. And she pioneered the innovative field we would now call social housing – which is where she came into contact with the business of rent collecting. She was perhaps the first social entrepreneur.

Octavia Hill was born in 1838 in Wisbech in Cambridgeshire into a well-off family of social reformers but, unusually, she had some direct experience of what it meant to be poor. Her father, James Hill, was a merchant banker who combined business with adventures into radical politics. He even went so far as to finance a number of socialist communes. He was, it turned out, a better radical than he was a businessman. His investments went awry and he was forced into bankruptcy in 1840, plunging him into depression and a nervous breakdown – and his family into financial hardship. It was a genteel poverty but it forced his third wife Caroline Southwood Smith, who had been governess to his older children before their marriage, to find a job. She told their daughter Octavia, then aged 12, that she must find employment too.

The family moved from Cambridgeshire to London where Caroline had been offered a job as manager and bookkeeper at the Ladies Guild, a craft workshop for unskilled women and girls. Octavia was accepted by the Guild for training in painting on glass and in 1852 began work at the age of 13. A year later the workshop expanded into making toys and took on a group of children from the nearby Ragged School[1] as toymakers. Fourteen-year-old Octavia was made their supervisor and put in charge of the toy-making workroom.[2]

As a youngster, not long after she learned to read and write, Octavia had spent time working with her grandfather, Dr Thomas Southwood Smith, who had become a public figure for his work to improve conditions in London's factories and his demands for wide-ranging reforms to the city's sanitation. Octavia had helped him by preparing copies of his correspondence on the condition of London's poor. Now she gained first-hand experience. At the workshop she learned something of the lives of the girls in her charge but occasionally she had to visit a child at home and was horrified by the grim tenements in which they were crammed eight or ten to a room. Her mother's work at the Guild brought the family into contact with an Anglican priest, Frederick Denison Maurice, an academic and the chaplain to Guy's Hospital, who was one of the founders of the Christian Socialist Movement. At home the Hill family often entertained the radical luminaries of the day; as well as Maurice regular visitors included John Ruskin, Charles Dickens and Hans Christian Andersen, and the anti-capitalist author Charles Kingsley, author of *The Water Babies*. Octavia wrote to her younger sister of an evening 'gathered around the fire', in which they 'talked of the Guild, of Ruskin, of the poor, of education, of politics and history'.[3] At 15 she was enthralled by Ruskin, saying of an encounter with him: 'to think that that was the man who was accused of being mad, presumptuous, conceited and prejudiced'.[4]

Two things inspired the initiative which was to prove Octavia's great contribution to the history of philanthropy. After hearing a lecture by Kingsley on the role women should play in improving the lives of the poor, she combed the parish of Marylebone to find accommodation for the family of one of the girls from her workshop, but was unable to find anything she regarded as tolerable. She decided the only solution was to become a landlord herself. When Ruskin's father died in 1864, leaving a substantial sum to his only son, the artist offered to finance Octavia Hill in a project to refurbish three dilapidated houses in Marylebone as accommodation for the very poor.

OCTAVIA HILL AND FIVE-PER-CENT PHILANTHROPY

Octavia Hill was not the first to establish a project for housing of a decent quality for working people in the capital. Bodies such as the Peabody Trust were already providing homes for the 'artisans and labouring poor of London'. But they only wanted to house what Hill called 'rather respectable, nice, working people'.[5] Parliamentary inquiries in the 1870s and 1880s pointed unmistakably to 'the utter failure of housing philanthropies . . . to reach the neediest and poorest of the slum dwellers', in the words of David Owen.[6] The Peabody Trust expected prospective tenants to provide a reference from their regular employer.[7] Octavia Hill, by contrast, wanted to provide dwellings for the families of labourers, casual workers, costermongers, hawkers and women who took in laundry. This 'class below' were far from being respectable in Victorian society.[8] The idea hatched by her and Ruskin was that he would receive a 5 per cent return on his loan, to be repaid from the tenants' rent. The idea of '5 per cent philanthropy' was born.

The first suitable houses she found were in the inaptly named Paradise Place. They had been in the hands of rapacious landlords who packed families into the tiny insanitary dwellings which, Octavia Hill wrote, 'swarmed with vermin; the [wall]papers, black with dirt, hung in long strips from the walls; the drains were stopped, the water supply out of order'.[9] Even the banisters were missing – having been burned by the previous occupants as firewood. Visiting the tenants, Hill found them to be so demoralized as to be 'beyond caring'. It brought on her the realization that it was not just buildings which needed to be restored. The women needed help to rebuild their self-respect and that involved learning to take responsibility for the state of their lives and homes. 'She saw to the repairing of old houses and the reforming of drunken and shiftless tenants', as one biographer put it.[10] She had the drains cleared and the houses repaired, thoroughly cleaned, ventilated and redecorated. She charged 4s. 6d. per family per week but gave them two rooms where before they had had only one. She collected the rents every week herself, later assisted by two lady volunteers who were tasked with checking on every detail of the premises but also of the family, especially the children. They were more like social workers than rent collectors. Octavia Hill gave them the name 'visitors' and set them two cardinal rules: one was 'that personal influence must be brought strongly to bear' on the tenants; the other was that they always 'must abstain from any form of almsgiving'.[11] Octavia had to overcome the initial hostility and suspicion of her tenants who, according to *The Times*, had 'sunk to the lowest depths of degradation' living in houses 'in an indescribable condition of filth and neglect'.[12]

At first her tenants would thrust out their rent money to her through barely opened doors. Slowly, however, she won their confidence. She offered the women cash incentives for cleanliness. She employed the older girls to wash and scrub the communal stairways and halls. She taught the boys how to mend shoes. She gave jobs to her out-of-work male tenants, plastering, painting and papering. She freely gave advice to her tenants on curtains and furniture and brought them flowers, teaching the women how to arrange them. She conducted singing lessons for the girls and organized fife-and-drum bands for the boys. She even bought a chest of tea to sell to her tenants more cheaply than they could buy it in the shops. She scoured the classified advertisements in the newspapers to find jobs for the men and then vouched for them to employers, saying 'I know them to be honest, I know them to be clean.'[13] She then assisted the wives in collecting the weekly wage from their husbands, before they could spend it in local ale houses. She set up a savings club. She even went to the local gaol to bail men out of prison if she felt that they had generally good characters. She spent hours chatting with her tenants over tea.[14] Only women could be rent collectors because such work demanded a feminine perspective: 'Ladies must do it, for it is detailed work; ladies must do it, for it is household work; it needs, moreover, persistent patience, gentleness, hope.'[15]

Octavia Hill was not alone in such a perspective. In 1869 the English feminist Josephine Butler made a distinction between masculine and feminine forms of philanthropy. The masculine variety was marked by 'large and comprehensive measures, organisations and systems planned by men and sanctioned by Parliament'.[16] But feminine philanthropy had more profound social and political consequences. Women engaged in charitable activism vastly outnumbered men. In 1893 as many as half a million women in England worked 'continuously and semi-professionally, in philanthropy', according to Frank Prochaska.[17] In the nineteenth century, he suggests, volunteering served as the principal occupation for bored middle-class women.[18]

As Octavia Hill's reputation grew, young women from all over England and Scotland came to work with her; she even had volunteers from the Netherlands, Denmark, Sweden and the United States. Hill devoted much of her time to training them. The socialist reformer Beatrice Webb later wrote that she 'first became aware of the meaning of the poverty of the poor' while staying with her sister Kate, who was a rent collector for Octavia Hill in the East End of London.[19]

The price Octavia Hill demanded for all her care and attention was that her tenants should pay their rent on time. Rent arrears were not tolerated, though those who were without work were sometimes permitted a fortnight's grace period. After that they paid up, or received notice to quit. One tenant was surprised to receive an eviction notice when Hill discovered he would not send his children to school and was overcrowding his rooms. When he protested that his rent was not in arrears, she told him that prompt payment was not the only criterion for occupying one of her properties.[20] She was resolute in her rules, insisting 'where a man persistently refuses to exert himself, external help is worse than useless'.[21] She repeatedly described her work in terms of adult education: she was training and disciplining adults who had been destructive and unruly as children. 'There is much of rebuke and repression needed, although a deep and silent undercurrent of sympathy and pity may flow beneath.'[22]

To Octavia Hill better buildings were merely a means to better citizens. It was a moral rather than an economic issue. When Sir Richard Cross, the chairman of a parliamentary select committee into the housing of the poor, asked about her plan for improving old houses, she corrected him by insisting that 'my particular plan has been that of improving tenants in old houses'.[23] In one of the many newspaper articles she penned in the hope of replicating her philosophy more widely she wrote: 'You cannot deal with the people and their houses separately.'[24] Hers was an unashamedly paternalistic approach. Influenced by the Social Darwinism of her time,* she held that 'the aborigines of the East End' lived in their unalterable squalor primarily because of their own moral weakness, and, without moral reformation, no amount of superior housing would permanently better their lot.

---

* See pages 338–340 below.

Her aim, writes David Owen, was to transmute 'improvident savages into solid citizens'.[25] Poverty and squalor revealed personal failure. 'There was something infinitely schoolmistressy about it all,' Owen pronounces. She, rather, saw herself as a liberator whose mission was to free poor tenants from bondage to 'tyrant vixen' landladies and . . . conscienceless landlords.[26]

Yet, as her Christian faith required, she was open to the possibility of redemption. 'I do not say I will not have drunkards,' she told a Royal Commission on the Housing of the Working Classes. 'I have quantities of drunkards; but everything depends on whether I think the drunkard will be better for being sent away or not.'[27]

Not all her contemporaries were enamoured of her approach. *Justice*, the journal of the Social Democratic Federation, despised what it regarded as 'her insufferable, meddling, patronizing, genteel do-goodism' and labelled her 'inquisitrix-general into the homes of the poor'.[28] Hill was untroubled, admitting 'it is a tremendous despotism, but it is exercised with a view of bringing out the powers of the people and treating them as responsible for themselves within certain limits'.[29]

More than that, she said, 'I have tried, as far as opportunity has permitted, to develop the love of beauty among my tenants. Taking her lead from her mentor, John Ruskin, she believed her tenants needed trees, gardens, playgrounds and flowers, among which the poor could satisfy their need of 'enjoying things that are lovely and quiet'.[30] This same impetus was later to lead her to campaign for the protection of green spaces in the city and to found one of Britain's most long-standing conservation charities, the National Trust. Beauty, joy and love were words which featured often in her vocabulary. 'The poor of London need joy and beauty in their lives,' she wrote.[31] Elsewhere she declared: 'I see no limit to the power of raising even the lowest classes if we will know and love them, deal with them as human beings, stimulate their hope and energy.'[32]

Most of her contemporaries admired and applauded her achievements. Her success snowballed. By 1874 Octavia Hill had 15 housing schemes with around 3,000 tenants[33] over which, one of her American admirers noted, she ruled 'with an iron sceptre twined with roses'.[34] Donors – royalty and aristocrats, two city financiers, leading figures from literature and the arts – offered her more money than she could cope with. In 1884 the Church Commissioners invited her to take over the management of a number of the embarrassingly run-down properties of which it was landlord. Hill was uncompromising in her response, so much so that the Bishop of London, Frederick Temple, later recalled of meeting her, 'When she talked to us for half an hour we were quite refuted. I never had such a beating in all my life!'[35] She insisted that the tenants should be involved in the process of rebuilding the estates, which must now incorporate open spaces. Together she and the tenants turned slum properties, notorious for poverty and petty crime, into model estates which paid her celebrated 5 per cent return on investment. They also featured art classes, music lessons, cultural outings and performances of Gilbert and Sullivan. There was even a military cadet corps for boys under 18. So delighted were the Church Commissioners, said Bishop Temple, that they proceeded to carry out similar plans on their other housing estates.

Yet for all its paternalism there was in Octavia Hill's approach an element of partnership and even mutuality which brought something new to English philanthropy. Like other humanitarian philanthropists and social workers, she was driven by the vision articulated in 1870 by Sir Charles Trevelyan when he declared:

> Since the beginning of this century the gulf between rich and poor has become fearfully wide. The rich have become richer and the poor poorer. The proposal is to close this gulf and to bring back the rich into such close relation with the poor as cannot fail to have a civilising influence and to knit all classes together in the bonds of mutual help and goodwill. Everything else would follow from this.[36]

It was a vision which had its limitations. Octavia Hill, like so many Victorian philanthropists, deplored dependence to the point where – in what she detected to be an age of creeping state and municipal socialism – she attacked housing for the poor erected by the London County Council and opposed free school meals and a universal old-age pension.[37] Such measures, she believed, undermined individual self-reliance and discouraged private enterprise – a belief that was challenged by the emergence of the welfare state. But she was, in the estimation of the historian and former Labour politician Tristram Hunt, 'one of the greatest social entrepreneurs in British history'.[38] Her holistic view of human needs, expressed in her campaigning conviction that beauty, art and nature were to be enjoyed by everyone, has clear affinities with twenty-first-century thinking. Although she was a child of her times she was possessed of a vision which transcended them. Towards the end of her life she was presented with a portrait of herself by her fellow workers. In her speech of thanks she said: 'When I am gone, I hope my friends will not try to carry out any special system, or to follow blindly in the track which I have trodden. New circumstances require various efforts, and it is the spirit, not the dead form, that should be perpetuated.'[39]

ROBERT OWEN AND PHILANTHROPY
WITHOUT RELIGION

The sense of mutuality and partnership at the heart of Octavia Hill's philosophy was an outworking of the idea of enlightened self-interest which had already taken root in eighteenth- and nineteenth-century Britain. From that point onwards the history of philanthropy became intimately bound up with the history of capitalism. Adam Smith had articulated the idea of enlightened self-interest in 1759 in *The Theory of Moral Sentiments*. There, and later in his *Wealth of Nations* (1776), he set out the idea that the self-interested actions of individuals frequently work out to be in the best interests of wider society:

> It is not from the benevolence of the butcher, the brewer, or the baker, that we expect our dinner, but from their regard to their own interest. We address ourselves, not to their humanity but to their self-love, and never talk to them of our necessities but of their advantages. Nobody but the beggar chooses to depend chiefly upon the benevolence of his fellow men.[40]

Yet though each individual looks out for himself, 'he is in this, as in many other cases, led by an invisible hand to promote an end which was no part of his intention'.[41]

The importance of this philosophical concept to the history of philanthropy was that it provided a clear basis for acts of benevolence and humanity – without any reference to religious motivation. A prominent example of this is the work of the industrialist Robert Owen, a man who lost his belief in Christianity in early youth

– his autobiography suggests it happened at the age of 10 – but who powerfully embraced the Enlightenment notion of the perfectibility of humanity. To Owen human character and behaviour are shaped far more by nurture than nature. He wrote that each man was 'the necessary result of . . . the conditions by which nature and society surrounded him'.[42] In this Owen was influenced by a combination of the doctrines of the French and Scottish Enlightenments and his own early experiences working in a cotton spinning mill in Manchester. Out of them he forged the first model industrial development of the nineteenth century – and a political creed which was to be the foundation of English socialism.

Robert Owen was born in 1771 in a small market town in Wales called Newtown. At the age of 10 he was apprenticed to a cloth merchant in Lincolnshire and three years later joined a clothing retailer in London before moving to a similar position in Manchester. That city was the centre of the English textile industry and there Owen became intrigued by the new cotton spinning machinery which produced what he was selling. At the age of 19 he borrowed £100 from his brother William and entered into a partnership with a machine maker, John Jones. Together they engineered a new version of a piece of machinery called a 'spinning mule' which created thread from cotton. The firm of Jones and Owen was a rapid success. But the Welsh youth had greater ambitions. In 1789 he sold his share of the business in return for three of the spinning mules and rented a new factory to start his own mill. Before long he was hired as the manager of a bigger mill – the first in Manchester to install the innovative Boulton and Watt spinning engine. He now had 500 employees in his charge. The quality of the thread he produced became renowned throughout the industry.[43]

But he also began to become concerned with the moral and physical welfare of his workforce. In 1793 he joined the committee of the Manchester Board of Health which had been set up to improve the working and living conditions of factory 'hands'. More significantly, at the age of 24 he was elected to the ranks of the distinguished Manchester Literary and Philosophical Society. There he began to imbibe Enlightenment notions that progress could come from industrialization and mass manufacture. Soon after joining he delivered a paper to the Mancunian sons of the Enlightenment entitled 'Remarks on the improvement of the cotton trade'. It was well received, so a month later Owen delivered a second, on 'The utility of learning'. The development of his thinking is revealed by the titles of other papers he delivered to the Society: 'Thoughts on the connection between universal happiness and practical mechanics' in 1795 and 'On the origin of opinions, with a view to the improvement of social virtues' in 1796. Four years later he attempted to put this Enlightenment theory into practice when he bought four water-powered cotton mills on the banks of the River Clyde not far from Glasgow. There at New Lanark he built the Industrial Revolution's first model community. He called it his 'social experiment'. It was a laboratory in which to test Enlightenment doctrines about material and spiritual progress. There he sought to combine industrial capitalism's drive to prosperity through technology with the improvement of humankind through care and compassion. In line with the teachings of Jean-Jacques Rousseau, Owen was convinced that if he created the right environment those who lived and worked in it would become good, rational and decent individuals.

Almost 2,000 people were employed in the four mills, including about 500 children who had been designated as paupers by the parishes of the Scottish Lowlands. Children as young as five were at work for 13 hours a day in what Owen later called 'the manufactories, which are often heated to a high temperature, and contain an atmosphere far from being the most favourable to human life'.[44] Its dark satanic mills thrived on 'a combination of vicious and inferior conditions'. He later told a House of Commons committee that when he first arrived:

I found that there were 500 children, who had been taken from poor-houses, chiefly in Edinburgh, and those children were generally from the age of five and six, to seven to eight. The hours at that time were thirteen. Although these children were well fed their limbs were very generally deformed, their growth was stunted, and although one of the best schoolmasters was engaged to instruct these children regularly every night, in general they made very slow progress, even in learning the common alphabet. I came to the conclusion that the children were injured by being taken into the mills at this early age, and employed for so many hours; therefore, as soon as I had it in my power, I adopted regulations to put an end to a system which appeared to me to be so injurious.[45]

Owen banned children under the age of 10 from working in his mills. He set up an infant school for them instead, as well as a secondary school for those over 10 to attend in the afternoon after their morning's work in the manufactory.[46] Corporal punishment, and even 'harsh critical words', were forbidden to the teachers since Owen believed that people were naturally good but were corrupted if they were treated badly. He instructed teachers to make learning interesting – by means of free discussion, question-and-answer, exploration of the countryside and extensive use of pictures, maps and charts. He discouraged the seating of children entirely in rows and encouraged them to believe 'that life may be enjoyed, and that each may make his own happiness consistent with that of all the others'.[47] New Lanark had the first workplace creche and the first adult night school anywhere in the world. Finding shoddy and expensive goods in the company store, he replaced them with food and clothes which he bought at wholesale prices and sold to the workers at cost. Prices dropped by a full 25 per cent. He instituted a scheme whereby workers set aside one-sixtieth of their wages for periods of sickness or injury and old age. When other mills laid off their workers during an American trade embargo, Owen kept his employees on full pay to maintain the factory machinery. He saw his employees as every bit as important to the success of his enterprise as the machines he owned. Workers elected twelve 'jurors' from among their number, who served for a year to maintain order in the community. Fines were imposed for drunkenness. Pilfering and absenteeism were reduced, though employees with illegitimate children were fined.

Yet, far from eating into his profits, all the social improvements only served to increase productivity. Owen used peer pressure to harness that. Above each machine in the factory he mounted a 'silent monitor' – a block of wood with a different colour painted on each face. Each day supervisors rotated the colours to reflect the output of the machine operator – black for poor performance, blue for indifferent, yellow for good and white for excellent. As his reforms progressed, the number of yellow and white markers increased.[48] Owen was the first factory-owner to manage rather than control or order his workforce; some have even called him, for that, 'the father of personnel management'.[49] As a result of this, and of Owen's undoubted technical expertise, profits at New Lanark were spectacularly good, with a return on investment of more than 50 per cent, even after all the money spent on social improvements. Owen's conscious calculation of enlightened self-interest was laid bare

in 1813 when he stated his intent to keep the factory workers' children
in school until the age of 12. His motives combined caring altruism
with an eye for cost efficiency, as he revealed when he wrote 'far better it
would be for the children, their parents and society that the first should
not commence employment until they attain the age of twelve, when
their bodies would be more competent to undergo the fatigue and
exertions required of them'.[50] Robert Owen, said one contemporary,
'was a remarkable instance of a man at once Tory and revolutionary'.[51]

Owen was certainly visionary. On New Year's Day in 1816 he
made a speech to his assembled workers in which he summarized his
non-religious Enlightenment dream:

> What ideas individuals may attach to the term 'Millennium' I know
> not; but I know that society may be formed so as to exist without
> crime, without poverty, with health greatly improved, with little,
> if any, misery, and with intelligence and happiness increased a
> hundredfold; and no obstacle whatsoever intervenes at this moment
> except ignorance to prevent such a state of society from becoming
> universal.

'Happiness' was a word of which Owen was fond; it appears in his
writings far more than it does in other Enlightenment texts.[52]

Robert Owen's social experiment attracted widespread support from
all across Britain and all over Europe. Philanthropists, churchmen, social
reformers, statesmen and royals – including the future Tsar Nicholas I
of Russia – visited New Lanark to study its operations and educational
methods. The model community attracted some 20,000 visitors between
1815 and 1825. The attention prompted Owen to shift his focus from
his own factories to those of the whole nation. His philanthropy turned
political. He announced that 'the chief object' of his existence would
be to make 'universal' the reforms he had achieved with his model
community in New Lanark. In 1813 he had written a book which he
hoped would persuade other factory owners to follow his example. He
had called it *A New View of Society: Or, Essays on the Formation of Human
Character, and the Application of the Principle to Practice.* But now his
vision was far more ambitious. When he published a second edition of
the book in 1816 he changed the subtitle to *Essays on the Formation of
Human Character Preparatory to the Development of a Plan for Gradually
Ameliorating the Condition of Mankind.* That same year he not only

reduced the working day in his factories by an hour, but he also tried to persuade Parliament to introduce a bill requiring similar improvements in all English factories. Its aim was to outlaw the employment of those under the age of 10, ban night shifts for all children, provide 30 minutes of education a day for workers under 18, and limit the working day to ten and a half hours. His rivals, however, killed his attempt at legislation. In reaction to this opposition his views became bolder still.

Until this point Owen had been a follower of the classic liberalism of the utilitarian philosopher Jeremy Bentham. The freedom of choice inherent in free markets, Owen believed, gave workers the right to move to another employer. This would release them from the excessive power of the capitalist mill owners. But other factory owners, he now realized, had failed to follow the example of his New Lanark experiment – and now they had killed off his attempts at parliamentary reform. So Owen began to make frequent visits to the philosophical anarchist and religious sceptic William Godwin, the husband of the woman generally considered to be Britain's first feminist, Mary Wollstonecraft, author of *The Vindication of the Rights of Women*. Owen grew steadily more radical.

By 1817 – a year of significant change for him – he had conceived the idea of an eight-hour working day and coined the slogan: 'Eight hours labour, Eight hours recreation, Eight hours rest.' The same year he came up with the idea of self-sufficient co-operative communes, proposing that 'villages of union' should be set up throughout the countryside. They would consist of communities of 500 to 1,500 people united by 'mutual and combined interest', which appeared to imply, in a spirit of proto-communism, that goods were to be held in common.[53] Something similar applied to children: Owen's idea was that each family should have its own private apartments and the responsibility for the care of their children until they reached the age of three, but thereafter, children would be raised by the community at large, with their parents only seeing them at mealtimes. In 1817 he also gave a series of speeches at the City of London Tavern – in front of hundreds of influential politicians, clergymen, economists and social reformers – in which he called for a general increase in taxation to pay for increased public spending and also declared that all religions were false. He then went on to announce the arrival of a secular millennium, or utopia.[54] Owen saw his communitarianism as a step towards Heaven on Earth – he called it the 'New Moral World'. At its heart was the vision he had set the year before in his New Year's Day address to the workers of New Lanark, where he had also referenced the millennium – a biblical concept, particularly popular at the time, which spoke of a time of peace and harmony after Jesus Christ returned when all evils would be cleansed from the earth. As the years passed, Owen increasingly began to use apocalyptic religious language.

All this was crystallized in 1820 when he published his *Report to the County of Lanark of a Plan for Relieving Public Distress, and Removing Discontent, by Giving Permanent, Productive Employment, to the Poor and Working Classes.*[55] In it he declared that a communitarian approach was needed, not only to remedy the plight of the working classes, but as an antidote to the polarizing effects of capitalism. It was the turning point in Owen's political development. His report declared that reform was not enough and that a total reorganization of society was needed. It rejected the quest for profit as an end in itself – and advocated of a system of fair wages aimed at justice for working people rather than maximum profits for owners and their middlemen. The report set out a set of doctrines which Owen called 'social science' but which others named 'socialism'. Robert Owen is often labelled 'the father of socialism'.

In the years which followed his focus on philanthropy fell away. He sold most of his interest in New Lanark in 1824 and moved to America where he founded a number of socialist communities, most famously at New Harmony in Indiana. The project consumed four-fifths of the entire fortune Owen had made in Scotland. And though in 1825 he addressed the American President, Senate and Supreme Court in the House of Representatives in Washington DC, his communitarian vision did not take in the United States. Owen returned to the United Kingdom in 1828.

Six years later in February 1834 he founded the Grand National Consolidated Trades Union, which within a few weeks had a million and a half members. 'Strikes broke out everywhere' as a result, according to A. L. Morton, author of *A People's History of England*, 'scaring the government into a belief that the revolution was at hand'.[56] It was not. Membership of Owen's grand union declined as rapidly as it had grown. By November that same year it had closed down.

Owen's next initiative, the following year, was to form the Association of All Classes of All Nations, later renamed the Universal Community

Society of Rational Religionists. Known popularly as the Rational Society, within two years it had grown 60 branches of Owenite socialists, mainly in Britain's industrial areas. The Owenite trading store in Rochdale gave birth to the Co-operative Movement. It was all immensely popular, so much so that Owen was presented to Queen Victoria by the Prime Minister, Lord Melbourne, in 1839. Owen's weekly newspaper the *New Moral World* was published for over a decade. As many as 50,000 people attended its weekly lectures, among them a young German mill owner from Manchester named Friedrich Engels.

But by 1848 Engels and his co-author Karl Marx in their *Communist Manifesto* had become highly critical of Owenite communitarian socialism – which they dismissed as 'utopian'. They argued that Owen's success at New Lanark had been due to good luck rather than good judgement. Marx and Engels dismissed the idea that society could be radically transformed by means of experimental communities in which property was held in common and economic transactions were conducted on a co-operative basis. Owen and his kind were 'bourgeois, idealistic and anti-revolutionary', despite the fact that this benevolent industrialist had been one of the first to see the inherent flaws in a capitalism which saw the labouring classes as mere 'hands'.[57] By 1850 Robert Owen's gentler British brand of communitarian socialism had been overshadowed by the harsher revolutionary internationalist socialism of the Marxist variety. Yet his role as a philanthropic pioneer, blending enlightened self-interest with idealistic altruism, should not be overlooked. On his deathbed in November 1858 a church minister visited him to offer religious consolation. It was rejected in no uncertain terms. Asked by the cleric whether he regretted wasting his life on fruitless projects, Owen replied: 'My life was not useless; I gave important truths to the world, and it was only for want of understanding that they were disregarded. I have been ahead of my time.'[58]

MIXED MOTIVES AND TITUS SALT

Robert Owen's deathbed judgement was undoubtedly correct. His views were extremely advanced when compared to the mainstream of Victorian philanthropy. The odd individual imitated his approach, in part at least. What Owen had begun with cotton in Manchester, Titus Salt emulated in wool on the other side of the Pennines. If Lancashire was the epicentre of industrial cotton, then Yorkshire was its equivalent for wool and Bradford was the national capital. Indeed, that city was the international centre of the trade in worsted wool – and Salt was the pre-eminent figure there.

His genius lay in perfecting new techniques to work with tangled *donski* wool from Russia and alpaca from Peru, both of which were considered unusable by the worsted wool industry. In 1839, after a series of experiments in secret, he found ways to combine the alpaca, and mohair, with cotton or silk, to create luxurious lustrous new fabrics. They were ideal for expensive dresses for fashionable ladies. Salt made a fortune. So successful was he that, in 1850, Salt decided he needed a huge new spinning mill. Alongside it he built a model village to house his 4,000 workers on the banks of the River Aire, three miles outside Bradford. It was to be far grander than Robert Owen's New Lanark. Grandiloquently, he called it Saltaire.

Salt's motives in this were obscure. He was a devoutly religious man; his family motto was *Quid non, Deo juvante* – 'With God nothing is impossible.' Like Robert Owen he believed that an attractive and healthy environment would encourage his workers to lead virtuous lives. He was undoubtedly a public-spirited man; his politics were those of a radical Liberal and he occupied almost every leading public office in the city – as alderman, mayor, chief constable, Member of Parliament and president of Bradford's chamber of commerce. Cynics, including John Ruskin, suggested that the houses for the workforce were merely an attempt by Salt to create a captive labour force. But Salt's grand vision went much further than would have been needed to secure a compliant workforce. The mill was the largest of its kind in the world when it opened in 1853 – its south front by design was the exact length of St Paul's Cathedral.[59]

But the site contained not just every necessary stage in the manufacturing process to turn alpaca into costly fabric, it also held 824 houses, each bigger than was the norm at the time. None of them were back-to-backs, the cramped style of building characterizing most houses in nineteenth-century Bradford. All were connected to the factory's gas supply, mains drains, and most had their own outside lavatory. Each had good windows to let in sun and light. The streets were open-ended and the entire complex, built 'in the Italian style', also had 40 shops, a series of schools, a library, a mechanics institute and community centre, and almshouses for the aged and infirm (who also received pensions). There were baths and a wash house, allotments, a park, and a Congregationalist church and a Methodist chapel. Salt required his workers to attend divine worship on Sundays. Swearing, gambling and drinking were frowned upon. All the large handsome public buildings were magnificently appointed – 'not unlike some Oriental temple,' a visitor commented in *Harper's Magazine* in 1872, adding, 'You half expect to see a gorgeously appareled procession of dervishes or swarthy priestesses issue from the ornate portals'.[60]

At the opening of the venture Salt told a visiting aristocrat that he had built the place 'to do good and give his sons employment'.[61] He had, said those around him, done 'all in his power to avoid evils so great as those resulting from polluted air and water'. These were no small measures in cholera-ridden Bradford, a city which had grown tenfold in the previous five decades. Instead, he 'hoped to draw around him a population that would enjoy the beauties of the neighbourhood, and who would be a well fed, contented, and happy body of operatives'. To that end 'he had given instructions to his architects that nothing should be spared to render the dwellings of the operatives a pattern to the country'.[62] In mapping out his community, David Owen writes:

> Salt showed an exceptional sense of scenic values, of vistas and squares, of the importance of well-arranged planting, and of the asset represented by the River Aire (whose course he changed so the prospect in from Saltaire would include graceful curves). Altogether this was a significant early achievement in town planning and noble expression of the philanthropic impulse – or of exceedingly enlightened self-interest.[63]

Small wonder that when Salt died in December 1876 his funeral was one of the great civic events of Victorian Bradford, with more than 100,000 people lining the streets.[64]

Yet if Titus Salt was enlightened, he was also self-interested. He might not have charged as much to his workers in rent as a commercial landlord would, so in that sense he was philanthropic, but his tenants were all, directly or indirectly, reliant on Salt for their livelihoods. Moreover, his new site overall proved a good return on his investment. Its location – on the banks of the Leeds and Liverpool canal and by the Leeds-Bradford-Skipton Railway – together with the increased efficiencies of the integrated one-site processing, made the new mill immensely lucrative. Profits were not only much larger, they flowed much more quickly. Treating all these factors together, his biographer David James says of Salt that, though his motives remain unclear, they appear to have been 'a mixture of sound economics, Christian duty, and a desire to have effective control over his workforce'.[65] Whatever its motivation, Saltaire caught the public imagination. It appeared to offer a practical answer to the pressing social question of the day: what should be the ideal relationship between capital and labour in a prosperous and caring society. Titus Salt came to be seen as embodying the best of Victorian capitalism. He was eulogized in the popular press of the day, decorated by Emperor Napoleon III, and made a baronet by Queen Victoria. Yet, as David James concludes, Sir Titus Salt offered no systemic solution to the problems of the new urban industrializing society. He offered only an escape from them.

ANGELA BURDETT-COUTTS AND OMNIVOROUS VICTORIAN PHILANTHROPY

Mainstream philanthropy in the Victorian era was rooted in a different approach. Men like Robert Owen and Titus Salt were the exceptions rather than the norm among the large number of Victorians who took to philanthropy. These men and women were inspired by a wide range of motives – religious commitment, humanitarianism, social idealism, civic patriotism and personal satisfaction – but their philanthropy was scattergun rather than systematic.[66] One woman sums up that approach in the sheer scale and range of her public benevolence: Angela Burdett-Coutts, the richest heiress of the era, who gave away more than £3 million – £350 million in today's money – in a philanthropic career which spanned 75 years. She inherited her 'addiction to philanthropy', to quote David Owen's *English Philanthropy, 1660 to 1960*, from her public-spirited but erratic father, the radical politician, Sir Francis Burdett.[67] But her huge fortune was inherited from the Coutts banking empire on her mother's side of the family. She used her considerable income to devote herself almost full-time to a wide-ranging philanthropy. Her career reflected the concerns of the time, making her, as Owen puts it, 'the premier Victorian philanthropist'.[68]

Angela Burdett-Coutts was only 23 in 1837 when she inherited the enormous Coutts fortune. Half the eligible bachelors in London threw themselves at her feet in eager hope. Hundreds of begging letters arrived in the post every day. The extent of her wealth would have taxed the business ability and wisdom of older heads, Owen suggests, but the young woman responded with a remarkably shrewd judgement and sense of organization. With her fortune, she acknowledged, came a great social responsibility and she set about spending her income on what *The Times* called, in her obituary, 'judicious charity'.[69] Burdett-Coutts was a religious woman and her initial acts of benevolence focused primarily on gifts to the various branches of the Church of England. She endowed a series of churches, church schools and vicarages, beginning in Westminster where her father had been MP for 30 years. She endowed colonial bishoprics in Cape Town, Adelaide and British Columbia. An enthusiast for Empire, and for what she saw as its civilizing Christian dimension, she funded numerous overseas missions. She supplied southern Nigeria with cotton gins. She sent hospital equipment and nurses to South Africa during the 1879 Anglo-Zulu war. She supported the Rajah of Sarawak in maintaining a model farm and even bought a gunboat for him.

In her giving to Anglican charities and imperial causes Angela Burdett-Coutts was advised by the old Duke of Wellington, with whom she had become friends in her youth. For over a decade they corresponded on her giving. Under the elderly politician's influence she began distinguishing what she called 'almsgiving' from 'charitable giving'. By the former she meant instant gifts without any overall plan. By the latter she meant donations aimed at reforming individuals with a distinctly moral agenda. Wellington at one point wrote to her:

> I have heard of the manner in which you dispose of your money, and indeed judging from the excessive demands upon myself, I am astonished that you have any left! You, like me, are supposed to be made of gold! And everybody supposes that it is only necessary to ask . . .[70]

The approach which Burdett-Coutts initially developed was for philanthropy tinged with moral reform and social control – something that, as we shall see, typified the giving of a large number of Victorian philanthropists. Under the tutelage of the old utilitarian Tory duke she began to take an interest in Ragged Schools – independent charity schools set up to provide free education, food, clothing and even lodging to children too poor to pay. The duke and his wealthy pupil hoped to inject into them a distinctly Anglican agenda.

Two years before she came into her huge fortune, however, at a dinner party she had met a young reporter named Charles Dickens. Angela Burdett-Coutts was inspired by his thirst for social justice. Dickens went on to broaden her horizons well beyond church projects.[71] The extent of his influence upon her is clear from their extensive correspondence, though only Dickens's letters have survived.[72] In them he gives her report of the field trips and enquiries he undertook in preparation for his novels. His letters gradually acquainted her with the reality of life in Britain's large industrial cities and the plague of moral and physical diseases threatening the working poor. The wealthy heiress was alarmed at Dickens's analysis of 'the condition of England'. But she was comforted by his suggestion that she could use her wealth to address some of the social tensions which threatened the stability of her country. The government was doing little to relieve distress and poverty, the novelist told her, and suggested that action from philanthropists like her were the nation's last resort.[73]

Dickens moved Burdett-Coutts away from the high Anglican philosophy in which the Duke of Wellington had schooled her. What was needed, the novelist suggested, was not support for religious teaching in Ragged Schools, since 'church principles did not always bring out the best in lower-class students when other needs were not fulfilled'. A better way to 'direct her generosity' was to provide school buildings or food on the table for the young students.[74] Dickens explained his approach in a letter to a friend:

> I sent Miss Coutts a sledge-hammer account of the Ragged Schools, and as I saw her name for two hundred pounds on the Clergy Education list, took pains to show her that religious mysteries and difficult creeds wouldn't do for such pupils. She writes back to know what the rent of some large airy premises would be, and what the expense of erecting a regular bathing or purifying place. I have no doubt she will do whatever I ask her in the matter. She is a most excellent creature . . . and I have a most perfect affection and respect for her.[75]

This led Burdett-Coutts into providing other kinds of assistance for neglected children. She established a Shoe Black Brigade to provide employment for young boys as they left the Ragged Schools. She prompted the flower girls of London to form a union and taught them how to stitch artificial flowers so they had something to sell when there were no fresh flowers in the winter. She backed a project for training homeless boys for the life of a seaman. She formed the Destitute Children's Dinner Society which soon had 50 centres where penny dinners were served; those children who were too poor to find even a penny had the cost borne by Angela Burdett-Coutts herself. She was one of the founders of the London Society for the Prevention of Cruelty to Children.

Charles Dickens, whose Christianity was of an evangelical variety, directed her towards those at the very bottom of society: fallen women, pauper families, chimney sweeps, flower girls and shoeshine boys – groups whose existence members of the upper classes rarely acknowledged. The Duke of Wellington did not approve. Like other high Tory Anglicans he believed poverty was ingrained in such people. Dickens persuaded Burdett-Coutts that, on the contrary, these folk were worthy of her sympathy and support. She still lent towards the notion that the poor, above all else, needed the spiritual comforts of conversion or redemption, but Dickens persuaded her that this went hand in hand with improving their material lives.

After some years the rich heiress began to desire a closer acquaintance with the poor. After reading *Oliver Twist* she asked Dickens to take her to Bethnal Green – the part of London where the novel's prostitute character, Nancy, lived. Dickens not only took her, he also encouraged her to meet Dr Thomas Southwood Smith – the grandfather of Octavia Hill – and an authority on public health and sanitation who knew the area well. Afterwards Burdett-Coutts and Dickens visited a model housing development off Gray's Inn Road and decided to build something similar in the East End. In 1862 she opened four blocks of flats, each containing 45 apartments, at Columbia Square in Bethnal Green. Each had two sets of rooms, with gas and water supplies, a boiler and oven. Several years later, at the heart of the development, she built a covered market named Columbia Hall which sold fresh fish and vegetables and was free from the tolls collected at other London markets so that it could sell food more cheaply to the poor.[76] She constructed it in the form of a huge neo-Gothic edifice complete with decorative windows, majestic vaulting and granite columns – which led it to be mocked in *The Times* as a 'cathedral of plaice and cabbage' far too exquisite for the ordinary wear and tear of a market.[77]

Perhaps the most celebrated collaboration between Dickens and the benefactrix was a home they devised for women and girls working the streets of London as prostitutes. This was a project which appealed to both Angela Burdett-Coutts's desire to promote moral reform and Dickens's concern to make material provision for those at the bottom of society. Burdett-Coutts had become aware of the problem early on. Shortly after she had received her unexpected inheritance she moved to her grandfather's house in Piccadilly. From her windows she could see prostitutes, night and day, making their rounds on the streets outside. One contemporary journalist estimated there were 80,000 fallen women on the streets of London. Prompted by Dickens, Burdett-Coutts decided to open a home to reform these unfortunate women.

There was another curious dimension to the project. In the 1850s newspaper reports and travellers' tales began to speak of the dearth of women in the British colonies in Australia, Canada and South Africa, particularly after the British courts stopped deporting prisoners, including prostitutes, to the colonies. The Bishop of British Columbia in Canada, George Hill, wrote to Burdett-Coutts to report that there was 'but one woman to every 20 men' in his colony. This unnatural state of affairs, he told her, might lead the colonies to fall into deprivation. By contrast, he wrote, he had read that there were '600,000 more women at home [in England] than there are men'. He asked his Anglican friends in London to promote emigration by 'some good respectable young women'.[78] The solution, it occurred to Angela Burdett-Coutts, was to reclaim prostitutes from the streets, transform them into respectable women, and then pay for their passage to the colonies.

This was more difficult than either she or Dickens had anticipated, as was clear from his letters. One of the women, Sesina Bollard, the novelist wrote, was 'the most deceitful little minx in this town – I never saw such a draggled piece of fringe upon the skirts of all that is bad . . . she would corrupt a Nunnery in a fortnight'. Sesina's friend, Isabella Gordon, concocted charges against the home's matrons and was sent away with half a crown and directions to another charity. Another girl, Jemima Hiscock, 'forced open the door of the little beer cellar with knives and got dead drunk' and began to use 'the most horrible language'. The beer must have been 'laced with spirits from over the wall', Dickens concluded in apparent bewilderment.[79] The Duke of Wellington had advised the woman he called 'dearest Angela' not to become involved.

As a High Tory he 'could not imagine that the lower classes had the potential or the wisdom to transform themselves or to redeem themselves into deserving poor or deserving individuals [even] when exposed to Christian benevolence'.[80] The prostitutes would not reform, he insisted, reproaching the heiress for providing such undeserving women with 'the means for going on . . . in the same vicious course'.[81] Later he changed his mind, deciding it was beneficial to the nation for such undesirables to be transported to the colonies, reformed or unreformed.

But in 1852 the Duke of Wellington died and then, in 1858, Angela Burdett-Coutts broke off her friendship with Charles Dickens – shocked that he had left his wife. Without the two great advisers who had shaped the first decades of her charitable activity her focus widened considerably. She adopted what David Owen has called 'something of the omnivorousness' characteristic of Victorian philanthropists.[82] The causes she espoused covered the entire spectrum of nineteenth-century humanitarian benevolence. They included a project to find work for unemployed silk weavers in Spitalfields; another to fund 1,200 jobless Scottish weavers to emigrate from Ayrshire to Australia; and during the potato famine in Ireland in the 1880s she donated the enormous sum of a quarter of a million pounds to buy seed potatoes (an act which embarrassed the British government into its own action). She also provided boats for the fishing industry in Ireland. After reading reports from Florence Nightingale about the 'sodden misery' of the constantly damp conditions in the hospitals at Scutari during the Crimean War, she commissioned an engineer to devise a machine which could dry 1,000 articles of linen in less than half an hour and sent it out to the Crimea. She financed the first proper mapping of Jerusalem to improve its sanitation. She sent aid to aboriginal peoples in Australia, to the Dyaks of Borneo, and to Turkish peasant refugees during the 1877 Russo-Turkish war. She supported the expeditions of David Livingstone and Henry Morton Stanley in Africa. She funded Charles Babbage in his work to develop the earliest computer. And she lifted her eyes beyond the poor and needy to create a middle-class residential community in the garden suburb of Highgate, to buy a set of sixth-century Greek manuscripts for a top London school, or provide church bells for St Paul's Cathedral. Among her various interests she supported the British Horological Institute, provided drinking fountains for dogs, erected the bronze statue of Greyfriars Bobby in Edinburgh and was president of both the British Beekeepers' Association and the British Goat Society.

Through all this, and much more, the name of Angela Burdett-Coutts became synonymous to the British public with philanthropy. In 1871 Queen Victoria bestowed upon her a peerage in her own right at a time when most aristocratic women merely used the title of their husband. More popularly, Burdett-Coutts was known as 'the Queen of the poor'.[83] She was so taken to the hearts of the people of London that her name became Cockney rhyming slang for 'boots'. At her funeral in Westminster Abbey on 30 December 1906 the eulogy was delivered by no less a person than the new monarch, Edward VII, who described her as 'the most remarkable woman in England' – apart from his mother, the late Queen Victoria.[84] 'She was not just admired,' wrote her biographer, Edna Healey,[85] 'she was venerated.'

SCIENCE AND PUNISHMENT: THE CHARITY ORGANISATION SOCIETY

Other Victorian philanthropists reacted against Angela Burdett-Coutts's splendidly haphazard inclusivity by attempting to make charity more scientific. In doing so they were tapping into a parallel tradition in philanthropy which had emerged in the Anglican Church in Ireland during the Great Irish Famine in the late 1840s and early 1850s. The four-year blight in the national potato crop, combined with the callous indifference of ideological free-market politicians in London, created a catastrophe of extraordinary magnitude. Nearly a million people died. Confronted by the scale of the need, a Christian stewardship campaign began in England which drew on principles which had been pioneered in Ireland itself. These sought to make philanthropic giving a regular habit rather than an occasional emotional response.[86] Wherever they had been tried, contributions among the Irish had on average 'increased fivefold in amount and tenfold in cheerfulness'.[87] The approach was transported to England where it chimed in with the new thinking in evangelical circles that individuals should be more systematic in their giving to charity. Thanks to the founder of Methodism, John Wesley – who had told his followers to 'gain all you can, save all you can, give all you can' – the doctrine of stewardship gained ground once more in the second half of the nineteenth century.[88] It insisted that self-serving motives for philanthropy corrupted its very purpose. Those who gave in order to gain credit from God, to increase their social status, or from fear of peer pressure, were acting from debased motives. 'If the motives are impure and unworthy, the offering will be valueless, and the deed itself will have aided the nature of sin.'[89] What was needed was a change 'from sentiment to system' so that giving was both 'systematic and proportional'.[90]

The decade after the Great Hunger in Ireland saw a flurry of evangelical essays and pamphlets on the issue of stewardship. It led to the foundation of the Systematic Beneficence Society, first in America in 1856 and then in Britain in 1860. Its aim was to promote the principles and practice of systematic giving and the duty of Christians 'to devote some stated proportion of their income to God for pious and charitable uses', and to address 'the glaring disproportion' between the wealth of Christians and the 'niggardly' amount they gave to charity.[91] As so often happens, however, the focus of this new movement soon switched from the donor to the recipient. It was the poor, it was decided, who needed systematizing rather than the rich. In 1869 The Society for Organising Charitable Relief and Repressing Mendicity was founded. A year later it changed its name to the more benign Charity Organisation Society (COS) but it retained the underlying fear embodied in its original title.

The philanthropists behind the Charity Organisation Society – whose supporters were drawn from the aristocracy and London elite – were consumed by the fear that cunning able-bodied paupers were able to exploit the generosity of charities and poor relief. Central to the COS's mission, therefore, was an attempt to make a distinction between the poor and the pauper. It was a return to the old notion of the deserving and the undeserving poor. The deserving poor included widows, orphans, the sick and the old. But the pauper, in the view of the COS, was an able-bodied person who could work but who preferred to subsist on charity handouts and poor relief. The word 'pauper' acquired negative connotations; 'pauperization' was the process by which such individuals were corrupted and debased by public and private charity. The COS, which tried to co-ordinate the activities of a wide range of charities, was undoubtedly the most powerful philanthropic institution of the late Victorian era.

The philosophy of utilitarianism which underpinned its thinking was crystallized in *Self-Help*, a book published by Samuel Smiles in

1859. It was a runaway bestseller among the middle classes, who found
it bolstered their prejudices about how deserving they were of their
privileged position in society. Smiles wrote:

> Help from without is often enfeebling in its effects . . . Whatever is
> done for men or classes, to a certain extent takes away the stimulus
> and necessity of doing for themselves . . . the inevitable tendency is
> to render them comparatively helpless.

Pauperism was therefore not an economic condition but a moral
disease. It undermined the 'manly independence' of the individual,
corrupted their family and community relationships, and damaged
the health of the general economy. It was a 'malady' capable of
infecting the entire society.[92] To the 'resident gentry' of the Charity
Organisation Society the solution to pauperism was to be found in
punitive and stigmatizing measures like the workhouse whose harsh
disciplines included eight-hour days of breaking stones. If that was
the only charity available then the able-bodied poor would put
themselves to work elsewhere.

So those at the top of the Charity Organisation Society took an
extremely dim view of charities which operated along more traditional
lines. They poured scorn upon the English cardinal, Henry Edward
Manning, when he raised nearly £80,000 through a Mansion House
Fund appeal to prevent the starvation of London's workmen during
periods of sharp unemployment. And they wrote a critical letter to
The Times to protest about a plan by the leader of the Salvation Army,
General William Booth, to launch a programme to help the poor and
needy. Cardinal Manning's funds were distributed for direct temporary
relief 'with little attempt to distinguish the bona fide unemployed
from the chronic loafers', according to an 1886 report of the COS
Committee on the Relief of Exceptional Distress.[93] And Helen Dendy
Bosanquet, one of the founders of the COS – who was open in her
detestation of the Salvation Army, repeatedly referring to the title of its
founder in inverted commas – said that its open-handed distribution
of charity to those who requested it, 'without any investigation into
their cases', was something which 'cut at the root of all the teachings
and endeavours of [the] 20 years' she had put into establishing the
philosophy of the COS.[94] 'General' Booth was hopelessly sentimental,

irresponsible and autocratic in his dealings with the poor. He might as well just hand out money to passers-by, another COS supporter wrote sarcastically in a letter to *The Times*.[95] Such ill-considered and unsystematic philanthropy was regarded by the COS as 'the chief source of pauperism'.[96]

So opposed was it to casual almsgiving that it devised a leaflet warning against passing a coin to a beggar. It carried the caption 'A penny given and a child ruined'.[97] The Society instructed its social workers that its 'scientific' philanthropy should not be 'indiscriminate' or 'promiscuous'. Charity distributed 'without regard to need or worth' could 'contribute to the very evil it was designed to remedy – the pauperization and demoralization of the poor'. True humanitarianism was an exercise in doing good, not feeling good.[98]

What was new about the Charity Organisation Society were the methods it used to distinguish between the deserving and undeserving poor. The COS claimed to use 'scientific principles to root out scroungers and target relief where it was most needed'.[99] This scientific approach involved a pioneering 'casework' approach to philanthropy. Detailed investigations of individual family circumstances were undertaken which laid the practical foundations for the development of twentieth-century social work. Out of a reactionary motivation there thus arose a progressive empirical method. The pioneering social casework of its special investigating committees created a series of special reports on 'the socially handicapped – the blind, the deaf and the mentally defective'.[100] Out of such work the COS set up many innovative projects for the sick, the children and the unemployed.

Yet its aggressive attitudes did not sit well with many who worked among the poor in a more empathetic way. To them the Charity Organisation Society 'became synonymous with much that was grudging, callous, dogmatic and reactionary'.[101] This was not so much enlightened self-interest as moralizing of an unenlightened kind. Its critics said COS stood for 'Cringe or Starve'.[102] Outside London, many Victorians rejected the COS as extremist and both public and private charity continued to be distributed largely on the basis of need, not 'character'.[103] Others were bewildered at its ideological opposition to old-age pensions or housing built for the poor by local government – something about which Octavia Hill wrote long and furious letters to *The Times*.[104] One critic at the time resorted to satire.

In 1886 Reverend Charles Latimer Marson, a curate at St Jude's in Whitechapel (who was later involved with various Christian Socialist groups), filled in a mock response to a COS application for relief submitted in the name of Jesus Christ. It began: 'Applicant stated that he lived almost entirely upon alms, principally obtained from women. He tramped about with a number of low fellows who sometimes did odd jobs, fishing and the like . . .' Then, after stating that the applicant's references were 'wholly unsatisfactory and inadequate', it concluded:

> Applicant appeared before the committee, and was rebuked for his utter want of thrift, industry, temperance and for the bad company he kept. He was offered a set of carpenter's tools by a lady if he would return to carpentry, but the Society refused to do anything for him, except recommend him to go to the infirmary, lunatic department, or to live a more business-like and practical life.[105]

Later critics suggested that, though the COS claimed the challenge it addressed was 'how to relieve poverty without pauperising', its real mission was 'how to prevent dependence upon public funds and stop giving relief'.[106] More problematic was its inability to recognize that the extent and depth of poverty were very much greater than the COS supposed at a time. The massive statistical surveys of the contemporary sociologist Charles Booth suggested that more than a third of the population of London lived below the poverty line.[107] Remedies to the problems of this 'great and appalling mass of human misery', wrote his namesake General William Booth of the Salvation Army, were 'well beyond the imagination of most of those who spend their lives in philanthropic work'.[108] William Booth's solution, set out in his 1890 book *In Darkest England, and the Way Out*, proposed homes for the homeless; training centres to prepare emigrants for overseas colonies; rescue homes for fallen women; homes for released prisoners; legal aid for the poor; and practical help for alcoholics.

To the dismay of the Charity Organisation Society, huge public support built up for his programme, a large amount of money was raised, and much of the scheme was carried out. The scorn which the COS had poured upon Booth was replaced by public acclaim and the active encouragement of King Edward VII – who even invited him to

be present at his coronation ceremony.[109] Social legislation, of the kind
COS officials had long opposed, began to be passed, crowned by the
National Insurance Act of 1911, which was to the COS 'the ultimate
aberration'.[110] The sway of the COS, with its progressive methods and
its regressive philosophy, was over.

A NEW JEWISH PHILANTHROPY — FREDERIC DAVID MOCATTA

The legacy of the Charity Organisation Society was more long-lasting
in one specific area. Its leaders declared war on charity malpractice. One
of the COS members most exercised about this was Frederic David
Mocatta, a Jewish bullion broker to the Bank of England, who was a
vice-president of the COS from its foundation. He also shared its general
concerns about pauperization. At the annual general meeting of the
Jewish Board of Guardians in 1889, he said 'it was not the province of
a great charity to aid the poor, so much as to render them independent.
A greater object still, was to prevent people from becoming poor. The
system of doles which used to find such favour was a very bad one.'[111]
Charity was needed, as his distant cousin Sir Alan Mocatta put it, 'to
help the ailing, the aged, the crippled and the mentally weak', but most
poor hard-working persons would be more grateful if they were merely
'enabled to bring up their families independently'.[112]

Frederic David Mocatta was personally generous in donating cash to
hospitals, schools and housing projects for the working poor of both
the general population and the Jewish community. But he also had
three areas of additional concern. He was troubled by the amount of
duplication and overlap by the plethora of different charities in London
at the time, which he thought created a non-scientific inefficiency; as
a result he oversaw the merger of bodies such as the Jews' Hospital
and the Jewish Orphan Asylum.[113] He was, secondly, particularly
disturbed by the number of charities that allowed their supporters a
vote to decide which candidates should receive their charity – a system
he regarded as immoral and irrational.[114] Relief should be granted,
he strongly believed, according to need and merit, which should be
carefully ascertained by experienced caseworkers rather than being
distributed according to the personal whims of donors. He not only
refused to contribute to any charity where such a voting system was in

force – excluding them from his will[115] – but he also worked for the abolition of the practice in other societies. But the third area which most preoccupied him was the attitude of philanthropists towards the Jewish immigrants fleeing persecution in Eastern Europe and arriving in England from the Continent, much as his own family had done seven generations before.[116]

Jewish philanthropy had developed significantly from the Judaic model outlined in earlier chapters, which survived through the Middle Ages right up until the eighteenth century. The shift in attitudes which had taken place in Christian circles after the Enlightenment had had its impact on the Jewish community too. Again the changes had begun in France. As part of Napoleon's attempts to centralize and control the Jewish community in Paris at the start of the nineteenth century the *Société d'Encouragement et de Secours* (Society for Encouragement and Relief) was formed in 1809. It was charged with supervising poor relief, monitoring the apprenticeships of young people, and organizing burials. The severe restrictions imposed upon poor relief by the elders of the community show that Judaism was riven by the same debates as were taking place in Christian circles.

From the outset the *Société d'Encouragement et de Secours* denied aid to those it considered drunks and idlers and, early on, assisted the French government in locating foreign indigent Jews for deportation. In 1820 it declared that no poor vagrant Jew was eligible for relief unless they had been resident in Paris for two years. The attitude soon spread outside the French capital. In Alsace-Lorraine one Jewish leader, Beer Isaac, declared that though Jews must look after infirm members of their own community, it was the job of the state to turn away Jewish vagrants. It was clear that this hardening of attitudes was caused by the Enlightenment, since those who were most draconian in their views were the Jews who were most progressively minded when it came to championing educational reform and social integration. They had clearly bought into the same linkage between piety and productivity which, as we saw in the previous chapter, characterized the Puritan Protestant vision in England from the early eighteenth century onwards. By contrast, Jews of a more conservative disposition still saw the poor as unfortunates in need of ungrudging charity, as the traditional religious approach demanded. The traditionalists criticized the new Jewish philanthropic practices as inhumane.

Similar distinctions emerged in the Jewish community in neighbouring Germany. Again it was the progressives who took the harsher view. Jewish beggars who arrived in the Jewish community from outside were compared by the radical Jewish reformer David Friedlander to sick and dangerous vagrants. He urged that 'all foreign incoming beggars be held back, by the strongest means . . . at the border of the Prussian state'.[117] The elders of the Berlin community, among whom Friedlander had great influence, imposed restrictions as severe as those of their co-religionists in Paris. Unmarried pregnant Jewish women were 'an extraordinary burden on the community and its charitable institutions', the Berlin Board of Elders complained.[118] In 1809 they asked the chief of police to keep poor pregnant Jewish women out of the city. Four years later Friedlander attempted a crackdown on children born out of wedlock by demanding the names of illegitimate children in receipt of assistance from the Jewish charity, the Talmud Torah, which provided traditional education to poor children. The more traditionalist Orthodox Jews who ran the organization refused to hand over the names. But the attitudes of the modernizers persisted and, as Derek Penslar records, Jewish newspapers in Germany were 'filled with hostile depictions of the Jewish poor as cheeky beggars and con artists – a "cancer", as one correspondent put it, that requires radical treatment'.[119] It was a metaphor which was to have more sinister overtones in that same country in the twentieth century. By the 1840s this new Jewish philanthropic ethos found harsh expression in proposals to establish 'industrial schools' for Jewish vagrants, which aimed to reform the poor through military discipline, hard labour and spartan living conditions. Children as young as five, like everyone else, were expected to work from 5 a.m. until 7 p.m., spending long periods outside in the cold. In the Bavarian city of Fürth, Jewish elders sent poor vagrant Jews to the Gentile workhouse where kosher food and sabbath rest were not available. The bodies of Jews who had committed suicide were sent to the local hospital's dissecting theatre, contrary to Jewish religious prohibitions.[120]

Harsh though these practices were, Penslar suggests, they were in keeping with the general tone of policies towards the poor among the Christian bourgeoisie in these places and at this time. In Berlin in 1837 a poor-care commission was established which brought together

representatives from all the Jewish charitable associations. It decided
that, while true invalids must be provided with charity, those capable
of work should be found employment. Every applicant for aid was
visited and examined by two of the commission's members – exactly
the same process which, two decades later, the Charity Organisation
Society was to put into practice in England. In fact, according to
David Owen, the rigorous techniques of the COS – thorough
investigation, detailed case records and home visiting – were being
used in London by the Jewish Board of Guardians 10 years before the
COS was founded – and 20 years before the great influx of Jewish
immigrants into Britain.[121]

When the flow of Jewish immigrants to London increased substantially
around 1880, Frederic David Mocatta found himself caught between
two impulses. On the one hand he was wedded to the orthodoxies of the
Charity Organisation Society with its insistence on viewing poverty as
a form of moral weakness, and its emphasis on the need for a scientific
approach to philanthropy. That had found expression in the running of
the Jewish Board of Guardians up until the 1870s. The board, which
David Owen says was managed with exceptional intelligence and
efficiency, was relieving something like half of the Jewish poor of the
metropolis at that point. But it was doing so by experimenting with
new services – medical care, sanitary inspection of the homes of the
poor, and loans rather than charitable gifts.[122]

But there was another side to Mocatta. His knowledge of international
Jewry was far more extensive than that of prominent figures in the
Charity Organisation Society, or even of many leaders of London's Jewish
community. The precarious situation of the Jews in Eastern Europe
was a source of personal anxiety to Mocatta. He devoted considerable
time to addressing the problem. He was vice-president of the Anglo-
Jewish Association, founded in 1871 to help obtain protection for Jews
being persecuted across the Continent. He also became a member of
the Alliance Israelite in Paris and a member of the committee founded
in London in 1872 to watch over the affairs of the Rumanian Jews.
In 1882 he took an active part in administering the Mansion House
Committee Fund for assisting Jews to leave Russia after a reign of terror
began in the south of the country, which was to last for almost three
decades.[123] The result was a movement of refugees of such proportion
that the Jewish population of London trebled between 1880 and 1914.

Applications to the Jewish Board of Guardians for assistance doubled in less than two decades. Around 90 per cent of the new applications came from these recent arrivals.[124]

The situation caused an acute dilemma for the leaders of the Jewish community, particularly since the heaviest inflow of Jewish refugees came at a time when the British labour market was already under pressure and there were few new jobs for the incomers. The public mood was inhospitable and Jewish leaders, anxious not to provoke the British government into imposing a limit on these desperate refugees, were in a quandary. Some prominent figures within the community urged prudence and discrimination. Despite the fact that the telegram address of the Board of Guardians was Rachmonem (the compassionate), it went to some lengths to warn prospective immigrants of the widespread unemployment in England.[125] But for Mocatta it was unthinkable that English Jews should do anything other than welcome and assist the refugees. He knew that, as a class, these poor Jewish incomers were sober, frugal and hard-working.[126] They were not poor because they were weak, shiftless, idle individuals, as the hard cocksure dogmatism of COS stalwarts such as Helen Dendy Bosanquet insisted. They were poor because of the circumstances of oppression and persecution from which they came.

Mocatta adjusted his thinking accordingly. In a series of letters in the 1880s to one of the founders of the Charity Organisation Society, C. S. Loch, Mocatta proposed a solution well outside of the normal COS orthodoxy. 'The care of suffering should be incumbent on society as a whole, and not left to chance as it is now,' he declared. He then went on to propose what amounted to a graduated income tax, to be paid by the wealthy to provide care for the poor. 'I am aware that such an idea will be called Communism, or Socialism, or that it may be considered as subverting every rule of political economy, but things must not be allowed to remain as they are.'[127] He later acknowledged that he realized his friends in the COS 'with whom I usually act and agree' would think him 'a little unsafe and crotchety on these points'. But he insisted that eventually 'I believe we shall "come to it", and that it will be the right thing'.[128]

As he got older Mocatta was more given to demanding aggressive action by the state on such matters.[129] And yet he also added a proposal entirely in keeping with the spirit of the late Victorian era, one which, as we have already seen, found favour with Octavia Hill and Charles

Dickens – that emigration was the solution to the chronic distress of the poor which, as Mocatta wrote in 1886, was not just chronic and destructive but also increasing. 'Nothing short of removing some hundreds of thousands of people can make things better,' he concluded like some latterday Malthus who could find no way out but the removal of vast numbers of poor people to the colonies. Enforced emigration did not happen, but the idea showed Frederic David Mocatta to be a man of his time, at once humanitarian and paternalistic. Small wonder he was regarded by his contemporaries as 'the *beau idéal* of the Anglo Jewish philanthropist'.[130]

QUAKER CAPITALISM – HOW PHILANTHROPY CHANGED BUSINESS

Perhaps the most profound shift in thinking on philanthropy in the nineteenth century came with Quakers such as the Cadbury, Fry and Rowntree chocolate-making families. Until this point business and benevolence were largely seen as parallel compartmentalized activities. Men like Frederic David Mocatta had spent the first part of their life making money, and the second part working out the most productive ways to give it away. With the Quakers that changed: business and philanthropy worked hand in hand. More significantly, their business methods did not influence their philanthropy; instead, their philanthropy changed the way that their businesses operated.

The Quakers, also known as the Religious Society of Friends, had first appeared in the mid-seventeenth century, as one of the radical religious groups which flourished in the aftermath of the English Civil War. They distanced themselves from the Anglican establishment, which is why they were known as Dissenters. The group, founded by George Fox, who preached that everyone could experience God directly in their own heart, were dubbed the 'Quakers' by a mocking magistrate in Derby after Fox, on trial there for blasphemy, suggested that the court should 'tremble at the word of the Lord'. When he was found guilty Fox fell to his knees 'to pray to the Lord to forgive' the magistrate. Justice Gervase Bennet thereupon 'got up into a rage and . . . ran upon me with both his hands and struck me'.[131]

As the years passed the Society of Friends lost none of Fox's boldness, enthusiasm and instinct for innovation. The law banned Quakers from positions in the Church, universities and professions, so they set up in business instead. In the early nineteenth century around 4,000 Quaker families ran 74 Quaker British banks and more than 200 Quaker companies.[132] Barclays and Lloyds banks were founded by Quakers, as were insurance and mutual assurance companies such as Friends Provident and Friends Life. Quaker finance underpinned a good deal of British industrial expansion. Under the 1661 Corporation Act,[133] Quakers were also barred from civic and professional life in cities established under a charter. So the largest city in England that did not operate under a charter of incorporation – Birmingham – became a centre for Quaker entrepreneurial activity.[134] It was there that the Cadbury Brothers, George and Richard, built Britain's most successful cocoa and chocolate business.

Quakers, it turned out, made particularly good entrepreneurs, not least because of the virtues which lay at the heart of the religious vision of the Society of Friends. As George Cadbury later spelled out, the Quaker ethos encouraged all 'the qualities most likely to lead to success in business . . . self-denial, rigid abstinence from all luxury and self-indulgence'.[135] Excessive preoccupation with riches, the founder George Fox had warned, would dim the Quaker 'inner light'. Business had a moral responsibility to create wealth but that wealth was to be put at the service of society. Personal wealth accumulation was seen as a 'snare'.[136] By contrast, service was seen as good for the soul of the individual but also for the spiritual health of the whole society. Quaker businesses therefore had a wider vision than making profit. Moreover, business was to be conducted ethically. Quakers refused to separate their commercial activities from the principles and disciplines governing their personal religious life. The Quaker emphasis on honesty led them to value the quality of the goods they sold. In an age in which haggling and bargaining were common business practices, Quakers' sense of fairness led them to pioneer a system of fixed pricing, explains Richard Turnbull in *Quaker Capitalism: Lessons for Today*.[137] As a result, among both business contacts and the general public, the early Quakers developed a reputation for quality, fairness and reliability, which turned out to be very good for business. Their religious principles also emphasized the importance of treating their workforce with decency and care.

Among the Quaker industrialists of the second half of the nineteenth century the figure of George Cadbury stands out. His father John had started the family firm in 1824 as a tea and coffee business which then branched out into the latest fashionable drink, cocoa. All three beverages were seen, in teetotal religious terms, as supporting the temperance movement by offering alternatives to alcohol. Old John Cadbury, a campaigner for total abstinence, was fond of saying that an abstainer could afford a good joint of beef on Sunday with the money not spent in the alehouse.[138] His was a puritan household and his sons Richard and George were brought up in a house where their father would not allow a piano nor even, until he was past the age of 70, sit in an easy chair. As a teenager George was sent as an apprentice to work in the grocery business of another Quaker, Joseph Rowntree at York, illustrating another strength of the Friends: their outsider status bonded them together in a network of mutual support, business linkages, capital flows and marriages.[139] In 1856 George returned to join his father's cocoa factory in Birmingham, but the business began to fail when the death of George's mother sent his father's health into decline.

In 1861, at the age of just 21, George and his brother Richard, who was a few years older, took control of the business, with the younger brother taking the lead. His willingness to innovate – which distinguished George from many of his competitors – led him to introduce a new cocoa press, the Van Houten, which removed excess oil from the beans, creating a finer cocoa powder. This was a far superior product to those of his rivals, who mixed potato starch, sago and treacle into the product to disguise the bitter taste of the excess oil.[140] The Cadbury Brothers marketed 'Pure Cocoa Essence' with the advertising slogan 'Absolutely Pure, Therefore Best'.[141] The firm were appointed cocoa manufacturers to Queen Victoria. Soon they were processing a third of all the cocoa imported into Britain.

It was more than a sense of religious duty which made George Cadbury focus on the need to improve life for his workers. Just two years after he took over Cadbury Brothers he began volunteering as a teacher with the Adult School Movement – and continued to teach in its Severn Street School until the age of 72 when he was still bicycling into the city at 6 a.m. on Sunday mornings to take a Bible class. Over the years, hundreds of Birmingham men learn how to read and write at his instruction.[142] More significantly, it brought Cadbury into first-hand contact with not just members of the respectable artisan class, but also with individuals whose lives were anything but respectable – vagrants,

ex-convicts and drunkards.[143] Sometimes Cadbury visited members of
his adult class in their small overcrowded homes, which opened his eyes
to the seamier side of working-class living. He later wrote:

> It was largely through my experience among the back streets of
> Birmingham [that] I have been brought to the conclusion that it is
> impossible to raise a nation, morally, physically, and spiritually, in
> such surroundings, and that the only effective way is to bring men
> out of the cities into the country and to give to every man his garden
> where he can come into touch with nature.[144]

His critics later accused George Cadbury of paternalism. But it is
unarguable that his concern brought many benefits to his employees.
Like his fellow Quaker, Joseph Rowntree, although he did not pay
wages above the market rate Cadbury did offer his workers savings
clubs, evening sewing classes, clothing clubs, dental treatment and one
sickness scheme to provide wages for staff who fell ill and another for
regularizing employment in a seasonal trade. He also reduced the length
of the working day and working week and introduced half-day and bank
holidays. All this, says David Owen in *English Philanthropy 1660–1960*,
'made Cadbury brothers almost unique in the British industrial world'.[145]

Yet George Cadbury did not see these merely as an additional
philanthropic outlay. In his book *Experiments in Industrial Organization*
he emphasized that business efficiency and employee welfare were
indivisible.[146] A cared-for and contented workforce was not a luxury
but an essential ingredient to business success because such workers
brought with them a spirit of co-operation and an ethic of hard
work.[147] But Cadbury wanted more than that. He did not only want
a contented workforce, he wanted one which was morally improved.
Yet 'how can [a man] cultivate ideals when his home is a slum and his
only possible place of recreation is the public house . . . To win them
to better ideals you must give them better conditions of life,' he said.[148]
George Cadbury was concerned that, in the sprawling slum conditions
of the Birmingham metropolis, it was impossible for ordinary people to
find the light, ventilation, space and decent living conditions which he
thought were prerequisites of moral improvement.

The opportunity to act came when it became obvious at the end
of the 1870s that the original Cadbury factory was inadequate to

the expanding firm's commercial needs. George and his brother hit upon the idea of moving their works to healthier surroundings in the countryside outside the city. A new site would allow the development of a new factory but also provide them with the opportunity of making a great social and economic experiment – the creation of a model village for their employees. They found the site, four miles away, in the rural setting of Bournville.

There George bought 300 acres of land. He had no existing template for the village community he wanted to establish – Robert Owen's venture at New Lanark had housed its workers only in six-storey tenements. Cadbury had in mind a rural idyll in an urban environment. He spoke of 'the advantages of outdoor village life, with opportunities for the natural and healthful occupation of cultivating the soil' where working men could 'enjoy fresh air and light'.[149]

George Cadbury's contact with the Birmingham workers he met through the Adult School Movement had convinced him, according to Cadbury's main architect William Alexander Harvey, that 'the greatest drawback to their moral and physical progress was the lack of any healthful occupation for their leisure'. Harvey continued, in his account of the project:

> His conclusion was that he must bring the factory worker out on to the land, that he might pursue the most natural and healthful of recreations, that of gardening . . . There was an advantage, too, in bringing the working-man on to the land, for, instead of losing money in the amusements usually sought in the towns, he saved it in his garden produce.[150]

George Cadbury believed that the benefits of gardening were physical, financial and spiritual. That was clear from his letter to his first architect, A. P. Walker. Cadbury set out practical details such as that each worker and his family were to have a cottage 'each surrounded by their own garden, not more than six to the acre'. But he also made clear that this vision was to be imbued by a religious dimension, telling the architect: 'I would not care for anyone to undertake it who did not enter into the spirit of the undertaking as a labour to the Lord . . . I am rather hopeful that this will be to a large extent a Quaker colony.'[151]

When the community at Bournville was built one-tenth of the village's total area was devoted to parks, recreation grounds and other open spaces. It had wide roads shaded with trees. The houses were built in a variety of designs using porches, bay windows, casements and gables, creating a multiplicity of different and distinct homes rather than rows of identical worker's cottages. It had a village green and a cricket ground, schools and shops, almshouses for the elderly and infirm, and a home for children with disabilities, places of worship and adult education facilities. When the families of the workers arrived they found a football field for the boys and a playground for the girls all ready for use. A key aim of the deed of foundation was to preserve the rural character of the village and provide a healthy environment for its inhabitants.[152]

The Cadbury paternalism was undisguised. Each new resident was supplied with a copy of George's *Suggested Rules of Health*, which offered advice on everything from sanitation to diet and clothing:

> The rules advocated, among other things: vegetarianism; avoiding intoxicating liquors, tobacco, pork, aerated drinks and drugs; the correct way to brew tea; single beds for married couples; cold and warm baths; outdoor exercise, particularly walking and gardening; good ventilation; sleeping eight hours in twenty-four; early rising; and the avoidance of tight clothing. The way of life advocated by George Cadbury was based upon his own, which espoused simplicity and thrift as acts of family worship. In the final statement of the rules, George Cadbury's evangelical Quakerism is most prominent when recommending that 'In a truly happy home Father and Mother will conduct family worship at least once a day when the Bible should be read and a hymn sung.'[153]

George's wife Elizabeth took it upon herself to offer maternal supervision and practical encouragement. As Richenda Scott's sympathetic 1955 biography put it: 'As the houses were completed and the families, shy and a little awe-struck at the unfamiliar open spaces, the great sweeps of sky, the clean freshly painted home, moved in, Elizabeth would come to welcome them, to learn their interests, and to help them find a niche in the village community.'[154]

Many Cadbury employees were members of the Religious Society of Friends, but the entire workforce, including non-Quakers, were expected to participate each day in acts of worship which involved reading aloud from religious texts in the factory's breakfast break. Originally, these consisted of a short Bible reading and a few minutes of silent prayer, but later the Cadburys introduced communal singing, not the usual Quaker tradition. The practice, according to Adrian Bailey and John Bryson, was 'an attempt to instil within the workforce a sense of unity, vocation, duty and diligence, alongside the more obvious opportunity of experiencing the presence of God'. It was another clear instance of what David Owen calls the Cadburys' 'fusion of philanthropy and higher self-interest', both of them, Owen thought, 'highly beneficial to the workpeople'.[155] By 1866 this daily worship had become known as the Morning Readings. It is some measure of the attitude of the workforce towards Cadbury paternalism that when, in 1870, the brothers decided to discontinue the readings the workforce petitioned them to change their mind.[156]

George Cadbury sold the first 143 houses built at Bournville to his workers on 999-year leases. The gardens were of such a size that, his plan was, the produce obtained from the garden, and the poultry which could be kept there, would cover the ground rent. But Cadbury had fixed the sale price at such a modest figure that a number of the buyers immediately resold the houses 'at a fancy profit'.[157] Alarmed at this, Cadbury – who was a champion of heavy taxation of land – built 227 more houses and turned Bournville into a charitable trust which rented the remainder of the properties rather than selling them. The rents were fixed at levels designed to show other factory owners that building decent housing for workers was a commercial proposition which could be made to yield a fair return on capital for those who were not obsessed with profit maximization. His desire to be able to test his ideas without interference from profit-chasing shareholders deterred him from making Cadbury Brothers a limited company (though later generations of Cadburys eventually reversed that policy, leading to the takeover of Cadbury by the multi-national conglomerate Kraft in 2010).

George Cadbury was a Quaker of an evangelical disposition who wanted to spread the message that Christianity in the mode of the Society of Friends had something to offer wider society. The model of Bournville was later copied by others, including Joseph Rowntree in York, and became an exemplar to the wider garden-suburb movement. 'It is impossible to overstate the local and international significance of Cadbury's model village at Bournville,' say Bailey and Bryson. Writing as recently as 2007, they declare 'it is still considered to be one of the most innovative housing developments'.[158]

What made George Cadbury singular as a philanthropist was his insight – way ahead of his time – that benevolence was not some kind of adjunct to ordinary life. Nor was it a way of achieving redemption for bad behaviour in commercial or political activity. Rather it was a quality which should inform the whole of the way that a good life is led. His business and philanthropic careers were so closely intertwined, as David Owen puts it, that it is 'difficult and unprofitable to classify some of his decisions' as one thing or another.

For George Cadbury his whole life was an adventure in philanthropy. That is clear from the breadth of his interests. Few good causes – political, social or religious – made requests of him in vain, Owen observed, especially if they seemed to hold promise for the future.[159] In addition to personal donations to religious institutions like the China Inland Mission and the London Missionary Society, he supported an agency formed to protect the natives of New Guinea from 'the crudest sort of commercial exploitation'.[160] At home he made substantial contributions to campaigns in support of old-age pensions and in opposition to sweated labour, demanding a minimum wage in sweatshops – which 'marked him as something of an alien spirit among late Victorian philanthropists and proclaimed his sharp deviation from the main tradition of Victorian philanthropy'.[161]

He also, unfashionably, opposed the Boer War. Finding that the British press was overwhelmingly shrill in its enthusiasm for military action, George Cadbury, who had already acquired four Birmingham newspapers to 'educate the public in civic affairs', in 1901 bought a controlling interest in a national newspaper, the *Daily News*. He instructed it to oppose the war in South Africa and call for it to be brought to an end through arbitration. Cadbury – a convinced Liberal who believed that men of substance, like himself, had a duty 'to encourage an enlightened public opinion and to guide the nation to upright high-principled decisions' – set up a trust to run the newspaper with the mission 'that it may be of service in bringing the ethical teaching of Jesus Christ to bear upon National Questions, and in promoting National Righteousness'.[162]

The newspaper lost money partly, perhaps, because of Cadbury's Quaker insistence that it did not run racing tips or carry advertising for strong liquor. But he was unconcerned about the need to subsidize it. George Cadbury gave away almost the whole of his income, keeping only what he required to maintain his fairly fugal lifestyle. He gave it away pretty much as he made it and was not concerned to leave a substantial inheritance for his large family. A strong believer in death duties and income tax, he put practically his entire income, beyond living expenses, into good works. 'I have seriously considered how far a man is justified in giving away the heritage of his children and have come to the conclusion that my children will be all the better for being deprived of this money,' he said on 14 December 1900, standing in front of the Friends Meeting House on the village green, declaring that he was giving away his wealth to the Bournville Village Trust. 'Great wealth is not to be desired, and in my experience of life it is more a curse than a blessing to the families of those who possess it. I have 10 children. Six of them are at an age to understand how my actions affect them, and they entirely approve.'[163] The *News* was directed to support the Liberal Party, campaign against sweated labour, and give voice to nonconformist views in general.[164] When, in 1912, he handed over the reins of the trust he had established to own the *Daily News*, he wrote a letter to the new chairman, his eldest son, Edward. In it he said: 'I have a profound conviction that money spent on charities is of infinitely less value than money spent in trying to arouse my fellow countrymen to the necessity for measures to ameliorate the condition of the poor, forsaken and downtrodden masses.' That could be done 'most effectively by a great newspaper'.[165]

Among the benevolent rich men of his day George Cadbury was, in the estimation of David Owen, 'the most creative and daring in his giving'. Inevitably, there were those who felt he had not gone far enough. The Socialist Quaker Society, in the first decade of the twentieth century, denounced him for 'favouring philanthropy to ease social ills rather than more radical steps'.[166] That is unfair. Cadbury clearly saw, certainly towards the end of his life, as he put it in 1912, that money spent on charities was 'of infinitely less value' than money spent on political reform. As well as funding newspapers to campaign for social change, he also gave financial donations to candidates for the Liberal Party and also to some from the Independent Labour Party. He knew the price he would pay for that – which was to be attacked from both right and left. As he handed over control of the *Daily News*

Trust, Cadbury wrote a letter to the new trustees in which he offered a warning from bitter experience:

> If you champion the cause of the poor who cannot do anything to recompense you, you must expect savage attacks from those whose interests may be affected. I have been bitterly attacked in Society papers, also, on the other hand, by anarchists who desire a violent revolution and who know that progressive legislation will make this impossible.[167]

But, more significant than his politics, George Cadbury developed what Owen calls 'seminal philanthropy'[168] – a conscious experiment which he believed others might emulate on a scale that could bring significant social change. As he grew older Cadbury became more and more convinced of the rightness of this. At the age of 73 he concluded: 'Much of current philanthropic effort is directed to remedying the more superficial evils. I desire [to be of service] in assisting those who are seeking to remove their underlying causes.'[169] George Cadbury's 'Quaker capitalism' was far more ethical than the corporate social responsibility of twenty-first-century shareholder capitalism, argues Deborah Cadbury, a non-Quaker descendant of the famous philanthropist.[170] At the turn of the twentieth century thoughtful philanthropists were being forced to the conclusion that voluntary private charity was just not equal to the problems being thrown up by an urban and industrial society. Joseph Rowntree, in York, came to the same conclusion as Cadbury, lamenting that 'much of our present philanthropic effort is directed to remedying more superficial manifestations of weakness or evil'. Indeed, he went further, adding that 'the charity which takes the place of justice, creates much of the misery it relieves, but does not relieve all the misery it creates'.[171]

The hard truth was that George Cadbury, this most radical of business-oriented philanthropists, was eventually forced to the conclusion that philanthropy on its own is unable to deliver the vision of social justice which he cherished. Poverty had a social dimension which ultimately only society could address. In the end Quaker philanthropists, even one like George Cadbury who gave away virtually his entire income, could not reform British capitalism. Opinion was now to polarize between those who saw the state as the solution and those for whom philanthropy became an adjunct to a capitalism more red in tooth and claw.

Interview: Trevor Pears on family philanthropy

Sir Trevor Pears and his brothers Mark and David are directors of a property business founded by their father and grandfather. Over a decade ago Trevor turned to philanthropy full-time, running the family's charitable trust, the Pears Foundation. The family has given over £250 million to causes which focus on issues of identity and citizenship and a wide range of programmes encompassing medical research, education, mental health and well-being, and projects to engage young people across the UK, in Israel and the developing world.

A decade ago you decided to make philanthropy a full-time career. What prompted that decision?

When our late Mum passed away in 1999, I felt confronted by some big questions, as I think you do when your second parent dies. My two brothers and I had worked in the family property business which our father had started with his father. I was in my mid-thirties, so still pretty young, but I'd been doing the same thing for 15–20 years. I began to ask questions of myself in terms of what I wanted to do with my life. I had this sense nagging away of something not being complete, and of a wider world I wanted to be more a part of. As a family we'd always given to charity, but it was in a fairly reactive way – giving when someone asked or when there was some disaster in the news. These values had been instilled in us from our parents but it was nothing remotely approaching anything strategic. So I thought I would carry on working in the business but give 10 per cent of my time to pulling our giving together in some way, and my brothers were happy with that idea.

So I embarked on a journey which, in hindsight, was like getting on a little boat, putting up a sail and letting the wind blow me without knowing where I was going. But once I'd started it became a compulsion. Looking back, a lot of it was about working out my identity; my Jewish identity, my British identity . . .

Does your religion consciously play a part in your philanthropy, either in your motivation or in the way you do it?

Being Jewish is a really important part of who I am, but I wouldn't have said or understood this when I set off 20 years ago. Back then it was about seeking answers to lots of questions. Who am I? What am I trying to achieve? What are my values? What does it mean to be Jewish? I had long struggled to find a way in to my Jewish identity. Some of the clarity I found along the way is best illustrated by my response to a question that I am frequently asked: 'What percentage of your family foundation's expenditure goes to Jewish causes?' Now, my answer is 'Every penny goes to Jewish causes, because being Jewish means to be involved in the world.'

Sometimes this question is then rephrased to ask about percentages given to Jewish recipients. One of our flagship programmes is a £1 million annual grant to the Hebrew University of Jerusalem. So you could say, 'That's clearly a Jewish cause or recipient.' However, the 24 students we support, who are doing their Masters degrees or Ph.Ds in agriculture, nutrition, global development or public health, come from Africa and Asia. None of them are Jews. The programmes take place in Israel because Israel has some of the best expertise in the world in these fields.

I would say that as the years have gone by it has surprised me to realize just how much wisdom and guidance I've taken from my Jewish roots that I had no idea about 20 years ago. Teachers from the ages, like Hillel and Maimonides, offer brilliant advice for philanthropy and for life today.

How do you choose the areas in which to give? Do you have a notional idea at the start of each year that you will spend so much on international development, so much on mental health, so much on youth development, so much on programmes to combat anti-Semitism?

We don't think in compartments like that. Many of the areas we support touch on each other. You might say that when we support the Scouts Association, or Girl Guiding, or the Duke of Edinburgh's Award, it is simply about supporting activities for young people. But these organizations could also be called mental-health charities, social-action charities and so on. Research indicates that adults who were part of these movements when they were children do better in well-being indicators in later life. Or your could say that these organizations are about another of our big interests, citizenship and British identity. Movements like the Scouts and Guides are building on all of this as well as being great for young people's personal development. And I haven't even mentioned the importance of the fantastic 300,000 adult volunteers who keep these organizations going! For me one thing touches on another and then touches on yet another.

Do you feel that this approach is strategic or organic?

It was organic, but is now a bit of both. Going back to that boat analogy, at first I pulled up the sail and was taken places by the wind, but after five or six years I acquired a rudder and as the rudder goes in, you start to get a sense of direction. This was the point when we started to recruit the foundation's small team of professionals.

You say that you were told by a seasoned philanthropist, 20 years ago when you first began to give more seriously, that 'it's hard to do good'. You said that this has proved to be correct. In what ways?

We are often engaged with deep, long-standing, possibly unresolvable issues that every generation, past, present and future, has to tackle. Recognizing this is important. I believe more progress is made when you park your ego rather than thinking you're blessing people with your wonderful beliefs and your money. We have learned that you have to listen to the diversity and variety of thinking out there – on what works, what's good, how to do it, and so forth. Having an attitude of 'I've already made up my mind, please don't confuse me with the facts' can lead to poor decisions and second-rate work being done. We can be our own worst enemies here. Over time our foundation developed three rules of philanthropy. Isaiah Berlin apparently said the first rule of philanthropy should be, do no harm. Our second rule is that there's no limit to what you can achieve if you're not concerned who gets the credit. Our third rule is to give with good grace. All three of those were born out of the journey so far and understanding how challenging the issues are.

And philanthropists have to watch out for unintended consequences of well-meaning acts?

Yes, for example, many years ago I visited a model-village project in Ghana where substantial, holistically conceived investments were being made to (rather than with) a number of villages. It was interesting. But it was also arbitrary. If you lived in a village that fell just outside of the area of the chosen villages in the project, you got nothing. The scheme therefore appeared to be causing ill will between neighbours and in addition was not working with the local population, but rather was imposing preconceived ideas on them by outsiders. A more regular example would be setting up a new initiative without seriously investigating whether there are already existing organizations and programmes doing the same work, and often doing it well.

How do you and your brothers balance business interests with philanthropy? Do you see them as separate compartments of your life, as the great philanthropist Andrew Carnegie did? Or does your philanthropy influence your business, like it did with the Quaker philanthropists, the chocolate-making Cadburys?

It's all connected and part of our collective endeavour. My brothers gave me their complete backing to go full-time, so what I'm doing is very much with their blessing. We're a family business and it's a family foundation. When moral dilemmas crop up in either area, it's the same people, and therefore values, driving the decision-making. On that basis I'd like to think we're closer to Cadbury, philosophically, than we are to Carnegie. Making money is important for us, but we value other things higher.

Who do you feel accountable to?

First of all, to myself. I'm my harshest critic. To my family. Then I've got a fantastic professional team at the foundation to try and square myself to. I feel a sense of responsibility to our grantees, my community and – though it might sound a bit grandiose to say it – to the whole country. I feel accountable to all these.

But you're not accountable in the way a politician is, to voters. Or a business is to shareholders. Or a charity is to the public who give it money.

No. But we try to be as transparent as possible. We publish details of our giving on 360Giving [a website on which charities can publish financial grants data in an open, standardized, easily understood way]. We publish many of our grants and our narrative in our annual accounts. We've got our own website where we are clear about our approach. We try to be as open as we can, whilst also acknowledging that we are an independent family foundation. Whilst I answered earlier that I do feel accountable, I also enjoy the benefits of independence as that freedom enables us to act faster, take a little bit more risk or take the longer-term view. Sometimes this freedom can make all the difference. One of the joys of philanthropy is that you can take a medium or long-term view. I don't need to do photo ops. I don't need short-term fixes or answers.

On your website you say that many philanthropists adopt a standard three-year sustainability model. It shows donations tapering off over three years. And it refuses to give money to cover the charity's overheads. Your approach is the opposite. Why?

We work with organizations we think are pretty good. They have people who are experienced. There's a collective narrative, knowledge and expertise that we're buying into. We are trusting and support them because we want them to do more of what they do – and they do well. So it makes sense to contribute to their core costs and it doesn't make sense to stop contributing after an arbitrary period. Rather than stop, as long as our aims and priorities continue to be in alignment, we often increase our funding over the years as we develop a sense of shared goals and partnership. The Foundation's expenditure has been steadily increasing over the past decade and this also has enabled us to maintain long-term relationships with our partners.

Many philanthropists think the opposite. They will only fund specific projects that they can put their name on.

The problem with short-term project funding is that there's a tendency for a charity to try to package up something to appeal to a donor or to accommodate a donor's demands. Sometimes this can actually take the charity a bit off-mission. They can expend resources and energy doing things that could be better spent on their core activities.

If you care very deeply about what a charity is doing, you want to go on the journey with them. We're not worried about getting credit for the Pears Foundation. Our focus isn't on some artificially created Pears three-year project where we closely follow predestined results because it's got our name on it. That's just nonsense. I'm not saying that every charity knows best but, certainly, I don't see the point of charities creating project-linked three-year funds just for the sake of it. We support their core efforts where they're already doing very good work and have clear strategic objectives.

We prefer to form long-term partnerships. We've been supporting the Duke of Edinburgh award for almost 20 years. We've been core-funders of the Trussell Trust and their food-bank model from their very early days. Most, though not all, of the organizations we work with have been partners for more than five, six, seven years. These are genuine partnerships. I view them, and ourselves, as part of the team. And we're simply a part of it, not apart from it. We're part of the journey long-term; amazingly in some cases, I'm on to my third or fourth CEO of some organizations we fund and it is not uncommon for Pears' institutional memory of an organization to go back longer than its CEOs.

But, of course, we do need to understand and, where possible, measure progress. We can be tough and critical friends. We're not walkovers. I don't believe that any organization we're involved with feels 100 per cent certain that we will automatically renew our funding. I'm sure that they hope we will, and work hard to try to make sure we do. I don't think anyone's sitting on their laurels thinking Pears will be here in 10 years' time so we don't have to bother. We'd be gone pretty quickly if they did. But most of the organizations we work with don't behave and think like that.

We do of course stop funding, from time to time. When we think organizations are going off-piste, or where's there's been a personnel change and we don't believe in the new leadership. Or simply when missions or priorities change. Then we do stop funding, and try to exit in a responsible way, but it always disappoints me when that happens because we believe in the general importance of the issues and their previous work. I get pleasure and confidence in seeing organizations going forward.

You say a philanthropist can take more risk. Give me an example.

We support a charity called Ambitious About Autism, which identi-fied that little was being done for young people with autism as they transitioned post-18 from education into life. Their language was about leaving school and 'falling off a cliff'. So they came up with an ambitious initiative to partner up with further-education colleges and access additional education funding to take some of these young people through to 25. It was to be education with a strong focus on life skills – to get them more ready for independent life and ideally for the world of work. The charity came up with a completely new model to do this. It was high risk, with no guarantees that it would work. But they asked us to back it and we said yes. Our decision was partially based on trust, as we had supported the charity and team there for several years; we knew they were really good at what they did. They're cracking good partners. But it wasn't plain sailing and several changes were required along the way. In the end it's been very successful and is making a huge difference to the lives of the students and their families. However, it was quite a high-risk venture and it could easily have just ended up not working. It required trust and honesty on both sides to move forward and develop the project.

You keep using the metaphor of philanthropy as a journey. Do you have any idea where you're going and what's the next thing in the journey? Are you just going to carry on doing more of the same, or do you want to develop in some way?

We think we've developed a good *modus operandi*. However, if I see a way of doing things better, I promise you we'll try and do that! We're trying to identify and work with the best organizations and people we can. I think the goal is to ensure we keep our values and principles intact whilst driving forward on all fronts!

We are also having more conversations as a family about endowing the foundation because at present most of our giving is coming from our corporate profits, which are then invested into the foundation.

Are you intending to pass it on to the next generation of the family?

Absolutely. I won't be disappointed, however, if the next generation wants to do very different things – so long as they maintain the *modus operandi* and underlying values. I'd be upset if they decided to change how the Foundation worked with others, especially in the listening and respect department. But they must make their own decisions. Agency is very important all across the board. If your aim as a philanthropist is to support people to have agency, to make their own decisions, that must certainly apply to your own children. It's a continuing journey, but it will be theirs to travel.

Chapter 9

Survival of the Fattest

Only at the very end of the play does the dead steelworker offer his final judgement. A musical about the life of Andrew Carnegie – the rags-to-riches philanthropist who started out the son of an impoverished Scottish weaver and ended as the wealthiest man in the world – was staged on the fringe of the Edinburgh Festival in 2016. In Ian Hammond Brown's musical *Carnegie: The Star-Spangled Scotchman* one of the seven workers killed during a strike at one of Carnegie's steelworks in 1892 is sent down from Heaven by St Peter to pronounce judgement on the great American industrialist as he lies on his deathbed. The worker, who died at the hands of the private police force Carnegie sent to supress the strike, has to decide whether his former employer should be admitted to Heaven or be sent down to Hell. The dramatic device on which the drama pivots penetrates to the heart of the great conundrum that seized philanthropy at the turn of the nineteenth and twentieth centuries: can epic acts of benevolence ever compensate for a lifetime of callous exploitation? Do the ends ever justify the means? Can philanthropy offer absolution or even redemption?

Andrew Carnegie has often been portrayed as a cut-throat businessman who, later in life, after some conversion experience, became the greatest philanthropist of the *fin de siècle* era. The truth is more complicated. Carnegie constituted a new departure in the history of philanthropy. Like so many philanthropists, he was a curious amalgam. Indeed, he was a man of contradictions. Andrew Carnegie grew up in Scotland in a family which had its roots in the Chartist reform movement of the 1840s. He was a man who wrote in support of the rights of workers, but who then resolved to smash the major trade union in his own industry. He was an opponent of slavery who was happy enough to exploit the ordinary folk in his own charge. He was an advocate of peace, who spent millions trying to prevent the First World War, while at the same time profiting from producing steel to build warships and armaments. He prioritized maximizing the bottom line in all his business dealings and yet was zealous about the business of giving his money away. Yet his philanthropic activity was not something separate from his entrepreneurial instincts. Where George Cadbury allowed his philanthropy to change his approach to business, Andrew Carnegie did the opposite: his business methods shaped his attitude to benevolence. He ushered in a new type of philanthropy – an era of foundations dedicated to 'the improvement of mankind'. His was the Golden Age of Philanthropy, or the Gilded Age as Mark Twain satirically described it.[1]

THE ROAD TO BECOMING THE RICHEST
MAN IN THE WORLD

Andrew Carnegie was born in 1835, the son of a handloom weaver from Dunfermline. His father wove fine damask linen on a large Jacquard loom which took up most of the ground floor of the modest family cottage. But even while the boy was at school his father's living was being gradually eroded by competition from Dunfermline's first steam-powered textile mill. One day, when Andrew was 12, his father came home and announced to his wife and children that he could get no more work. They decided to sell the family furniture to pay for tickets to sail to the United States.

The life Andrew Carnegie embarked upon, after the family arrived at the home of his uncle who had earlier emigrated to Allegheny in Pennsylvania, was to embody the American Dream. His first job was as a bobbin boy in a local textile mill where he earned $1.20 a week. But, after learning double-entry bookkeeping at night school, he became a messenger boy for a telegraph company, where he swiftly learned to decipher Morse code messages by ear and was promoted to become secretary to the railroad superintendent. A year after he arrived he wrote to a relative back in Scotland: 'It is far better for me that I came here . . . In Dunfermline I would have been a poor weaver all my days, but here I can surely do something better than that, if I don't it will be all my own fault, for anyone can get along in this country.'[2]

America, midway through the nineteenth century, was undergoing its second industrial revolution. The first had transformed New England into a centre of textile manufacturing, but elsewhere the United States remained primarily an agricultural nation. Now, on the eve of the American Civil War, the rapid expansion of factory production, mining and railroad construction began the vast nation's transformation into a mature industrial society.[3] The young Carnegie, under the tutelage of the railway superintendent, Thomas Scott, began to invest his wages – and later money he borrowed – to buy shares in railroads, bridges, iron, oil and steel.

Carnegie's entrepreneurial skill had been evident even as a child when he persuaded his schoolfriends – in an episode which sounds like something from *Tom Sawyer* – to gather dandelions and clover in the woods to feed his rabbits in return for being allowed to choose the names of the animals' offspring.[4] In the US his first investment was to buy 10 shares in the company which eventually became American Express. An investment in a sleeping-car company for the railroad was soon bringing him an annual income of $5,000. When the Civil War broke out in 1861, Scott and Carnegie were seconded to the War Department in Washington to organize railroad and telegraphic services. Carnegie used the inside information that the enemy were burning wooden railway bridges, and jeopardizing troop movements, to invest in the Keystone Bridge Company which produced bridges made of iron instead. He invested his dividends in an oil company which was rapidly worth $5 million.

When the war ended in 1865, Carnegie was offered a job as head of the Pennsylvania Railroad Company. He turned it down to concentrate on his investments. Two years later Carnegie formed the Pullman Pacific Car Company and travelled to Europe where he earned $3 million in commission from selling railroad and bridge bonds to Europeans. In Europe he met the inventor Henry Bessemer, who had come up with a converter which made the mass production of steel far more economic. As the age of iron was giving way to the age of steel, Carnegie was in the forefront of the advance. His Carnegie Steel Company soon had plants all round the country using the new technologies which made the production of steel easier, faster and more profitable. Andrew Carnegie swiftly assembled an economic empire which ensured he owned or controlled every step of the industrial process – from raw materials to ships and railroads for transporting the goods, even coalfields to fuel the steel furnaces. He ran his companies with a hand of steel. His factories operated non-stop, with two twelve-hour shifts every day of the year except for the Fourth of July. Every other Sunday he demanded that his employees work a danger-prone 24-hour shift.[5] He was utterly unsentimental about business matters: when his old mentor, Thomas Scott, went bust, the pitiless Carnegie refused to help him.[6] Andrew Carnegie's entrepreneurial skill, nose for an investment, political friendships, manipulation of favourable government tariffs, together with ruthless mergers and acquisitions, soon made him one of the most powerful men in America.

CAPTAINS OF INDUSTRY OR ROBBER BARONS?

Carnegie was not alone. He was one of a coterie of industrial and financial titans which included Cornelius Vanderbilt, John D. Rockefeller, Andrew W. Mellon, Russell Sage, Henry Clay Frick, Jay Gould, J. P. Morgan and Henry Ford. Their admirers called them 'captains of industry' but their detractors accused them of unscrupulous and underhand behaviour, manipulating stocks, insider trading, and bribing judges and politicians. They all made money out of the American Civil War. As a young financial speculator J. P. Morgan was implicated in the sale of faulty weapons to the Union army at six times their value. Later he had a telegraph line installed in his Wall Street office so he could buy and sell gold on the back of news developments about the war before anyone else had the information.[7] In 1867 the journalist E. L. Godkin coined the term 'robber barons' for this new generation of businessmen, after the feudal lords in medieval Germany who imposed tolls higher than those authorized by the Holy Roman Emperor on travellers using rivers or roads passing through their territory – and who also often resorted to the robbery and kidnap of passing merchants. 'The America of the post-Civil War era was a paradise for the entrepreneur, untrammelled and untaxed,' wrote Matthew Josephson in his 1934 book *The Robber Barons*.[8]

But amassing huge fortunes was not enough. This new generation of the mega-wealthy wanted to flaunt it. At first they did it by lavish spending. In New York, in prominent places such as Fifth Avenue, they built palatial mansions in the style of French châteaux, to which they added preposterous features like – in the case of the steel magnate Charles M. Schwab – a belfry with chimes.[9] The mansions were fitted with luxurious furnishings. Matthew Josephson, in *The Robber Barons*, recorded a bedstead carved from oak and ebony inlaid with gold, an enamel wall, and carvings, tapestries, staircases and ceilings ripped from the medieval castles of Europe and transported to nineteenth-century Manhattan.[10]

Even that was not sufficient. In addition to buying fine art, racehorses and yachts, the new rich gave ostentatious parties. Those of the Vanderbilts were so extravagant that members of the public flocked to the street outside their mansion to gawp – in such numbers that the police were sometimes called to keep order on the street. It was to describe such flamboyance that Veblen invented the phrase 'conspicuous consumption'. When extravagance would not suffice, the newly moneyed resorted to mockery of those who lacked their advantages. Josephson records one party described on the invitations as a 'poverty social' – to which guests came dressed in rags and were served scraps of food on wooden plates. 'The diners sat about on broken soap boxes, buckets, and coal hods. Newspapers, dust cloths and old skirts were used as napkins, and beer served in a rusty tin can.'[11] When such degenerate and morally bankrupt pleasures no longer proved satisfying the robber barons turned to philanthropy.

Andrew Carnegie was not interested in lavish parties. He only attended them when it would help him do some business deal. His attitudes to philanthropy and commerce were interwoven. He was profoundly influenced by the English philosopher Herbert Spencer, regarded by his contemporaries as the greatest thinker of the Victorian era. Spencer was a pioneer of what came to be known as Social Darwinism. Where Charles Darwin had described natural selection and the survival of the fittest as the mechanisms of evolution in the animal kingdom, Spencer saw a similar dynamic at work in human society; indeed, the phrase 'survival of the fittest' is Spencer's, not Darwin's.[12] Those who rose to the top of this genetic hierarchy were inevitably the best, he argued. In the pre-industrial 'barbarian' age, those men who flourished were physically strong and brave; but after the Industrial Revolution those who did best were the cleverest and most hard-working. Famine and war, Spencer said, following Malthus, were the social forms of natural selection. Helping the poor interfered with that. People needed to compete for resources if society was to advance: 'without struggle, there is no progress,' Spencer wrote. As for the disabled, 'it is best they should die'.[13]

This most notorious line of Spencer's is echoed by the hard-hearted Scrooge in Dickens's *A Christmas Carol* when the miser rejects an appeal for charity for people so poor they might die: 'then let them do it and decrease the surplus population'. Carnegie, and other robber barons, saw in Spencer's thinking a justification of their own material success. In his autobiography Carnegie later wrote of his first encounter with Spencer: 'I remember that light came, as in the flood, and all was clear. Not only had I got rid of theology and the supernatural, but I had found the truth of evolution.'[14]

Others were more venal. To John D. Rockefeller thinking like Spencer's proved that there was no 'evil tendency' in business, 'merely the working out of a law of nature and a law of God'.[15] The railway magnate James Hill was more specific: 'the fortunes of railroad companies are determined by the law of the survival of the fittest'.[16] The admiration was mutual. On a visit to America in 1882, Spencer addressed a group of his extraordinarily well-heeled supporters in Delmonico's restaurant in New York, many of whose portly figures seemed to give credence, rather, to a doctrine of the survival of the fattest. They were served no fewer than twenty-five courses of food and a dozen different kinds of wine (see first set of illustrations). Spencer told them that their nation would eventually produce 'a more powerful type of man than has hitherto existed', and when that happened 'the Americans may reasonably look forward to a time when they will have produced a civilisation grander than any the world has known'.[17] That was the theory, at any rate; in practice Spencer was rather grumpy about the places he actually visited, saying of the cradle of industrial America, Pittsburgh, 'six months here would justify suicide'.[18]

SOCIAL DARWINISM AND THE GOSPEL OF WEALTH

The philosophy of Herbert Spencer was enough to allow the robber barons to recast philanthropy in their own image. The rich had proved, by their very material success, that they were the best-equipped members of society to make decisions. Industrial tycoons must therefore know better than everyone else how to address and solve major social problems. Carnegie made public his own personal philosophy in 1889, as he approached the age of 60, in an essay entitled *Wealth*, later more famously republished as *The Gospel of Wealth*.[19] 'The problem of our age is the proper administration of wealth,' he began, adding that it had to be managed in such a way that 'the ties of brotherhood may still bind together the rich and the poor in harmonious relationship'.[20] But that relationship was rooted in a tension, he acknowledged. 'Under the law of competition, the employer of thousands is forced into the strictest economies', as a result of which 'often there is friction between the employer and the employed'. Yet while this 'may be sometimes hard for the individual, it is best for the race, because it ensures the survival of the fittest in every department'. Inequality, he added, is 'essential to the future progress of the race'. The best interests of the race inevitably means wealth is given to the few. The key question was: how should this wealth best be used? At their deaths rich men could leave their fortunes to their families. Or they could bequeath their wealth 'for public purposes'. Carnegie approved of neither. His preferred option was that it should be administered for the good of all by rich men during their lives.

On the first idea, Carnegie argued, if men left great fortunes to their children out of affection, this was a misguided affection. 'It is not well for the children that they should be so burdened.' There are a few examples of 'millionaires' sons unspoiled by wealth, who, being rich, still perform great services to the community'. But they are exceptions rather than the rule. 'I would as soon leave to my son a curse as the almighty dollar.'

Yet neither did he approve of those who died leaving large sums to the taxman. Of all forms of taxation, death duties seem the wisest, Carnegie said, but it was far better for a rich man to dispose of his wealth during his own lifetime. Some might argue that such wealth should be distributed in small quantities among the people over the years. But money distributed in that way, Carnegie argued, 'would have been wasted in the indulgence of appetite, some of it in excess'. Instead, he insisted 'even the poorest can be made to see . . . that great sums gathered by some of their fellow citizens and spent for public purposes, from which the masses reap the principal benefit, are more valuable to them than if scattered among themselves in trifling amounts through the course of many years'. And it would be 'better for mankind that the millions of the rich were thrown into the sea than so spent as to encourage the slothful, the drunken, the unworthy'. While temporary assistance to the needy could do genuine good, in general 'neither the individual nor the race is improved by almsgiving'.

It follows from all this, Carnegie concluded, that 'the duty of the man of wealth' was first 'to set an example of modest, unostentatious living, shunning display or extravagance'; then to provide moderately for his dependants; and then to consider the rest of his income 'simply as trust funds', which he has the responsibility to administer to produce what will be, in his judgement, the most beneficial results for the whole community. The man of wealth thus becomes 'the mere trustee and agent for his poorer brethren' and brings to their service 'his superior wisdom, experience and ability to administer, doing for them better than they would or could do for themselves'.

In Carnegie's judgement 'the best means of benefiting the community is to place within its reach the ladders upon which the aspiring can rise – free libraries, parks, and means of recreation, by which men are helped in body and mind'. Prominent among these will be works of art 'to give pleasure and improve the public taste' and 'public institutions of various kinds which will improve the general condition of the people'. The vast bulk of a rich man's fortune should be spent in this way since, Carnegie concluded, 'the man who dies . . . rich dies disgraced'. As a philosophy it was a new Darwinian determinism which mingled elitism and altruism with unapologetic capitalism and an early variant of trickle-down economics. But it advocated a new form of giving, moving into new areas, with new methods, and with the wider ambition of improving 'the general condition of the people'.

By no means everyone was enamoured of Carnegie's new thinking. His declaration in his *Gospel of Wealth* that he was going to give away his entire fortune – and his insistence that other rich individuals must do the same – received as much criticism as it did praise. The year after the essay was published – even before its title had been prefixed with the word *Gospel* – it was attacked by one of the great orators of the era, the Methodist preacher, Reverend Hugh Price Hughes, not merely as 'an anti-Christian phenomenon' but also as 'a social monstrosity and a grave political peril'.[21] Hughes was outraged by the high protective tariffs on steel imports imposed by Carnegie's political friends in the US government, which allowed the steel magnate to charge a high price for his goods free of any competition from abroad. Carnegie and his fellows were 'the unnatural product of artificial social regulations': they were untrammelled by any laws on a minimum wage for their workers, or by legislation protecting their right to organize in trade unions, or even by income tax, which the US Supreme Court ruled in 1895 was unconstitutional. All these constituted, to the fiery Methodist preacher, unjust freedoms for the industrialists. The fortunes of millionaires were paid for by paupers at the other end of the social and economic spectrum.

William Jewett Tucker, a professor of religion who later became president of the Ivy League university, Dartmouth College, was more measured in his language but equally critical. Tucker praised Carnegie's 'independence, business sagacity, breadth of view, and generous motive', but insisted that the 'vast system of patronage' Carnegie advocated would, in the end, 'create a more hopeless social condition'. The millionaire's assumption that 'he can administer [his wealth] for the community far better than it could or would for itself' avoided 'the whole question of economic justice'. In the United States, at that time, Tucker suggested, 'more than one half of the wealth of the country is in [the] possession of less than fifty thousand families'. Carnegie was avoiding 'the ethical question of today' which centred around 'the distribution rather than the redistribution of wealth'. Tucker concluded: 'I can conceive of no greater mistake, more disastrous in the end to religion if not to society, than that of trying to make charity do the work of justice'.[22]

Carnegie had not formulated his philosophy late in life. At the age of just 33, in 1868, the year when his annual income first reached $50,000, Andrew Carnegie had written a memo to himself setting out a massive new resolution on New Year's Eve. It was not found until after his death in 1919, but it showed that he resolved, even then, that, however much he earned in future, he would confine his expenditure to this $50,000 limit and use the surplus 'for benevolent purposes'. Indeed, in this note-to-self he actually planned to 'cast aside business forever' in two years' time and acquire an education in Oxford, then settle in London to purchase a controlling interest in a newspaper which he would use to lobby for the 'education and improvement of the poorer classes'. Thereafter he would devote himself full-time to philanthropy. Revealingly, he noted, 'whatever I engage in, I must push inordinately'. He would choose 'that life which will be the most elevating in its character'. The amassing of wealth 'is one of the worst species of idolatry – no idol more debasing than the worship of money'. To be overwhelmed by business cares and to continue to focus wholly on making money would 'degrade me beyond hope of permanent recovery'.[23]

It did not work out quite like that. It was another five years before Carnegie made his first big public charitable donation. In 1873 he built a swimming baths in the place of his birth, Dunfermline. In those early years his philanthropy was very much a sideline to his commercial activity. Throughout the 1870s and 1880s he built Carnegie Steel into the largest pig-iron producer in the world and a manufacturer of structural steel for the building of America's new skyscrapers, elevated railroads and electricity pylons. By 1892 Carnegie steel was worth $25 million. But philanthropy was now a constant presence in his thinking. In 1880 he built a library for Dunfermline and the year after offered a free library to Pittsburgh, though local city regulations prevented the million-dollar venture opening till 1890. In 1885 he gave $50,000 to establish the first medical research laboratory in the United States at Bellevue Hospital in New York. In 1888 he paid for children to go to Paris to be treated by Louis Pasteur.

The trigger for Carnegie to finally switch his primary focus from business to benevolence was the death of his formidable mother, Margaret, in 1886. The Scottish-American industrialist was so devoted to the woman who had mortgaged her house to give him the money for his first major US investment that he refused to marry while she was alive; indeed, he had three times, apparently at his mother's behest, broken off his engagement to the woman who was eventually to become his wife – Louise Whitfield, the daughter of a New York merchant. The year after Margaret's death they married, with Louise later declaring that Margaret Morrison Carnegie was 'the most unpleasant woman she had met in her life'.[24]

The switch in his allegiance from mother to wife marked a similar shift in Carnegie's professional life. After he married, at the age of 51, with more money than he knew what to do with, Andrew Carnegie began to focus less on his investments. He worked only in the mornings and put the operation of his businesses under the control of his senior managers. The most important of these was Henry Clay Frick, a businessman whose company had supplied Carnegie's steelworks with smelting coke and who then entered into partnership with the tycoon.

Increasingly, Carnegie left the day-to-day running of the Carnegie Steel Company to his junior partner.[25]

Instead, Carnegie busied himself with philanthropic projects of which his top priority was the establishment of libraries – he eventually built almost 3,000 across the world. Borrowing books had been the chief mechanism by which the young Carnegie had educated himself. His father was one of five weavers in Dunfermline who gathered together the few books they had and formed the first circulating library in the town.[26] As a boy in Scotland, Andrew's uncle George Lauder had introduced him to the works of Scotland's greatest poet, Robbie Burns, and to the plays of William Shakespeare, paying the boy a penny every time he learned a great section of their works. As a messenger in America the teenage Carnegie had been fortunate to encounter Colonel James Anderson, an iron manufacturer who opened his personal library of 400 volumes to working-class boys of Allegheny. Carnegie was able to borrow a book from him every Saturday; he carried it about with him all week to read 'in the intervals that could be snatched from duty'.[27]

But the business principles and practice Carnegie had established over the previous four decades were not set aside. When he opened his library in Dunfermline he had chiselled over the doorway the words 'Let there be Light' – a motto which was to be inscribed over the entrance to every one of his libraries. But though he built the library he refused to buy any books or pay for the operation of the building. Some Dunfermline town councillors, piqued at this apparent parsimony, turned their back on him as he was speaking at the library's opening ceremony, but Carnegie insisted that the project was a partnership and that those he helped had to be prepared to help themselves. The council must buy the books.[28]

Other robber-baron philanthropists followed Carnegie in insisting that their new philanthropy must be governed by rigorous business principles. The idea that the prime purpose of philanthropy was to shift resources from the rich to the poor gave way to the notion that its task was rather to shift resources from the rich to the wider community.[29] Carnegie's fellow tycoons fell into line with his belief that they could best improve society by establishing a civic infrastructure of libraries, universities, public parks, art galleries, museums, concert halls and meeting halls which would enable the poor to elevate their aspirations. The result was celebrated buildings like New York's Carnegie Hall, which opened in 1891 and which became one of the most prestigious venues in the world for both classical and popular music. Social justice was entirely absent from Carnegie's agenda.

ANDREW CARNEGIE'S CALLOUS CONTRADICTIONS

What drew attention to that omission, in the most glaring way, were the events which unfolded at the Homestead Steelworks in 1892, three years after publication of *The Gospel of Wealth*. The great industrialist had previously been eloquent in his defence of workers' rights. Six years earlier he had written: 'The right of the working-men to combine and to form trades-unions is no less sacred than the right of the manufacturer to enter into associations and conferences with his fellows, and it must sooner or later be conceded.' Indeed, he added, 'my experience has been that trades-unions, upon the whole, are beneficial both to labor and to capital.'[30] Unions educated working men and the better informed that workers were, the fewer contests they had with employers, he insisted. He even argued against the practice of hiring 'scab' labour to break strikes.[31]

But such progressive considerations went out of the window when he was confronted with the need to cut costs to maintain profits. Only a few years after he had written those words, he decided to introduce a sliding scale of wages in his steel factories to guarantee profits so that, if the price of steel fell, the cost of production would fall too. Employees at his Homestead steelworks in Pittsburgh were presented with a new contract with pay cuts of up to 35 per cent. The men walked out on strike and Carnegie told his managers to 'shut down and wait . . . until part of the men vote to work.'[32] So relaxed was he that he went off to Scotland. In his absence his junior partner Henry Clay Frick decided, however, not to starve the strikers into submission but to bring in a private police force from the Pinkerton National Detective Agency to drive the strikers out of the mill. He sent a telegram to Carnegie in Scotland which read, cryptically: 'Small plunge, our actions and position there unassailable and will work out satisfactorily.'[33]

The Pinkerton men arrived at Homestead in the early hours of 6 July 1892, floating down the river to the mill on a barge. The workers, who had been tipped off, were lying in wait. They fired on them with old Civil War blunderbusses and rolled explosives down a hill to the river on a railway car.[34] A twelve-hour battle ensued in which seven strikers and three Pinkerton men were killed. Eventually, the Pinkertons laid down their guns and surrendered and were marched through the town where they were attacked by both strikers and townsfolk.

News of the battle flashed around the world, with initial reports suggesting that as many as 20 men had died. Meanwhile at Braemar, in Scotland, Carnegie was besieged by reporters and, unusually for him, refused to speak to them. The next day he sent a telegram in reply to Frick. It read: 'Cable received. All anxiety gone since you stand firm. Never employ one of those rioters. Let grass grow over works. Must not fail now. You will win easily next trial – only stand firm – law and order – wish I could support you in any form.' In public, however, he was saying the opposite. That same day Carnegie told a reporter from the *New York Herald*: 'The strike is most deplorable, and the news of the disaster, which reached me at Aberdeen, grieved me more than I can tell you. It came on me like a thunderbolt in a clear sky.' After that he told another reporter: 'I have given up all active control of the business, and I do not care to interfere in any way with the present management conduct of this affair', but then added, ambiguously, referring to the strikers: 'The men have chosen their course and I am powerless to change it. The handling of the case on the part of the company has my full approbation and sanction.'[35]

The strikers' victory was short lived. On 10 July, at Frick's request, the state militia was ordered into Homestead. Four thousand state troopers, with 2,000 more in reserve, marched in and surrounded the plant. Within twenty minutes they had ousted the strikers and restored the company officials to their offices.[36] After just a few days parts of the steel plant were back in operation, employing new workers along with those of the old workforce who were deemed not to have been troublemakers and who were prepared to accept new terms and conditions including a No-Strike clause. The Amalgamated Association of Iron and Steel Workers maintained the dispute in name only for several months before eventually calling off the strike officially in November.

But if Carnegie and Frick had won the battle they had lost the war. Effigies of the two men were hung on telegraph poles throughout the town.[37] The steelworkers' union did not re-emerge as a serious power in the industry for almost four decades, and employers used the example of Homestead to drive wages downwards across the country, but there was a price to pay for that. Carnegie was fiercely attacked in the press on both sides of the Atlantic. Such was the public outrage that the House of Representatives felt obliged to send investigators to Homestead. The governing Republican Party lost the presidential election – ousting the sitting president, Benjamin Harrison – and blamed the fact on Carnegie's handling of Homestead.[38]

Carnegie's emerging reputation as a philanthropist was instantly and seriously damaged. Trade unionists in Pittsburgh petitioned the city council to return a $1 million gift from Carnegie, with one local labour leader declaring: 'I would sooner enter a building built with the dirty silver Judas received for betraying Christ than enter a Carnegie library.'[39] The lampooning by newspapers was ferocious. One cartoon, in the *Saturday Globe*, depicted two Carnegies, joined at the hip – one, smiling, handing out a library and a cheque, the other holding a notice telling workers that their pay had been slashed. The caption read: 'As the tight-fisted employer he reduces wages that he may play philanthropist.' Another cartoon called him 'The Modern Baron with Ancient Methods' and showed him standing on top of a castle-like steelworks ready to pour hot tar on invaders.[40] The editorial comments were even more scathing than the cartoons. The *St Louis Post-Dispatch* printed an unsigned editorial, which was widely reprinted. It cut a deep wound in Carnegie's philanthropic pride, stating:

> Three months ago, Andrew Carnegie was a man to be envied. Today he is an object of mingled pity and contempt . . . One would naturally suppose then if he had a grain of consistency, not to say decency, in his composition, he would favor rather than oppose the organization of trade unions among his own working people at Homestead. One would naturally suppose that if he had a grain of manhood, not to say courage, in his composition, he would at least have been willing to face the consequences of his inconsistency. But what does Carnegie do? Runs off to Scotland out of harm's way to await the issue of the battle he was too pusillanimous to share. America can well spare Mr Carnegie. Ten thousand Carnegie Public Libraries would not compensate the country for the direct and indirect evils resulting from the Homestead lockout.[41]

The *Forum*, in which Carnegie had published his progressive labour ideas, came out hard against him. In London the *Financial Observer* witheringly declared: 'Here we have this Scotch Yankee plutocrat meandering through Scotland in a four-in-hand [coach], opening public libraries, receiving the freedom of cities, while the wretched . . . workmen who sweat themselves in order to supply him with the ways and means for this self-glorification are starving in Pittsburgh.'[42]

But Frick was unrepentant. He had lowered unit-labour costs by 20 per cent. He later boasted in a letter to Carnegie that they had taught the workers 'a lesson they will never forget'.[43] Frick was even uncowed by an assassination attempt; on 23 June an anarchist called Alexander Berkman attacked Frick in his office, shooting him twice and stabbing him. He was not a competent assassin. The hard-nosed industrialist received treatment in his office and continued to work, sending a telegram to Carnegie which said: 'Was shot twice but not dangerously. There is no necessity for you to come home. I am still in shape to fight the battle out.'[44]

Even in Scotland, however, Carnegie realized the damage that had been done to his standing. (Frick had sent him a detailed report, newspaper clippings, and copies of his correspondence with lawyers, the sheriff and Robert Pinkerton.) Carnegie wrote to the British Prime Minister, William Gladstone, in a hasty stream of consciousness: 'This is the trial of my life . . . Such a foolish step contrary to my ideas – repugnant to every feeling of my nature. Our firm offered all it could offer, even generous terms . . . The false step was made in trying to run the Homestead works with new men. It is a test to which workingmen should not be subjected – it is expecting too much to expect poor men to stand by and see their work taken by others – their daily bread.' He told Gladstone he had written an alternative plan of action but that, alas, his letter did not reach Frick to whom he referred as 'my young and rather too rash partner'. But there is no record or reference to any such letter or cable, according to Carnegie's biographer David Nasaw.[45]

Carnegie was more frank with his cousin Dod Lauder, telling him that trying to land the Pinkertons by boat was a grievous error by Frick – as was the decision to start up production too soon with scab labour. Frick had broken the union but had made too many mistakes along the way. Had he shown more patience they might have won without loss of life or the avalanche of negative publicity which followed.[46] Eventually, Carnegie and Frick were to fall out, with the younger man writing to the older: 'for years I have been convinced that there is not an honest bone in your body. Now I know you are a goddamn thief.'[47]

The damage to the reputation of Andrew Carnegie, and by association his fellow tycoon philanthropists, was long-term. A decade later the satirical magazine *Puck* carried a cartoon showing Carnegie poring over a document entitled 'Plan for the Carnegie Library' while by the door an elderly couple stand in the cold winter wind and snow. The caption says: 'Books are already so cheap and libraries so abundant that even the poorest man has all the literature he wants. Now, why not provide respectable homes for the people who are too old to work and who were never able to save anything from their scanty wages – and so keep them from beggary.'[48]

Two years after that, a drawing by a different cartoonist in the same magazine shows the figure of Puck tugging at the coat-tails of Carnegie, as he and John D. Rockefeller pile money bags around the base of a statue labelled 'Fame' as they seek to endow libraries and universities. Puck, by contrast, suggests they could do more good for society by endowing a Home for Consumptives: 'You have qualified thoroughly as modern philanthropists, now why not do some good?'[49] Prose writers were more direct. Three years after the Homestead Strike and Lockout an article by Reverend Washington Gladden, a leader of the Social Gospel Movement, was published. Entitled 'Tainted Money' it attacked the benefactions of 'robber barons', 'Roman plunderers', 'pirates of industry' and 'spoilers of the state'. He did not mention Carnegie by name but few had little doubt about his target. The same year, in a sermon to the National Conference of Charities and Corrections, Gladden questioned whether a church or university should take offerings of money made in morally reprehensible ways. 'Is this clean money?' he asked. 'Can any man, can any institution, knowing its origin, touch it without being defiled?'[50] In the event some 225 communities spurned Carnegie's offer of a free library because of his labour politics.[51]

Carnegie was hurt, but only to some extent repentant. He later said it was the only business episode in his life that he looked back on with regret. 'Nothing I have had to meet all my life, before or since, wounded me so deeply. No pangs remain of any wounds received in my business career save that of Homestead,' he later admitted.[52] But it was not, for Carnegie, a critique of his general approach to business and philanthropy. He revealed that in a speech at the dedication of his Pittsburgh library at the end of 1895. It was justifiable for any employer to maximize profits, even if this involved work practices which reduced pay and conditions for its employees. That way he would have more money to spend on philanthropy, he said. Even if he could have shared some of his profit with his workers without damaging the viability of the business, he argued, it would be neither 'justifiable or wise'. Revealing that he still retained his elitist view that ordinary citizens did not know what was good for them so much as a successful businessman did, he declared:

> There are higher uses for surplus wealth than adding petty sums to the earnings of the masses. Trifling sums given to each, every week or month – and the sums would be trifling indeed – would be frittered away, nine times out of ten, in things which pertain to the body and not the spirit; upon richer food and drink, better clothing, more extravagant living, which are beneficial neither to rich nor poor. These things are external and of the flesh: they do not minister to the higher, the divine, part of man.[53]

But his business cravings were no longer enough. By 1896 Carnegie Steel was fully vertically integrated. Carnegie controlled every level and phase of the business – the mining of ore, of coal, the smelting coke ovens, limestone deposits, the railways to move them, and every level of manufacturing from blast furnaces to steel rolling with the most technologically advanced facilities in the world. All this was creating an annual profit of $40 million by 1900. By the end of the decade he was making almost half the steel produced in America, and had accumulated a fortune worth hundreds of millions of dollars. With little more to achieve he sold his business to his main competitor, J. P. Morgan, who controlled the United States Steel Corporation. The sale left Andrew Carnegie, in the words of the man who bought him out, 'the richest man in the world'.

FAMILY MAN PHILANTHROPY

Now in his mid-sixties, Carnegie decided to spend the rest of his days as a family man – his only daughter Margaret had been born three years earlier – and as a full-time philanthropist. In 1898 he bought and restored a castle at Skibo in the Scottish Highlands, at the request of his wife Louise. From there he expanded his philanthropic efforts to build libraries. An avid reader since his boyhood, he saw free libraries as 'the best agencies for improving the masses of the people because they only help those who help themselves. They never pauperise, a taste for reading drives out lower tastes.'[54] By the time of his death in 1919, Carnegie had opened 2,811 libraries around the world at a cost of over $60 million.[55] Now he expanded into other areas of his personal interests too. The Carnegie Hero Fund was established in America in 1904, and then in Britain in 1908, after a colliery disaster near Pittsburgh where two men gave their lives in attempted rescues after an explosion in which 181 men died. In 1905 came the Carnegie Foundation for the Advancement of Teaching, a body set up to fund research into teaching methods and education policy. In 1906 his Simplified Spelling Board aimed to reform the spelling of the English language.

But Andrew Carnegie's overriding passion in the final years of his life was how to prevent the world war which he sensed was looming. 'There is still one evil in our day, so far exceeding any other in extent and effect,' he told the students of the University of St Andrews in his address as Rector in 1905. 'There still remains the foulest blot that has ever disgraced the earth, the killing of civilized men by men like wild beasts as a permissible mode of settling international disputes.'[56] In 1906 he laid the foundation stone for a Peace Palace at The Hague, to be managed by the $10 million Carnegie Foundation, as a home for the Permanent Court of Arbitration, and later the International Court of Justice. He endowed it with one of the largest legal libraries in the world, in an attempt to bring peace through law. Carnegie spent more than $25 million in an unsuccessful attempt to prevent the onset of the First World War. It was one of the bitterest regrets of the closing years of his life that he did not succeed.

Finally in 1911, after a decade of philanthropic endeavour, Andrew Carnegie, now aged 75, realized he would be unable to supervise the spending of the $150 million which remained from the sale of his businesses. As a result he entered into a new departure in philanthropy. His previous foundations had used conventional legal structures. But now he created a perpetual corporate structure in the form of the Carnegie Corporation of New York to which he transferred most of his remaining wealth with instructions on how it should distribute his fortune after his death. That year, and the year after, Carnegie gave the corporation $125 million, making it the largest single philanthropic

body ever established. In addition he made it his residual legatee, so
that the remainder of his estate went to it after the other bequests in
his Last Will and Testament were discharged. The trustees were charged
with making gifts in the spirit of the man who was at that point the
biggest philanthropist the world had ever seen.

By the time of his death Carnegie had given away at least $350
million. Just as significantly his corporation had a market value of $3
billion a century later. Over that century the reputation of Andrew
Carnegie has been distinctly chequered. The Homestead affair cast a
long shadow over the good name of Carnegie. A righteous indignation
fuelled his many critics and this extended into a wider criticism of
philanthropy, so that George Bernard Shaw spoke for many when he
declared, 'He who gives money he has not earned is generous with
other people's labour'.[57] Shaw also cast doubt upon the motives of the
wealthy: 'A millionaire does not really care whether his money does
good or not, provided he finds his conscience eased and his social
status improved by giving it away'.[58] Such a view persisted until the
era of Ronald Reagan and Margaret Thatcher, which ushered in an
intellectual reclamation of Carnegie and his fellow robber barons.

In the two decades that followed the Reagan/Thatcher era, a number
of biographies appeared which sought to restore the reputations of the
philanthropists of the Gilded Age, portraying them as maligned and
misunderstood. But after the global financial crisis of 2007–8 criticism
of them has returned. Today Carnegie and his peers are once more
treated with ambivalence as they are frequently compared to the super-
rich philanthrocapitalists of the late twentieth and early twenty-first
century. Ian Hammond Brown, the writer of the 2016 musical *The
Star-Spangled Scotchman*, said: 'When I began writing, two years ago, I
took a real dislike to Carnegie. But as the process went on I changed.'
In his musical the actor playing the part of Carnegie, Joe Whiteman,
turned out to be – with extraordinary serendipity, and only after he had
been cast in the role – the great-great-great-grandson of the American
mega-tycoon. During rehearsals Whiteman was approached by a man
in a pub who asked him: 'How does it feel to have a ruthless bastard for
a grandfather?' The author, having set himself the question of whether
Carnegie should go to Heaven or to Hell, at the end of the musical
begrudgingly allows him through the Pearly Gates. 'He may have been
"a ruthless bastard" but he did a lot of good – by contrast with plenty

of other ruthless industrialists in that era who were only exploitatively self-serving and did no good at all.'[59]

PHILANTHROPY'S SHIFT TO THE ARTS

Two wider issues arise out of the philanthropic innovations of Andrew Carnegie. The first is the shift in philanthropy's focus – away from helping the poor and towards supporting social infrastructure in the arts, education and science. That is a legacy which continues to shape the outlines of twenty-first-century philanthropy. The second is Carnegie's establishment of the corporate foundation. This too has had a profound impact upon the direction of philanthropy since his death, and it continues to be a key influence today.

Philanthropists through the ages have sought to marry their public duty with their private interests. One of the things that was new about Andrew Carnegie was the emphasis upon literacy and libraries, which he felt had been so formative in his own self-directed education. The sheer scale of his donations influenced his fellow tycoons in also supporting the creation of a civic infrastructure of literature, science and the arts which would be, in Carnegie's words, 'ladders upon which the aspiring can rise'.[60] This was philanthropy not for the poor and destitute, but for the able and industrious.

Not everyone welcomed his approach. In Britain the socialist activist and designer, William Morris, repeatedly claimed it was useless for philanthropists to try to impart their values to workers through the provision of works of art and literature. Most workers had neither the time, money nor education to appreciate them. 'Though public libraries and museums and picture exhibitions are good . . . if you are tempted to look upon them as substitutes for decent life in the workshop and the home . . . they may become dangerous snares to well-meaning, middle-class philanthropists,' Morris wrote.[61]

But there was another objection. There was a qualitative shift from old-style philanthropy, which might reward a benefactor with a warm glow of altruism after making a donation to the needy; by contrast, a rich person giving to the arts might experience a more direct enjoyment, perhaps when hearing a new piece of music which they had commissioned or meeting celebrity actors in a theatre they had sponsored. Traditionally, the arts did not figure in conventional views of philanthropy. As we saw in Chapters 5 and 6, Anglo-Saxon attitudes to philanthropy were shaped for centuries by the Preamble to the 1601 Statute of Charitable Uses, which defined charity in terms limited to the care of the sick and vulnerable (including the founding of schools to care for orphans) and the wider preservation of public order. The arts – and science, research and higher education – were not included.

It was only in 1891, with what became known in Britain as the Pemsel case, that the House of Lords declared that charity consisted of four principal categories: 'trusts for the relief of poverty; trusts for the advancement of education; trusts for the advancement of religion; and trusts for other purposes beneficial to the community'. It was under the last of these categories that the arts and higher education became included in the definition of charitable purposes. One of the law lords responsible for the ruling, Lord Edward Macnaghten, went so far as to spell out that the fact that wealthy people themselves benefited from the arts – in a way they did not from most other forms of charitable activity – made them no less charitable. The judge argued that the rich benefited from every kind of charity, either directly or indirectly. The case also provided the basis for charities to be exempt from the payment of income tax.[62] The direct impact of this ruling was immediately felt in England, but its influence also spread throughout the English-speaking world.

In London and in some of the great provincial cities – Liverpool, Manchester, Birmingham and Newcastle – some of the most conspicuous gifts of Victorian philanthropy took the form of endowments to museums, art galleries and universities. This was an age in which benefactors liked to immortalize their generosity in bricks and mortar in grand buildings which still bear their names. The Walker Art Gallery in Liverpool stands out as a glorious example of that in a city filled with Grade-One-listed monuments to an era of philanthropic and civic pride. Andrew Barclay Walker was a local brewer whose line of business – he owned the city's largest chain of alehouses – made him a controversial figure at a time when the moral high ground was occupied by the Temperance movement and nonconformist religion exercised considerable influence in English cities. Many in Liverpool saw his 1873 proposal to build a great art gallery in the city as an attempt to buy respectability. Others saw it as a move by Walker, a Conservative, to ensure his party's dominance over the Liberals in the city council.[63] Some accused him of trying to curry favour with metropolitan artistic elites. Others saw his support for the arts, which appears to have come out of nowhere, as nothing more than an attempt 'to buy a knighthood through showy displays of philanthropy'.[64]

Resistance to accepting Walker's donation came from those who saw a great public cause being perverted for private benefit,[65] and from religious zealots who plastered the city with placards and billboards associating the gallery, both before and after its opening, with prostitution, violence and drunkenness. The walls of the new building were covered in chalk slogans setting out drink-related crime statistics: '23,556 drunkards' and '472 brothels known to police' along with the legend, 'All these will I give for a baronetcy?' The elegant neoclassical statues at the gallery's entrance were replaced by depictions of a common prostitute and a drunkard in rags, while the statue above the gallery's cornice was replaced by the figure of the Devil.[66]

Walker quickly discovered that to be successful philanthropy has to be perceived as a disinterested act aimed at the public good. If it is seen as a device purely for partisan or personal advantage, the act of philanthropy loses its political purchase. To succeed it has to create for the donor a universally accepted narrative that presents him or her as a benevolent, selfless servant of the polis, dedicated to the common good. The danger was that – in the words of James Moore, an academic who has chronicled the saga around the founding of the Liverpool gallery – what 'should have become a monument to his benevolence' was threatening to become 'a prison for [Walker's] vanities'.[67]

The controversy highlighted an ethical dilemma at the heart of ostentatious business philanthropy. The public authorities lacked the finances to provide a municipal art gallery for the local population. Should they, then, deny the city an elevating institution because of their reservations about the motivation of the donor and the alleged dubiety of the ways in which he had raised the money? The city councillors felt they had to make a public case for why the city needed such an institution, especially since the operational costs of the gallery, once it opened, would be borne by local taxpayers. Unless they depicted the gallery as a public institution designed for the enjoyment and education of all classes of Liverpudlians, the civic leaders felt they would be too open to criticism. So a prominent member of the art gallery committee, Benjamin Herdman Grindley, launched an attack on those who saw art as merely the hobby of the rich.[68] Culture and refinement, he argued, was required at all levels of society, especially since much of the adult population had become 'so sensual in their nature, and so low and debased in their pleasures' that what they needed was 'not so much education, as cultivation'.[69] Politicians were now being forced to endorse and reinforce the arguments of the tycoon philanthropists.

In a further attempt to strengthen their position the city councillors persuaded a prominent opponent of Walker, the Liberal politician Philip Henry Rathbone, to take on the choosing of paintings and sculptures for the gallery. This would ensure that its art collection represented the artistic consensus of the whole city, rather than simply the taste of one dodgy brewer. Rathbone's brief was to develop a collection of Victorian art that was both high in quality and popular to the visitor. The ordinary Liverpudlian must feel both represented and inspired by the art on show. Ironically, in doing so, the Liberal politician enhanced the public reputation and political standing of his Conservative rival. Walker got his knighthood and his name became associated with an important symbol of Liverpool's cultural identity – the Walker Art Gallery. Liverpool acquired a prestigious home for what went on to be lauded as one of the country's leading regional art collections. Carnegie's gospel of wealth had become an international orthodoxy in which 'tainted money' and political distaste for controversial business methods could be laundered by judicious philanthropy.

The power imbalance implicit in much philanthropy – by which a gift carries conditions requiring the recipient to adopt the values of the giver – is more explicit with philanthropy in the arts. Donors inevitably favour the forms of activity which they enjoy. Popular low-brow forms of entertainment do not attract donations in the way that forms of 'high art' do. That would be uncontroversial if it were just a matter of personal choice, but because charitable donations now attract tax relief in many countries the personal whims of philanthropists are, in effect, subsidized by every taxpayer. We shall consider this further in Chapter 14.

But it is worth noting here that this is a legacy of the philanthropic innovations of Andrew Carnegie and his fellow tycoons. It became less of an issue in Britain when governments began to subsidize the arts after

1940 as the government-funded Committee for the Encouragement of Music and the Arts (which later became the Arts Council) was set up, with John Maynard Keynes as its chairman. But twenty-first-century austerity has brought public spending cuts which have increased the role for philanthropy in the arts. The disproportionate influence of the personal interests of philanthropists in this field is revealed by the statistics which show that, though the arts receive only 1 per cent of the total charitable donations in the UK, they receive a disproportionate 7 per cent of all higher-rate taxpayer donations over £1 million.[70] Although the arts and higher education make up a small proportion of public spending, they are significant beneficiaries of major gift philanthropy. Philanthropists know what they like and like what they know. Since Andrew Carnegie, philanthropy has sought to impose cultural as well as moral and social change on the societies in which the donations are made.

THE RISE OF THE PHILANTHROPIC FOUNDATION

The other innovation of Andrew Carnegie and his fellow tycoons which has left a lasting legacy is the creation of the philanthropic foundation. This goes beyond the idea of a charitable trust established to fulfil a narrowly defined purpose. Many of Carnegie's initial trust funds – such as his Hero Fund, Foundation for the Advancement of Teaching or Endowment for International Peace – were established in a more traditional format which aimed to promote some particular personal interest of the donor. In the early years of the twentieth century other rich individuals, like John D. Rockefeller and Olivia Sage, established a series of similar foundations.[71] But the Carnegie Corporation of New York – established in 1911 with an endowment making it at that point the biggest charity in the world – was structured entirely differently. That structure was copied by the foundation which soon dwarfed it, established by John D. Rockefeller, a man whose name became the byword for enormous wealth in the early twentieth century.

Rockefeller had made his money in the oil industry where, like Carnegie, he drove out rival firms through cut-throat competition, arranging secret deals and fixing prices; like Carnegie he established a vertically integrated monopoly, which meant that eventually he controlled 90 per cent of America's oil industry from the drilling, refining and storage to the distribution. His Standard Oil company became the largest and most valuable company in the world, and his wealth peaked in 1916 when he became the world's first billionaire. Unlike Carnegie, Rockefeller was a devout Christian. The example of his mother, together with his strict Baptist upbringing, brought Rockefeller to philanthropy early on. He began giving in 1855 at the age of 16, when his personal books showed that 6 per cent of his earnings went to charity. In parallel with building up Standard Oil he gave away millions of dollars to found and develop the University of Chicago, support Baptist missionary activities at home and abroad, finance medical research, expand educational opportunities for poor children in the American South, and a host of other charitable initiatives. But every gift prompted literally hundreds of requests for further donations.

A history of the Rockefeller Foundation records: 'At the office, in church, on the road, and even at his dinner table, Rockefeller was besieged with requests for charity.'[72] Letters arrived by the hundreds in Rockefeller's offices at 26 Broadway in Manhattan. 'The good people who wanted me to help them with their good work seemed to come in crowds,' Rockefeller later remarked. According to Frederick Gates, the Baptist clergyman who was the philanthropist's chief adviser, 'Mr Rockefeller was constantly hunted, stalked and hounded almost like a wild animal.' At one time, Gates counted 50,000 such requests within the space of a month. He later wrote: 'Few were answered, but everyone was opened for a glance as to its character.' Even with Gates, Rockefeller could not keep pace with the need to give money away. Gates eventually wrote to Rockefeller to say: "Your fortune is rolling up, rolling up like an avalanche! You must keep up with it! You must distribute it faster than it grows! If you do not, it will crush you, and your children, and your children's children!'[73]

But even when Rockefeller was devoting more time to his philanthropy than to his oil business, he could not keep up with the requests or the distribution of cash. As a result he and the Reverend Gates devised a plan for a foundation with a much wider brief than the charitable enterprises he had funded in the past. The notion had been forming in Rockefeller's mind for over a decade. In 1899, speaking on the tenth anniversary of his founding of the University of Chicago, he addressed other men of great wealth: 'Let us erect a foundation, a trust, and engage directors who will make it a life work to manage, with our personal cooperation, the business of benevolence properly and effectively.'[74] Its purpose was to be no less than:

> To promote the well-being and advance of the civilization of the people of the United States and its territories and possessions and of foreign lands in the acquisition and dissemination of knowledge; and the prevention and relief of suffering and in the promotion of any and all of the elements of human progress.

Such a generalized brief would allow Rockefeller, and the staff he hand-picked to run the foundation, to undertake virtually any project they deemed worthy. Rockefeller transferred to his new entity, the Rockefeller Foundation, 70,000 shares in his company, worth more than $50 million (around $1.3 billion in today's values).[75] He then soon found himself 'laying aside retail giving almost wholly, and entering safely and pleasurably into the field of wholesale philanthropy'.[76] He earmarked a further $50 million transfer to bring the total endowment to $100 million. Never before had philanthropy been practised on such a scale. But the Reverend Gates was a shrewd and worldly wise adviser, for a clergyman, and he warned Rockefeller that the funds at the disposal of the foundation were 'so large that their administration would be a matter of public concern, public enquiry, and public criticism'.[77] They decided to seek official endorsement for the foundation. This would require, they assumed, something bigger than the approval of New York state, which frequently capped philanthropic endowments at $3 million and insisted upon narrowly defined purposes.[78] So Gates recommended that Rockefeller look beyond the boundaries of the state and approach the US Congress to obtain a bill to give the foundation corporate status. Yet instead of finding approval in Washington, Rockefeller encountered fierce hostility. After Carnegie's Homestead debacle the name of philanthropy had become contaminated. Prominent international figures such as G. K. Chesterton were openly taking pot shots at Rockefeller by name. Chesterton wrote:

> Philanthropy, as far as I can see, is rapidly becoming the recognizable mark of a wicked man. We have often sneered at the superstition and cowardice of the mediaeval barons who thought that giving lands to the Church would wipe out the memory of their raids or robberies;

but modern capitalists seem to have exactly the same notion; with this not unimportant addition, that in the case of the capitalists the memory of the robberies is really wiped out. This, after all, seems to be the chief difference between the monks who took land and gave pardons and the charity organisers who take money and give praise; the difference is that the monks wrote down in their books and chronicles, 'Received three hundred acres from a bad baron'; whereas the modern experts and editors record the three hundred acres and call him a good baron. . . In the case of Rockefeller . . . his philanthropy is . . . offered as a defence or expiation of his alleged commercial methods. If we were to set that philanthropy as a virtue over against his vices, then we would have a right to ask if it is really virtuous . . . the question is whether he got his millions by tyranny or fraud . . . I confess that I object to this particular style in which the millionaire is whitewashed.[79]

The criticism in Washington was more direct. The former US President Theodore Roosevelt remarked: 'No amount of charities in spending such fortunes can compensate in any way for the misconduct in acquiring them.'[80] The sitting president, William Taft, archly condemned the proposal as 'a bill to incorporate Mr Rockefeller' rather than his foundation. And the president of the American Federation of Labor, Samuel Gompers, scathingly observed: 'The one thing that the world would gratefully accept from Mr Rockefeller now would be the establishment of a great endowment of research and education to help other people see in time how they can keep from being like him.' Instead of endorsing Rockefeller, Congress decided to investigate him. The Federal Commission on Industrial Relations, which had been set up by Congress in 1912 to scrutinize US labour law, was asked to consider whether self-perpetuating private foundations posed 'a menace to the Republic's future'. Testifying before the commission Reverend John Haynes Holmes, later chair of the American Civil Liberties Union, declared that such a foundation 'must be repugnant to the whole idea of a democratic society'. The commission's chairman, Frank Walsh, went further, calling the huge philanthropic trust 'a menace to the welfare of society'.[81] Rockefeller's friends and allies lobbied in vain; despite an offer to limit the size of the foundation and require it to spend its entire capital within 50 years, Congress refused to pass the bill.

In the end, Rockefeller managed to persuade New York state to incorporate the foundation, but the objections raised by Congress constituted a critique which may usefully be applied to twenty-first-century global philanthropists. There are four areas of concern. First, questions will inevitably be raised about the source of a foundation's funding, especially where there is controversy about the business methods by which the funds were first accumulated. The eighteenth-century philosopher Immanuel Kant had insisted that individuals cannot claim to be beneficent when their wealth is a product of direct or indirect injustice, asking: 'Under such circumstances, does a rich man's help to the needy, on which he so readily prides himself as something meritorious, really deserve to be called beneficence at all?'[82] Or as the contemporary philosopher of philanthropy, Rob Reich, puts it more colloquially: 'If I steal your wallet and decide to donate its contents for a good cause rather than purchase things for myself, my philanthropic aim does not excuse the initial theft.'[83]

A second problem area is that of accountability. Foundations are unaccountable, both politically and in terms of the disciplines of the market: they are governed by trustees who are elected, not by the public, but by existing trustees. In this sense they are profoundly anti-democratic. But neither are they answerable to consumers in the marketplace as commercial businesses are. Nor are they, generally speaking, in competition with other foundations. Their accountability to the state's charity regulators is limited; no one can question their grant distribution so long as they stick within very broad charity guidelines. This means that philanthropy is a form of the exercise of power. Such 'soft power' is often used in a way which maintains the legal, political, social or economic dominance of the elite to which philanthropists belong.[84]

The third concern is that mega-donations expose deep tensions between philanthropy and democracy. Large-scale gifts become a mechanism by which donors can convert their private wealth into public policy. This can be done consciously or unconsciously. The foundations created by the robber barons rarely tackled the direct alleviation of poverty – perhaps because poor relief might have been seen to offer workers an alternative to the very low pay and dangerous work of the unregulated factories of the early industrialists. It also meant these first foundations were disposed to support the work of those think tanks which presupposed that industrial capitalism was a necessary framework for progress.[85] These were the foundations which later were so enthusiastic in their support for the major studies of philanthropy by W. K. Jordan and David Owen who, as we saw in Chapter 5, nurtured the dubious notion that Protestantism created a bridge between feudal attitudes to charity and the scientific philanthropy favoured by the foundations of the robber baron philanthropists, most of whom were evangelical Protestants.[86]

Finally, these first foundations were self-perpetuating. They had no inbuilt time limit – about which serious questions had been raised as far back as the Enlightenment by the French economist Turgot and the English philosopher John Stuart Mill. Both argued that the state should be allowed to intervene in the operation of private endowments. 'No work of man is made for eternity,' wrote Turgot.[87] 'Private corporations do not exist for themselves but for the interests of society. They must cease to exist whenever they cease to be useful', since society does not always have the same needs.[88] The idea of a perpetual foundation was untenable in an age which believed in the possibility of social and moral progress, said Mill. He wanted foundations to be wound up 'no more than two or three generations' after the death of the founder.[89] We will see how these four areas of concern apply to modern philanthrocapitalism in Chapter 16.

Carnegie and Rockefeller were remarkably different in their approach to their foundations. Carnegie maintained a controlling hand until his death in 1919; by contrast, Rockefeller was hands-off from the outset, seeing his task as empowering others. Carnegie regarded the trustees of the Carnegie Corporation as 'working executives', according to the historian Robert Kohler. He paid them a salary and dominated board discussions in the manner of an executive chairman, so that the corporation functioned in its early years 'more like an old-fashioned family charity than a modern foundation'.[90] Carnegie's letter of gift in setting up the corporation declared that its trustees had 'full authority to change policy or causes', but, in reality, they were more governed by his preferences.[91] Although the endowment said that the trustees would 'best conform to my wishes by using their own judgement', initially the corporation's gifts followed the patterns Carnegie had already established with grants for public libraries, church organs and educational institutions. Only after Carnegie died did the foundation branch out, though its strategies largely remained focused on education and science, 'as a logical sequel to Carnegie's preoccupation with libraries as "the university of the people"'.[92]

Rockefeller ran his foundation differently from the start. He refused to take an interventionist role. Although he was a member of its board for years, he never attended a meeting. His son John D. Rockefeller Jr followed his father's example; when he was chairman of the Rockefeller Foundation, he routinely deferred to the expertise of his fellow board members and the staff. He even moved the foundation offices away from the Rockefeller business headquarters to emphasize its independence. The day-to-day running was overseen by the foundation secretary Jerome Greene, who pursued a policy of replacing Rockefeller family members with new trustees who would understand 'the changing conditions and needs of future generations'.[93]

But Carnegie and Rockefeller, for all their differences of governance, held a common belief on how their foundations should operate. Both men wanted their organizational strategies to mimic the rigorous business methods with which their founders had made their vast fortunes. Decision-making was to be driven by empirical evidence and data, and administered by skilled staff trained in commercial disciplines and the handling of corporate stock. And both also abandoned the idea that philanthropy was about directly relieving the hardship of the poor and needy. Rather, they averred, they wanted to tackle misery at its roots rather than merely addressing its symptoms. They wanted 'a more scientific spirit and method in philanthropy'.[94] Both men felt that charitable handouts might unhelpfully interfere with the free workings of the market economy. In this both Carnegie and Rockefeller put great faith in the notion that 'a reasoned, scientific approach to problem solving could make the world a better place'.[95] Research, particularly in departments of science and social science, were the chosen means. The 1909 Rockefeller Sanitary Commission's almost totally successful campaign to eradicate hookworm was seen as an exemplar of good practice. The inauguration of college teachers' pensions, also in 1909, by the Carnegie Foundation for the Advancement of Teaching, led the way for pensions for other workers.

This new 'scientific philanthropy' promoted the development of public health systems and sought to strengthen medical education to provide the human capital needed to make these public health systems successful. The Rockefeller Foundation focused on attacking the barriers that prevented millions of people from gaining access to basic and, in many cases, life-saving health care. Like many scientific internationalists, writes Eric Abrahamson, Rockefeller and the Reverend Gates believed that the practice and promotion of science in society would also shape patterns of social behaviour and support the values of reason, restraint, moderation, idealism, tolerance, compassion, devotion and discipline. Indeed, they hoped that medical research would eventually unlock the secrets of human behaviour to control the human impulse to destruction.

The impact of Carnegie and Rockefeller on philanthropy was massive. Carnegie personally gave away $350 million and Rockefeller $530 million – worth respectively over $9 billion and $14 billion by 2020 standards.[96] But their most long-lasting contribution was the creation, through their foundations, of institutions capable of distributing private wealth with greater intelligence and vision than the individuals could ever have achieved on their own. It was a crucial step in the professionalization of philanthropy, but it marked another shift in focus away from compassion for the individual.

Interview: Rajiv Shah on the philanthropy of foundations

Dr Rajiv J. Shah is President of the Rockefeller Foundation in New York, which was founded in 1913 by the oil magnate John D, Rockefeller, often said to have been the richest man in modern history. A devout Baptist, Rockefeller used his vast wealth to establish a foundation dedicated to improving the well-being of humanity around the world. Raj Shah, who trained as a medical doctor, joined the foundation after a career which began with the Bill & Melinda Gates Foundation. After that he joined the Obama administration and ran America's massive international aid programme, USAID. There he reshaped the agency's $20 billion operations, elevating the importance of innovation, promoting public-private partnerships, and securing bipartisan support from Democrats and Republicans alike for the US aid programme. He founded Latitude Capital, a private equity firm focused on power and infrastructure projects in Africa and Asia. He has been an academic at Georgetown University.

After training to be a medical doctor, what attracted you to join the Gates Foundation?

I had spent time before medical school working on a health project in a rural village in southern India. I hoped that becoming a doctor would be a way to serve such people. While I was training to be a paediatrician I took some time off to work on Al Gore's presidential campaign and there connected to Bill Gates. I thought of the opportunity to work with him as a chance to get exposed again to global health efforts. When I joined the Gates Foundation, I thought I was just doing this to help for a while and was going to go back to medicine. I ended up doing that for eight or nine years.

They got you hooked, because you're still in philanthropy.

Yes. The very first time I was in a group setting with Bill everyone was debating whether or not to stand with Bono at the 2001

Davos.* I found it interesting to be part of that debate – and you see what has happened, with that partnership between Bill and Bono, over the decades. It was a special point in time.

When you look back at your time at Gates, what's the thing you're most proud of?

One thing is the work we did on vaccines and global health. Working with Bill was all about setting the bar much higher than before. He started by asking: 'If these vaccines really work and they're super cost-effective, how do we make sure that every single child on the planet gets the full range of what immunization science has to offer?' That led to: 'What do we know about the vaccine industry and how it's structured? What do we know about global vaccine financing? What do we know about the outcomes on the ground? Could we use new types of contracting structures to create a viable long-term vaccine industry that would serve low-income countries that are squeezed out by the present structure of the industry? And can we do all of that while serving the least fortunate kids in the whole world?' It was being dropped into a cauldron of insanely high expectations and ambitions – with a commitment to be analytic and business-like in how we deconstructed that problem and tried to solve it.

You came up with some innovative financing mechanisms. That must have been a steep learning curve, because finance was a new area for you.

Yes, it was. One of the things about Gates – and the Rockefeller Foundation, and also in government – is that you have access to the smartest people in the world. With them you can come up a steep learning curve fast. We pulled together a group of capital markets experts in New York and began learning about the structure of the vaccine industry and its financing. We found we could use different types of financial tools to restructure that industry. We came up with a $6 billion International Finance Facility for Immunization. Bill and

---

* Bono and Bill Gates made a joint appeal at the World Economic Forum in Davos in 2001, calling on government, industry and not-for-profit organizations to substantially increase funding for global health. It was the start of a long and fruitful partnership which over the past two decades has brought about large-scale improvements on HIV/Aids, malaria and polio worldwide.

I would go and meet with Gordon Brown and Nicolas Sarkozy* and would shuttle back between them, and we built a coalition of European finance ministers who were willing to stick their necks out and try something super-innovative.

But then you moved from Gates to government and ran the United States' entire aid programme. What made you make that move and how did you have to adjust your philanthropic framework?

At Gates, alongside the vaccines work, I was part of the team that set up the Alliance for Green Revolution in Africa (AGRA), along with a set of science investments with American universities and large biotechnology food-production firms. We created the largest agricultural research investment programme in the world with some of the capital that Warren Buffett gave to the Gates Foundation. We felt that was the highest-leverage way to fight hunger around the world. That led to my becoming focused on agriculture for a while.

Anyway, I got a call one day to ask me to join the Department of Agriculture as the chief scientist, so I joined the Obama administration. Then, within a few months of being in that role, President Obama asked me to move over and lead USAID.

That was a massive job. You went with a big plan and then had to throw it out of the window because of the emergency in Haiti.

Within the first week was the Haiti earthquake and that became a 24/7 commitment. We mounted the largest humanitarian response ever – with a food distribution to three million people a day, water brought in on a day-to-day basis, and we sent the US armed forces to rebuild the airport and perform something like 22,000 surgeries, including limb reattachments for children and women who had been crushed under the rubble. America was enmeshed in a series of conflicts around the world at the time that caused a lot of people to look to our country and question our intentions and how we use our power. President Obama felt that this was an opportunity to demonstrate what American power can look like when it is used for good.

---

* Gordon Brown was the British Chancellor 1997–2007 and Prime Minister 2008–10. Nicolas Sarkozy served as the French Minister of Finance during this period (2004) and was elected President of France in 2007.

When you look back on your time at USAID, is Haiti the thing that sticks out in your mind or is it more to do with the new systems you put in place? What stands out?

Certainly Haiti. The floods in Pakistan the year after that. I spent almost a month in Afghanistan on the front lines of that conflict and ended up being the highest-ranking US official to go to Mogadishu since Black Hawk Down* in 1993. The work we did in fragile states and in conflict or post-conflict environments, including the Ebola effort in West Africa, were all deeply meaningful opportunities to advance American national interests and protect some of the weakest and most fragile parts of our world. Those are the memories that really stick with you.

The other thing was that we did effectively restructure the agency. We doubled the size of our foreign service. We moved 50 to 60 per cent of our activities into public-private partnerships that were more results-oriented. We launched big efforts like Feed the Future that ultimately moved 19 million people out of poverty, re-engaging American companies and public investment in African agriculture and energy production.

The decision to focus on aggressive internal restructuring came after a long conversation with Tony Blair,† who said: 'If you look at the last 20 years of public policy, the big shift has been a real embracing of public-private partnerships and a focus on results, metrics and measurement.'

So it was time to do it on aid as well?

Yes. That was consistent with my own observations, my own experiences with AGRA and the International Finance Facility on vaccines.

You called it a new model for development. And you managed to build support for that not just from Obama's Democrats, but also among Republicans.

It was not easy, but eventually some of the strongest support for building a vibrant global development effort came from some of the most prominent conservative politicians in America. They had a deep passion for serving people who are vulnerable – so long as we were doing it with the focus on efficiency, results and business-like

---

* When two US helicopters were shot down during an attempt to seize a Somali military leader in 1993. It led to a humiliating withdrawal of US forces from Somalia.
† Tony Blair was British prime minister from 1997 to 2007.

partnerships. And this bipartisanship has remained strong. Every year the Trump administration proposes shutting down our global development investment, including USAID. And every year a bipartisan group of members in Congress protect both the investments and the way we were doing it. The bipartisanship has survived, but the noise at the top sometimes makes that hard to see. It's survived not just among politicians but among corporate CEOs, faith-based institutions on the left and the right, and among a generation of young people who have been inspired by Geldof, Bono and the ONE campaign. Youth activism in global development is more important now than ever.

When you moved to the Rockefeller Foundation what of this did you bring with you and what did you leave behind?

The big advantage of the Rockefeller Foundation is that we have had a way of making really big bets that has persisted over a hundred years. When I joined I felt we should return to our roots and bring together innovation, science and technology with new partners and bigger aspirations. So we restructured the institution and today we focus on three or four really big bets. The first is that we believe we can end energy poverty in our lifetime.

What do you mean by energy poverty?

Access to reliable electricity, 24-7, allows human beings and businesses to be more productive. Without it, you simply cannot have upward mobility and a chance at inclusive growth. Every person should have per-capita energy consumption of over a thousand-kilowatt hours a year. Globally, there are probably two billion people who don't have that – and they remain stuck under a couple of dollars a day in income. We are not talking about just a couple of lightbulbs in the home; we are talking about the energy to unlock human potential and upward productivity and mobility.

The light bulb is important, though. It allows students to read and people to work outside the hours of the sun. But what else do they need to be able to do?

Everything that improves productivity. A woman who is able to use electrified post-harvest processing then has time for other activities that create value. A flour miller who's able to process grain from his neighbours' farms is creating economic value for the poorest communities at scale. A woman who runs a manual sewing machine finds an electrified machine is transformational.

Light at night is a driver of economic productivity as well as improving the quality of life. Just a couple of weeks ago I was walking through rural villages in Bihar in India where the government power went out at 5.30 p.m. and everything would have just stopped. But because we've invented this low-cost mini-grid model of renewable energy for these types of villages, the lights went back on and the carpenters were doing their work, and the market was active with people still selling food. There is a very nascent industry we think we can create that will help electrify the world's bottom two billion people – using the science of new energy-storage technologies and big-data analytics of remote energy management systems.

What are the other big bets you're aiming for?

To end preventable maternal and child death. While there's been huge declines in deaths from pneumonia, diarrhoea and malaria, you haven't seen really strong progress on the deaths of mothers and children during the first month of life. Most such deaths come from high-risk pregnancies. We think the way to solve that problem is by using predictive analytics to identify high-risk pregnancies before a woman is pregnant, or right when she becomes pregnant – and then get her the right antenatal care and postnatal support for her and her child – by giving community health workers the predictive analytic tools that let them identify high-risk pregnancies.

In Mali in the 1970s and '80s everybody thought diarrhoea could only be treated by doctors in clinics. But they overturned that script by inventing an oral rehydration solution that a mother could give a child. It saved millions of children. In the same way, we think if we can flip the script and use the data science revolution to empower community health workers, and mothers themselves, we can identify high-risk pregnancies and avoid all preventable maternal and child deaths. That's our second big bet.

The third?

The third one is around food and agriculture. The big insight we've had there is that if you look at the future burden of disease – 15, 20, 30 years from now – it is almost all diet-related chronic disease. Even today, eight of the ten fastest-growing diseases around the world are fundamentally about diet. The horrible diets that people have around the world – and they're worse for lower-income people – are going to crush the population with diabetes, cardiovascular disease and diet-related cancer. We believe that much of that is preventable by rethinking the food system. So we are investing in science to better understand protective foods and to make sure that more communities consume the target levels of things like legumes, leafy green vegetables, nuts, omega three fatty acids and foods rich in that. There's a lot of data that shows that once you hit these target consumption patterns, you can actually have very steep and significant reductions in pre-diabetes.

You've got to persuade people to change their diet first.

Yes, and in food there's a very large ingrained industry that convinces people that once you get a few dollars a day, shifting your diet to processed foods – and experiencing the convenience of what they produce – is a sign of both luxury and growth. It's probably going to cause more diabetic disease in the next 20 years than we've ever seen before. There's a big opponent in that space.

When you are making these decisions on what to prioritize, who does the Rockefeller Foundation feel accountable to? To the founders' vision? To the priorities of the elected government? Or to the people out there that you're trying to help? What are your systems and your mechanisms of accountability?

Our most important accountability is that we are stewards of an historic institution which focuses on helping vulnerable families. That remains our most important accountability. Accountability to the people we serve is how we interpret it. Our founders started by saying: 'How could you best apply modern science to lift up the most vulnerable communities around the world at the greatest scale?' That led to the invention of modern public health in the United States and around the world. In agriculture it led to the Green Revolution. I feel like we're very true to the founder's vision, but our core accountability is to those we serve.

Was that the same in both the Gates and the Rockefeller foundations? Or did you detect a difference in approach or outlook?

Bill Gates has explained how much he's learned from the Rockefeller Foundation's model of philanthropy: setting a big long-term aspiration; being willing to make long-term high-risk investments in science and technology and innovation; partnering with others; building operating structures that reach the world's poorest; measuring results and learning from them. I believe the Gates Foundation represents that model to a very high degree of excellence because of Bill's and Melinda's personal willingness to learn, their depth of knowledge and their extraordinary talent and commitment.

They have learned and changed over the decades, as we'll see later in this book – and quite significantly.

I used to marvel at the fact that people like Bill and Melinda, who could be doing anything with their time, would go and walk with me, and others on their teams, through the fields of Nigeria – and sit with farmers in very poor places and swat away the flies in order to really understand the lives of some of the poorest families in the world. Melinda's last book[97] comes out of all that learning, and it is brilliant. Having that ability to constantly learn, and the humility to do it, is a great example from them and we try to live that every day as well.

So one generation of philanthropists stands on the shoulders of another?

Yes, absolutely. Without question. And we are proud to work together sometimes and proud to be complementary sometimes.

The more extreme advocates of philanthrocapitalism disparage what they call the old-style philanthropy of foundations like Rockefeller. They accuse you of 'a lack of strategic thinking'[98] and insist that the techniques they used to create huge fortunes in business can just be transferred across uncritically to philanthropy.

Well, Bill Gates and John D. Rockefeller and those in their tradition do not articulate it that way. It's hard to comment on others – but if you do one thing and it's wildly successful and you've made $30 billion doing it, and everyone around you has succeeded by following your leadership, you tend to believe in that way of working. There are some good attributes to that – they want to be results-oriented, want to push hard, want to win at scale on behalf of the people they serve. I just think the ones that are best at doing it have the humility to learn from the past and observe what's out there and listen carefully to people on the ground who are both living these issues and doing this work.

That's where I find the biggest distinction. It's less about where your skill comes from – and more about whether you are willing to sit with a teacher in a tough school and listen to what her or his life is like on a day-to-day basis, engaging with their students.

I think there are too many people perhaps that look at all that and say, 'Oh, that's not working. We're going to do it our way and our way is better and smarter because it worked in technology or it worked in real estate or something like that.' That's unfortunate.

That sense of two-way, of listening, and preserving an awareness of the other person, is lacking in hard-edged philanthrocapitalism.

To me, the word 'philanthrocapitalism' tends to capture both the Gates-Rockefeller approach and some other things I'm not so sure about. So I don't know whether I'd lump everything under that phrase. I've seen too many people just not have the time or the inclination to really respect the fact that a hard-working teacher, in what they might think of as a failing school, in a city like Detroit or New Orleans, actually has a whole lot to offer and learn from. The people on the ground have some really important insights. So we should listen as we try to create change. It's hard, both to make the time and to create the systems that really help you learn and listen to those you're trying to serve. Not everybody's going to want to spend the amount of time that a Bill Gates will spend doing that. In some social circles, it's a little easier to go to dinner parties and talk about it than it is to get out in the communities you're trying to serve and really listen.

Our world, over recent years, has become even more unequal. There are even more pools of capital that are massive and in private hands. And there's more despair and struggle amongst those who go without. We need to fix that through philanthropy, but also through real policy changes that transform the nature of our society.

The twenty-first century is facing massive challenges. Are you saying that they can't be addressed by individual sectors, but that there needs to be a partnership between philanthropy, government and the business sector to deal with problems of the scale that we're facing?

Yes. If you're really trying to structure solutions for inequality in our society (which is what our work in health, power and food is all about), or if you're trying to solve the climate crisis (which our work in power and food in particular touches on heavily), you're only going to solve those challenges by building large-scale, public-private partnerships. They have to include governments at all levels. They have to include private innovators and technical institutions and universities and scientists. And, ultimately, they have to include the people who are serving in communities all around the world. There is no way of making our world more equal for billions of people, or reducing the climate stress that we place on our planet, without large-scale collaborations. Just going in alone against challenges of that scale will simply not be successful.

Given the scale of those problems, is there an argument for an organization like the Rockefeller Foundation spending all its resources at once, now, rather than carrying on as a permanent perpetual foundation?

Well, I actually think that's a very fair and appropriate question. My natural inclination is to think you get the highest return on investment on your philanthropic spend by spending it well now. We're not trying to perpetuate institutions. Our goal is to solve these problems. If we see a solution and expanding our financial commitment would threaten our long-term viability but solve the problem, that's probably a higher return on investment that I'd be open to. And I am.

On the other hand, I think our world will always need a few special institutions that are just committed to bringing other people to collaborate to solve the world's toughest challenges. The Rockefeller Foundation today is not the wealthiest individual institution, but it is perhaps the most respected as a long-standing institution that really tries to reach out to others and build collaborations. I believe that maybe there is a role for an institution like that to perpetuate over time – so long as it stays true to that vision.

But the opportunity to end energy poverty for billions of people within a one- to two-decade time-frame is a once-in-a-generation opportunity. You've got to have the science and the technology, the manufacturing and the price points, and the mindsets, and everything has to come together at one time. So if we saw an opportunity to go beyond our annual spend and make a very significant investment to really accelerate that process – and launch a revolution that really tackled poverty in a fundamental way – I would be absolutely willing to go to my board and say: 'This is our opportunity to make history. Let's take it.'

Chapter 10

Cradle to Grave – Philanthropy and the Welfare State

Even Oscar Wilde could sense that the tide was turning. The author best known for the elegant frivolity of *The Importance of Being Earnest* may seem an unlikely early advocate of socialism. On the face of it, the Irish wit and playwright was the personification of capitalist decadence, with his knee breeches and velvet jacket, his purple coat lined with lavender silk, his Byronic collar with its green carnation, his cuffs trimmed with frilled rich lace at the wrists, and the smoke curling insouciantly from the opium-tipped cigarettes he favoured with his champagne. And yet this dandy aesthete numbered, among celebrated writings filled with coruscating wit, a single political essay. Oscar Wilde, in *The Soul of Man under Socialism*, attacks philanthropy and charity as degrading and demoralizing to the poor. 'Their remedies do not cure the disease: they merely prolong it. Indeed, their remedies are part of the disease,' he wrote in his 1891 essay. Philanthropists waste their time by tackling the symptoms of capitalism's shortcomings when what is needed is to address the causes by trying 'to reconstruct society on such a basis that poverty will be impossible', in which 'there will be no people living in fetid dens and fetid rags, and bringing up unhealthy, hunger-pinched children in the midst of impossible and absolutely repulsive surroundings'.[1] In its place Wilde offers a curious vision of individualist libertarian socialism.

The term 'socialism' meant different things to different people as the nineteenth century turned into the twentieth – and their views on the significance of philanthropy varied accordingly. To the internationalist followers of Marx and Engels socialism was a revolutionary creed which had no time for the 'philanthropists, humanitarians, improvers of the condition of the working class, organisers of charity' and other 'reformers'.[2] By contrast, to Fabian thinkers like Beatrice and Sidney Webb, socialism would mean a more organic and evolutionary transition to a more 'civilised life' which would offer 'sufficient nourishment and training' to the young, a 'living wage' to the able-bodied, 'treatment when sick, and modest but secure livelihood when disabled or aged'.[3] It was a prototype for the welfare state, whose originator, William Beveridge, worked as a researcher for the Webbs on the Royal Commission on the Poor Laws for four years from 1905. It had little time for philanthropy and charitable volunteering, except as a junior partner to their socialist enterprise. Christian Socialists such as Frederick Denison Maurice, Charles Kingsley and others, who saw socialism as an instrument of both social reform and moral regeneration, were better disposed towards philanthropy.

But others in this period used 'socialism' loosely. When the leader of the Conservative Party, Lord Salisbury, proposed in 1883 to offer low-interest government loans to subsidize housing for the poor, the scheme was condemned as 'socialistic' by his Liberal rival Joseph Chamberlain. 'Social legislation', protested the next leader of the Conservatives, A. J. Balfour, is not the same as 'Socialist legislation'. Indeed, he insisted, 'it is its most direct opposite and its most effective antidote'.[4] But the mood of the times was less precise. 'We are all socialists now,' the prominent Liberal politician, Sir William Harcourt, is reported to have said in 1888. The sentiment became so commonplace that it was even repeated by the Prince of Wales.[5] 'The wave of opinion carrying us toward Socialism and utter subordination of the individual is becoming irresistible,' Herbert Spencer wrote gloomily to Andrew Carnegie.* What all these wildly differing views had in common was a shared sense that the old poor law was not working and that philanthropy was simply incapable of coping with the scale of the problems of an urban and industrial society.

That sense was reinforced by the haphazard nature of much philanthropy. The duplication of charities, among whom rivalry and petty jealousy abounded, often caused confusion and muddle. There were literally 'hundreds of agencies that work over the same ground without concert or cooperation or the slightest information as to each other's exertions,'

---

* See page 272 above.

according to the historian J. R. Green.[6] Not all the ministrations of these philanthropists were well appreciated, especially those like the Charity Organisation Society which determined that what the poor needed, before all else, was social workers. Frank Prochaska tells the story of a beggar in Yorkshire, fed up of being pestered by social workers, responding to one lady district visitor who asked if he could read or write. The man replied: 'No, Ma'am, I can't . . . and if I'd known as much when I was a child as I do now, I'd never have learned to walk or talk.'[7]

Prominent philanthropists themselves contributed to the growing disillusion. Joseph Rowntree, in York, pronounced in 1904 that 'much of the current philanthropic effort is directed to remedying the more superficial manifestations of weakness or evil, while little thought or effort is directed to search out their underlying causes'.[8] His fellow Quaker, George Cadbury in Birmingham, agreed. So did General William Booth of the Salvation Army. Faced with the 'great and appalling mass of human misery' charitable approaches were inadequate; 'to drain the whole bog is an effort which seems to be beyond the imagination of most of those who spend their lives in philanthropic work,' he wrote.[9] The socialist aristocrat, the Countess of Warwick, who supported the Russian Revolution, described philanthropy as a mere 'plaster'. Even that powerhouse of Victorian philanthropy, the Charity Organisation Society, which had long opposed interventions by local or national government, finally admitted in 1886 that there were 'permanent causes of distress which it is impossible for philanthropy alone to cope with or even in any sufficient degree to palliate by schemes of direct relief'.[10] The very statistics it and other progressive philanthropists compiled to justify their activities – statistics of which the COS was so proud – only provided ammunition for those who felt the problem was so large that only the state could address it.

Philanthropy might even have been making things worse. The great English constitutionalist, Walter Bagehot, wrote in 1872: 'Great good, no doubt, philanthropy does, but then it also does great evil. It augments so much vice, it multiplies so much suffering, it brings to life such great populations to suffer and to be vicious, that it is open to argument whether it be or be not an evil to the world'.[11] And even Joseph Rowntree wrote: 'Charity as ordinarily practised, the charity of endowment, the charity of emotion, the charity which takes the place of justice, creates much of the misery which it relieves, but does not relieve all the misery it creates'.[12] He went further: 'The problem of the distribution of wealth is, in this country, much more urgent than the problem of its creation.'[13]

Philanthropy had lost any claim to be better than the charity over which later Victorian philanthropists had claimed superiority. A thirst for social justice was replacing the impulse to charity. Philanthropy – patchy in its coverage, condescending in its attitudes, and insufficient in its resources – must, from now on, step aside and make way for the state. The focus had shifted from what could be done to relieve the distress of the poor to what could be done to abolish their poverty. A consensus was emerging, with increasing shared conviction, that the state was better placed than philanthropy to offer solutions. Henceforth the history of philanthropy was to be rewritten as a prelude to the history of the welfare state. What was there left for philanthropy to do?

POOR-TO-POOR PHILANTHROPY

Yet the change was not that sudden. In many ways philanthropy in the latter half of the nineteenth century unconsciously paved the way for the welfare state. The idea grew that the answer to social problems lay in common action. Philanthropy was not just the largesse of the affluent towards those beneath them. It also contained elements of that common action. What Prochaska has called 'the philanthropy of the poor to the poor' was significant.[14] Much of this was informal: 'caring for ageing relatives, assisting kin in times of adversity, the provision of Sunday dinners, visiting sick friends, taking in washing, helping with rent, dropping a coin in a hat in . . . the pub to support an unemployed neighbour or someone who had lost a purse'.[15] But working people also organized their own mutual aid societies, trade unions, Sunday schools and benefit clubs; soup kitchens, milk schemes, goose schemes and penny dinner societies; wash houses and sewing classes; boot and clothing clubs, blanket clubs and coal clubs, sick clubs and holiday clubs; Ragged Schools, slate clubs and book clubs; lying-in and maternity charities, mothers' meetings and visiting societies; temperance societies and advice bureaux each with a poor man's lawyer.[16]

Women often played the dominant role in all this. Mothers' meetings were more than emotional support groups; the women – many of whom were illiterate – shared information on cooking, diet, nutrition, health, housing, childcare, and any issue with domestic implications. These included venereal disease, child abuse and votes for women.[17] The poor made cash contributions to voluntary schools and voluntary hospitals.

Many of the more prosperous working-class families in the 1890s even made cash contributions to charity each week.[18] 'Although the workers cannot really afford to give charity on the same scale as the middle class, they are nevertheless more charitable in every way,' wrote Friedrich Engels, who had little time for middle-class philanthropy.[19] Indeed, at the start of the twentieth century one English clergyman observed: 'It is largely this kindness of the poor to the poor that stands between our present civilisation and revolution.'[20] All this certainly gave ordinary people a very real measure of control over their own affairs and their immediate environment – an autonomy which the welfare state was to undermine. These voluntary efforts by individuals and groups, self-supporting and self-governing, carried on their work with little interference from public authorities.[21]

In parallel to all those private initiatives, however, the state had been moving steadily into areas of social action. Previously the nation's schools had been voluntary organizations, funded by individual subscriptions and churches. Now the state had become increasingly involved in regulating them, through its concerns for the literacy and discipline of the population. From the 1870s it also took control of many educational institutions, though it was still voluntary organizations such as the National Society for the Prevention of Cruelty to Children which pressed the government for better care of the young. Often the state entered into these arenas only reluctantly and after being prodded by such lobby groups.[22] In 1886 Whitehall encouraged local government to set up work projects for the jobless, and in 1905 the Conservatives passed the Unemployed Workman Act, which helped the jobless with small cash handouts or temporary work. At the turn of the century a mixed economy of welfare had grown up in which both philanthropic and state initiatives complemented one another.

But it was the welfare reforms of the Liberal government of David Lloyd George, just before the First World War, that produced a massive gear change in the balance between the voluntary sector and the state. Lloyd George had a variety of motives for the raft of reforms which followed. Pure humanitarianism was mixed in with the need to fend off the electoral challenge from the emerging Labour Party. There were also considerations of national economic efficiency. Whatever the political motivation, the impact was far-reaching.

In 1906 children were provided with free school meals, partly out of a sense of public decency and partly because army recruiters during the

Second Boer War (1889–1902) were alarmed at how undernourished and unhealthy the British working classes were. The 1907 Probation Act provided an alternative to prison for young offenders while the Children and Young Persons Act of 1908 imposed punishments on those neglecting children or forcing them to sell tobacco or play in the street. An old-age pension was introduced in 1908. The year after, the Labour Exchanges Act created centres in which employers could post advertisements for jobs to be seen by those looking for work. The Liberal government encouraged local councils to pay a fair wage. Public works programmes, including shipbuilding, digging new sewers and establishing water works, were financed to create jobs. The construction of unhealthy and overcrowded back-to-back houses – the staple design for the working classes in Victorian times – was banned. New regulations were introduced outlawing the use of poisonous leads to protect workers in the paint and textile industries. In 1911 the National Insurance Act introduced compulsory health insurance for the low-paid, financed by three-way contributions from workers, employers and government. The scheme paid out weekly sums for a six-month period to those who fell ill.

The Lloyd George government passed what it called a People's Budget, which taxed the rich to subsidize the low-paid, ill and injured. Lloyd George, in commending the budget, said he was committed to an 'implacable war against poverty and squalidness'.[23] The Liberal reforms – some of the most ambitious welfare programmes in British history – moved the state squarely into territory which had once been the exclusive preserve of philanthropy.

PHILANTHROPY'S PARTNERSHIP WITH THE STATE

But philanthropy, as embodied in a range of voluntary organizations, did not entirely wither. Indeed in the early years of the twentieth century the state and volunteer activists work closely together. The innovative state measures, such as old-age pensions and unemployment insurance, were mainly administered by voluntary bodies – non-profit working-class mutual associations including friendly societies and trade unions. This was, in part, because it was cheaper for the state to use the existing administrative structures of the societies and unions rather than setting up a separate new bureaucracy.

But the Liberal government also believed that voluntary action – with people giving their own time and money to help others – was an essential component of a good society.[24] Philanthropy, in its activist mode, may have lost its leading role in the mixed economy of welfare but it had not been completely excluded. During the First World War, and throughout the 1920s and 1930s – as the activity of the state grew in housing, health, education and much else – the administration of welfare was channelled through both local government and voluntary organizations, which were now given government funding.

In the interwar years various schemes were introduced to co-ordinate public and private welfare. In that way, big issues could be tackled by breaking the problem down 'into little pieces', to quote Edward, Prince of Wales, patron of the National Council of Social Service, in a speech about unemployment in the Albert Hall in 1932. In response to his call for citizens to act as 'good neighbours' some 2,300 projects were initiated within the year by individuals and voluntary groups. Some of them were started by the unemployed themselves. Altogether more than a million people were found jobs.[25]

A reciprocal relationship developed between the state and philanthropic sectors. Maternity and child health clinics, run by volunteers, received state subsidies; but at the same time lobby groups set up by the same activists brought their influence to bear upon government legislation. The National Council for the Unmarried Mother and Her Child persuaded Parliament to make absent fathers financially responsible for their children and strengthened the legal rights of mothers and children.[26] The Society for the Promotion of Birth Control Clinics lobbied for working-class women to be given guidance on family planning. Citizens Advice Bureaux helped poor people negotiate welfare regulations. In 1934 a leading social worker, Elizabeth Macadam, wrote a book analysing the growing interdependence of statutory and voluntary services and called it *The New Philanthropy*. It called for a more professional and effective partnership between philanthropy and the state, accepting that government was now in the driving seat on welfare but emphasizing the importance of the charitable volunteers who gave their time without charge.[27]

There were those who took a contrary view. Many socialists in the 1930s still regarded philanthropy as 'an odious expression of social oligarchy and churchy bourgeois attitudes'.[28] The 1929 Local

Government Act had imposed upon local councils some responsibility for meeting the needs of the voluntary hospitals in their areas, yet despite it, at the outbreak of the Second World War in 1939, many of these hospitals were on the verge of bankruptcy. Nurses were routinely seen in the streets on their days off soliciting charitable donations on regular flag days. It was a sight which offended the man who went on to become the founding father of the National Health Service, Aneurin Bevan. Attacking 'the caprice of private charity', in a speech on the second reading of the NHS Bill in 1946 he said:

> I believe it is repugnant to a civilised community for hospitals to have to rely upon private charity. I believe we ought to have left hospital flag days behind. I have always felt a shudder of repulsion when I have seen nurses and sisters who ought to be at their work . . . going about the streets collecting money for the hospitals.

VOLUNTEERING – A GREAT BRITISH TRADITION

During the Second World War the tradition of philanthropic activism in Britain continued. Some organizations continued to wither as volunteers became involved in war work and funds dried up, but volunteering was encouraged elsewhere. The Women's Voluntary Service was set up to help the victims of bombing, supervise the evacuation of children and keep services running amid the destruction of war. Its contribution was so vital that it became an auxiliary to more than 20 government departments.[29] The work of the National Council for the Unmarried Mother and Her Child was subsidized by the wartime government to cope with servicewomen and war workers who became pregnant outside wedlock.[30] The Citizens Advice Bureaux dealt with around ten million enquiries during the war.[31] Indeed, volunteering has continued, in parallel to the welfare state, as one of the prime areas of philanthropic activity in Britain ever since.

Throughout the 1950s married middle-class and upper-class women constituted the backbone of many volunteer-driven civic organizations. Volunteering became fashionable among younger people in that decade and through the 1960s. Voluntary Service Overseas was founded in the 1950s to provide opportunities for young people to work in developing countries before or after leaving university, though organizations like that now prefer to recruit mainly older experienced professionals in search of a career break or taking early retirement.[32] As the British population has aged, with improved healthcare and increasingly active lifestyles, the number of older volunteers has increased. People over 65 now make up a substantial proportion of UK volunteers. As many as 30 per cent of the over-60s volunteer regularly, in addition to their informal help for relatives, friends and neighbours. Such volunteering was estimated in 2011 to be worth £10 billion a year, a cost which would otherwise fall on the taxpayer. Informal volunteering – such as unpaid caring for the disabled and elderly, which might otherwise have fallen on the social services budget – is valued at £34 billion.[33]

Today, as many as four out of ten Britons engage in voluntary activity – in everything from the Girl Guides to running the local food bank – during their spare time.[34] The model of philanthropist-as-activist has also been diversified beyond volunteering into membership of single-issue groups. These often cross the boundary between charity and social or political campaigning – running the local Oxfam shop; fundraising for conservation groups; lobbying to change social attitudes on race, gender or sexuality; or supporting victims of domestic violence in women's refuges. Many of these are on the liberal-left of the political spectrum but conservatives, who favour a small state and advocate public-spending cuts, are also enthusiasts for increased volunteering in public bodies such as the National Health Service. More than half a million people volunteered to assist the NHS in 2020 as the COVID-19 pandemic began. The commitment to voluntary action remains a constant in British public life, even as the population shifts demographically and charities reconfigure themselves to fill gaps in state provision.

But the Second World War was also responsible for one of the major paradigm shifts in twentieth-century British politics. After the high levels of poverty and unemployment of the 1930s, the change in social attitudes which occurred, in a war effort involving the entire nation, was profound. During the war expanding government intervention – imposing new controls and introducing new services – shifted public attitudes towards the state. Politicians from the Labour Party, which had overtaken the Liberal Party as the main political opposition in the 1920s but which had never formed a majority administration, were seen to have been effective members of a national coalition government.

Even the leaders of the Church of England – which was often referred to as the Conservative Party at prayer – warmed to the idea of universal state benefits promised by wartime planning.[35] In 1941 William Temple, who became Archbishop of Canterbury the following year, argued that the welfare state – to use the term then coming into fashion – was an expression of national benevolence. He declared: 'The state is a servant and instrument of God for the preservation of Justice and for the promotion of human welfare.' The change, he pronounced, was 'epoch-making in its consequences'.[36]

The following year William Beveridge's seminal report, *Social Insurance and Allied Services* (known as the *Beveridge Report*), laid the foundations of that welfare state.[37] In it, Beveridge, an early member of the Fabian circle, recommended state care 'from cradle to grave' – with benefit payments to the sick, unemployed, retired and widowed. It would introduce a minimum standard of living 'below which no one should be allowed to fall'. He recommended that after the war the government 'on the road of reconstruction' should find ways of fighting what he called the 'five giants' of Want, Disease, Ignorance, Squalor and Idleness. Included in his proposals were a National Health Service. Interestingly, Beveridge, who later joined the Liberal Party, also recommended preserving the work of the voluntary sector to provide additional services for the sick, elderly, unemployed and others in need. But his inclusion of philanthropic volunteering was overshadowed in the public and political focus on the welfare state.[38] . In 1945, with the war over, the Labour Party won a surprising landslide over the Conservatives under Winston Churchill. The Labour government of Clement Attlee established the welfare state. More than a thousand voluntary hospitals, which had been struggling to survive through private giving, were taken into public ownership in the National Health Service. The state also took over responsibility for education. The initiative was wildly popular. The public response was summed up by the Anglican hierarchy at the 1948 meeting in Lambeth with a resolution which stated:

> We believe that the State is under the moral law of God, and is intended by Him to be an instrument for human welfare. We therefore welcome the growing concern and care of the modern State for its citizens, and call upon Church members to accept their own political responsibility and to cooperate with the State and its officers in their work.[39]

Taxation, not philanthropy, was now seen as the vehicle for social justice, and the payment of taxes became the prime civic duty. State spending on social services was soon to dwarf donations to charities, which began to dry up as donors came to believe that the state had, quite properly, taken over responsibility for such activities. Other voluntary organizations suffered more directly; friendly societies lost their role in administering social insurance when it became clear that their performance was uneven. This effectively destroyed them.[40]

Key figures in the Labour Party paid lip service to the preservation of philanthropy. Clement Attlee became president of Toynbee Hall, a social work charity in the East End of London much favoured by Labour Party members. Speaking of it he said: 'We shall always have, alongside the great range of public services, the voluntary services which humanise our national life and bring it down from the general to the particular.'[41] Beveridge came to much the same conclusion in a later report, *Voluntary Action*, in 1948, in which he said he did not believe that 'state' and 'society' were opposed. He preferred the term 'social service state' to 'welfare state', which he felt smacked of dependency. His new report considered the role of parish societies, women's voluntary work, children's charities, mutual aid, Citizens Advice Bureaux and concluded that the 'vigour and abundance of voluntary action outside one's home, individually and in association with other citizens, for bettering one's own life and that of one's fellows, are the distinguishing marks of a free society'. They have been, he added, 'outstanding features of British life'.[42] In the House of Lords the following year he insisted:

> The State has now taken over many things which these voluntary agencies did in the past, but . . . however much the State has done or may yet continue to do, Philanthropy will still be needed . . . It will be needed to pioneer ahead of the State. The State has taken over many things which occupied the philanthropists of the early nineteenth century – elementary education and housing, for example. That means merely that there is a perpetually moving frontier for philanthropic action.[43]

But the document had much less impact than Beveridge's previous report. Within the Labour movement there remained a strong strain of hostility to charity which, according to Pat Thane, Professor in Contemporary British History at King's College London, had been experienced by many working people as demeaning. Voluntary action belonged to the past, many Labour members felt, and had no part in the new post-war world order. Charity had merely created 'a patch-quilt of local paternalisms', in the words of Aneurin Bevan, who added: 'There is no worse enemy to . . . intelligent planning.' Charitable giving was driven by 'warm gushes of self-indulgent emotion' and turned the benefactor into 'a petty tyrant' who sent instructions along with his cash.[44] Philanthropy, writes Frank Prochaska, was now 'a repugnant remnant of a tribal past'.[45]

But the predictions of the death of philanthropy, before and after the Second World War, were premature. New activist charities were created in response to the welfare state as it became clear that groups like the elderly, the disabled and people with mental illnesses were being overlooked by the new institutions of the state. Others were formed in response to the decolonization which marked the end of the British Empire. Overseas aid organizations, such as Oxfam, expanded from specific wartime roles to alleviate famine relief. Now they broadened out into wider economic and social development in the world's newly independent nations. In the 1960s, as society grew increasingly prosperous, it also became aware of the yawning gap between the affluent and a class of people living with economic disadvantage and hardship; new domestic charities, such as the Child Poverty Action Group, and the campaigning housing charity, Shelter, came into being. The voluntary sector was reinvigorated and the philanthropy which supported it was drawn less from wealthy individuals and more from wider appeals to the generosity of the general public. The relationship between statutory authorities and the voluntary sector now became more complex and intertwined.

FOUR MODELS OF PHILANTHROPY

When it comes to working out how to balance the state against philanthropy there are four models on offer. They reflect the four categories of European capitalism drawn up by the influential Belgian economist André Sapir.[46] The Anglo-Saxon model is found in the UK and Ireland, and also in the United States. The Rhineland model holds sway in most of continental Europe – Germany, Austria, France, Belgium, Luxembourg, Poland, Hungary and the Czech Republic. The Mediterranean model prevails in Italy, Spain, Portugal and Greece. And the Nordic model is to be found in Sweden, Denmark,

Norway and Finland. The systems try, in different ways, to balance the objectives of high employment and low poverty; each approach addresses one of these better than the other – the Anglo-Saxon and Nordic approaches are better for jobs and the Rhineland and Nordic models do better on eliminating relative poverty. The details do not need exploring here,[47] but what is significant is that each produces a different approach to philanthropic activity and its relationship to the way the state operates.

In the Anglo-Saxon model charitable activity – by organizations or individuals – is seen as a counterweight to the actions of government. It is part of what creates pluralism in society. Philanthropy offers alternatives. It more easily fosters innovation. It can, by word or example, offer effective criticism of the way the state does things. It can advocate for reform. It has a strong culture of volunteering. Public trust in charities and philanthropic foundations is relatively high compared to levels of trust in the politicians and bureaucrats who run the state. Donations and gifts are stimulated by the tax advantages the state confers upon charitable giving. That, at any rate, is the theory.

At the other end of the spectrum, the Mediterranean model is dominated by a separation of State and Church, with the latter as the main vehicle for charitable activity. These southern European economies came relatively late to the welfare state, during the 1970s and 1980s. Social assistance payments there are low but the state is strong on pensions. Trust in politicians is poor. But the Church, on financial matters at any rate, enjoys greater public confidence. This can lead to considerable tension. Politicians feel the need to control voluntary organizations either politically, by placing their own representatives on boards, or through legal measures, as with the attempts in Italy to bring community-owned banks under political jurisdiction.[48] This reached a low point in 2019 when the anti-migrant populist government in Italy opened a 'war on ten fronts' against the Catholic Church and its charities for their work with migrants and refugees. It cracked down particularly on non-governmental organizations which rescued migrants in danger of drowning in the Mediterranean.[49] Catholic scholars, including Stefano Zamagni – Professor of Economics at the University of Bologna and President of the Pontifical Academy of Social Sciences – hit back, accusing the government of having 'contempt for the poor'.[50] Some politicians also resent the work of philanthropic volunteers, accusing them of taking work from the unemployed. And when charities exercise any kind of critical scrutiny of the state, they are often challenged by politicians who question their mandate to tread on what is perceived as political territory. Only a relatively small percentage of Italians give to charity, though those who do, give healthy amounts. Generally, charity in Spain and Greece has been affected by Europe's migrant crisis, in which those countries are on the front line. Individual giving by Spaniards has dropped 47 per cent in the last eight years, in what is thought to be a combination of hard economic times, welfare cuts, and hostility to charities spending their resources on new arrivals from Africa and the Middle East.[51]

Perhaps the healthiest balance between state and philanthropy is found in the Nordic model. In Scandinavian countries businesses are taxed and regulated by the state very lightly, to encourage them to create jobs and wealth; by contrast, individuals are subjected to high rates of income tax, with the money used to provide an extremely strong welfare system. Traditionally, the citizens trust the government and pay taxes fairly willingly. The role of charity is to fill the gaps in the state system. Charitable organizations often identify a need which is then addressed by state welfare. Nordic countries have a particularly strong tradition of philanthropic activism and voluntary service. All this makes for a strong complementary role between the state and philanthropy, which is not afraid to criticize government.

In the Rhineland model, of which Germany is the great exemplar, the state is by far the more dominant partner. These continental societies are more highly regulated than the UK. Decisions are more long-term. Big business, the trade unions and the government co-operate in industrial planning. Charities and other civil society organizations[52] often receive contracts from the government, particularly in health and education. This transforms them effectively into sub-contractors to the state. The advantage of this is that there is significant co-ordination between government and the voluntary sector. But it also weakens the ability of charities to subject government actions to independent critical scrutiny. Tax relief for charitable donations is not significant, but Germany has the largest number of philanthropic foundations in Europe, some of them extraordinarily wealthy.[53]

The most significant development in philanthropy in the UK during recent decades has been a shift from the traditional Anglo-Saxon model to a more continental one. Since the time of Margaret Thatcher, the state has increasingly pressed charitable organizations into acting as deliverers of government services. The process, which began in a big way under Mrs Thatcher, continued under Tony Blair, Gordon Brown, David Cameron and Theresa May. Although charities did not figure highly in the early priorities of the administration of Boris Johnson, some leading British charities now receive 80 per cent or more of their income from the state,[54] in a way which compromises their independence and curtails the traditional function of charities as watchdogs on government.

THE PHILANTHROPIC CONTRADICTIONS
OF THATCHERISM

In the late 1970s with the arrival of Margaret Thatcher as leader of the Conservative Party, and later British prime minister, it seemed that philanthropy might be about to enjoy a new golden age. Mrs Thatcher ushered in a new aggressively free-market era in British politics. Previous Conservative leaders, in the one-nation tradition, had followed economic policies which did not depart greatly from those of the post-war Labour government. One of the party's most influential policymakers in the 1950s and 1960s, Rab Butler, wrote that 'modern conservatism' required 'strong central guidance over the operation of the economy',[55] later adding 'a good Tory in history has never been afraid of the use of the state'. Harold Macmillan, the Conservative prime minister from 1957 to 1963, quipped that 'Toryism has always been a form of paternal socialism.'[56] But Margaret Thatcher was different. She wanted a smaller state with a greater role for the private sector and charities. At the outset she invoked the example of Victorian philanthropy. 'It is noteworthy that the Victorian era – the heyday of free enterprise in Britain – was also the era of the rise of selflessness and benefaction,' she said in a speech in 1977.[57] A free society, she added, 'is morally better because it entails dispersal of power away from the centre to a multitude of smaller groups, and to individuals'. By contrast, 'the concentration of power in large groups, and in the hands of the State . . . corrupts'. Included in those small groups, she later spelled out after becoming prime minister, were volunteering charities:

> The voluntary principle is important for reasons which are far beyond economics . . . The willingness of men and women to give service is one of freedom's greatest safeguards. It ensures that caring remains free from political control. It leaves men and women independent enough to meet needs as they see them, and not only as the State provides. And that's why voluntary organizations . . . can only exist effectively in a free society.

In case cynics might sneer that this was just a convenient cover for cuts in public spending, she added:

> So this enthusiasm for voluntary help is therefore not the need to reduce Government spending. The fact is that it's as important in times of expansion and economic growth as it is during a recession. There are those who . . . imply that the volunteer is just a cheap substitute for a salaried staff, but quite the contrary. I believe that the volunteer movement is at the heart of all our social welfare provision.[58]

Mrs Thatcher was not a politician to be troubled by internal contradictions. As Frank Prochaska pointed out, in a review of the compatibility of Mrs Thatcher's advocacy of the voluntary sector and her espousal of 'Victorian values':

> Given Mrs Thatcher's tributes to the voluntary sector for promoting freedom and benevolence, one might have expected her administrations to offer rather more inducements to giving. Many in the voluntary sector looked forward to changes in the tax system to encourage charitable contributions. It was not until 1987 that the Conservative government introduced a 'give as you earn' scheme. But with tax relief set at a ceiling of £240 on donations, it was far too modest to make much of a difference. For all the upbeat talk about a return to charitable giving, Mrs Thatcher's support for reducing the tax burden on the sector had strict limits.[59]

This was not Mrs Thatcher's only inconsistency on philanthropy. Even as she made severe cuts in the budgets of local councils, she boosted state funding for charities. But this was a double-edged sword. As part of her move to shrink state bureaucracies in health and social services, she handed out contracts to charities – to care for old people, assist the unemployed, supervise released prisoners, and much else – to run public services in ways that she hoped would be more innovative and more efficient. Government grants to charities more than trebled – from £93 million to £293 million in the decade after she took power in 1979.[60] Some of her supporters objected to this on principle; Digby Anderson of the Social Affairs Unit argued that what Thatcher was doing constituted a 'hidden expansion of the welfare state' through 'the permanent subsidy of voluntary bodies by the central and local state'.[61] A few charities, uneasy at their dependence upon the government, severed relations with the state, but most were only too pleased to accept the substantial government grants without fully realizing the extent to which it compromised them. The spending of the state was not being reduced so much as disguised.

There were two problems with this increase in state funding of the voluntary sector. The first was that politicians are not reliable allies. Their horizons, governed by the fast pace of political events and fluctuations in the economic cycle, are far more short-term than those of charities committed to long-term solutions and sustainable programmes. The Alzheimer's Disease Society discovered that in 1987 when, after two years of government grants – which constituted half its income – it was told to merge with Age Concern or reform its management structure if it wished to continue receiving public funds.[62] When Mrs Thatcher's ideological enthusiasm for volunteering came into conflict with her plans for reducing public spending, it was not philanthropy which triumphed. In 1984 charities, like those working with the Manpower Services Commission on training and job-creation schemes, found themselves the victims of sudden cutbacks. The result, as Prochaska outlines, was confusion and bitterness.

But there was a second difficulty. One of the roles routinely cherished by philanthropic activists is their ability to lobby and campaign on behalf of those they serve. On occasion, this means criticizing government policies which impact negatively on charities' clients.

Although Mrs Thatcher's rhetoric linked voluntarism with enterprise and liberty, she bridled when that liberty was exercised in criticism of her policies. A particularly acute example of this occurred when she decided to overturn Nye Bevan's long-standing prohibition on hospitals engaging in fundraising. She even offered them interest-free loans from the Exchequer to finance their appeals. At a stroke, writes Prochaska, 'it gave what amounted to charitable status to statutory bodies and turned NHS administrators into fundraisers'.[63] Charities were outraged. The director of the National Council for Voluntary Organisations, Sir Nicholas Hinton, protested at what he said was 'the most damaging blow suffered by the voluntary sector for many years'.

Charities whose staff and volunteers worked inside the NHS were forced to compete in fundraising with 'the largest, most heavily financed enterprise in the whole field of social welfare', whose fundraising drives were financed by the Treasury.[64] To the Victorians one of the great virtues of philanthropy was its independence from political control. Yet Margaret Thatcher, despite her rhetorical espousal of Victorian values, used charities to further the centralization of power in the hands of government. In his book *Accountable to None: The Tory Nationalisation of Britain*, Simon Jenkins observes: 'Of all the paradoxes of Thatcherism none is greater than this: that more open government should have been used, not to enable the public to participate more fully in democracy, but as a tool of state centralism in its quest for national efficiency'.[65] Under the guise of Victorian liberalism, concludes Frank Prochaska, 'Mrs Thatcher carried forward the very collectivist agenda that she disavowed'.[66]

TURNING CHARITIES INTO AGENTS OF THE STATE

Despite their ideological and political differences, Margaret Thatcher's successors continued very much in the same vein. Tony Blair adopted a very different rhetoric from that of Thatcher. Where she saw philanthropic activism as an expression of enterprise and liberty, he saw it as necessary for community renewal and contributory citizenship. In part, also, his embrace of the voluntary sector was one of the symbolic ways in which he signalled to voters that his New Labour project rejected the socialist collectivism of his party's past. That history was more recent than felt comfortable to him. In the final year of the Thatcher government the man who was to become Tony Blair's Chancellor, Gordon Brown, had disparaged charity as 'a sad and seedy competition for public pity'.[67] A decade later Blair, outlining his New Labour philosophy, asserted an entirely different attitude to voluntary activity:

> Human nature is cooperative as well as competitive, selfless as well as self-interested; and society could not function if it was otherwise. The grievous twentieth-century error of the fundamentalist left was the belief that the state could replace civil society and thereby advance freedom. The new right veers to the other extreme, advocating wholesale dismantling of core state activity in the cause of 'freedom'. The truth is that freedom for the many requires strong government. A key challenge of progressive politics is to use the state as an enabling force, protecting effective communities and voluntary organisations and encouraging their growth to tackle new needs, in partnership as appropriate. These are the values of the Third Way.[68]

Soon Gordon Brown was singing from the same hymn sheet. Launching a campaign to reinvigorate charitable service and civic spirit, he wrote: 'Politicians once thought the man in Whitehall knew best. Now we understand that the . . . mother from the playgroup . . . might know better.'[69] New Labour was happily hijacking the idea that society was bound together by a whole host of voluntary associations which the father of conservatism, the philosopher Edmund Burke, had as far back as 1790 called the 'little platoons' of society. But, although the language had changed, the same Thatcherite vision of an increasingly centralized powerful state dominated Blair's thinking. The state was still seen, as the passage above showed, as 'an enabling force, protecting effective communities and voluntary organisations'.

Like Thatcher, and prime ministers after him, Blair persisted in the notion that philanthropic activism was something which could be enlisted at the government's bidding, rather than as an expression of autonomous citizenship in its own right. The independent intermediary 'little platoons' of civil society were being transformed into agencies of the state. To Blair, service delivery was again the main point of the voluntary sector; its sensitivity to local needs merely made it more efficient in discharging that task. The cart was, as with Mrs Thatcher, being put before the horse. Charities were becoming mere fingers on the hand of government. By the end of Blair's time as prime minister the percentage of their incomes which charities derived from the state had risen even higher.[70]

The next Conservative prime minister, David Cameron, employed a different rhetoric. His general election manifesto in 2010 was entitled *Your Invitation to Join the Government of Britain*. It promised the creation of a Big Society which would put more decision-making into the hands of ordinary citizens. This would bring about 'a massive transfer of power from Whitehall to local communities'.

When Cameron came to power, in coalition with the Liberal Democrats that year, he promised that ordinary people, as individuals and working as volunteers in groups, would be given the power and information they needed to work with local government to 'achieve fairness and opportunity for all'. Philanthropic activists would be given the right to bid to take over local state-run services. The new government would take 'a range of measures to encourage volunteering and involvement in social action'. It would also 'encourage charitable giving and philanthropy'. It would 'support the creation and expansion of mutuals, co-operatives, charities and social enterprises'.[71]

The reality proved rather different and by 2013 Cameron had quietly dropped his Big Society slogan. By then his political opponents, and many members of the public, saw his pro-philanthropy talk as little more than a fig leaf to cover cuts in state spending – in the vain hope that volunteers would step in to fill the gaps being left in public services. But the electorate had undergone a tectonic shift in attitude, as the public-policy historian Glen O'Hara wrote at the time: 'In general it seems as if the public simply do not want to take part in state provision. That is what they elect politicians for; that is what their taxes pay doctors, nurses, teachers and policemen for.'[72] More gravely, for philanthropic organizations, government spin about the Big Society masked 'a real shrinking of the voluntary sector', according to Pat Thane, with a third of charities fearing that their level of service would decrease due to cutbacks, and the speed with which they were being imposed.[73] The philanthropy of civil society was shrinking after years of expansion.

But worse was to come. The years of increased dependency upon the state had left charities implicitly compromised by what had become their reliance upon government funds. 'No one is rude to his rich uncle,' one senior figure in the charitable sector had earlier ruefully observed to Frank Prochaska.[74] But now that implicit threat became explicit. Already in 2013, in a report by the Independence Panel of the Baring Foundation, senior figures in the academic and charitable sector had warned of the serious social consequences this trend was causing:

> The situation is dangerous. When independence is lost by a significant number of organisations, trust in and public support for the whole sector may end up being eroded and even organisations with strong independence may feel the cold. Society will certainly feel the impact, with diverse voices becoming increasingly silent, narrowing political debate, and charities looking to their contract terms rather than their mission when vulnerable people turn up on their doorstep for support.[75]

By 2014 the government had become by far and away the largest provider of funding to charity, handing out some £14 billion in contracts and grants.[76] Of the larger charities, 80 per cent depended on this one main income stream. Among smaller charities, 38 per cent received state funding.[77] The aims of charities had become compromised, argues Prochaska, to the extent that they often did what the government paid them to do rather than following the mission for which the charity had been founded.[78] The first sign that things were about to unravel came when a hard-right Conservative MP, Priti Patel, launched an attack on Britain's leading international development charities, complaining about the number of aid agency chief executives whose pay now exceeded £100,000 a year.[79] Despite the fact that their salaries were in the bottom quartile of pay for senior managers running comparable-sized organizations in the private sector – with thousands of staff and budgets in the millions – considerable political outrage was generated. The following month it became clear this was more than an outlier from an eccentric extremist on the Tory backbenches. The coalition government's new charities minister, Brooks Newmark, at his first public event as Minister for Civil Society, said that charities should 'stick to their knitting' and stay out of the 'realm of politics'.[80]

A year later it was revealed that contracts issued by the government to charities now contained a clause warning them that they must 'pay the utmost regard to the standing' of the government. They also had to agree not to do anything that might 'damage the reputation' of the government or 'attract adverse publicity'.[81] Charity leaders attacked these as 'gagging clauses' intended to prevent outsiders from whistleblowing on government inefficiency or on policies which the charities felt were harmful to their clients. David Cameron was unrepentant and persisted in the policy. Indeed, he went further. Six months after the end of the coalition, when Cameron was prime minister in a majority Conservative government, it was announced that charities working on government contracts were to be barred from attempting to influence parliamentary, government or even party policy. The National Council for Voluntary Organisations described the move as 'tantamount to making charities take a vow of silence'. Opposition Labour Party politicians condemned 'an outrageous attempt to further curb the independence of charities' – not an issue which had concerned them overmuch when they were in government. The move, charity leaders insisted, was contrary to everything Cameron had said in his first speech as leader of the Conservative Party. Then he had declared he wanted to 'set free the voluntary sector' to deal with the problems 'that blight so many of our communities . . . drug abuse, family breakdown, poor public space, chaotic home environments [and] high crime'. Charities had a right, indeed a duty, he averred, to campaign on behalf of their clients 'regardless of any relationship, financial or otherwise, which may exist' with government.[82] Five years later the reality was hitting home that he who pays the piper calls the tune.

Under Cameron's successor as Conservative prime minister, Theresa May, the policy continued of insisting that charities and other sub-contractors working for government departments were made to sign non-disclosure agreements. At the end of 2018, after a terrible fire in a large block of flats, Grenfell Tower, in London's North Kensington, during which 72 people died, *The Times* undertook an investigation into the government's use of these clauses. The journalists found that Cabinet ministers had banned 40 charities, and more than 300 contracted companies, from criticizing them or their departments.[83] The restrictions applied to a wide range of activities, from commercial firms involved in the refurbishing of

Grenfell Tower to 22 voluntary groups and charities implementing the rollout of a controversial new welfare scheme called Universal Credit. Responding to a public outcry, Theresa May wrote to the National Council for Voluntary Organisations to insist that the government 'recognises the importance of the voice of charities and social enterprises in speaking out on behalf of beneficiaries'. But, she added, government contracts with those charities must include 'provisions to ensure that providers adhere to the high standards we expect'. These, she insisted, covered 'dangerous, unfair or unethical practices', and were not an attempt to 'prevent charities from campaigning' or from 'fairly criticising' the government.[84] Charities were unconvinced. Vicky Browning from the Association of Chief Executives of Voluntary Organisations described the Conservative policy as 'anti-democratic'.[85] The government of Boris Johnson, which succeeded Theresa May's, signalled no departure from attempts by the state to increasingly control the charitable sector.

The overall trend is clear. Since the Second World War, governments of both Britain's major political parties have paid lip-service to the importance of philanthropic activism and voluntary organization. Yet when confronted with a choice – between allowing philanthropy freedom and increasing centralized government control – those in power always chose to strengthen their own authority rather than tolerate the existence of rival centres of influence. In the late 1970s a mere 10 per cent of the income of the nation's charities came from the state;[86] at the start of the twenty-first century the proportion was approaching half[87] – with the government by far and away the largest provider of funds to British charity – some £14 billion in 2012–13. And once on the payroll of the state, charities had less of an incentive to raise funds privately. Precise figures are hard to come by, though the 2016 annual almanac of the National Council for Voluntary Organisations suggests this may have fallen slightly as Conservative government policies of public-spending austerity tightened in the years to 2020. [88] But it is estimated that about 41,000 charities, about a quarter of all those registered in the UK, have a direct financial relationship with the state – and more than half of these receive more than three-quarters of their income from government sources.[89] The government is now the largest single contributor to Britain's philanthropic causes.

RECOVERING THE MORAL PURPOSE
OF PHILANTHROPY

Critics complain that this government domination of charities influences the nature of philanthropic work. Charities do not, as a result, merely mute their criticisms of government; they also often absorb the view of welfare favoured by the state. Certainly, there is an obvious incompatibility between the ethos of the managerial state and that of philanthropic activism. Governments are largely driven by considerations of efficiency; charities by a sense of moral purpose. Governments consider trends and statistics; charities meet individuals face to face. Governments favour approaches which are systematic, comprehensive and rule-bound; charities can be selective, innovative and are more free to improvise. The state almost always yearns for centralized control whereas charities are rooted in a profound sense of independence.

Voluntary associations, in Frank Prochaska's words, ought to be 'the nurseries of democracy'. They provide opportunities for 'grass-roots participation, a moral training, and lessons in decision-making and organization'.[90] The hijacking of a charity so that it becomes an agent of the state, therefore, does not merely impair that charity's vision; it is also bad for a healthy democracy. Charitable autonomy has a virtue in itself. If politicians understood this then they would dramatically increase tax incentives to giving. The fact that they rarely do this indicates how low a priority that is, whatever the latest form of political rhetoric a government adopts to disguise the fact.

The problem with such heavy state involvement in philanthropy is that the traffic is largely one-way. Were politicians to listen to front-line charity workers, and modify their policies in the light of grassroots experience, there would be clearer advantages to a partnership between philanthropy and the state. Sound welfare requires both systematic efficiency and emotional empathy. The tension between the voluntary and compulsory approaches to public services can be problematic but it could also be fruitful – if the relationship between the two is respectful and the charities are not seen as the lesser partner. The schematic approach of the state can be enriched if politicians allow their systems to be humanized by charities which have direct contact with the people served by public services. Policymakers and civil servants rarely have the insight to fully understand how policy dreamt up in Whitehall impacts ordinary citizens on the ground.

But for that to happen would require politicians to view the critiques offered by the third sector as a help rather than a hindrance. Philanthropic innovation arises from hands-on experience rather than abstract policy. That is clear in everything from the chimney-sweeping machine invented to prevent boys being sent up chimneys, and the eight-hour factory day pioneered by Quaker industrialists, to the introduction of pension schemes and the invention of food banks. The direct contact of volunteers also allows the voices of the excluded, marginalized and victimized – of minorities and dissenters – to be heard in the corridors of power in a way which is healthy for democracy. The philosopher John Stuart Mill understood all this long ago when he wrote: 'A people . . . who expect to have everything done for them . . . have their faculties only half developed.' The only check on the authoritarian tendencies of the state, he said, is the development of an 'intelligence, activity and public spirit among the governed'. And Mill added that what he called 'voluntary cooperation' is 'the great school of that public spirit', which is 'the distinctive character of the public of free countries'.[91] That is the spirit which needs to be recovered in the relationship between the state and philanthropy.

The change in attitudes which had occurred at the end of the nineteenth century had been driven, as noted above, by a sense that the scale of poverty in a heavily industrialized urban Britain was just too big to be tackled by philanthropy. The statistical surveys of sociologists such as Charles Booth had contributed to that conviction. There seemed to be something structural in the social economy which had to be addressed in a scientific and comprehensive way. And only the state was adjudged to be large enough to do that. Yet as the prominent philanthropist Josephine Butler had argued, as early as 1869, the large legislative welfare systems which would be required were essentially 'masculine' in character.[92] Such an approach was in stark contrast to that of the nineteenth century, in which philanthropy had been dominated by a distinctly female sensibility. At the beginning of that century only about 10 per cent of charitable subscribers were women; by the end of it that figure was over 60 per cent.[93] The shift can be attributed to the growing number of middle-class women, who were excluded from employment and politics, and for whom involvement in charity was their best form of self-fulfilment. But it was about more than numbers. For many philanthropy had become an intensely personal experience. That was summed up in lines from Elizabeth Barrett Browning's epic novel-in-verse, *Aurora Leigh*, published barely a decade before Josephine Butler's remarks. Browning wrote:

> You weep for what you know. A red-haired child
> Sick in a fever, if you touch him once,
> Though but so little as with a finger-tip,
> Will set you weeping! But a million sick . . .
> You could as soon weep for the rule of three,
> Or compound fractions.[94]

This whole phenomenon has been described by Frank Prochaska as 'the feminisation of philanthropy'.[95] Such gender stereotypes were, of course, merely nominal. Another woman, the early socialist Beatrice Webb, took the opposite attitude. She was countering Mrs Browning's point – and wilfully inverting a line from the poem when she asserted: '"A million sick" have always seemed actually more worthy of self-sacrificing devotion than the "sick child in a fever" preferred by Mrs Browning's Aurora Leigh.'[96] But many of the voluntary traditions of Britain were deeply rooted in female culture. Those traditions were abandoned as the state gradually came, more and more, to take over social welfare. There have been, of course, huge advantages to that. The 'patch-quilt' of health and other services, varying from one area to another in different places, which existed before the welfare state, has largely been abolished; where disparities do occur, they are routinely condemned as a 'postcode lottery'. Few would want to go back to the old system. Yet something of the human touch, which came from the sensitivities of personal ministration, has been lost – something that might be rediscovered were philanthropy to be accorded a less junior role in relation to the welfare state. How should that balance best be restored?

FINDING A NEW BALANCE

In 1899 Pope Leo XIII issued a document which he called *Rerum Novarum* (Of New Things). What was new about it was that it was the first attempt by the Catholic Church to address the social problems which arose from the Industrial Revolution. Great wealth was being created across the Continent, but so was abject poverty for many ordinary people. The growing gap between the rich and the poor alarmed the Pope – as did the rise of communism with its accompanying atheist materialism. A new way of thinking about the world was needed. *Rerum Novarum* was to prove the first in a series of social encyclicals issued by a succession of popes over the next 120 years. The document was filled with moral outrage. It condemned the situation in which a 'tiny group of extravagantly rich men have been able to lay upon the great multitude of unpropertied workers a yoke little better than that of slavery itself'.[97] The language was so powerful that – despite its critique of socialism – the document was itself condemned as socialist at the time.[98] Yet what has emerged from more than a century of Catholic Social Teaching is something which seeks to offer a classic middle way between unfettered free-market capitalism and the collective planning of full-blooded socialism. The thinking which the Church evolved may offer an insight into how to balance the roles of government and the voluntary sector with regard to the welfare state.

At the heart of Catholic Social Teaching is the assertion that all human beings possess an intrinsic dignity. Yet how are the interests of individuals to be balanced against those of the collection of individuals we call society? Its answer lies in the notion of the 'common good'. The idea has its roots in the thinking of the great medieval theologian Thomas Aquinas, who synthesized the thought of Aristotle and St Augustine to bring together two great traditions of Western culture. The idea of the common good goes well beyond the assertion of the eighteenth-century utilitarian philosophers that society should be ordered to produce 'the greatest happiness for the greatest numbers'.[99] In contrast, the Catholic Church defines the common good as 'the sum total of social conditions which allow people, either as groups or as individuals, to reach their fulfilment more fully and more easily'.[100] It does away with the black and white distinction between individual good and collective good. In doing so it abolishes the distinction between selfish and altruistic action.

The common good is produced by nurturing a sense of human solidarity which acknowledges the mutual interdependence – economic, cultural, political and spiritual – existing between all people.

'Solidarity is not a feeling of vague compassion or shallow distress at the misfortunes' of others, Pope John Paul II said in 1987. 'On the contrary it is a firm and persevering determination to commit oneself to the common good; that is to say, to the good of all and of each individual.' It means 'we are all really responsible for all' – not only as individuals but communally.[101]

Yet solidarity, left to itself, can exert unhealthy pressure towards collectivism, points out the religious commentator Clifford Longley.[102] Untempered, solidarity can give rise to the idea that only the state can properly organize the comprehensive mutual responsibility which the community requires. So solidarity has a centralizing, and therefore disempowering, tendency. To balance this Catholic Social Teaching has developed the idea of a countervailing force which it calls 'subsidiarity'. This principle, set out by Pope Pius XI in *Quadragesimo Anno* in 1931, on the fortieth anniversary of *Rerum Novarum*, declares that 'it is gravely wrong to take from individuals what they can accomplish by their own initiative and industry and give it to the community'.[103] The state should not take over what local government can do – and a local council should not perform tasks which could be done by voluntary groups, charities and civil society organizations. Decisions should be taken at the lowest level compatible with good government. So subsidiarity gives ordinary people a greater say in their lives by allowing them greater participation in the processes of government. It empowers both individuals and voluntary groups. It helps defend the role of philanthropy against the excessive intrusions of big government. The better subsidiarity is applied, 'the happier and more prosperous the condition of the State'.[104]

Subsidiarity and solidarity exist in a kind of tension, but one which is necessary to the preservation of the common good. So far as the welfare state is concerned, solidarity insists on effective safety nets for the disadvantaged while subsidiarity insists that these must not create disincentives to work. But the idea of the common good poses other challenges. Welfare programmes have become a mechanism for attaining social, rather than individual, good. Thinking about welfare has largely lost the sense of the intrinsic worth of the individuals who find themselves dependent upon social assistance. Calculations about welfare budgets have become mere cost-benefit analyses about whether the cost of welfare outweighs the social costs of neglect. Our values have ceased to be transcendent and become utilitarian. Such a value shift imperceptibly alters society's attitudes to the individuals caught in poverty traps, so that the state begins to treat them differently.

All this stems from what Pope John Paul II called 'a purely economic conception of man'.[105] That narrow approach needs to be broadened so that the state instead looks for value in a wider range of qualities than the mere economic. An imperfect product made by a person with disabilities, for example, may be accorded a greater intrinsic value than a superficially superior object made by mass-production methods. Welfare-to-work programmes might profitably widen their definitions of what constitutes 'work' to include voluntary, charitable or caring activities which existing social-security regulations exclude.[106] Philanthropy can play a key role here.

Imaginative suggestions for such modifications are less likely to come from government than from Edmund Burke's 'little platoons' – charities and voluntary groups, but also churches, schools, clubs and sporting associations, campaigning groups and trade unions. All these, writes Burke's biographer, Jesse Norman, are institutions which 'trap and store knowledge'. Through their 'myriad private interactions, traditions and practices . . . the social order becomes a repository of shared knowledge and inherited wisdom'.[107] What this suggests is that, although there may be short-term advantages for governments in turning charities into compliant agents of the state, such an approach does long-term damage to the vibrancy of a democracy.

So how is this better balance between philanthropy and the state to be arrived at? Part of the solution lies in realizing that the state does not just dominate economically. It also has a tendency to change the philanthropic agenda. Once governments provide money to charities, they feel entitled to control them. Of course, politicians have a duty to make sure that taxpayers' money is spent wisely. But it is now the state which defines what 'wisely' means. As we have noted, it has a tendency to see the problem rather than the person. The little platoons are increasingly regulated by drill sergeants hired by the state. The independent spirit of civic society risks being killed off by a culture of homogeneity which is intolerant of those who offer alternatives to the state's received wisdom. Something similar happened in the transition from the medieval to the early modern period when philanthropy shifted from a religious paradigm to one shaped by the emerging nation state. In the sixteenth century the state became the sole arbiter of what people could believe, a phenomenon which became called Erastianism; the danger is that, in subverting the independence of charities, the modern state is imposing a subtle form of ideological supremacy in a similar vein. When that happens much of the initiative and enterprise of philanthropy is crushed. Innovation rarely comes from government.

The hospice movement offers a good example of how new approaches arise from an alternative worldview. The modern hospice evolved out of the insights of a British nurse, Cicely Saunders. Just after the Second World War, while she was working with the dying, her deeply held Christian beliefs opened her to the insight that 'as the body becomes weaker, so the spirit becomes stronger'.[108] Slowly it dawned on her that the terminally ill needed palliative care which addressed their spiritual fears as well as their physical pain. This brought into play an entirely different worldview from that of the medical profession, which at the time was focused exclusively on physical healing. 'In the hospitals of the 1940s, the dying were regarded as medical failures, and the doctors gave up on them,' wrote the *Church Times*, comparing Saunders after her death to Florence Nightingale.[109] 'Pain relief was given only when the pain was already unbearable.'

Volunteering at St Luke's Home for the Dying Poor in the late 1940s, Cicely Saunders developed a conviction that 'holistic care, physical, mental and spiritual' was as necessary as continuous pain relief 'to enable people to live their last days conscious and aware, without fear, and surrounded by love'.[110] Working tirelessly for almost twenty years she raised the money to establish the world's first purpose-built hospice, St Christopher's in south London. Today Britain's 200 hospices every year support more than 200,000 people as they approach the end of life. Those hospices now receive around one-third of their funding from the state but still raise 67 per cent – more than £1 billion a year – from philanthropic fundraising. Their 40,000 paid staff are outnumbered by more than 125,000 volunteers.[111] Many of these are motivated by their religious faith and the hospice movement is still very much rooted in a Christian ethos, though it assists suffering individuals of all faiths and none. But it seems significant that the instincts which prompted the growth of something as distinctive as the hospice movement drew on a worldview which was entirely different from that of the state. So much so that, if hospices were to begin drawing most of their funding from the state – and were put under pressure to dilute their religious ethos for fear they might be seen as not inclusive in a pluralist society – it is easy to see how their nature could begin subtly to change.

The religious tradition is merely one of those intermediary institutions which, to borrow Jesse Norman's phrase, 'trap and store shared knowledge and inherited wisdom'. There are many others which offer equally distinct non-state worldviews and philosophies: professions like the law; trade unions as they protect the interests of their members; lobby groups such as environmental activists; the founders of the fair trade movement; the food banks which have sprung up across Britain as a spontaneous grassroots response to seeing people struggle to find enough to eat as the state cuts their benefits. All these have developed out of a way of looking at the world which is different from that of the state.

Governments need now to encourage such alternatives, rather than seeking to contain or constrain their influence. Not all ideas should, or can, be derived from the state. The English approach to law is that everything is permitted except what is prohibited; the state should take a similar approach to the alternatives put forward by other worldviews. Philanthropic activism provides an essential training in civic virtue which the state itself cannot nurture. Philanthropy is, to recall the words of John Stuart Mill, 'the great school of that public spirit' essential to the maintenance of a healthy society. Politicians, despite their seemingly insatiable thirst for control, need the independent spirit of philanthropy more than they might suppose.

Interview: Ian Linden on charity and the state

Ian Linden was Director of Policy for the Tony Blair Faith Foundation until 2016. For 15 years before that he was Director of the Catholic Institute for International Relations (CIIR), an international development and education charity which was in receipt of substantial funding from the British government. It later changed its name to Progressio and closed when British government funding was withdrawn. A member of the Christian-Muslim Forum, he has lived and worked in Africa. He has strong connections with the Labour Party. As an academic historian he has focused on issues of economic development, religion and conflict. He has been an associate professor in the Study of Religion at the School of Oriental and African Studies (SOAS) in the University of London. He was awarded the CMG for his human rights work in 2000.

For much of the 20th century it was assumed that philanthropy was a thing of the past – and that only the state could provide the answer to social disadvantage. Why did that attitude change?

Clement Attlee, who became the prime minister of the Labour government after the Second World War, spoke of cold charity versus the warm state that would embrace the poor. Britain emerged from that war with a very centralized powerful state that was co-ordinating almost everything from growing carrots to providing effective fighter airplanes. Having inherited such a state, people after the war said: 'That worked, we actually got through this horror.' So the state was a bloody good thing, especially when you had a charismatic figure like Churchill to embody what the state was supposed to be doing.

As late as 1988 a Labour politician from a different generation, Gordon Brown, was still disparaging charity as 'a sad and seedy competition for public pity'. What changed attitudes on the left?

Between 1989 and 1991 the Berlin Wall came down and the Soviet Empire collapsed. A mass of states, most importantly and obviously

Russia, were now required to embrace market economics, capitalism and democracy. But you can't really do market economics in a social democracy if you don't have a civil society, with significant institutional bodies, and an informed electorate.

Many socialists until that point had failed to understand the impact charitable institutions had on society. Charities and voluntary groups created a cadre of supporters and members who had a deep understanding of whatever the charity was all about. You got a bunch of people that knew quite a bit about education, homelessness, alcohol abuse, and other poverty issues, and were able to lobby for state provision to change in those spheres. The work of organizations like Oxfam played an important role in creating an informed electorate on issues of international development. Such an informed lobby acts as a bulwark against the populist platitudes of a reactionary government. One important role of philanthropy is that it provides the money to make the wheels of civil society turn.

But in the second half of the twentieth century in Britain it was the government, rather than philanthropy, which began to pour funds into the charities that were a key part of that civil society. Margaret Thatcher centralized the state by slashing the local government funding – and then handed out money to charities to do the jobs which councils had previously done. Funding for charities trebled. Subsequent prime ministers – of both parties – have continued this approach. How did this affect you?

Well, the first and obvious impact was an excessive dependence on state funding, which was dangerous because the state could give, and the state could take away again. Also, because however much the charities talked about their moral independence from the state, it was perfectly obvious that they would at some point become constrained in their advocacy – not least because you have a Charity Commission coming along which says 'this is the sort of thing you can do under your articles of association' and 'these other things you can't do'.

But did it ever go beyond that?

Yes. In the 1970s, in the years before the fall of the fascist dictatorship in Portugal, CIIR was doing advocacy work on human rights after the Wiriyamu Massacre – when Portuguese commandos killed between

130 and 300 men, women and children in Mozambique after accusing them of sheltering rebel guerrillas. The massacre had been uncovered by a British missionary, the Catholic priest, Fr Adrian Hastings. His account was printed in *The Times* a week before the Portuguese prime minister, Marcelo Caetano, was due to visit Britain to celebrate the 600th anniversary of the Anglo-Portuguese alliance. CIIR had set up a committee to scrutinize the working of Portuguese colonialism and especially the manner in which it was prosecuting its colonial wars. Fr Hastings was a member of that committee. Just ahead of the visit someone who was clearly from MI6 popped up and said, 'We're not at all happy with you doing this. Could you please shut up?'

What happened?
We didn't shut up and nothing happened.

So charities didn't feel too constrained about speaking out, despite their government funding?
We didn't. But we were small fry – with a budget of just £4 million. It was a very different ballgame for bigger charities like Oxfam. Small charities had more freedom precisely because we were a bit below the radar. We were able to work on South Africa during apartheid in ways which were not in line with the British government's policy. Having said that, CIIR was never able to seriously increase its official funding much above £4 million.

There were two distinct elements to the work of CIIR. On the one hand there was the advocacy and lobbying as you've just described. But there was also a programme to send British volunteers overseas to share their skills in developing economies. It was much easier to get official funds for the skillshare than for the advocacy.
Absolutely. The big money came through that.

The two halves were supposed to complement one another. The advocacy gained added legitimacy because CIIR had volunteers on the ground who knew the local situation first hand. And the allocation of volunteers to particular places and projects was informed by the intelligence gathered by the advocacy teams.
Yes. They fed off each other.

Was there a danger – with the government making funding more available for one side than the other – that the tail was wagging the dog?

Yes. And then about 20 years later CIIR, which had changed its name to Progressio, folded because DfID (the government's Department for International Development) took away the money.

That does show the danger of a charity being over-reliant on political sources of funding.

Yes, though the government could argue that they took away the money because there was a larger Catholic development agency, Cafod, doing similar advocacy and education work – and there was another huge British organization, VSO (Voluntary Service Overseas), which was government-funded and was doing a much bigger skillshare job and doing it very well. We were squeezed at both ends.

So is private money from a philanthropist the answer?

In my experience the sort of person who is a philanthropist has generally had a high level of experience of entrepreneurial money-making and the big global league. They, therefore, come to their charitable giving with that under their belts. The problem is that most philanthropists have not got the remotest idea about how effective poverty-alleviation actually works. They tend to have hobby horses which they want the money focused on. If you go to a big rich donor you stand a pretty good chance of having to do what the donor wants you to do – which may not be the best thing, though it can be better than nothing, as it were.

How did the Tony Blair Faith Foundation address these issues?

When Tony Blair left Downing Street, after he had been to see the Queen and given his final speech in Parliament, he got on the train back to his constituency in the North-East and said to one of his aides, Ruth Turner: 'OK, let's plan the Faith Foundation.' That's how keen he was on doing it. Bill Clinton had rung him up and said: 'Take your time, Tony: don't make a big decision immediately.' But Blair was clear about what he wanted to do; his experience of the Northern Ireland peace process had taught him that you couldn't really neglect faith in the big movements for peace in the world.

Anyway, he consulted widely with the Archbishop of Canterbury and various cardinals, the Chief Rabbi and many more, on what exactly the foundation should do. When he asked me I said he should build on his legacy with the Africa Commission, Gleneagles, the work he did on debt relief, on promoting the Millennium Development Goals, and on child poverty in Britain.* A couple of months later I got a call to ask me to come to the Faith Foundation to explore the role of faith leaders in implementing the millennium goal on health provision.

What made you say Yes? Did you hesitate because of the opprobrium that was attaching to Tony Blair as a result of the war in Iraq?

Obviously, I thought, Iraq's going to hang over it – and I knew there was a risk my reputation would get tarnished because of that. But I'd done some work for the British government on Muslim development agencies. The Department for International Development (DfID) was anxious to even up the support it was giving to Christian development agencies, but after 9/11 there were anxieties that things could go wrong with the Muslim agencies. DfID asked me to write a report, so I looked at Muslim Aid, Muslim Hands, and so on and so on, and I visited projects that they had in different parts of Africa. It was very clear that they were doing absolutely excellent work – and reaching areas other aid agencies couldn't go. While at CIIR I had wanted the organization to get involved with Muslim organizations in the area of interfaith relations and international development, but this had not proved possible. So when I got the offer from the Faith Foundation I thought this was my chance to do what I'd spent years scrambling for money to do. Now somebody with money was saying to me, would I like to do something I've wanted to do for about the last 10 years. So I said yes.

Was Blair just trying to make amends for Iraq, or did he have a genuinely innovative vision for economic development in Africa?

It was a great programme. In Sierra Leone we got to five million people with the messages of malaria prevention using faith leaders. At

---

*Tony Blair had set up the Commission for Africa in 2004 in partnership with African politicians and economists to discover longer-term solutions for the Continent's economic development. It resulted in increases in aid and debt relief at the 2005 G8 summit of world leaders at Gleneagles.

baptisms priests would talk about how the water of baptism was good but water on the ground where mosquitoes breed is bad. There was similar material for Muslim sermons, some of which I helped write.

I heard stories about people who were very anti-vaccination until the local imam persuaded them that inoculations weren't a Western plot to undermine the Muslim population.

That's right. When primary health-care workers went to Kano in Nigeria they were accompanied by senior imams from Egypt to tell the local people that inoculation wasn't a plot to sterilize Muslims. And they countered rumours that there was pig serum in the vaccine in violation of Islamic dietary laws. But to be convincing they had to be highly respected faith leaders, backed by lots of Islamic scholarship, to convince the local Nigerian imams that they knew what they were talking about.

In Sierra Leone we were able to build on an existing tradition of interfaith relations. After the civil war* the country was so devastated that the only game in town was the different religious institutions. There was an amazing imam there who got together with the Christian leaders, and together they formed a sort of interfaith national reconstruction body. So when we arrived and said, 'How about you guys working on malaria together?', it was a low-hanging fruit. And don't forget who gave British troops permission to shoot up the guys who were zonked out on drugs, who were chopping off people's arms and legs.

Tony Blair's role in authorizing British troops to end the civil war in Sierra Leone was a factor?

Absolutely. British troops had a peacekeeping mandate from the United Nations. But it was a mandate to sit there and behave like the Dutch did in Srebrenica – doing nothing, just watching† – and they basically said they didn't want to do that. So they went through to Blair and said they couldn't just sit there watching these guys run around. The rebels

---

* The Sierra Leone Civil War (1991–2002), in which 50,000 people died, ended after British troops repelled rebel forces attempting to overthrow the elected government.
† The International Appeals Court in the Hague found that Dutch soldiers acting as UN peacekeepers were partly liable for the deaths of about 300 Muslim men massacred by Bosnia Serbs near Srebrenica during the Yugoslavian civil war. The Dutch government resigned in 2002 after acknowledging its failure to protect the refugees.

were so drugged out of their heads that the British commander said his troops could mop them up in a week – if they had permission from the British prime minister. Blair gave them that permission – and the British forces mopped them up in a week. In Sierra Leone people constantly came up to me to talk about Tony and say: 'You know that man saved our nation.' And he actually did.

As well as his Faith Foundation programmes he had others under what was called the Tony Blair Africa Governance Initiative.

That was a brilliant conception and he managed to get brilliant people to do it. He recruited some really talented young people, the type who would otherwise have ended up in corporate philanthropy in J. P. Morgan, young men and women in their late twenties with a bit – and sometimes a lot – of corporate experience under their belt. Tony hired real experts in various areas. He'd figured out, because of his work with heads of state, that one of the fundamental problems in Africa, which NGOs couldn't tackle – and which most of the programmes of intergovernmental co-operation couldn't address – was to turn excellent policy plans into implementable, and implemented, programmes of work on the ground. The problem was the transmission belt, from head of state through to ministers through to local workers in health, education and so on. If there was a transmission belt at all, it just broke down. So you'd have these wonderful policy documents sitting there – and everybody spouting about how wonderful the policy documents were – but nothing was happening. What the Blair Africa programme did was put in a facilitating person, somebody who knew how to get a transmission belt working, and do it in a way that could transmit that learning and information and skills right through the ministries. It has made a fundamental difference to the effectiveness of the state in a number of places.

In the Health Ministry in Sierra Leone it has done wonderful work which achieved an entirely new programme of women's and under-fives' health. It was so successful that they began to have problems because so many people were coming across the border to participate in it.

The programme recruited excellent people. They put them either into the president's or a senior minister's office. In Rwanda the initiative put someone in the President's office. In Sierra Leone our people went into various ministries, including health – which is where I worked directly with them to bring the faith leaders into the programme. The Africa

Governance Initiative also put first-rate people into the ministry to support the Minister and the leaders of the national malaria programme in implementing the policy.

Why could a philanthropy foundation do that – when rich donor governments, international organizations, and NGOs couldn't?

Others hadn't thought of it. And also because getting funding for that kind of idea was not easy. Funders could be leery of it, saying that some African regimes were pretty corrupt. But the counter-argument was that such regimes could be made less corrupt by putting in good civil servants in key posts. It was high risk. But because the people Blair put into these key positions were very good – because they knew how not to be 'the big white bwana coming in to tell Africans what to do', because they were discreet and sophisticated – they could turn things round in an amazing way. You got major national programmes developed in co-operation with the people on the ground.

They were operating like classic McKinsey-style management consultants?

Yes, but with a level of commitment and dedication that you don't usually get with top international consultants. And because it had Tony Blair written on it – and his track record on Africa was so outstanding – the African governments were willing to play ball. He gave the access.

What has all that taught you about the key function of philanthropy in terms of its relationship to the state?

The most important thing in my book would be that philanthropy provides the funding for a vibrant civil society. A vibrant civil society is important because it has people with direct and in-depth expertise in the different areas that are of concern to government – health, education, the alleviation of poverty, social policy, international development and so on. Those people are able to contribute a great deal of precise knowledge into the debate about, to give a domestic example, what is the best way to get knife crime down. That wouldn't be the case if such organizations didn't exist. Everybody would be in the state sector. The capacity to get into that level of knowledge on the ground would simply not be there. And philanthropy has a key role in funding that.

Chapter 11

The Staggering Successes of Philanthrocapitalism

People left from the little railway station at Irlam. It was not a place at which many people arrived. For thirty years the buildings on the platform had stood derelict, a sad reminder of the former glory of the town which has now been absorbed into Greater Manchester. When Neil McArthur was born there in the 1950s everyone had a job. Many, like his father, were employed in the local steelworks, or on the nearby Manchester Ship Canal, or in Irlam's oil-processing, soap, candle, margarine, basket, rope and boiler-making factories. Thousands of people poured in to their places of work each day from trains which busied the little station. The line was so well used that there were plenty of locomotives for the boy Neil to enter into his trainspotter's notebook. It was a hobby which made the station one of his favourite places.

But the manufacturing industries which had been the town's lifeblood slowly died, and finally the steelworks closed in 1979. Irlam, once an industrial boom town, went into decline. The station was now used mainly by those travelling from Irlam rather than to it. Each morning local people left to commute, east to Manchester or west in the direction of Liverpool. The only way for an ambitious young man to succeed was to leave. Young Neil, who had not passed his 11-plus scholarship and failed to get a place at grammar school, obtained an apprenticeship as an electrical engineer with British Nuclear Fuels in nearby Warrington. Later he moved south, to university in Essex, to study telecommunications, after which he set up a series of companies.

The final one was Opal Communications, which eventually became the major home-broadband supplier TalkTalk. When it was sold for £103 million in 2002, Neil McArthur, at the of age 46, found himself a very wealthy man. After making all the luxury purchases expected of a newly wealthy businessman, including homes in Spain and Barbados, he looked around for something more fulfilling to do.

The Irlam boy refused to believe that his home town was dead. He bought what he told a local journalist was 'six acres in the middle of a moonscape' and spent £8.5 million building offices to house his firm's technology division in Irlam.[1] Although he had sold the business he had kept working there as its innovation director. Poignantly, the site he chose was the wasteland where the steelworks had once stood and in which his father had once worked.

A property advisor in London told him he was mad: 'What the hell do you want to build it in the middle of Beirut for?' It was not difficult to see why an outsider would make an unflattering comparison with Lebanon in its war-torn days. The closure of the steelworks had impacted upon the whole local economy. Irlam looked down-at-heel. A third of the shops were boarded up. Only the brothel and the betting shop were doing a healthy trade. The little railway station, where the young McArthur had spent many happy hours, was derelict.

McArthur decided that revitalizing the steelworks site was not enough. He determined to devote a good portion of his new wealth to regenerating his home town. In 2004 he began buying every empty shop in the neighbourhood. After smartening them up, he let them out at low rents to businesses of which he approved – florists, curtain-makers, carpet-fitters, optometrists, and beekeepers making honey from the flowers of Chat Moss, the giant peat bog to the north of the town. He bought so many shops that he lost count. Yet he refused to rent them out to bookmakers and takeaway food outlets, choosing only services he felt would improve the feel of the area. 'If you buy three shops in a row and do them up really well, it isn't long before the neighbours get the paintbrush out,' he told the northern editor of the *Guardian*, Helen Pidd, who observed, 'Irlam now boasts that rarest of beasts, especially in the working-class north: a high street with next-to-no empty shops.' That was only the start. McArthur bought up five pubs and then went on to donate millions towards a new sports centre, a new rugby club and a new sixth-form college. He gave dozens of smaller grants to the local Scouts, a synchronized swimming group, market-garden allotments and an array of public art projects all round his home town.

Over the past two decades Neil McArthur has donated £23 million to this otherwise forgotten suburb of Salford. Some £11 million has been channelled through his North Cheshire Developments, which he calls a 'quasi-commercial' regeneration company, and £12 million has gone into a charity he founded. Characteristically, he has not named it after himself but from a combination of old family names, as the Hamilton Davies Trust. Perhaps most symbolically he contributed more than £1 million to the refurbishment of the station building to turn it into a museum to his childhood hobby – with vintage memorabilia from the heyday of the railways and a thriving community café, well used by local people who hire it for special occasions such as weddings, christenings and family celebrations. None of the railway travellers passing through would now look out of the window and think about war-torn Beirut.

So successful has the station regeneration been that the local transport authority is planning to engineer a similar transformation in 96 of its other railway stations, turning them into 'multi-purpose community hubs'. Whether that can happen without someone like Neil McArthur battling on their behalf is another matter. The energy he devotes to his philanthropy is as important as his money. Dealing with planning regulations and local councils takes commitment as well as cash. To get the station building reopened he says he had as many as 100 meetings with the railway authority, Network Rail. You need, as he put it with characteristic northern bluntness, to be able to 'grind the buggers down'.

The philanthropist does not hesitate to exploit his high-level contacts to get things done. When he had the idea of reopening the station to trains he was able to secure a meeting with the chairman of the national rail authority – a meeting which a local councillor would almost certainly have found it far more difficult to arrange. 'You've got to start top-down,' said McArthur, 'otherwise you've got no chance.'

The extent of Neil McArthur's wealth and influence makes some wary. The *Guardian* raised the question as to whether it was healthy for one person to own so much of a town. Some allege he has a political agenda: when he offered to contribute millions to a new health clinic for Irlam, left-wing politicians feared it might be part of a creeping Conservative plan to privatize NHS healthcare. McArthur's answer to them was direct: 'I'm a bigger socialist than you are. I just believe in making the pie bigger before I share it out. That's capitalism working well with socialist principles.' Other critics assume he is using his power to increase his fortune – an accusation McArthur dismisses. 'No one with any knowledge of property would think for a minute I invest in these things to make money,' he said. 'I make a net loss in the regeneration business.' He sees his commercial redevelopment company and his charitable trust very much in the tradition of the philanthropy of great northerners like Titus Salt and Joseph Rowntree.

'The reason you had Victorian philanthropy is that you didn't have high taxation, so the public sector didn't have the money to build universities and schools and hospitals. So it was expected that the wealthy people would build these things.' The growth of the state, as we charted in the previous chapter, reversed that expectation. But McArthur feels that British society now needs to rethink that. Many on the left are open-minded to the idea. The socialist mayor of Salford, Paul Dennett, takes a pragmatic view of McArthur's activities. 'For me, it's a great model for delivering in a climate of austerity, where our budgets have been cut by 50 per cent,' he told The *Guardian*. 'Far better than building via the dreaded Private Finance Initiative, which has seen councils saddled with massive long-term debt . . . I'm not suspicious of him at all'.

The consensus on the streets of Irlam is that they are very fortunate to have a local-boy-made-good who sustains such a commitment to his home town. Since McArthur's initiatives began the economy of Irlam has turned a corner, according to a report by the Greater Manchester think tank, New Economy.[2] Total employment in Irlam has increased and a greater variety of jobs are available with more people working in professional occupations. The number of locals with no qualifications has fallen. Thousands of new homes are being built; house prices are rising; and the number of privately rented properties is increasing. The image of Irlam as a place to live is distinctly improved, the report concludes. The only sadness it expresses is that the 'unique contribution' to all this of Neil McArthur's company and charity means that the regeneration is not a model for other depressed towns unless they are fortunate enough to find their own local philanthropist. McArthur is convinced of the solution. Wealthy people in other areas should give of their money, their time and their expertise to bring about wider social transformation: 'It should be an expectation, shouldn't it?'

THE RISE OF THE PHILANTHROCAPITALIST

Philanthropy in Britain underwent a gear change after the election of Margaret Thatcher as prime minister in 1979. The post-war political consensus of a 'mixed economy', in which the public and private sectors co-existed in a 'one nation' tradition, was shattered. Thatcher, like her friend and contemporary President Ronald Reagan in the US, embraced neo-liberalism as an economic and political ideology. It favoured free markets, a small state, less government, lower taxes, cuts in public spending, deregulation of the financial sector, the privatization of state-owned companies, flexible labour markets and curbs on the power of trade unions. We saw in the last chapter how this impacted on the collective philanthropy of charities, which were co-opted to become agents of the state, with their independence often compromised. But neo-liberal ideology had a significant impact upon direct philanthropic giving too.

Under Thatcher, and Reagan, taxes on the rich were slashed on the grounds that they were a disincentive to investment, risk-taking and hard work. The result was a massive growth in the wealth of the very rich, accompanied by a marked increase in inequality as the burden of the economic changes fell on poorer members of society: in 2017, Oxfam estimated that eight men now owned more wealth than the bottom half of the world's population.[3] The explosion in financial services, and the rise of new communication technologies, created a new class of moneyed entrepreneurs, a number of them mega-rich. A new generation of philanthropists was created as a result. Not all the rich gave. Almost two-thirds of the newly wealthy gave nothing at all. According to the British tax authorities less than 40 per cent of those earning more than £250,000 in the 2016–17 tax year listed a charitable donation on their tax return.[4] The median level of giving among the ultra-rich is just £240 a year.[5] Only 5 per cent of those with more than £10 million gave away more than 0.25 per cent of it each year, according to the wealth management consultancy, the Scorpio Partnership.[6] That is very low compared with the US, where wealthy Americans routinely give 3.5 per cent of their investable assets to charity and take pride in sponsoring buildings and enterprises named after them.[7] But a few wealthy Britons did make substantial donations. The *Million Dollar Donors Report* for 2014 suggests that charitable causes in the UK received close to 300 gifts of more than £1 million, totalling £1.6 billion.[8]

These new philanthropists had large amounts of money in their pockets. Some also had an increased awareness of the growing gap between rich and poor, combined with a conviction that their own business acumen might offer solutions to the world's deep-rooted social problems. The economist Michael Green and the journalist Matthew Bishop coined a new phrase to describe this new philanthropy. They called it 'philanthrocapitalism'.[9] We have detected a number of its salient features in the story of Neil McArthur. These 'new philanthropists' were not just wealthy, they were possessed of enormous personal drive and commitment. Their philanthropy was driven by the quirks and flukes of their own life story, personal experience, political convictions or business interests. This 'new philanthropy' was met with a mixture of public applause, tempered by suspicion and occasionally overt criticism.

The transition from philanthropy to philanthrocapitalism can be illustrated by contrasting the giving of David Sainsbury with that of the British businessmen and women who have more recently followed in his footsteps. Sainsbury has been said to be the single most generous individual philanthropist in the UK over the past five decades. He wrote his first philanthropic cheque, for just £5 – plus 110,000 Sainsbury's shares – in 1967 to establish the charitable trust which, by its 50th anniversary in 2017, had given away more than £1 billion. Part of what makes Sainsbury different from the philanthrocapitalists who followed him was the tender age at which he began his philanthropic career.

David Sainsbury was aged only 26 when he inherited a vast shareholding in what was then the UK's leading supermarket chain, Sainsbury's, founded by his great-grandfather in 1869.[10] His fortune exploded in value when the company floated on the stock market in 1973. But the young Mr Sainsbury didn't just inherit money. He also inherited a family tradition of philanthropy. The Sainsbury family has no fewer than 17 different grant-making trusts established and run by members of three generations of what is now a philanthropic dynasty. Each trust is an independent legal entity with its own board of trustees actively led by an individual member of the Sainsbury family. Each follows their own particular interests, priorities and ways of working. David Sainsbury's is the Gatsby Charitable Foundation, named after F. Scott Fitzgerald's celebrated novel set among the seductive perils of the extravagant wealth set of the Gilded Age of Philanthropy in 1920s America.[11] Unlike Fitzgerald's flamboyant flaneur, David Sainsbury's Gatsby has always functioned discreetly and out of the public eye. So, despite having given away £1 billion of his own money, Sainsbury himself is so little known to the general public that, unlike US mega-philanthropist Bill Gates, he can go about his daily life unrecognized. His interview for this book (see page 231) is a rare example of him making public comment about his philanthropy.

The breadth and depth of his philanthropy prompted the British government to ennoble Sainsbury in 1997. 'This is not one-off giving,' said John Low, chief executive of the Charities Aid Foundation, which partners the *Sunday Times* in producing its Giving List.[12] 'This is a family making a lifetime decision. They have been hugely committed to philanthropy, giving systematically over a long period. Such consistent giving has a profound social impact and builds the capacity to change things in the world.' The former prime minister Gordon Brown was equally unequivocal in his tribute: 'David Sainsbury's 50 years of outstanding philanthropic work has unlocked social progress in a unique way – venturing into areas where no one has gone, testing ideas no one has thought of, sponsoring lifesaving and life enhancing innovations no one has championed and by investing in the best of causes his charities have transformed conditions for millions.'[13]

THIS IS YOUR LIFE

What marks the change from philanthropy to philanthrocapitalism? Philip Beresford, who established the *Sunday Times* Rich List in 1989, chronicled a significant shift. In 1989, he noted, 75 per cent of giving came from those with inherited wealth and only 25 per cent from individuals who had made their fortunes themselves. By 2005 those proportions were completely reversed. Many of this new generation of philanthropists had created considerable riches and had done so very rapidly. Some, like the dot.com billionaires, had done so on the back of technological advances. Others were investment bankers, takeover specialists and financial speculators who had made their fortunes in a booming financial sector. Most of them were seized with the conviction that the skills, acumen and techniques which had brought them such success in business could now be transferred to benevolent activity; they began to use terms like 'venture philanthropy', 'social investment' and 'strategic giving' which sought to bridge what they saw as an old-fashioned gap between the private and voluntary sectors. They dismissed as outmoded the idea that a successful businessman or woman would 'give something back to the community' merely by writing a cheque to a worthy cause.

Yet, for all that, they shared with philanthropists of previous eras a propensity to focus their giving on causes with which they had some personal connection or particular interest – their old school or university which had given them the skills and character to make big money; the hospital which had provided them with life-saving treatment; a charity conducting research into the disease which a relative suffered; their favourite arts or sports organization; or some other serendipitous encounter.

The business guru Charles Handy set out in his 2007 book *The New Philanthropists* to encounter a cross section of these new givers, with revealing results.[14] For some the seeds were sown in childhood. The billionaire David Ross, the co-founder of Carphone Warehouse, who was in 2008 named as one of the hundred richest people in the UK, links his interest in philanthropy back to the vision of education which formed him. The independent boarding school Uppingham required Ross and his fellow pupils to distinguish themselves in four ways: academically, in the arts, in sport, and by making a contribution to the society in which they lived. Those four aspects became embodied in his philanthropy. He has made donations to his old school and university. He has created his own opera festival. He has given time and money to support a football club, Leicester FC, and served on the organizing committee of the 2012 London Olympic Games. He has been a prominent donor to the Conservative Party.

School also impacted, in a rather different way, on the philanthropic activism of Sir Peter Lampl, a Briton who made his fortune in the US as a management consultant but later set up his own private equity and leveraged buyout firm, Sutton. Returning to the UK a very rich man in the 1990s, he visited his old grammar school in Reigate, where he had been a pupil in the 1960s. He discovered that what had been a state-funded school had now become a private one. Many students who had been there in his day, like his best friend who was a farm labourer's son, would now be excluded because their parents were unable to pay. 'A lot of the kids who had gone there with me wouldn't have been able to go there any more,' he told Handy[15]. He found the same problem when he returned to his old Oxford college, Corpus Christi. Two-thirds of the students there had come from state schools in his day, but it too had been transformed into a fortress of the affluent middle classes. Now more than half the students came from fee-paying schools. 'I was appalled,' he recalled. Lampl's response was to establish the Sutton Trust to counter educational disadvantage. He set up 60 summer schools for inner-city state school teenagers to give them the skills to get into top universities and increase social mobility throughout British society.

Others have been shaped in their philanthropy by experiences later in life. Christopher Purvis became wealthy as an investment banker with Warburgs, first in London and then in Japan. Upon discovering that he had become so rich that he never needed to earn any money again, he turned from investment to philanthropy. Having developed a love of Japanese culture in his time running Warburg's operations in Tokyo, he sponsored a series of ventures to foster good cultural, artistic, sporting and business relations between Britain and Japan. Handy includes in his survey of philanthropists the footballer Tony Adams, a former captain of England and the youngest ever captain of Arsenal, who despite his popularity and acclaim became an alcoholic – a problem which even a spell in prison for drink-driving did not solve. Adams gave all the royalties from his autobiography to start Sporting Chance, a clinic to help sportspeople with problems of addiction. The charity, Adams told Charles Handy, 'is also part of my own recovery programme'. Another philanthropist, the merchant banker David Charters, who built his fortune at Deutsche Bank where the bonuses were bountiful, offered Handy a candid explanation for his involvement with the charity Action for Blind People: 'It is my personal nightmare – going blind.'[16]

What is clear from example after example is that private philanthropy depends to a very large extent on the particular life experiences of givers. Philanthropy is very often governed by the random interests or enthusiasms of individual donors. Ironically, then, this newest breed of modern philanthropy is as haphazard and unsystematic as the medieval almsgiving was criticized for being. It may perhaps be even more arbitrary. That might not matter if philanthropy were considered to be nothing more than a way for rich individuals to support pet causes, enhance their reputations, or make their mark in the elite society into which they have moved. The American philosopher Richard Miller, Professor in Ethics and Public Life at Cornell University, defends such an approach. The wealthy have the moral right to choose how to dispose of their money, he argues.[17] But donors are not just giving away their own money. Thanks to the system of tax incentives put in place to promote philanthropy – by successive governments in Britain, throughout Europe, and in the US – the personal choices of philanthropists are being subsidised by taxpayers. We shall examine the thorny problem of tax and accountability in Chapter 15.

PHILANTHROCAPITALISM VERSUS CORPORATE SOCIAL RESPONSIBILITY

When the seminal book *Philanthrocapitalism* by Matthew Bishop and Michael Green was first published in 2008 it carried the subtitle *How the Rich Can Save the World and Why We Should Let Them.*[18] The dominant characteristic of the new phenomenon of philanthrocapitalism, the book claimed, is that the new billionaires and multimillionaires are changing the face of giving by applying to philanthropy the same keen business techniques and attitudes which had enabled them to accrue such vast fortunes so swiftly. Rather than simply writing a cheque, the ultra-wealthy are now becoming personally involved, starting their own philanthropic ventures, helping directly run them, and applying market-based solutions to the causes they take up. They deploy business jargon to talk of 'effective philanthropy' as a 'social investment' – and want to invest their time and energy as well as their cash. They talk of a new model of 'strategic grant-making'. In one sense there is nothing new in this: Carnegie and Rockefeller, as we have seen, were doing much the same thing at the beginning of the previous century. They too were self-made men who had earned huge sums in an unregulated sphere of the economy and had done so early in life before turning to philanthropy to find fulfilment. They too had been driven by the conviction that their ambition, business acumen and strategic mindset made them more qualified to decide how their philanthropic gifts should be spent than were the recipients of their largesse. And they too were determined that their profit-making strategies should govern their philanthropy. 'It is well to remember,' chastized Andrew Carnegie in 1899, 'that it requires the exercise of no less ability than that which acquired the wealth, to use it so as to be really beneficial to the community.' Bill Gates, a century later, was doing little more than echoing that sentiment when he told the graduating class of Harvard in 2007: 'To turn caring into action, we need to see a problem, see a solution and see the impact.'[19]

All this goes well beyond the notion of Corporate Social Responsibility (CSR) – the idea that companies must conduct their business in a way which takes account of their impact on everyone the business touches. It is worth briefly comparing philanthrocapitalism with corporate philanthropy. CSR developed in the 1950s and 1960s. By the 1990s it had become widely accepted in the business world. Interestingly, it was subject to many of the same ambiguities as philanthrocapitalism. It too was perceived as having mixed motives. CSR was thought to improve the general reputation of the company and thereby induce customers to buy products. It was seen as a way of stealing a march on competitors. It was thought it might attract or motivate its employees. Business leaders hoped it might forestall government attempts at regulation or increased taxation. A report by the Committee Encouraging Corporate Philanthropy in 2006 found that companies engaged in CSR had motivations which were typically 54 per cent charitable, 35 per cent strategic and 11 per cent commercial.[20] In a survey by McKinsey in 2008 almost 90 per cent of senior executives admitted that their firm sought business benefits from their corporate philanthropy.[21]

Like philanthrocapitalism, corporate philanthropy uses a variety of techniques: direct cash grants, in-kind support, secondments and placements, payroll giving (matched pound for pound by the company), staff fundraising, and employees volunteering to work with good causes. Like philanthrocapitalists, corporate philanthropists set up their own foundations, funded directly by contributions from the firm. This allows the business to time and control the tax efficiency of its donations, giving more when company profits are high. Companies with reputational problems are often particularly prominent in pursuing CSR approaches. Six of the top ten corporate philanthropists in the UK in 2017 were in the banking or finance sector, which had still not recovered its reputation after the global banking crisis of a decade earlier. It is perhaps no coincidence that at a time when Goldman Sachs was making enormous profits, during a time of economic downturn, the bank announced a $100 million programme to provide business training to women in developing nations, knowing, as the *Financial Times* put it, that 'philanthropic work such as this tends to soften a bank's image'.[22] Drug companies – often controversial for their large profits – are particularly prominent in CSR activity; Merck and Johnson & Johnson are among the six corporations which provide almost two-thirds of the CSR spend in the US, while AstraZeneca and GlaxoSmithKline were two of the four companies accounting for more than three-quarters of the British total.[23]

Like philanthrocapitalists, corporate philanthropists are open to the accusation that the causes they prefer are very much determined by the personal whim of the man or woman at the top. The personal interests of the CEO and board members have by far the greatest weight in determining the focus of company philanthropy, according to a McKinsey survey. This can produce unstrategic shifts in philanthropic practice: when Hank Paulson, a noted environmentalist, was the chairman of Goldman Sachs, the firm championed the environment as their major philanthropic focus, but when Paulson's successor, Lloyd Blankfein, took control, the bank switched to supporting business training for women in developing countries. The personal preferences of senior executives seem far more influential than any link to the core competency of the firm. That creates 'potential for abuse', warns Thomas W. Dunfee, Professor of Social Responsibility in Business at Wharton Business School.[24] 'GSK, Merck, Altria and Bayer are among the many firms that make major contributions to the arts. Why global pharmaceuticals or tobacco companies as organizations would have special insights in this domain is not clear,' Dunfee observes.

Suspicion of corporate motives comes from both the left and right, as it does with philanthrocapitalism. Critics on the left insist that, whatever the rhetoric, any proclaimed desire to improve the social good will always be subservient to business strategies. Critics on the right insist that it is not the job of big companies to get involved in philanthropy at all – a criticism which dates back to an essay by Milton Friedman in 1970 attacking the new phenomenon of corporate social responsibility.[25] Friedman denounced CSR, saying that the only social responsibility of business is to create wealth and profit. Once a company has made money for its shareholders they are then free to dispose of their profits to charity if they so desire. CSR was, to Friedman, a form of hypocritical window-dressing which undermines the free market. Those who claim that business is not concerned 'merely' with profit but also with promoting desirable 'social' ends are, according to Friedman, 'preaching pure and unadulterated socialism'. That is not a view much in fashion today, perhaps because most shareholders understand that corporate philanthropy can enhance long-term profitability. Or perhaps it is because there is a wider understanding of corporate social responsibility, which focuses not only on what a company does with its profits but also on how it makes those profits in the first place. Stressing out your workforce but then offering them sports facilities to relax and de-stress in is no longer seen to add up in moral terms.

LESSONS PHILANTHROPY MUST LEARN FROM BUSINESS

The most recent developments in Corporate Social Responsibility offer a useful model for the enrichment of philanthrocapitalism. Today there is an increased tendency to allow philanthropic concerns to impact upon business models, in what Michael Porter and Mark Kramer in the *Harvard Business Review*[26] call 'corporate social profitability'. This next stage of CSR is typified by a project in which Danone yoghurt teamed up with Grameen Bank in Bangladesh to develop a low-cost yoghurt that provides 30 per cent of a Bangladeshi child's recommended daily nutrients. Porter and Kramer speak of 'shared value' and creating a win-win result in which a company creates economic value for itself in a way that also creates value for society. 'Businesses must reconnect company success with social progress,' they write, rather than leaving important social issues at the periphery of CSR. Such shared-value partnerships are on the rise, with 87 per cent of leading charities and 93 per cent of leading companies exploring opportunities in this area, according to the 2013 Company Giving Almanac.[27]

Perhaps the best example of this in Britain is the continuing partnership between the pharmaceutical company GlaxoSmithKline and the international development charity Save the Children. The scheme, which three years running has been voted the most admired partnership between business and charity,[28] was renewed to run for another five years from 2018. It sets out to combine the expertise of the business and voluntary sectors in an attempt to save the lives of some of the 15,000 children under the age of five who die – every day – from preventable causes.

Using GSK's global expertise in research and development of medicines and vaccinations and Save the Children's experience of delivering healthcare to remote and marginalized children and families, the partnership reached over five million people in its first five years, including 2.8 million children under five in 45 countries. A million children were screened and treated for malnutrition. Some 187,000 children were treated for diarrhoea, malaria or pneumonia. The training and equipping of health workers and health centres in the poorest countries has been extensively improved as a result.

Most innovatively, the pharmaceutical giant and the charity worked together to reformulate chlorhexidine, the antiseptic in a GSK mouthwash. They turned it into a gel to prevent the fatal bloodstream infection sepsis which kills 400,000 newborn babies a year in developing countries. The gel, which is applied to the stump of the umbilical cord after it has been cut, has been designed for use in remote communities. It is heat-stable and comes in single-use tear-open sachets so it can be easily administered by health workers and mothers in the communities who most need it. In addition, GSK employees raised £3.3 million for the charity through voluntary fundraising efforts. The relationship between the business and charity is only one of a number developed by Save the Children under the leadership of its former chief executive, Justin Forsyth. Such ambitious strategic partnerships, which draw on the expertise both of donor and recipient, offer a useful paradigm for philanthropy.

So, too, does another model developed out of corporate social responsibility, the concept of fair trade – the idea that companies in the rich world should pay a price to producers in the poor world which, at a minimum, covers the costs of production and which therefore makes it more likely that they are able to afford the essentials of food, education and healthcare. Retailers who want their products to carry the accredited Fairtrade mark must also pay an additional premium to help producers improve their businesses and the communities in which they work. The movement, which has grown rapidly since the 1980s, also sets out to develop a relationship of partnership between buyer and seller which has affinities with the relationship between donor and recipient. As concern for the environment has risen up the social and political agenda, fair trade has also come to embrace the notion of sustainability.

A pioneer in this in the UK has been the Co-operative supermarket chain, which was founded 170 years ago out of the need to eliminate the exploitation of workers and customers alike in the infancy of industrial capitalism. With shops in every postal district in the UK, it has made Fairtrade products accessible to its 8 million customers throughout the nation. In the 1990s it began selling Fairtrade coffee. By the start of the twenty-first century it had expanded its Fairtrade offering to a wide range of products – from sugar, tea and cocoa to bananas, blueberries, roses and even cotton wool. Today it has a 100 per cent Fairtrade chocolate confectionery range and became the first retailer to launch its own-brand Fairtrade range of wines – of which it is now the world's largest retailer. In addition, the Co-op has a Beyond Fair Trade scheme which enables the supermarket chain to make supplementary investments in the local communities in which its producers live and work. Fair trade has become big business, with fair trade products available in most British supermarkets.

The UK is the market leader in selling fair trade products – with around £2 billion sold in 2017 – but sales are also strong in Germany and the US, with the latter now accounting for more than $1 billion of total global sales of more than $9 billion.[29] Fair trade grew more than 8 per cent in the previous twelve months. More than 30,000 different products with the fair trade-certified label, produced by 1.6 million farmers and workers, are now available in 150 countries worldwide. The value of all this to producers in developing countries is clear, but fair trade has also been an important component in the Co-op's boosting of its own brand in a highly competitive marketplace. The partnership is a clear example of a win-win exercise in corporate philanthropy. It is clear that corporate social responsibility, for all its mixed motives and variable delivery, has real potential to contribute to the social good. This model of true partnership is, as we shall see, one which needs to be developed in much contemporary philanthropy.

BILL GATES AND THE LAST REALM
UNTOUCHED BY CAPITALISM

The models at work in philanthrocapitalism, by contrast, are frequently not so consultative. This new breed of philanthropists, according to the authors of *Philanthrocapitalism*, Matthew Bishop and Michael Green, insist that 'effective giving is about more than the money'. It must also be 'strategic', 'market conscious', 'impact orientated', 'knowledge-based', often 'high engagement', and always driven by the goal of maximizing the 'leverage' of the donor's money.[30] The new generation of self-made men and women – though they are largely men – implicitly assume that the world of good causes to which they have turned their attention is ineffective. It is, they believe, in desperate need of reshaping. And that is best done by taking the secrets and techniques they used to build their business empires – and applying them to philanthropy. They therefore seek to improve the efficiency, effectiveness, capacity and accountability of charity through hard-nosed strategy, performance metrics and cost-benefit calculus. They see their benevolence in terms of an investment targeted at a specific problem to which they can bring a specific solution.

'They do not see a difference between the way they look at their investment portfolios and the way they look at their philanthropy,' writes the fundraising consultant, Susan Raymond.[31] Their vocabulary is full of terms like 'rigorous due diligence', 'scalability', 'return on capital', 'leveraging the investment', 'accountability to stakeholders', 'agreed targets', 'excellence in delivery' and 'accurately measured outcomes'.[32] Their background as successful entrepreneurs also leads them to become more deeply involved in their charities than do traditional philanthropists. They go so far, says Dr Raymond, as to 'co-mingle commercial investments with donated dollars to get the job done'. So confident are they in their own business acumen that they prefer 'giving while living' rather than endowing foundations in perpetuity as did the philanthropists of the Carnegie and Rockefeller era. Linsey McGoey, author of *No Such Thing as a Free Gift: The Gates*

Foundation and the Price of Philanthropy, says these red-in-tooth-and claw entrepreneurs 'want to revolutionise the last realm untouched by the hyper-competitive, profit-oriented world of financial capitalism: the world of charitable giving.'[33]

One of the favourite phrases of this new generation of donors is 'strategic philanthropy'. A leading advocate, Paul Brest – a former Dean of Stanford Law School who was for 12 years president of the $10 billion Hewlett Foundation – defines strategic philanthropy as 'the setting of clear goals, developing sound evidence-based strategies for achieving them, measuring progress along the way, and determining whether you were actually successful in reaching the goals'. Philanthrocapitalism, with billions of dollars at its disposal, he argues, should not merely distribute cash to worthy causes but target major problems and then work scientifically and strategically to address them using those innovative business techniques.

Undoubtedly the greatest exemplar of this is Bill Gates who, with his wife Melinda, has impressively pledged to give away as much as 95 per cent of their wealth in a fight against global poverty and ill-health. In a TED talk in 2009 Gates set out his philosophy on the need for philanthropy to correct the failure of the free market to address major global issues. 'There's more money put into baldness drugs than are put into malaria. Now, baldness, it's a terrible thing,' he said, provoking laughter among his audience. 'And rich men are afflicted. And so that's why that priority has been set.' Ten times more is spent on treatments for baldness than is spent on fighting malaria.[34] By contrast, malaria, which once infected most of the globe, has been eradicated from rich countries. 'So this leads to the paradox that because the disease is only in the poorer countries, it doesn't get much investment.'[35] His response was to found the Bill & Melinda Gates Foundation which, since it began in 2000, has given away more than $45 billion.[36] Its work includes a Global Health programme which has helped virtually eradicate polio, is combatting malaria and tuberculosis, and has taken on treating HIV/AIDS in the developing world. Gates's gifts have – without doubt – saved tens of millions of lives. Anyone doubting the tremendous success which philanthrocapitalism can have needs look no further than the Gates Foundation. 'I am an optimist,' he told the audience. 'Any tough problem, I think it can be solved.' We will look in detail at the work of Gates in the next two chapters.

Gates is not the only philanthropist to think that what worked in business must work in philanthropy. The strategy which made Warren Buffett one of the world's most successful investors was to carefully select companies he thinks have a particular expertise and then invest in them, often for decades. When it comes to philanthropy, he adopts a similar technique. Rather than becoming involved in a hands-on way personally, he chose to make a massive philanthropic donation – approximately $30 billion worth of shares in his business, Berkshire Hathaway – to the Gates Foundation in 2006. When asked why the man who was then the world's second-richest man was giving away his money to the world's richest man rather than giving it to the government to dispense in aid, Buffett replied: 'Bill and Melinda will do a better job than . . . the federal treasury.' Philanthropists 'should seek out talent to distribute their money just as they sought out talent to acquire it'.[37] He had chosen to give it to Bill Gates because, when it came to philanthropy, he is the 'best in the business'.[38] As a gift it was said at the time to be double the total given away by Carnegie and Rockefeller put together.[39]

In Britain a key exponent of the philanthrocapitalist approach is Sir Christopher Hohn. He has gone a step further with the philanthrocapitalist model by setting up a hedge fund in 2003 which he named the Children's Investment Management (TCI) Fund. Part of its profits were automatically channelled into a charity – the Children's Investment Fund Foundation which was chaired by his then wife Jamie Cooper-Hohn. This was a revolutionary financial structure. It brought together the most aggressive, opaque and secretive form of contemporary capitalism with the new desire to use business methods to further laudable social aims – an amalgam which *The Economist* characterized as 'the combination of ruthless profiteering and philanthropy'. To hammer home the point it added: 'charity and rapacity sit surprisingly comfortably together, both in Mr Hohn's person and in his business'.[40]

Sir Christopher – knighted in the Queen's Birthday Honours in 2014 'for services to philanthropy and international development' – has a fierce reputation in the world of finance. Hedge funds developed a mechanism traditionally used by investors to hedge against risk and turned it into an instrument to make extravagant profit. They greatly increase the potential for money-making but also increase the risk of loss. The sophisticated databases they establish enable their managers to find out more about individual companies than the average investor can. They then buy enough shares to get a vote on the company's board and press those companies to sell off less profitable divisions – or force them to buy back their own stock and improve the value of the hedge fund's shareholding.

Chris Hohn's 'activist' style as a hedge fund manager has involved him in a series of prolonged takeover battles, asset sales and mergers which have made him 'powerful' and 'feared', *The Economist* wrote. His role in derailing an offer from the German Stock Exchange to take over the London Stock Exchange in 2005 led to the ousting of the Deutsche Börse's long-serving chief executive, Werner Seifert. Afterwards the German financier wrote a book entitled *The Invasion of Locusts* – with Hohn as the 'leader of the swarm'.[41] Hohn's activities heightened concerns about the way in which activist investors can determine the fate of the world's largest corporations. In 2007 he launched an attack on the Dutch bank ABN AMRO that helped trigger its sale. (One of the junior partners in Hohn's hedge fund at the time was Rishi Sunak, who became a multimillionaire through TCI and in 2020 went on to become Chancellor of the Exchequer in the Conservative government of Boris Johnson.)[42] In 2008 he engaged in a tussle with the Japanese electricity firm J-Power which helped push its main fund to a 40 per cent loss.[43] In 2012 he sued the Indian government for pricing coal below international market prices and thereby reducing the profits that Hohn could expect from the shares his fund held in the world's largest coal company, Coal India, which was state-controlled.[44]

In 2013 Hohn became embroiled in a controversy over the privatization of Royal Mail when it emerged, just two weeks after the British Coalition government had put the postal service up for sale, that Hohn had acquired a large number of the shares which critics said the government had sold too cheaply.[45] The Business Secretary, Vince Cable, had claimed that the shares would be sold by the government to 'long-term, blue chip' institutional investors. But Hohn's fund, by 'buying ferociously', acquired more than 5 per cent – some of which he sold at a huge profit just three months later.[46] In 2016 the man now described as 'Europe's most aggressive activist investor' wrote to executives at the embattled German car maker Volkswagen. He had just built up a €1.2 billion stake in the company. His letter unveiled what Hohn called Volkswagen's 'dirty secret': excessive pay for managers had encouraged aggressive management behaviour which resulted in the scandal of Volkswagen installing illegal software in its diesel engines to mask their excessive levels of nitrogen oxide pollution.[47] This was 'corporate excess on an epic scale' in which 'management has been rewarded for failure,' he claimed.[48] And so he has continued. At the end of 2018 he called for the ousting of managers at Ireo, an Indian property developer with links to US president Donald Trump, after they were accused of stealing vast amounts of investors' cash.[49] Over the years Hohn has boldly picked fights with governments and companies across the world in pursuit of higher returns.

Yet, for all his financial ruthlessness, Christopher Hohn never forgot something he saw early in his career. After studying accounting and economics at Southampton University, Hohn, the son of a Jamaican car mechanic who grew up in Surrey, took a banking job in the Philippines. The image of children scavenging on rubbish dumps for food there stayed with him. After the Philippines he went on to graduate from Harvard Business School and then worked his way up the ladder in Wall Street where he ended up working for the renowned hedge fund investor Richard Perry. Over seven years Hohn produced outsized profits while managing $1 billion of assets for European investors.

At a party in Harvard he had met his future wife, Jamie Cooper, who was studying public administration as a prelude to working for various charitable organizations. When he decided to go it alone as a fund manager, the couple, over dinner at a London restaurant, devised a plan to combine his financial acumen with her philanthropic expertise. Hohn came up with a unique business/charity hybrid in which a hedge fund would channel a proportion of its fees and profits into a charity to improve the lives of children in developing countries. Hohn secured funding for the plan from pension funds, insurers and prominent universities including Yale. In the first three years of its operation it provided returns of more than 40 per cent – thanks to Hohn's skilful choice of investments and successful campaigns to force change in a variety of companies. In 2006 Hohn donated £230 million to the foundation, making him that year Britain's most generous philanthropist.

The Children's Investment Fund Foundation is now one of the UK's largest charities and proclaims itself to be 'the world's largest philanthropy that focuses specifically on improving children's lives'. With offices in London, Nairobi and New Delhi, it works with a wide range of partners in areas such as nutrition, education, maternal and child health – including de-worming – adolescent sexual health and tackling child slavery and exploitation. It also supports 'smart ways to slow down and stop climate change'. The language it uses on its website to describe its approach offers a classic illustration of the philanthrocapitalist technique of applying a corporate psychology to the philanthropic sphere.[50] 'I want to solve problems, not make grants,' it begins, quoting Chris Hohn. It continues:

> Our programmes are designed to support bold ideas to seemingly intractable problems . . .
>
> We know that the returns on smart investments in areas such as children's early development and adolescent girls are especially high. So we aim to play a catalytic role as a funder and influencer to deliver urgent and lasting change at scale.
>
> We place significant emphasis on quality data and evidence. For many of our grants, we work with partners to measure and evaluate progress to achieve large-scale and sustainable impact.

The buzz words are clear: 'bold ideas', 'returns on smart investments', 'catalytic role', 'funder and influencer', 'change at scale', 'quality data', 'measure and evaluate', 'sustainable impact'. The organization has a 'grant portfolio tool' and deploys 'smart philanthropy' with 'a rigorous business-like approach'. As the 2020 coronavirus pandemic took hold, Hohn, ever the problem-solver, gave £3 million to fund the development of a rapid diagnostic detection device.

His then wife, Jamie Cooper, explained the approach to an interviewer: 'We wanted to publicly make the statement that if you're making these kinds of profits, getting these kinds of management fees, you should be doing more than writing a few cheques.'[51] The foundation selects its targets rigorously. One of its programme interventions came after evidence emerged of a gap in which children were being neglected in programmes treating adults with HIV/AIDS in developing countries. By underwriting the cost of children's antiretroviral medications, the foundation helped create a market in an area of children's health which had been long neglected. The number of children who were properly treated for HIV increased and the gap between AIDS treatment offered to adults and children was reduced.

But the work of the foundation only begins when they make a donation. Like venture capitalists, venture philanthropists 'do as much, if not more, afterwards. It's an evidence-based approach to both the need, and the intervention,' Cooper added. So, after the donation has been made, the foundation monitors and evaluates progress early on. As a result it often 'changes course, sometimes quite radically, if we're not on target'. The whole approach, Cooper told the *Guardian*, is 'just like a business: constant assessment, constant course correction. Finding the algebraic equation that will get us to where we need to be.' The approach is what she calls 'management through to success'. The whole process takes time:

> You spend ages researching areas and find they're not right for what you want to achieve – but something else is. So, you want to improve literacy in a developing country, which means improving school attendance. Turns out the cheapest and most effective way to do that is de-worming. But for de-worming to work, it has to be national. And that takes time, drawing up a national programme with a government. But if you want a quality return, it has to be done.

Encouraged by the ambitious scale of Chris Hohn's approach to investment, the Children's Investment Fund Foundation thinks big. In 2012 it was the driving force behind a summit in London, hosted by Prime Minister David Cameron and attended by prime ministers from Africa and the Indian subcontinent, designed to tackle children's malnutrition all around the world.[52]

Links between Hohn's hedge fund and the foundation, of which his wife Jamie was the chief executive, have been unravelled since the couple divorced acrimoniously in 2014. Jamie Cooper-Hohn reverted to the name Jamie Cooper and stood down as chief executive of the charity. The fund no longer donates money to the foundation on a contractual basis, though there is provision for it to do so on a discretionary basis. The couple remain as trustees of the foundation but Ms Cooper has set up a new charity, Big Win Philanthropy, with a similar brief to 'invest in children and young people in developing countries'. It gave out grants totalling £1.3 million in 2017, according to accounts filed in 2018. The couple's battle in the divorce courts, which lasted a fortnight in the High Court in London, afforded a rare glimpse into the world of the secretive hedge fund manager. Hohn, who has avoided media interviews throughout his career, described himself to the judge as one of the world's 10 best investors and 'an unbelievable moneymaker'. Yet he insisted: 'I don't really care about money, I gave away all the money

I made to charity.'[53] His words seemed to bear out the judgement of *The Economist* from seven years earlier that Chris Hohn 'has never gone in for the trappings of wealth' but rather 'seems driven less by greed than by a desire to be proved right, and to win . . . the money is simply evidence that he won'.[54] The divorce judge in 2014 observed that the couple lived a 'Swatch lifestyle rather than Rolex one'[55] and awarded Ms Cooper what was then the largest divorce settlement ever made in the English courts, ordering Hohn to pay his ex-wife £337 million, around a third of his accumulated wealth.[56] The court judgement in the divorce estimated that Hohn's total donations to the foundation had topped $4.5 billion.[57]

Despite the divorce both the billionaire and the charity have continued to flourish. Even after a year of negative results in 2016, when the whole hedge fund industry was plunged into crisis, strong growth in 2017 made Hohn one of the six highest-earning hedge fund managers in the world and one of the UK's highest-paid businessmen.[58] No one suggests that he is anything but sincere in his philanthropy – indeed close friends say he is passionate about his charity in private[59] – but the foundation may have proved useful protection at a time when the reputation of hedge funds was under attack and Hohn cut his pay by almost a quarter in 2017 – to £215 million – despite a sharp increase in profits at his hedge fund.[60] Still, his total personal wealth at the end of 2019 was estimated by *Forbes* magazine at $3.1 billion. In 2020 the *Financial Times* reported that hedge funds had just had their best annual performance in a decade with Hohn, whom it described as 'back in the top 20 managers of all time', as one of the top performers.[61]

The value of the philanthropic foundation's endowment had by 2020 now grown to $5.2 billion, according to its website. It has 'a growing portfolio of charitable grants with a value of over three-quarters of a billion dollars'.[62] In the 2017 financial year it gave out grants totalling $208 million. According to the *Sunday Times* 2020 Giving List, Hohn donated £348 million in the twelve months to May 2020.[63] The charity maintains the same distinctive approach. When the foundation advertised for an Executive Director of Finance and Operations recently, the recruitment pack described the charity as 'flexible and innovative with a high appetite for risk'. It added: 'We strive to be nimble and take risks where the potential pay-off is big. We are not afraid to "fail fast", learn and try something new.' The foundation is 'entrepreneurial and performance-led'. And it concluded:

> As part of our commercial DNA, we will always be clear about how we intend to manage performance and we expect our partners to do the same. We always seek to clarify and align incentives (political, financial and intrinsic) to increase the probability of success.

The Children's Investment Fund Foundation is the complete archetype of the approach of contemporary philanthrocapitalism.

HOW THE RICH CHOOSE THEIR CHARITY

Hedge fund philanthropy may be the quintessence of philanthrocapitalism, but there is a wide range of other specialist types. As well as venture philanthropy the new generation of givers talk of 'managerial philanthropy' or 'entrepreneurial philanthropy'. All are business-oriented, but they demonstrate almost as many variations as there are benevolent business people. Managerial philanthropists donate their organizational expertise without contributing any cash. Entrepreneurial philanthropists, who offer both human and financial capital, specialize in assisting with start-up charities. Other philanthropists offer a combination of all these approaches.

All these new givers are bolstered in their ideas by a new class of philanthropy professionals. Although many philanthropists choose their charities based on their life experiences, others are impelled by a general urge to 'give something back' and then need help in choosing their charity. There is now a philanthropy industry designed to assist both philanthropists in search of good causes and charities that want to discover the best ways to approach the rich for money. One such website proclaims: 'Every philanthropist is different, so our Centre for Philanthropy will work out a tailor-made approach for you. Our flexible vehicles allow you to have the maximum impact.'[64]

This 'consumption philanthropy', as it has been dubbed by Paul Schervish of the Center on Wealth and Philanthropy at Boston College,[65] is supported by a raft of professionals inside the banking industry in both the UK and US. Barclays, Standard Chartered and J. P. Morgan now offer specialist philanthropy services to their wealthier clients. So does Coutts & Co, the private bank in which the Queen of England keeps her money.

As many as 28 per cent of professional advisory firms offer some form of philanthropy advice, according to Philanthropy Impact, a membership organization working to inspire philanthropy and social investment.[66]

But there are growing numbers of increasingly specialized bodies to service the new philanthrocapitalism industry. Some, like New Philanthropy Capital, offer donors advice on their giving. NPC was founded by two Goldman Sachs bankers, Gavyn Davies, then its chief economist, and Peter Wheeler, who developed an interest in philanthropy but decided one day, chatting in the Goldman Sachs canteen, that there wasn't enough 'hard-headed, independent, high-quality' information available to allow them to make an informed decision on where their money might have maximum impact. What was needed was the charity equivalent of the kind of data and intelligence produced in the banking world by an equity-research firm. Davies and Wheeler founded New Philanthropy Capital to fill the gap they saw in the philanthropic marketplace. The aim was to produce reports on charities which would act like those that provided bankers with 'buy' recommendations in the commercial sector. It gathers information direct from Britain's 162,000 charities but also from the increasing number of academics who work on philanthropy issues.[67] NPC is now only one of a number of similar research organizations which service the philanthropy industry. Individual would-be philanthropists often approach such bodies when they first think about giving.

When John Stone sold Lombard International Assurance in 2004 for £124 million he had what he described as 'a fairly modest lifestyle'.[68] He decided he wanted to give away more than £100 million of his newly acquired fortune.[69] But he had no idea to whom he wanted to give it. So he approached NPC. 'John and his wife Vanessa weren't particularly issue-focused,' said a member of NPC's staff. 'He didn't know what an NGO (non-governmental organization) was. So we drew up a list, and they chose a pilot portfolio of ten charities, very different, in water, girls' education, microfinance, in India, Africa, Asia. Over the next three years, they visited them all.' Stone later described the process to Beth Breeze of the Centre for Philanthropy at the University of Kent:

When we began, we didn't have a passion for any particular cause, we really started with a blank piece of paper. We sought advice, from Coutts and New Philanthropy Capital, who asked us lots of questions and got us thinking about how we could achieve the biggest effect with the money we had. We developed some criteria for our giving: we wanted to give hand-ups, not hand-outs; we were more inclined to support developing countries where there's no welfare state and our money can achieve more; and we decided to focus on three areas: children, clean water and microfinance. We don't want to start our own charities; we'd rather support others doing good work than re-invent the wheel. We'd also rather support smaller organisations as I can relate to their entrepreneurial outlook and it's easier to get involved with them than with bigger more bureaucratic charities. But our initial 'pilot portfolio' of ten projects includes investments in organisations that are small, medium and large, because we decided to experience being involved in all types of charities.[70]

As a result of their travels the couple decided that water and sanitation were at the root of so many other problems in the developing world. NPC identified three countries – Tanzania, Cambodia and Zambia – where their money would do most good. It analysed organizations capable of productively spending £1 million over three years. The Stones made more visits and, after monitoring the outcomes of their donations, scaled up their giving to £5 million a year. By 2019 it was up to £9 million.[71]

'It's unashamedly a business-like approach,' Stone said. 'NPC works like a stock-market analyst examining and tracking a sector . . . I'm certainly trying to run my giving like a business, as far as possible. Some NGO people think we shouldn't, but really every [enterprise] is the same, bar the profit principle.'[72] By 2011 Stone looked back and reflected: 'It has taken me five years to scale up my philanthropy to be able to make significant grants. I wanted to be sure that my money would be put to the best possible use and have the biggest impact on those I chose to help. It does take time to give strategically in this way, but I believe it is better to proceed slowly and carefully, to ensure that philanthropic donations are committed wisely, which should bring more long-term benefit to society and, as others will be more inspired by seeing money well-spent, it should eventually result in bigger funding for charities.'[73]

The professional advice and patient groundwork paid off. By 2017 John Stone, and his stepson Charlie Edwards, were running their family foundation with complete self-assurance. 'Our trustee meetings,' Stone told the Coutts *Million Pound Donors Report* in 2017, were now run 'a bit like the board of a private equity company, which is fairly unusual. Charitable organisations generally talk about "beneficiaries". We hate that word, we find it very patronising, so when we are providing access to safe water and sanitation, we talk about providing WASH [Water, Sanitation and Health] solutions to households, to consumers, not "beneficiaries".' Their largest investment – more than $10 million over five years – has been into market-based solutions in Asia. 'We've seen access to sanitation in rural Cambodia grow from 20 per cent when we started to over 55 per cent today, on track to reach 100 per cent by 2030. A total transformation.'[74] The idea that solutions must be 'market-based' is important to them. Initiatives which rely upon unending donor funding are unsustainable. 'Africa is littered with thousands of water pumps that don't work, because they don't generate revenue to pay for maintenance. So years later they are broken with no money to fix them,' Stone laments.

They have even developed the confidence to embark upon riskier activities. Charlie Edwards talks proudly about their sponsorship of The Boxing Academy, an 'alternative education provider' that takes children who have been excluded from state schools and are about to be sent to a Pupil Referral Unit. 'Its innovative model evolved around boxing and providing role models for young men, but it was in a pretty precarious state when we came across it,' Edwards told the 2017 *Million Pound Donors Report*. The Stone foundation provided £75,000 a year of unrestricted funding to the school, which was recently awarded 'free school' status by the state-school inspectors. 'It's now very stable and doesn't need external funding – and they're looking to roll the model out.' His stepfather added:

> That highlights a general philosophy of ours, which is to support pioneering and innovative developments. We have a much higher risk profile than many philanthropists, which is fine because we are small and, as I am an entrepreneur, we can make decisions quickly. I made my money from taking risks in business, so am much more inclined to take risks philanthropically in a sector which is generally very conservative and risk-averse . . . Because we're prepared to take risk, we expect things to go wrong, which most charities hate. We make it very clear: we know things go wrong, so don't cover it up – come and talk to us about it. It's about openness and mutual trust.[75]

Another business method which John Stone has been keen to import from the commercial world is the practice of 'leveraging' their donations – obtaining promises from other funders that they will match his contribution to a particular project. 'You have to feel that the people you work with are going to make your pound go further,' says Charlie Edwards.

One of the biggest of his co-funders is Impetus-PEF, a trust founded in 2013 by two groups of City of London financiers with backgrounds in private equity and venture capital. Impetus-Private Equity Foundation offers another model within the range of philanthrocapitalism strategies. It too seeks to pioneer a new way of working with 'a long-term approach, rigorous performance management, a focus on impact, and the capacity to scale high-performing organisations'. But for every £1 it gives out in grants as 'seed money', it provides between £3 and £4 of practical support from both its in-house investment managers and external experts. Impetus-PEF specializes in assisting charities which work with children who are disadvantaged by poverty, discrimination, poor school performance, or limited access to university or employment. To support them it has assembled a pool of some 350 experts in 40 organizations – including top law and accounting firms such as Ashurst, Blackstone, Clifford Chance, Deloitte, McKinsey, PwC and Warburgs – offering world-class management consulting or professional services. Free of charge, they provide hands-on management support to charity chief executives and senior managers. Their in-house investment team work hand in hand with those who manage charity finances. Highly skilled volunteers from the extensive Impetus-PEF network work, without being paid, alongside charity staff to improve business plans, strategic reviews, financial systems, fundraising and IT systems. They also conduct leadership coaching. In 2016 these volunteers provided £1.4 million worth of expertise to more than 40,000 young people.[76]

Their work is precisely targeted. 'Our research shows that children on free school meals are twice as likely to be out of education, employment and training when they leave school as their better-off peers,' says Samantha Windett, the director of policy at Impetus. Worse than that, 'even if they get the same qualification as their better-off peers, they are still 50 per cent more likely to be out of education and employment'. Worse still, they then fall into what she calls 'a youth jobs gap, which shows that young people from disadvantaged backgrounds are actually being locked out of the labour market'.[77] The charities which Impetus supports attempt to deal with this disadvantage in a variety of ways. One, Magic Breakfast, delivers food and support to 480 schools directly and to more than 1,800 schools through government-funded partnership with another charity, Family Action. This means a healthy breakfast is provided every day for 280,000 children who go to school hungry.[78] The children who get fed make the equivalent of two months extra progress every year. Another Impetus charity, ThinkForward, provides additional coaching at school to pupils from the age of 13 to 18 who are deemed to be most at risk of never finding a job. And a third, Football Beyond Borders (like The Boxing Academy) works with alienated teenagers, attempting to re-engage them by developing their football skills alongside a more conventional education.[79]

PHILANTHROPY THAT CHANGES LIVES

The impact of this help on the lives of disadvantaged young people can be totally transformative. That is clear from the moving accounts related by individuals who have profited from the help of the many charities which Impetus supports in education, training and preparing for the world of work. The Impetus-funded charity the Access Project tells the story on its website of a student named Zein who was having difficulties at secondary school. English was his second language; he had arrived from war-torn Lebanon where his life had been in danger; and his father was dying of cancer. Then the Access Project arrived in his school and offered him additional tuition. 'I met my tutors twice a week,' he says. 'They go to work with you. They help you understand your course better. It's such a beautiful feeling'. The result was a place at Warwick University. As well as particular problems the project addresses systemic disadvantage. A second Access Project student, Salimah, had always wanted to go to university but, she says, 'I didn't know many people who had come from Hackney and ended up in Oxford'. Only 2 per cent of the intake at England's most selective universities are students from low-income backgrounds. 'Access to university, and making access fair, is a huge issue, nationally,' says Andrew Berwick, one-time director of the project. 'Impetus have been an amazing support for us over the last couple of years.' Before Impetus-PEF began working with the charity, 30 per cent of their students were accepted to top-tier universities; two years later the percentage had risen to 56 per cent.[80] 'They've given us the tools and the support to become a more impactful and effective organisation,' says Berwick. 'It really makes a difference down to the individual student level. What it means for someone like Salimah is we are able to identify exactly what kind of support she needed.' Salimah herself recalls: 'Sometimes I was all over the place, disorganized. Being part of the project really gave me a sense of direction.'[81] She got As in all her A level exams and a place at Oxford to study French and Arabic.

There are similar stories from the world of work. A young woman named Fisa had done well at school but became withdrawn at college after her brother died. For two years she ceased communicating with her family. 'I stopped talking to everyone. It was the most blank phase of my life,' she says. Then one day her social-security benefits officer introduced her to a programme called Spear run by the charity Resurgo which is also funded by Impetus-PEF. 'That was the first time since everything went wrong in my life that someone had sat there and spoken to me about my situation and asked me whether I was just OK,' she recalls. The charity worker helped her with her CV, her interview training and much more. 'They kind of became my family,' says Fisa, who now has a job with the NHS and her own home. 'If I hadn't gone to Spear I would have gone from job to job, place to place until I ended up with the wrong crowd. I never thought I'd have a good job and my own place. I just never dreamed to be where I am today.' What is clear from these few personal accounts is that philanthrocapitalism can have a direct transformative impact on huge numbers of lives.[82]

Interview: Richard Branson on entrepreneurial philanthropy

Sir Richard Branson founded Virgin Records in 1972 and then built Virgin into a global brand with more than 400 companies in a wide variety of fields, from airlines to telecoms, financial services to health care, even a commercial space company. Even after the COVID stock market crash he is worth £3.6 billion according to the 2020 Sunday Times *Rich List. His philanthropy has supported dozens of causes, most prominently The Elders, Carbon War Room, The B Team and the Branson Centre for Entrepreneurship, through the foundation Virgin Unite. Once a year he invites some of the world's wealthiest people to gather at his home on Necker Island in the British Virgin Islands to dream up philanthropy on a global scale under the banner of Audacious Ideas.*

What was the first act of philanthropy that you can remember?

When I was just turning 16, I started a magazine for young people called *Student*. We started getting lots of letters from young people all over Britain with different problems – gay people who didn't know where to meet other gay people, somebody who had venereal disease, somebody who needed contraception advice . . . So we set up the Student Advisory Centre to offer free advice and help people.

You conceived of that as an act of public good rather than as part of your business?

Yes. The magazine was funded from advertising. The centre was a not-for-profit organization. It was also a good education for all of us who were working at *Student*. I certainly learned a hell of a lot. This was the 1960s, with a lot of free love taking place, and therefore a lot of people who needed some help.

So it was part of the Sixties holistic zeitgeist rather than two separate spheres of activity.

Yes. I started off *Student* magazine because there was the Vietnam War, there was the Biafran War, the Provos were marching,* and so on. I didn't start with it with an idea of making money. I started it as a vehicle to campaign on issues I and other young people felt strongly about. But obviously it was necessary to earn enough money to pay the bills, so in a sense I stumbled into being an entrepreneur. It was like when we went into the airline business: nobody thought we'd make any money out of it. People thought we were daft, but I just felt if we could get into what was a very badly run industry and improve it, we'd have a chance of surviving. And that applies to a lot of the businesses that we've launched over the years.

If you look at your philanthropy from then till now, it's very eclectic. Have you ever had any kind of strategic plan? Or has it just evolved from the situations and the people that you've encountered as your life has progressed?

It was definitely more of an evolution than a massively detailed plan. The Elders came about at the time when America and Britain were talking about invading Iraq in 2003, and we wanted to see whether there was any way that we could stop the invasion and the war. I had come to know King Hussein of Jordan quite well when we'd flown in supplies for refugees there. I spoke with him and he said that he would be happy to try to bridge the gap between Saddam Hussein and the West. So we sent Saddam Hussein a letter asking whether he would consider stepping down to avert the invasion, avoid his almost-certain death, and go and live in Libya. And he sent a message back saying that he would certainly consider it but wanted Nelson Mandela and Kofi Annan† to fly in and fly out with him to guarantee safe passage. I talked to Kofi Annan and Nelson Mandela, and they both agreed to go. But then the bombing started and the meeting never took place.

---

* A counter-cultural protest movement which began in Holland and inspired hippies in San Francisco and London.

† Nelson Mandela was President of South Africa from 1994 to 1999. Kofi Annan was Secretary General of the United Nations from 1997 to 2006.

But that got myself and Peter Gabriel* thinking that if one could potentially avert a war by two elders going and seeing somebody like Saddam Hussein and finding a way out, then there may well be other situations in the world where elders could help. So, with Nelson Mandela we created The Elders with Kofi Annan, Archbishop Desmond Tutu, and Graça Machel, Mandela's wife. One of the first things they did was to go to Kenya where a civil war was on the verge of breaking out. They took Kenyan leaders out to a game reserve for two weeks. The meeting helped bring about a coalition government which ultimately ended the hostilities. Initially, Nelson Mandela chaired The Elders. Then Archbishop Tutu took over, followed by Kofi Annan, who sadly died in 2018. And now Mary Robinson chairs the group.[†]

They have worked on conflict resolution all over the world since then – in Ivory Coast, Cyprus, Egypt, Iran, Israel and Palestine, the Korean Peninsula, Myanmar, Sri Lanka, Sudan and South Sudan, Syria and Zimbabwe.

Yes. And they'll speak out on issues like climate change. They were at the Paris Climate Conference trying to push an agreement through. They've taken action on nuclear proliferation, which is something people have forgotten about but is actually frightening in the way that it's ramping up again. It's particularly disturbing. Anyway, so they've got a lot of work on their hands, but The Elders is an organization that's now been going for 13 years.

Do you get involved in it at all or are you just funding it?

The Elders have an advisory board of people like me who join most of their meetings. We sometimes go on trips and try to help in the background. But The Elders are a completely independent group of leaders. They have full autonomy and I think that's important.

---

* Peter Gabriel, the former lead singer of Genesis, and human rights activist.
[†] The inaugural members of The Elders were Nelson Mandela and Kofi Annan plus Jimmy Carter (President of the United States 1977–81), Desmond Tutu (Archbishop of Cape Town 1986–96 and Chair of South Africa's Truth and Reconciliation Commission 1996–8), Mary Robinson (President of Ireland 1990–7 and UN High Commissioner for Human Rights 1997–2002), Graça Machel (Education Minister of Mozambique 1975–89), Muhammad Yunus (founder of the Grameen Bank) and Li Zhaoxing (Foreign Minister of China 2003–7).

We've set up a number of organizations like The Elders using our entrepreneurial skills. We find a fantastic chief executive and help them recruit a really great team of people around them. The B Team, which is a group of 27 of the most influential business leaders in the world,* is almost like a business version of The Elders.

The aim of that is to try to pioneer a better way of doing business, which prioritizes the well-being of people and the planet as well as profit?

Yes. I co-founded it with Jochen Zeitz. We've now stepped back and Paul Polman of Unilever has taken over as Chair. The idea is to speak out on issues like climate change, gay rights or a whole lot of other issues that the business community in the past seemed reluctant to speak out on. Then we've formed other organizations like the Carbon War Room, which is now merged with the Rocky Mountain Institute, to try to help businesses become green and show them how it can be done and how it can actually be profitable by and large to turn green. And the Global Commission on Drug Policy is something which I'm very much involved with, to try to get governments to treat drugs as a health problem, not a criminal problem. Portugal, which used to have a massive heroin problem, did this in 2001 by decriminalizing personal possession and use of all drugs. If you are struggling with addiction, you are given the medical support you need, not a criminal sentence. As a result, overdose deaths dropped dramatically, as did HIV and hepatitis infections. People feel much more confident to step forward and seek help, as the threat of criminalization has been removed. It gets them on the path to becoming useful members of society again.

You describe yourself as a serial philanthropist and once said: 'I find it difficult to say no to projects that I feel are important.' But how do you fix upon the causes you back?

Some years ago, we introduced something into Virgin we call 'Circles'. If we have a new person joining Virgin, we'll sit them down and say,

---

* The founding B Team leaders include: Sir Richard Branson, Mo Ibrahim of Celtel, Guilherme Leal of Natura, Strive Masiyiwa of Econet Wireless, François-Henri Pinault of Kering, Paul Polman of Unilever, Ratan Tata of the Tata Group, Zhang Yue of Broad Group China and Jochen Zeitz of The Zeitz Foundation.

look, the first thing to do is to draw a circle around yourself and make sure that everything within that circle is healthy and that you feel good about yourself. Am I meeting my fitness goals? Have I got my alcohol intake right? Have I got my work-life balance right? Then you increase the size of the circle. Make sure your family or your friends, and then the people in your street, are covered, and do everything you can to help them and make a difference there too. Then try to get your neighbours to draw circles as well, so you have circles that overlap. Then if you set up a business and your business grows, and you have a factory somewhere, you draw a circle around the factory. If every small company could draw a circle around itself, and attend to the problems within that circle, most of the problems in this world would be resolved.

Within the circle we've drawn around Ulusaba, our Game Reserve in Africa, we've created clinics, schools, orphanages. We also involve guests who come to our Game Reserve in this work. When you become an international company, you should have circles that encompass the world and you should take on issues like climate change or conflict or drug reform and other big issues.

Where did you get the idea from for these circles? Was it an idea from outside? Or did it just grow organically from the way that you run your business?

From the way that Virgin works, really.

That's interesting. Because over the centuries philosophers who have thought about how philanthropy should work – from Aristotle and Confucius, the Christian Church Fathers, the medieval Jewish sage Maimonides – have all had the idea that giving requires those kinds of circles or hierarchies of priority. Your philanthropic and your entrepreneurial activities have interwoven. They've not been separate things?

They haven't been. I think that if you're a successful entrepreneur, extreme wealth can come with it – and with extreme wealth comes extreme responsibility. We need to have a world where the vast majority of the wealth of billionaires is reinvested back into society, either whilst they're alive or when they die. I don't think that their families should inherit billions.

Capitalism is the only economic system, in my opinion, that works. But if you are a capitalist and you're lucky enough to create extreme wealth, you must get that balance right in your lifetime or when you die, so the vast bulk of that money is used in really, really constructive ways.

Why do you use the word extreme when you talk about wealth?

Because we live in a world where – if you develop Microsoft or Cisco – the wealth that attaches to individuals who develop those ideas is extreme. There's no question. It's many, many, many, many, many, many times more than the average person, which is fine, as long as that money ultimately goes back into society and doesn't just spoil one or two rich kids, grandkids or great-grandkids. It's getting that balance right.

Presumably you've had conversations with your own children about what they will inherit. How do you come to a conclusion about how much should kids inherit, what's good for them, and what's bad for them?

It's a balancing act for different families. My kids do not expect to receive billions from me when I die. They would think that would be absolutely wrong. What I will do is work out some kind of system to make sure that they will be able to continue the lifestyle that they've led as they grew up – and that if they need medical help or education, they can get those sorts of things. Exact numbers, we're still working out what the balance would be, and I would never make that public. But we all agree that the vast majority of the billions of value that Virgin has created over 50 years will be spent on good causes and charity.

The last thing you want is to ruin your kids. My daughter became a doctor and now chairs our foundation. My son makes feature documentary films. They've got the satisfaction of doing their own thing and not the satisfaction of having big sums of money in the bank.

Your daughter is helping you spend the money philanthropically already?

Yes, and they both will take that challenge on in the years to come.

So you're hoping that they will inherit philanthropy as well as inheriting money.

I hope that they have been brought up to get more satisfaction from making a difference in the world than from partying. I believe that I'm lucky enough to have had two grounded kids who feel exactly the same way that I do.

So how do you put the money back into the good of society if you've got extreme wealth? You said somewhere that if the wealthy don't contribute philanthropically, they deserve to pay hefty taxes. What should go in philanthropy and what should go in taxes?

First of all, I think that individuals and companies should be encouraged to be entrepreneurial, to create considerable wealth, to make a real difference in the world. Most of the improvements in the world have come, I think, from entrepreneurs. But if they are one of the lucky few who have made extreme wealth from it – and I'm talking of billionaires – and they don't use that wealth in a positive way, then I think large taxes should be imposed. Ideally, though, I think it will be much more satisfying for entrepreneurs to agree to make that difference themselves than leave it to the taxman to spend the money.

So you're saying that income tax shouldn't be so high that it is a disincentive to wealth creation. But that inheritance tax should be high if people haven't given their money away philanthropically when they die.

Exactly.

What do you say to the complaints that Virgin Care has failed to pay any corporation tax in the UK despite making over £15 million in profit from NHS contracts over the past two years? When people say you're a ruthless capitalist and you don't pay taxes, how do you respond?

Let me begin by saying that we've made it very clear that we've never taken a penny out of Virgin Care, and we never will. One hundred per cent of any Virgin Care profits (after we have our investment back) will be reinvested in the NHS. Virgin Care is not something we plan to make a penny from or take a penny out of.

Are you saying that you see it as a public service rather than a business?

Exactly. It was Gordon Brown who approached me to see whether we could use the expertise that we had learned through Virgin Atlantic in the National Health Service.* It was he and the Labour Party that came up with the idea that private companies could come in and help operate bits of the NHS, on the strict basis that they cut the costs but improve the quality. That is exactly what Virgin Care has managed to do. So far from taking millions out of Virgin Care, we've actually invested nearly £60 million into Virgin Care, and are really proud of what the team are doing.

The great thing about Virgin Care is that the NHS is being preserved. It's going to forever be a free service, but hopefully, bits of it will be improved in quality. It's very difficult to get that message across to the public. People are cynical about anybody that touches the health service. I suspect of all the things that we've done, it's the one thing that we will always get thrown back at us, and we'll never get our message completely across. Anyway, as far as we're concerned, we're proud and pleased with what we're doing.

It's often said that the public are cynical of philanthropy in general, assuming that there must be some kind of ulterior motive or a tax dodge behind it? There's a constant suspicion about it.

I agree 100 per cent. If I look back at my life, any time we do anything which is purely philanthropy, we generally find we'll get some cynical comments about it. Any time we talk about launching a new business, we don't get that cynicism. But some newspapers will always try to find fault with philanthropists. It's a pity, and I hope it doesn't discourage people from being generous.

What's the boldest philanthropic project you've undertaken?

We've set up an organization called Audacious Ideas with Chris Anderson from TED.† Once a year, we'll bring together some of the world's wealthiest people here on Necker Island. In the 12 months prior, we'll do research into what are the most audacious things that could be done to fix the world and the big, big challenges we face.

---

* Gordon Brown was Chancellor of the Exchequer 1997–2007 and Prime Minister of the UK 2007–10.
† Chris Anderson is a British-American businessman who is the head of TED, a non-profit organization that provides idea-based talks across a wide range of disciplines. It has hosted tens of thousands of short talks, many of which are posted on the internet.

What kind of thing?

There was an organization called the One Acre Fund that improves the productivity of every acre of agricultural land by nearly twofold and operates in quite a few African countries. They were given $100 million to expand it into a number of other countries. Another example is that methane emissions from the digestive systems of animals and other sources are a major cause of global warming. There was an organization that submitted an audacious idea to put satellites up to see where those methane emissions were taking place, so that governments and companies could be alerted, because methane is 18 times worse than carbon for the atmosphere. The annual Audacious Ideas meeting, over a three- or four-day period, pledges maybe just short of half a billion dollars to a big cause like that.

Something that a business wouldn't do, or a government couldn't do on that global scale, but philanthropy can do.

Exactly. Governments could do it, but they typically have thousands of things on their plate to deal with. As they move from one election cycle to the next, few government ministers are in office long enough to think strategically and plan for the long term. So they have just not got the time to think about the big-picture issues.

The urgent squeezes out the important too much in politics.

Yes, I think it does, sadly. But the good thing is that you can have the best of both worlds, where you have a democratically elected government which then can draw on experts outside government, entrepreneurs and other people, to help them solve some of these problems.

What are the big challenges of the twenty-first century which are particularly susceptible to being addressed by philanthropy rather than by business or government?

Before I answer that it's worth thinking about how, every decade, the numbers of children dying from starvation, women dying from childbirth, kids who have no access to education, or girls who are forced into child marriage – every single one of these things is improving. On most indicators, we've seen steady improvements. Quite a lot of that is down to philanthropies like the Bill & Melinda Gates Foundation in Africa and others.

Bill Gates has saved millions of lives.

Yes, literally millions of lives. And will save millions more.

But looking forward to the challenges of the twenty-first century, climate change is arguably the biggest. We've been spending a lot of time and energy trying to think about what, if we were in government, we would do to address climate change. We're now submitting ideas to the Australian government, the British government, to the US government and others, saying from a business perspective, this is what we think you should do to deal with it.

Basically, what we're saying is that a carbon tax often hasn't worked as intended. In Australia, the government fell because it was unpopular with the public and with business. In France, when President Macron tried to increase fuel prices, his government nearly fell and you had massive demonstrations.

Our idea is that, instead of a carbon tax, you create a framework for investment, something I'd like to call a clean energy dividend. You force companies to invest the same amount of money they'd have to invest under a carbon tax. But, instead of just handing that over to government, they'll invest directly in initiatives to reduce carbon – in renewable energy like wind and solar, and in other innovations. For instance, I'm an investor in Beyond Meat and Memphis Meat. Those two companies have developed great products which will replace the need for the livestock that does so much damage to the planet by emitting methane and clearing the rainforests.

The reason we think this will be successful is that it will encourage and unlock far greater investment in green innovation, to the tune of trillions. The companies would benefit because they'd be able to receive a return on investment – the dividend. The public will benefit because prices of energy would drop. And governments will get on top of climate change much more quickly. It's a simple idea, but sometimes it's simple ideas that can make the difference.

Chapter 12

The Serious Shortcomings of Philanthrocapitalism

The children's television show *Sesame Street* was a hit from the outset, thanks in no small measure to the Muppets. The human-sized puppets – in their vivid colours of all shades, shapes and sizes – seemed to engage more directly with the pre-school children who were the programme's audience than did the human actors who appeared alongside them on the screen. So much so that, within a few years, a survey showed that 95 per cent of all American pre-schoolers had watched the show before they reached the age of three. In 2019 it celebrated 50 years on screen, in which time it has won 189 Emmy Awards – more than any other children's television show.

There was, of course, something more to it than entertainment. The idea for the show was dreamt up at a dinner party in 1969 when Lloyd Morrisett, an educational psychologist working for the Carnegie Corporation, got into conversation with a TV producer from America's Public Broadcasting Service (PBS). Together they came up with an innovative idea – that a kids' TV show could be used to close the educational gap between children in poor black communities and those in middle-class suburbs. A group of broadcasters, writers, educators and researchers came together in an organization called the Children's Television Workshop (CTW) to produce the programme. Educational goals and the kindergarten curriculum shaped the show's content, which used tunes, based on commercial television's catchy advertising jingles, to teach the young children to count and become familiar with the alphabet. 'The goal was to have children entering school prepared to succeed,' said Morrisett. It had another provenance. 'The show came out of the civil rights movement. We were going to change the world,' said the Latino actress, Sonia Manzano, who interacted on screen with the Muppets for 44 years. The range of colours and shapes of the puppets sent out the message to children of colour that Sesame Street was 'a place where no matter who you are or what you look like, you're welcome'. She was speaking at an awards ceremony to mark the programme's half century where *Sesame Street* was said to have 'revolutionized how we think about childhood and the world'.[1]

SESAME STREET AND METRICS MADNESS

The pioneering programme was funded by two philanthropic foundations, the Carnegie Corporation and the Ford Foundation. Yet despite the show's huge international success it failed in terms of the specific objective the two foundations had set, points out Garry W. Jenkins in his essay 'Who's afraid of philanthrocapitalism?'[2] It did not succeed in closing the gap between poorer black students and those from the more affluent white middle classes. This was because, ironically, *Sesame Street* was so effective as a teaching tool that it raised educational standards for all the children who watched it – black and white, rich and poor, alike. 'Disadvantaged children who watched the programme did surpass the children who did not watch', according to an academic symposium which was held to assess its impact. But children from all backgrounds were attracted to it, 'neutralising the potential for any compensatory effect'.[3] Indeed, one study suggested that because 'white children watched *Sesame Street* more than black children, the program exacerbated the education gap' it had set out to reduce. Jenkins raises the example of *Sesame Street* in the course of a study of the differences between traditional philanthropy and philanthrocapitalism. Intentionally or not, he observes, philanthrocapitalism believes itself superior to old-style philanthropic foundations, portraying them as 'crisis-prone, desperately poor, starry-eyed, even witless do-gooders'.[4]

The benefits of philanthrocapitalism are clear enough. Its downsides are less immediately obvious. There are ideological critiques from both the right, who see it as interfering with the operations of the free market, and the left, who suggest philanthropy can undermine the politics of democracy. More pragmatically, critics like Garry Jenkins have pointed out that the particular characteristics of philanthrocapitalism – with its emphasis on targets and measurement – can sometimes mean that the tail wags the dog. At the heart of business lies the maximization of profit; at the heart of philanthropy lies an altruistic concern with the betterment of humankind. The two models of thinking do not always overlap. Philanthrocapitalism's preoccupation with measurement can, in some circumstances, undermine the wider outcomes philanthropy sets out to achieve.

Jenkins spells out why. Philanthrocapitalism's rigid metrics have their own different shortcomings. They can focus too narrowly on specific targets and lose sight of the bigger picture. They can prioritize what is easily measured over what is most important. They can create perverse incentives for charities to ignore groups or people who are thought too difficult to reach. What Jenkins calls 'measurement frenzy' can start out as a disciplinary tool but end up undermining the relationship between donor and recipient.[5] In the hands of a stern manager such metrics can inhibit creativity, expression, compassion, justice and community empowerment. 'Under the philanthrocapitalism model, Children's Television Workshop might have had its funding cut off because of its failure to deliver the promised results,' Jenkins observes. Instead, because it was funded under the old philanthropy model, the programme was continued and raised standards across the nation, and across the world.

Sometimes the problem lies, not in the effectiveness of a charity's work, but in the narrowness of the philanthrocapitalist metric. That was clear from a project in the UK started with the intention of reducing teenage pregnancy at a time when Britain had the highest number of teenage mothers in Western Europe. Teens & Toddlers, founded in the year 2000, brought a group of teenagers to a nursery in Southwark in south London for two hours, twice a week. Half the teenagers were studying for a qualification in healthcare, but the other half were drawn from those most at risk of being excluded from school. Each teenager 'adopted' a toddler and, throughout each session, spent time playing with them and dealing with their problems, tantrums and accidents. The idea was to teach teenagers 'how demanding it is to be with a child' and how much 'their energy depleted after just a couple of hours'.[6]

The project reported big changes in the troubled teenagers in a very short time. Peter Hein, then the facilitator of the project, described it as 'a great joy to see how teenagers with disruptive behaviour change when they get into a relationship with toddlers and are then able to transfer it into their relationships with the rest of the world'. They derived a real sense of self-esteem from being looked up to by the toddlers; and the toddlers loved having a special friend. Diana Whitmore, president of the Psychosynthesis and Educational Trust, who launched the project, noted that being an example to the children had an immediate effect on the teenagers.

'When they are in the classroom, it is a job to control them,' she said. 'However, the minute they go into the nursery they change dramatically. We have never had an incident with the teens in the nursery. From this we point out to them that they have a choice about how they behave.' The problem was that the project demonstrated no direct causal impact on the rate of teenage pregnancy. What was overwhelmingly clear, however, was that the scheme had an immense impact upon the self-esteem of all the teenagers who participated. Some of them, who had previously been deemed no-hopers at school, then continued on to higher education. Only 3 per cent of those who went through the programme did not find a job or a place in further education or training, according to Porticus, the organization which funded Teens & Toddlers from 2011.[7] Porticus – the family trust of the multibillionaire Brenninkmeijer family, whose businesses include the international fashion chain C&A – were happy to see the emphasis of the project switch from preventing pregnancy to raising the self-esteem and aspirations of young people from a disadvantaged part of the inner city. It is a shift which has continued under Impetus-PEF, which has injected £850,000 into the programme over the last ten years. Impetus has also given the project strategic management support which has helped the charity weather cuts in funding from local authorities. Using extra finance from social impact bonds, it has expanded the scheme to Manchester and the north of England.

Today the Teens & Toddlers website defines the purpose of the project as working with young people, aged 13 to 17, who are at risk of not achieving their academic potential because of low self-esteem, behavioural issues, poor attendance, a history of exclusions, poor attainment, disengagement from school and engagement in risky behaviour. Teenage pregnancy is nowhere mentioned. 'Over time we have learned more about how the programme works,' says Joanne Hay, the current CEO of Teens & Toddlers. 'We did a "theory of change" exercise and used this to explain the process of change and linkages to short and long-term outcomes. We also changed the way we describe the problem.' One way and another, funding for a very useful project has been sustained thanks to the flexibility of a series of funders who were not over-rigid in their use of targets.

THE PHILANTHROPIST AS DICTATOR

There are downsides to taking risks. And it is not the philanthropists who suffer. One night, in November 2008, Bill and Melinda Gates hosted a gala event in their home in Seattle for some of the most senior figures in education all across the United States. The next morning, after what one of the guests[8] described as 'a well-fed evening at their fabulous home', this education elite – of around 130 schools chiefs, senior civil servants, education charities, teachers' union leaders and presidential advisors – gathered in the Seattle Sheraton for what Gates called 'A Forum on Education in America'. There the world's richest couple made a surprise announcement.

Although Bill and Melinda Gates are best known internationally for their work on global healthcare, in the US their Gates Foundation began by investing large sums in trying to improve state education. Bill Gates, who likes to call himself America's most successful college dropout, was greatly exercised by the number of young people failing to graduate from high school so they never even get to college. The problem was, he decided, that the nation's high schools were too big. Between 2000 and 2008 his foundation spent around $2 billion replacing 2,602 large high schools with smaller ones. The aim was to improve teaching quality. Nearly 800,000 students in 40 school districts were involved. At the 2008 meeting in Seattle the couple's shock announcement was that their massive philanthropic investment had not been a success. 'We had a high hope that just by changing the structure, we'd do something dramatic,' Gates said. But it hadn't worked. They were scrapping the scheme and embarking on an entirely new strategy.[9]

Earlier that year Bill Gates had formally stepped down from his leadership post at Microsoft – the giant computer software corporation which had made his billions – and turned his attention to full-time philanthropy. In the run-up to that change he had appointed a new director of education at the Bill & Melinda Gates Foundation. She was Vicki Phillips and she had immediately launched a strategic review of Gates's education policy. She brought with her research, based on a study of 150,000 students in Los Angeles, conducted the year before at Harvard. It had developed a method of evaluating the quality of teachers against the exam performance of their students. Top teachers, it seemed to show, could close the infamous gap between black and white students in terms of their educational performance. Based on this study, the Gates Foundation came up with a plan: the top 25 per cent of teachers should have their pay increased, whereas those at the bottom should be fired.[10] Not every educationalist was convinced. But Bill Gates was clearly persuaded – perhaps because he had a similar incentive structure at Microsoft, where employees were ranked as top, good, average, below average and poor. Those at the top received bonuses and promotions; those at the bottom got nothing or were dismissed[11].

The new approach was 'not a 360-degree turn by any means', insisted Vicki Philips after the change of strategy was announced at the Seattle forum. Some of the education experts present were enthusiastic: Chester Finn, the head of the conservative education think tank, the Fordham Institute, which was funded by Gates, gave 'two cheers' to Bill and Melinda's new plan.[12] But others were not so impressed and asked: Would it work any better than Bill Gates's last bright idea? They were even less impressed when it became clear how messy the aftermath of his first education initiative would be. The funding for it was ended abruptly. Schools closed, sometimes in districts where the programme had been running less than three years and the schools had not been given enough time to demonstrate any improvement. In Colorado, where Denver's Manual High School shut down when the Gates funding was pulled, the former students were shipped to other schools around the city. Only 52 per cent of them went on to graduate, having left a school which previously had a graduation rate of 68 per cent.[13] Criticism was fierce. After visiting Milwaukee, where $15 million of the Gates money had been spent, William Schambra of the Bradley Center for Philanthropy and Civic Renewal commented scathingly: 'For Gates it's fine to say, well, that was an interesting experiment and it didn't work out, and walk away from it. But for Milwaukee . . . those are real children that we're talking about. For the folks in Seattle it's an "oopsie", but for the folks in Milwaukee it's a major disruption.'[14]

What all this highlights is the extent to which the personal convictions of an individual philanthropist can determine public policy – and how vulnerable to sudden change that policy can be. A number of outside experts suggested that Gates had simply 'misread the numbers' on the effectiveness of small schools. The smaller a school, the more likely its overall performance could be skewed by a small number of excellent, or very poor, students, pointed out the academic statistician Howard Wainer.[15] The distinguished historian of education – and former US Assistant Education Secretary – Diane Ravitch, was more precise: 'The Gates Foundation's mistake was in believing that there is a silver bullet to solve the problems of inner-city schools, which enrol large numbers of students who are poor, have limited English language proficiency, and are more likely to require special education . . . and many students have health problems and issues related to their family's poverty that even the smallest of schools can't solve.'[16] It was not until 2010 that Bill Gates himself finally acknowledged he had got it wrong. He candidly admitted that 'many of the small schools that we invested in did not improve student achievement in any significant way'.[17] A year after that, in a 2011 interview with the *Wall Street Journal*, he conceded that on 'the measure we care most about – whether you go to college – it didn't move the needle much. So we did a *mea culpa* on that.'[18]

But that is not the end of the story. The Gates Foundation then spent $355 million to develop better tools to track teacher performance. They analysed videos of teaching in individual classrooms to discover which approaches seemed to produce the most improved performance by students.[19] Gates-funded grassroots organizations lobbied state authorities to adopt this 'value-added modelling' (VAM) to determine a teacher's efficacy.[20] The respected Brookings Institution published a study in 2010 which supported this approach. But the consensus was not universal. A study the same year by the US Department of Education found that VAM was subject to high levels of random error. They could misclassify teachers as much as 26 per cent of the time. David Labaree, Professor of Education at Stanford University, asserted that 'the evidence for the validity of the Gates value-added measures is weak'.[21]

Analysis of the Gates data by the economist Jesse Rothstein of the University of California at Berkeley showed that 40 per cent of the teachers Gates placed in the bottom quartile scored in the top half when an alternative method of measurement was used.[22] Howard Wainer, the statistician who spotted the mathematical fallacy behind the small-schools-are-always-better theory, was also sceptical about this second Gates education initiative. 'It's conceivable you could get a value-added score to work at an elementary level, but how can you do it at a high school?' he asked. 'How should my Physics score match against your French score? Was Mozart a better musician than Babe Ruth was a hitter?'[23] And Kevin G. Welner, the Director of the National Education Policy Center, published a study which suggested that the statistics 'undermine rather than validate value-added based approaches to teacher evaluation'.[24] Many educationalists were, therefore, not surprised when in 2014 the Gates Foundation announced it was also suspending its teacher evaluation programme.[25]

My purpose in giving all this detail is not to debate the rights and wrongs of the Gates education analysis. It is simply to illustrate the problems that can arise with top-down philanthropy. This is not an isolated example. Rather it is characteristic of business-oriented philanthropy. Philanthrocapitalism, as Garry Jenkins puts it, 'defines the problem, sets the agenda, devises the strategy, and determines how long it should take to solve the problem'. Then 'it goes out to find or create organizations to execute its agenda.'[26] It is not that the Gates Foundation fails to consult with experts. It does that, and then makes its decisions in 'a closed internal process', only after which do they contact organizations with grassroots experience 'to execute their vision after the fact'.[27] Those charities selected to receive grants thus become little more than sub-contractors, much as are those charities, as we saw in Chapter 10, who are selected by the state to receive government grants and contracts.

BILL AND MELINDA CHANGE THEIR MINDS

To be fair, as the shifts on education policy demonstrate, Bill and Melinda Gates have shown a willingness to change their mind when the evidence suggests they have made a mistake. Even Diane Ravitch, who dismissively refers to the new-style philanthropists as the Billionaire Boys Club, acknowledges that. In her book *The Death and Life of the Great American School System* she criticizes Gates for exerting 'vast power and unchecked influence' over American education. Yet she also concedes: 'We must give the Gates Foundation and its founders credit for their honest self-scrutiny. Most proponents of education reform defend their ideas against all critics, regardless of what evaluations show.'[28] Even a critic as hostile as Linsey McGoey admits the Gates' willingness to change their mind 'is a rare and commendable trait', adding that 'the opposite reaction – stubborn refusal to admit that well-intentioned ideas can reap unplanned negative consequences – would be far more troubling.'[29]

To Bill Gates mid-course corrections are an inevitable part of good business practice. In an open letter on the Foundation website, he and Melinda write: 'We think an essential role of philanthropy is to make bets on promising solutions that governments and businesses can't afford to make. As we learn which bets pay off, we have to adjust our strategies and share the results so everyone can benefit.'[30]

Part of that willingness to change comes from the distinctive input the husband and wife have to the conduct of the huge foundation. Melinda says that while her husband takes a data-led approach, her attitude is more people-oriented. 'I think what I've taught him is to take that data and meet with people on the ground to understand: can you actually deliver?', she says.[31] The primacy of people over doctrine in her own outlook is clear from the fact that, though a practising Catholic, she has defied her Church's teaching on contraception and pledged the foundation to give $560 million towards a campaign to get 120 million women access to contraception. Contraception, she says, is one of the 'greatest anti-poverty innovations in history'.[32]

But when the world's biggest philanthropic organization changes direction it is only because the rich individuals at the helm have changed their minds. It is not because others have pressed that change upon them. There is, rather, a reluctance to challenge them. 'Never in the history of the United States was there a foundation as rich and powerful as the Gates Foundation,' writes Diane Ravitch. 'Never was there one that sought to steer state and national policy in education and never before was there a foundation that gave grants to almost every major think tank and advocacy group in the field of education, leaving almost no one willing to criticize its vast power and unchecked influence.'[33]

One person was willing to challenge the Gates top-down style of philanthropy. He was an ordinary schoolteacher. Anthony Cody, a science and maths teacher at a high-needs middle school in Oakland, California, had become alarmed at the growing tendency 'to turn education into a quantifiable commodity'. It was an approach which he regarded as 'fundamentally misguided because there is so much learning that you can't measure on test'.[34] Yet a new consensus on tests-for-teachers was being articulated everywhere – in a new Paramount documentary feature film, *Waiting for Superman*, and in reports from a series of research groups. Cody decided to investigate to see what linked those behind this new thinking – and discovered that the Gates Foundation was funding many of them. Cody told the *Washington Post*: 'I find it remarkable that an education reform project built around the concept of "accountability" has no mechanism, no means by which we, the public, can hold its sponsors accountable. We have "bad teachers" who must be held accountable. Schools and students that must be held accountable. But Bill Gates himself? Who holds him and his employees accountable for the devastating effects their reforms have had?'[35] His questions were directed at Bill Gates, but they could be asked of any philanthrocapitalist: 'To whom are you accountable?'

The legal answer to that question is that a charitable foundation is accountable only to its trustees. The website of the Gates Foundation lists only three – Bill Gates, Melinda Gates and Warren Buffett – who in 2006 pledged 10 million shares in his company Berkshire Hathaway, then worth around $30 billion, to the foundation, to be paid in annual instalments.[36] Such a small group of trustees is not untypical. A Charity Commission survey in the UK showed that the average board of trustees in 2017 had just 5.9 members, with the typical trustee being white, male and over the age of 60. Just under half were, or still are, users of the services provided by their charity.[37] But if that is the legal position, where lies the social and moral obligation?

HOLDING THE SUPER-RICH ACCOUNTABLE

'No matter how smart or experienced the Gateses and Buffetts are, they are wrong to think they will get the best ideas from such a small board,' says the philanthropy scholar Pablo Eisenberg. Philanthrocapitalists need to realize 'they don't have all the answers'. They should 'listen more to community groups and the constituencies they serve to figure out where money is most needed'.[38] Instead, Eisenberg laments, the trend points in the opposite direction. Sixty per cent of the 86,000 foundations in the US today do not accept unsolicited proposals from charities and community groups. Of those that do accept outside input, for 'every grant approved by a foundation, eleven more are declined'.[39] Philanthrocapitalism, asserts Eisenberg, is 'saying a few of us know what's best for non-profits, their constituencies, and the greater good'. This is unacceptable, given the enormous tax subsidies these donors receive. It constitutes 'a dangerous shift of the balance of power in the non-profit world'.[40]

There is a particular irony in this, given the business-oriented philosophy of philanthrocapitalists. Their command-and-control approach to philanthropy is hardly compatible with the values and virtues of the free market. In practice the more extreme forms of 'strategic philanthropy' are narrow and elitist. Rather than promoting the open-minded innovation generally associated with effective free markets, philanthrocapitalism has a tendency to 'lead only to a concentration of power and decision-making in the hands of business elites', as Garry Jenkins puts it.[41] If philanthropy is to 'save the world' – as that original book by Matthew Bishop and Michael Green suggested – philanthrocapitalists must attune their preferences to the needs and desires of broader society. Their approach needs to be less directive and more consultative if they are to avoid the accusation that their giving is self-serving and suspect. It is true, as Bishop and Green suggest, that as 'hyperagents' the super-rich can do things to help solve the world's problems that traditional power elites cannot: 'They do not face elections every few years, like politicians, or suffer the tyranny of shareholder demands for ever-increasing quarterly profits, like CEOs of most public companies. Nor do they have to devote vast amounts of time and resources to raising money, like most heads of NGOs. That frees them up to think long-term, to go against conventional wisdom, to take up ideas too risky for government, to deploy substantial resources quickly when the situation demands it – above all, to try something new.'[42]

But that strength is also a weakness. 'This trend of charitable ultra-wealthy individuals taking over the role of government is quite alarming,' points out the *Berkeley Economic Review*. The super-rich are not accountable to any public body for their choices and can therefore invest and divest 'with little consequence'.[43] The good causes they support can find their funding axed on a whim. More seriously, perhaps, they can distort democratic decision-making processes. Both local and federal governments have modified their policies to fit in with the Gates Foundation's initiatives. They have diverted public money from other priorities to match-fund the donations given by Gates.[44] As a result the mistakes made by Gates were then echoed and amplified by the US Department of Education.[45] So philanthrocapitalism suffers from more than a lack of accountability; it can also subvert the democratic process. Its massive grants, and ability to influence public spending, have created what Diane Ravitch calls 'a new era' in philanthropy.[46] The philanthrocapitalist approach, based on market principles, favours solutions grounded in competition and individualism. This stands in contrast to a public policy which is generally rooted in communitarian principles which emphasize social solutions grounded in co-operation and collective action. Such a conflict in values raises tensions between philanthropy and democracy.

PHILANTHROPY AND CIVIL SOCIETY

What would be healthier is a philanthropy which does not arrogate to itself the functions of government but, rather, offers an alternative to both private and public sectors. The value of philanthropy lies not simply in the achieving of results. It also lies in the way that philanthropy, by supporting charities and non-profit organizations, helps foster the values which hold a society together. In this way the best philanthropy helps build the complex networks of institutions, customs and relationships which Edmund Burke saw as essential to the functioning of a healthy and dynamic society. 'Such responsibility cannot be turned over to an unelected class of corporate chieftains (even well-intentioned ones) no matter how grateful we may be for their generosity,' as Garry Jenkins observes.[47] Left to its own devices, philanthrocapitalism intensifies the voice of those who already have substantial influence, access and power – rather than strengthening charities in their role of giving a voice to those who would otherwise go unheard. Enabling those who are politically marginalized to be part of the public conversation is, ironically, one of the virtues of the old style of philanthropy which philanthrocapitalists dismiss as outmoded.

The contrast between the two approaches was highlighted by Steven Lawry of the Hauser Center for Nonprofit Organizations at Harvard University in a study of Muhammad Yunus and his Grameen Bank in Bangladesh.[48] Yunus, an economics professor at Chittagong University in the 1970s, observed that poor people could never borrow money from banks because they lacked any assets, such as land or houses, to put up as security against a loan. He came up with an idea to get round the problem. Yunus's brainwave was that the bank should make the loan to a small group of friends and neighbours, who would allocate the money to one individual. The social pressure that occurs naturally in such groups would ensure that the individual paid the loan back. Yunus went to the Ford Foundation's office in Bangladesh and persuaded them to put up $800,000 to back the idea. It was such a success that Yunus won the Nobel Peace Prize and initiated what turned out to be the microfinance movement.

Yet the Ford Foundation's approach is one of those singled out for its 'lack of strategic thinking' by enthusiasts for philanthrocapitalism.[49] The Ford Foundation had been the largest American philanthropic institution since the 1940s when, on the death of its founders, Edsel Ford and Henry Ford, it had acquired most of the shares of the Ford Motor Company. Its approach was wide-ranging. It supported economic development, scientific research, agricultural reform, education, human rights, democracy and empowerment in the developing world. The new philanthrocapitalists decried its approach as scatter-gun. Yet what was clearly on display with Yunus and his bank for poor people is the benefit of responding to an initiative proposed by someone with direct on-the-ground experience rather than the philanthrocapitalist dreaming up the idea and then looking for a charity on the ground to implement it. The Ford Foundation funding was vital, but it was the grant recipient who led the way. Yunus had the idea, based on his experience with poor people at the grassroots; he developed it and provided the expertise to offer a solution to a social ill. Lawry comments: 'Foundations should open their doors wide to the potentially powerful ideas of people like Yunus – entrepreneurs who come from outside of philanthropy and can test and champion their ideas in the complex social, economic and political environments in which they live and work.' The job of the philanthropist is to seek out 'people distinguished for their powerful ideas and their practical understanding of what it takes to bring about meaningful change in their societies – and then fund their work with the fewest possible constraints.'[50]

Such individuals and groups are to be recommended not simply because of their local knowledge, insights and understanding of their communities. They should also be supported because empowering organizations and communities on the ground is vital to promoting a strong civil society. It is on values like participation, empowerment, problem-solving, relationship-building and community-strengthening that the foundations of democracy rest. Those are the qualities which teach citizens the skills of self-government.

Michael Edwards is someone who has direct experience of that, from a number of perspectives. He worked in senior management positions in Oxfam and Save the Children in the UK and then the World Bank before joining the Ford Foundation, where he worked on the links between economic development and civil society. He insists that 'market values and democratic value are not just different; they can at times pull in opposite directions'.[51] Philanthrocapitalists may well be right when they say that 'technology + science + the market = results' in the search to produce new vaccines against malaria and HIV. 'But there is no vaccine against poverty and inequality, violence and alienation, corruption and poor governance,' Edwards adds.[52] Those problems can only be solved by promoting the development of civil society, an activist citizenry, government accountability and the regulation of markets.

For some of our most pressing social problems – on the environment, social housing, educational disadvantage, human rights, or care of the elderly – market-based approaches are not helpful. The self-confident short-term assumptions of philanthrocapitalism can erode something fragile in the wider social ecology from which grow the very values on which philanthropy relies.[53] Quaker industrialists such as Cadbury and Rowntree understood that in a previous century. Business, they insisted, should become more like philanthropy – and not the other way around. Philanthropists need to foster more co-operation, not competition. They need to look more to collective than individual action. And they must show a greater willingness to work together to change the fundamental structures that keep many people poor rather than seeking merely to address the symptoms.

That means encouraging philanthrocapitalists to take a broader view. They must temper their top-down entrepreneurial enthusiasms with the humble recognition that there are sometimes other answers. They must stop seeing charities as sub-contractors and view them as partners in a relationship where both sides are willing to learn and improve together. Philanthropy is better than no-philanthropy, and results and impact are important. But so too are the values of listening and respect which promote a strong civil society. Democracy needs philanthropy, but philanthropy also needs democracy, for it creates the culture in which the best kinds of philanthropy can thrive.

Interview: Chris Oechsli on giving it all away

Chris Oechsli is the CEO of Atlantic Philanthropies, the foundation set up by Chuck Feeney, the Irish-American businessman and the pioneer philanthropist who inspired Bill Gates and Warren Buffett who says Feeney is 'my hero'. Known as the James Bond of philanthropy, because he operated entirely anonymously for over a decade, Feeney made his fortune from duty-free shopping. His great innovation was his determination to give away all his money while he lived, rather than leaving a foundation when he died. At the age of 88 he has given away $8 billion over 35 years, in 23 countries on five continents, focusing on health, human rights and higher education. In 2002 Feeney and his board decided to spend all the foundation's assets by 2016 and to wind down the entire operation by 2020.

How did Chuck Feeney first hit upon the idea of Giving While Living which made him the role model for a whole generation of philanthropists like Bill Gates?

It was a combination of factors. He saw opportunities to make a difference and apply his wealth. So why wait? He also had an aversion to setting up a large formal structure. And there was the personal drive of wanting to get engaged in this activity himself – and doing it in what he calls a 'big-bet way', deploying significant resources to really make a difference.

When did he switch from business to being a full-time philanthropist?

I don't know that there was ever a formal switch. In 1982 he decided to set up a charitable foundation. In 1984 he made the decision to sign over the entire business to it. But he continued to focus on the business – to build up the resources for his philanthropy. At first he spent around 10 to 20 per cent of his time on his philanthropy. But then in the mid-'90s, when we sold his major operating business – Duty Free Shoppers (DFS) – his philanthropy began to take up around half of his time. By the end of the '90s, when we had sold most of his business assets, his philanthropic endeavours took more like 80 per cent or 90 per cent.

But many of his business instincts carried through into his philanthropic work. He never lost his entrepreneurial, cost-conscious, impact-oriented, bang-for-the-buck perspective.

At first all his giving was anonymous. It was so secretive he was called 'the James Bond of philanthropy'. When did that change, and why?

His giving came out in 1997 as a result of litigation over the sale of DFS. So Chuck felt that was an appropriate time to unmask himself.

Did he ever regret that? Did he prefer being anonymous or was he happy with the change?

I think on balance he recognized it was the right thing to do. He liked being able to move around without undue attention to himself. It allowed him to get closer to people, programmes, projects and organizations, and have more authentic discussions and observations. And he's just not somebody who needs or feels comfortable getting a lot of personal attention. But I don't think he regretted it.

It meant that he became a great exemplar for people like Bill Gates and Warren Buffett who have both cited Chuck as their inspiration.

Absolutely. Bill Gates told him: 'You were the example. You did this well before we all did.' Chuck was part of the initial meeting of wealthy individuals that gathered at David Rockefeller's offices in 2009 to draw up the Giving Pledge.* They wanted him to be one of the first signatories, but he said: 'Well, I've already done it. So it's a bit disingenuous of me to sign.' He signed two years later once it was off the ground. But the Pledge is a promise to give away half your wealth before you die – and though he was very supportive of the effort – he also wanted to champion people giving away more, and sooner.

What does Chuck see as the advantages of 'Giving While Living' versus setting up a perpetual foundation?

Well, from a personal standpoint, he gets satisfaction from engaging with giving. From a strategic standpoint, the theory is: 'A stitch in time saves nine.' If you can fund research to save lives you had better do it right away. The argument *for* perpetual foundations is that the challenges

---

* See pages 548–550 below.

of our time are complex and perpetual foundations are best situated to invest in those complex long-term problems. But Chuck's response to that is to say: 'It's our responsibility to do something sooner. Others can take it up and continue the effort long-term'. But Chuck is not a finger-wagging person. He's not saying everyone has to follow his lead; he's just saying, this is a valid approach and it's definitely one where you can make a significant difference.

So how did he decide which areas to get involved with? In his letter to the Giving Pledge he says: 'Begin with what you know.'

I think that's right. Begin with what – and who – you know. It's about proximity, being close to the people and places that you want to engage with – as opposed to just the intellectual exercise of working with an idea that you're not close to or familiar with. A lot of Chuck's initiatives grew out of personal experience and contacts. He started with higher education because of the opportunities it had given him at his university, Cornell. That widened to higher education in Ireland and also in Vietnam and Australia – places where Chuck had had awareness and contacts.

Why Vietnam?

A combination of things. A general sentiment of Chuck's that Vietnam had been hard done by. He picked up a newspaper article about a very small non-profit organization called East Meets West. It was based in the San Francisco Bay Area and was doing little projects in villages – one-room schoolhouses, wells, some small micro-finance work. They were going out of business, so he gave them some very modest amounts. Then a friend, who had worked with Chuck at DFS, who was visiting Vietnam, met the people there and reported back that they were a very good group. Chuck dipped his toe in the water with several grants to the organization. From that he got a sense that this was a country that was on the upswing, with industrious people looking for opportunities. Then he spotted that the nearby University of Da Nang needed a library, which aligned with Chuck's higher education interests. And that led to discussions with other universities in Central Vietnam. Next he heard that East Meets West was supporting families with children with heart defects so they could go down to Ho Chi Minh City for surgery. In the process, Chuck got to know the place that did the surgery, and the needs there, and started to invest in hospitals.

One thing just led to another.

Correct. He developed a sense of the leaders of these institutions. It was always about the people and Chuck's appreciation of their abilities and approach. Getting close to the people, and having a sense of who they were, and how they worked, and what their needs were, drove a lot of his early choices.

Some of his causes were quite political: native and indigenous peoples in the US and Australia, people of colour in America and South Africa, refugees in the US, the Affordable Care Act, Vietnam, both sides in the Irish peace process.

I don't think 'political' is the right word. I think it is driven by certain values – supporting people who were under-appreciated, undervalued, who didn't have the support to do what they were capable of.

A champion of the underdog?

Chuck would use that phrase. Not just the underdog, but the underdog who is dynamic and enterprising and who could benefit from added wind in their sails, as he would say, to be able to do well or better. And Chuck has an orientation towards reconciliation, an aversion to conflict, and an urge to explore how you resolve conflict.

One of the things that is unusual about Chuck Feeney as a philanthropist is his decision to spend everything in his charitable foundation before he dies. So much so that you put in place a programme to wind up Atlantic Philanthropies by 2020. Has that altered the nature of your philanthropy in this final phase?

Those are questions we've given a lot of time to: how to wind down on the grant-making side, and how to deploy the final resources. It has all been driven by building on Chuck's values and approach – the notion of being able to make a difference, betting on good people and institutions who are capable of driving solutions and change. We worked off of Atlantic's existing geographies and themes. Then we spent a lot of time talking with our major grantees about how they thought Atlantic should end. Of course, we couldn't be responsive to everybody's recommendations, but some themes emerged. Almost $3 billion of the $8 billion we have given in grants has been for physical facilities. A lot of recipients of those grants said: 'What we need now is an investment in the people to populate those facilities.' That led us towards betting on the development of good people.

Have you always done that, or was it a shift in emphasis?

It was a shift in emphasis but a rather significant one. Our final grants are to seven fellowship programmes and a host institution. Their work will be co-ordinated by a new institution, the Atlantic Institute, based in Oxford, to support the seven fellowship programmes over a 15-to-20-year period. It will be a partnership with the Rhodes Trust. I know there's some legacy issues associated with the Rhodes name, but the trust itself is about investing in young people who are public-spirited and who, in Rhodes's words, are 'going to fight the world's fight'. That's a 100-year-old phrase that we translate into making a difference in the lives of disadvantaged and vulnerable people based around themes of global significance.

Will it be a permanent foundation?

Our funding will provide a guaranteed 15-plus years of operation of the institute and the fellowship programmes. Whether they continue after that depends on whether it makes sense for them to continue and whether they can find the funds to do that.

You've always been keen on leveraging money from elsewhere. I've read Chuck Feeney saying: 'I'm the catalyst, but the money's going to come from elsewhere in the end.'

Yes. It's almost formulaic for him that a percentage comes from Atlantic Philanthropies and a percentage comes from other private donors, and in some cases from government. The anonymity principle has worked well there because Chuck has been willing to forgo the naming of a facility so that another donor could be attracted with the prospect of having the building called after them.

I gather that Chuck has refused to allow his name to be given to any of the buildings his $8 billion has been spent on.

That's right. There are a few places in the world where somebody has put up a plaque that acknowledges Chuck or Atlantic, but they were not done at our request or approval. There are no buildings that are named after Atlantic or Chuck. That really summarizes Chuck the person. It just didn't hold appeal for him. His satisfaction has come from being engaged and seeing his investment making a difference.

Are the Atlantic Fellows part of the wind-down, or have you had them all the way through?

They are part of the wind-down. We started our first programme three or four years ago. This was part of the decision on how to end – by betting on dynamic promising enterprising people. The seven fellowship programmes are hosted at different organizations, but the underlying theme is equity and fairness. Several of them are focused on issues of health. One of the first was the investment at the Global Brain Health Institute, which grew out of our programmes on aging. Chuck has had a very strong interest in neurocognitive health, issues of ageing, the increased incidences of Alzheimer's and dementia and their disproportionate impact on disadvantaged communities.

Who does Chuck feel he is accountable to – for how all this money is spent? Who do you feel that you've got to answer to?

That's a profound question. I think Chuck's highest sense of accountability was to himself and a sense of moral and personal responsibility that wealth was to be effectively used for the benefit of others. It just did not sit well with him to accumulate or consume wealth for personal benefit.

He is famous for his frugal lifestyle, carrying his papers in a plastic carrier bag, and he famously wears a Casio watch that cost $10 rather than a Rolex.

That's him. I think it's a fundamental moral sense that you have a responsibility to put your wealth to use for the benefit of others – and that this is both a moral thing and a personally enriching activity. His childhood was in Catholic schools. I'm sure that influenced his moral compass. He's not a religious person in the sense of a practising or proselytizing religious person, but I think the ethics and morality certainly have roots in his early life. His mother was very influential. She was a nurse and a very giving person. I think Chuck inherited this sense of moral responsibility from her.

So his higher sense of accountability is first of all to himself. But then, after that, what?

I don't know that he felt accountable to the public in an explicit sense. I think it was really just driven, principally, internally. But he brought in a board of directors to be part of the process. Chuck did not control all the decisions on grant-making; he intentionally brought in others. Sometimes it was a very compatible and synergistic relationship, and sometimes it wasn't.

How did he handle that? There's a famous story about George Soros saying, 'It's my money. I'll decide.'

[Laughs] I think Chuck expected others to have the same sense of personal accountability that he had for himself. He felt you had to be clear about what you're trying to achieve: that the money had to be used wisely, with clarity of purpose, and the recognition that you had certain advantages, being a large funder, as to how to do that. He sometimes derogatorily referred to 'sprinkle philanthropy', which was people giving away lots of little grants. If you were working with significant sums, you should use the money in ways that smaller donors can't.

He favoured 'big bets' and 'impact' . . .

Big bets. Impact. Clarity of purpose. Effective use of funds. Not getting too big as an organization. Keeping costs reasonable. When the board for a period of time, in his opinion, didn't adhere to that approach, he was very unhappy, and changes were made.

Aren't there tensions between that approach to philanthropy and democracy, between what a big donor like Chuck wants and the priorities of the people and the government they elect?

Absolutely. There are tensions. The negative end of the spectrum is that big resources are in the hands of a few who are making decisions that can affect a broader public. And is that fair? But the flip side is that it strengthens civil society if you have big resources that are not controlled by the government – especially if that government is not always responsive to the public good. Then civil society has a role in challenging and offsetting what government does.

You make that point in one of your website pages where you talk about the election of Donald Trump.

[Laughs]. There are some pretty precise examples. The same debates are being had in the UK and other countries as well. Democracy is a good thing. But is democracy always responsive to the public good? The role of philanthropy is to keep that tension going, ideally in a constructive manner. There are benefits to having resources outside the hands of publicly elected officials.

Especially if those public officials have a view like 'America First', and somebody like Chuck has a view of a more universal kind of humanity.

Absolutely. I also fully recognize and appreciate the tension of having a few people around like that – whether it's someone on the left like George Soros* or the Koch brothers† on the right. The tension is real but it's a tension that we're going to be living with. The extreme solutions are to eliminate philanthropy – by taxing the wealthy and not giving them any tax breaks for charitable activity. The other way is to put in far more rules that restrain what philanthropy is allowed to do. What the existing situation does, I think, is place responsibility on those who do have resources to be more inclusive and public-spirited.

Do you think the current rules are about right? What do you think about the idea that they should be changed so that you should get more tax breaks if you give your money to soup kitchens for the poor rather than opera houses for the rich?

The problem with rules is that people always find ways around them. My own view, and this is personal, is that people who have tremendous resources probably should be paying more taxes – and also giving back to the public systems that have helped them gain their fortunes. But the idea that politicians should be able to control philanthropic decisions is a tough one. Chuck would say, 'I'm not going to tell somebody what they can do with their money, but I hope that they will recognize that using their money for public benefit and philanthropic purposes is a very satisfying and appropriate use of wealth.' That's more a question of educating and sharing than dictating.

One final thing. Chuck always joked that he was so committed to giving everything away before he died that he wanted his last cheque to bounce. Will it?

Atlantic Philanthropies' last cheque certainly will not bounce. But if Chuck's last cheque were to bounce, he'd take great pleasure in that.

---

* See pages 554–558 below.
† See pages 576–592 below.

Chapter 13

Philanthropy Goes Global

It began with a painful wrist, something that was more than merely uncomfortable for a professional art photographer. After surgery for a pinched nerve, Nan Goldin was prescribed a powerful opioid painkiller. It had a similar effect as taking morphine. 'Though I took it as directed, I got addicted overnight,' she later wrote.[1] When the doctor insisted that she came off the medication, Goldin – who had entered a clinic thirty years earlier after sliding into depression and hard-drug abuse[2] – went onto the black market and purchased it there. The drug was called OxyContin. It was manufactured by Purdue Pharma, a company owned by the Sackler family, best known internationally for its generous philanthropic donations to the arts.

Goldin's three pills a day turned into eighteen.[3] She was forced back into rehab. Eventually she broke the habit. That was in 2017, and she has been free of the addiction ever since. But from that time she has campaigned continually to hold the Sacklers responsible, not just for what had happened to her, but for the deaths of more than 200,000 people attributed to opioid overdoses.[4] Goldin was celebrated for her gritty portraits of sexual hedonism, AIDS, drug dependency and domestic violence in the late twentieth-century subculture of New York's Lower East Side. But now she turned protest into her new art form. Using social media, she organized demonstrations inside those art galleries that had received donations from the immensely rich Sackler family, which first made its fortune by popularizing Valium through direct marketing to doctors. She and her followers showered galleries with fake prescriptions or filled the floors with empty pill bottles. The publicity was considerable. But the art establishment, which had been in receipt of significant sums of Sackler money for more than 50 years, simply ignored it. Until, that is, early in 2019, Nan Goldin told the National Portrait Gallery in London that she would pull the plug on their major retrospective of her work – unless the gallery turned down a £1 million donation on offer from the Sackler Trust.[5]

THE SACKLER SAGA AND REPUTATION LAUNDERING

The pressure had been building elsewhere for some time. The Sackler family, which was estimated to be worth $13 billion,[6] had denied responsibility for the opioid crisis. But Goldin discovered that in 2007 three Purdue executives – including its president and its top lawyer – had pleaded guilty in a federal court to criminal charges that they misled regulators, doctors and patients about the drug's risk of addiction and its potential to be abused. The company agreed to pay some $600 million in fines and other payments, one of the largest amounts ever paid by a drug company in such a case.[7] Members of the Sackler family were not directly implicated. But then, in January 2019, papers filed in a Massachusetts lawsuit, containing dozens of internal Purdue Pharma documents, suggested the family was far more involved than the Sacklers had long contended.[8]

Nan Goldin had founded a pressure group called Pain – Prescription Addiction Intervention Now. When she heard that members of the Sackler family had been personally named in the lawsuit she decided that the best way to bring the company and family to account was to target the Sacklers' philanthropy. She adopted a double focus. She aimed to embarrass public institutions which had accepted Sackler funds. And she demanded that the family's philanthropic donations be redirected to 'fund various treatment models: rehab centers, medication assisted programs, harm reduction, relapse prevention, and holistic approaches'. She also called for Purdue to introduce more effective labelling of its products, indicating the addictive potential of the drugs.[9]

Within two months she had succeeded. In March 2019 one of Britain's most celebrated British art institutions released a statement which said: 'The Sackler Trust and the National Portrait Gallery have jointly agreed not to proceed at this time with a £1,000,000 gift from the Sackler Trust.' The Sackler Trust also issued a statement saying: 'The allegations against family members are vigorously denied, but to avoid being a distraction for the NPG, we have decided not to proceed at this time with the donation.'[10] Two days later the Tate Gallery announced it too would no longer accept money from the Sacklers. The next day the Guggenheim Museum in New York did the same. Three days after that the Prince's Trust – the charity set up by the Prince of Wales to help young people into education, training and work – renounced future Sackler donations. That same day the Sackler Trust said it would temporarily cease all philanthropic giving in the UK.[11]

But the dominos continued to tumble. The following day Purdue Pharma and the Sackler family agreed to pay $270 million to the state of Oklahoma to avoid a televised trial over the company's role in the opioid epidemic.[12] Two days later New York state prosecutors filed a lawsuit against the company – and the family – alleging that they fraudulently transferred funds out of Purdue Pharma.[13] The drug company, and the family which owned it, were now facing more than 1,600 lawsuits.[14] Company executives began exploring the possibility of filing for Chapter 11 bankruptcy, to insulate the pharmaceutical giant from a raft of crippling court judgements.[15] Several major universities – the Sacklers have given millions to Harvard, Yale, Oxford, Cambridge, Stanford, Columbia, Tufts, UCL, King's College London, Washington, Edinburgh, Tel Aviv and the Royal College of Art – announced that they would no longer take their money.[16] Next, two months later, the *New York Times* reported that the Metropolitan Museum of Art in New York had announced it too would stop accepting gifts from the Sacklers – 'severing ties between one of the world's most prestigious museums and one of its most prolific philanthropic dynasties'.[17] In July 2019 the world's most famous museum, the Louvre in Paris, removed the name Sackler from its collection of Persian and Levantine artefacts housed in what had been known since 1997 as the Sackler Wing of Oriental Antiquities. The authorities acted in such haste that many of the Sackler signs in the museum were simply covered up with grey tape.[18] Their philanthropy appeared to be becoming the means of the Sacklers' undoing. By August 2019 the family was talking of settling $11.5 billion to end lawsuits which would mean the once mega-wealthy Sacklers losing most of their money, though it would still leave them with over a billion dollars.[19] A month later the Sacklers' one-time cash-cow company, Purdue Pharma, filed for Chapter 11 bankruptcy.[20]

The Sackler saga illustrates several significant developments in the history of philanthropy. It reveals how globalized philanthropy has become; actions and reactions on either side of the Atlantic influenced the progress of the affair internationally. But it also exposes the extent to which philanthropy has become subject to a critical scrutiny which recalls some of the suspicion and hostility that John D. Rockefeller encountered a century before when he failed to persuade the US Congress to endorse his plan to incorporate what was to become the world's biggest philanthropic foundation.

Until this point twenty-first-century philanthropy had had a good press. According to one media analysis, 99 per cent of all stories about philanthropy published between 1990 and 2004 were positive in tone.[21] But now philanthropy was being viewed more critically than it was just a generation earlier. Then major donations were commonly greeted by public applause and admiration; now even mainstream enthusiasts for private giving, like Phil Buchanan, president of the US Center for Effective Philanthropy, became ambivalent. Writing in the *Financial Times* in April 2019, he condemned the Sacklers as donors 'who appear to have used their philanthropy to burnish their reputations with one hand while fanning the flames of the opioid epidemic with the other'.[22] Others were even more direct in their criticisms. Mike Moore, a former attorney-general in Mississippi, who had become one of the lawyers suing Purdue, condemned Sackler philanthropy as mere 'reputation laundering'. The lawsuit filed by New York state directly linking the Sacklers' business and their philanthropy declared: 'Ultimately, the Sacklers used their ill-gotten wealth to cover up their misconduct with a philanthropic campaign intending to whitewash their decades-long success in profiting at New Yorkers' expense.'[23] Nan Goldin was most graphic of all: 'They have washed their blood money through the halls of museums and universities around the world.'[24]

But the criticism extended beyond the Sacklers. A spotlight was now focused first upon sponsorship throughout the arts, and then on modern philanthropy more generally. Veterans of the scene did their best to defend the old ways. They knew that corporate and philanthropic sponsorship of the arts was filling the gaps created by cuts in public funding over recent decades. Professor Christopher Frayling, a former Rector of the Royal College of Art and erstwhile chairman of the Arts Council England, lamented that a 'moral panic' had arisen. This was a new puritanism with rigid moral guidelines that would seriously damage the arts, which had become increasingly reliant on major donors. 'It is one of the iron rules of fundraising that companies with an image problem are the people you go to first of all, because they're the ones who have some ground to make up,' he told BBC Radio. 'Some of these companies smell a bit [but] isn't it great that they are giving their money to the arts rather than to anything else. Lots of good things have happened as a result.' It would not do to be 'too squeamish', he concluded.[25]

But Sir Charles Saumarez Smith, former chief executive of the Royal Academy, conceded that things were now tricky for recipients. 'It's become more of a minefield,' he told the BBC. 'It used to be relatively straightforward . . . you could take money from charitable foundations because charitable foundations are set up to do good in the world. That has been the rule and the advice of the Charity Commission – that it's not for arts institutions themselves to make moral judgements. But that is changing.' Previously, he said, looking back over two decades as a museum director, 'you looked at the good to which the money was put, rather than the bad by which the money might have been made – because once you start asking questions about how money is made it opens a can of worms'. But changes in the business world, and at universities, where ethics committees have been set up to perform due diligence checks, had since migrated into the arts world. The culture had changed. 'Now it's obviously sensible to look at where money is coming from,' he concluded.[26]

Such precedents opened the door to more demanding critics. The Sackler scandal 'raises the question of whether the Gallery will now apply the same standards to its BP sponsorship deal or continue to promote a fossil fuel company in the midst of a climate crisis,' declared Jess Worth, co-director of the campaigning organization Culture Unstained. 'Waved through with minimal scrutiny in the past, BP sponsorship now – like the Sackler donation – looks ethically untenable.'[27] Later in 2019 a group of prominent artists wrote to the National Portrait Gallery calling on it to sever its 130-year links with the energy company.[28] Activists from Art Not Oil also made a public protest about BP's partnerships with the Royal Shakespeare Company. One of the country's most celebrated actors, Mark Rylance, resigned as an associate artist of the RSC in protest. 'I do not wish to be associated with BP any more than I would with an arms dealer, a tobacco salesman or anyone who wilfully destroys the lives of others alive and unborn,' the actor said.[29] Six months later the RSC axed its sponsorship deal with the oil company – which offered cut-price tickets for 16 to 25-year-olds – four years before it was due to expire.[30]

But the focus widened beyond the arts. Peggy McGlone in the *Washington Post* declared that 'concerns about income inequality have challenged the very notion of allowing billionaires to gild their reputations by making tax-deductible gifts that result in their names being etched in stone'.[31] Other critics used the affair to attack the propensity of philanthropists to support the social and cultural activities from which they personally benefit. 'McGlone is on to something,' wrote Mike Scutari in *Inside Philanthropy*. 'One of the big knocks against modern mega-philanthropy is this idea of "elites supporting elites",' he added.[32] Charitable efforts by the rich are increasingly caricatured as self-protective ruses, conceded Phil Buchanan.[33] Philanthropy is just another way for the wealthy to exercise power, wrote Anand Giridharadas in his 2019 polemic, *Winners Take All: The Elite Charade of Changing the World*.[34] The Sackler saga was part of 'a growing awareness that gifts to the arts and other good causes are . . . a way for ultra-wealthy people to scrub their consciences and reputations'.[35] The rich should stop talking 'about all these stupid philanthropy schemes' and 'start talking about taxes', proclaimed the Dutch historian Rutger Bregman, speaking to an audience of the wealthy and powerful at the World Economic Forum in Davos.[36] The attack went viral on social media. We will consider later how fair all this criticism was. But what it all tells us is that in the twenty-first century philanthropy has gone global – and so have the criticisms of it.

MASSIVE GIVING IN AN AGE OF INEQUALITY

The rich are today richer than ever before. London has more billionaires than any city in the world, according to the *Sunday Times* Rich List. At a national level only the United States and China have more of these super-rich individuals than Britain does.[37] Not everyone is so lucky. The bottom half of the population in the US earn only half of what they did in 1980 as a percentage of national income. By contrast, the top 1 per cent earn double.[38] The picture in Britain is similar. In 2007 the bottom 90 per cent of the population earned only 57.4 per cent of the nation's income – the least pay they had taken home since 1929, the year of the Wall Street Crash that began the Great Depression, according to Danny Dorling, Professor of Geography at the University of Oxford.[39]

But the extravagant wealth at the top also produced extravagant displays of generosity. Charitable donations, which had totalled around $13 billion in 1996, now accelerated to the hundreds of billions of dollars.[40] In the decade before and after the millennium, praise for the new generation of mega-philanthropists grew as did their mega-donations. In 2006 Warren Buffett, widely regarded as one of the most successful investors in the world, pledged more than three-quarters of his massive fortune – approximately $30 billion – to the Bill & Melinda Gates Foundation. His gift crowned the first decade of the twenty-first century as 'a new golden age of philanthropy'.[41] Revealingly, perhaps, the last Golden Age of Philanthropy, in the Carnegie and Rockefeller era, also saw extreme levels of social and economic inequality – and that Golden Age, as we saw in Chapter 10, turned out to be merely gilded.

Now, once again, at the start of the twenty-first century, philanthropy and inequality grew together. In 2014 Oxfam International published a report showing that the world's richest 85 individuals had the same combined wealth as the poorest half of the global population – some 3.5 billion people. Yet that year the 50 most generous philanthropists in the US gave only $7.7 billion to charity – a fraction of the $358 billion given by the rest of the population. The relationship between inequality, philanthropy and taxes will be one of the subjects of this chapter.

Not all the rich give. Far from it. Fewer than 9 per cent of the world's billionaires are serious philanthropists, according to Beth Breeze, director of the Centre for Philanthropy at the University of Kent.[42] Only one in ten of the UK's richest 18,000 people – those worth £10 million or more – give anything to charity at all, according to a report by the Beacon Collaborative, a group of philanthropists campaigning to encourage their peers to increase their annual charitable giving by £2 billion collectively.[43] The total amount donated by those on the *Sunday Times* Giving List 2019 was £3.75 billion. Top of the list was Jonathan Ruffer, who runs an asset-management company in the City of London. He gave away two-thirds of his personal fortune in a single year – some £320 million – much of it to drive the regeneration of the run-down former mining community of Bishop Auckland, not far from where he grew up.* But the world's biggest givers are in the US. They are led

---

* See his interview on page 73.

by Bill and Melinda Gates who have personally given more than $45 billion over the last three decades.[44] Their philanthropic foundation – by far the world's largest – is a colossus. It holds assets of $51 billion[45] with more to come, and disburses nearly $5 billion a year in grants.[46] Over the next few decades the Gates Foundation alone is projected to disburse more than $150 billion.[47]

HOW BILL GATES BECAME THE WORLD'S BIGGEST PHILANTHROPIST

Bill Gates has been on a long journey. In 1997 the founder of the software giant Microsoft was the richest person in the world, and had been for some years.[48] Yet he was regarded by his fellow billionaires as a bit of a miser.[49] That year the media mogul Ted Turner gave a $1 billion donation to the United Nations. In the speech in which he announced it Turner singled out Bill Gates by name as a rich man who was not giving enough.[50]

Like many newly wealthy people, Gates began his philanthropy in a random manner. As news of his mega-wealth spread – in 1995 he was already said to be worth $12 billion – he became inundated with requests for charity. His father, a lawyer, suggested he should set up a foundation to figure out which of the entreaties were really deserving. The William H. Gates Foundation was established with an initial gift of $94 million. A second philanthropic body, the Gates Library Foundation, followed. Gates gave it $200 million to build on an earlier programme, begun by Microsoft, which aimed to connect all US library computers to the internet. The donation raised eyebrows. 'This doesn't even count as philanthropy. It is seeding the market. You're simply lubricating future sales,' Gates was chided by the historian Theodore Roszak.[51]

What changed things dramatically was a trip to Africa which Bill and his then fiancée, Melinda French, took with a group of friends ahead of their wedding. It was a three-week safari in Zaire, Tanzania and Kenya – the longest time Bill had ever taken off work from Microsoft. But it was not the wildlife which made the greatest impression on them. 'In the middle of the trip it just started hitting us . . . that people were living in huts with no running water, no electricity,' Melinda later said.[52] 'I would see these women carrying huge piles of things on their heads, and they'd often have a baby on their back and one in front, walking to market [and] I'd think, "OK, the women don't have any shoes on." You just start

asking a series of questions.' The experience, she says, helped set her on
'this learning journey', adding, 'it continues to be a learning journey'.[53]

For Bill Gates, who is very data-driven in his philanthropy, that
journey continued when, in an article about diseases in the developing
world, he read that millions of children under the age of five die routinely
every year from diseases that were wiped out a century earlier in the
rich world. Yet despite that, less than 10 per cent of the world's health
research budget was spent on combating global diseases which afflicted
90 per cent of the global population.[54] As he later told a meeting of the
World Health Assembly in Geneva, he and Melinda 'couldn't escape
the brutal conclusion that – in our world today – some lives are seen as
worth saving and others are not'.

The couple merged Gates's two existing foundations into a new one –
the Bill & Melinda Gates Foundation. In 2000 they endowed it with a
massive $1.6 billion, making it instantly one of the largest foundations
in the world. It prioritized the then unfashionable cause of global
health – funding research into vaccines, offering incentives to scientists
to pioneer unusual methods, and subsidizing research into neglected
tropical diseases. Almost overnight Bill Gates had become the world's
most generous philanthropist. By the time he was 44 he had given away
four times more, in real terms, than John D. Rockefeller had done in
his entire life.[55] What Gates had done, by allocating $1.5 billion to
buy vaccines, was create an incentive for drug companies to invest in
research on the diseases of the poor world. His investment told Big
Pharma that if they created the product, they were sure to find a buyer.
The number of manufacturers involved in vaccine research jumped from
just three to 12.[56] The Global Alliance for Vaccines and Immunization
(GAVI), which Gates heavily supported, guaranteed to buy millions of
doses of vaccines when they were developed. It also ran programmes to
assist poor countries to immunize more people with existing vaccines.
Within the first five years, 99 million people were vaccinated – averting
an estimated 1.7 million deaths.[57] Thanks to Bill and Melinda Gates, it
is estimated that eight million more children have been saved from an
unnecessary death in the years up to 2020.[58]

Over the next five years, the Gates Foundation expanded its projects
to address a list of the poor world's top killer diseases – diarrhoea,
HIV/AIDS, malaria, pneumonia and tuberculosis. Gates's aim was
to reduce decisively the 25-year gap in life expectancy between the

poor and the rich worlds. But the philanthropic ambition of Bill and Melinda Gates went further. They next developed the structure of their foundation to span four international programmes: Global Health; Global Development; Global Growth and Opportunity; and Global Policy and Advocacy – plus a fifth programme to increase educational opportunities for poorer Americans. The concerns of philanthropy had come to mirror those of a globalized world.

In 2005 Bill and Melinda Gates, along with the international rock star Bono, were named by *Time* magazine as Persons of the Year for their 'outstanding charitable work'. The citation mentioned Bono's role in organizing the Live 8 concerts which had focused the world's eight richest governments on the severity of global poverty. Bill and Melinda Gates were cited for the scale of the work of their foundation. Bono seized the occasion to highlight the work of Melinda. 'It wasn't called the Bill & Melinda Gates Foundation by accident,' he said. 'From the start, Melinda's vision has been as important as Bill's in shaping the organization. For all she's already achieved, her focus on empowering women is going to be fundamentally transformative.'[59] Melinda herself set out the complementarity of the couple's approaches. She knew that, however comprehensive was Bill's planning on the science and logistics of vaccination, it would not be a success unless they could work out how to persuade individuals to have their children inoculated. 'Because the delivery is every bit as important as the science,' she said.[60] The billionaire philanthropist Warren Buffett understood that too – which is why he pledged three-quarters of the shares in his company to the Gates Foundation – doubling its endowment and making it by far the largest philanthropic body in the world. Gates, he insisted, was a man who could deliver.

As a result of all this the first decade of the twenty-first century was widely hailed as a new 'golden age of philanthropy'. The prominent moral philosopher, Peter Singer, Professor of Bioethics in the Center for Human Values at Princeton University, declared that 'Bill Gates and Warren Buffett are changing the world like no other humans in history'. They and Melinda Gates, he added, 'really live up to the idea that every human life has equal value whether it's the life of an impoverished person in a developing country or the life of one of their fellow Americans'.[61] A few months after Buffett's mammoth donation, Bill Gates left Microsoft and became a full-time philanthropist with his foundation. In 2007 he set out his philosophy on giving. He was addressing graduates at Harvard University, from which he had dropped out in 1975 before going on to build one of the world's most successful businesses. It is worth quoting at some length:

> I left Harvard with no real awareness of the awful inequities in the world – the appalling disparities of health, and wealth, and opportunity, that condemn millions of people to lives of despair.
>
> I learned a lot here at Harvard about new ideas in economics and politics. I got great exposure to the advances being made in the sciences. But humanity's greatest advances are not in its discoveries – but in how those discoveries are applied to reduce inequity. Whether through democracy, strong public education, quality health care, or broad economic opportunity – reducing inequity is the highest human achievement . . .
>
> For Melinda and for me, the challenge is the same: how can we do the most good for the greatest number with the resources we have.
>
> During our discussions on this question, Melinda and I read an article about the millions of children who were dying every year in poor countries from diseases that we had long ago made harmless in this country: measles, malaria, pneumonia, hepatitis B, yellow fever. One disease I had never even heard of, rotavirus, was killing half a million kids each year – none of them in the United States.
>
> We were shocked. We had just assumed that if millions of children were dying and they could be saved, the world would make it a priority to discover and deliver the medicines to save them. But it did not. For under a dollar, there were interventions that could save lives that just weren't being delivered.
>
> If you believe that every life has equal value, it's revolting to learn that some lives are seen as worth saving and others are not. How could the world let these children die?' The answer is simple, and harsh. The market did not reward saving the lives of these children, and governments did not subsidize it. So the children died because their mothers and their fathers had no power in the market and no voice in the system.
>
> But you and I have both. We can make market forces work better for the poor if we can develop a more creative capitalism – if we can stretch the reach of market forces so that more people can make a profit, or at least make a living, serving people who are suffering

from the worst inequities. We also can press governments around the world to spend taxpayer money in ways that better reflect the values of the people who pay the taxes.

If we can find approaches that meet the needs of the poor in ways that generate profits for business and votes for politicians, we will have found a sustainable way to reduce inequity in the world.

This task is open-ended. It can never be finished. But a conscious effort to answer this challenge will change the world. I am optimistic that we can do this.[62]

GATES AND THE DREAM OF GLOBAL HEALTH

That speech encapsulates the philosophy of the Gates Foundation over the last two decades. It displays a vivid sense of outrage at the injustice of inequality. It raises awareness. It sees a role for philanthropy in making good the failures of the market and of governments. It calls for a more creative capitalism but asserts the importance of democracy, education, healthcare and the broadening of economic opportunity. It seeks win-win situations. It embodies a call to action. And it is imbued with a sense of optimism. The size of the fortune which Bill Gates has accumulated enables him to take all that forward on a massive scale. The Gates Foundation now spends more annually on global health than does the wealthy government of Germany.[63] When the foundation made its first big grant for malaria research, it nearly doubled the amount of money spent on the disease worldwide. That typified the Gates approach: find an intervention that works, pour in large amounts of money – $2 billion in this case – then scale up the response with techniques taken from best business practice. It also involves learning from experience. 'When we first started learning about malaria,' Bill and Melinda wrote in their 2019 annual letter, 'we thought the world would never make real headway on the disease until someone invented a long-acting vaccine. But thanks to bed nets and other measures, malaria deaths are down 42 per cent since 2000.'[64]

They used the same approach with polio. In 1988 a thousand children a day were paralyzed by polio, but 30 years later – after Gates contributed $3 billion to an $11 billion initiative by the World Health Organization – two and a half billion children have been vaccinated and cases of polio have been cut by 99.9 per cent. Perhaps the greatest achievement has been to eradicate the disease among the 1.3 billion population of India,

which will soon be the most populous country on the planet.[65] There
the Gates Foundation partnered with the government in a campaign
to wipe out the disease. Three decades ago more than 150,000 polio
cases were diagnosed in India in one year alone. But in February 2014
the Indian government was able to declare that 'India became polio-
free last month on January 13th, three years after its last victim was
diagnosed with the disease in West Bengal.'[66] It almost certainly would
not have happened without the Gates Foundation.

The campaign had been run along the philanthrocapitalist lines beloved
of Microsoft's founder. As the Gates Foundation website spelled out: 'A
number of factors contributed to India's success: highly targeted, data-
driven planning; well-trained and motivated staff; rigorous monitoring;
effective communications; mobilization of trusted community and
religious leaders; political will at all levels; and adequate funding.'[67] Gates
hailed the Indian government's eradication of polio as the greatest health
achievement he had seen. Its Gates-assisted campaign had deployed two
million staff to vaccinate 170 million children throughout the country
in just two days to help finally extirpate the disease. The mission would
have failed if India, home to one in six of the world's population, had
not vaccinated every single child in the country on those dates. It was a
mammoth task. 'India may be the hardest place on the planet to vaccinate
every child,' Gates said. 'The country has some of the most densely
populated urban areas in the world, making it a challenge to track [the]
children polio workers have [already] immunised.'[68] The approach is
now being used as a model to tackle polio in the few countries where it
now remains – including Nigeria, Afghanistan and Pakistan. Worldwide,
polio has now been virtually eliminated.[69]

But the Gates Foundation's philanthropy was still expanding.
Out of its Global Health programme grew a Global Development
programme. It extended Bill and Melinda's concerns to maternal and
child healthcare, hygiene, family planning, gender equality, nutrition,
agriculture, financial services, clean water and sanitation. Gates, ever
in search of technical fixes, launched the *Reinvent the Toilet Challenge*
to bring sanitation to the 2.5 billion people in the world who do
not have access to mains drainage. Gates tasked researchers with
developing innovative, and financially profitable, systems to manage
human waste. The toilets had to work without mains water, at a cost
of less than five cents a day, so they could be used in urban slums.

In 2015 Gates shared a video of himself drinking a glass of water from a system which converts human sewage into water, electricity and ash. The film produced much mirth among commentators, but it registered the serious point that 88 per cent of the world's fatal diarrhoeal illnesses are caused by unsafe water and poor sanitation – and that there were ways to make this safe. Diarrhoea, the second biggest cause of death for the under-fives, kills more children than AIDS, malaria and measles combined. More than a million children died that way in 2000; by 2015, thanks in large part to the investments of the Gates Foundation, that figure had halved. To the delight of data-conscious Bill, every $1 he invested returned around $5 in higher work productivity, lower health costs and fewer missed work days.[70]

The key to his success, Bill Gates insisted, was focus. 'We don't build roads,' he said. 'Our deep, deep areas of expertise are health and agriculture. Our initial focus was global health and US education. In global health, overall, we've done a great job, we feel more impact than we expected.'[71] What Bill Gates called 'catalytic philanthropy' – 'innovating where markets won't and governments can't' – made the Gates Foundation one of the leading forces for improved health on the planet. As Bono put it in 2017: 'That's 122 million kids saved since 1990. That's crazy . . . that's over 13,000 a day . . . It's an enormous thing.'[72]

CAN PHILANTHROCAPITALISM REALLY SAVE THE WORLD?

Bill Gates was not alone. The role of private philanthropy in international development has increased dramatically over the past two decades. At the beginning of the twenty-first century the flow of philanthropists' cash to developing countries was so small it didn't warrant a separate entry in the statistics of the Organization for Economic Co-operation and Development. By 2011 philanthropy had made its way into the official OECD figures as a separate item – accounting for about half as much as aid from the rich to the poor world[73]. It was considered so significant it even figured in the organization's official *communiqué*. That same year the G20, the group of the world's leading economies, asked Gates, as the most celebrated of the new philanthropists, to write a report on how to finance the Millennium Development Goals – the targets set by the world at the end of the twentieth century to eradicate extreme poverty and hunger by the year 2015. Matthew Bishop and Michael Green, the authors of *Philanthrocapitalism*, observed with a touch of cynicism that the eagerness of big governments for a 'new global partnership' with philanthropists may have been driven less by admiration for the innovative methods of the new humanitarians – and more by the need to find additional cash to finance politicians' goals.[74]

Certainly the input of the Gates Foundation is very substantial. It is now the second largest donor to the World Health Organization (WHO); only the US government gives more.[75] Enthusiasts claim that philanthrocapitalism promises to develop poor nations faster than most governments and intergovernmental organizations ever could. Philanthropy, they say, is capable of 'remaking the landscape of international development assistance'. It has the ability to 'resolve the tension between society and the market that has lain at the core of the century-old debate on how to reduce world poverty'.[76] Critics, on the other hand, say that philanthropy alone will never do this without collaboration with governments, the private sector and grassroots communities.

Certainly, as the philosopher Peter Singer argues, philanthropy is free of the constraints that voters place upon governments and which geopolitics place upon United Nations agencies. Government aid programmes, which are often proclaimed as acts of benevolent altruism, are in reality often tied to the requirement to purchase goods produced by the donor nation. 'Wheat for Africa must be grown in America, although aid experts say this often depresses local African markets, reducing the incentive for farmers there to produce more,' Singer wrote in the *New York Times*. 'In a decision that surely costs lives, hundreds of millions of condoms intended to stop the spread of AIDS in Africa and around the world must be manufactured in the US, although they cost twice as much as similar products made in Asia.'[77] Private donors need not comply with such political pressures. They can more easily avoid dealing with corrupt or wasteful governments. They can adopt innovative high-risk approaches which politicians and aid agencies would avoid for fear of being told by the public that they were 'wasting our money'.

Justin Forsyth – who has worked in all three of the political, charitable and international spheres – says that the big lesson he drew from a decade working in the private office of the British Prime Minister, then as the chief executive of Save the Children, and then as Deputy Executive Director of the United Nations Children's Fund, was that coalitions working across the usual boundaries could be remarkably effective. 'The halving of child deaths in recent decades is a remarkable story that wouldn't have happened without the power of the Gates Foundation, and innovation from the private sector, and NGOs and governments. We can't stop dangerous climate change, end extreme poverty or end child deaths from malaria and diarrhoea without everybody playing their part,' he says. That means charities co-operating with philanthropists and their businesses. Speaking while at Save the Children he said:

> We also want to harness the business and research power of companies. We don't just want cash from the private sector; we want to work with them to change how they do their everyday activities so their core business becomes transformational. We work with the pharmaceutical company GlaxoSmithKline, to stop newborn babies dying of sepsis.* We have a similar core business partnership with Reckitt Benckiser Group on diarrhoea – the biggest killer of children – and they have invented two new products. For me, the lesson from Gates is not just the power of money but how Bill and Melinda Gates use their power to lever wider change ... So when companies like Unilever, GSK or RB step up, we should back them and when billionaires follow the lead of Bill and Melinda Gates and use their wealth for good, we should urge others to follow.[78]

But the lead of Bill and Melinda Gates on global health has also been questioned in three key areas. The first is that Bill Gates's personal intuitions can lead to him to target 'easy-fix solutions' and to avoid the more complex issues which cause far bigger problems for poor people in the developing world. The second is that his huge influence can unbalance global spending, not just on health but in other areas such as agriculture, promoting an over-reliance on Western technology which has been dubbed philanthropic colonialism. The third is that there is an incoherence between the grants given out by the Gates Foundation and the investments it holds, creating what we might call philanthropic contradictions. Let us examine these in turn.

---

* See page 427 above.

PHILANTHROPIC ARROGANCE

Several of the criticisms levelled against Bill Gates for his early philanthropic activities on education reform in the United States are also levelled at his globalized philanthropy. The critique applies to philanthrocapitalists in general, but Gates, as the most powerful figure in the field, often bears the brunt of the public concern. The resources of the Gates Foundation are so considerable – both financially and in terms of its founder's public profile – that it negotiates on equal terms with governments. Gates gives so much to the Global Alliance for Vaccines and Immunization (GAVI) that his foundation gets a seat on the board.[79] That gives him far more influence than he would get, for example, by giving a grant to the World Health Organization.[80] But it also draws the criticism that such influence is unhealthily exercised on the basis of Bill and Melinda Gates's personal intuitions – or on what Britain's prestigious medical magazine, the *Lancet*, cuttingly called 'a whimsical governance principle'. This was an oblique reference to the first guiding principle of the Gates Foundation, set out on its website; it declares that its activities are 'driven by the interests and passions of the Gates family'.[81] Critics say that Gates is inclined to define the problem, set the agenda, devise the strategy, and then find or create organizations to execute its agenda.[82] The leading US philanthropy commentator Pablo Eisenberg says this top-down style discourages policymakers from considering 'a broader range of ideas'. He accuses Gates of 'philanthropic arrogance'.[83] Certainly such an approach causes problems in the field of health, as it has in that of education.

Specific allegations were made in 2008 when the director of the WHO's malaria programme, Dr Arata Kochi, wrote a memo to the director-general of the organization. In it he complained that the growing dominance of the Gates Foundation over malaria research was stifling a diversity of views among scientists on the issue. Gates had increased the total spending on malaria research – from $84 million a year in the late 1990s to around $1.2 billion by 2008. That made the Gates Foundation the world's biggest donor. But the large influx of Gates money, Kochi warned, could have 'far-reaching, largely unintended consequences'. So many of the world's leading malaria scientists were now being funded by Gates that they were now 'locked up in a cartel' in which the research funding of many of the scientists was linked to maintaining the approval of others within the group, Kochi claimed. 'Each has a vested interest to safeguard the work of the others,' he told his boss. That meant getting independent reviews of research proposals 'is becoming increasingly difficult'. The Gates Foundation's decision-making, said Dr Kochi, was 'a closed internal process, and as far as can be seen, accountable to none other than itself'. He cited an example. Some outside experts were warning against the vaccination of babies with a preventative anti-malaria drug, Fansidar – which has rare but deadly side effects. But their warnings were being met with 'intense and aggressive opposition' from Gates-backed scientists who were increasingly prey to 'group think'.

Dr Kochi was not alone. The Gates Foundation has surrounded itself with an 'aura of uncriticizability', claimed the medical anthropologist Katerini Storeng, who conducted a study of Gates healthcare for Oslo University's Centre for Development and the Environment, and the London School of Hygiene and Tropical Medicine.[84] The power of the Gates Foundation and other big funders 'is so great that some researchers feel inhibited to offend them', according to Colin Butler, who in 2019 conducted a review of Gates's work for Australia's National Centre for Epidemiology and Population Health.[85]

But there is a wider criticism. The personal preferences of philanthropists can also unbalance the way money is spent. Areas of major importance were being neglected because they did not match the particular interests of individual donors. The accusation is general but again Bill Gates – such is the scale of his generosity – was the focus of the criticism. In 2009 the *Lancet* published an evaluation of Gates's grants from 1998–2007 conducted by a team led by David McCoy, now Professor of Global Public Health at Queen Mary University London. It acknowledged that a massive boost to global health funding had been provided by the Bill & Melinda Gates Foundation since its inception – particularly on immunization. But the study showed a heavy bias in funding towards malaria and HIV/AIDS, with relatively little investment into tuberculosis, maternal and child health, and nutrition (an imbalance which the Gates Foundation has since partly addressed). Chronic diseases were almost entirely absent from its spending portfolio. The *Lancet* editorial spoke of an 'alarmingly poor correlation between the Foundation's funding and childhood disease priorities'. Grants made by the foundation did 'not reflect the burden of disease endured by those in deepest poverty'.[86] Worse than that, 'a focus on malaria in areas where other diseases cause more human harm creates damaging perverse incentives for politicians, policy makers, and health workers,' the editorial insisted. 'In some countries, the valuable resources of the Foundation are being wasted and diverted from more urgent needs.' In 2019 Professor McCoy was updating his research. It suggested that, despite some improvements in the pattern of funding, several of the 2009 criticisms remained valid.[87]

What causes such a blind spot on the part of a philanthropist as sophisticated as Bill Gates? It lies perhaps in his preference for technological rather than social approaches. Gates's penchant for technical solutions, such as new vaccines, has a tendency to squeeze out cheaper or quicker options, claims Linsey McGoey, a former advisor to the World Health Organization.[88] The foundation's prioritization of vaccine solutions also reflects the Gates preference for interventions with quick measurable and visible solutions.[89] This ignores a long-standing debate among healthcare experts, which has been going on for over a century, over whether what they call a 'vertical intervention' – focusing on a single disease – can ever succeed without a complementary 'horizontal' programme to create a competent healthcare system to deliver the vertical initiative. Bill Gates is keen on technical solutions but less interested in strengthening the healthcare infrastructure needed to deliver vaccination on the ground. The Gates Foundation had 'a very loud, vocal voice, saying that we do not *believe* in the strengthening of health systems', one GAVI insider told Katerini Storeng, recalling that Bill Gates often told him in private conversations that 'he is vehemently *against* health systems'. He claims that Gates told him that supporting health infrastructure was 'basically . . . a complete waste of money, that there is no evidence that it works, so I will not see a dollar or cent of my money go to the strengthening of health systems'. A repeated refrain was: Health systems do not kill people – diseases do. 'Mr Gates himself . . . believes that the world can be cured by technology.'[90] (Gates was to significantly change his mind on this after the Ebola emergency in Africa in 2015. But his warnings on the need for change to prevent a global epidemic, which eerily predicted the 2020 COVID-19 coronavirus pandemic, went unheeded).*

---

* See pages 500–501.

Grassroots groups in Africa have criticized the Global Alliance for Vaccines and Immunization for following what they call this 'Gates-approach'. In response GAVI has included extra cash to strengthen health infrastructure. But still, under the influence of Gates, only 10 per cent of GAVI's spending between 2000 and 2013 has been dedicated to that – compared with 78 per cent being spent on vaccine support. Today the Gates Foundation continues to be 'disproportionately supportive of vertical health programs, focusing on a range of individual diseases, and a few syndromes, rather than seeking to improve health systems', according to Colin Butler's 2019 report for the National Centre for Epidemiology and Population Health. No money seems directed at improving continuing education for health professionals in poor countries. To make its philanthropic interventions more successful, says Butler, the Gates Foundation needs to invest 'a small fraction of its budget to reward, retain and equip dedicated, locally trained staff, not only of doctors and nurses, but also outreach workers and laboratory staff'. A broader strategy is needed to achieve Bill and Melinda Gates's goal of eradicating extreme poverty.

PHILANTHROPIC COLONIALISM

Such criticisms are not restricted to the Gates's work on health. Similar complaints are made about their initiatives to combat hunger by improving agriculture, according to a major report in 2016 by the Global Policy Forum, a consortium of German development agencies which work largely in Africa.[91] Philanthropy is skewing policy on agriculture as well as health. Big philanthropy organizations, like the Gates Foundation, have such influence that they are persuading governments and international development agencies to follow their lead in setting up public-private partnerships with agro-industry and pharmaceutical companies. These often promote environmentally damaging styles of corporate farming, the report warned. Big foundations often have a policy which requires governments to contribute half the funding for the projects instigated by the philanthropists. Governments are then faced with a hard choice: to turn down the philanthropist's money or to divert funds from another public priority to the project which fits with the philanthropist's preferences. By insisting that 'he who plays the piper calls the tune', foundations can subvert normal decision-making by democratically elected governments, the report complains.[92] The 'sheer size' of philanthropic grant-making can thus undermine national governments and international agencies such as those of the United Nations. 'So far there has been a fairly willing belief among governments and international organisations in the positive role of philanthropy,' the consortium concludes. But the evidence is mounting, 'in light of experiences in the areas of health and agriculture', that 'a thorough assessment of the impacts and side-effects of philanthropic engagement' is now necessary.

How valid are such criticisms? Consider agriculture. Both the Gates and Rockefeller foundations regard technological innovation as the solution to hunger in Africa. In 2006 they jointly launched the Alliance for a Green Revolution in Africa (AGRA).* Since then the Gates Foundation, which has taken the leadership, has given more than $3 billion to support 660 projects intended 'to increase agricultural productivity among smallholder farmers in Sub-Saharan Africa'. Yet, although the vast majority of grants focus on Africa, more than 80 per cent of the money goes to organizations based in the US and Europe. Only 4 per cent went to groups based in Africa. And only 12 per cent of the research grants went to universities and research centres based there.[93] The Gates Foundation replies that this is simply because Western innovation and technology are the most effective means to increase African agricultural productivity. 'The world has already developed better fertilizer, and crops that are more productive, nutritious, and drought- and disease-resistant,' Bill and Melinda Gates have written.[94] 'With access to these and other existing technologies, African farmers could theoretically double their yields. With greater productivity, farmers will also grow a greater variety of food, and they'll be able to sell their surpluses to supplement their family's diet with vegetables, eggs, milk, and meat.' Their answer, therefore, is to fund research on biotechnology, synthetic fertilizers, irrigation systems and hybrid seeds – including the controversial kind which are genetically modified.

Bill Gates sees no controversy in genetically modified organisms, or in the scientific jargon GMOs. In 2015 he stated: 'There is quite a bit of improvement still available with conventional breeding but in this timeframe the GMO-derived seeds will provide far better productivity, better drought tolerance, and salinity tolerance, and if the safety is proven, then the African countries will be amongst the biggest beneficiaries. I

---

* See the interview with the Rockefeller president, Rajiv Shah, on page 367.

think most of Africa will see this as a way of improving its productivity.'[95] Warren Buffett's son Peter, who has established his own foundation, is critical of this. He condemns the tendency for 'transplanting what worked in one setting directly into another with little regard for culture, geography or societal norms'. He calls it 'philanthropic colonialism'.[96]

But Africa needs a lot more than technology to solve extreme hunger. Interestingly, Bill and Melinda Gates now accept this. Their 2015 annual letter acknowledges that other limitations 'keep Africa from feeding itself'. These include the lack of roads and transport, lack of access to markets, gender disparities, and government policies that do not serve the interests of farming families. Moreover, they accept that 'wealthy countries also need to make policy changes, like opening their markets and cutting agricultural subsidies'.[97] Yet despite that, when it comes to making grants on agriculture, the Gates Foundation focuses almost exclusively on advanced technologies. It hardly addresses structural barriers to agricultural development – such as import tariffs and trade liberalization agreements which are loaded against poor countries and in favour of rich ones. Instead, the Gates approach involves persuading African farmers to buy commercial patented seeds, rather than relying on their own traditional varieties. 'Under the guise of eliminating hunger in Africa', the Global Policy Forum says, such philanthropy is merely 'a tool to open African markets to US agri-business'.[98] Worse than that, Gates is allowing agribusiness giants such as Monsanto 'to corporatize Africa's genetic riches for the benefit of outsiders,' complains Phil Bereano, Professor Emeritus of Technology and Public Policy at the University of Washington.[99] Instead, these critics say, the foundation should be prioritizing green agro-ecology approaches.[100]

PHILANTHROPIC CONTRADICTIONS

There is a third area of criticism. The intensity of Bill Gates's focus can sometimes be too narrow. In 2007 the *Los Angeles Times* highlighted what it saw as the inconsistency of Gates funding a polio and measles vaccination drive in Nigeria, while at the same time holding investments in oil companies which were polluting the Niger Delta. The industry's sooty gas flares – containing benzene, mercury and chromium toxins – were blamed by local doctors for an epidemic of bronchitis in adults, and asthma and blurred vision in children.[101] Oil bore holes, filled with stagnant water, created a breeding ground for the mosquitoes that spread malaria, one of the diseases Gates was targeting. And the region's oil workers, and the soldiers who were protecting them from rebel guerrillas, were a magnet for prostitution. That contributed to a surge in HIV and teenage pregnancy, both of which were targets of Gates campaigns. His foundation's health initiatives were being undermined by its own investment policies.

Some 41 per cent of Gates Foundation investments – totalling around $8.7 billion – was held in companies whose work was incompatible with the foundation's charitable goals, analysts for the *Los Angeles Times* reported. These included pharmaceutical companies which priced their drugs too highly for poor people to afford. The *LA Times* criticized the 'firewall' that the Gates Foundation erected between its grant-making and its investing. 'The goals of the former are not allowed to interfere with the investments of the latter,' it claimed. In response the foundation's chief operating officer, Cheryl Scott, said it did not invest in companies whose core activities 'we find egregious'. That was why Gates did not own tobacco stocks. But more generally, she wrote, 'the Foundation is a passive investor' because it wants to stay focused on its philanthropy and diverting staff to scrutinize the foundation's investments in close detail would distract the staff from its core work.[102]

But later the Gates Foundation modified its approach. According to Dr Colin Butler's 2019 review, it has substantially reduced its investment in fossil fuel companies.[103] It has also sold the $23 million-worth of shares it bought in Monsanto in 2010,[104] though in 2018 Warren Buffett revealed that his Berkshire Hathaway company – in which the Gates Foundation holds almost 60 million shares – had increased its holding in Monsanto to shares worth $2.2 billion.[105] And the Gates Foundation remains one of the world's largest single investors in biotechnology for farming and pharmaceuticals.[106] There is also 'a revolving door . . . between the Gates Foundation and pharmaceutical corporations', according to the Global Policy Forum report. It names a number of the foundation's staff who have also worked for pharmaceutical companies.[107] And Colin Butler's review criticizes Gates for ignoring 'ecological or planetary health' in its grant-making.

Not all the criticisms levelled at Gates are consistent. Right-wing critics have attacked the fact that someone as rich as Bill Gates receives tax subsidies on his donations. In Britain the populist *Daily Mail*, reporting on a joint initiative on malaria announced in 2016 by the

British government and the Gates Foundation, complained that 'British taxpayers will foot most of the bill' for an ambitious project dreamt up by 'Microsoft tycoon and philanthropist Bill Gates'.[108] The British Chancellor, George Osborne, and Bill Gates had unveiled a £3 billion plan for a five-year project for research into drugs, diagnostics and insecticides to eliminate the mosquito-borne disease. The conservative tabloid was outraged by the fact that the British government was contributing three times more than the Gates Foundation – as if it thought that one man had a greater responsibility than an entire nation.

Attacks from the left have been more concerned with issues of accountability and the fact that – though governments must answer to voters and companies to shareholders – philanthropists are obliged to answer to no one. The philosopher Peter Singer, writing in the *New York Times*, said: 'Much as we may applaud what Gates and Buffett are doing, we can also be troubled by a system that leaves the fate of hundreds of millions of people hanging on the decisions of two or three private citizens.'[109] We will address this issue in the next chapter, but it is worth noting here that, with regard to global health and agriculture, there are those who argue that philanthropy may even impede real development – which has been described by the Nobel economist Amartya Sen as being about increasing freedom and well-being, not just raising incomes.[110] The barriers to change aren't necessarily technology, or even lack of funds: they're more often political, argues the radical development activist Deborah Doane.[111] Philanthropy can only promote real lasting change if rich givers are prepared to nurture the growth of a range of small organizations such as charities, voluntary groups, neighbourhood organizations, pressure groups, community development associations, and the other 'little platoons' that make up civil society. Such are the mechanisms by which ordinary people hold the powerful to account. Without them changes in the structure of power can never occur. To this end the *Lancet* offered the Gates Foundation 'five modest proposals':

> First, improve your governance. Visibly involve diverse leaders with experience in global health in your strategic and operational stewardship.
>
> Second, be more transparent and accountable in your decision-making. Explain your strategy openly and change it in the light of advice and evidence.

Third, devise a grant award plan that more accurately reflects the
global burden of disease, aligning yourself more with the needs of
those in greatest suffering.

Fourth, do more to invest in health systems and research capacity
in low-income countries, leaving a sustainable footprint of your
commitment.

Finally, listen and be prepared to engage with your friends.[112]

BILL GATES LEARNS THE LIMITS OF TECHNOLOGY

Bill and Melinda Gates themselves appear to have learned some lessons
when it comes to health systems. In 2010 Melinda conceded that
'women and children have a continuum of needs, and we must design
health programmes accordingly'.[113]

But it was in 2015 that Bill really changed his mind about health
infrastructure. What brought about this sudden conversion was his
experiences funding the fight against the 2014 African Ebola epidemic,
in which more than 11,000 people died. That became clear from a
paper he wrote for the *New England Journal of Medicine* in which he
warned that the next epidemic could be far worse.[114] He summarized its
contents in the *New York Times*, warning:

> As awful as it is, Ebola spreads only through physical contact, and by
> the time patients can infect other people, they are already showing
> symptoms of the disease, which makes them relatively easy to identify.
> Other diseases – flu, for example – spread through the air, and people
> can be infectious before they feel sick, which means that one person
> can infect many strangers just by going to a public place. We've seen
> it happen before, with horrific results: in 1918, the Spanish flu killed
> more than 30 million people. Imagine what it could do in today's
> highly mobile world.[115]

In a TED talk in Vancouver in 2015 he warned of the danger of 'a virus
where people feel well enough while they're infectious that they get on
a plane or they go to a market'.[116] It was an uncanny foreshadowing of
the coronavirus pandemic which hit the world five years later in 2020.
It led Gates to call on the world's politicians to create not only a global
warning and response system for epidemics – along military lines – but
also the creation of better health infrastructure in the developing world

Business has now discovered the advantages of philanthropy. In 2013 the luxury fashion house Fendi gave €2.2 million to restore the famous Trevi fountain (*above*) in Rome. Fendi is part of the Paris-based multinational conglomerate LVMH, run by Bernard Arnault, the richest man in Europe, for whom it produced what the *Financial Times* called 'juicy tax breaks'. When the restoration was complete a glass runway was laid over the waters of the 300-year-old fountain down which top models glided in 2016 for a Fendi fashion show.

Chuck Feeney, who made $8 billion from duty-free shops, is the 'James Bond of philanthropy'. For years he gave his fortune away anonymously before announcing his philosophy of 'Giving while Living'. This inspired Bill Gates and Warren Buffett to devise the Giving Pledge to persuade their fellow billionaires to give away at least half their fortunes before they die. Feeney (*left*) hired Chris Oechsli (*right*) to give his away. It is almost all gone. Feeney lives simply – and says he wants his last cheque to bounce.

In 1993 Microsoft magnate Bill Gates and his fiancée Melinda French went on safari with a few friends ahead of their wedding. But it was not Africa's animals which left an indelible impression on the couple. When they returned they told close friends that the poverty and struggle of the ordinary people there had been traumatising. It was the catalyst to turn Bill and Melinda Gates into the world's biggest philanthropists.

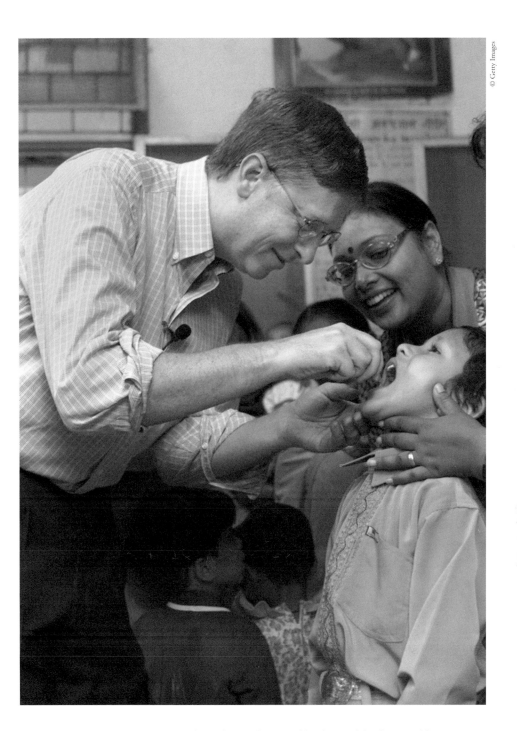

Philanthropy is now on an epic scale in the modern world. The wealth, drive and business acumen of tech titans like Bill Gates have brought huge benefits for humankind. Cases of polio, which once paralyzed a thousand children every day, have been cut by 99.9 per cent worldwide thanks to vaccinations funded by Gates – seen (*above*) administering polio vaccine to a child in India where the disease has now been declared eradicated. Gates is the great exemplar of philanthrocapitalism which seeks to apply business methods to the charitable sector. Its successes are self-evident – but it has its downsides too.

Among the dozens of causes supported from the £3 billion personal fortune of Richard Branson is The Elders – a group of senior international statesmen and women inaugurated by Nelson Mandela (*above*), Kofi Annan, Jimmy Carter and others to broker peace in the world's trouble spots. Branson's giving has not saved him from criticism over the fact that he has paid no personal tax in the UK for 14 years.

Britain's leading philanthrocapitalist, Sir Christopher Hohn, has donated over $5 billion to children's causes. Known in the City for his secrecy and financial ruthlessness, Hohn never forgot the sight of children scavenging for food on rubbish dumps when he was a young banker in the Philippines. He invented a unique hybrid to channel his hedge fund profits into a charity – the Children's Investment Fund Foundation – creating a 'remarkable combination of ruthless profiteering and philanthropy'.

A recent revival of the 18th century tradition of activist philanthropy has seen celebrities like Angelina Jolie (*above, after the 2005 Pakistan earthquake*) donating not just money but time, harnessing their fame to draw forgotten emergencies into the international spotlight. Over the last 20 years Jolie has dragged a photo-hungry media with her on 60 trips to refugee camps in 30 countries. Other 'agitator philanthropists' like Bono and Bob Geldof have sustained campaigns for the world's poor over three decades.

Philanthropists can develop a long-term vision which eludes governments. After funding the fight against Ebola in 2014, Bill Gates gave a TED talk in which he warned that a more infectious pandemic could kill 10 million people. He repeated the warning every year, publicly (*including above in 2018*) and in a private meeting with President Donald Trump in 2019. The world took no notice – until the deadly COVID-19 coronavirus struck. Then, while governments floundered, Gates pumped billions into the search for a vaccine.

Is all philanthropy political? Many of those who give to 'good causes' also give to political parties. But their political influence goes well beyond electoral politics. The energy billionaires and brothers, Charles (*centre*) and David Koch (*above right with opera singer Samuel Ramey*) have given hundreds of millions of dollars to fund right-wing lobbyists and academics who promote climate change denial.

By contrast the multi-billionaire financier George Soros, who grew up under both Nazi and Communist totalitarianism, has given over $18 billion to promote democracy, human rights and accountable government. Soros (*pictured below with Archbishop Desmond Tutu*) began by funding scholarships for black South Africans in 1979. For 40 years he has supported liberal democracy and opposed authoritarian regimes. Political philanthropists of both right and left raise the question: Is philanthropy compatible with democracy?

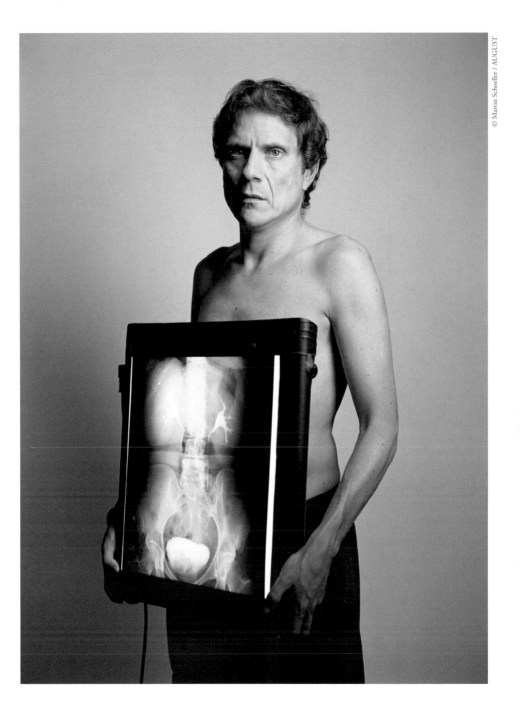

Zell Kravinsky (*above*) gave away $45 million – almost everything he had – but it wasn't enough. So he donated one of his kidneys to a total stranger. Kravinsky is one of the most extreme devotees of the philosophy of Effective Altruism which is embraced by many philanthrocapitalists. EA enthusiasts say that human choices should be made merely by using data to measure efficiency. Giving should be purely rational, not emotional or sentimental. The approach works well on simple problems, but on complex issues it can be dehumanising. It ignores the social, psychological, aesthetic, empathetic and spiritual dimensions to life which philanthropy should embrace and celebrate.

At its best philanthropy involves donors listening to recipients and entering into relationships of mutual respect. For over a decade the NoVo Foundation, run by Jennifer and Peter Buffett (*above with his father, Warren*) was a model of this approach. It married strategic and reciprocal philanthropy – giving $700 million to pioneering projects to empower black women and combat domestic violence. But it was funded out of Warren's company profits. When these slumped in the 2020 COVID-19 stock market crash, NoVo reverted to a top-down model of philanthropy. It made cuts which its partners condemned as the opposite of what the crisis required.

In 2015, to mark the birth of their first child, Facebook chief Mark Zuckerberg and his paediatrician wife Priscilla Chan pledged to give away 99 per cent of their Facebook shares – then worth $45 billion – in the biggest act of philanthropy in world history. But they did not set up a traditional charitable foundation to do it. Instead they used more opaque financial models – a limited liability company and secretive donor-advised funds. Will these be more efficient vehicles for better philanthropy – or new methods of plutocratic manipulation?

where such an epidemic would wreak greatest havoc. It was a complete reversal of his previous rhetoric, though he accompanied it with more familiar advocacy for increased research and development on vaccines and diagnostics. But he now insisted that Africa's Ebola outbreak had underlined 'the urgent need to strengthen health systems in the world's poorest countries'. He added, in a clear change of message, 'Health systems – which encompass everything from rural clinics to community health workers to hospitals – are the best protection against epidemics'.[117] Sadly his warning went unheeded by the world's governments.

But it changed policy within the Gates Foundation. The following year, in 2016, a Gates spokeswoman, Leonora Diller, insisted that in all its grant-making the Gates Foundation was now 'guided by the evidence and by the deep research and expertise of our partners and grantees'. She added: 'We continue to try to do all we can to be transparent and accountable [on] our investments and our decision-making'.[118]

And in 2019 Bill Gates admitted to the *Financial Times*: 'Ten years ago, we were pretty naïve. We hoped if you invested and developed new technologies, the world would applaud and figure out how to get them into [the field].'[119] But the adoption of vaccines had been sluggish, so he had learned that he needed to place greater emphasis on management, politics and health systems. Now, he knew, he needed to listen more to those already working at the grassroots. The foundation, he revealed, which now has more than 1,500 staff in its Seattle headquarters, has eased its centralized control and expanded regional offices in places such as South Africa.

Even so, his philanthrocapitalist enthusiasm for data is undiminished. Speaking of how he had become much more hands-on in seeking to eradicate polio from one of its few remaining outposts in Nigeria, he said: 'We look at the delivery systems, the supply chain, the metrics. We have a dashboard with the latest data, and several times a year I have a video conference with Nigerian state governors. We are making it a super-measured field.' Apart from anything else, he insisted, using data to focus on technical solutions with clear measurable outcomes was essential to encourage donations by other philanthropists. 'It's important to shine a light on progress. People are motivated by success. The fact that the world has cut child deaths in half in just 20 years – that gets people excited and makes them think about what else can be accomplished. It's not easy for a leader to prioritize investments for which the pay-off isn't immediate. Elections are rarely won because vaccination systems were strengthened, even though a strong vaccination system underlies a healthy, productive society.'[120]

Some development experts were not entirely convinced. A month later Jean-Jacques Schul, chair of IDAY, a Brussels-based network of 600 civil society organizations in francophone Africa, responded in the *Financial Times*. Bill and Melinda Gates, he wrote, were still 'driving poor countries on a non-sustainable development path'. He wrote that 'supporting costly solutions with foreign donations may offer short-term solutions, but generous donors also create longer term problems and cannot claim therefore to put the recipient countries on a sustainable development path'. Take malaria. It is true that foreign aid has succeeded in reducing the number of worldwide malaria deaths by three-quarters. But, he added, 'despite annual donations of about $3bn, malaria deaths have been flat stagnant since 2016, with more than 800 African children still dying every day and no hope of bringing this to an end with the current costly methods supported by the rich donors. Countries like India and Mozambique, which had come close to eliminating the disease, have seen malaria rise again after foreign aid was withdrawn.'[121]

Britain's aid budget has long seen civil society organizations as 'key partners' in delivering effective development. Only grassroots organizations 'hold governments to account' because they 'give voice to marginalised groups'.[122] Such groups are best at delivering services to the poorest and most vulnerable but are also essential to empowering ordinary people. They are crucial in scrutinizing the activities of bureaucrats and politicians who often cloak their activities with a veil of secrecy behind which corrupt practices all too easily flourish. To be fair to the Gates Foundation it does, unlike many other philanthrocapitalist institutions, at least acknowledge this. Its spokeswoman, Leonora Diller, has said:

> The problems affecting the world's poorest are complex and we believe that solving them requires the close collaboration of governments, NGOs, academic institutions and for-profit businesses. Governments and international organizations provide the leadership and resources. The private sector has access to life-saving innovations and we believe that the role of philanthropy is to take risks where others can't or won't. Our investments are substantial, but just one piece of the puzzle.[123]

But philanthropists need to put their money where their mouth is, insists Myles Wickstead, a former British ambassador to Ethiopia and head of the secretariat at Tony Blair's Commission for Africa. Philanthropists, like governments, need to form direct relationships with civil society organizations. 'NGOs, international or national, need resources. Philanthropists, international or national, have them.' By working together, philanthropists and civil society groups have a better chance of making real progress on poverty, inequality and sustainability.[124]

Many philanthropists will be resistant to this idea. They will share the common Western presumption that it is up to donors to determine how their money is best spent – not recipients. For most of the last century it has been a commonplace that rich countries should impose conditions on poor countries over the spending of foreign aid. In recent decades aid experts have begun to suggest, rather differently, that poor nations should be empowered and allowed to set their own priorities. The rich nations' club, the OECD, in 2005 even went so far as to agree that wealthy donors would henceforth 'respect partner country leadership and help strengthen their capacity to exercise it'.[125]

The reality often falls short of such rhetoric. A civil servant at the top of a health ministry in one east African government, when asked what would be his country's health priorities in five years' time, recently replied: 'Don't ask me, ask Bill Gates.' The alternative to that is set out by the radical grassroots activist Deborah Doane, who has made a series of recommendations for ways in which philanthropists can demonstrate their authenticity and integrity:

> Set up an independent entity; don't sit on the board; set some guidelines about tackling root causes like corporate power or tax justice; ensure smaller organizations have access to the funds without jumping through excessive hoops; make sure it's governed openly by a broad group of stakeholders, representing gender, race, class, none of whom can sit on the board indefinitely and finally, agree to relinquish control.[126]

But there may be other ways to keep philanthropy true to its avowed mission. In the next chapter we shall examine the attempt by a number of celebrities to do that.

Interview: Ngaire Woods on philanthropy, aid and the global economy

Ngaire Woods is Professor of Global Economic Governance at the University of Oxford. As an academic at Oxford and Harvard she has specialized in international relations with a particular focus on the developing world. Professor Woods has served as an advisor to the board of the International Monetary Fund, the African Development Bank, the UNDP Human Development Report, and the Commonwealth Heads of Government. Since 2011 she has been the founding Dean of Oxford's Blavatnik School of Government which seeks to improve government across the world through research and the training of current and future politicians and civil servants. More widely, she has researched the challenges of globalization and the role of international institutions in global economic governance. Awarded the CBE in 2018, she sits on the board of several philanthropic organizations including the Mo Ibrahim Foundation and the Rhodes Trust.

What is the place of philanthropy in the global economy?

There are two very different rationales for redistribution in the world. One is rooted in a recognition that all humans depend upon one another. If you're a company and you want to work profitably, you need access to roads, to people who are well-educated, to a healthcare system so all your workers don't die of epidemics. That's why in many countries, there's a tax system and there are priorities for providing for those public goods. People have a duty to recognize what it takes to make their enterprise and society work and to contribute to that. That's why they have an obligation to pay taxes and to contribute to the public good.

Some people see philanthropy as an alternative to that. But philanthropy, for me, is rooted in something else. It comes from the human desire to make a difference, to give to others and to help them. There's quite a consistent set of studies that tell us that a very important source of human happiness and self-worth is what we do for others. Philanthropy is an extension of that. I walked past a homeless woman yesterday in London who had just been given a punnet of strawberries and she reached out and offered me one. That's a philanthropic act: I'm going to share what I've got because that might make your day better, as well as mine.

On the international level, then, is aid to poor countries – from governments or from philanthropists – a kind of taxation or a kind of generosity?

The rationale for aid is a combination of both these arguments. One argument says that we depend for our prosperity and progress on other countries. We wouldn't have access to the resources that we need for our economy to work – the trade routes, the sea routes, the natural resources, the human resources – were it not for our engagement with other countries. So we have a duty to make some provision, which is global, for collective goods, like measures to combat climate change or epidemics. Without working together and helping other countries, we ourselves will suffer.

That sounds like self-interest rather than a moral duty or a charitable impulse?

I think it's an enlightened self-interest. It says: 'I have to make this work, because otherwise I can't do my own job.' That's different from philanthropy and the desire people have to help others.

So the philanthropic impulse is something which co-exists with a sense of duty. They're not alternatives?

That's right. The two co-exist. But sometimes they clash. Some people say: 'No, I don't want to pay taxes. I would rather give my money to the Royal Opera House and to a homeless charity.' But if everybody did that, if everybody defected from the system in that way, you couldn't get off base-camp. You wouldn't have public hospitals, you wouldn't have public roads, you wouldn't have public education systems.

But what if you didn't have philanthropy at all? If you only had duty and taxation? Some socialists take that position, arguing that philanthropy is outdated – and that the state should provide everything. What would be the downside of doing that?

Well, I think you would risk squashing the impulse people have to help others. In my view that impulse should be encouraged in every walk of life, from the simplest actions of mutual kindness to the larger acts of philanthropy. But acts of philanthropy should not be seen as an alternative to paying taxes and contributing to the basic infrastructure necessary for societies to work.

So what contribution does philanthropy have to make – in giving aid to poor countries – that taxation and governments can't?

Something that individual philanthropists can do in international development is to tackle issues government are afraid of. For example, in the early days of the HIV/AIDs crisis, many communities shied away from offering treatment and support to affected communities such as men having sex with other men and sex-workers. In many countries, politicians were reluctant to cut across social taboos. Politicians in donor countries often worry too much about tabloid newspaper headlines.

Are philanthropists good at filling that gap? Or do they fall prey to the same temptation of going for the easy options?

Philanthropists can play an important role. Bill Gates is an example of somebody who's done this. In India when the HIV/AIDs crisis was not being recognized by the Indian government, the Gates Foundation sponsored the Avahan initiative to work with vulnerable at-risk populations which included female sex-workers, men having sex with other men, and transgender people. Gates is an example of someone who thinks that if there's an evidenced-base for doing something, he'll go ahead and do it regardless of what people around him say.

Global health was out of fashion philanthropically until Gates took it on.

I think so.

He's been an innovator in lots of ways.

Yes. That's the plus side. The Gates Foundation very deliberately took on issues such as neglected diseases affecting the poor. But it's a huge mistake to think that you can solve health problems only through philanthropy. You also need to improve government on the ground. Too often people take for granted the provision of roads, educated health-workers, sanitation and toilets, clean water and nutrition, all of which are preconditions for health. These things need to be provided in a highly co-ordinated way which is beyond philanthropists. That's why they also need to think about how they work with governments and how their actions can either strengthen or weaken the prospects of better government.

Philanthropists can also get it wrong because they believe they know what is best and how best to deliver it, without properly understanding the context in which they are working. Take the example of an international foundation that decides that fighting Ebola should be its top priority. It goes to the Democratic Republic of the Congo and says: 'We're going to give you x million to fight Ebola, but only if you match it with x million of your own.' Then you start seeing a clash between a kind of philanthropic approach and a public-interest approach – because that government then has to take money out of other parts of its health budget. That might divert money from maternal healthcare, or malaria, which might be things that actually kill more people in that country.

It will also provoke resistance in that country, as it's done with Ebola in the Democratic Republic of the Congo, with Congolese saying: 'Why are you ignoring all the deaths from other causes? Why are you privileging Ebola? Why are you bringing in foreigners to do all the jobs that we used to do? Why are you building a health clinic above a river to deal with an infectious disease which could affect the river?'

We really need to be listening to communities about what their main problems are. I've seen this play out in so many countries. In Vietnam there was a clash at one point between those in the international community arguing for resources to go on HIV/AIDS and the domestic folk arguing that they needed to go into road safety as road deaths were killing far more people than HIV/AIDS. These are really hard decisions.

This is where government comes in. Decisions about scarce resources need to be made by people who can justify their right to make such a decision. In part it might be because they are elected by a community or held to account in some other way. Equally, though, it is because they have access (as a government) to information and evidence about the community being served.

That's the significance of the school of government that I sit in. It's governments that have to make the absolutely heart-rending decisions. Foundations can say: 'We're doing this and we're doing good.' The private sector can say: 'And we are doing that and we're doing good.' But it's the public sector that, each time, has to say: 'We can only afford one hospital this year and it's going to be in this region – not that region.' Every decision that a government makes on allocation is a decision which advantages some and disadvantages others.

So when a philanthropist offers a million pounds to combat a fashionable disease which sounds particularly scary from afar, governments sometimes have to say: 'Thanks. But we can't match it with a million pounds of our own because we've got to spend on something else'?

It's really hard. But the golden rule of development assistance is ownership. Whatever you're doing has to be owned by the local community and recognized as being important to it. My test of ownership is threefold. First, where did this idea or proposal originate? Did it originate in the World Bank headquarters in Washington DC or did it originate in the community for which it's being planned or proposed? Second, what resources are the local community putting into it? Are they putting in their own time, their own effort, their own resources? However meagre those might be, if they are dedicating some of their own resources to the issue, that's usually a clear sign of how important it is for a community. Third, who gets to decide whether to continue this project or this programme or not? Who makes that decision? Ownership is the holy grail of development assistance. Because projects that people really think are important – and invest with their own time, sweat, money – and that they have the power over deciding whether to continue or not – those are the projects that are by far most likely to work.

Over the years as I've studied development assistance, time after time after time, I've seen well-intentioned development agencies and philanthropists going into countries with what they think they know will work – and imposing it in that community. And it doesn't work. It gets 'tissue rejection' in the local community. The lesson about effective philanthropy or effective development assistance actually is always the same. You have to ask, about any project: 'Is this something that those who have the problem really rate as terribly important and are willing to put themselves into solving?'

Let's look at the issue down the other end of the telescope. Here at the Blavatnik School of Government you have been a recipient

of philanthropy. How does philanthropy look when you're sitting at the other end of the table?

Building this School has relied hugely on philanthropy, almost entirely on philanthropy, which has made it possible to do fantastic things.

You're not just talking about paying for this extraordinary building. Philanthropy has provided scholarships to make it possible for students from poor countries – which are often most in need of better government – to study here. How important is that, from your own experience – because you first came to Oxford from New Zealand as a young student on a scholarship?

I came to Oxford as a Rhodes Scholar in 1987. There was no way I would have been able to even imagine studying at Oxford without a scholarship. When I went for my Rhodes interview, the scholarship committee said: 'How do you feel about taking Rhodes money?' It looked to the committee that I might find it controversial, because I was full of anti-colonial liberationist ideas. My answer is that Cecil Rhodes in his time was one of many Europeans making huge amounts of money from what we would think of as exploitative practices abroad. But where most of his contemporaries put their money into building themselves huge castles and such like, he actually gave his to a public trust and used it philanthropically.

That's why I think we should continue to call it the Rhodes Trust. Because we're not saying Rhodes was a saint. What we're recognizing is the act of philanthropy. What we're recognizing is that he, unlike many of his peers, chose to put this money to the public good, instead of just investing it in himself or his own comfort. That doesn't mean that you're saying everything the man did or stood for is good. It's saying his act of philanthropy was transformative and deserves some recognition.

That's out of line with much of the contemporary discourse which is unmitigatedly critical of philanthropy.

One great philanthropist always says to me, 'No good deed goes unpunished.' [Laughs]

You have to have a thick skin to be a philanthropist today . . .

We're in a world where everyone wants just to scream at each other and find a reason to hate each other and that includes hating philanthropists.

I just think it's quite important for people to pause and to ask what is the philanthropist supporting and what it is you're recognizing and how. Oxford always recognized acts of philanthropy by naming buildings: the Radcliffe Camera, the Bodleian Library, the Weston Library and so on all round the university. This is the Blavatnik School of Government, and I think it's absolutely appropriate to recognize an act of philanthropy in that way.

I think it sends a signal, which is actually if we want to build great things, everybody should step up to the plate. If you are one of the world's richest top 1 per cent, you should be stepping up to the plate. Other people contribute in non-financial ways. They give their time. They volunteer. They mentor our students. They take the time to stop and advise us on things. There's all kinds of support that make this kind of institution possible.

But none of that would be possible without the initial philanthropic gift from the billionaire businessman Leonard Blavatnik.

That's right. Yes.

Yet taking the Blavatnik money has caused some controversy.* How do you respond to these reputational blowbacks on donors like Blavatnik? Or Stephen Schwarzman, who just gave the biggest donation ever to the University of Oxford, and then found students at the university asking questions about what due diligence had been done on him?†

I don't think there's ever been a donor who hasn't immediately been accused of having an ulterior motive or not being a perfect human being

---

* Sir Leonard Blavatnik is a Ukrainian-born businessman who earned billions from privatized industry and oilfields in post-Soviet Russia and has built a $25.7 billion empire which has diversified into the chemical and music industries. His philanthropic foundation has donated $700 million to institutions such as Harvard, Oxford and Tate Modern since 2009. He gave £75 million to set up Oxford's Blavatnik School of Government, which opened in 2012. In 2017 its professor of government and public policy, Bo Rothstein, resigned after Blavatnik made a personal donation of $1 million to the Donald Trump inauguration committee. See Devon Pendleton, 'The meteoric rise of billionaire Len Blavatnik', *Bloomberg*, 26 April 2019.
† See pages 552–3 and 630–1.

or having made their money in a way which not everybody approves of. Steve Schwarzman is just the latest.

I don't start from the proposition that all human beings are perfect. I start from the proposition that we are all flawed and we all spend our lives trying to do a little better. That means owning up when we make mistakes and having generosity towards others when they own up to making mistakes and then moving on together.

When philanthropists step forward and make possible institutions that are for the public good, it's fine for people to question them and ask tough and difficult questions. That's just part of being a public figure of any kind – people will ask questions, spread rumours, throw insults. That's part of the terrain of being in the public eye. But it's important to recognize acts of philanthropy and to focus on what they make possible.

Take this School. We are able to run a truly astonishing world-class programme of study and to select 120 people from around the world to do it, 85 per cent of whom are on scholarships provided by a variety of organizations, foundations, governments or philanthropists. For me, that's not trivial at all. Would those who question accepting the gifts of philanthropists rather that we excluded all those from less advantaged backgrounds and took in only wealthy students who can pay their own way? I came to Oxford on a scholarship and that scholarship helped me to have more impact. It helped me to help other people, a lot more.

Schwarzman is interesting, because his motivation in giving £150 million to Oxford to create a new humanities block is that he thinks such an interdisciplinary centre is the best place to focus on learning about how artificial intelligence is going to change the world in the coming decades.* That's not self-interested; it's genuinely public-spirited.

I think he's a visionary, and not just on this. He created a college in China, long before Trump began his trade wars with China, because he could see a serious problem. We have two superpowers in the world, China and the United States, and they need to understand each other. As Mrs. Merkel† says, 'You can either talk to each other or you can

---

* See pages 647–9.
† Angela Merkel, Chancellor of Germany, 2005–.

go to war.' Those are the only two choices. So, a decade ago he built Schwarzman College at Tsinghua University in Beijing as a way to get a large group of Americans to begin to understand China better. His programme funds students to spend a year in the heart of a Chinese university, where they can learn (or improve) their Mandarin, and learn about China, so that the next generation can work with and deal with China in a more educated way. I think that was visionary.

So you're saying that even if a philanthropist's fortune may have been built by dubious methods, their money can still be cleansed by doing good with it?

No, I disagree with the way you use 'dubious' and 'cleanse'. I think you cannot take money that's illegally made and we don't as a university. Now, on money that is legally earned, human beings have a lot of views. Some argue that bankers are overpaid, and therefore their money is immorally gotten. The case some students have made against Steve Schwarzman is not that he ever acted illegally. It's that his investments did not meet the ethical standards of those students. There's always going to be an argument about that. I can't imagine any donation not provoking some questioning if some people think the donor hasn't paid enough tax, or should have paid their workers more, or paid more attention to homelessness. But I welcome the scrutiny. We're in the business of taking philanthropy and using it for transformative purposes. But what people should also scrutinize is what we are doing with the money, whether we are actually using it for transformative purposes.

So you should be held accountable, as well as the philanthropist?

Yes. We produce a report every year on what we're doing, precisely because we think we should be accountable. And we should be accountable for any money we get – whether it's government money, private sector money or philanthropy.

In the big challenges of the twenty-first century what role can philanthropy play that is different from the private sector, government or the academic world?

I see the big challenge is that the world needs better government. In a world which is becoming more and more polarized – where inequality is huge, and trust is being smashed – people need to find ways to cooperate at every level, from the local community, to global politics. When humans can't cooperate, their lives become poorer and shorter and nastier. The possibilities of doing good business are quickly extinguished.

Everyone has to step up at this time. Philanthropists, with their business hats on, need to pay their taxes and undertake their business in ways which would make their grandchildren proud. Instead of lobbying government for the right to pollute or to take dangerous risks, they should help governments to work better and build a better future. With their philanthropic hats on they can help societies build terrific institutions which last for centuries, they can focus on neglected issues or issues too sensitive for politicians to handle. They can lead in shining a light on those in their society who need help, support, and opportunity. Their positive legacy will be shaped by both their acts of philanthropy and how they undertake their core business.

Chapter 14

Celebrity Philanthropy

Before Angelina Jolie became the most beautiful woman in the world she was a wild child. As part of a Hollywood dynasty – her father was the 1970s film star Jon Voight – she seemed in her youth to feel entitled to erratic and self-indulgent behaviour. Her early history was one of self-harm, eating disorder and experiments with, as she put it, 'just about every drug possible, cocaine, ecstasy, LSD and, my favourite, heroin'.[1] Celebrity profiles made much of her sex life, emphasizing her bisexuality and interest in sadomasochism, and dwelt on her fascination with knives and blood. When she married her first husband, Jonny Lee Miller, in 1996, her wedding outfit consisted of black rubber trousers and a white T-shirt on which she had written the groom's name in her own blood. At the Oscars in 2000 she kissed her brother in such a way as to start tabloid rumours of incest. When she arrived with her second husband Billy Bob Thornton for a film premiere later that year, he announced on the red carpet that 'we fucked in the car on the way here' – an announcement to which the apparently spaced-out Jolie nodded approval.[2] Her publicists decided that her wild image had got out of hand. So when Jolie was filming her 2001 blockbuster *Lara Croft: Tomb Raider*, shot at the Angkor Wat temple in Cambodia, one of her publicity team, Michelle Kydd Lee of the Creative Artists Agency, suggested the film star should visit a refugee camp in the war-ravaged country.[3]

What had been planned as image enhancement became a turning point in Angelina Jolie's life. The shock of what she saw in that camp made the movie star contact the United Nations High Commissioner for Refugees when she got home to find out what she could do to help improve the conditions of the displaced people she had met. A few months later she returned to Cambodia to spend two weeks in the camps. She then discovered that the plight of refugees extended far beyond a single country. That same year she visited camps in Sierra Leone and Tanzania and then travelled to meet Afghan refugees living in exile in Pakistan and donated $1 million to an emergency UN appeal there. It was the largest donation UNHCR had ever received from a single individual.

Jolie was generous with her money, but she was more generous with her time. She began to visit refugee camps all across the world, dragging a photo-hungry media with her to places she called 'forgotten emergencies' which were normally well outside the international spotlight. Cynical UN staff, who had bet with one another about how much luggage she would bring and whether she would turn up in the field wearing high heels, were surprised by her determination not only to travel and live as they did but also on her insistence on paying her own way. Within a year UNHCR had named her an official Goodwill Ambassador. Over the next two decades she made nearly 60 visits to 30 countries – including Thailand, Ecuador, Kosovo, Kenya, Namibia, Sri Lanka, Russia, Jordan, Egypt, Chad, Lebanon, Haiti, Costa Rica and India – to meet refugees and displaced people, donating millions of dollars of her own money. She travelled to dangerous war zones including Darfur, Syria, Iraq and Afghanistan. She also used her fame to pay calls upon the political elite, observing: 'In my early 20s I was fighting with myself. Now I take that punk in me to Washington, and I fight for something important.'[4] She appointed her own full-time adviser on international affairs, telling an audience of the powerful at Davos that 'celebrities have a responsibility to know what they're talking about and be in it for the long run'.[5]

'She's moved into this in a highly professional way,' says Professor Andrew Cooper of the Centre for International Governance Innovation. He calls her activities 'celebrity diplomacy'. 'She knows she's not formally educated and acknowledges that she needs advice. She didn't speak for six months; she researched silently and took professional advice.'[6] But after she found her feet, she was unafraid to become involved in politics. In Arizona she visited detained migrants who had illegally crossed the border from Mexico. In response to what she saw she paid for a free legal-aid system for asylum-seeker children; it is now the principal provider of *pro bono* lawyers for immigrant children in the US.[7] In 2012 she fronted a campaign with the British Foreign Secretary,

William Hague, against sexual violence in war zones. That same year she became the first celebrity ever to represent UNHCR at the diplomatic level. After being named a UNHCR Special Envoy, she addressed the United Nations General Assembly in 2019.[8] 'The fact that she is willing to address aspects of the issue which are politically sensitive in the US – speaking about refugees from Mexico, visiting Iraqi refugees when no one else would – buys her credibility,' says Professor Cooper. 'It shows there's an integrity to her vision; she's not just picking easy causes.'[9]

FROM AUDREY HEPBURN TO ANGELINA JOLIE

Angelina Jolie's activist philanthropy was not a new invention. It was very much in the tradition of the activist philanthropists of the eighteenth century. The first man ever to be described in English as a philanthropist – John Howard, the great penal reformer of the eighteenth century – was, in a different way, a celebrity philanthropist. As we saw in Chapter 7, Howard became a celebrity through his philanthropy; Angelina Jolie, by contrast, used her celebrity to bring a new dimension to philanthropy. She is not alone. In recent decades celebrity has become a new mechanism by which to hold to account those who wield power, whether through wealth or political office. It was no coincidence that when Bill and Melinda Gates were named on the cover of *Time* magazine in 2005 as Persons of the Year, they were part of a triumvirate under the headline 'The Good Samaritans'. The third person, the rock star Bono, embodied this new nexus, linking together the worlds of celebrity, politics and philanthropy.

Celebrity philanthropy in the modern era began in the 1950s and 1960s when the film stars Danny Kaye and Audrey Hepburn became the first famous 'goodwill ambassadors' for the UN children's agency, Unicef. Hepburn, one of Hollywood's most celebrated leading ladies of those decades, took on the role when her acting career was over; she dedicated the remainder of her life to helping impoverished children in the poorest nations, continuing her field visits even after she had begun to suffer seriously with the abdominal cancer that took her life in 1993. Other stars have picked up the mantle with less success. Sophia Loren turned up for a UN appointment in a brown Rolls-Royce that matched her fur coat. Geri Halliwell, aka Ginger Spice, made just one relatively high-profile trip to the Philippines to promote contraception and AIDS awareness before she fell off the radar, with UN officials opining privately that she was 'not up to the job'.[10] Paul McCartney and Heather Mills's work for Adopt-a-Minefield suffered a major setback when the charity's two patrons decided to get divorced. The footballer George Weah, Fifa's World Player of the Year in 1995, visited his native land, Liberia, as a Unicef goodwill ambassador but later suspended his work to run as his country's president.[11]

But what moved celebrity philanthropy into a different gear was the activity of an Irish rock star with the energy of a human tornado. In 1984 Bob Geldof, the lead singer of a comparatively little-known band from Dublin called the Boomtown Rats, was at home in his Chelsea town house watching the television news when a report came on from Ethiopia. A devastating famine had gripped the land and countless numbers of people were dying. The nation was shocked. So was Geldof. But what was unusual about him was that he determined to do something, and do something as big as he could. He telephoned all his fellow pop stars to ask them to appear on a charity record to raise funds for famine relief. They recorded a single called 'Do They Know It's Christmas?' Thanks to the firmament of stars Geldof assembled, and the cause in which they had come together, it became the biggest-selling record in UK history. A record in the United States followed, 'We Are the World.' It too went to the top of the music charts. Then on 13 July 1985 the Irish singer, through a feat of gargantuan proportions, organized a marathon 16-hour concert which took place in UK and the US simultaneously and was broadcast live across the world on television and radio. Its cast list included most of the biggest names in international rock music.* The concert was watched by 1.5 billion people around the world and in the West raised £150 million – and also inaugurated a new vehicle of public philanthropy.

THE LIVE AID DIVIDEND

There was more to Live Aid than fundraising. As Geldof began to inquire into how the money should be spent, he decided to embark on a trip across the Continent and invited me – then *The Times* correspondent in Ethiopia – to accompany him. We travelled through

---

* See the interview with Bob Geldof on page 273.

one African country after another in which the vast majority of people
lived so close to the edge of subsistence that drought turned rapidly to
famine – and on an unimaginable scale. As many as a million people
perished in Ethiopia alone.[12] All across the continent we found African
nations in huge debt to international organizations and Western banks.
For every pound donated in aid, ten times as much was leaving Africa
in loan repayments – money that ought to have been invested in the
development of the Continent's own peoples. And these countries were
only allowed to trade with the rich world on terms which were loaded
against the poor. Many African states had been left with unbalanced
economies after the colonial era, during which countries were developed
in ways designed to extract minerals or grow crops primarily to sell
cheaply to the West. That imbalance had never been righted. Geldof,
who received a knighthood in 1986 for the extraordinary achievement
of Live Aid, gradually thereafter became involved in campaigning for
more aid, debt relief and fairer terms of trade for the nations of Africa.
Geldof's role as an activist swiftly overtook his career as a pop musician.

A decade later one of the younger rock stars who had featured on
the original Band Aid record underwent the same education on global
injustice. Bono, the lead singer of U2, who were becoming the most
popular band in the world, began in the 1990s to quiz Geldof on the
origins and mechanics of global poverty. Bono, a Christian, had begun
to take an interest in a campaign being promoted from the mid-1990s
onwards by a group of British church activists under the name Jubilee
2000. It took its inspiration from the biblical concept of Jubilee set out
in the Book of Leviticus, decreeing that every 50 years a Jubilee was to
be declared in which all debts were to be wiped away. The concept had
been highlighted in relation to international debt relief in my 1990 book
Bad Samaritans: First World Ethics and Third World Debt.[13] The new
campaign floated the idea that what was now needed was a Jubilee in the
Year 2000 which would wipe away the massive swathes of Third World
Debt. It was a steep learning curve, as a campaigning document later set
out, describing the journey that Geldof and Bono made together:

> It was not an easy issue to get to grips with. They discovered first how
> the debt had come about. They learned how the money had been loaned
> by the West, knowingly, to corrupt dictators during the Cold War
> to keep them on our side rather than going over to the Soviets. They

learned how the rich world shares the blame for much of the problem, which began with irresponsible lending by Western banks awash with oil-money they needed to lend-on after the oil price-hikes in the 1970s.

They learned how interest rates had soared and, simultaneously, prices for Third World commodities had plummeted on world markets, meaning the debts could never be repaid. They discovered how the International Monetary Fund had said it would lend to African nations so they could pay the interest on the old loans – but only if they made cuts in their health and education budgets for millions of the poorest children.

All this was despite the fact that most African countries have actually paid back what they borrowed. Nigeria, for instance, originally borrowed about $17 billion; it has repaid $18 billion but, thanks to the wonder of compound interest, still owes $34 billion.

And that was just the start.

They then learned about international trade. And how – through a complex web of rules, taxes, tariffs and quotas – the rich world takes far more from the poor than we give them. For every $1 we give in aid, we take $2 back through unfair trade.

We like to think we are generous to the poor, but the net flow of money is not from the rich world to the poor, but the other way round.[14]

Bono's attention also focused on the rising AIDS pandemic, which in the West had at first been considered a disease of gay men and drug addicts, but in Africa had spread uncontrollably in the general population infecting tens of millions of people. Bono and Geldof – together with Jamie Drummond, an activist from the Jubilee 2000 Drop the Debt campaign – set up an anti-poverty advocacy organization called DATA. Its initials spelled out their concerns – Debt, AIDS, Trade, Africa. The new lobby group aimed to arm the celebrities with the facts and analysis they needed to urge world leaders to take action on specific issues to help the eradication of poverty in Africa. The goal was to create a political constituency to achieve the UN Millennium Development Goals to combat disease, poverty, and other pressing development problems.

DATA needed political heft and it needed funding. Bono partnered with the American lawyer, Bobby Shriver, a member of the Kennedy family who had excellent connections with Democrats on Capitol Hill, and then approached Bill Gates, who was initially sceptical. The world's richest man and one of the world's biggest rock stars met at the Waldorf-Astoria in New York in 2002. 'I was kind of amazed that he actually knew what he was talking about,' Gates said much later, 'and had a real commitment to making things happen. It was phenomenal. After that, we've been big partners in crime.'[15] Shortly after that initial meeting the Gates Foundation made its first contribution to DATA, the first donation of tens of millions of dollars. Another billionaire philanthropist, George Soros, was also persuaded to support the fledgling group thanks to Bono's persuasive powers.[16]

Two years later DATA morphed into ONE, a grassroots organization which now has nine million members dedicated to lobbying 'to end extreme poverty and preventable disease, particularly in Africa'.[17] Its mission statement insists 'the fight against poverty isn't about charity, but about justice and equality'.[18] It is now one of the most authoritative and professional lobbying organizations in the development world. 'Through it Bono shifted the core of his attention to lobbying the state at the heart of the global system, the United States,' says Professor Andrew Cooper of the Centre for International Governance Innovation.[19] Gates has continued to support DATA and then ONE. 'What ONE did was take the evidence of where things were working, find the politicians who really cared about this issue and gave us a chance to get to know them,' Gates said in 2017, looking back on the organization's work, and the role he and Bono played together. 'We've both been coming down from the learning curve on this . . . but we have 15 years of great progress . . . We are a lot less naïve now about how tough it is to get these things out than we were when we first met . . . Assuming generosity stays strong, we'll have another great 15 years.'[20]

BOB GELDOF — FROM CHARITY TO JUSTICE

Back in England, Bob Geldof was also institutionalizing his activism. In 2004, 20 years on from the Band Aid record, Geldof – who had now branched out from pop music into television production and publishing – had returned to Ethiopia to visit friends. There he learned that feeding camps had been set up again in the northern highlands, just as they had been 20 years before during the great famine of 1984 and 1985. He drove north to see for himself. Angered at what he discovered, he returned to Addis Ababa and rang Tony Blair in

Downing Street. The call was patched through to Evian in France, where the prime minister was attending a summit of the world's eight most powerful nations.

'It's happening again,' Geldof exploded.
'Calm down, Bob,' said the prime minister, 'and come and see me when you get back.'

A few weeks later Blair announced a Commission for Africa made up of seventeen Commissioners, the majority of them African, from the worlds of government, business and the development sector. They included two prime ministers, a president and two finance ministers. To ensure the independence of the enterprise they invited Geldof to join too. They did not quite know what they were letting themselves in for – though neither did he.[21] Geldof and the other commissioners immersed themselves in a year-long study of Africa's problems. With the help of a team of 40 of Britain's best civil servants – drawn from four different government departments – they trawled exhaustively through all the existing research on Africa, to discover what had worked in the past and what hadn't. Then the commissioners consulted on the ground in Africa. In March 2005 the Commission reported. It came up with 90 detailed proposals based on just two conclusions: that Africa needed to change, to improve its governance and combat corruption; and that the rich world needed to support that change in new ways. This meant doubling aid, delivering debt cancellation and reforming trade rules. The Commission drew up a detailed plan of how that could be done.[22]

But as the weeks and months went by, and the meeting of the leaders of the rich world at the G8 summit at Gleneagles in Scotland in July that same year grew nearer, Geldof (as he relates in his interview for this book on page 540) became increasingly anxious that the recommendations of the Commission would not be implemented. The Commission report had contained a whole section headed 'Broken Promises'. It listed pledges of aid made, but not delivered. Targets for health or education – set and ignored. Reform of farm subsidies – neglected. Subsidies on rich countries exports to be phased out – but then increased. Changes to trade rules planned – then aborted. Now Geldof feared the same thing was happening to the Commission's 90 proposals; they were never going to be implemented. Gleneagles was creeping steadily closer – and the deal on Africa was being blocked at every turn. The United States was refusing to sign up to the necessary finance package. When Bono told the US Secretary of State, Condoleeza Rice, privately, that during U2's tour of the States he would incite 10,000 fans a night to call the White House to complain, she simply shrugged and replied: 'We can take the calls.' The Germans and the Italians said they had no money. The Canadians were dragging their feet. The Japanese seemed immovable. Geldof brooded more and more. Almost all the pledges of the Millennium Development Goals – to get children into school, prevent avoidable deaths and end extreme poverty – were on target to be broken. Had all the efforts of the Commission for Africa been wasted?

What was needed, he concluded, was the creation of a new international lobby for Africa. Not one Live Aid concert, but eight – one in each of the countries of the G8 leaders – to force them to turn the Commission's recommendations into the blueprint for a Gleneagles debt, aid and trade package. The Live 8 concerts took place simultaneously in the first days of July 2005 in Berlin, Ontario, Moscow, London, Paris, Philadelphia, Rome and Tokyo, with additional events in Johannesburg and at the Eden Project in Cornwall. Most of the biggest names in pop music performed. 'The only person we haven't got is Elvis,' Geldof quipped. Nearly a million people attended the concerts in person. They were watched on television by 3.8 billion people – more than half the population of the planet. As a result Bono and Geldof were invited to one-to-one meetings with the leaders of the United States, Germany, Canada, France and Britain. The leaders of the rich nations, meeting at Gleneagles less than a week after the Live 8 concerts, agreed a package financing 50 of the 90 recommendations of the Commission for Africa.

The outcome was widely praised. The UN secretary general, Kofi Annan, called it 'the greatest summit for Africa ever'. The leading economist Jeffrey Sachs described it as 'an important, if incomplete, boost to the development prospects of the poorest countries'. Kevin Watkins, now the head of Save the Children, said it was 'a major breakthrough on debt'. Oxfam said 'no previous G8 summit has done as much for development, particularly in Africa'. But, Oxfam added, it was 'disappointed that in the light of undisputed need and unprecedented popular pressure and expectation' the G8 had not gone much further. On aid, Oxfam said, the outcome was a 'welcome and a clear victory for campaigners'. But it needed to be delivered faster and the total promised would still 'fall far short' of what was needed to meet the Millennium Development Goals. On debt, Gleneagles had achieved 'a serious step forward in ending the debt burden of the poorest countries'. But many countries had been left out of the deal and strings were attached to the relief in a way which could harm the poorest people. On trade, Oxfam concluded, the G8 had 'failed to substantially move forwards on creating a more just world trade system'.[23]

More radical critics went far further. Bianca Jagger memorably accused Bono and Geldof of 'sleeping with the enemy', adding that she felt 'betrayed by their moral ambiguity and sound-bite propaganda, which has obscured and watered down the real issues'.[24] John Coventry, of War on Want, declared that Geldof had 'got too close to the Government and he got burnt'.[25] The media academic Muhammad Idrees Ahmad accused Bono and Geldof of presiding over 'a comical revival of the "white man's burden"', claiming that the 'ageing pop stars ignored the legitimate voices of Africa and turned a global movement for justice into a grand orgy of narcissistic philanthropy'.[26] For Renate Bloem, of the Conference of Non-Governmental Organizations, Gleneagles illustrated a wider problem with celebrity philanthropy. 'It embodies a very Northern perspective. Civil society in the global South has other concerns. Celebrities are heard at the expense of alternative voices from the South and also the anti-globalization or social justice movements in the North.'[27]

Geldof himself was unrepentant. Accusing his critics of a lack of understanding of how the real world of politics worked, he insisted: 'The package backed at Gleneagles outlined a way to put the MDGs back on track. Those of us involved always knew it would be a long, incremental process.'[28] Getting involved in the mechanics of government through the Commission for Africa, it was clear, had recalibrated his ambitions: after two decades as the quintessential campaigner he had ceased to ask for the ideal and settled for the politically possible. It was on similar grounds of *realpolitik* that Olly Buston, the former European director of DATA, defended the wider practice of celebrity philanthropy at an international conference in The Hague in 2008. Although the world's top politicians had yet to deliver on all the promises they made at the summit in Scotland, 'what they have already coughed up constitutes 400 times more than Geldof raised through the original Live Aid,' Buston said. More than that, Geldof's lobbying of top politicians – in the Conservative coalition led by David Cameron and George Osborne which followed the Labour

administrations of Tony Blair and Gordon Brown – persuaded the British
government finally to commit to the UN target to give 0.7 per cent of
national income to international development.[29]

What all that highlighted was the complexity of this new interface
between politics and philanthropy. 'In the United States, celebrity
diplomacy is attacked from the right as part of a liberal-socialist
Hollywood agenda,' observed Andrew Cooper of the Centre for
International Governance Innovation. 'In Europe, it is attacked from
the left because celebs, being results-orientated, tend to crowd out
the public intellectuals of the left who are more analytically critical.'
Celebrities are unelected, the left says, so what gives them the right
to impose their own views? The response to that of the philanthropic
activists is once again pragmatic. 'In a perfect world we would have a
democracy in which everyone is perfectly informed, everyone's voice
is heard, and public policy reflects the collective best interest,' Buston
noted. 'But the world isn't like that. It is a world of media moguls,
corporate lobbyists and powerful interest groups like the National Rifle
Association – which has a $200m annual budget – all of which have a
disproportionate influence. More than that, the rich nations are over-
represented at the IMF, World Bank, the G8, the UN Security Council
and other global institutions. Our democratic institutions don't deliver.
What we're trying to do is redress the balance.'[30]

A CALL FOR BONO – IT'S THE POPE

The phone rang in the recording studio. An assistant answered it. It
was a call for Bono. The record producer, Brian Eno, one of the great
experimental gurus of the pop industry, exploded in anger. He had
given strict instructions that they were not to be interrupted in the final
touches of recording 'Love and Peace or Else' for U2's 2004 album *How
to Dismantle an Atomic Bomb*. He changed his mind when he heard who
was on the line asking for the U2 frontman.[31] It was Pope John Paul II.

Bono and Geldof had gone to Rome in 1999 to persuade the Pope to
give his backing to the Jubilee 2000 Drop the Debt campaign. The way
the two Irish rock stars conducted themselves in the Vatican offered an
interesting insight to exactly how celebrity philanthropy works. After the
papal audience at the Pope's summer residence, Castelgandolfo, the two
men met the media. Geldof, for all the informality of the outfit he had

chosen to meet the Pontiff – mismatched brown jacket, check trousers and T-shirt – focused professionally on the job in hand, saying of Pope John Paul: 'I just hope that the spirit of humanity that guides him could move politicians. Then the final push of political will to eradicate this unnecessary tragedy would be easily achieved.' Bono, by contrast, reported that he had told the leader of the world's 1.2 billion Catholics that 'he was a great showman, the first funky Pontiff'. He claimed that the Pope had pinched his wrap-around rock-star sunglasses and tried them on. 'The Pope's legged it with my goggles,' he joked.[32] While Bono was giving his masterclass in reminting his story afresh for every media interview 'with a potent combination of charm, sincerity, wit and conviction', Geldof was discussing strategy with Jubilee 2000 campaigners. Soon afterwards Pope John Paul publicly endorsed the campaign – a gesture to which Bono later paid tribute, calling him 'a street fighter and a wily campaigner on behalf of the world's poor'. The pop star later said of the pontiff: 'We would never have gotten the debts of 23 countries completely cancelled without him.'[33] The Pope was clearly impressed enough to stay in touch with Bono for years after their meeting.

Bob and Bono, as the pair became known in the media, were 'an extremely odd couple', according to the rock critic, Neil McCormick, who accompanied them on their trip to meet the Pope. 'Bono is an upbeat, optimistic idealist motivated by a profound and long-lasting commitment to Christianity; Geldof is a belligerent, pessimistic atheist cynic who seems compelled to do good work almost despite himself.'[34] Andrew Cooper described their *modus operandi* differently. 'Bono is the quintessential fixer. He's the ultimate networker, charming and persuasive,' he argues. 'Geldof is more of an anti-diplomat, a provocateur . . . a shock-jock deploying irreverent or sometimes offensive language to attract attention.'[35] Geldof acknowledges the contrast, self-deprecatingly describing himself and Bono as 'the Laurel and Hardy of Third World Debt'. The duo, he says, 'play soft cop, hard cop because in the end I always lose my patience and he's always eminently reasonable'.[36]

There is more to it than that. Geldof, an individual of considerable intellectual sophistication, has built up a deep understanding of global poverty. He has spent at least two days a week, year in, year out, campaigning behind the scenes for more than 30 years. His instincts for the realities of global geopolitics impress the world's most senior politicians and their advisers when they meet privately. Bono, eight years his junior, sees Geldof as an emotional and intellectual godfather whose analysis he solicits before making any major move in international politics. The two men consult each other regularly.

Geldof, for his part, knows that his compatriot has strengths he lacks. 'Bono is the point man. He's got far more fame than me, particularly in the States where celebrity equals access,' says Geldof. 'He is a really smart person. Since Band Aid he has been interested in the issues, but he got involved at the time of Jubilee 2000. Bono is a Christian and Jubilee 2000 was largely driven by the churches and the unions.' The younger man's faith was crucial a few years later in the United States when the pair went to court the administration of President George W. Bush on their Aid, Debt, AIDS, Africa agenda. Their contact with the conservative US establishment did not go down well within the rock world. Bono's U2 colleague, the guitarist known as the Edge, argued that 'all this Third World stuff is ferociously uncool'. It was threatening to damage the band's street-cred. He particularly pleaded with Bono not to 'hang out with the conservatives'. When Bono began to engage with one of America's most extreme right-wing senators, Jesse Helms, there were some in music circles who stopped speaking to Bono and Geldof entirely.[37]

Jesse Helms, then chairman of the Senate Foreign Relations Committee, was Washington's biggest opponent of American funding for the fight against AIDS. A conservative Christian, he believed that AIDS was God's judgement on homosexuals, drug takers and prostitutes, all of whom were 'perverts' or 'weak morally sick wretches' who had fallen prey to 'a gay disease'.[38] Bono was not deterred. He asked for a meeting with Helms at which, drawing on their common faith background, he reached out to the arch-conservative politician. The 40-year-old Irishman pointed out directly to the 80-year-old American that more than two thousand verses of the Bible referred to the poor and yet Jesus speaks of judgement only once – and that too is about poverty, not sexual morality. Bono quoted from the Gospel of Matthew, Chapter 25, in which Jesus says on the Day of Judgement: 'I was naked and you clothed me, I was sick and you visited me . . . As you did it to one of the least of these my brothers, you did it to me.' Then he asked Helms: 'How could addressing this disease not be at the centre of Christ's mission?' Opposing government funding to fight AIDS meant that millions of HIV-positive women in Africa were transmitting the virus to their unborn children. Helms welled up.

Not long after, the conservative senator wrote an op-ed article in the *Washington Post* declaring that his conscience was 'answerable to God' and adding 'perhaps, in my 81st year, I am too mindful of soon meeting Him'. The man who had once denounced foreign aid as a 'rathole' now ended his 30-year Senate career by calling for the US government to allocate $500 million in aid to focus on eliminating mother-to-child transmission ofʲ the AIDS virus in Africa. Not only did Helms change his mind on AIDS funding, but he lobbied the White House himself. 'Dick Cheney came into the Oval Office and said, "Jesse Helms wants you to listen to Bono's ideas"', an amused President Bush revealed in his speech announcing the aid package.[39] Helms later told Bono that he was 'so ashamed' at his previous attitude. He even became a fan of U2, attending concerts 'like they were revival meetings'. Washington insiders were taken aback. Bono's liberal friends, including bandmate the Edge, were appalled.[40]

BOB & BONO – SUPPING WITH THE DEVIL

Bono and Geldof were unrepentant. 'People go on about us supping with the devil,' Geldof said with exasperation at the time:

> . . . but what's the point in supping with God; he's already on the side of the angels. If the devil wants to cool down the temperature in hell a little to make the lives of the world's poorest people more bearable, then I say: 'Pull up my chair to the table.' It's a balancing act. We're constantly debating: 'Should we do this, or that, or have our photo taken with this individual.' We do what we feel is right. I don't to want be hubristic but our little lobbying group is proving to be quite potent. Attitudes in Washington are shifting.

The Bush government, he adjudged, was 'an administration really in search of a foreign policy'. This was particularly so post-September 11. 'The Americans are asking: where did this come from? Why do people not like us? Why don't they see our point of view? But the key thing is they're open to persuasion so long as you're not asking them to do anything which hurts US interests.'[41]

For Geldof, celebrity philanthropy is about using his fame to gain access to world leaders to present them with unarguable facts. 'They are wide open to coherent intellectual argument. We work on deep info, we make sure we're really across the detail so that we have the answers to whatever arguments the politicians or civil servants come up with.'[42] He is not exaggerating, senior politicians say. 'There is nothing quite like them,' one US senator said. 'They're polite, prepared and persistent.'[43] For Bono, celebrity philanthropy is as much about personal relationships. He said, after his interactions with Jesse Helms, 'when you have a person who may appear rigidly opposed to something, [you must] look for ways to widen the aperture of their narrow idealistic view . . . We found a way to deal with the supposed "opposition" by taking them out of caricature.'[44] Between them the two musicians found a way to build a bi-partisan coalition between a Democrat Congress and a Republican White House. The administration increased US programmes to combat AIDS fivefold.[45] When President Bush unveiled his $5 billion aid package in a speech on the White House lawn, Bono was by his side flashing a V for Victory sign and pronouncing: 'This is an important first step, and a serious and impressive new level of commitment.'[46] Bush looked pleased. The president appeared to be seeking the approval of the pop star – not the other way round.

The template for celebrity philanthropy which Geldof and Bono established has proved resilient as the years have passed – with Bono now taking over the lead from Geldof. The younger man has continued his charm offensive with senior politicians. At the opening of Bill Clinton's memorial library in Arkansas in 2004 – attended by Presidents George Bush senior, Jimmy Carter, Bill Clinton and George Bush junior – Bono went out of his way to speak of something positive that each of them had done for Africa, before serenading them, unplugged and in the pouring rain, with U2's 'The Hands that Built America.' The collective presidency preened itself in response to the Bono formula: a few facts, a few stories, some good news and praise in plenty – to ready his listeners for his next request. But Bono's network has extended much further. He has established partnerships with top academic economists, such as Jeffrey Sachs of Columbia University, struck up fruitful relationships with Presidents Clinton and Obama, and continued to make alliances with top religious figures. In 2018 he met Pope Francis to discuss how business might be harnessed to serve the United Nations' Sustainable Development Goals – giving the Pope his views on clerical sex abuse in his native Ireland on the side.

Perhaps Bono's most long-standing partnership is with Bill Gates. When the two men, along with Melinda Gates, were named *Time*'s 'Persons of the Year', the magazine praised them all for being 'shrewd about doing good, for rewiring politics and re-engineering justice, for making mercy smarter and hope strategic and then daring the rest of us to follow'.[47] The *New York Times* drew attention to Bono's success in enlisting powerful allies from a diverse spectrum of leaders in government, religious institutions, philanthropic organizations, popular media, and the business world, as well as for spearheading new organizational networks that bind global humanitarian relief with geopolitical activism and corporate commercial enterprise. Bono, the newspaper declared, was 'the face of fusion philanthropy'.[48] In 2011 the *National Journal,* the Washington DC politics and policy magazine, ranked celebrity activists and suggested that this fusion philanthropy made Bono 'the most politically effective celebrity of all time'.[49]

Not everyone agrees on the implications of this. Matthew Bishop, the great enthusiast for philanthrocapitalism, is broadly positive, saying of Geldof and Bono: 'They have learned a lot, realized how naive and ineffective their earliest efforts were, yet they have stuck to their mission and driven themselves to find better ways to achieve it. Along the way, they have inspired millions of people around the world to be more altruistic and given many more the chance of a better life.'[50] Andrew Cooper acknowledges that 'their ability to gain extended face-time with prominent national leaders is unprecedented'. He sees it as a win-win situation. 'The attraction is two-way: in celebrities, world leaders find a populist recognition and legitimacy they are unable to cultivate on their own; while celebrities find that access to the world's most powerful leaders helps advance their activist agendas.'[51] Some critics have suggested that Geldof and Bono were giving unwitting support to the policies of Tony Blair and George W. Bush, though in fact it was the G8 leaders who accepted Geldof's agenda, rather than the other way round. The Italian prime minister, Romano Prodi, at the next G8 summit in Heiligendamm, went into the bathroom with an aide and emerged with an improved aid offer as Geldof and Bono were about to walk out of a private meeting in his hotel room.

But other commentators were less unqualified in their criticism. 'Celebrities don't raise the more philosophical questions,' complained Renate Bloem. That means they defuse, drain or stifle more radical forms of protest.[52] The British environmental campaigner George Monbiot declared that Bono and Geldof had turned a political campaign for justice into a philanthropic movement. 'The good these two remarkable men have done is in danger of being outweighed by the harm,' he wrote.[53] New York University's prominent aid sceptic William Easterly compared Bono unfavourably to John Lennon, concluding that Lennon was a rebel who challenged power, whereas Bono is a conformer interested more in technical and policy solutions. 'There is something inherently noble about the celebrity dissident, but there is something slightly ridiculous about the celebrity wonk,' he wrote condescendingly in the *Washington Post*.[54] Post-colonialist academics such as Ilan Kapoor go further, suggesting that 'celebrity humanitarian heroes' help 'legitimate late liberal capitalism' and thereby increase global inequality. Celebrity activists, he claims, promote their own brand and the image of 'caring' Western nations, while, in reality, they are helping promote corporate capitalism and justifying the very global inequality they say they want to redress.[55] In one outlandish intellectual conceit he even claims that Bono causes the deaths of African children – and then celebrates them.[56]

A few critics choose to play the man rather than the ball. The most common of these *ad hominem* attacks on Bono centre on a decision by U2 to relocate part of its corporate base from Ireland to the Netherlands to minimize the taxes the band pays. Heribert Dieter, of the German Institute for International and Security Affairs, wrote: 'Of course, Bono can do with his money whatever he likes, but some of his key commercial decisions would appear to sit uncomfortably next to his antipoverty politics.'[57] Bono had chastized politicians for failing adequately to fund anti-poverty efforts in Africa, several critics said, but U2 had then carefully minimized its finances to avoid paying the very taxes Western governments required to help poor nations. The move had come in 2006 when the Irish ended the tax exemptions that had enabled U2 to collect their songwriting royalties tax-free. The band moved the relevant part of their financial empire to Holland where royalty income remains untaxed. 'Celebrities need integrity. They must walk the talk,' Dieter told the international conference on celebrity diplomacy in The Hague in 2008.[58] Bono's supporters have offered the defence that Bono as an individual is bound by the collective interests of his band. More recently, a U2 official spokesman told the *Financial Times*: 'Bono and U2 pay millions in tax. Given the entertainment industry is a global one, Bono works and therefore earns all over the world, and pays his taxes all over the world, including in Ireland.'[59] But Bono himself, who still lives much of the time in his native Dublin, has declined to wave off the critique. 'I hear about things down at the pub, all right,' he told *Fortune* magazine.[60]

BONO AND FUSION PHILANTHROPY

Rock music to me is rebel music. But rebelling against what? In the 50s it was sexual mores and double standards. In the 60s it was the Vietnam War and racial and social inequality. What are we rebelling against now? If I am honest, I'm rebelling against my own indifference. I am rebelling against the idea that the world is the way the world is and there's not a damned thing I can do about it.[61]

One thing Bono is not rebelling against is capitalism. Indeed, as the years have passed, Bono, the doyen of celebrity philanthropism, has become increasingly open in his embrace of capitalism. In 2012 he made an appearance at the f.ounders tech conference in Dublin – a gathering known as 'Davos for geeks' – where he spoke about what he had learned over the previous three decades. He talked of music but also of his campaigning for Africa and how it had been 'a humbling thing for me' to realize the importance of capitalism and entrepreneurialism in philanthropy, particularly as someone who 'got into this as a righteous anger activist with all the clichés'.[62] Aid is just a bridge, he told an audience of two hundred leading technology entrepreneurs and investors. Job creators and innovators are the key. Then in 2015 he told students at Georgetown University that real economic growth, not government aid, is what lifts people and countries out of poverty long-term. Entrepreneurial capitalism is the key to prosperity. Then, holding his forehead with his right hand, Bono said, 'Rock star preaches capitalism – wow. Sometimes I hear myself and I just cannot believe it. But . . . aid is just a stop-gap. Commerce, entrepreneurial capitalism, takes more people out of poverty than aid.'[63]

The speeches were treated by conservative commentators as a massive conversion.[64] It was nothing of the sort. On both occasions Bono was acknowledging the need for aid as essential to a compassionate capitalism in areas where the market had failed. 'Capitalism can be a great creative force but it can be a destructive force. It is not immoral but it is amoral, we need to give it some instructions,' he said at Davos, calling for the world's business leaders to raise ethical standards to help fight against global poverty.[65] He repeated the message in 2019 at the same top people's get-together. Capitalism is the best economic system for wealth creation, but it can come at a cost. 'It's a wild beast, and if not tamed, can and has chewed up a lot of lives,' Bono said at the 2019 World Economic Forum. It has taken large numbers of people out of extreme poverty but it has caused a lot of harm, he said. 'We need to re-imagine it, repurpose it, remake it, in our own image and the image of this new generation coming through that really, really want their world back.'[66]

Bono appears to be attempting to put that into practice with a fusion capitalism to match his fusion philanthropy. On the conventional financial front, he has invested his U2 earnings in a private equity firm, Elevation Partners – named after a U2 song. It made large private investments in Facebook and Yelp several years before they went public and later invested in Forbes Media, Palm and MarketShare and, through another investment vehicle, in Airbnb, Uber and Sonos. Today the main fund is worth $1.9 billion.[67] In 2013 Bono joined the board of the guitar makers Fender at the invitation of its chairman Bill McGlashan, who was so impressed by the musician's ability to think strategically that, a year later, he invited Bono to become a partner in his multi-billion dollar global investment group, TPG Growth.[68] As a result of all these conventional investments Bono was said, in 2019, to be worth $600 million.[69]

The fusion element came with Bono trying to use his fortune to pursue his anti-poverty campaign goals. The year after he set up Elevation Partners he also launched an eco-friendly fair-trade fashion label with his wife Ali Hewson and designer Rogan Gregory. Called Edun – 'nude' spelled backwards to suggest products which were natural and whose name was supposed to conjure the Garden of Eden – it set up the Conservation Cotton Initiative Uganda to supply the label's raw materials. The aim of the $20 million investment was to suggest that fair trade, rather than aid, should be the model for relations between the West and the developing world. It set out to provide funding, training and enterprise support to cotton farmers to help build sustainable businesses in Northern Uganda. It also worked with weavers and clothing workshops in Rwanda, Kenya and South Africa. The goal was to prove that it was possible to run a profitable business 'where everybody in the chain is treated well', as Ali Hewson said at the launch.[70] But it was not a success, closing its store in Manhattan when its French luxury goods partner LVMH pulled out of the business in 2018, by which time Edun had lost a total of $80 million.[71] Failure is part of philanthropic enterprise, its enthusiasts argue: if you never fail, you are not taking enough risks or not trying hard enough. Bono moved on.

His other commerce/philanthropy hybrid initiative was more successful. In 2006 he and Bobby Shriver launched Project (RED) to raise money for the Global Fund to Fight AIDS. The (RED) brand was licensed to major international corporations including American Express, Apple, Converse, Motorola, Microsoft, Dell, Gap and Giorgio Armani. The licence allowed each company to create a (RED) version of one of its best-selling products in return for a percentage of the profits going to the Global Fund. The aim of this 'shopping for a better world' scheme was to raise both funds and also awareness of the fight against AIDS – and to do so by tapping into the marketing budgets of the giant corporations, which were far bigger than their corporate philanthropy allocations. Before (RED), the private sector had given a mere \$5 million to the Global Fund; through (RED), businesses have generated over \$600 million for the fight against AIDS. So far over 140 million people have been reached with prevention, treatment, counselling, and care services through (RED) grants.[72]

Not content with that, Bono is thinking bigger on the philanthro-capitalism front. A year after he joined TPG Growth, the private equity fund set up a new partnership. TPG-Saya was a joint enterprise with the Sudanese telecoms billionaire and philanthropist Mo Ibrahim after he had visited Bono in his Dublin home.[73] Its aim was 'to find smart investments that can ethically operate at scale, creating jobs along the way'.[74] The idea, Bono said, was to make business investments which also delivered social value – and from which, he announced, he would not take any profit. Next, in 2016, Bono and McGlashan – and the businessman and philanthropist Jeff Skoll, who made his fortune from eBay – joined forces to set up the Rise Fund. This is a \$2 billion social impact fund to invest in businesses involved in working towards the UN's Sustainable Development Goals on poverty, inequality, climate change, environmental degradation, economic prosperity, and peace and justice. Bono has also set up a new company called Y Analytics to develop methods of measuring the social and environmental success of such investments. The aim is for economists and researchers to work with investors to make decisions that benefit society while also bringing them high financial returns.[75] All this perhaps explains why Bono has called himself an 'adventure capitalist'.[76]

Fusion philanthropy seeks to bring business, politics, finance, philanthropy and the charitable sector into alliance with one another to generate results which none of them could produce alone. Bill Gates understands that. In conversation with Bono, the Microsoft magnate turned full-time philanthropist, said:

> Philanthropy is a pretty small part of the world economy. Even in the US, where we have very broad base giving by people of all levels, it is [only] worth two per cent of the economy. But it can play a very special role. Sometimes you have problems that no one from the private sector can solve, like malaria. Often these problems require creativity and risk-taking that governments aren't necessarily the best at. Philanthropy can fund some really great solutions.

Gates cited, as an example, his foundation's work on vaccines which both the market and governments had neglected. Then he continued:

> But when it comes to delivering at scale – [on] education for girls, agricultural systems, stability, justice – we are totally dependent on governments. So, the big factors in this world are the private sector and governments. Philanthropy, you know, that's my life, but in the grand scheme of things it's only a footnote, it's running pilots that can help the two big sectors work better.[77]

'ROCK STARS, IS THERE ANYTHING THEY DON'T KNOW?'

Celebrity philanthropy clearly has a role to play in motivating change at different levels of the modern world's social, economic and political systems, which in many ways seem unaccountable to ordinary people whether as citizens or consumers. Celebrities might be thought to lack a proper mandate, since they are not elected to public office but are selected through the more amorphous mechanism of public acclaim in their chosen field. And those who become activists are self-selecting. Yet, as Raymond Cohen, Professor of International Relations at the Hebrew University of Jerusalem, told the conference in The Hague, in the crisis of legitimacy which characterizes our unaccountable globalized society, 'in an odd way celebrities have become democratised – they speak for the common man'.[78] Professor Geoffrey Wiseman – for 15 years a diplomat in the Australian Foreign Service before working for the UN and then teaching diplomacy and security in the School of International Relations at the University of Southern California in Los Angeles – concurred. Celebrities such as Geldof and Bono, he argues, 'have a degree of legitimacy which grows primarily from the cause they espouse and the transparency of what they do – [and] are accountable because they go to the media and are interviewed about it. They also clearly have expertise.'[79]

The lobbyist Olly Buston offers a more direct defence. While acknowledging that celebrities like Geldof and Bono can claim no more legitimacy than anyone else, 'the fact is that it works,' he told that conference. 'George Bush wouldn't meet the heads of aid agencies, but he will see Bono and Bob and when he does the media cover what is said. Just doing this for 25 years, and refusing to go away, has given them legitimacy – and the more top politicians they meet adds to that.' World leaders use celebrities as conduits to one another in the way that previously only professional diplomats facilitated. 'Because celebs don't have national interests to represent, they are seen to represent the voice of the public, and they amplify it.'[80]

What is needed now is a new generation of celebrity activists, says Jamie Drummond, who has worked with Bono and Geldof for over two decades. 'They're coming through, and interestingly it's a different gender as well as a younger generation,' he says. They also emphasize different areas of activism – like education for girls and concern over climate change. 'Malala Yousafzai and Greta Thunberg have become celebrities by sheer force of authenticity and integrity. That's massively to be welcomed.' What is needed over the next 10 years is for stars with massive social media followings, like Beyoncé or Taylor Swift or Katie Perry and whoever succeeds them, to share with their followers their thinking on the social and political changes which society requires. 'Society desperately needs that. We also need to hear far more from a new generation of global stars from the global south. That's especially true of Africa because, though it has been much talked about in recent times, its voice is only heard second-hand. Changing that is the vision of those, like Bono, who have invested in a Lagos-based artist management firm called Mavin, which is aiming to help the immense talent across the continent go global.'[81]

'Rock stars,' Homer Simpson once sighed, 'is there anything they don't know?' Perhaps, the answer is that when it comes to holding the world's politicians, corporations and philanthropists to account, they may know – and do – a good deal more than the cynics might suppose.

Interview: Bob Geldof on philanthropy and political power

After Live Aid had raised £150 million for famine relief and economic development in Africa, Bob Geldof switched focus from fundraising to politics. He spent over a year working on the Commission for Africa with 17 eminent African and other world leaders, drawn together by Prime Minister Tony Blair. It drew up a blueprint to double aid to Africa, wipe away unpayable debts, strengthen good government and fight corruption, attract investment and boost economic growth across the continent. Geldof then lobbied the world's eight most powerful nations at the G8 summit held in Gleneagles outside Edinburgh to implement this agenda. To maximize public pressure on the politicians he organized Live 8 – eight simultaneous live concerts in London, Paris, Berlin, Rome, Philadelphia, Ontario, Tokyo and Moscow – with another in Johannesburg which was addressed by the South African president, Nelson Mandela. The concerts were watched by three billion people worldwide. Afterwards Geldof joined the Africa Progress Panel to monitor the implementation of the Gleneagles package. Most recently, he has set up a private equity company, 8 Miles – named after the distance between Europe and Africa at the Straits of Gibraltar – to attract overseas financiers to invest in business development in Africa.

'Famine is nothing to do with hunger; famine is to do with economics . . . and politics,' you said. What was it that shifted you from simply raising money for the victims of famine to trying to bring about economic and political change?

In 1990 you wrote: 'For all his skill as a populist Bob Geldof could not shift the agenda from one of charity to one of justice.'[*] I was really piqued, but it was the spur for me to change tack. I was already kind of there with the understanding that famine was about economics – you don't die from a lack of food if you have money. And I'd had a brush early on with Margaret

---

[*] Paul Vallely, *Bad Samaritans: First World Ethics and Third World Debt*, London, 1990, p. 244.

Thatcher over her government refusing to waive the VAT on the Band Aid record. All the publicity was allowing me access to top politicians – which meant that I was able to pressure them early on to lift the tax on the record. I understood the power of the public lobby. That's sort of my job as a pop singer. I played the naïf at first. I used to take my small dog, Growler, into the meetings to disarm the politicians and civil servants. But after we got to see Thatcher and Mitterrand and Kohl, and Ted Kennedy and George Bush senior,* I twigged that we could really leverage this.

I realized this called for an entirely different approach. In 1999 Bono rang me and said we should do another record and concert to call for Third World debt relief. I said it's too esoteric; it's opaque economics. You can't whip up popular sentiment at a concert for that. It would just end up being another gig. And why compromise the memory of Live Aid, which still resonated and gave us access. You should never repeat the unrepeatable: Jeffrey Archer's concert for the Kurds raised some money but who remembered it? 'Free Nelson Mandela' was a great song and gig, but did it free Nelson Mandela? No. 'Will another concert bring debt relief?' I said. 'No, it won't.' We needed to do something different.

To change things you have to engage with the agents of change who, whether you like it or not, in our world, are politicians. Economics changes through politics. So if we were serious we needed to fully engage. That meant understanding the issue in all its complexity or else we wouldn't be taken seriously. So we got top economists – like Amartya Sen, Joe Stiglitz, Paul Collier and Ann Pettifor – to give us some lessons. I decided that what was needed was not another concert but some sort of 'think tank', some sort of political lobby, with people writing research papers and coming up with new ideas. That would provide us with the evidence and arguments and logic we needed. It was a strange time. But through a combination of celebrity and credibility we could leverage access to the top politicians and persuade them and their advisers that debt relief was not just the right thing to do but easy to do. And it was imperative if they wanted to bring Africa and its peoples inside the global economic commonweal.

Bono asked what we should call this new body? And I said I'd already thought of that: Daft – Debt, Aid, Free Trade. And Bono said, I can't

---

* François Mitterrand, President of France; Helmut Kohl, Chancellor of Germany; Senator Edward Kennedy; President H. W. Bush.

fucking have something called Daft. I started laughing and said actually the name I'd thought of was Data – Debt, Aid, Trade, Africa. Someone else said that it could also stand for Democracy, Accountability, Transparency, Africa. So it was perfect. Data was scientific, it's empirical, it's not all pop-starry. Now it's 'get serious' time.

But then in 2004 you went back to Ethiopia on the twentieth anniversary of the 1984 famine and found that things were slipping backwards. And structural issues, like debt, were the problem.

I went to Downing Street to see the Prime Minister, Tony Blair, and I asked him why – with the world economy changing so dramatically with globalization – why was Africa left outside everything? They were being lumbered with this debt which they could never repay – and on which they spend the little money they have which should be going on health and education. The money was an impossible sum to them, but so paltry as to be virtually meaningless to us. How can that be in anyone's interest?

'It's not,' he said.

'Why don't you do something?' I asked.

'Like what?' he replied.

I'd been thinking about the Brandt Report, which had been written in 1980 by a group of eminent retired politicians led by the former German Chancellor, Willy Brandt. It had offered a new blueprint for relations between the rich world and the developing world. Trouble was, it had been written by people who were now out of power. It just became a wish list. What we needed, I said to the PM, was a new report, a twenty-first-century version – but one written by people who were in power *and* who had a chance of implementing it this time.

We sat and talked for half an hour and then he called in Alastair Campbell* and some special advisers and civil servants, and I went through my pitch again and Alastair said: 'We just don't need to do this, Bob.' And the civil servants asked what possible good would another report do?

I knew Britain was hosting the next G8 meeting in the UK in two years' time. So I asked, was Africa on the agenda. I was told it hadn't

---

* One of Tony Blair's closest advisors and Director of Communications at 10 Downing St.

been decided yet. So I said: This new report could be a template. You commission the report, world leaders make up the commission and write and agree their conclusions, the UK makes it policy, and you bring it to the other seven at our G8. And Britain has this worldwide success for fuck-all money.

So Tony turned to a civil servant and asked: 'How much could this cost? And he said £5 or £6 million. And Blair said: 'Right, we'll do it.' There was some low-volume grumbling and then Blair said: 'None of the others will want to do this. I know, I've often talked to them about Africa. They are simply not interested. They need to be pushed. So Bob, I'll do the politics, but you have to do the public. We need them to agree. I can't afford a failure.'

I said: 'Right, I'll do the public.'

And he said: 'Don't let me down.'

And I said: 'I won't, but don't you let us down.'

And that was the beginning of the Commission for Africa.

Tony Blair pulled together 17 prominent figures including presidents, prime ministers, economists, intellectuals and business people – and you. After a year it produced a report which offered a new blueprint for economic development that proposed massive debt relief, improved aid and new ways to improve trade and economic growth.

It was a fine piece of work. One of the key things was that it looked at the problem through African eyes rather than the usual Western ones. So that's the first thing. But then at the launch Blair spoke, Brown spoke, I spoke, and then you asked a question at the press conference and said: 'Prime Minister will this be the British policy for the summit you will be hosting for the G8?' – which was the question we agreed you'd ask.

And he said: 'We haven't fixed that yet.'

And I blurted: 'Yes, it will.' And he looked at me and said 'Gosh, well, if Bob's going to make the policy, I guess that's what it is.' And he said afterwards, 'Did you put Vallely up to that.' And I said: 'Noooo.' But that became the policy. Unbelievable. From the Band Aid Christmas Record and the Live Aid concert it had taken 20 years, but eventually the boys and girls with the guitars got to write the policy.

But as the months went by you became afraid that this piece of work, that you were so proud of, was just going to sit on a shelf gathering dust?

Richard Curtis had come up with the idea of a mass movement to press the G8 to action.* He called it Make Poverty History. I didn't want to get involved because I knew it would just lead to endless internal arguments among the NGOs. So I kept out of it. Eventually, Richard and Bono realized it wasn't going to do the job on its own so they said, you've got to do Live Aid again. And I said no. The second time is always a failure. But they kept coming back. I told them: 'You do it on your own – you know how it's done.' But they kept saying: 'You're the one who does this best. You can get people, they believe you; they won't believe us.'

So what changed your thinking?

They kept on and on at me, but literally it was when Bono said he had this idea for the opening number – twenty years after the Live Aid concert. He said: 'Thing is Bob, you're Sgt Pepper. And it *was* 20 years ago today. So the stage opens, and there's Paul McCartney, backed by U2, and he's singing: "It was 20 years ago today." When he said that I knew it could be one of the great rock 'n' roll moments and I really wanted to see it, so I said: 'OK, fuck it, I'll do it.'

What did Tony Blair say when he heard? After all, he and Gordon Brown had always said they were children of Live Aid. And now you were going to do not just two concerts simultaneously but eight – in each of the home countries of the Western world's eight leading economic powers.

Tony asked what we were doing ahead of the G8. So I said: 'I'm doing a 6-part documentary series trying to show people the real Africa, not the hobbled, hopeless place so often portrayed in our media – so people understand what you are trying to achieve. It'll be on BBC prime time in opposition to the nation's favourite soap – *Coronation Street*. I have to say he wasn't overly excited by that. Then there's the Make

---

* Richard Curtis is a filmmaker and television screen writer. His films include *Notting Hill, Bridget Jones's Diary* and *Love Actually*. His TV comedies include *Blackadder, Mr Bean* and *The Vicar of Dibley*. He was a key driving force behind Comic Relief, Make Poverty History and Live 8.

Poverty History march on Edinburgh. Again, he wasn't over-impressed. But he finally perked up when I said I was going to do Live 8 and I told him about Sgt Pepper and U2. To put some punk into it, I said I was going to call on all British school kids to walk out of school and descend on Edinburgh. I said Richard Branson was giving us a fleet of jets to fly activists from the other side of the Atlantic (which he did). And I said we were organizing a flotilla of boats to do Dunkirk in reverse: we were sending British boats across the Channel to collect all the activists from Europe, all the NGOs, all their supporters, who were coming over here. And he said: 'Have you arranged that?' And I said: 'Yes, I've been in touch with all the clubs and I've asked Dame Ellen MacArthur* to get involved.' I had to rush down afterwards to some port and have my photo taken by a newspaper, sitting in a bloody rowing boat in a gulch on the south coast to make it look like I really had organized it all. But it stirred up the necessary publicity, which is vital to pushing through difficult stuff. It was also a laugh. And we needed a laugh.

You called it _The Long Walk to Justice_, to echo the title of Nelson Mandela's _Long Walk to Freedom_. You said, 'We'll have a million people there', and I said, 'What happens if a million don't turn up?' And you said: 'It doesn't matter now. I've said it. They don't have to come, but what matters is that everyone thinks they're coming.'

Anyway, there was a million kids on the streets of Philadelphia and Berlin and countless hundreds of thousands in the other six capitals. So we did what I had promised Blair. We gave them the public. And he delivered too on the politics.

Some critics said you'd become intoxicated by proximity to power.

Not in the least. Doesn't do it for me at all.

So why do you think people say that?

Because they see you with the powerful – but that's a requirement if you want to lobby successfully. And I found I liked some of the individuals,

---

* Ellen MacArthur, the solo long-distance yachtswoman, who earlier in 2005 had broken the world record for the fastest solo circumnavigation of the globe, and had been made a Dame in recognition of her achievement.

but that's different. You're only intoxicated by power if power is what you want for yourself. I have no interest in political power for myself. That's why I always said No when people asked, 'Why don't you stand for Parliament?' Why would I? Hmmm . . . Gosh, let me see. Sit in parliament as one of 650 ignored people or leap around a stage in front of thousands of people, beautiful women, cash, drugs, posh hotels, playing music. Difficult choice, that! Anyway, what most people find when they achieve the summit is that democratic power, of necessity, and thankfully, is extremely limited. You're so hemmed in by the checks and balances, as nearly all of them have found to their great frustration. Thank God.

Being outside that allows me to say whatever I want. I'm a free agent, I can say what I like, I don't give a fuck what anyone else thinks. For what I'm interested in doing, there is more juice in being outside of the structures than there is within it.

Perhaps that explains why, whenever I saw Bono with Bush and you with Blair, it always seemed to me that the politicians were the ones who were in awe. You were the celebrities and they were the fans. Was there that kind of power dynamic?

As campaigning politicians they wanted to be seen with Bono because huge numbers of people had bought his last album. And they thought: 'I could do with those numbers.' But they also liked and respected him. I found the confusion of politicians really interesting. They felt they had to see us. But we had to learn about their jobs too. The negotiations on these meetings were tortuous. At the Heiligendamm meeting of the G8, the staff of George W. Bush – who we now knew in a 'hail fellow well met' sort of way – asked beforehand: 'Are you going to smile for the cameras when you meet the President?' We said: 'We're not going to smile until he's made some concessions on the important issues.' They said: 'Well, the President thinks there ought to be a smile.' And this went on and on. But eventually they agreed there would be no smiling. So Bono and me walked from the meeting with the Italian President, Romano Prodi, in his little hotel bedroom to the presidential suite – it was like moving from the Travelodge on the ring road to Claridges – and as we walked across the courtyard all the press photographers were there clicking away. So there was me and Bono with our 'serious with purpose' faces on. Next minute the door of the presidential suite burst open and down the steps bounds Bush going: 'Guys!' – grinning away at us. And we're going: 'That fucking bastard, we agreed no smiling!' The last thing Bono wants is George Bush hugging him in front of all the cameras. He said, 'This wasn't agreed, Mr President.' And Dubya just laughed and said: 'Well, you know . . .'

He put one over on you there.

Yeah. But he was more attuned to our arguments and in terms of US commitments to the poor of Africa he did pretty good. So we lost the Smile Wars but several presidential commitments were made. That's a good trade-off from our perspective. But they talked to us. Why? I think because they trusted us. Because having done this for so long they realized we knew what we were talking about. And because we never blabbed about our private conversations. We didn't diss them, when they hadn't done anything diss-able. And when they'd done something good, we bigged them up. It allowed us to speak truth to power. Equally they understood that we would speak truth *about* power should that be necessary. Ultimately I think – and this might sound laughable – that they respected us. They certainly listened.

But even after you successfully lobbied the G8 at Gleneagles, and got aid doubled, and huge amounts of debt written off, you didn't call it a day. You joined the body which was set up to make sure the G8 leaders kept their Gleneagles promises.

We put in the Commission report that there had to be an oversight committee to monitor progress. Blair stalled and stalled but finally said: 'OK, we'll set up the Africa Progress Panel. I've got Kofi* to chair it.' And I said, 'Fucking grey hairs – we'll be back to Brandt and the impotence of politicians out of office.' But I was wrong. I learned so much. They were fucking brilliant. Kofi was such a hero. Such a great man. A wonderful man. If I'd thought I had some access to the top before, this was uber-access. We got wherever we wanted. Kofi used to take me along to private meetings with heads of state so I could play bad cop to his good cop. Kofi used me all the time like that, as the bad cop, while he remained quiet and reasonable.

---

* The former UN Secretary General Kofi Annan.

After all this have you not got to the point where you think: 'That's it – I don't need to do any more'? How much time, today, do you spend on philanthropic activism versus your business interests versus your music?

It's about equal. It adds up to around a third of the week on each. Music is a constant. There's a daily Band Aid conversation online about some project. On business, part of that is my own ongoing business interests, but separately part of it is about trying to attract investment into Africa.

You're now chairman of a private equity firm called 8 Miles – named after the closest distance between Africa and Europe. It invests in mid-level African companies. Is that business or philanthropy?

It came out of a conference I was asked to speak at, in China. It was for investors in China who between them had $13 trillion under management. (I didn't know that otherwise I would have shit myself; that's more or less the size of the EU GDP.) I talked to them about Africa and said: 'Why are you looking to invest in China when China has gone off and invested in Africa. Can't you join the dots? And why are you asking me about corruption in Africa, where it is an average of 6 per cent across the continent, when it is 13 per cent here in China? Why are you querying human rights violations in Africa when China is the most repressive authoritarian regime currently in the world? And this is not Geldof, the pop singer, telling you this; it's all from McKinsey's Lions report.'*

That was my general theme. Afterwards a group of them said they would provide funds for me to set up a private equity company for investment into viable companies in Africa. I really didn't want to do that. The last thing I am interested in is finance. I knew it would take up so much time. I wanted to make albums and go on tour, not be a bloody 'master of the universe'. But just as I'd been annoyed by your comment about not being able to resolve the politics of development, so too the constant accusation hurled at Bono and me – that we were naïve and imagined aid alone could resolve the economic problems of Africa – irritated me too. From the outset, as the acronym DATA had

---

* McKinsey Global Institute, 'Lions on the move: the progress and potential of African economies', June 2010; 'Lions on the move II: realizing the potential of Africa's economies', September 2016.

indicated, we knew it was about Debt, Aid and Trade. We'd done the first two with Gleneagles. Now here was chance to show that the third, Trade, could be done. So eventually I said yes.

We started with a vineyard and wineries in Ethiopia. I go down to Addis and visit the vineyards, and I see the clinic, and the school and the proper houses we built there, and the water we cleaned up – and the proper trade unions and proper local managers and executives – and a booming company and the pride that they achieve in that. The pride with which they wear their work clothes and keep them spotless. And I absolutely love it! Far from the 'hopeless, helpless, poor Africans', like any other person in the world, give them a shot and they go for it. They only need the stuff we have relatively easy access to – cash. And decent laws and good government because capital will only go where it is safe.

We partner with six companies in Africa, typically investing between $15 million and $25 million in each business employed across Africa. Combined, the companies employ about 10,000 people, which in turn directly affects roughly 150,000 others. That is phenomenal if you consider the impact upon those lives. Decent schooling, healthcare, nutrition, clothing, etcetera, and all because of a regular pay packet from a viable job.

The chairman's job is to conduct the board, manage the managers and hold them to account – and act on behalf of the investors – and I very much enjoy it. I've never had a fucking cent out of the whole thing. And I never will have. But it's building robust businesses in Africa with all that that implies. I love it.

What motivated you to do it yourself, again, rather than just urging others?

With all of this, at every turn, an avenue opens up each time and you see the opportunity. And then what do you do? Say 'No, fuck it' and walk away and go back on tour? After the Band Aid record became an unexpected phenomenon I felt obliged to take it further to keep more people alive. After Live Aid the political consequences became clear. We could have stopped and just spent the money. But, again, once it became clear it could go further, the responsibility I felt was there yet again. Then Live 8 brought a global audience of three billion. And I thought I could use that to turn the needle a bit more. So you take it to the top table of politics and economics at the G8 and you get the achievement of Gleneagles.

And so at that dinner in China the same thing happened. I really, really did not want to do it. I knew it would be years of boredom and responsibility and travel and grief – and it has been. But to have refused either the offer or the challenge would have been to renege on everything that had gone before. The idea that many lives could be bettered, or opinions changed or investments attracted to growing economies – all that was part of the blueprint set out by the Commission for Africa. Instead of just talking about it I wanted to show it could be done.

So why have I not stopped? Because I see it working. When we started there were only around three democracies in Africa; now most of the continent has some kind of democracy, or at least has to pay lip service to it. Their economies are growing hugely. As a result you get an improvement in health and education. Infant mortality is crashing. Malarial deaths are crashing. All through a combination of aid, debt relief, business investment, the philanthropy of people like Bill Gates, and the entrepreneurial genius of the African peoples. Why have I not stopped? Because it works.

Chapter 15

Geeks Bearing Gifts – Philanthropy and Politics

At 3 p.m. on Tuesday 5 May 2009 just over a dozen of the world's richest people met in strictest secrecy in New York in the aftermath of the 2007–8 global financial crisis. They were responding to a summons from Warren Buffett, Bill Gates and the financier David Rockefeller Jr. Almost everyone they had asked had accepted the confidential invitation to gather, behind closed doors, in the President's Room at Rockefeller University for what turned out to be a long meeting extending through to a dinner. Several of them had flown in from California to attend. The meal, one newspaper later wryly recorded, was to cost them billions.[1]

Each of the billionaires was given 15 minutes to deliver a presentation on how they saw the future global economic climate – and what role philanthropy might play in it. Among those who contributed – in addition to Bill and Melinda Gates, Buffett and Rockefeller – were the billionaire investor George Soros, the television celebrity Oprah Winfrey, the pioneer philanthropist Chuck Feeney, the media mogul Ted Turner and the mayor of New York, Michael Bloomberg. Others around the large conference table included the banker David Rockefeller Sr; the real estate developer Eli Broad and his wife Edythe; the founder of the Blackstone private equity firm Peter G. Peterson; the hedge fund manager Julian H. Robertson; the former chairman of the technology giant Cisco Systems, John P. Muggeridge, and his wife Tashia; and the former CEO of the Gates Foundation, Patty Stonesifer. According to one of those present, Gates was the most impressive speaker of the day, Turner the most outspoken, and Warren Buffett the most insistent on his agenda for change. Oprah Winfrey was said to be in 'listening mode'. Over the next year the secret group met twice more. At the second meeting, in a private room in the New York Public library, Warren Buffett praised the wife of a Wall Street investment banker for coming up with what he called the best idea he had heard – that each person needed to sit down, work out how much their children would need, and then decide how to give away the rest of their money. The debate continued at a third meeting in a hotel near San Francisco. But Bill and Melinda Gates were keen that the idea should be expanded beyond the United States. So they hosted a dinner in London, and Bill Gates subsequently travelled to India and China to sound out billionaires living there.[2] By the start of 2010 the group had devised a plan to tie down the world's richest individuals to some kind of public philanthropic pledge.

WHAT WAS DECIDED AT THE SECRET MEETING OF THE WORLD'S RICHEST MEN

The idea was launched in June 2010. The Giving Pledge would commit the billionaires who signed it to give away at least half of their wealth during their lifetime, or in their wills. It was not a new idea. Gates and Buffett had been inspired by the example of an Irish-American named Chuck Feeney, the former billionaire who had given away practically his entire fortune almost completely unnoticed.* Both Gates and Buffett named him as their role model. Presenting Feeney with a Lifetime Achievement Award for Philanthropy in 2014, Buffett called the shopping magnate 'my hero and Bill Gates's hero'. By the time Feeney's foundation was spent up in 2020, it had handed out $8 billion to promote education, human rights, science and healthcare around the world. No one before had ever given away the entirety of such a large fortune while they were still alive.[3]

Chuck Feeney's motto 'Giving While Living' was the inspiration for the Giving Pledge. It was to be a moral commitment rather than a legally binding one. Within two months 40 billionaires had signed the Pledge. They included the Star Wars film-maker George Lucas and the Texas oil man T. Boone Pickens. The exclusive billionaires club

---

* See interview with Chuck Feeney's CEO, Chris Oechsli on page 468 above.

provided what Gates called 'a forum for some of the world's most engaged philanthropists to discuss challenges, successes and failures, and how to be smarter about giving'.[4] Three years later the Pledge went global. Signatories from Australia, Germany, India, Malaysia, Russia, South Africa, Ukraine and the United Kingdom brought together an international group committed to exchange knowledge on how to give 'in the best possible way'.

The initiative signalled a significant shift in the history of philanthropy. The focus was on philanthropic investment in global projects. 'American philanthropy used to be all about giving locally,' Anne Petersen, the president of the Global Philanthropy Alliance, told the *New Yorker.* 'But there's been a dramatic trend toward international giving, and that's only going to continue.'[5] Yet the Giving Pledge was not greeted with open arms everywhere. When Gates and Buffett travelled to China – the country which has the second-largest number of billionaires in the world – and invited 50 members of the Chinese super-rich to a meeting to discuss the Pledge, several turned down the invitation amid grumbling about efforts to impose Western philanthropic values on China.[6] Self-aggrandizement, Gates was told, was contrary to the Confucian tradition. Giving by the rich in China was customarily in the form of private donations to relieve immediate needs rather than in pursuit of long-range strategic goals. A similar reluctance was encountered in India. The country's wealthiest citizen, Mukesh Ambani, declined to meet the American philanthropists because he wanted to go to a cricket match. To overcome the resistance Gates returned to India a few months later, but this time he made sure that two rich Indians co-hosted the meeting. Ratan Tata, chairman of the Tata conglomerate, and software entrepreneur Azim Premji also signalled their willingness to take the lead in establishing their own informal network of high-net-worth Indian givers.[7] In 2013 Premji became the first Indian to sign the Giving Pledge.

Other more recent signatories include the Paypal founder Elon Musk, the Facebook chairman Mark Zuckerberg and his paediatrician wife Priscilla Chan, and MacKenzie Bezos, who in 2019 became the world's fourth richest woman after her divorce from the founder of Amazon, Jeff Bezos (who has pointedly not signed). British billionaires who signed the Pledge included Richard and Joan Branson, Christopher Hohn, David Sainsbury, the oil and gas entrepreneur Ian Wood, and the Sudanese-British telecoms billionaire Mo Ibrahim. By May 2019 a total of 204 billionaires in 23 countries, ranging in age from 30 to 90, had added their names. They promised to give money to a diverse spread of issues from poverty alleviation, refugee aid and disaster relief to global health, education and the empowerment of women and girls, as well as to medical research, arts and culture, criminal justice reform and environmental sustainability.[8] Between them they pledged to give away a total of more than $500 billion.

The call to generosity was spread still further. Warren Buffett, who declared himself to be 'having more fun than any 88-year-old in the world', called on the next generation to get involved in the business of philanthropy even earlier in their lives. Today's Silicon Valley billionaires, he said, had got rich quickly and therefore had a responsibility to give 'to benefit others who, through the luck of the draw, have received the short straws in life'.[9] Buffett practises what he preaches. His lifestyle is comparatively modest. He lives in the same house he bought in Omaha, Nebraska, in the 1950s when he ran a tiny investment partnership, and works at the desk his father used 75 years ago.[10] The rich, he insists, need to acknowledge that their money has come largely through their good fortune:

> My luck was accentuated by my living in a market system that sometimes produces distorted results, though overall it serves our country well. I've worked in an economy that rewards someone who saves the lives of others on a battlefield with a medal, rewards a great teacher with thank-you notes from parents, but rewards those who can detect the mispricing of securities with sums reaching into the billions. In short, fate's distribution of long straws is wildly capricious.[11]

For that reason he intended to give away at least 99 per cent of his accumulated wealth. These young tech titans 'have gotten their ideas capitalised at a very fancy value very early on,' he told the *Financial Times*. 'They didn't have to grind it out the slow way.'[12] They should, therefore, resolve to become major philanthropists not out of guilt, 'but rather gratitude'.[13]

Buffett would probably be pleased to know that his example is being emulated well below the billionaire level. In the UK a global organization named the Founders Pledge was launched in 2015. It encourages young entrepreneurs as they start out to make a commitment to sign a legally binding promise to give to charity at least 2 per cent of the profits they realize when they sell their business or list it on the Stock Exchange. Like the Giving Pledge for billionaires, its goal is to 'send a powerful signal' to entrepreneurs engaged in start-ups. The signal is that philanthropy 'should be the norm, not the exception' even among those who are only just launching a new business. The Founders Pledge offers them a raft of support and research services to help them choose how, what and when to give. By 2020 it had 1,360 members who had pledged future earnings to a value of $2.05 billion.[14]

Individual giving under the Founders Pledge is at a far smaller level than the Giving Pledge of Buffett and his peers. One of the successful graduates to the Founders Pledge is Alex Depledge, who in 2012 set up an online marketplace *Hassle.com* (now known as Helpling) to help householders instantly find pre-vetted domestic cleaners in their area. Within a year she had been included in a list highlighting British entrepreneurs who were expected to lead their firms to £100 million revenues within five years. She was named Entrepreneur of the Year by TechCity Insider in 2014 after scaling up her start-up from just three employees to a staff of 57 and expanding into major cities across Europe. A year later she sold the business for £27 million and was one of the first members of the Founders Pledge to fulfil her promise. She said afterwards:

> Here I was – suddenly wealthy – and all I felt was guilt that I didn't deserve it. Founders Pledge was a balm to that. A strange kind of therapy. What I most liked about the process was that I was locked in. Sounds daft or even slightly scary, I know, but how many times do you think, 'Oh I am totally going to do that,' and then it somehow falls down your priority list, and you never get around to it. I know if I hadn't signed the Founders Pledge, that would have been me too.[15]

Instead, the organization helped Alex Depledge through the process of becoming a philanthropist:

> The deployment team listened to what I was most passionate about (Mental Health and Sex Slavery of Women), went away, and then came back with a comprehensive research report that highlighted the best way I could support those charities. They identified the best

charities in terms of outcomes, data-driven giving and transparency. I now know that the money I've donated will actually help to free women from sexual slavery.[16]

It also inspired her to begin working on a philanthropic project that she could run herself, intended to get 'children from underprivileged backgrounds' into computer coding. 'We have a great dearth of digital literacy in this country,' she told the *Financial Times*. 'Start-ups desperately need engineering talent, and at the same time there are talented kids from challenging backgrounds who don't have prospects.'[17]

WHEN PHILANTHROPY IS GOOD FOR BUSINESS

Not all this philanthrocapitalist giving is purely altruistic. There can be solid business reasons – both national and international – for personal and corporate philanthropy. When the US financier Stephen Schwarzman made a massive $100 million donation out of his $12 billion personal fortune[18] to fund American students to study in China, he did so, he said, to address the imbalances and tensions that will inevitably arise as China's economy races past that of America and the rest of the world in the coming decades. 'I realize that China is not going to slow its growth just to convenience others,' he said. 'The chance that you won't have more friction over time strikes me as low.' There are eight Chinese students in America for every American student in China, and as a result 'most Americans know next to nothing about China'. The aim of the scholarship is 'to educate future global leaders about China'. Some, like Professor Ngaire Woods, the Dean of the Blavatnik School of Government at the University of Oxford, have praised Schwarzman's initiative as 'visionary'.* Others are more suspicious. *The Wall Street Journal* noted that the scholarships were for Tsinghua University, which trains many of China's top leaders, including current President Xi Jinping and his predecessor Hu Jintao. This kind of gift, the newspaper observed, has 'become a standard way for foreign investors to curry favour with Chinese authorities and generate positive publicity in the state-controlled media'.[19] A seat on a Tsinghua advisory board offers Western executives an opportunity to mix with Chinese elites. Schwarzman is co-founder

---

* See interview with Ngaire Woods on page 512.

of Blackstone, one of the largest alternative investment companies in the world. It manages assets of over $500 billion.[20] The donation was made at a time when Blackstone was stepping up investment in the Chinese property sector, and after its giant sovereign wealth fund, China Investment Corp, raised its stake in Blackstone to 12.5 per cent. Schwarzman's generous personal donation, which leveraged donations from others totalling $575 million,[21] will certainly do Blackstone's business interests no harm.

Other mega-donations are more tangential in their self-interest. After the large-scale fire at Notre-Dame in Paris in 2019, even before the flames had been extinguished, a donation of €100 million had been offered towards the cathedral's reconstruction. The donors were the Pinault family, whose Artemis holding company control some of the most famous Paris-based luxury brands, including Yves St Laurent, Boucheron and Balenciaga, as well as other top fashion houses like Gucci and Alexander McQueen. Not to be outdone, within hours, the rival Arnault family doubled the figure by offering a €200 million contribution to the restoration fund. The family patriarch, Bernard Arnault, is the richest man in Europe, thanks to his Paris-based multinational conglomerate LVMH, which controls top brands such as Louis Vuitton, Christian Dior and Moët Hennessy. Within three days more than €700 million had been pledged.[22] Both the Pinault and Arnault families, noted the *Financial Times*, made much of their fortunes in a sector synonymous with the pride and heritage of 'Made in France'. They knew that the cathedral was a major symbol of French history, culture and identity.[23]

Notre-Dame was not a one-off occurrence. In 2016 LVMH staged a fashion show for its Italian luxury brand Fendi in which the models glided down a glass runway constructed over Rome's 300-year-old Trevi fountain, which had been restored with donations from the company. French and Italian luxury groups have taken the lead in restoring other famous European monuments. Bulgari has supported the refurbishment of Rome's Baths of Caracalla and the Spanish Steps. The Venetian businessman Renzo Rosso, founder of the fashion brand Diesel, donated €5 million to the restoration of the Rialto bridge across the Grand Canal in Venice. And Diego Della Valle, chairman and owner of the Italian leather goods company Tod's Group, embarked on a €30 million restoration of the Colosseum in Rome.

In all this, the donors benefited not just from the publicity associated with the restorations but also from what the *Financial Times* called 'juicy tax breaks'. In France donors can benefit from a 60 per cent tax refund on their gifts to charity; in Italy the refund is 65 per cent.[24] It was perhaps no coincidence that the big donations for Notre-Dame came at a time when France was riven with disputes between the government and the grassroots *gilets jaunes* movement, which staged violent street demonstrations against, among other things, inequality and the perception that President Emmanuel Macron was a 'president of the rich'. The protesters were quick to object to the large Pinault and Arnault donations, indignantly proclaiming that 'the oligarchy gives to Notre-Dame' and pointing out that the country's elite did nothing to alleviate the poverty of ordinary people while 'they can mobilize a truckload of cash in one night for Notre-Dame'.[25] So shaken were the Pinault family that they announced they would not claim the tax refund for which their donation was eligible. Tax is a subject to which we will return in the next chapter.

GEORGE SOROS — WHY ALL PHILANTHROPY IS POLITICAL

The majority of philanthropists would insist that they are more high-minded. Yet the evidence shows that modern giving is increasingly shaped not just by the personal preferences of individual philanthropists, but also by their political inclinations. All philanthropy is political, according to the Rockefeller Foundation. 'Because most philanthropy seeks to change society, it is inherently political,' it argued in the celebration of its centenary.[26] But philanthropy is even more political when it is aimed at influencing bureaucrats and politicians – national and international – and persuading them to change public policy. Many philanthropists are totally open about this. Ted Turner, the founder of the cable news network CNN, in 2001 pledged $250 million to establish the Nuclear Threat Initiative, a not-for-profit group, to work for the safe disposal of nuclear, biological and chemical weapons after the break-up of the Soviet Union. In 2019 it was working to reduce the ballistic missile arms race in Iran and the Middle East in opposition to the policies of the government of Donald Trump.[27] Likewise Warren Buffett has been unafraid to venture where governments fear to tread. A supporter of Turner's nuclear threat initiative, Buffett gave $50 million to the International Atomic Energy Agency's plan to establish a 'fuel bank' to supply nuclear reactor fuel to countries which signed nuclear non-proliferation agreements. In an indication of the extent to which one philanthropist's money can leverage decisions by governments, Buffett's money was later matched by more than $100 million in contributions from the United States, the European Union, the United Arab Emirates, Norway and Kuwait.[28] In a globalized economy the concerns of philanthropy can be global too.

Politics is personal for philanthropists also. The causes to which the billionaire financier George Soros subscribes very much reflect the story of his life. He was brought up a non-observant Jew, and when, at the age of 14 in 1944, Nazi Germany occupied Hungary, his family escaped the Holocaust by purchasing documents indicating they were Christians. After the war he lived briefly under the sway of Soviet Communism before emigrating to England to study at the London School of Economics. Having grown up under both Nazism and Communism he developed a horror of totalitarianism. In 1956 Soros emigrated to the US, where his investment career took off, eventually turning his Quantum Fund into the world's largest hedge fund in the late 1990s[29]. But comparatively early on, in 1979, horrified by apartheid, he began funding scholarships for black South Africans. At the age of 50, after a career in merchant banking and then hedge fund investment, he decided he was wealthy enough never to need to earn any more money for the rest of his life – and turned increasingly to philanthropy. To date he has given away around $32 billion to humanitarian, pro-democracy, anti-totalitarian and free-market causes.[30]

'I underwent a kind of midlife crisis,' he told an audience drawn from the world's political and business elite in Davos in 2019. 'Why should I kill myself to make more money? I reflected long and hard on what I really cared about.'[31] The result was the creation of his Open Society Fund, whose objective was 'helping open up closed societies, reducing the deficiencies of open societies and promoting critical thinking'. In the 1980s, as the first cracks began to appear in Communist control of Eastern Europe, he began funding the new non-violent movements fighting for freedom in Hungary and its Communist neighbours. In 1984 he established the first of his Open Society foundations, over the years transferring $18 billion to finance them from his multi-billion-dollar fortune.[32] They were dedicated to promoting democracy, human rights and economic, legal and social reforms in the former Soviet sphere of influence.[33] His philanthropy played a part in the collapse of Communism in central Europe and then the Soviet Union.

Soros continued to make financial trades, most famously betting against the British pound in the early 1990s – and earning him \$1 billion when the UK devalued its currency and withdrew from the European Exchange Rate Mechanism (ERM) in 1992. Soros was, inaccurately, dubbed 'The Man who Broke the Bank of England'. But the financial crisis which spread across Asia in 1997 was so severe that it prompted a rethink for Soros. The man who had made his fortune through the untrammelled operations of the free market began to argue that greater regulation was needed – a conviction which was only reinforced when the global financial crisis struck in 2007. Soros was rethinking politically too. After President George W. Bush decided to invade Iraq in 2003, in response to the events of 9/11, Soros turned completely against Bush's Republican administration. Soros's Open Society foundations, classified under US law as nonpartisan organizations, are not allowed to make donations to political parties or contribute to candidates' campaign funds. So Soros began to make donations out of his own pocket. He gave an unprecedented \$20 million to the Democrat campaign which tried unsuccessfully to block the re-election of President Bush, whose neo-conservatism Soros denounced as a 'crude form of social Darwinism' that would plunge America into a 'permanent state of war'. He was then an early backer of Barack Obama, contributing to the campaign which saw America's first black president elected in 2008. Soros became a committed backer of the Democrat Party, supporting Hillary Clinton's campaign in 2016. Soros reacted to the election of President Trump, whom he dismissed as the 'ultimate narcissist', by contributing tens of millions of dollars to help Democratic candidates at federal, state and local level in the 2018 mid-term elections.

As a result George Soros became a bogeyman to the American right.[*] Open Society's support for the reform of immigration policies, prisons and the criminal justice system only confirmed the conviction of conservatives that Soros is a dangerous liberal. So did its mentoring programmes for black and Latino young men, along with its support

---

[*] See the interview with Patrick Gaspard, president of Soros's Open Society Foundations, on page 597 below.

for the Black Lives Matter movement. The reactions of the right cover a spectrum from mere criticism to totally outlandish fantasy. The American conservative conspiracy theorist Alex Jones has called Soros 'fundamentally evil'. Anti-Semites call him a 'Jewish puppet master' intent on building 'a New World Order'. His activism has made him a villain to conservative groups and the target of anti-Semitic smears. The actress Roseanne Barr called him a Nazi in an infamous social media posting. Even Donald Trump joined in, alleging that 'some people say' Soros financed the large caravan of South American migrants which was travelling towards the US/Mexican border in 2018–19. Words have consequences. In 2018 a Trump supporter from Florida planted a pipe bomb in the letterbox of Soros's home in New York state.[34]

But Soros did not just take on the American right. He also used his foundations' funds to champion the values of democracy, pluralism and individual rights further afield. In the early 2000s he backed the revolutions that erupted in Georgia, Ukraine and Kyrgyzstan. The Russian president, Vladimir Putin, who retaliated in 2014 by seizing Crimea, saw Soros as part of a Western plot to drive him out of the Kremlin. Putin turned the Russian propaganda machine, with its bogus social media accounts and internet bots, on Soros.[35] When a large wave of migrants arrived in Europe in 2015, provoking political crises in several European nations, Soros's foundations spent $12.5 million supporting migration-related initiatives. The move provoked the ire of Viktor Orbán's nationalist government in Hungary, which closed down a university Soros had founded. Orbán has taken Soros-baiting to a new level, erecting thousands of anti-Semitic billboards featuring a cackling Soros, warning Hungarians not to let him 'have the last laugh'.[36] In Italy the hard-line interior minister, Matteo Salvini, declared on television: 'Soros would like Italy [to become] a big refugee camp because he likes slaves.'[37] In Turkey, President Erdoğan called him 'a man who assigns people to divide nations and shatter them'.[38] And in Britain, Soros angered Eurosceptics by donating £800,000 to the Best for Britain campaign set up to fight for a second referendum to reverse the plebiscite which in 2016 had voted to take the UK out of the European Union.[39] 'Old voters have overruled young voters who will have to live with the consequences of Brexit for decades ahead. This is aggravating the disillusionment with democracy among young people,' he said.[40] Pro-Brexit politicians complained that, through Soros, the global liberal elite was attempting to subvert the will of the British people. The populist Brexiteer Nigel Farage called him 'the biggest danger to the entire Western world'.[41]

Undeterred, Soros continued to increase his social activism and philanthropy. In 2017 he transferred $18 billion from his company to his foundation – making it instantly the second-largest philanthropic organization in the US after that of Bill and Melinda Gates.[42] The wealth of the foundation now dwarfed his own personal fortune which, as a result of the massive gift, was reduced to a comparatively meagre $7 billion, according to Bloomberg's Billionaires Index which tracks the fortunes of 2,800 billionaires on a daily basis.[43] The Open Society Foundation now operates through a network of more than 40 smaller foundations and offices in countries from Afghanistan to South Africa – funding refugee relief, public health efforts, and programmes including a mobile court for war crimes in the Democratic Republic of the Congo and advocacy also for rights of the Roma, one of Europe's largest ethnic minorities. 'I find the current moment in history rather painful,' Soros said at Davos. 'Open societies are in crisis, and various forms of dictatorships and mafia states, exemplified by Putin's Russia, are on the rise. In the United States, President Trump would like to establish a mafia state, but he can't, because the Constitution, other institutions, and a vibrant civil society won't allow it.'[44]

The elderly Hungarian-American appears indefatigable. In 2019 he was at Davos again. At the age of 88, a *Sunday Times* reporter noted, George Soros does not shy away from making powerful enemies. That year at the annual dinner he hosts in the Hotel Seehof, one of the oldest and grandest venues in the Swiss resort, the billionaire hedge-funder turned his fire on the Chinese president, Xi Jinping. That country's new social credit system, Soros warned, will use artificial intelligence and other hi-tech surveillance techniques to keep tabs on the nation's 1.4 billion people. For Soros, who has not forgotten the scars left by living under totalitarian regimes as a young man, this was an unacceptable assault on individual liberty. 'China isn't the only authoritarian regime in the world, but it's undoubtedly the wealthiest, strongest and most developed in machine learning and artificial intelligence,' he told his audience of tycoons, prime ministers and journalists. 'This makes Xi Jinping the most dangerous opponent of those who believe in the concept of open society.'[45] His voice may have been quiet and shaky but George Soros's message was as loud and strong as ever.

PRIVATE MONEY AND PUBLIC ELECTIONS

Other philanthropists are more direct in their political interventions, seeking primarily to exert influence on which politicians get elected. One of the first big donations by the Amazon boss, Jeff Bezos, who enjoyed what could be the most rapid personal wealth surge in history, was to fund With Honor, a group dedicated to getting military veterans elected to the US House of Representatives in 2018. Its aim was to break the stranglehold of career politicians. A condition of his donation was that the candidates had to be committed to working with like-minded politicians in the opposing party – a development which irritated both Republicans and Democrats.[46] Another political philanthropist was the tech designer Tim Gill, who became rich after selling his Quark publishing software company. Gill has donated $422 million to the promotion of LGBTQ rights – more than any other person in America. Gill came out as gay to his parents in his first year at the University of Colorado, where he volunteered for the campus gay liberation group and later supported local AIDS awareness. But he did not become seriously engaged as an activist until, a decade later, the Christian right in Colorado helped pass an anti-gay initiative and Gill decided – as the wealthiest openly gay man in the state – that he had to fight back. He started the Gill Foundation to underwrite academic research, polling, litigation, data analytics and political organizing at grassroots level to oppose anti-gay candidates in elections to Congress. In 2006 his organizations defeated 50 of the 70 candidates they targeted. His fight is not over, since in many US states it is still legal to discriminate against LGBTQ people in housing, employment, restaurants, hotels and restrooms. In some states two lesbians can marry in the morning and be fired that afternoon for bringing a photo of their new spouse to work. Gill envisages continuing to campaign for another two decades and plans to spend every last dollar that he has donated to his foundation's coffers.[47]

Some philanthropists venture even more directly into party politics. In Britain almost half the individuals in the top 50 of the *Sunday Times* 2020 Giving List also made political donations. But unlike big givers in the United States, their political leanings almost all tended in one direction. Among those who gave generously both to charity and to a political party all but three gave to the

Conservative and/or Brexit parties.[48] The three exceptions gave to the Liberal Democrats. One of them, surprisingly perhaps, was the philanthropist and former Labour government minister Lord David Sainsbury, who gave £8 million out of his own pocket to the LibDems, as well as £170 million to charitable causes. Not one gave to Jeremy Corbyn's Labour Party. There was one small donation to the anti-Tory coalition in Wales.[49]

Giving and politics are otherwise kept separate largely because charity law forbids philanthropic foundations from making political donations, though occasionally a charity will fall foul of the rules. That happened to one of the largest philanthropic charities in the country – and in the world – the Garfield Weston Foundation. The charity is funded directly by shares in the Weston family's giant worldwide food and retailing operations, which owns household brands such as Ryvita and Twinings, along with high street giants Primark. The trust was set up by Garfield Weston, a Canadian biscuit manufacturer and British baker, who founded the family business. The charity's structure is unusual, since it holds the majority stake in the family business empire, Wittington Investments Ltd. The foundation in 2020 controlled assets of £10.5 billion[50] – almost half of all the funds controlled by all the philanthropists named in the 2020 Giving List. It practises old-style philanthropy rather than the more fashionable philanthrocapitalism. In 2018 it gave a total of £69 million to 1,917 projects. A few of these were major donations, like the £25 million it gave to Oxford University for the refurbishment of its 1930s New Library, which was reopened in 2015 as the Weston Library.[51] Most of its grants in 2018 were amounts of less than £20,000 to grassroots charities for small projects like a new roof on a village hall. But Weston also ventured, ineptly as it turned out, into politics. In 2010 it was reprimanded by the government regulator, the Charity Commissioners, after an investigation found that Wittington Investments Ltd had given £100,000 to the Conservative Party each year from 1993 to 1999. It had also made donations to a right-wing think tank, the Centre for Policy Studies, and to Eurosceptic political lobby groups. Such donations were in breach of charity law and Weston was officially reprimanded. Part of the money was repaid.[52]

MAYOR BLOOMBERG — BUSINESS, POLITICS
AND PHILANTHROPY

Similar laws exist in the United States. They were used to force the dissolution of the Donald J. Trump Foundation by the New York attorney general, Barbara Underwood. After a two-year investigation she filed a lawsuit alleging that it was engaging in 'a shocking pattern of illegality'. It was 'functioning as little more than a checkbook to serve Mr Trump's business and political interests' and unlawfully co-ordinating with his 2016 presidential campaign.[53] President Trump denied the claim but his lawyers later acknowledged the illegality in court, and at the end of 2019 a New York judge ruled that Trump had 'breached his fiduciary duty' by allowing funds raised for US veterans to be used for the Iowa primary election in 2016. He was ordered to pay $2 million to charity as a penalty.[54] The way round such legal restraints for a politically engaged philanthropist is exemplified in the approach of Michael Bloomberg, the sometime mayor of New York. Bloomberg, like David Sainsbury in the UK, has a portfolio of interests which, unusually, involve him directly in business and politics and philanthropy. Throughout his career – in which he has amassed a fortune which made him in 2019 the ninth richest person in the world – he has pursued these three spheres of activity more or less simultaneously. Where most other billionaire philanthropists have first built a business empire and then moved into politics or philanthropy, Bloomberg has allowed his commercial activities, political ambitions and altruistic impulses to interact and reinforce one another.

Mike Bloomberg, a bookkeeper's son who put himself through college by working as a parking lot attendant, began as a securities broker with Salomon Brothers in 1966. Fifteen years later he lost his job when the firm was taken over. But instead of looking for another post he resolved to start his own business. He created a computer system to provide rapid feeds of financial data for the global finance industry. His small start-up was launched in one room in 1981, but grew into a global company that employs nearly 20,000 people in 176 locations across 120 countries.[55] It expanded into a mass media company offering not just real-time market data and analytics but also running a news network, radio stations and magazines like *Business Week*.

Bloomberg's philanthropy began comparatively early in his career. He made his first contribution to public life in 1968, two years after he graduated from Harvard Business School and moved to New York. He and a friend started a small programme in Harlem to help children with their homework. It was funded with $5,000 from his employers, with a matching amount from a law firm. Bloomberg's philanthropy grew with his business. By 1990 he had installed 8,000 terminals for Wall Street traders; the profits were enough to allow him to endow the William Henry Bloomberg Professorship at Harvard with a $3 million gift in honour of his late father. Bloomberg made clear that he had inherited his understanding of the interaction between business and philanthropy from his father, of whom he said: 'throughout his life, he recognized the importance of reaching out to the non-profit sector to help better the welfare of the entire community'.[56]

The profits from Bloomberg's business enabled him to venture into his third area of activity, politics. In 2001 he ran for election as mayor of New York. Because New York City laws restrict the amount of campaign contributions a candidate can accept, Bloomberg opted to finance his own campaign. Unbound by their restrictions, he spent $73 million of his own money on his electioneering – five times more than his opponent was able to spend.[57] The reform of public education was his top political priority once elected, and it subsequently became one of his favoured philanthropic areas of activity. But Bloomberg augmented his public policy with private donations to favoured organizations. He provided money to hundreds of small neighbourhood arts and cultural groups but also to support groups for people living with cancer and to similar good causes. Yet he did so, not in his own name, but through the Carnegie Corporation of New York. It listed him only as an 'anonymous donor' in the years from 2001 to 2010 when he gave amounts ranging from $5 million to $20 million a year.[58] By 2011, when the donations became public, Bloomberg was listed among the Top Ten American Philanthropists in the *Chronicle of Philanthropy*. His generosity drew praise from grateful recipients, but also occasioned rebukes from critics who believed he was using his fortune to buy political favours.

Bloomberg financed his own mayoral campaign again in 2005, this time spending even more, $78 million, which included funding a phone bank to seek volunteers for his re-election campaign. Once again the commercial, political and voluntary sectors were intermingled. During his overall tenure as mayor, from 2002 to 2013, Bloomberg brought his innovation-driven approach to city government. He turned around a broken public school system by raising standards and paying good teachers more. He stimulated economic growth and revitalized old industrial areas, encouraging entrepreneurship, supporting small businesses, and strengthening key industries such as new media, film and television, bio-science, technology and tourism. Bloomberg's economic policies created record numbers of private sector jobs in formerly depressed neighbourhoods, even in the wake of a deep national recession.

During his third mayoral term, which began in 2009, the main political aims he set out – gun control, education reform, and developing a New York City plan to reduce greenhouse gas emissions – were to prove the themes he would pursue as a philanthropist after 2014 when he left office. As mayor he established a scheme to plant a million trees throughout the city. He reduced pollution to produce the best air quality in the city of New York in more than 50 years, increasing residents' life expectancy by three years.[59] He also networked with mayors in other major cities across America to reduce carbon emissions nationally. His concern with health led him to outlaw smoking in the city's restaurants, bars and parks – a measure that he told the *Financial Times*[60] was his greatest achievement in office – and which he later pursued through his philanthropy. He insisted that calorie counts be added to menus at restaurant chains; and he banned artery-clogging trans-fats, forcing fast food giants such as McDonald's and Dunkin' Donuts to change their recipes – all of which led to the criticism that he was turning New York into a 'nanny state'.

His philanthropy continued in parallel. In 2010 he signed the Giving Pledge, committing to give away at least half his wealth in his lifetime – and the rest through his foundation in the lifetime of his two daughters.[61] In 2011 he donated $50 million through Bloomberg Philanthropies to a Beyond Coal campaign run by the environmental group, the Sierra Club, which is pushing to accelerate the closure of coal-fired power plants across the US. He gave the campaign another $30 million in 2015. In a further synergy between his politics and philanthropy, he has given away around $100 million to support both Republican and Democrat candidates who share his views on tougher gun control and education reform.[62] He planned, according to *Forbes* magazine in 2019, to spend at least $500 million to try to defeat Donald Trump in the 2020 US presidential elections.[63]

Then, late in 2019, Mike Bloomberg declared his intention to run for president himself, announcing he was joining the race to become the

Democratic Party nominee. He would, he said, offer voters a pragmatic option to unseat a president who 'represents an existential threat to our country and our values'. Bloomberg's 'unique set of experiences in business, government, and philanthropy' would enable him, he declared, to 'win and lead'.[64] He announced: 'I offer myself as a doer and a problem solver – not a talker. And someone who is ready to take on the tough fights – and win.' Bloomberg declared that he would not accept any political donations to his campaign, and would work for just $1 a year if elected president. He fought an unconventional campaign, bypassing the earliest primaries and focusing instead on the big Super Tuesday primaries in March 2020.[65] It was not a successful strategy. Despite spending a colossal $900 million of his own money on television ads, Bloomberg performed badly in the candidates' TV debate and did not win the nomination of a single state; he swiftly withdrew from the race.[66]

As a philanthropist, like Bill Gates, Michael Bloomberg has fixated on data, impact and evaluation. 'He's very focused on measurable results, even though that's not always the easiest thing to do in the arts,' says Rocco Landesman, the head of ArtPlace, a charity that uses the arts to help revitalize neighbourhoods.[67] Like Gates, Bloomberg is thorough in his initial research into a problem. Before Bloomberg handed over $50 million to the Sierra Club for its campaign to accelerate the closure of coal-fired power stations, he went through their plans with a fine-tooth comb. Carl Pope, former head of the group, says he had never before experienced the degree of due diligence sought by the Bloomberg Family Foundation before it committed its cash. It took three years to develop a campaign which Bloomberg was convinced would reduce the country's 500 coal stations by 30 per cent by 2020. A formal agreement took another nine months, as a team of Bloomberg staff and Sierra Club officials drew up a plan. 'They wanted a predictive model to anticipate which coal-fired plants would be retired early and why, and to automatically shift our emphasis and put more resources into more promising targets. We'd never seen anything like it,' Mr Pope told the *Financial Times*. But he now understands the logic, since the result has been that closures of the dirty plants are currently ahead of target.

Not everyone is so supportive of the Bloomberg approach. His donations to US education reform, rather like those of Bill Gates, have been criticized for using metrics which can sometimes be over-simplistic and authoritarian. Education specialists criticize Bloomberg's single-minded focus on upgrading the quality of teachers and ignoring factors such as the need for smaller class sizes, better infrastructure, computer-aided learning or social disadvantage among students.

Where Bloomberg differs from Gates is that, once he has given his approval, his approach is much less hands-on. Bloomberg is adept at delegation. 'My approach is to look at the overall objectives, pick a course and delegate a lot more than others might [on] the actual implementation. What I'm good at is picking people and giving them authority.'[68] In the days when his profile as a philanthropist was being kept low as the 'Anonymous Donor' via the Carnegie Foundation, Bloomberg never demanded that Carnegie provide him with a single detailed report on how his money was spent. He would simply send a single cheque for tens of millions of dollars every December. Nor did he require any application process, which freed the groups from the red tape and paperwork that often accompany grant-seeking, but also caused some political resentment as to why some groups received money and others did not.[69]

Just as his third term as mayor of New York ended, Bloomberg funded a report entitled *Risky Business* with former US Treasury Secretary Hank Paulson and hedge fund billionaire-cum-environmentalist Tom Steyer. The initiative set out to depoliticize the climate change debate and focus instead on the economic risk that global warming poses to US businesses. The report – written by a bipartisan group of former presidential cabinet officers, lawmakers, corporate leaders and scientists – asserted that climate change could cost the country billions of dollars over the next two decades.[70] Six months after its launch Bloomberg joined with two Californian environmentalist philanthropists, Liz Simons and Mark Heising, to finance a $48 million programme to help US states ditch coal-fired electricity – the biggest contributor to the US carbon footprint – and switch to cleaner sources of energy such as solar and wind power. The money was allocated to dozens of local and national organizations to assist states with their energy planning.[71]

At the end of his third term of office as mayor of New York, in December 2013, Michael Bloomberg became a full-time philanthropist. But he continued with his singular mix of business, politics and philanthropy even after leaving public office. He ramped up his giving to a level where, since leaving City Hall, he has given away more than $6 billion to a wide variety of causes and organizations.[72] The way that the money was spent revealed the degree to which Bloomberg had learned from the cross-fertilization of the private, public and philanthropic sectors. It was evident too in the first annual report of his Bloomberg Philanthropies Foundation in 2013, which set out the six synergies its founder had learned in that cross-over:

- The first was to 'lead from the front'. Fear of controversy could often be a stumbling block to progress. Good philanthropy should put 'results first, not public opinion'. Bloomberg's work to 'end our nation's coal dependency' had been unpopular in many parts of the country. But his $50 million commitment to clean energy had led to the closure of more than 130 dirty coal plants 'improving air quality for millions of Americans and accelerating the transition to cleaner alternative energy sources'.
- The second was 'spreading solutions that work'. Here he cited his anti-smoking measures and claimed that 60 countries had emulated his approach, passing comprehensive tobacco control laws which should save four million lives.
- Bloomberg's third key principle was 'following the data'. He wrote: 'Data is the driving force behind my company's value to the financial services industry – and it is the driving force behind our problem-solving efforts at City Hall. Bloomberg Philanthropies is no different. It harnesses the power of data to assess opportunities, understand impact, evaluate results, and improve performance.' This was the classic philanthrocapitalist mantra on the importance of metrics. 'In God we trust; everyone else bring data,' he quipped.
- But his fourth golden rule ventured outside that area by recognizing the need for his foundation's partners to be empowered. 'Writing checks isn't enough to achieve lasting and necessary change,' he wrote. 'Often, that requires empowering individuals and organizations to advocate for themselves. Bloomberg Philanthropies will help organizations be effective advocates in both swaying public opinion and government officials in order to sift policies and advance progress.'
- Partnerships were his fifth principle. 'The challenges we face in America and around the world are increasingly complex, and

neither the private nor the public sector can solve them alone. Public-private partnerships have been a hallmark of my time in City Hall, and I have witnessed their efficacy and impact. Bloomberg Philanthropies brings together people, ideas, and resources from across sectors toward a common purpose.'

- The sixth principle was to think globally but act locally by focusing on cities. 'The change that happens in cities can change the world. Cities are the global centres of communication, commerce and culture. And whether it is facilitating the spread of good ideas between cities to help mayors tackle some of their toughest challenges, or leading a global coalition of large cities to take real action against climate change, Bloomberg Philanthropies leverages the power of cities to create lasting change – especially when national and international bodies refuse to act.'[73]

After a brief period as a full-time philanthropist in 2014, Bloomberg reassumed the position of CEO at Bloomberg LP at the end of the year. That did not prevent him from being ranked as the third-largest philanthropic donor in America in 2015.[74] One of the biggest recipients of his largesse was his old university, Johns Hopkins, to which he had given $1.1 billion over the years, and to which in 2018 he was to add a further gift of $1.8 billion – the largest private donation in modern history to an institute of higher education.[75] But he also continued his political activism, taking up a role for the United Nations Secretary General Ban Ki-moon as his first Special Envoy for Cities and Climate Change in 2014. He was tasked with building a global coalition of mayors and city officials committed to reducing greenhouse gas emissions.[76] A year later he was asked by the governor of the Bank of England, Mark Carney, to lead a new global task force to help the financial markets understand the growing risks of climate change.[77]

Again Bloomberg's politics were augmented by his philanthropy, as he offered $15 million to help implement the Paris climate accord which had been signed by President Barack Obama – and from which his successor Donald Trump has withdrawn. 'In the US, emission levels are determined far more by cities, states, and businesses than they are by our federal government,' said Bloomberg. 'The American government may have pulled out of the Paris agreement but American

society remains committed to it.'[78] Bloomberg demonstrated his own
commitment to that when, in 2019, he pledged another $500 million
to shut remaining coal-fired power plants by 2030 – and reduce carbon
emissions in other ways. His politics and philanthropy continued
hand in hand on health too. In 2016 he accepted a role as the World
Health Organization's ambassador to reduce deaths from preventable
diseases, traffic accidents, tobacco, obesity and alcohol. A few months
later Bloomberg Philanthropies announced an additional $360 million
to allow campaigners in 110 countries to monitor tobacco use, lobby
for strong tobacco control laws, and create mass media campaigns to
educate the public about the dangers of tobacco use. All the while his
business empire and investments grew so that in 2019 his net worth was
estimated at $55 billion.[79] At that point he had given away $6.4 billion
and committed to $1.8 billion more.[80]

Philanthropy, business and government do more than complement
one another, insists David Sainsbury who, like Bloomberg, is unusual
in having operated in all three spheres. Each brings something specific
to bear on social problems. Lord Sainsbury's time in public office
confirmed his conviction that charitable spending could never be a
substitute for social welfare. Philanthropy – which totalled around
£3.16 billion in the UK according to The *Sunday Times* 2020 Rich
List[81] – can never provide sufficient resources. In major areas of public
spending, David Sainsbury believes, there is no evidence that charities
could do better than the state in the allocation of resources. What
charities do better is take risks and innovate. They are also better
able to learn from their mistakes – which politicians find hard to do
for fear of being accused of U-turns or flip-flopping. One thing that
government does very badly is that if it has an initiative that is not
going well, ministers have a tendency just to throw up their hands,
Sainsbury reveals, 'and say, "forget it, we'll do something else"'. But in
business, and philanthropy, 'you say what's going wrong and why it's
going wrong – and try and correct it'.[82] You have 'got to be prepared
to have "course corrections" . . . to change direction halfway through
a project'.[83] (Lord Sainsbury expands on this in his interview for this
book, pages 234–5.)

Active involvement in politics revealed to Lord Sainsbury another
advantage which philanthropy has over government. The year after
he became science minister, in 1999, environmental activists began

to issue public protests at his philanthropic and business support for companies involved in genetically modified food. While politicians must take account of lobbying by voters and short political electoral cycles, philanthropists can afford to take a different perspective. The time horizon of government projects is limited by the length of the five-year parliamentary session. David Sainsbury prefers to fund projects for the long term: 'I think if you are going to change something significant, you probably need ten years of concerted effort,' he says.[84] That remark carries within it both the advantage of philanthropic agility and also the disadvantage of the democratic deficit that philanthropy can embody, as we will consider in the next chapter.

FAKE NEWS AND ACTIVIST CINEMA

Some philanthropists steer away from party politics towards wider political causes, though these can be no less controversial. One big donor who has been unafraid to venture into partisan areas is Craig Newmark, who made his fortune from launching the advertising website Craigslist. It began, in 1995, as a regular email to friends listing social events in the San Francisco Bay Area, but it then morphed into a website of classified ads which now covers 70 countries worldwide. This digital revolution syphoned off the advertising on which much of the newspaper industry relied, assisting the decline of the printed press – a decline which, ironically, Newmark then lamented. The social media that replaced it is so unreliable, he complained. Alarmed by the disinformation campaigns and false reports that had plagued the 2016 US presidential election Newmark decided to fund a five-year journalism ethics programme focused on verification, fact-checking and accountability in journalism.

'I just want some news I can trust,' the Craigslist founder told the *San Francisco Chronicle* in 2016, announcing a million-dollar donation to the Poynter Institute for Media Studies to combat 'fake news'.[85] A year later Newmark teamed up with Facebook and Mozilla to finance a $14 million News Integrity Initiative to give the general public the skills to distinguish fact from fantasy.[86] The following year the Craigslist founder gave the online news magazine *Mother Jones* another $1 million, hoping to boost the investigative journal's ability to combat disinformation campaigns aimed at deceiving the American people.[87]

Supporting trustworthy journalism is Newmark's mission statement. 'At a time when factual information is under attack, we especially need trustworthy and rigorous investigative reporting to inform and empower people from all backgrounds,' Newmark said.[88] By 2019 the Craigslist founder had written cheques totalling $85 million[89] to the American Press Institute, the Ground Truth Project, Wikimedia, New York Public Radio and Berkeley Journalism School. He created the Craig Newmark Center for Journalism Ethics and Security at Columbia University, declaring 'a trustworthy press acting in good faith is the immune system of democracy'.[90] He was not alone in this belief. In 2017 Jeff Bezos gave away $1 million of his Amazon profits to the Reporters Committee for Freedom of the Press. Many saw his purchase of the *Washington Post* in 2013 as a form of philanthropy – using his wealth to support important journalism.[91]

Jeff Skoll, who became a billionaire twice over after selling his shares in eBay – where he was the first employee – has turned his political and private passions into a philanthropic business. Skoll has combined liberal social activism with his enthusiasm for cinema to produce what has become known as 'social impact entertainment'. He uses films as vehicles to promote causes such as civil rights, campaigns against inequality and calls for action on climate change, along with myriad more specialist causes. Over the past 15 years his company, Participant Media, has made more than a hundred movies, accumulating 73 Academy Awards nominations and winning 18 Oscars. Championing the philosophy that 'a good story well told can help change the world', his movies include *An Inconvenient Truth*, *Fast Food Nation*, *The Kite-Runner*, *Standard Operating Procedure*, *He Named Me Malala*, *Spotlight* and *Deepwater Horizon*. In 2019 one of his movies – *Roma*, a black-and-white film focusing on the plight of a domestic worker in Mexico – was pipped at the post for the title of Best Picture by another of his movies, *Green Book*, about a black musician's trip with a white chauffeur through the segregated states of the Jim Crow Deep South in 1960s America. *Roma*, which did win the Oscar for best director for Alfonso Cuarón, had a website which directed users to organizations representing domestic workers in Mexico and the US. It also urged them to sign a domestic workers' bill of rights.

Skoll is relentless in the subjects he pursues. *Roma* was foreshadowed by his 2007 film *The Visitor*, in which the protagonist befriends undocumented immigrants in New York; it was launched in partnership with the American Civil Liberties Union, which used screenings to educate audiences about immigrants' rights. In 2011 his movie *The Help* first explored the themes of racial prejudice developed in *Green Book*. It too was set in the 1960s, in Mississippi, and told the story of a Southern society girl who returns from college with dreams of being a writer – and brings turmoil to her small town by interviewing the poor black women who have spent their lives taking care of rich white families and their children. More recently, Skoll's 2016 film *Hidden Figures* told the little-known story of three female African-American mathematicians who were vital to NASA's space programme. The movie prompted its distributors 21st Century Fox to fund science and engineering scholarships for women.

Persistence is a virtue in social impact education, Skoll believes. One of his first films was the 2006 global warming documentary *An Inconvenient Truth*, made by Al Gore, which helped earn the former US vice-president the Nobel Peace Prize. Skoll initially believed that – once the film had exploded the myths of climate change deniers, and presented audiences with a raft of ideas for how they could minimize their carbon footprints – his job would be done. But, years later, when asked to name his biggest philanthropic mistake, he pointed to the Al Gore film and said: 'We figured the scientists and public opinion would take care of it from there. But the fossil fuel industry fought back . . . Lesson One, if you're going to do a campaign about something, be in it for the long haul.'[92] Skoll also devotes much of his conventional philanthropy to the same cause. Organizations campaigning on climate change feature prominently in the list of grants handed out by the Skoll Foundation, which he endowed with $1 billion of eBay's stock at its formation. The largest single charitable donation of the Skoll Global Threats Fund to date has been a $30 million contribution to the Climate Reality Project.[93]

GLOBAL WARNING – PHILANTHROPY AND CLIMATE CHANGE

Anyone tempted to judge by media reports might imagine that funding action on global warming is a top priority among philanthropists. Michael Bloomberg was not alone in keeping the topic in the political headlines. Nat Simons, who runs a major hedge fund in San Francisco, created headlines of his own in 2013 when it was revealed that, for almost a decade, he and his wife Laura Baxter-Simons had quietly been giving $500 million to clean energy companies and climate change action groups. Through their Sea Change Foundation they have been pressing for public policies and private investments into those changes in behaviour and technologies which they reckon will reduce the most substantial sources of greenhouse gas emissions. In 2017 they signed the Giving Pledge and declared that climate change was the most pressing problem facing the world. In a public statement they said:

> About ten years ago, we began to seriously consider how we should approach philanthropy. We decided that we wanted to create a foundation that would focus on what we felt was the most pressing problem facing the world. At the time, we had young children and were (and remain) deeply worried that the world they will inhabit will be fundamentally compromised due to unchecked greenhouse gas emissions. We also appreciated the long-term benefits associated with moving toward a low carbon economy and determined that this issue needed to be urgently addressed, regardless of politics. As such, our efforts to date have been primarily focused on climate change and clean energy policy in the US and internationally.[94]

The couple said that they intend to give away between $50 million and $75 million a year to promote climate mitigation work and the development of clean energy.[95] In the United States, where climate change scepticism is more widespread than in the UK, Nat Simons' activism has made him a target for conservative critics, some of whom have claimed, without offering any credible evidence, that his Sea Change Foundation is a conduit for Russian funding of the US environmental movement.

The fears of such conspiracy theorists are no doubt reinforced by the philanthropic activism of another Californian hedge fund billionaire. In 2012 Tom Steyer quit his company to devote most of his time to campaigning on global warming. His firm, Farallon Capital Management, was named after a group of islands near San Francisco known for their shark-infested waters – an ironic homage to Steyer's reputation as a highly aggressive investor. After signing the Giving Pledge, the billionaire and his wife Kat Taylor gave $25 million to establish NextGen Climate to encourage more young people to vote. 'Eighty per cent of people under 30 in the United States want an accelerated move to clean technology,' he told the *Financial Times*. 'It's one of a handful of issues on which they are very engaged.'[96] Yet young people are also less likely to vote. He set up a NextGen Climate political action committee (PAC) to raise and distribute campaign funds to support environmentalist candidates seeking political office. It attacks politicians who are climate change deniers. And it mobilizes environmentalist student voters to lobby members of Congress and lead protests.[97]

Steyer's campaigning is seen in the US as highly political, since the amount of philanthropic dollars directed towards support for democratic systems is tiny compared with the funds flowing into mainstream philanthropic causes such as healthcare and education. Of the $54 billion in grants which US charitable foundations make every year only around $1.4 billion goes to supporting the health of democratic systems.[98] Steyer became even more of a bogeyman to the American right when he later rebranded his group as NextGen America and in 2017 announced its mission was being expanded to also 'promote American values and standing up to Donald Trump and the Republican Party's assault on our way of life'. He even launched a television advertising campaign to impeach Trump, declaring that there was 'no limit' to what he was prepared to spend to fight him.[99]

More conventionally, in 2015 a group of top philanthropists – including Bill Gates, Jeff Bezos, Mark Zuckerberg, Richard Branson and Jack Ma, founder of the Chinese e-commerce company Alibaba – got together on the first day of the Paris climate change summit to launch the Breakthrough Energy Coalition. This global group of private investors declared their intention to 'invest early, invest broadly, invest boldly, invest wisely and invest together'. They want to fund scientists, engineers and entrepreneurs to invent innovative technologies to limit the impact of climate change by providing affordable and reliable energy to everyone.[100]

They were not alone. In 2017 the Hewlett Foundation, America's largest institutional funder of philanthropic action on climate change, gave $128 million towards tackling the problem. In 2018 the Swiss entrepreneur Hansjörg Wyss pledged that he would give $1 billion for conservation causes, including more marine reserves, wildlife refuges and national parks. A survey of the 50 top philanthropists in 2019 listed several big donations to environmental causes.[101] Mike

Bloomberg announced that his Beyond Carbon initiative now aimed to shut down all America's coal plants over the next 11 years as part of his campaign for a 100 per cent clean energy economy. Bob Fisher, whose parents founded the Gap clothing empire, runs the Pisces Foundation with his wife Randi. It focuses on water resources and environmental literacy; among their grant recipients is the Pulitzer Prize–winning *InsideClimate News*, an organization dedicated to debunking climate change scepticism. Darren Walker, president of the Ford Foundation, has committed it to join eight other groups in a $459 million programme to protect rainforests, the land rights of indigenous peoples, and to promote sustainable agriculture.

Another prominent climate change philanthropist is Yvon Chouinard, founder of the outdoor clothing company Patagonia, which already donates 1 per cent of company sales to environmental causes. In 2018 it announced that it would be giving $10 million to combat global warming. What added political piquancy to the donation was that it represented the sum the company had saved as a result of the tax cuts – from 35 to 21 per cent – introduced in the US by climate change sceptic Donald Trump. 'Taxes protect the most vulnerable in our society, our public lands and other life-giving resources,' said Patagonia's CEO Rose Marcario. 'In spite of this, the Trump administration initiated a corporate tax cut, threatening these services at the expense of our planet . . . Instead of putting the money back into our business, we're responding by putting $10 million back into the planet. Our home planet needs it more than we do.' Yvon Chouinard went further. 'Our government continues to ignore the seriousness and causes of the climate crisis. It is pure evil,' Patagonia's founder said in a press release. 'We need to double down on renewable energy solutions. We need an agriculture system that supports small family farms and ranches, not one that rewards chemical companies intent on destroying our planet and poisoning our food. And we need to protect our public lands and waters because they are all we have left.'[102]

Yet despite all these well-publicized donations, total giving by philanthropists to combat the heating of the planet is surprisingly small. A decade ago prospects for climate philanthropy looked positive. In the United States the number of climate-change-related grants doubled in the eight years after 2000. By 2008 they totalled almost $900 million thanks to the Hewlett Foundation and a few other big funders.[103] But after the 2007–8 global financial crisis, donations for work on the environment plunged.[104] In 2015 the heads of the two charitable foundations which had taken the lead on climate action in the US called upon fellow philanthropists to join them in greater action: Larry Kramer of the Hewlett Foundation and Carol Larson of the Packard Foundation rang the alarm in a jointly authored article for *The Chronicle of Philanthropy* headlined 'Foundations Must Move Fast to Fight Climate Change'.[105] They revealed that less than 2 per cent of all philanthropic dollars were being spent in the fight against global warming. By contrast, half of all donations from individuals with an income of over $1 million a year went on health and education, with 17 per cent going to religion and 15 per cent to the arts and culture. Only 4 per cent went on meeting the basic needs of the poor. But climate action got the least amount of all.[106]

The picture in the UK seems depressingly similar. In 2019 a group of the top climate scientists in Britain wrote to the nation's top 100 philanthropists and charitable foundations, complaining that just 3 per cent of their grants went to combat climate change or wider ecological priorities. Out of a total of more than £4 billion given out in grants, only £105 million went on environmental causes. This was largely because, Dr Joe Smith, director of the Royal Geographical Society, told the BBC, 'the remit of many charities, trusts and foundations was set decades ago'.[107] The scientists – including Professor Myles Allen, head of the climate dynamics group at the University of Oxford; Professor Piers Forster, director of the Priestley International Centre for Climate at the University of Leeds; Professor Joanna Haigh of the Grantham Institute for Climate Change and the Environment at Imperial College London; and the British government's former chief scientific adviser Sir David King – called for a change of gear by philanthropists to tackle what they called 'the extraordinary ecological collapse' now under way.[108] 'The work to counter these threats is desperately under-funded,' they wrote. 'Last year's IPCC report advised that we have 12 years to cut global emissions by 45 per cent or face an existential threat, while this month's UN report on biodiversity revealed that human activity is threatening the existence of over a million plant and animal species,' the scientists wrote. Evidence is growing rapidly on the impact of climate change and the urgency of the crisis. Polls show that 85 per cent of the British public are now concerned about climate change.[109] Even in the US nearly 70 per cent of Americans, including a majority of Republicans, want the government to take 'aggressive' action to combat climate change, a

2019 Reuters/Ipsos poll showed.[110] The World Health Organization estimates that climate change will cause 250,000 additional deaths per year from malnutrition, malaria, diarrhoea and heat stress between 2030 and 2050.[111] Yet, despite all that, the heating of the planet appears to be of limited interest to most billionaire philanthropists.

Perhaps that is changing. In July 2019 three US philanthropists pledged $600,000 – with the promise of tens of millions more to follow – to Extinction Rebellion, the activist group staging disruptive protests against the scale of governmental inaction on global warming. One of the three, Trevor Neilson, was galvanized into action when he was forced to flee his house in California during a wildfire. 'Something about throwing my two-year-old and wife in the car and evacuating from the worst fire in the history of southern California brought the issue into a new type of focus,' he said. Together with members of the Kennedy and Getty families, he set up the Climate Emergency Fund to fund 'non-violent direct action protests'. But most 'of the world's biggest philanthropists are still in a gradualist mindset,' he added before declaring: 'We do not have time for gradualism.'[112] At the United Nations Climate Action Summit in September 2019, Bill Gates announced that his foundation was working with the World Bank and some European governments to provide $790 million to help millions of the world's small farmers adapt to climate change. The Gates Foundation pledged $310 million of that total.[113] But Bill Gates is ahead of the philanthropy field on the urgent need to address climate change, though others are becoming alive to the issue. In 2020 Jeff Bezos, who had previously threatened to dismiss employees who complained about his company's carbon footprint – thanks to Amazon's fleets of diesel-guzzling trucks and high use of packaging – announced that he was donating $10 billion to create the Bezos Earth Fund to begin distributing grants in the summer of that year in a global initiative to fund scientists, activists, NGOs and any other effort 'that offers a real possibility to help preserve and protect the natural world'.

HOW THE KOCH BROTHERS FINANCED
CLIMATE-CHANGE REJECTION

In fact, there is more than a lack of interest or urgency at play. There is also a significant group of individuals who seek to undermine the scientific consensus on climate change by encouraging scepticism and even denial. Perhaps the most prominent of these have been Charles and David Koch, who became fabulously wealthy thanks to the success of Koch Industries, America's second-biggest private company, which employs more than 120,000 people. It is an oil and gas conglomerate which owns refineries, pipelines, fertilizer factories, and coal and cement transport systems. According to an investigation by the *New Yorker*,[114] the Koch brothers have, over the past two decades, given millions of dollars to conservative think tanks and academics who have sown doubts about climate change, criticized environmental regulation, and campaigned for minimal taxes for industry. A Koch Industries spokesman responded by insisting that the brothers were merely facilitating 'an open and honest airing of all sides' on the climate debate.[115] But Greenpeace, which estimates from an analysis of Koch tax returns that they have spent at least $88 million doing this, calls Koch Industries the 'financial kingpin of climate-science denial'.[116] The brothers' cash funds a network of think tanks, lobbyists, politicians, pundits, public relations agencies and university professors, who together constitute what Greenpeace calls 'the most formidable obstacles to advancing clean energy and climate policy in the US'. The Koch brothers, said *The Economist*, are 'villains accused of using their billions to subvert the will of the people'.[117]

Their determination to cast doubt upon the research which shows that the heating of the planet is caused by human activity is rooted in two factors. First, their $100 billion business empire centres on the exploitation of the fossil fuels which most scientists blame for climate change. More than that, the US Environmental Protection Agency has ranked Koch Industries as one of only three companies in America which is simultaneously a top-ten polluter of air, water and climate.[118] Greenpeace additionally accuses Koch Industries of having a long history of 'pollution cover-ups, union-busting, and fights against wage and benefit improvements'.[119] But the Kochs' strategy also plays into the brothers' libertarian conservative political ideology – which conveniently aligns with their corporate self-interest.

When their father, Fred Koch, died after a heart attack in 1967, he left his sons enormously wealthy. Charles Koch, who was to become the driving force behind what was then just a medium-sized family oil firm, renamed it Koch Industries, in honour of his father. David Koch, who went on to oversee the brothers' giving to a wide range of conservative and artistic causes, made a wry joke about their fabulous inheritance:

> Let me tell you a story. It all started when I was a little boy. One day, my father gave me an apple. I soon sold it for five dollars and bought two apples and sold them for ten. Then I bought four apples and sold them for twenty. Well, this went on day after day, week after week, month after month, year after year, until my father died and left me three hundred million dollars![120]

That sum was enhanced by their father's clever planning to avoid death duties. One of his strategies was to set up a 'charitable lead trust' which enabled him to pass his estate down to his sons without inheritance taxes – so long as the sons donated the interest the trust accrued to charity for twenty years. As their biographer, Jane Mayer, put it: 'to maximize their self-interest . . . the Koch boys were compelled to be charitable'. Tax avoidance was thus the original impetus for the Koch brothers' extraordinary philanthropy. As David Koch later explained, 'So for 20 years, I had to give away all that income, and I sort of got into it.'[121]

The Koch boys inherited their father's politics as well as his fortune. Fred Koch had been one of the 11 founders of the John Birch Society, an ultra-conservative movement which opposed the civil-rights activists who challenged racial segregation in the 1960s. 'The colored man looms large in the Communist plan to take over America,' Fred Koch had written in 1960. Charles Koch was a member too, but he resigned a year after his father's death and adopted a more sophisticated form of conservative philosophy. After graduating from MIT with degrees in nuclear and chemical engineering, Charles got a job as an energy consultant. But, after what he described as an intellectual epiphany brought on after attending a conference on free-market capitalism, in the evenings he would read political theory. He became deeply influenced by the writings on freedom of conservative thinkers such as Friedrich Hayek.[122] The ideas exhilarated him. None more so than a small 1962 tract from the relatively obscure British scientist Michael Polanyi entitled *The Republic of Science: Its Political and Economic Theory*. The paper argues that science should function like an economic market, with research dollars flowing to the very best scholars and ideas, as determined by scientific consensus. For Koch, reading it was a seminal moment which was to lead him and his brother to give more than $200 million to colleges and universities to further academic research in line with their own free-market and libertarian instincts.

The rationale for what was to prove a 50-year strategy was set out by a corporate lawyer and champion of the tobacco industry, Lewis Powell, who had inveighed against the growing scientific evidence linking smoking to cancer. He wrote a confidential memorandum entitled *Attack on the American Free Enterprise System*. It became a blueprint for conservative business interests as they planned to snatch the national political agenda back from the liberals and progressives that the conservatives liked to brand as socialist or even communist. Powell, who was soon afterwards appointed to the Supreme Court by Richard Nixon, feared that what he saw as an undermining of Americans' faith in enterprise was a slippery slope to socialism. His 5,000-word memo set out a plan for a broad attack on the liberal establishment. The most disquieting enemies were not 'the Communists, New Leftists and other revolutionaries', but instead 'come from perfectly respectable elements of society: from the college campus, the pulpit, the media, the intellectual and literary journals, the arts and sciences, and from politicians'.[123] To take back control of the agenda conservatives must first regain control of these institutions. The first step was to restore 'openness', 'fairness' and 'balance' by insisting upon equal time for conservatives. 'This is a long road and not one for the faint-hearted,' Powell concluded.

All this resonated with Charles Koch. He cited Lewis Powell by name in a 1974 speech in which Koch focused particularly on college campuses. 'We have supported the very institutions from which the attack on free markets emanates, partly through taxes,' he said.

> We have also contributed voluntarily to colleges and universities on the erroneous assumption that this assistance benefits businesses and the free enterprise system, even though these institutions encourage extreme hostility to American business. We should cease financing our own destruction . . . by supporting only those programs, departments or schools that contribute in some way to our individual companies or to the general welfare of our free enterprise system.

At a conference that he paid to convene in New York City in 1976, Koch suggested that he and his peers must focus on 'attracting youth', because 'this is the only group that is open to a radically different social philosophy'.[124] Another Koch affiliate at the conference suggested that

Hitler's creation of a youth movement was key to the Nazi capture of the German state; libertarians, he said, should organize university students to create a similar group identity.[125] The Kochs' initial approach was cautious, starting with just seven colleges in 2005. But, pleased by their growing influence, the brothers increased their donations at an exponential pace. By 2014 they had spread to 361 campuses, according to Greenpeace's analysis of the Koch Foundation's annual tax returns.

In parallel with their assault on academia, the Kochs launched an onslaught on public policy to shift the general consensus there back to the right. In addition to the $200 million they spent on universities, the Kochs funnelled huge amounts into conservative think tanks. In 1974 the Charles Koch Foundation was set up, changing its name two years later to the Cato Institute. It campaigns for a smaller role for government in both domestic and foreign affairs; it lobbies for the scrapping of the minimum wage; it campaigns against curbs on child labour; it opposes universal healthcare and wants to limit state schooling; it calls for the privatization of government services. It embodies the Kochs' radical right-wing libertarianism which insists that nothing should stand in the way of free enterprise. Its influence has been considerable. In 2017 the Cato Institute was named as one of the top ten think tanks in the United States.[126] It is not the only such Koch-supported body. Others include the Heritage Foundation, Americans for Prosperity and Freedom Partners, a network of donors fostered by the Kochs. They also supported literally dozens of other lesser-known outfits promoting the libertarian credo. All this forms what *The Economist* has called the 'Kochtopus'.[127] Its tentacles have slowly pulled American politics toward their own arch-conservative, pro-business, anti-tax and anti-regulatory agenda.[128]

Those tentacles constantly sought out new avenues. One of Koch's early ultra-libertarian advisers, George Pearson, suggested that traditional gifts to universities didn't guarantee enough ideological control. Instead, writes Jane Mayer in *Dark Money: The Hidden History of the Billionaires Behind the Rise of the Radical Right*, Pearson advocated funding private institutions located within prestigious universities. In that way the Kochs could influence hiring decisions and exert other forms of control 'while hiding the radicalism of their aims'. They did this by using 'ambiguous and misleading names' to 'obscure the true agenda' and 'conceal the means of control'. So the Kochs funded or created bodies with neutral-sounding names – like the Centre for the Study of the Philosophy of

Freedom or the Institute for Economic Inquiry – on dozens of campuses. They received six-, seven- and eight-figure donations.[129]

In addition to this strategy to seize control of the underlying political culture the Koch brothers also ventured out into conventional electoral politics. In 1980 the reclusive Charles, who runs the Koch business out of Wichita in Kansas, persuaded his more urbane brother David, who had settled in New York and become the public and political face of the pair, to stand as the vice-presidential candidate of the Libertarian Party. The brothers regarded Ronald Reagan, who was running for president that year, as too liberal. David Koch in his electoral campaign called for the abolition of all federal income taxes. He proposed closing the government agencies responsible for collecting taxes, protecting investors, regulating drugs and protecting the environment. He even wanted to scrap the FBI and CIA. The Libertarian Party also opposed public education and healthcare. 'At the time . . . such views were considered kooky even by most conservatives,' the New Yorker later observed.[130] The voters were unimpressed. Despite spending $2 million of his own money, David Koch got only 1 per cent of the vote. His brother Charles told a reporter that their venture into conventional politics had left him disillusioned. He resolved to return to his backroom strategy for advancing his libertarian agenda. 'Our movement must destroy the prevalent statist paradigm,' he declared.[131]

BARRACKING OBAMA

Still, they could not resist returning to the fray when America's first black president, Barack Obama, came on the scene. A year after he was elected, in 2009, his attempt to introduce universal healthcare galvanized the Kochs and their fellow arch-conservatives into action. After Obama's Affordable Care Act was passed in 2010, conservative legal groups mobilized to challenge the constitutionality of the law. In the forefront was the Cato Institute. Broader opposition to Obama came from the rise of the populist Tea Party, which purported to be a grassroots expression of discontent with the political establishment, but which, reporters discovered, was very much the creation of the Koch brothers at least in terms of its funding. Because Koch Industries was a private company, unlisted on the Stock Exchange, it had been for decades able to operate away from public scrutiny. David Koch joked it was 'the largest company that you've never heard of'. But with its moves against Obama, and with the growing prominence of the Tea Party, the brothers found it harder to deflect scrutiny. They found themselves in the firing line from the White House as President Obama took aim at the Kochs' political network. In a speech he warned the American public against big companies which hide behind groups with harmless-sounding titles. The Koch brothers were left in no doubt who he meant when he declared: 'The names always sound very benign – it's "Americans for Prosperity", "Committee for Truth in Politics", "Americans for Apple Pie" – I made that last one up. None of them will disclose who is paying for these ads. You don't know whether it's some big financial interest; you don't know if it's a big oil company . . .'[132] Obama's chief political strategist, David Axelrod, went further. In an op-ed in *The Washington Post* he singled out the Kochs as the billionaire oilmen who were secretly funding the Tea Party while pretending it was a grassroots movement for change.[133] They disliked the publicity, but the Kochs must have been pleased with the outcome of the mid-term elections. It was reported that as many as a third of the candidates backed by the Tea Party were victorious in the election.[134] When Republicans forced through historic spending cuts after retaking Congress in 2010, Tea Party insurgents got most of the credit.

Meanwhile, behind the scenes, the Koch brothers continued donating to support institutes and academics working to foster doubts about the global scientific consensus on climate change. Toward the end of 2010 they sent out invitations to the latest of their secret strategy meetings with other wealthy tycoons, designed to work out 'how we can retain the moral high ground and make the new case for liberty and smaller government that appeals to all Americans, rich and poor'. The invitations, one of which was leaked to the *New York Times*, spelled out the detailed agenda. It included countering what Charles Koch called 'climate change alarm', resisting Obama's 'move to socialized health care' and 'the regulatory assault on energy', and making donations to higher education to further the libertarian agenda. It boasted of the success of the tactics the group had approved at its previous meeting, six months earlier, to 'activate citizens against the threat of government overspending and to change the balance of power in Congress'. The success of the Republicans in the November 2010 mid-term elections showed how successful their plan had been.[135] A report by Greenpeace at the end of 2010 catalogued both the millions that Koch Industries had spent to elect 'polluter-friendly politicians' and the tens of millions more they had contributed to 'polluter lobbyists' in Washington DC. Between 2005 and 2008, the report claimed, Koch Industries had spent three times more than Exxon Mobil funding organizations of the 'climate denial machine' and its 'forceful stream of misinformation'.[136] Such publicity, combined with their elevated profile as a result of their attacks on Barack Obama, brought the Koch brothers uncomfortably into the public spotlight.

But the Kochs were one step ahead of their opponents. From 2008 they had stopped making publicly traceable contributions to climate-change-denial organizations, it was revealed, five years later, by an academic studying the anti-climate change movement. In 2013 Professor Robert Brulle, an environmental sociologist at Drexel University, published a study of the funding of climate change denial groups and academics.[137] It revealed that the Koch brothers, who had been heavily involved in funding climate change denial organizations in the first years of the decade, ceased to make major donations after 2008. By odd coincidence, however, clandestine funding for climate change sceptics increased dramatically at exactly the same time. This was done through secretive new bodies named donor-advised funds. These DAFs had been originally established as mechanisms to offer medium-sized donors the same tax advantages which major philanthropists gain when they set up their own foundations. But philanthropic foundations are subject to rules and regulations – and levels of government scrutiny – which do not apply to donor-advised funds. DAFs operated anonymously, like numbered Swiss bank accounts.[*] They had two key advantages to big givers like the Kochs who prefer to keep their activities out of the public eye. They created a veil between the donor and the recipient. And they also allowed the wealthy to obtain tax relief immediately, without being required to specify where and when their gifts would eventually be spent.

These opaque funds were seized upon by conservative philanthropists who wanted to hide their funding of controversial causes. Between 2003 and 2010 some $78 million was donated to climate sceptics, Brulle's researches revealed. It was moved, anonymously, through two of these funds, Donors Trust and Donors Capital. It was through the

---

[*] See pages 667–670 for a detailed discussion of donor-advised funds.

latter that Koch money was funnelled.[138] The majority of donations to the climate counter-movement were now 'dark money,' or concealed funding, said Brulle. 'Most funding for denial efforts is untraceable. Despite extensive data compilation and analyses, only a fraction of the hundreds of millions in contributions to climate change-denying organizations can be specifically accounted for from public records. Approximately 75 per cent of the income of these organizations comes from unidentifiable sources.'[139] The use of donor-advised funds in this way constitutes a new milestone in the modern history of philanthropy. It raises with greater urgency questions of whether philanthropists are answerable to anyone for their actions. As Robert Brulle writes:

> The real issue here is one of democracy. Without a free flow of accurate information, democratic politics and government accountability become impossible. Money amplifies certain voices above others. It gives them a megaphone in the public square. Powerful funders are supporting the campaign to deny scientific findings about global warming and raise public doubts about the roots and remedies of this massive global threat. At the very least . . . voters deserve to know who is behind these efforts.[140]

Climate change sceptics spend ten times more, he revealed, than do environmental groups and the renewable energy sector.[141]

THE KOCH KICKBACK

Back in the public eye the Koch philanthropic dollars were next directed towards opposition to Barack Obama. In 2012 they helped to raise an estimated $400 million to oppose the re-election of President Obama, who they considered to be a seriously misguided socialist. Charles Koch, in a newsletter to his employees, even compared Obama to the self-professed Marxist leader of Venezuela, Hugo Chavez.[142] The move transformed the brothers from libertarian outsiders to influential conservative powerbrokers, *The Economist* pronounced. But at a cost. The Kochs, who had for years operated beyond public scrutiny, also became public figures and the subjects of widespread vilification. When one of their grant recipients, Americans for Prosperity, spent millions on a television advertisement criticizing the president, the Obama campaign retaliated by purchasing airtime of its own to run an ad criticizing the 'secretive oil billionaires' attacking the president. Obama's campaign manager named them as 'the same Koch brothers whose business model is to make millions by jacking up prices at the pump'.[143] One US Congressman, Harry Reid, took to the Senate floor to call them 'un-American' and attack the Republican Party for being 'addicted to Koch' (the family name is pronounced 'coke').[144]

Just as alarmingly for the Kochs, their long-term strategy of stimulating a right-wing revolution in America's universities also came under public inspection. A row erupted at Florida State University when it was alleged that it had received a Koch grant which carried stipulations about the kind of teachers who could be hired and fired by the school's economics department. One undergraduate, Jerry Funt, complained that on the university's introductory economics course 'we learned that Keynes was bad, the free-market was better, that sweatshop labor wasn't so bad, and that the hands-off regulations in China were better than those in the US'. Their economics textbook, he said, argued that 'climate change wasn't caused by humans and isn't a big issue'. The Kochs responded that the students were merely being introduced to 'fresh' thinking.[145]

An even bigger controversy followed at the Catholic University of America when the new Charles Koch Foundation pledged $1 million to support the study of 'principled entrepreneurship' at the university's new business school. Instead of being greeted with the expected praise, the announcement was met with an objection by 50 Catholic scholars highlighting the 'stark contrast' between the donors' libertarian ideology and the traditional teachings of the Catholic Church.[146] The unregulated laissez-faire economic theories advocated by the Kochs are precisely those which have been condemned by every Pope since Leo XIII issued his seminal encyclical *Rerum Novarum* in 1891. Those criticisms have been reiterated even by conservative popes such as John Paul II and Benedict XVI. To the embarrassment of the Catholic University, just a week after the announcement of the Koch donation, Pope Francis issued his first written document, *Evangelii Gaudium*, which denounced those who 'deified' the market, attacked supply-side economics, and condemned the 'new tyranny' of unfettered capitalism. The 50 scholars wrote:

> The Koch brothers are billionaire industrialists who fund organizations that advance public policies that directly contradict Catholic teaching

on a range of moral issues from economic justice to environmental stewardship . . . Catholic social teaching articulates a positive role for government, an indispensable role for unions, just tax policies, and the need for prudent regulation of financial markets in service of the common good . . . while the Koch brothers lobby for sweeping deregulation of industries and markets. Pope Francis has criticized trickle-down economic theories, and insists on the need for stronger oversight of global financial markets to protect workers from what he calls 'the dictatorship of an economy which is faceless and lacking any truly humane goal'.

We are concerned that by accepting such a donation you send a confusing message to Catholic students and other faithful Catholics that the Koch brothers' anti-government Tea Party ideology has the blessing of a university sanctioned by Catholic bishops.[147]

The university brushed aside the objections, insisted the Kochs would have no veto over the appointment of academics, and pocketed the large donation. In a rare interview Charles Koch later said that he was not trying to close down academic debate but to widen it. Students should study Marx – he would even be open to funding Marxist research, he suggested (though, as the *Washington Post* drily observed, there is no evidence of him ever having done so). But he wanted greater diversity, he insisted. His philosophy was: 'Let a hundred flowers bloom. We love it. That's what we want.'[148] Many on the campuses did not believe him.

The elevated public profile of the Koch brothers brought protests in other areas too. In 2013 David Koch – who also had a $400 million track record of major donations to pioneering medical and scientific research at institutions like the world-leading Massachusetts Institute of Technology[149] – gave a $100 million donation to New York Presbyterian Hospital. That too generated demonstrations, this time by trade unions, objecting because the Kochs also funded groups opposed to the Affordable Care Act and the expansion of Medicaid. Such a stance, the protesters insisted, ran counter to the hospital's mission of making healthcare accessible for all. They paraded with banners which read 'Quality Care, Not Koch Care'.[150] The following year the brothers' $25 million donation to the United Negro College Fund, to finance scholarship for black students, was greeted with mixed responses. Some praised the gift, but others denounced it. One protester wrote: 'UNCF

Literally Sells Their "Souls To The Devil" Accepting Checks From The Koch Brothers'. Others spoke of 'tainted money'. The charity was unmoved. Its president, Michael Lomax, said that such public criticism was a small price to pay to help minority children realize their dreams of a college education.[151]

It was in higher education that the pressure was felt most. At the end of 2014 a campaign spread through American universities calling itself *UnKoch My Campus* as students and lecturers kicked back against the Koch strategy to 'crush campus commies with capitalism'.[152] The anti-Koch movement pointed out that many of the Koch-funded academics questioning climate change were economists who lacked scientific credentials.[153] It called for universities to make public any conditions the Kochs attached to their gifts. The critics insisted that the billionaires had too much influence in the appointment of academics and the content of the curriculum. Alarm was expressed at the revelation that, at Florida State University, the Koch donation had created an advisory board which gave the Kochs the ability to veto the hiring of academics. An economics professor, Tim Salmon, revealed that he had sat on the appointments committee for two positions underwritten by the Kochs. He said the committee forwarded the names of 40 potential candidates to senior university officials – who crossed off 25 of the names because, he was told, those candidates would not be acceptable to the Kochs. He also claimed that the Koch Foundation conducted its own interviews with the Florida State candidates.[154] Universities elsewhere in receipt of Koch philanthropy insisted that they would reject gifts which came with uncomfortable strings attached. However, their critics noted, no academic institution had so far turned down a Koch gift.

Then in 2018 the Senate of Montana State University, which two years earlier had accepted money from the Charles Koch Foundation, voted to overturn a decision to accept a $5.7 million Koch grant. The money was to establish a 'Center for Regulation and Applied Economic Analysis' to fund research critical of the idea that government should set industry standards. The University Senate was almost evenly divided on the issue but voted 13 to 12 not to accept the cash. Eric Austin, an associate professor of political science, who voted No, said he did not have any concerns about the quality of the research the Koch-funded academics were doing. But, he said, 'the Koch Foundation has

a well-documented history and philosophy and aim, going back almost
20 years, of seeking to produce research that supports their aims rather
than testing whether it holds in reality. They seek to influence peer
review and the tenure process (in ways) inconsistent with the values
of the university.'[155] There was mounting concern in academic circles
about this. At another university the director of the school of history,
philosophy and religious studies left his post 'sickened' by the events
which led to the establishment of a Koch-funded School of Civic and
Economic Thought and Leadership. Professor Matthew J. Garcia quit
Arizona State University saying that the Charles Koch Foundation
had circumvented rules preventing interference in the appointment of
professors to existing departments in universities and colleges across the
country. They did this 'by financing the creation of new schools and
departments that contain only professors that share their conservative
views. These are troubling trends.'[156]

Professor Garcia was not alone. The row over the Catholic University
of America resurfaced in 2019 – when it emerged the Kochs had upped
their donation from $1 million to $10 million. Again there was alarm
that donors such as Charles Koch were exercising undue influence over
academic recruitment. 'Koch money has been used to start academic
institutes on campus, such as the Institute for Human Ecology (IHE),'
wrote the leading Catholic commentator Michael Sean Winters in the
international Catholic journal, *The Tablet*. 'The institutes hire people
outside the normal channels, and pay the salaries, at least initially.
However, these professors are assigned to a department and eventually
become regular employees. The list of fellows at the IHE is a "Who's
Who" of right-wing academics.'[157] The Koch brothers insist this is
simply about adding intellectual variety to a higher-education system
currently indoctrinating young people with a liberal worldview. But
their critics fear that what the Koch brothers want is not balance but a
new order in which their own arch-conservative perspective dominates.
Higher education is just the first cog in their political machine, says
Kalin Jordan, a co-founder of *UnKoch My Campus*.[158] Courses designed
by Arizona University's Koch-funded Centre for the Philosophy of
Freedom are now filtering down to state schools.[159] The response of
Charles Koch to all this criticism was to redouble his efforts. In 2014
alone he directed $27 million in grants to 300 universities to back
libertarian ideas stressing the virtues of markets and the downsides of

governments.[160] Higher education had been hit by public-spending cuts and university administrators were eager, or at least content, to take the proffered grants.

PHILANTHROPISTS FOR TRUMP

But success behind the scenes could not distract the Koch brothers from their concerns about the vituperation and vilification now greeting much of their public philanthropy. Koch Industries brought in a public relations guru, Steve Lombardo, to limit the damage to the Koch corporate brand. He launched a multi-million-dollar advertising campaign 'featuring smiling minority employees and cinematic sequences of Americana'.[161] Inside the company, however, all was far from smiles. At the start of 2015 a group of senior political operatives arrived at the Koch factory in Kansas for a meeting. They were in the pay of the Freedom Partners, an umbrella group of 200 wealthy conservative businessmen who work to support the Republican Party. The Koch brothers had been big supporters of Freedom Partners. The politicos had arrived with a plan to spend big in the run-up to the 2016 US presidential elections to make sure that Donald Trump did not secure the Republican nomination. They and the Kochs – all champions of free trade for both ideological and pragmatic business reasons – did not like Trump's protectionist rhetoric. But they were in for a surprise.

When they arrived at the meeting it was full of corporate executives from Koch Industries as well as Koch's political advisers. Those from the corporate side of the Koch empire were alarmed at the damage being done to the company's corporate brand by the brothers' political activities. They argued that after all the effort in securing a Republican victory in the Senate in 2014, federal policy had changed very little in ways which would benefit Koch Industries. And now all the public reaction against the Kochs' work inside universities was threatening to undermine the company's reputation too. The activists from Freedom Partners looked to Charles Koch to overrule his corporate underlings. But he did not. After spending millions intervening in American elections for many years, it seemed that Charles and David Koch had lost their appetite for party politics. As part of the company's damage-repair strategy Charles Koch began to give more interviews. In one of them, when asked to choose between Donald Trump and Hillary Clinton, he replied that it was like being asked to choose between a heart attack and cancer. His preferred candidate for president had been Mike Pence.

Into the vacuum stepped a Koch associate whose libertarian views were regarded by many as even more extreme.[162] Robert Mercer, a hedge fund manager, was one of the top funders of America's new conservative policy infrastructure.[163] Mercer, a supporter of the National Rifle Association, was a cultural hardliner who financed the opposition to building an Islamic Center near Ground Zero.[164] A climate change denier, he had given more than $5 million to the Heartland Institute between 2008 and 2015, according to his tax returns.[165] Mercer's views were well to the right of even conservative Republicans. In 2011 he had invested $11 million in the news website Breitbart.com, which *Time* magazine said 'pushed racist, sexist, xenophobic and antisemitic material into the vein of the alternative right'.[166] Under its driving force, Steve Bannon, no publication did more 'to legitimize the kind of xenophobic and race-baiting viewpoints that Trump embraced to fuel his rise,' wrote David Callahan in the journal *Inside Philanthropy*.[167]

Soon after that Mercer invested $5 million in a British data-science company named SCL, which offered highly sophisticated micro-targeting efforts to locate voters in political campaigns. Mercer, who early in his career had worked at IBM, where he developed speech-recognition programmes, was fascinated. 'There's no data like more data' is a favourite saying of his. He made his quantitative hedge fund fortune by amassing huge amounts of data on human behaviour which enabled him to predict, for example, that markets moved in a certain direction when it rained in Paris. It allowed him to make extremely precise and lucrative financial bets.[168] So Mercer was intrigued at SCL's claim to be able to manipulate voter behaviour through something called psychographic modelling.

In 2013 SCL launched an offshoot it called Cambridge Analytica, a name which became notorious after it was discovered that it had purloined the personal data of up to 87 million Facebook users to exploit in its operations. In 2014 the company claimed it was involved in 44 political contests in the United States and the following year undertook data analysis for Ted Cruz's Republican presidential campaign. In 2016 Mercer, and his daughter Rebekah who managed much of his political philanthropy, poured over $13 million into supporting Ted Cruz for president.[169] When Cruz failed to obtain the Republican nomination, the Mercers were persuaded by Steve Bannon, who was now on the board of Cambridge Analytica, to back Donald Trump. The Mercers rushed in where the Koch brothers had feared to tread. In 2016 Cambridge Analytica – which was already working for Leave. EU, one of the organizations campaigning in the referendum that saw a narrow majority of Britons vote to leave the European Union – began working for Trump's presidential campaign. (Criminal investigations into its activities were later begun in both countries.) The Mercers became one of Trump's biggest financial supporters. Among other things, the Mercer family became major patrons of the Government Accountability Institute, which launched an unrelenting attack on Hillary Clinton in the run-up to the 2016 US presidential election.[170] So substantial was their contribution that Rebekah Mercer secured a spot on the executive committee of the Trump transition team.[171] Steve Bannon was subsequently appointed as chief strategist in the Trump administration. Rebekah Mercer also secured a place on the Trump team for the pollster Kellyanne Conway, who had previously worked for the Mercers.[172]

Despite the Kochs' opposition to Trump on free trade and immigration, when Trump was elected, with Pence as his vice-president, the brothers were not too unhappy. A smiling David Koch was seen at Trump's election victory party at the Hilton hotel in midtown Manhattan. Various lobbyists and political operatives working for Koch Industries were in Trump's transition team. They drew up the first blueprint for the Trump administration's repeal of regulations on clean air and climate put in place by Barack Obama.[173] The man put in charge of neutering the Environmental Protection Agency (EPA) was a prominent climate change denier. Myron Ebell had worked at the Competitive Enterprise Institute, a think tank bankrolled by the Kochs.[174] The tentacles of the Kochtopus were already encircling the Trump administration even before it had officially taken power. When Trump finally took office in January 2017 he appointed as head of the EPA Scott Pruitt, a militantly anti-regulatory attorney general from Oklahoma, who had previously been heavily supported by the Kochs. In turn Pruitt placed Patrick Traylor, a lawyer for Koch Industries and other fossil-fuel companies, in charge of the EPA's enforcement of key anti-pollution laws. Mike Pompeo, later appointed by Donald Trump as Secretary of State, was the biggest single recipient of Koch campaign funds in Congress. No fewer than sixteen high-ranking officials in the Trump White House had ties to the Kochs.[175]

If the Kochs' image had earlier been tarnished, their profitability had not. Koch Industries, which in 2005 had been worth $9 billion, had increased in value tenfold: by 2015 their 'dirty business of oil refining and petrochemical production' was worth $85 billion.[176] By 2019 it was estimated to be worth $110 billion.[177] Although David Koch died from prostate cancer that year, his brother Charles, generally reckoned to be the driving force behind the Koch philanthropy, remained at the helm. The brothers' political empire, with its foundations and academics, operatives and lobbyists, appears to be as formidable as ever.

The Kochs are undoubtedly the most prominent example of right-wing philanthropy at work. But there are scores of others, most particularly in America, who embrace causes which many find controversial and even distasteful. Art Pope has used the fortune he has amassed from his North Carolina discount-store chain to push for a tightening of the law to prevent fraud in elections, even though such fraud, is negligible in the United States, maintains David Callahan in *The Givers*, a study of philanthropy and power in modern America.[178] Pope's move, which would require voters to show ID at the polls, effectively disenfranchises the 10 per cent of the electorate who lack photo ID because they are too poor to own a car and are unlikely to go to the expense of getting a driving licence simply to vote. Such voters – many of them black – were unlikely to vote for the arch-conservatives that Art Pope smiles upon.

A few philanthropists espouse causes which others regard as downright dangerous. Hedge fund manager and philanthropist Bernard Selz and his wife, Lisa, have long donated to causes regarded as orthodox in the world of philanthropy – the arts, culture, education and the environment. Slightly more eccentric were their donations to the promotion of homoeopathy. But over the past eight years their private foundation has also donated more than $3 million to fund groups that question the safety and effectiveness of vaccines. The director of one of these groups, the Informed Consent Action Network, which promotes the idea that government officials have colluded with the pharmaceutical industry to cover up side effects, declared: 'They should be allowed to have the measles if they want the measles.'[179] He insisted that measles was 'a trivial childhood illness', despite the fact that one in every thousand children infected with measles dies from complications.

The idea that a philanthropist like Bernard Selz can obtain tax relief on donations to a cause which directly contradicts advice promoted by the public health officials representing those same taxpayers is clearly problematic.

A DECADE OF DELIVERY — OR DISASTER

Warren Buffett says he does not regard donations of this kind as philanthropy.[180] It is possible to make a distinction between 'benevolent' and 'malevolent' philanthropy, argues Jamie Drummond, who founded DATA with Bono and Bill Gates, and who then ran the ONE campaign, an advocacy organization with nine million members who lobby politicians for action to combat global poverty. 'The world has agreed some norms like the Universal Declaration of Human Rights, the Paris Agreement on climate change, or the UN Sustainable Development Goals – which have been agreed by every nation on earth,' Drummond says. 'So it seems reasonable to say that philanthropy which broadly pushes in this direction is good and that philanthropy which pushes in the opposite direction is on the dark side.'[181] Drummond has a particular vision for how political philanthropy can be most effective. It derives from merging the approaches of George Soros and Bill Gates, both of whom have funded DATA and ONE:

> George has a heavily political vision in favour of open societies, influenced by the philosophy of Karl Popper, but which also derives from the experiences he has undergone in his own life. Bill's approach is entirely different. His view is: 'Let's scale smart technocratic solutions to specific problems without worrying too much about society as a whole or systems at large.' Both approaches have a lot of validity to them. But for me the sweet spot lies in finding a place where the Gatesian specificity fits with the Sorosian societal analysis. What you need to do is politicize the Gates worldview, and make the Soros worldview more specific and evidence-based. The work we do tries to fit into that overlap. Bono talks about 'factivism' – evidence-based activism for social change.[182]

Drummond has the ambitious aim of bringing together an alliance of major philanthropists to fund a global advocacy movement to achieve the UN's global goals for sustainable development and to combat global warming, which he sees as the great challenge of the twenty-first century. 'We need a mega-financing strategy to shift society firmly and determinedly towards building a future which works for people, which includes the poorest, while preserving the planet and is sustainable,' he says. He insists that people and planet face what he calls A Decade of Delivery or Disaster:

> All of the extraordinarily wealthy people who are somewhere between fairly alarmed and extremely alarmed about the state of the world need to come together to start working at a different level. They can provide the money to build a mega-coalition between groups working on climate, gender and equality (who are the most dynamic of the next generation of activists) and get them working more effectively together to build some alliances.
>
> We've got the agreements. We've got lots of policy consensus on what's important and the right thing to do. But we are not implementing them. We have trillions in tax havens while key innovations languish and lack scale as they can't find risk-taking investors. Adam Smith would see this as a moral market failure which can easily be fixed if society wills it. We have to build political support for implementing this shift. The role of philanthropy in doing that will be massively important.[183]

Philanthropy, Drummond argues, must turn its attention now to promoting not just changes in government policy but also to changing the lifestyles of ordinary people. 'We need individual behaviour change, but scaled to a societal level, and that's going to be really hard to do. Philanthropists have a massive role here. They need to take advocacy far more seriously than they do.' If the years from 2020 do not offer a decade of delivery, disaster will take the form of 'the medium-to-worst-case scenarios on greenhouse gas emissions, damaging biodiversity loss, a demographic boom, especially in Africa and the Middle East which will bring mass movements of people within Africa – and a migration to Europe which will far exceed the Syrian Exodus which so destabilized international politics'. Put all that together with the governance challenges of the online world, global organized crime and the rise of populism, Drummond says, 'and you can easily point the way to, not a decade of disaster, but decades of disaster, as all these overlapping trends reinforce each other'.[184]

Instead, with a few honourable exceptions, since the 2007–8 global financial crisis and the 2020 coronavirus pandemic, most philanthropists have pulled back from such involvement, preferring to fund individual projects.[185] Most philanthropists nowadays would rather dig a well or open a new clinic than fund advocacy. Drummond sees that as a false dichotomy:

> Well, I'm actually in favour of both. Humans want to give to specific other humans to deliver specific things that will make a difference in their lives. I think that's fine and good. But if it's all you do, then that's a very limited form of compassion. Suppose you really want people to have access to clean water, and somebody comes along and says, 'Look, would you support this legislation that will provide funding and policy to make sure that all the people in Malawi or Ethiopia get clean water – not just the people in the village where you paid for the well.' And suppose it costs the same amount of money to fund this advocacy campaign as it would to dig another well in another village. Then why not fund the advocacy campaign?[186]

Such is the rationale, Drummond argues, for political philanthropy.

Yet the arguments which can be used to justify what he calls 'good' philanthropy can also be applied to justify 'bad' philanthropy. The donations given to colleges and universities by the Kochs are the epitome of philanthropic gifts. That poses a philosophical difficulty for enthusiasts of philanthropy like David Nasaw, the biographer of Andrew Carnegie. 'I might applaud the work of the Rockefeller, Carnegie, and Gates foundations,' he wrote:

> But I might be considerably less enthusiastic about a torrent of private money unleashed on educational campaigns to outlaw abortion and birth control, de-fund the public schools, abolish inheritance and income taxes, end gun control, and withdraw funding from the United Nations and international organizations. You might disagree; either way neither of us should be sanguine about a future in which billionaires play a larger and larger role in determining social policy without any say from the rest of us.[187]

Such big philanthropy, says David Callahan, makes it harder for the voices of ordinary citizens to have due influence. 'When it comes to who gets heard in the public square, ordinary citizens can't begin to compete with an activist donor class,' Callahan writes – and yet these ordinary citizens, are paying, via their taxes, for a sizeable chunk of the philanthropists' gifts.[188] The fact that both liberals and conservatives exploit this tax advantage is, he adds, no real consolation.

Philanthropists like the Koch brothers throw into stark relief a series of questions which have surfaced in previous chapters. Who holds philanthropists accountable for the ways they spend their money? Should their gifts be subsidized by taxpayers? Are the tensions between philanthropy and democracy now increasing to the point where they must be addressed? In the next chapter we turn our attention to those issues.

Interview: Patrick Gaspard on political philanthropy

Patrick Gaspard is president of the Open Society Foundations (OSF), the world's largest private funder of independent groups working for justice, democratic governance and human rights. It was founded by the international financier George Soros. A former US ambassador to South Africa from 2013 to 2016, Gaspard has had a career at the intersection of government, political campaigns and social justice movements. The Open Society Foundations take their name from Karl Popper's 1945 book The Open Society and Its Enemies. *George Soros so far has donated a total of $32 billion to philanthropic causes.*

What is the basic brief which George Soros gave to his Open Society Foundations?

OSF concerns itself chiefly with the rights of the most marginalized communities in the world. We invest in helping those communities and citizens hold their governments to account – in a way that enables the most marginalized voices to be included in the political debate.

That has been, right from the outset, a very overtly political approach to philanthropy, which a lot of philanthropists shy away from. Did George Soros see the work as political from the outset?

I'm rather astounded whenever anyone engaged in the business of philanthropy seems to dance around the big key question, the political question. Any institution that is taking up the fundamental question of the use of power and the allocation of resources in society is inherently engaged in a political effort.

The philanthropy of George Soros was influenced from the outset by the philosophy of Karl Popper, under whom he studied at the London School of Economics. Popper had the simple, basic notion that repressive regimes could be overturned through the flow of transparent information that could hold them to account. That was the bricks and mortar of George's early philanthropy. Then, not too long into his journey, he came upon Aryeh Neier,* who is a legend in the human rights community and who became the first president of OSF in 1993. Aryeh and George together shaped this new political philanthropy that continued to have the emphasis on the dissemination of information but also began to take on the promotion of institutions fighting for individual rights and the public good in defence of those rights. That's the early evolution of the philanthropy.

The next development came with the global recession of 2007–8 when George and OSF began to take on questions of economic inclusion. Having the right to vote means very little to individuals who have no economic power. So we embarked on a third iteration of OSF which addresses economic dislocation, and also issues like climate change. OSF has become very concerned about the pressure on public resources that can be exploited politically by tyrants of every stripe.

At the end of 2019 George Soros published his book *In Defence of Open Society*. In it he acknowledges that, after decades of movement towards more open societies, there has been a setback. We have seen the rise of nationalist and populist demagoguery all across the world. It's the era of 'fake news' rather than improved information flows. The book talks of how 'the tide has turned'.

Something has happened, which appears to have shifted that in reverse. We're not entirely sure what this moment means now. There's still the distinct possibility that what we're experiencing could lead to a rejuvenation of democratic practice. But we are certainly experiencing a distortion – or even a perversion – of democratic practice right now. So OSF's philanthropy is making every attempt, in our very modest way, to take on this question of improving the flow of information within democracy at a time when the global economic downturn, and the illiberal moment that has followed it, has forced all of us into our own hall of mirrors. Social media allows us to constantly find absolute validation for our own views. There is less and less pressure to engage with communities that hold different values, ideologies and philosophies to your own.

---

* Aryeh Neier (b. 22 April 1937) is an American human-rights activist who co-founded Human Rights Watch and was National Director of the American Civil Liberties Union from 1970 to 1978. He was president of George Soros's Open Society Foundations from 1993 to 2012.

There's less real dialogue.

Yes. It's an era of less real dialogue and vanity dialogue. And this era of great migration in the world has created a sense of fragility within some communities. That fragility, along with the economic dislocation, and with the tools of misinformation, have all spiralled together to create what seems to be the greatest existential threat to democratic inclusion, democratic practice, and the public good in quite some time.

Some of that threat has got very personal. George Soros has become the bogeyman of the paranoid Right. The attacks on him have got very anti-Semitic. He's had a bomb sent to his home.

Absolutely. And we're seeing those attacks repeated in so many countries of the world, most especially in the United States.

When George first launched into his work it was in the latter stages of the Cold War and his philanthropy enjoyed bipartisan support in the US. Republican leaders in Congress embraced George's leadership and spoke openly about the need for there to be a community of philanthropists who were investing in the opening of spaces that had been previously closed off behind the Iron Curtain.

George enjoyed a partnership with political figures who were not entirely completely aligned with every aspect of his vision but who did embrace his notion of openness, transparency and government accountability. It was widely accepted that there was a common thread that united us all along the lines of the Universal Declaration of Human Rights and a civic republicanism.

So what changed?

There is the fact that George Soros at one point – acting as an individual, and quite separate and distinct from his philanthropic institutions – made a decision that he was going to invest significant personal resources in opposing the re-election of George W. Bush as president because he saw him as a great threat to open society practice in the US. At that point some of the moderate mainstream Republicans who had allied with Soros, in his work opening up the former Soviet states, turned against him and then eventually turned against his philanthropy.

So it was his shift from political philosophy to party politics that was problematic?

That may have been a factor. But it also got injected with a significant dose of anti-Semitism. That is under-examined in the attacks against George Soros. We have seen moments in the past – during economic cataclysm and times of migratory pressure – where the Jewish community has been depicted as the threatening Other. Individual Jewish leaders have been depicted as being multi-tentacled controllers of aspects of governance and the economy. This is a very, very old trope. George Soros, as a consequence of his success as a financier, is an easy target for such tropes which are greatly magnified thanks to the political distortion that comes with the social media platforms.

Is anti-Semitism the cause or is anti-Semitism just the weapon that they use against him?

Given the number of other philanthropists and foundations that are also involved in the question of human rights, and who do not receive this level of vitriol, my inclination is to believe that anti-Semitism is a cause and not just a weapon.

George would be quick to say that he's at a place where he's comfortable and actually proud of the enemies that he seems to have made – because one can trace from Erdoğan to Salvini to Orbán to Donald Trump* a set of actors who, through corrupt means, have lifted up an illiberal politics that is toxic. It flies in the face of the Universal Declaration of Human Rights, the work on sustainability by the United Nations, and the accepted norms of democratic practice in our societies. But we'll keep on with this work, and George will continue to be proud of the organizations that we support in these challenging places.

You talked at the beginning of this conversation about 'fighting for the public good'. But how do you define 'the public good'? Can't the arguments you use to justify George Soros's brand of political philanthropy also be used by right-wing lobbyists, like Charles Koch, to justify what they do? Or is there a difference in how you define the public good?

---

* See pages 557–8 above.

Given that we are the Open Society Foundations, I would be quick to defend the rights of the Koch brothers and those on the Right if they are making investments that are governed by the law. Having a political philosophy that's different from our own does not make what they are doing invalid. We believe in a robust federalism, and that's why we invest in all the places that we do.

There are so many varying definitions of the public good. But if you look at the work of the Open Society Foundations in Ethiopia, in North Macedonia, in Baltimore, I think you'd find that it's informed by the classical definitions of the public good: the sense that one has an obligation to work to reconcile and balance the rights of the individual with the needs of the many, the needs of the community. Our notion of the public good also has as its springboard, some of the ways that it's been interpreted through the American classical period. James Madison*, for instance, suggested that the public good needs to embody a notion of individual and collective justice – which is very different than thinking of the public good merely in terms of broadly shared prosperity.

As hugely influential philanthropists like Charles Koch on the libertarian right might?

It's not just about prosperity. It's not just about access to material resources, but access to something more elusive, more ephemeral, that Madison defined as justice – which we interpret today as collective and individual rights being extended fully to the most marginalized communities who lack voice, agency and resource.

Give me an example . . .

Well, the greatest industrial force in the world today is the cyber industry. That raises a new question about what constitutes public space and what constitutes the public good. We have to take up the question of individual privacy rights there in a much more nuanced, much more sophisticated, fashion to expand our notion of the public good. Because the diminishing ratio of individual privacy is contributing, I believe, to the diminishment of the collective public space, and ultimately, the public good as well.

------

* James Madison was a founding father of the United States and the fourth president of America from 1809 to 1817.

More widely, the way Madison linked the question of the public good to the question of justice is reflected in the 40 advisory boards that OSF holds itself accountable to. We have advisory boards on our work on economic inclusion, in West Africa, in Central Europe, in Latin America – and they all take up the question of this inchoate thing that we call justice. They interpret it for their local setting in a way that informs our central notions of justice, rights and public collective good.

What's the opposite of the public good? Is there such a thing as socially damaging philanthropy?

I'm sure there is. But I'm not going to wag my finger. But I will say that I'm proud to work for an organization that is not in the business of making charitable contributions in spaces without proper reflection on systemic impact and influence. When I look across the 35 years of investments that have been made by George Soros and the Open Society Foundations, it is rare to find an instance where there isn't always a commensurate consideration of systemic change. Philanthropy, particularly in emerging economies, can make investments that can influence democratic debate, and we've always attempted to influence that debate as it relates to structural change.

What about the Koch brothers' funding for climate change scepticism? Would you describe that as philanthropy? How would you categorize that in comparison with what you're doing?

I think that there are individual donors and institutions that provide resources to support ideas through a philanthropic lens that I personally, vehemently, disagree with. It stands in opposition to the very notion of the collective public good that we should be defending in our democracies. That does not mean that they are not engaged in philanthropy. I might define it as a philanthropy that works to defend interest groups that already are steeped in a kind of corrupt exclusive power. It's a kind of philanthropy, but it is not a philanthropy that is intended to increase inclusion and to protect those who are most fragile.

You mentioned your advisory groups in Africa and other emerging economies. In situations like that, can philanthropy be in tension with the requirements of democracy? Suppose a philanthropist comes in and says: 'Here's this great idea we've got. We're going

to put money into this. We want your government to put money in as well.' There the philanthropist is using his money to influence the political priorities of the local society.

It's always difficult to speak of the work of others. But for ourselves, we pride ourselves in a philanthropy that takes local knowledge as its point of orientation. From the beginnings of OSF George Soros has embraced Karl Popper's idea that we should all recognize our own fallibility. That forces us into a humility which does not just require us to lean on the opinions of our local advisory boards but also to grant to them a level of autonomy that is rare and perhaps even unprecedented in philanthropy.

If you went right now to an advisory board meeting of our foundation in Skopje, you would find a group of a dozen individuals around a table with a budget that was decided and allocated by me and our global board, thousands of miles away. But the decisions about how to use that resource belong entirely to that autonomous advisory body. The same is true if you go to a meeting of our advisory board in Dakar in Senegal.

That actually flies in the face of the caricature of George Soros and OSF of having this kind of puppet-master control. I think that those who know little about us would be astounded at the level of local control from boards made up of civil society leaders who are steeped in activism, steeped in academia, or who sometimes are former figures from government who are making a new contribution.

Yes, there are instances where a local foundation inside of OSF will leverage our resource to say: 'Here is this fantastic idea that has come up from the Dalit community in New Delhi to turn around the delivery of goods and services in a way that would protect their rights.' And they may say: 'We're prepared to invest in it – and if local or federal government will meet us halfway, we think that we are much more likely to have success.' But that is not about the imposition of notions from on high; instead it is investing in ideas from the grassroots. It's not a philanthropy that parachutes in, with 'best practices' that are not indigenous, and which runs the risk of hubris and an arrogance that will work against success over time.

What accountability mechanisms have you put in place to ensure that does not happen?

First of all, in all the places where we are engaged in grant-making there are, of course, local laws that we must adhere to. So there's, first and foremost, accountability to the rule of law in every single place that we work. Second, we are accountable to our local and thematic advisory boards. I don't sit here, in my office in New York, and cook up strategy that we then farm out to Addis, to Cleveland or wherever. Instead, we work modestly to curate discussions with our advisory boards and with our staff to try to determine what are the most effective interventions for OSF, with our resources, in ways that will advance open society democratic values, in spaces where we are invited to work by civil society.

In addition to all that, we believe, essentially, in transparency. We think that kind of transparency is another measure of the public accountability that's essential for philanthropy. That is in contrast to private and public companies which are largely unaccountable, except to their boards who focus less on the question of governance and more on profitability margins.

It sounds like you have come a long way from that early story* of George Soros saying in a meeting: 'It's my money. I'll decide.'

Frankly I've never experienced that George Soros, and I don't think there's anyone in the foundation – even some of my colleagues who have worked here since its inception 30 years ago – who have experienced that George Soros. Last year, I was with George in Cape Town in South Africa, the country where he started his philanthropy in the late 1970s at the height of apartheid. There were grantees there who had received a scholarship from George 25 years ago who had had no contact with George after their first initial request for resources. They came back and described the extraordinarily transformative things that they had done on equal access to housing, to antiretroviral medications, and pushing advocacy for the LGBTQ community in South Africa. George thanked them and said that he had always hoped and assumed based on their reputations, their biographies, and his instincts about them, that they would use the resources in ways that accrued to the benefit of minorities and an open society.

It was an extraordinary thing to see. George's lack of ego there was absolutely incredible, so I hear the anecdote of George saying 'it's my money and I get to decide' but it's actually never been his approach. He really and truly has been a subscriber to Popper's notion of fallibility. George fears the authoritarian in all of us, so he's been radical in ceding

---

* See pages 612–3.

control. I know based on conversations that I've had with leaders in the Roma community in Bulgaria, for instance, that from the moment George signed cheques over to organizations, to local foundations, he never then made any attempt to dictate in any way how those resources were to be applied – other than to say that this was for the open dissemination of information to push back against dictatorship and create platforms of local agency and voice.

What are the big challenges of the twenty-first century – is it climate change or nationalism and populism – and what role can philanthropy specifically play in dealing with them?

I believe very strongly that philanthropy will not determine outcome in democratic societies. But it can make some meaningful contribution to forming debate and including the voices of the most marginalized – to give them a fighting chance of being heard. Perhaps the greatest challenge that open societies now face is the challenge of information democracy and the distortions that we're experiencing now in the hall of mirrors created by social media platforms.

The ways big data is being used, along with the emergence of artificial intelligence in governance, are encroaching on democratic decision-making everywhere from the United States to China with the emerging cryptocurrency and with the way in which the Uighurs are being managed and governed. Right now at the border of India and Pakistan, in Kashmir, we're seeing the ability of a government to control the flow of information through cyberspace – and having a powerful negative influence on the right to mobilize and the right to a collective conversation that can lead to collective action. I think that the information democracy question is existential and powerful.

The question of climate change, and the impact and pressure it's going to have on public resources, is inescapable – and terribly important for philanthropists to consider. It's a space that the Open Society Foundations is moving into as we consider what equable transitions look like as climate impact becomes more and more evident.

We are also taking up the question of how to keep alive the issue of economic inclusion and justice in a world that is growing increasingly illiberal. The fundamental defence of democratic values can no longer be taken for granted. So we have to rally with other like-minded actors in philanthropy to address that.

Chapter 16

Is Philanthropy Bad for Democracy?

Some rich individuals can be deeply eccentric in their generosity. The New York hotel magnate Leona Helmsley, known in her lifetime as the 'Queen of Excess', left $12 million to her dog – and excluded two of her grandsons from her will. The lapdog, a fluffy white Maltese, was aptly named Trouble. A judge later reduced the inheritance to a mere $2 million on the grounds that 'the greater amount exceeded that necessary to care for the dog'.[1] David and Cheryl Duffield were slightly more expansive after their beloved miniature schnauzer Maddie died of cancer. They pledged $200 million to find a home for every stray cat or dog in the United States.[2] Such idiosyncrasy is not confined to America; in Britain the Devon Donkey Sanctuary received £23.3 million in legacy income in 2017, more than the Royal British Legion and Save the Children.[3] Then there was Ruth Lilly, 87, an heir to the Eli Lilly pharmaceutical fortune, who submitted several poems to *Poetry* magazine in the 1970s and was rewarded only with handwritten rejection notes from the editor. They were clearly very nice notes since in her will she left the little magazine – a tiny but prestigious publication with a staff of four and circulation of 12,000 – an astonishing bequest worth more than $200 million. It transformed the struggling journal, which was little known outside literary circles, into one of the world's richest publications. That immediately earned it a bill for 15 years back-rent from the Chicago library which had rented it offices, but the bequest ensured the magazine's survival in perpetuity.[4]

It is easy to dismiss such cases as quirks. But, in their oddity, they highlight something integral to all philanthropy. The late Paul Allen, who co-founded Microsoft with Bill Gates, said of philanthropy that 'it always comes back to what you are passionate about'. Through philanthropy, he said, 'you are transmitting your hopes, and keeping them going in the future'.[5] Those hopes are deeply personal, as the legacies to the Maltese lapdog, the Devon donkeys and the tiny poetry magazine show. But they reveal more than personal passion. They show that philanthropy, whatever else it may be, is always an expression of power. So much of it depends on the personal whims of super-rich individuals. Sometimes these coincide with the priorities of society, but at other times they contradict or undermine them. Increasingly, questions have begun to be raised about the impact these mega-donations are having upon the priorities of contemporary society.

There is a popular assumption that philanthropy involves a transfer of funds from the rich to the poor. The facts show otherwise, as previous chapters have shown. Barely a fifth of philanthropy from the richest Americans goes to the poor. A lot goes to the arts, sports teams and other cultural pursuits.[6] But half goes to education and healthcare. At first glance that seems to fit the popular profile of 'giving to good causes'. But dig down a little. The biggest donations in education go to the elite universities and schools from which philanthropists themselves personally benefited, according to a 2019 investigation into philanthropy and tax avoidance by the *Financial Times*. Michael Bloomberg, as we have seen, gave his *alma mater*, Johns Hopkins University, a total of $1.8 billion. The banker Sandy Weill donated $250 million to Cornell University for a medical school. The billionaire hedge fund manager, Ken Griffin, gave $150 million to create scholarships in his name at Harvard. Thanks to such endowments this most famous of American universities is now worth $39 billion – more money than most US states spend on their schools.[7] As the *Financial Times* data analyst, John Burn-Murdoch, puts it: 'The top 20 Ivy League colleges . . . the most elite higher education institutions in the US . . . account for only one per cent of college places in the US, but [receive] 28 per cent of these philanthropic donations.' The wealthy, when they do give, largely direct their money to sectors from which they benefit themselves. 'Philanthropic giving is good. But if that money is being given to the pet causes of the wealthy – and that money . . . would otherwise have gone into government coffers through taxes, and been distributed more evenly – then, for me, that's something we've got to look at,' the *FT* journalist says.[8] It is the same in Britain. In the UK in the ten-year period to 2017 more than two-thirds of all millionaire donations

– £4.79 billion – went to higher education, according to the *Coutts Million Pound Donors Report*. Almost half the philanthropic donations to Britain's 110 universities go to just two of them – Oxford and Cambridge.[9] When the rich and the middle classes give to schools, they give more to those attended by their own children than to those of the poor.[10] Millionaires' spending on the arts in the UK was £1.04 billion. Just £222 million went to the needy.[11] The *Financial Times* investigation, by Burn-Murdoch and the *FT*'s statistical analyst, Federica Cocco, provides evidence to counter the common assumption that philanthropy automatically results in a redistribution of money or power. A lot of elite philanthropy is about elite causes. Rather than making the world a better place, it largely reinforces the world as it is. Philanthropy very often favours the rich – and no one holds them to account for it.

PHILANTHROPY AND POWER

These new critiques echo the attacks made on 'robber baron' philanthropists such as Andrew Carnegie and John D. Rockefeller at the turn of the previous century. But in the intervening period little was heard from that critical perspective until comparatively recently. Academics like Robert Arnove, looking back on the robber barons' legacy in 1982, revived the notion in academic circles. 'Foundations like Carnegie and Rockefeller and Ford have a corrosive influence on a democratic society; they represent relatively unregulated and unaccountable concentrations of power and wealth which. . . establish an agenda of what merits society's attention,' he wrote in *Philanthropy and Cultural Imperialism*. Such foundations benefit the interests of the 'ruling class' and act to delay and prevent 'more radical structural change'.[12] (Carnegie, ironically enough, might have agreed; unless philanthropists spent on social welfare, he once wrote, the alternative would be socialism.[13]) Left-leaning scholars began to study philanthropy as an exercise in power, applying the critique of the Marxist thinker Antonio Gramsci and suggesting that charity by the mega-rich was one of the forms of 'soft' social control which elites use to maintain their social and economic dominance. Philanthropy was one of the tools which they used to project the ideological world view of the rich and turn it into the common sense of wider society.[14]

But it was a philanthropy professional, Teresa Odendahl, formerly of the National Network of Grantmakers, who first gave this critical perspective a wider currency. In her 1990 book *Charity Begins at Home* she interviewed 150 wealthy philanthropists and was the first to demonstrate that the rich primarily support upper-class charitable interests and neglect basic human services. Elite American philanthropy therefore serves the interests of the rich more than it does those of the poor disadvantaged or disabled. 'Philanthropy is essential to the maintenance and perpetuation of the upper class in the United States,' she concluded.[15] Philanthropy is part of the nexus of a modern power elite. Leftist critics began to portray elite philanthropy as a symptom of the new dominance of neo-liberal ideologies and economics.

Perhaps the most recent example of this is Anand Giridharadas, a New York-based journalist whose *Winners Take All: The Elite Charade of Changing the World* (2019) is a one-sided polemic which spells out all that is wrong with contemporary philanthropy without acknowledging any of its benefits. He derides the repeated tendency of philanthropists to assume that they are always the answer and sees them as part of the problem. Society's winners are all too ready to tell the rest of us what we are doing wrong – and think they know better than everyone else how to address and solve public problems. Giridharadas scorns the philanthrocapitalist habit of using business language, like speaking of proposed solutions as a win-win: 'That phrase sounds great. Who could be against win-win? But, in fact, win-win is a darkly powerful way of suggesting that the only kind of progress worth having is the kind that lets the winners win – in tandem, supposedly, with empowering others.'[16]

But giving by the mega-rich, he complains, is merely a mask for entrenching existing privilege. It is a nonsense to look for solutions from the very system which created the problems in the first place. Instead of challenging the rich to do more good, society should be insisting they do less harm. Philanthropists should be asked to give away, not more money, but more power, Giridharadas writes. But philanthropists will never cede control; the boards of trustees of their foundations are drawn from members of the same elite. Their shallow desire to do good never asks questions about matters such as taxation, redistribution, labour laws and mining regulations.[17] Thanks to Giridharadas and others, the fashionable mode for talking about philanthropy in some circles is now suspicion, hostility and even outrage.

More significantly, perhaps, the tendency to view philanthropy as an expression of power has spread beyond those who are ideologically opposed to capitalism. David Callahan, for example, is an enthusiast for philanthropy. He is the founder and editor of *Inside Philanthropy*, a US website which covers the world of giving by wealthy individuals and foundations. Yet even he admits that 'an ever larger and richer upper class is amplifying its influence through large-scale giving in an era when it already has too much clout'. And he predicts: 'Things are going to get worse, too'. Callahan wants a reform of philanthropy, 'so that it's more aligned with American values – and especially the egalitarian ethos so core to our national identity'.[18] One of the most thoughtful contemporary defenders of philanthropy, Professor Rob Reich, director of the Center on Philanthropy and Civil Society at Stanford University, concedes that 'philanthropy is a form ... of power', since he defines it as 'the deployment of vast private assets towards a public purpose, frequently with the goal of changing public policy'.[19] Moreover, he adds, it is a form of power that is largely unaccountable, untransparent, donor-directed, protected in perpetuity and lavishly tax advantaged. Philanthropy therefore deserves critical scrutiny rather than automatic gratitude.

Increasingly, that power is global in its reach. Globalization has transformed philanthropy. That change is both structural and one of sheer scale. The United States is the most philanthropic nation in the world. There, for the past half-century, the share of disposable income which goes in charitable giving has remained steady at about 2 per cent.[20] In the UK the proportion is only half that, less than one per cent of GDP, with rich Brits giving less than a quarter of their investable assets to charity.[21] But, where 40 years ago just 4 per cent of donations went through foundations, that figure rose to 11 per cent by 2010. The balance of charitable giving has altered. It has become less individual and more institutional. It has also grown exponentially. For every foundation that existed in 1930 there are now five hundred. The assets they hold have soared from less than $1 billion in 1930 to more than $800 billion in 2014. Almost all these foundations are controlled by rich philanthropists and their peers – and are almost entirely unaccountable to anyone else.

Some operate in almost total secrecy, as the magazine *Bloomberg Businessweek* discovered in 2014 when it launched an in-depth investigation into the philanthropy of three highly secretive hedge fund managers. Despite running what was effectively the fourth-largest charity in the US, the three men were almost totally unknown even within philanthropy circles.[22] The three financiers had given around

$13 billion via private foundations to human rights and environmental causes and to medical research into disorders like Huntingdon's disease. But they did it using a complicated web of financial tools to shield themselves from public view. The magazine figured out their identities, and the extent of their donations, by combing through the database of the tax authorities and uncovering the men's private foundations. They held more than giant funds like that of the Rockefeller Foundation.

The three men – David Gelbaum, Andrew Shechtel, and C. Frederick Taylor – had in 1989 co-founded a successful and low-profile quantitative hedge fund, TGS Management, which uses computer algorithms to invest. TGS 'left virtually no public footprints' – until the *Bloomberg* investigation.[23] Their philanthropy was hidden, using a network of trusts, companies and lawyers, in a dozen private foundations, two of them the Gabriel Trust and Endurance Funding Trust. By piecing together the jigsaw, *Bloomberg* discovered that some $1.8 billion had been handed out in grants, including more than $700 million to find a cure for Huntington's disease, a cause favoured by Andrew Shechtel. Another $1 billion had gone to opaque donor-advised funds. Billions of dollars were yet to be dispersed, the investigation suggested. All three men declined to talk to the magazine, which speculated that the donors' elaborate matrix of secrecy may not have been entirely altruistic: 'They're also avoiding public scrutiny of how they made their fortunes, and how they've chosen to give them away.'[24] But the amounts of money involved, *Bloomberg Businessweek* suggested, were large enough to influence the spending priorities of the state and did so with neither transparency nor accountability. It was further proof that the scale of modern philanthropy, as the philosopher Peter Singer warned, can leave 'the fate of hundreds of millions of people hanging on the decisions of two or three private citizens'.[25] The implication was that philanthropists should not have complete discretion over their giving when it has such consequences for other people and for society in general.

SHOULD THE TAXPAYER SUBSIDIZE PHILANTHROPY?

Most Western governments offer generous tax incentives to encourage charitable giving. Governments, in effect, declare that they are happy to forego the tax due on part of the income of a rich person if they give the sum to an approved charity. In Britain, for example, in 2019 an individual earning up to £50,000 a year paid 20 per cent of it in income tax. On earnings over that, individuals paid 40 per cent. Those who earned more than £150,000 paid 45 per cent.[26] But gifts to registered charities are not taxed. So a gift of £100 would cost the average taxpayer only £80, with £20 being paid by the government. The same gift would cost the higher rate taxpayer only £60, with £40 coming from the state. The highest rate taxpayer would need to pay out only £55 because the state would provide the other £45. Super-rich philanthropists, therefore, find themselves in a position where a large percentage of their gift is matched by the taxpayer. With such a subsidy from the state it becomes far less clear whether the money philanthropists give away can rightfully be regarded as entirely their own. If taxpayers contribute part of the gift, why should they not have a say in which charity receives it?

All these subsidies to philanthropists cost the state huge sums in lost taxes. In Britain the total cost to the state of the various tax breaks to donors in 2012 was estimated by the Treasury at £3.64 billion.[27] The United States Treasury lost $51.6 billion in 2014 – an amount more than three times the annual budget for temporary assistance to needy families.

The sums lost by governments are growing year by year.[28] There is an added complication. That picture is not static. The rich do not just get more in the way of tax breaks than everyone else; the amount they get is increasing year on year. In the US in 2000 the wealthy got only 30 per cent of all tax relief on charitable donations; by 2017 they got 52 per cent.[29] That means questions about philanthropy and tax allowances are likely to become more pressing.

Yet the idea that a philanthropist's money is his own to do with as he pleases is deep-rooted. Some philosophers argue precisely that each individual has full ownership rights over his resources – and that a philanthropist's only responsibility is to use his resources wisely.[30] Certainly that is how most philanthropists see it. Mark Dowie in his book *American Foundations* gives a good example of that. Not long after the billionaire philanthropist George Soros set up his Open Society Institute (OSI) – in defence of democracy across the globe – a protracted argument took place within the institute's inner circle over the allocation of funds. Dowie records:

> Finally, an impatient Soros exerted his authority by saying, 'This is my money. We will do it my way.'

'No, it isn't,' objected a junior member of the staff. A hush fell over the room, and he finished the sentence in a quiet voice: 'Half of it is ours.'

'What are you talking about?' asked Soros.

'If you hadn't placed that money in OSI or another of your 25 or so foundations, sir, about half of it would be in the Treasury,' explained the tremulous youth. 'It would be ours.' Soros ignored the interruption and proceeded with the meeting.[31]

The junior staff member did not last long in Soros's employ, Dowie suggests, but Soros registered his message. The OSI later morphed into a network of Soros organizations now known as the Open Society Foundations (OSF) in which practices are very different (see the interview with Patrick Gaspard, President of OSF, on page 604 above).

So what is the rationale for tax relief? Tax exemptions for charities have existed in the UK since income tax was introduced in 1799, though charities had been largely exempt from certain taxes since the Elizabethan age. Tax incentives for charitable giving have existed in the US federal income tax system since 1917, with individuals, corporations and the states allowed to give away as much as half their annual income to qualified non-profit organizations without paying any tax. In both countries, and elsewhere, the idea is that tax relief will encourage the rich to give to causes of which the state approves. Gifts were exempt from taxation in the US so long as they were for 'religious, charitable, scientific, or educational' purposes, as were donations to societies for the prevention of cruelty to children or animals.[32] The categories and forms of tax relief were altered and expanded over the years, but the system is still in force. Other countries followed suit, with Sweden becoming the last country in Western Europe to introduce such a mechanism in 2012.[33] Today the US and the UK retain generous tax exemptions.[34] Both countries offer additional incentives where donations are made to endow a foundation; that enables a philanthropist to escape liability for tax on the donation yet also retain control over how the money is spent, within the constraints of charity law.

The effect of this is to give the wealthy control in matters that would otherwise be determined by the state.[35] The problem is that giving by the super-rich is not closely aligned with the spending choices of democratically elected governments. This is because the wealthy have demonstrably different values from the rest of the population, according to *The Economist*.[36] They are socially more liberal but economically more conservative. A major research study in 2013 reveals that the richest one per cent of Americans are considerably more right wing than the public as a whole on issues of taxation, economic regulation and especially welfare programmes for the poor. The richest 0.1 per cent – individuals worth more than $40 million – hold even more conservative views. They want to cut social security and healthcare programmes. They oppose a minimum wage. They favour decreased government regulation of big corporations, pharmaceutical companies, Wall Street and the City of London. All that may well explain the gap between the rich and the rest of us when it comes to making donations to those in need; the rich give only a fifth of their philanthropy to the poor, whereas for the general public the proportion is almost double that. Rich people do have different values to the rest of society.

'There is good reason to be concerned about the impact on democracy if these individuals are exerting influence through their philanthropy,' writes Benjamin Page, the lead academic on the 2013 study.[37] The disproportionate influence of the mega-wealthy may explain, it concludes, why certain public policies appear to deviate from what the majority of citizens want the government to do. The choices made by philanthropists tend to reinforce social inequalities rather than reduce them. In which case, should the state be giving tax relief to philanthropists at all?

All this may explain the suspicion – or even hostility – which characterizes the attitudes of sections of the British public towards philanthropy. That is particularly true on the left of the political spectrum. Newspapers such as the *Guardian* can be 'negative, even snide', one of its own writers admits.[38] The paper's coverage of big givers is full of unspoken inferences and unarticulated questions about how the donors obtained their money – and in particular whether they gained it by exploiting their workers. The often unspoken assumption is that philanthropists are only giving to look good, or to somehow 'redeem themselves'.[39] That mistrust provokes impatience among some academic experts on philanthropy. Dr Beth Breeze, Director of the Centre for Philanthropy at the University of Kent, complained to the *Guardian* that such attitudes formed 'a barrier to giving': 'It's strange: we approve of charity, but disapprove [when] the money comes from rich individual donors.'[40] The business guru Charles Handy is even more direct: 'We should not sneer . . . society is the richer. They provide a social justification for the free enterprise system that it has often lacked.'[41] Society, he says, should be cheering philanthropists rather than sniping at them.

Yet this does not address the charge that the money donated by philanthropists might be put to better use if it were collected as taxes and spent according to the priorities of a democratically elected government. Beth Breeze's answer is that there is no joy in paying tax but philanthropy does provide real satisfaction to people with surplus money and benevolent visons of what to do with it. In any case, she asks, 'what kind of tax level would we need for there to be no room for extras? Even if the hospital's perfectly equipped, who'll pay to send the clowns into the children's ward?'[42] Her research suggests that rich donors value tax relief, not because it offers some hidden benefits to them, but because it increases the value of the gifts to the causes they choose to support.[43] The philanthropist John Caudwell, who amassed a £1.5 billion fortune through his mobile phone business, Phones4U, makes a similar point when he says:

> I feel I've made a big contribution. I've paid a lot of tax . . . I've created something like 20,000 jobs. I certainly don't feel guilty. Still, you know, something felt like it was missing. Business gives you a massive high. Doing a great deal, coming up with an inspirational solution . . . It's very addictive. But it doesn't last long. In isolation, it's a bit sterile. It doesn't reward the soul.[44]

Caudwell, who claims he has paid more than £300 million in taxes over the past 10 years,[45] is now steadily giving his fortune away, much of it to disabled children through his foundation, Caudwell Children. But he insists that it would not be so good for society if what he does voluntarily was done by the state through taxation. 'Taxes aren't the way to go,' he says. 'They strangle the economy; you wouldn't create the wealth. And nothing squanders money as well as a government. What we need is to encourage rich people to give.'[46]

Yet such exhortations do not get round the fact that tax relief imposes an additional responsibility upon the philanthropist – because he is not merely spending his own money, he is also spending that of the taxpayer.

THE CASE FOR TAX REFORM

Some have suggested that the solution lies in abolishing tax relief. This is not a new notion. In 1863 William Gladstone, then Chancellor of the Exchequer, told the House of Commons that the working man should not have to pay higher taxes in order to enable the rich to get tax relief on gifts which had already brought them 'credit and notoriety'.[47] But Gladstone's attempt to end tax relief failed after Britain's charities launched a campaign to protect their privileges, which resulted in *The Times* thundering at Gladstone for his 'perverse boldness'.[48]

Today there is renewed support for doing away with tax relief, from both left and right, in both the UK and the US. Wealthy donors do not need tax exemptions, argued a prominent right-wing libertarian, Daniel Mitchell, of the Cato Institute – the think tank funded by the conservative philanthropist Charles Koch. With the country's finances in a mess, the state simply cannot afford to be so generous about rewarding charitable giving, Mitchell wrote in the *Wall Street Journal*.[49] In any case, he argued, tax breaks lead people to make bad choices about giving. Scrapping tax relief would do a lot less harm than raising taxes because philanthropists would carry on giving anyway, since 'many of them would still get nice perks for doing good – like seats at the opera or buildings named after them'. (There is no consensus on this. According to a 2010 Indiana University survey, more than two-thirds of high-net-worth donors said they would decrease their giving if they did not receive tax relief. But research by Beth Breeze in the UK suggests that rich donors are not motivated by tax advantage.[50] Warren Buffett agrees; he has said that tax concerns are largely irrelevant to his giving, and that the same is true of many of his super-rich peers.[51]) The best way to help charities, continues Mitchell, is not through tax exemptions but by boosting economic growth, which would provide everyone with more money to donate.

At the opposite end of the political spectrum, Professor Fran Quigley, a human rights lawyer at Indiana University, has argued that charitable tax deductions should be stopped because they transfer decision-making from democratically elected bodies to rich individuals. 'The tax deduction for a donation to an institution that serves the wealthy is money that could have been spent on proven government-assistance programs [for the poor] like food stamps, unemployment compensation, and housing assistance,' says Quigley. 'Getting rid of the charitable tax deduction would mean billions of dollars in increased revenue each year,' he writes. Quigley's arguments are not just financial; they are also moral. Scrapping tax relief would 'also help dispel the illusion that discretionary charity . . . constitutes an effective and adequate response to hunger, homelessness, and illness'. Philanthropy is a 'moral safety valve' which prevents the rich from facing up to the fact that benevolence is no substitute for taxation.[52]

Yet attempts by politicians even to limit the amount of tax relief – let alone abolish it entirely – have met with public disapproval. The British government tried to address the issue in 2006. Its Charities Act introduced a requirement that, to be eligible for tax relief, a charity had to be able to demonstrate that it offered 'a public benefit' rather than merely falling into a general charitable category established back in the days of Elizabeth I. But more robust attempts at reform in both the UK and US – when Chancellor George Osborne and President Barack Obama both attempted to limit the amount of tax relief that the rich could claim on their giving – failed. In 2012 the proposal was made on both sides of the Atlantic to cap tax relief so that rich taxpayers got only the same percentage as standard ratepayers. But both politicians ran into opposition from philanthropists, the press and a mass outcry from charities.[53]

An alternative solution to the dilemma raised by some academics is that restrictions should be imposed upon the kind of cause for which tax exemptions can be claimed. 'Donations to college football teams, opera companies and rare-bird sanctuaries are eligible for the same tax deduction as a donation to a homeless shelter,' complains Quigley, who wants the government to make distinctions between different kinds of charity.[54] Rob Reich of Stanford University agrees. He points out that California's wealthiest school district raises more private donations per child than the state's poorest districts spend in total on their pupils.[55] Tax breaks would have greater credibility, he argues, if they were designed to incentivize only the more 'useful' sorts of charity, especially those focused on reducing poverty.[56] Reich, who also insists that it is 'indefensible' for higher-rate taxpayers to get far more tax relief than do ordinary taxpayers, wants donations to soup kitchens to get greater tax subsidies than gifts to wealthy private schools. All this resonates particularly strongly in America where the idea of increasing taxes on the super-rich is gaining popularity among voters of all parties, as we will see below.* In Britain too the Labour Party under Jeremy Corbyn talked of removing charitable status from fee-paying schools.[57]

The problem comes in finding a mechanism which would better align charitable giving with generally agreed conceptions of the common good. Tax relief in Britain is still largely confined to the categories of charity set out in Queen Elizabeth's 1601 Charitable Uses Act. It lists four categories of charity: relief of poverty; advancement of education; promotion of religion; and 'other purposes beneficial to the community'. There are even fewer limitations on bodies wishing to become tax-exempt charities in the US, beyond a requirement not to engage in party politics. That is why a donkey sanctuary receives the same tax relief as a shelter for victims of domestic abuse. It might be argued that governments could establish a hierarchy of priorities for charitable tax deductions in the UK. One criterion might be to favour charities which finance activities whose cost might otherwise fall on the state. So parents might feel that donations to a private school and a publicly funded one should be treated equally, but if the state school relies on public finances, where the independent school does not, then society might see a greater incentive in granting tax subsidies to the school for which it has financial responsibility.

But other nuances might be harder to pin down. Addressing human hunger might be considered more socially valuable than feeding donkeys. But how does the state distinguish between an organization that feeds the hungry, a university where students study the problem of hunger, and a think tank devoted to downplaying hunger as a social problem? There are other thorny questions: Who should decide what is a good charity? And on what grounds? (see the interview with Rowan Williams on page 197). What about charities with high administration costs? Or bodies like donor-assisted funds which are so operationally opaque that it is impossible to make a reliable assessment of their public benefit? Considering the whole issue, *The Economist* expressed the fear that any alternative might weigh charities down with government bureaucracy, discourage the entrepreneurial instincts of donors, and quash the vitality which characterizes the best philanthropy. Perhaps the status quo, it was forced to conclude, was 'the least bad option'.[58] But that leaves unanswered

---

* See page 636.

the basic question posed by Gladstone: Why should the rest of us face a bigger tax bill simply because a rich individual chooses to give to charity?

THE DANGERS OF PLUTOCRACY

There are other tensions inherent in the relationship between philanthropy and democracy. For all the huge benefits modern philanthropy can bring, as we have seen in examining the giving of Bill Gates, the sheer scale of contemporary giving can skew spending in areas such as education and healthcare to the extent that it can overwhelm the priorities of democratically elected governments and local authorities. Then there are the huge spends on lobbying from individuals like the Koch brothers on the right, or George Soros on the left, which can succeed in altering public policy. David Callahan estimates that more than $10 billion a year is devoted to such ideological persuasion in the US alone.[59]

Democracy, rule by the people, is in tension with plutocracy, rule by the rich. The word plutocracy is also borrowed from the ancient Greek but it is a distinctly contemporary phenomenon. The giant Wall Street financial corporation, Citigroup, has even coined a twenty-first-century variation combining plutocracy and the economy into 'plutonomy' – an economic system where the rich get richer by persuading the government to manipulate the economy to their advantage – and ignoring the growing inequalities this creates. In two confidential reports written for the exclusive use of their richest clients, global strategists at Citigroup described the American, British and Canadian economies as plutonomies in which the fortunes of the very rich had grown exponentially. This, explained the first report, *Plutonomy: Buying Luxury, Explaining Global Imbalance* (2005), had been brought about by new technology and a class of rich and educated financial innovators encouraged by capitalist-friendly governments.[60] Under the heading *Riding the Gravy Train*, the report predicted that this trend was set to continue – in contrast to 'egalitarian Japan and continental Europe'.[61] Some commentators had spoken of these growing inequalities as 'scary global imbalances', but Citigroup told its investors that in reality these inequalities were 'quite unthreatening'.[62] 'The rich are getting richer; they dominate spending'. This trend 'looks unlikely to end anytime soon'.[63] By contrast the 'non-rich' account for 'surprisingly small bites of the national pie'.[64]

The following year the Citigroup researchers were congratulating themselves on their prescience. Their second report, *Revisiting Plutonomy: The Rich Getting Richer* (2006), revealed that 'asset booms, a rising profit share and favourable treatment by market-friendly governments have allowed the rich to prosper and [corner] a greater share of the economy in the plutonomy countries'.[65] The top one per cent of the US population had 'benefited disproportionately' from globalization at the relative expense of the ordinary working people. The top earners were 'likely to get even wealthier in the coming years'.[66] This was the wealth from which the new super-philanthropists were giving.

Some philanthropists began to grow uneasy at all this. The late German billionaire shipping magnate and philanthropist, Peter Kramer, in a 2010 interview with *Der Spiegel*, criticized philanthropists including Gates and Buffett.[67] 'These guys have so much power through their wealth that they, instead of the government elected by the people, can decide what's good and what should be promoted and subsidized. That can be dangerous.'[68] Donors are taking the place of the state. 'That's unacceptable,' he said. The result was 'a bad transfer of power' from the state to billionaires. 'So it's not the state that determines what is good for the people, but rather the rich who decide. That's a development that I find really bad. What legitimacy do these people have to decide where massive sums of money will flow?' Billionaire philanthropists were 'indulging in hobbies that might be in the common good, but are very personal'. Gates and Buffett would have been better giving the money 'to small communities', as Kramer did. The German philanthropist took his lead from the wishes of those in receipt of the grants he gave out to build schools in Africa. At one point he told a newspaper in Rwanda, where he had built and financed the running of 100 schools, that he would love to invest more into Rwanda's education sector but only when 'given a green light from the government'.[69] Such an approach is in distinct contrast to that of Bill Gates, who funds major health initiatives but often wants his contribution matched by the government of the host country. This can mean it has to divert resources from the priorities of the local community.

Some critics go further, accusing philanthropy of being not just non-democratic, but anti-democratic. In one sense there is nothing new in this. As long ago as 1796 George Washington used his farewell speech as US President to warn that civic groups which operated in parallel to the democratic process, however plausible their original purpose, would eventually attempt to put their will above the will of the nation:

> They are likely, in the course of time . . . to become potent engines, by which cunning, ambitious, and unprincipled men will be enabled to subvert the power of the people and to usurp for themselves the reins of government, destroying afterwards the very engines which have lifted them to unjust dominion.[70]

In our own time a similar warning was given, less dramatically but more analytically, by the United Nations General Assembly in 2015 when it told governments and international organizations they 'should take into account the diversity of the philanthropic sector and assess the growing influence of major philanthropic foundations, and especially the Bill & Melinda Gates Foundation, on political discourse and agenda-setting'. Governments, before taking money from philanthropists, 'should analyse the intended and unintended risks and side effects of their activities'. They should be particularly concerned about the fragmentation of global governance, the weakening of representative democracy and institutions such as parliaments. They should also worry about 'the unpredictable and insufficient financing of public goods, the lack of monitoring and accountability mechanisms, and the prevailing practice of applying business logic to the provision of public goods'.[71] Small civic groups involved with huge philanthropists should carefully evaluate the impact and side effects of these initiatives and 'potentially reconsider their engagement'.[72] George Washington could not have predicted the enormity of the scale on which the power of philanthropy has developed since his day, nor the implications of its recent adoption of the business matrixes of modern philanthrocapitalism. But his warning was more prophetic than he could have imagined.

Certainly the democratic process seems to be undermined by activities such as the Koch brothers' funding of lobbyists to deny climate change, or Art Pope's campaign to tighten voter identification in a way which excludes black people from elections. But do such philanthropic activities manipulate the democratic process any more than do George Soros's campaigns to promote liberal values? Or Tom Steyer's funding a movement to encourage more young people to vote on climate change? Or Craig Newmark's attacks on fake news?

All these are funded by rich individuals motivated to intervene by something arising from their own lived experience. By what yardstick can we suggest that some are more legitimate than others? David Callahan puts it this way:

> When donors hold views we detest, we tend to see them as unfairly tilting policy debates with their money. Yet when we like their causes, we often view them as heroically stepping forward to level the playing field against powerful special interests or backward public majorities . . . These sort of *à la carte* reactions don't make a lot of sense. Really, the question should be whether we think it's OK overall for any philanthropists to have so much power to advance their own vision of a better society?[73]

Arguments against philanthropy can all too easily become muddled with arguments against the specific policies of certain philanthropists. Critics often take aim against the former when in reality they only oppose the latter.

Rob Reich, a political scientist whose background is in philosophy, published a study in 2018 on the ethics of modern charity, *Just Giving: Why Philanthropy is Failing Democracy and How it Can Do Better*. It examines giving in the light of the two great principles of Western political philosophy: freedom and equality. Reich concludes that philanthropy fits well with contemporary ideas of liberty, not least in the way it enhances the freedom of donors. But this is outweighed, in his view, by the way it undermines equality – because rich donors give mainly to causes which enhance the interest of their own socio-economic class and because the higher up the income ladder they go, the less likely donors are to direct their giving to the poor.[74] By undermining equality, philanthropy undermines justice and fails democracy.

PHILANTHROPY AND INEQUALITY

Inequality is fast becoming the great new political problem of our time. The rising gap between the rich and everyone else has fuelled unrest and instability across the world, producing the election of Donald Trump in America, the Brexit crisis in the UK, the rise of populist nationalism across Europe, and extensive migration from the world's poorer countries.[75]

Thomas Piketty's bestselling 2014 blockbuster, *Capital in the Twenty-First Century*, brought the subject of economic inequality to the top of the international social science agenda. The increase in inequality and the increase in philanthropy are almost certainly linked. Let us consider why.

In Britain the gap between the very rich and the rest is wider than in any other large country in Europe. Society is the most unequal it has been since shortly after the First World War.[76] There are many ways to measure inequality, but perhaps the most telling is to look at annual income. This is because, says Professor Danny Dorling of Oxford University, 'it is income that gives us respect and the freedom to do everything from buying a bus ticket to securing a mortgage'.[77] The richest one per cent in Britain have seen their income almost triple in the last four decades.[78]

'We live in times of peak inequality,' writes Dorling, who in 2010 published a major study entitled *Injustice: Why Inequality Persists*. 'It pervades almost every aspect of our lives in Britain in ways that we now accept as normal. Like goldfish in a bowl of dirty water we have adapted to think that our tank is normal. But it isn't.'[79] A British child is twice as likely to die before the age of five as one in Sweden, where the gap between rich and poor is far lower. 'Since 2015 we have seen a statistically significant rise in infant mortality across Britain: no other state in Europe has experienced that.' Ever greater numbers of people have recourse to food banks – 1.3 million parcels were given out in the year to April 2018. Yet as recently as the 1990s there were no food banks anywhere in the UK, just as there were no soup kitchens. Those had not been seen since the 1930s – the last time inequality reached current levels.

From the 1930s inequality was steadily reducing. Its low point in Britain was in 1978. The rich still took a greater share of national income than everyone else that year. But the bottom 90 per cent of the population were paid 72 per cent of the nation's take-home pay. By 2007 that had fallen to 57 per cent – the lowest since 1929 during the Great Depression. The causes of the change were global. Financial institutions were deregulated in the UK and US in the 1980s. The financial sector expanded hugely. The globalization of the world economy accelerated. Low-paid jobs migrated abroad. Trade unions lost influence and membership, which reduced their bargaining power, lowering wages in real terms. The income of the wealthy increased.[80] Globally, the richest one per cent have never held a greater share of world wealth than they do today. By contrast the share of the other 99 per cent has fallen steadily in the last five years, with more and more people in debt, especially the young. 'Income inequality has now reached a new maximum and, for the first time in a century, even those just below the richest one per cent are beginning to suffer, to see their disposable income drop,' Dorling wrote in 2014.[81] (The richest one per cent are those who live in households with a pre-tax income of more than £160,000 a year.) In 2018 he published his volume *Peak Inequality*, suggesting that living with these constantly increasing divisions would lead to disaster.[82] Its subtitle was *Britain's Ticking Time Bomb*. Inequality, he believes, has the potential to undermine democracy.

Inequality in America, home to the world's biggest philanthropists, is even worse. Income inequality there has doubled in a generation. 'Today, the United States has less equality of opportunity than almost any other advanced industrial country,' wrote the Nobel Prize-winning economist Joseph Stiglitz, who in 2012 published *The Price of Inequality*. The typical chief executive in a top US company, who would have earned 20 times more than his average worker in 1965, today earns 312 times more. By contrast the wages of ordinary workers have barely increased.[83] It is the same in Britain where, 20 years ago, the average top chief executive earned 47 times as much as the average worker; today they earn 145 times as much. But earnings for low-paid workers have barely risen at all in two decades.[84] The number of staff represented by unions has halved in both the UK and US.[85] Some 40 million people in the US – one-third of them children – live in poverty. One person in eight depends on food stamps. Five million Americans live in the kind of abject deprivation normally associated with developing countries.[86] Inequality is worse now than in the time of 'robber barons' like Carnegie or Rockefeller.[87] At the same time the super-rich have a bigger share of household wealth than at any time since the start of the Great Depression in 1929.[88] The richest eight men on the planet in 2017 owned as much as the bottom half of the human race.[89]

Before examining the relationship between philanthropy and inequality it is worth considering what constitutes 'excessive inequality'. (Richard Branson speaks of 'extreme wealth' and incentives in his interview on pages 448–450.) Some inequality of income and wealth is inevitable. It may even be necessary. If an economy is to function well, people need incentives to work hard and innovate. The problem for society and governments is to find a balance which increases social justice without excessively blunting incentives.[90] Philanthropy can have a role to play in this.

WHY IS PHILANTHROPY NOT NARROWING THE GAP BETWEEN RICH AND POOR?

The links between the rise in philanthropy and the rise in inequality were demonstrated a decade ago by the economist Kevin Laskowski of the National Committee for Responsive Philanthropy. He showed that the huge increase in giving between the 1970s and 2000s correlates with an increase in inequality. Correlation is not causation, of course. But it was enough for Laskowski to write: 'Philanthropy's golden age did not emerge fully-formed from the wallets of a new breed of strategic grantmakers. The forces that drove increasing inequality similarly powered philanthropy's rapid rise.' Rising inequality increases surplus wealth – and the chance that some of that surplus will be given in charity.[91] The philanthropist Peter Buffett, son of Warren, makes the same linkage. 'There are plenty of statistics that tell us that inequality is continually rising,' he wrote in the *New York Times*. At the same time philanthropy has grown at a far greater rate than have the business and government sectors. 'It's a massive business, with approximately $316 billion given away in 2012 in the United States alone and more than 9.4 million employed.'[92]

Many philanthropists do not like to talk about inequality for fear that it turns the spotlight back on them. Even those who address it prefer to speak of poverty rather than inequality, noted the *Financial Times*, adding wryly: 'Big philanthropists are never part of the problem. They are always the solution.'[93] But a growing number of rich givers, noted Buffett Jr, were keen to talk about the need to 'level the playing field'. That fits with classic views of altruism, suggests Rob Reich, who says in *Just Giving*, 'for many people and in many historical traditions, philanthropy has something to do with providing for the poor and disadvantaged'. What follows from that, Reich says, is that 'if we ask ourselves what kind of philanthropy a liberal democratic society might wish to produce, a focus on equality could lead us to believe that public policies should structure philanthropy so that it assists the poor and disadvantaged'.[94]

Interestingly, a scholar from the opposite end of the political spectrum agrees. In *Why Philanthropy Matters: How the Wealthy Give, and What it Will Mean for our Economic Well-Being*, Zoltan J. Acs argues that philanthropy by its very nature reduces inequality and promotes social mobility. Professor Acs, who teaches at George Mason University, which has been funded by the Koch brothers to the tune of $50 million,[95] succinctly summarizes his thesis thus:

> America has faced this question of what to do with wealth and debated it for 300 years. America wanted rich people but it did not want a class structure. In other words, America wanted to become rich but America did not want wealth to remain in the same hands. So America invented philanthropy.
>
> Philanthropy has long been a distinctive feature of American culture, but its crucial role in the economic well-being of the nation – and the world – has remained largely unexplored. *Why Philanthropy Matters* takes an in-depth look at philanthropy as an underappreciated force in capitalism, measures its critical influence on the free-market system, and demonstrates how American philanthropy could serve as a model for the productive reinvestment of wealth in other countries. Factoring in philanthropic cycles that help balance the economy offers a richer picture of capitalism, and a more accurate backdrop for considering policies that would promote the capitalist system for the good of all.
>
> Philanthropists strengthen American-style capitalism in two ways. The first is that philanthropy, when targeted to universities, research and other productive uses, lays the ground work for new cycles of innovation and enterprise. The second way philanthropy strengthens capitalism is that philanthropy – like creative destruction – provides a mechanism for dismantling the accumulated wealth tied to the past and reinvesting it to strengthen the entrepreneurial potential of the future. . . Philanthropy is a partial answer to the question of what to do with wealth, which must be recycled to create social stability and opportunity for all.[96]

Professor Acs asserts that the mega-wealthy are uniquely positioned to create social change by using their resources and networks to change public policy – and then provide the money to deliver those policy changes. 'What is required to sustain American-style capitalism into the 21st century?' he asks, and then answers his own question: 'A global philanthropic revolution! Through philanthropy, the unequal distribution of wealth can be channelled into creating opportunity for future generations.'

What unites both left and right here is the theoretical insistence that philanthropy needs to focus more on helping the poor – even if they disagree about the best way to do that.

A far bigger problem is that the great growth in philanthropy in recent decades has not made much impact in reducing economic inequality. 'We should expect inequality to decrease somewhat as philanthropy increases . . . It has not,' writes Laskowski. Indeed, as Albert Ruesga, president and CEO of the Greater New Orleans Foundation, has noted, 'the collective actions of 90,000+ foundations . . . after decades of work . . . have failed to alter the most basic conditions of the poor in the United States'. Laskowski calls on philanthropists to direct more of their giving directly to charities which address inequality and specialize in advocacy for disadvantaged groups. But sadly many supposedly philanthropic foundations, he laments, are often primarily investment companies for whom charity is merely a way of handling the excess cash flow of the mega-rich.

More cynical critics, such as Anand Giridharadas, suggest philanthropy's failure to address inequality is wilful. He quotes a line from *The Leopard*, a nineteenth-century Italian novel in which one of the aristocratic characters declares: 'If we want things to stay as they are, things will have to change.' Philanthropy, Giridharadas asserts, is one of the myriad ways adopted by elites to 'change things on the surface so that in practice nothing changes at all'.[97] These elites make only 'small-scale changes', which do not threaten their own socio-economic status or challenge 'any of the larger dynamics of power and sexism and prejudice'. Their philanthropy is, rather, about making 'winners feel good'.

That is unfair. A few philanthropists have begun to talk about the need to address inequality. Peter Buffett reports that inequality is now the fashionable topic of conversation among liberal philanthropists in New York. The Ford Foundation has moved inequality to the centre of its philanthropy. Nearly two-thirds of foundation leaders named inequality as the most pressing issue of coming decades, in a 2016 survey conducted by the Center for Effective Philanthropy.[98] Yet many appear to be paying lip service rather than devising effective strategies to address the gap between the super-rich and the rest of society.

David Callahan has offered a series of insights as to why the philanthropic sector in the United States has had so little success in combating persistent inequality.[99] In part the problem is that it is just too big a job; philanthropy, for all the huge sums trumpeted in the media, accounts for just 5 per cent of US GDP in a nation of 320 million people with a $19 trillion economy. And many of the large structural forces, like technological change and globalization, which have boosted philanthropy have also helped to drive inequality. But, Callahan points out, 'the forces of plutocracy and of conservatism have been better than progressives' at understanding all that. Philanthropists concerned about poverty tend to focus on alleviating its symptoms rather than addressing its causes. Very little philanthropic funding, Callahan reveals, has ever gone to strengthen regulatory oversight of the financial industry.[100]

By contrast, liberals have never understood the importance of cultivating ideas to influence 'key public policy debates, especially around economics, regulation and entitlements' in the way conservatives have. Nor do they invest in media, legal and academic networks of key opinion-formers to the same degree as right-wing donors. Instead, mainstream and liberal funders tend to focus on community-based efforts to build wealth, create jobs and housing, and improve human services. But all that good work can be wiped out by public spending cuts, predatory lending or exploitative low levels of pay. They are, Callahan says, 'nurturing saplings while the forest is being clear-cut'.[101]

A key element in inequality is poorly paid jobs at the bottom of the labour market. Philanthropists who attempt to address this invest in education and training to equip workers for better jobs. 'Upskilling workers can allow some people to exit bad jobs,' Callahan says, 'but millions of other workers will remain stuck in a labor market that inflicts mass hardship and makes a mockery of the core American value that if you work hard, you'll get ahead.' Yet mainstream philanthropists have been reluctant to finance policy solutions to address why so many jobs are, in Callahan's words, 'crappy'. They should, he says, be lobbying to raise the minimum wage, intervene in public policy or help with union organizing. They could fund think tanks to press for changes in corporate culture to favour greater sharing of the fruits of prosperity. But these kinds of interventions are at present favoured only by conservative philanthropists.

Only a few top philanthropic foundations such as Ford, Kellogg and George Soros' Open Society give grants to groups working in such areas. Most see them as too political. Many of the new givers coming out of business may be disinclined to back groups that challenge how American capitalism operates. What they ought to be doing, Callahan says, is lobbying to change tax and fiscal policies currently tilted in favour of the wealthy. Right-wing philanthropists are happy to lobby in the opposite direction without any compunction about being 'too political'.

PHILANTHROPY AND JUSTICE

Does philanthropy undermine justice? That is the other weighty accusation made by Rob Reich in *Just Giving*. It is not a new question, as we saw in Chapter 9 featuring Andrew Carnegie and the great industrial philanthropists of the early twentieth century. For all their munificence they were accused of avoiding 'the whole question of economic justice'. Then, as now, a huge percentage of wealth was in the hands of a tiny few. Carnegie and his fellows, their critics said, neglected 'the ethical question of today', which was about 'the distribution rather than the redistribution of wealth'[102]. His greatest critic, William Jewett Tucker, as we noted, concluded there is 'no greater mistake . . . than that of trying to make charity do the work of justice'.* Carnegie built a network of libraries and other institutions to help the poor elevate their aspirations, but social justice was entirely absent from his agenda. More than that, he and the other 'robber baron' philanthropists faced questions on the source of the money with which they were so generous – for it had been accumulated through business methods of a new ruthlessness. Many of today's tech titans have also amassed their vast fortunes through a relentless pursuit of monopolies.

But does that devalue the gift itself? Can good philanthropy redeem bad business? In a previous era some thought so. When General William Booth, who founded the Salvation Army in 1865, was asked about the ethics of accepting charitable donations from questionable sources, he is supposed to have replied: 'The trouble with tainted money is t'aint enough of it.' Others took the view that a donation can be a form of

---

* See page 342 above.

atonement which brings redemption for the donor.[103] The ostracism of the Sackler family as leading international art philanthropists in 2019 and the boycotting of BP's cultural sponsorship* suggests that the contemporary answer to that question is increasingly no. Media coverage of those controversies repeatedly quotes Teddy Roosevelt's judgement on John D. Rockefeller that 'no amount of charity in spending such fortunes can compensate in any way for the misconduct in acquiring them'.[104] Hardliners such as Anand Giridharadas go further, asking: 'Should anyone working to help families affected by President Trump's immigration policies take money from Mark Zuckerberg, whose soft-pedalling of Russian interference in the 2016 election allowed anti-immigrant hate to spread and potentially helped Mr. Trump gain votes? Should any health institution take money tied to Pepsi or Coca-Cola?'[105]

Yet there are counter-arguments. The case of Stephen Schwarzman throws these dilemmas into sharp relief. The billionaire financier, one of America's richest businessmen, has donated hundreds of millions of dollars to libraries, universities and hospitals from the fortune he amassed as chairman and CEO of Blackstone Group, the world's largest private equity firm and biggest property landlord.[106] We saw in the last chapter that his $100 million donation to create scholarships for American students to study in China was seen by some as a vehicle to curry favour with the Chinese government. By contrast his massive donation to the University of Oxford – the biggest it had received since 1438 – seemed more genuinely disinterested.[107] We shall consider this in more detail below.†

But Schwarzman's philanthropy has only served to draw the attention of critics to his company's controversial business methods. Shortly before his large donation to Oxford was announced, the United Nations issued a report into the international housing market, which singled out Blackstone for 'wreaking havoc' among local communities and helping to fuel a global housing crisis. Schwarzman's company was accused of 'aggressive evictions', massively inflating rents, and imposing an array of heavy fees for ordinary repairs – all creating 'devastating consequences' for many tenants in countries around the world.[108]

---

* See pages 476–481 above.
† See pages 647–9 below.

Blackstone and other corporate landlords had bought, at heavily discounted prices, hundreds of thousands of ordinary family homes left empty after their owners defaulted on mortgage payments after the 2007–8 banking crisis. Blackstone responded that it was merely trying to help build the rental market in countries with a housing shortage after the financial crash. But Schwarzman's reputation was damaged by the accusation from such a high-level source as the United Nations that Blackstone was maximizing profits by pushing low- and middle-income tenants from their homes, constantly hiking rents by as much as 50 per cent, and ruthlessly evicting tenants.[109]

That was not all. Schwarzman's company was revealed to be avoiding large amounts of tax. A BBC investigations team, following up a huge batch of documents leaked from the offshore law firm Appleby, uncovered advice from accountancy firms to Blackstone. They outlined the use of trusts in the tax haven of Jersey, and a complex structure of companies in Luxembourg, to avoid £60 million in tax on big property deals in London and Glasgow. The tactics were perfectly legal but were publicly denounced by campaigners from the Tax Justice Network as an 'economic fiction'.[110]

Defenders of philanthropy would point to a mitigating factor. Allegations of this nature could be levelled against a host of ruthless financiers, most of whom do not make any attempt to compensate by engaging in philanthropy. Rather they spend their money on another Rembrandt, ocean-going yacht or Learjet. By comparison, it can be argued in extenuation, that even a 'robber baron' philanthropist deserves some credit when he donates huge sums for causes in the public interest. It is hard to argue that philanthropy of this kind does not offer some mitigation against the allegation of injustice.

There is another aspect of the relationship between philanthropy and justice. Philanthropy, said the American theologian Reinhold Niebuhr, is 'the perfect illustration of the curious compound of the brutal and the moral which we find in all human behaviour'.[111] It is charged with ambiguity. The trumpeting of the personal generosity of a company boss may be seen as reputation laundering or a cover for dubious business practices. But it can also be a form of reparation. Holding on to the idea that both these things might be true at once sounds contradictory, but it is a good example of what the philosopher Gillian Rose means when she writes of 'the broken middle'.[112] Rose rejects binary oppositions between inner morality and political pragmatism. She does not seek to cover up differences and disagreements, nor pretend that they do not exist, nor suggest that they do not matter. Rather, she insists that real life is about living in 'the broken middle' where moral positions can be both tarnished and yet serviceable. That accepts the impossibility of reconciling different positions, but refuses to declare one side self-serving and the other selfless. Instead, Rose wants to reconcile the separations of civil, moral, collective and individual life. This is unsettling but it enables us to engage ethically, politically and socially, and arrive at what she calls a 'good enough justice'.[113]

The idea that philanthropy is a form of reparation is taken further by Chiara Cordelli, a political philosopher who specializes in the ethics of philanthropy. Reparation does not just cover the duty of individuals or companies to repair damage caused by their dodgy dealings. The rich may acquire reparative responsibilities even without directly benefiting from injustice, she argues.[114] She builds this conclusion on the work of John Rawls's celebrated Theory of Justice. Rawls, one of the most influential moral philosophers of the twentieth century, sees justice as a matter of fairness. He argues that citizens discharge their moral responsibility when they contribute their fair share of the taxes which governments use to take care of the poor and vulnerable. The better-off are then free to dispose of the rest of their income as they like. But when governments cut fair provision to needy citizens, things change. The rich benefit because their taxes fall, while the suffering of the poor increases. So, in those circumstances, the rich have a duty to do more.[115]

This is not just theory. The rich have benefited in practice in both the UK and US in recent decades from government policies which cut both taxes and welfare benefits. Evidence of that is set out in Anthony Atkinson's 2014 book *Inequality*, which charts the extent to which the rich have benefited from the withdrawal of public services in the US.[116] As a result, wealthy citizens in a democracy have a moral duty to do more to help the poor. If they do not, Cordelli argues, governments should reform tax relief so that it channels charitable donations to meet public needs rather than philanthropists' private preferences.

A number of philanthropists agree with this. Warren Buffett says that he has an obligation to give back to society because society is responsible for much of his wealth. His fortune was not based entirely on his own efforts and acumen. He was lucky in the genes he inherited; Buffett calls it 'ovarian roulette'. But most of all, his success was rooted in a whole social infrastructure. 'Society is responsible for a very significant percentage of what I've earned. If you stick me down in the middle of Bangladesh or Peru or someplace, you'll find out how much this talent is going to produce in the wrong kind of soil. I will be struggling 30 years later.'[117] Buffett was quoted to this effect in *I Didn't Do It Alone: Society's Contribution to Individual Wealth and Success*, a report produced by a group called Responsible Wealth.[118] One of the other rich entrepreneurs quoted in it, Martin Rothenberg, founder of Syracuse Language Systems, spelt out the extent to which public investment makes private fortunes possible. 'My wealth is not only a product of my own hard work. It also resulted from a strong economy and lots of public investment, both in others and in me,' he said. The state had given him a good education. There were free libraries and museums for him to use. The government had provided a graduate scholarship. And while teaching at university he was supported by numerous research grants. All of this provided the foundation on which he built the company which made him rich. Such effective public infrastructure had been paid for out of taxes, said Warren Buffett, adding:

> I have absolutely no complaints about these taxes. We work in a market-based economy that rewards our efforts far more bountifully than it does the efforts of others whose output is of equal or greater benefit to society . . . If you are a terrific nurse, this world will not pay a lot for it . . . Taxation should, and does, partially redress this inequality.[119]

Such public investment capital plays a huge part in most private sector success, says the Nobel Prize-winning economist and social scientist Herbert Simon. He reckons that 'social capital' is responsible for at least 90 per cent of what people earn in wealthy societies like the US, UK and northern Europe. Entrepreneurs rely not only on their own abilities but also on the technology and organizational skills in the community, and the presence of good government. That, says the philosopher Peter Singer, undermines the argument that the rich are entitled to keep their wealth because it is all a result of their hard work.[120]

It is not only some members of the very rich who embrace the notion of a 'social contract' which obliges those who have created wealth to give back in order to support the society which made that wealth creation possible. Lower down the entrepreneurial chain in the UK, Julian Richer, founder of the hi-fi chain Richer Sounds, transferred 60 per cent of the ownership of his £9 million company to his employees in a partnership trust in 2019. Asked why he had made this decision, he replied that the staff had demonstrated loyalty over four decades, so he was now 'doing the right thing' because that way 'I sleep better at night'.[121] Another intriguing example of a successful entrepreneur with a philanthropic impulse, at the opposite end of the wealth scale, can be found across the globe in India, where Shaffi Mather quit a successful career to set up a free ambulance service for the poor.[122] Mather, who ran a real estate business before working for two of India's largest communication corporations, had his life changed by a perilous ride to hospital with his mother. Afterwards he left his job to found an ambulance business which employed a 'fair trade' model, providing free services to the poor by charging rich customers extra.

Philanthropy, such examples show, can be perfectly compatible with justice. But it requires a conscious effort on behalf of philanthropists to make it so. The default inclines in the opposite direction. Reinhold Niebuhr in *Moral Man and Immoral Society* indicates why: 'Philanthropy combines genuine pity with the display of power [which] explains why the powerful are more inclined to be generous than to grant social justice.'[123]

'JUST STOP TALKING ABOUT PHILANTHROPY – AND START TALKING ABOUT TAXES'

Anyone now searching the internet to find a copy of Citigroup's 2005 and 2006 reports on *Plutonomy* will have some difficulty. They will keep encountering the message: 'This content was removed at the request of Citigroup, Inc.' Perhaps the giant banking group is now embarrassed by the gleeful tone of its analysts' advice on how to take advantage of the fact that the rich are getting richer and the poor poorer. Or perhaps what disquiets them is the second document's prediction that the widening gap between the rich and poor would eventually lead to 'a political backlash against the rising wealth of the rich'. This might take the form, the analysts envisaged, of higher taxes on the rich, increased regulation of the corporate sector, or a more general 'push-back on globalization'. This could lead to politicians clamping down on immigration. Or they might start trade wars to protect their own citizens – in ways that would hamper international trade. 'We don't see this happening yet, though there are signs of rising political tensions.'[124]

And so it came to pass – with the rise of new forms of national populism and demagogy across the world. The rich and the powerful began to fear things might get even worse. In 2019 the Dutch economic historian Rutger Bregman addressed an audience at the annual gathering of the international elite in Davos. 'Ten years ago, the World Economic Forum asked the question: what must industry do to prevent a broad social backlash?' he reminded them. 'The answer is very simple. Just stop talking about philanthropy. And start talking about taxes. We can invite Bono once more, but we've got to be talking about taxes,' he said. 'Taxes, taxes, taxes. All the rest is bullshit, in my opinion.'[125] A video clip of his outburst went viral all round the world on social media. It was hailed as a moment when truth was at last spoken to power. 'I hear people talking the language of participation, justice, equality and transparency, but almost no one raises the real issue of tax avoidance – and of the rich just not paying their fair share.' Addressing an audience which was there to discuss how to bring about a fairer society, he said that he felt as if he were at a fire-fighters' conference where 'no one's allowed to speak about water'.[126]

Is philanthropy just a way of avoiding tax? The month after the Davos meeting the *Financial Times* undertook an analysis of corporate tax avoidance around the world. It totalled at least $500 billion. Was the corporate world trying to hide this behind its philanthropic giving, the newspaper asked.[127] It examined the Amazon boss, Jeff Bezos, who had over the previous 10 years donated a total of $2 billion through his philanthropic foundation. Over the same period Amazon's tax bill was $1 billion – less than 4 per cent of the profits it made, thanks to clever – and entirely legal – tax avoidance schemes. Had it paid taxes at the going rate it would have handed $9.5 billion to the US Treasury. So, even allowing for Bezos's generous $2 billion giveaway, Amazon was $6.5 billion better off. The *FT* did a similar calculation with Bill Gates. To date he has donated the staggering sum of $35 billion to his charitable foundation. But his company Microsoft has been keeping $142 billion offshore on which no tax has been paid. Had that money been declared as profits in the United States the company would have paid $49.7 billion in tax. Hence, the *FT* analysts calculated, the money Gates donated was '$14.7 billion less than he had taken out of the system in the first place'. America was the capital of corporate tax avoidance with $189 billion in unpaid tax. That sum, the *Financial Times* estimated, was equivalent to the country's total budget for education and child nutrition. Interestingly, Europe did not figure in the top tax avoidance destinations; China was second with $67 billion, then Japan with $47 billion and next India with $41 billion.

Higher taxes on the rich could well be the next demand arising out of the widespread populist discontent spreading across developed countries. The idea of wealth taxes, which have always been part of the palette of political options in much of Europe, is gaining ground in America too. Polls there have suggested for some time that the majority of people want the rich to pay more taxes. But by 2019 there were signs of a significant increase in this feeling. An opinion poll early that year revealed that support had increased substantially to 74 per cent of US voters – including 65 per cent of Republicans. An OECD survey showed that, right across developed countries, people wanted their government to increase taxes on the rich in order to help the poorest in society. It was, said the OECD secretary-general, Angel Gurría, 'a wake-up call for policy makers'.[128] In France the *gilets jaunes* street protesters demanded more taxes on the rich. In Portugal and Greece almost 80 per cent of people called for their governments to impose higher taxes on the wealthy.

Political impetus increased in the United States in the run-up to the 2020 presidential elections. Several leading Democratic politicians called for more taxes on the rich. The presidential candidate Senator Elizabeth Warren proposed a tax on *assets* – at 2 per cent a year for anyone worth more than £50 million, and 3 per cent on billionaires. The plan would raise $2.75 trillion over 10 years and 'provide millions of families with a better shot at the American dream'. Another candidate, Senator Bernie Sanders, offered a different variation: an *inheritance* tax of 45 per cent on estates over $3.5 million, rising gradually to 77 per cent for those who died leaving more than $1 billion. A third option, a tax on the *income* of the super-rich, was proposed by the firebrand Congresswoman Alexandria Ocasio-Cortez, who chided that 'a system that allows billionaires to exist, when there are parts of Alabama where people are still getting ringworm because they don't have access to public health, is wrong'.[129] Her proposal, for a 70 per cent tax on all earnings above $10 million a year, was backed by 59 per cent of voters in one poll.[130]

Many big business people reacted to all this with alarm. At Davos the computer magnate and philanthropist, Michael Dell, was dismissive of Rutger Bregman's call for 'taxes, taxes, taxes'. When asked – to the sound of laughter in the room – if he supported the Ocasio-Cortez tax plan, he replied that he didn't. 'My wife and I set up a foundation about 20 years ago, and we would have contributed quite a bit more than a 70 per cent tax rate on my annual income,' he said. His figures on that were unclear. The Michael and Susan Dell Foundation has given away over $1 billion to children's and community initiatives in the US, India and South Africa over the past two decades, but Dell is still worth $30 billion and is the eighteenth richest man in the world.[131] 'I feel much more comfortable with our ability as a private foundation to allocate those funds than I do giving them to the government,' he said. Name a country, he asked rhetorically, where such a high tax rate had not discouraged enterprise and economic growth? The answer came immediately from another member of the same Davos panel, the MIT economist Erik Brynjolfsson, who replied: 'The United States . . . from the 1930s to the 1970s, the tax rate averaged about 70 per cent. At times it was as high as 95 per cent – and those were actually pretty good years for growth.'[132]

More than pretty good. The data from the twentieth century suggests that, not just the US economy, but economies all over the world experienced their strongest periods of growth when taxes on the well-off were high. Starting in 1980, however, President Reagan made huge cuts to the top marginal income tax rate – down from 70 per cent to 50 per cent in 1982, and then again to below 30 per cent.[133] Economic growth began to slow and the gap between rich and poor began to widen. President Trump's controversial 2017 Tax Cuts and Jobs Act cut corporate tax from 35 to 21 per cent and income tax to 37 per cent.[134] The result, as the billionaire Warren Buffett pointed out, is that his secretary pays tax at a higher rate than he does.[135] Trump's tax changes meant that, at a stroke, charitable deductions went from being a tax break which benefited the middle class to one skewed heavily towards the very rich. In addition, said the *Financial Times*, 'the ultra-wealthy and their advisers continue to be adept at making the most of the charitable deduction by controlling the timing and structure of philanthropic donations, to the point that vast fortunes created in tech start-ups, for example, can be significantly shielded from capital gains tax – something that does not seem fair.'[136]

Conservative philanthropists began a fightback. Increased taxes are a threat to their business bottom line but also offend them ideologically. Many super-rich libertarians, like the Koch brothers, prefer to give money to charity rather than see it spent by government. In support of this they cite the political philosopher Robert Nozick, whose *Anarchy, State and Utopia* insisted that the state had no right to force the wealthy to help others.[137] Taxation takes away their freedom to choose to be virtuous. And forced virtue is no virtue at all. But the fightback against increased taxes on the rich also took less high-minded forms. Art Pope and other Koch associates funded an organization which hired electronic billboards in New York's Time Square that attacked Alexandria Ocasio-Cortez.[138] And the Koch-funded political action committee Americans for Prosperity launched a campaign to protect right-wing Democratic politicians from challenges by left-wing insurgents like Ocasio-Cortez and the other radical ethnic-minority congresswomen whom Donald Trump attacked in language which was widely condemned as racist.[139] Two of the women, Alexandria Ocasio-Cortez and Ayanna Pressley, both pressed for policies on a Green New Deal which would have caused difficulties for Koch Industries.[140]

But other mega-rich philanthropists backed the new idea that they, and the rest of the super-rich, should pay more taxes. Warren Buffett had for many years consistently called for higher taxes on the wealthy. In 2011 he had written a piece for the *New York Times* in which he demanded a tax rise for everyone making more than $1 million a year – and an even bigger hike for those making more than $10 million a year. He explained:

> Some of us are investment managers who earn billions from our daily labors but are allowed to classify our income as 'carried interest', thereby getting a bargain 15 per cent tax rate.

I know well many of the mega-rich and, by and large, they are very decent people. They love America and appreciate the opportunity this country has given them. Many have joined the Giving Pledge, promising to give most of their wealth to philanthropy. Most wouldn't mind being told to pay more in taxes as well, particularly when so many of their fellow citizens are truly suffering . . .

My friends and I have been coddled long enough by a billionaire-friendly Congress. It's time for our government to get serious about shared sacrifice.[141]

The idea that higher tax rates discourage investment was wrong, Buffett said. 'People invest to make money, and potential taxes have never scared them off.' His fellow billionaire philanthropist, Bill Gates, was equally at ease with the idea of higher taxes. In an interview with the BBC in 2014 he backed the idea of an inheritance tax and higher taxes on unearned income. He added: 'I've paid more taxes than any individual ever, and gladly so. I should pay more . . . but I've paid over $6 billion in taxes.'[142] Some conservatives sneered at this, saying that if philanthropists wanted to give the government more money they 'should just write a check and shut up'.[143]

But the attitude of Buffett and Gates was shared by many of the newly rich, highly educated knowledge workers who had benefited from public services like education, scientific research and infrastructure. 'They wish the public sector was more nimble and effective, but they're not anti-statists and they don't mind paying higher taxes,' concluded David Callahan after his survey of new givers.[144] A group of America's richest citizens endorsed this in an open letter designed to make inequality and a wealth tax part of the political agenda for the 2020 election. George Soros and 17 other billionaires – five of them leading philanthropists – wrote: 'America has a moral, ethical and economic responsibility to tax our wealth more.' They called for a 'moderate' tax on assets of the wealthiest 0.1 per cent. They wrote: 'A wealth tax could help address the climate crisis, improve the economy, improve health outcomes, fairly create opportunity and strengthen our democratic freedoms.'[145] One of the signatories, movie industry heiress Abigail Disney, told the *Financial Times*: 'I'm choosing to be a traitor to my class'.[146] That same week another billionaire philanthropist, Eli Broad – the only individual ever to have created two Fortune 500 companies in different industries – wrote a piece in the *New York Times* with the headline: 'I'm in the 1 Per Cent. Please, Raise My Taxes'. In it he declared:

> Two decades ago I turned full-time to philanthropy and threw myself into supporting public education, scientific and medical research, and visual and performing arts, believing it was my responsibility to give back some of what had so generously been given to me. But I've come to realize that no amount of philanthropic commitment will compensate for the deep inequities preventing most Americans – the factory workers and farmers, entrepreneurs and electricians, teachers, nurses and small business owners – from the basic prosperity we call the American dream.
>
> I have watched my wealth grow exponentially thanks to federal policies that have cut my tax rates while wages for regular people have stagnated and poverty rates have increased.
>
> So ... I invite fellow members of the 1 per cent to join me in demanding that they engage in a robust discussion of how we can strengthen a post-Trump America by reforming our tax code.[147]

THE MAGIC PORRIDGE POT OVERFLOWS

What adds to the pressure on the rich is that they are constantly getting richer. Investment returns are swelling the fortunes of ultra-rich philanthropists faster than they can give their money away. Much faster. The annual return of the US stock market over the 20 years, before the coronavirus crash, has been more than 8 per cent,[148] but the investment portfolios of the rich have almost certainly generated far more because they have access to hedge funds beyond the reach of the ordinary investor. When the market value of Microsoft pushed past $1 trillion in April 2019, Bill Gates, who was worth $54 billion in 2010 – the year he signed the Giving Pledge – found himself worth over $100 billion.[149] And that is despite having already personally donated $35 billion to his foundation.

Warren Buffett's wealth also nearly doubled to $90 billion, despite annual transfers of stock from his company to the Gates Foundation and the four foundations controlled by his three children. Although Michael Bloomberg ramped up his philanthropy in 2014, at the end of his third term as mayor of New York, his fortune has increased by 50 per cent to $48 billion. Philanthropists like Chuck Feeney, the billionaire who really has almost totally succeeded in giving all his money away, are the exceptions. (Feeney gave away $8 billion, leaving himself with only $1.5 million to see out his days.[150]) Philanthropy industry expert David Callahan has estimated that the world's wealthiest people are sitting on $4 trillion and accumulating money much faster than they can give it away.[151] The situation reminded a *Financial Times* writer of the fairy tale of the Magic Porridge Pot whose owner forgets the words to make it stop producing porridge. At Warren Buffett's company, Berkshire Hathaway, 'every working day, $100m rolls in . . . cash from its subsidiaries, dividends from its shares, interest from its treasuries. Something must be done with it all. The porridge is starting to overrun the house.'[152]

Among the ranks of the rich there are those who have begun to become very alarmed. The South African billionaire and philanthropist, Johann Rupert, founder of Richemont, whose brands include Cartier and Montblanc, revealed to his fellow manufacturers of luxury goods at a conference in Monaco that he feared that one day the poor might rise up in revolt at inequality. Artificial intelligence and automation could lead to job losses on a scale which will cause deep social unrest. Conflicts between social classes could make selling high-end fashion and jewellery more tricky, he told a *Financial Times* summit on the Business of Luxury. The time could come when the rich will want to conceal their wealth, he said. 'We cannot have 0.1 per cent of 0.1 per cent taking all the spoils,' he added. Rupert, who is worth $7.5 billion, said: 'We are destroying the middle classes . . . and it will affect us . . . That's what keeps me awake at night.' The former investment banker concluded gloomily: 'We're in for a huge change in society. Get used to it. And be prepared.'[153]

Some of the ultra-rich took such predictions so seriously that they have taken steps to protect themselves in the event of riots. Robert A. Johnson, a former hedge fund manager at Soros Fund Management, told the World Economic Forum in Davos: 'I know hedge fund managers all over the world who are buying airstrips and farms in places like New Zealand because they think they need a getaway'. Many of his rich acquaintances were saying to one another: 'You've got to have a private plane. You have to assure that the pilot's family will be taken care of, too. They have to be on the plane.' A more sensible response, Johnson suggested, would be for the wealthy to adopt a greater 'spirit of stewardship' – an openness to policy change that could include, for instance, a more aggressive tax on inheritance. 'Twenty-five hedge fund managers make more money than all of the kindergarten teachers in America combined,' he told the *New Yorker*.[154] 'Being one of those twenty-five doesn't feel good. I think they've developed a heightened sensitivity.' Analysis by the National Bureau of Economic Research showed that half of American adults have been 'completely shut off from economic growth since the 1970s'. Around 117 million people in the US earned, on average, the same as they did in 1980, while the typical income for the top one per cent has almost trebled. 'If we had a more equal distribution of income, and much more money and energy going into public school systems, parks and recreation, the arts and healthcare, it could take an awful lot of sting out of society,' Johnson said. But 'we've largely dismantled those things'.

It is not only in America that philanthropy is seen as a way to head off such potential unrest. In the UK Giuseppe Ciucci, chief executive of Stonehage Fleming, which manages the wealth of rich families, has told the *Financial Times*: 'Giving should be done in a far more public way. Unless people demonstrate that they give to charity, they may be targets of jealousy, envy and crime.'[155] Lord Davies of Abersoch, chairman of the Lord Mayor's Appeal charity in 2016, said increasing social pressure was 'turning up the heat' on rich families in the UK to demonstrate that they are paying taxes and giving back to society. 'It doesn't matter if it's public or private. The important thing is that wealthy families give their money away' and are seen to do it.[156]

In both the UK and the US a mounting uneasiness with income inequality is growing. A new economic populism is spreading which refuses to regard the concentration of wealth charitably. The golden age of philanthropy is over, declared the American historian of philanthropy, Benjamin Soskis.[157] Philanthropists, henceforth, must expect to be regarded with a critical, or even a jaundiced, scrutiny. 'There is definitely a philanthropy backlash underway,' says Beth Breeze in the UK.[158] 'Philanthropy should, of course, be scrutinised as well as celebrated, but as our study of media coverage shows, ill-chosen words cannot only hurt the donors but also possibly put them off donating again – and helping those in need – in the future.' She and the historian of philanthropy Hugh Cunningham have researched the adjectives used to describe philanthropists. References in *The Times* during the nineteenth century included derogatory terms such as 'puffing', 'pseudo', 'sham', 'false' and 'unscrupulous'. The twenty-first-century adjectival equivalents are not the same, but are just as pejorative: 'ruthless', 'tax-ruse', 'sinister', 'status-seeking' and 'self-righteous'.[159] The common factor is that wealth and power seem always to provoke reactions which are, at the very least, ambivalent.

The extensive interviews Breeze has conducted with rich donors over more than a decade suggest that such journalistic cynicism takes its toll. Many major philanthropists are confused and hurt by the widespread suspicions about their motives. Other studies bear this out, with one prominent British donor asking researchers: 'Why are the media nasty? They don't do good news. They are snide and they pander to jealousy.' Another said: 'You need to accept from the outset that whatever you do will be rubbished in newspapers.' A third commented: 'I am afraid of the media, it's always negative . . . They have great power and there's no right of reply.'[160] The accusation that philanthropy is some kind of tax dodge is particularly common, yet critics routinely fail to concede that, whatever the tax breaks, giving still involves the philanthropist laying out a significant amount of their own money. 'It's mathematically impossible for an individual to be better off after making a donation,' Breeze writes.[161]

Much of the criticism is 'knee-jerk' in its assumptions about philanthropists' intentions, Beth Breeze says, citing the public reaction to the swift announcements of donations which followed the fire at Notre-Dame in Paris, which sent shock waves through the French nation. The man who, within hours, announced a €200 million donation to the rebuilding fund, Bernard Arnault, was taken aback by the negativity of the public response. Arnault – who briefly became the world's second-richest man in July 2019 – later told a shareholder's meeting: 'It's pretty dismaying to see that in France you are criticized even for doing something for the general interest'. Sceptics pointed out that, in France, companies can get tax relief of 60 per cent on donations, up to a maximum of 0.5 per cent of their annual turnover. But Arnault's luxury goods company, LVMH, had already reached the ceiling on this tax relief, so its Notre-Dame donation would cost it the full €200 million.[162] Cynics were still not satisfied; one compared the donation to repair the cathedral to the medieval purchase of indulgences: 'As soon as gold in the coffer rings, the rescued soul to heaven springs.'[163] Their scepticism was fuelled by the fact that three months after the fire only €10 million of the big donors' money had materialized for the preparatory clean-up operation. Critics conveniently chose to ignore the fact that Olivier de Challus, chief guide and architectural expert at Notre Dame, said: 'It doesn't matter that the big donors haven't yet paid because the choices about the spire and the major architectural decisions will happen probably late in 2020. That's when the large sums of money will be required.'[164]

Others shifted the ground of their criticism. It was not that philanthropy was wrong, but that billionaires had given to the wrong cause. Workers' organizations complained that it was galling that funds could be found for a cathedral when they had not been found for social problems. 'Millions for Notre Dame, what about for us, the poor?' read one placard carried by *gilets jaunes* street protesters. 'Everything for Notre Dame, nothing for Les Misérables,' said another.[165] 'The rebuilt cathedral will be a monument to the gigantic hypocrisy of austerity politics,' declared one leftist commentator.[166]

Such indignation chooses to ignore the undoubted benefits achieved by philanthropists in so many areas. Those criticisms cannot outweigh the achievement of cutting worldwide cases of polio by 99.9 per cent – a virtual eradication which would not have happened without the $3 billion in donations from Bill Gates. 'It seems to be OK to be a local giver, raise money for charity, give a bit to Comic Relief. But as soon as you add a few zeroes, people start thinking: What's in it for them?' says Beth Breeze.[167] As Justin Forsyth, when he was chief executive of Save the Children, said of Bill Gates: 'Are we supposed to like him less than other people because he's able to do more than other people? That seems perverse.'[168] So does the fact that philanthropists come in for far more critical fire than do global billionaires who never give a penny. Beth Breeze estimates that there are a mere 9 per cent of global billionaires who are serious philanthropists. She asks: 'So why all the focus on their motives and actions, rather than the other 91 per cent?' Why place emphasis 'only on the alleged culpability of those who give, while non-givers – choosing mega-yachts over mega-donations – are curiously absent from the discussion'.[169]

It is hard not to conclude that much of the hostility and generalized cynicism directed against philanthropists is, in fact, misplaced outrage at the exponential growth of the wealth of the ultra-rich. Since it is now less fashionable for the mega-rich to flaunt their wealth by conspicuous consumption, philanthropists are the most prominent members of the billionaire class regularly in the public spotlight. 'Critics seem to have conflated their unhappiness with a system they believe taxes the wealthy too lightly, with a critique of giving that they believe is designed to distract from that system,' writes Phil Buchanan. He is president of the Center for Effective Philanthropy in the United States, where suspicion of philanthropists is a far more recent phenomenon than in Britain. The danger is that this scepticism 'threatens to erode cultural norms about helping others' and about the importance of charity. 'Of course, critique is vital. But a cynical, generalized dismissal goes too far. Why give if all you get is grief?'[170]

THE REDEMPTION OF PHILANTHROPY

There are two ways in which philanthropy is vital to democracy, argues Rob Reich. It enables innovation. And it can nurture the variety of voices essential for an effective democracy. Reich calls these two Discovery and Pluralism.

Those who rail against unelected billionaires, accusing them of letting loose their neo-missionary impulses across the globe, often overlook one of their singular advantages. They can make good the failures of both the market and government. The private sector mainly offers private goods for which consumers are prepared to pay. Governments use taxes to provide public goods – services from which everyone benefits, such as defence, sewers, street lighting, policing, and the basic public education essential to create the educated workforce on which modern economies depend. But some services do not fall neatly into either camp. Global health is a classic example. The whole world benefits from the eradication of polio or malaria, but no one government can afford to foot the bill. Nor is there enough profit to incentivize drug companies to research drugs which are needed mainly by people too poor to buy them.

Enter Bill Gates & Co. Philanthropists like him are also often the only ones who are prepared to make investments with sufficiently long time horizons. Companies will not do that because they are owned by shareholders who want a quick return on investment. Governments do not do it because global problems seem too distant from the daily lives of voters – and politicians usually will not look ahead further than the next elections. By contrast, philanthropists are accountable to no one. The downside of that, as we have seen, is that they can plough money into ill-advised projects, as Gates and Zuckerberg did in education. But the upside is that they can invest in innovative or high-risk schemes that might not bear fruit for decades – which is what the Rockefeller Foundation did in funding the research that eventually produced a vaccine for yellow fever, once one of the world's most dreaded diseases. They can even allow themselves to fail, as Bono did with his fair-trade *haute couture* fashion project Edun.* Such 'discovery', Reich suggests, is something that philanthropists are uniquely fitted to fulfil in modern market democracies.

There is more to this than a philosopher's theory. The evidence shows that philanthropy does indeed promote innovation and flexibility. It can also leverage additional sources of finance which the private and public sectors fail to provide. The international community acknowledged this when a gathering of heads of state, finance ministers, UN officials, and prominent business and civil society leaders came together in Addis Ababa in 2015. They met to draw up plans for financing economic development in the developing world. Afterwards they declared:

> We welcome the rapid growth of philanthropic giving and the significant financial and non-financial contribution philanthropists have made towards achieving our common goals. We recognize philanthropic donors' flexibility and capacity for innovation and taking risks and their ability to leverage additional funds through multi-stakeholder partnerships.[171]

Bill Gates, who stepped down from his role in Microsoft to become a full-time philanthropist in March 2020, has led the philanthropic field in taking risks on new approaches – and his ability to raise matching funds from other sources is clear from the way that the US sharply increased spending on fighting infectious diseases like malaria, but only after the Gates Foundation put them back on the global public-health agenda.[172]

Just how innovative philanthropy can be is evident from the example of Thomas Siebel. The US software billionaire, after a decade of conventional

* See pages 532–3 above.

philanthropy, became concerned about the rampant use of the drug methamphetamine in his home state of Montana. Meth is a highly addictive and physically destructive drug which had become a particular problem in rural America. In 2005 Montana had the fifth worst level of meth abuse in the US; half of its prison inmates were jailed for meth-related crime. But rather than writing a cheque to a local drug-abuse charity, Siebel decided to find out why people become addicted to meth.

After learning that first-time users were typically teenagers who were unaware of meth's risks, Siebel created the Meth Project to change teenage perceptions about the drug. He hired a major San Francisco advertising agency to develop a hard-hitting campaign that reached 80 per cent of Montana teens at least three times a week. The ads were world-class, directed by an Oscar-nominated director, with production budgets of up to $1 million each, winning over 40 awards in national and international advertising competitions. The 30-second mini-movies were gut-wrenching. 'Teens are shown attacking and robbing their own families, prostituting themselves, or dying from an overdose,' wrote Mark Kramer in the *Stanford Social Innovation Review*. 'In one ad, a boy describes how his mother has always been there for him, while the screen shows him stealing her purse, hitting her, and kicking her away as she screams and desperately tries to grab his leg while he runs out the door.'[173] The stark ads captured teenage imaginations. Over the next two years meth use in Montana dropped 45 per cent among teens and 72 per cent among adults. Meth-related crimes fell by 62 per cent. Awareness of the dangers of meth among teenagers rose from 25 per cent to 93 per cent. Six other states then adopted the Montana method. Siebel showed how philanthropic innovation can expand the tool kit of remedies available to wider society.

A good example of the longer-term perspective which philanthropy can enable is the investment in university research on the ethics of artificial intelligence at Oxford and MIT by the billionaire financier, Stephen Schwarzman. For all the controversy around Schwarzman's business methods, there can be little doubt that his work on the rise of AI is genuinely in the global public interest. Schwarzman's curiosity about AI was sparked on a visit to China when he got stuck in the notorious Beijing traffic with the Chinese technology tycoon and philanthropist Jack Ma, founder of the Alibaba group which is the biggest online retailer in the world. In the course of their 90-minute delay Ma – whose company is one of the largest investment corporations and venture capital firms in the world – told Schwarzman about the role AI was playing in his gigantic business, and of its expanding future prospects. 'It's going to be astonishing,' Ma told Schwarzman, but added 'there's a lot of bad stuff that could happen, like huge unemployment as you replace people with machines'.[174] Back home, Schwarzman discussed the new phenomenon with US tech experts and concluded there was a risk of America falling seriously behind in AI because it hadn't invested anywhere near as much as had the Chinese. He decided to donate \$350 million to establish a new college at the leading US applied science research university MIT. The new institute would work on future technologies in computing, data science and AI.

But that was not enough. Schwarzman was not just exercised by the technology but also began to worry about the impact it could have on society if automation and artificial intelligence throw millions of skilled workers and middle-class professionals out of a job. While all this had been going on Schwarzman had been in conversation with Oxford University, whose vice-chancellor, Louise Richardson, had approached him for a donation to a new centre for the humanities to foster interdisciplinary research across the arts. The billionaire told her that Oxford's proposal was not ambitious enough and sent her off to draw up bigger plans. Schwarzman wanted not only to create new linkages between the humanities disciplines of literature, history, philosophy, theology, linguistics, languages, arts and music, he also wanted their input into a new Institute to study the Ethics of Artificial Intelligence to be housed in Oxford's department of philosophy. 'I went to a conference, and there was an AI computer making paintings, and there's going to be AI music,' Schwarzman told *Forbes* magazine. Oxford's world-leading humanities departments were the ideal place for 'figuring out what's important to be human' – because that understanding 'is going to be challenged [by] the introduction of AI'.

Oxford was initially hesitant, but grew to embrace the idea – along with the huge Schwarzman donation. 'What I hope to achieve [as] part of this dialogue [is] to try and help the system regulate itself so innocent people who're just living their lives don't end up disadvantaged. If you start dislocating people, and your tax revenues go down, your social costs go up, your voting patterns change . . . You could endanger the underpinnings of liberal democracies,' he told *Forbes*. 'Most governments' laws and regulations get created after there's a problem. They're for the most part responsive to crisis.' What he wanted with the introduction of artificial intelligence 'is to just not have the crisis happen'.[175]

Schwarzman's artificial intelligence initiative is interesting for another reason. It shows how complicated are the motives which drive philanthropists. Exploring the moral implications of the introduction of future technologies – and the political and social policies which will be required to address the higher levels of unemployment AI will bring – is undoubtedly in the public interest. It will further the common good in ways which are very much in the tradition of classic philanthropy.

Yet Schwarzman clearly sees that his Oxford project to develop the liberal arts is also vital to the future of the business world in which he has made his vast fortune. 'Our education system all started with the humanities, and that needs to be strengthened,' he said in the *Forbes* interview. Schwarzman, who studied culture and behaviour at Yale, sees the benefits of an arts education to those who work inside his company managing $512 billion in investment assets. 'You're taught to think a certain way, which is sort of multi-matrix type of thinking. When things change, you instantly move, re-sort what's important, use your logic, and that enables you to adapt to the real world,' Schwarzman believes. 'If you went around the table at our management committee, we all had the same background . . . we all were trained for that level of ambiguity, change, commitment.'[176]

HOW PHILANTHROPY CAN STRENGTHEN DEMOCRACY

How completely can any government represent the diversity of views of the whole population? Philanthropy, in all its eccentric variety, lets a thousand flowers bloom. So although it doesn't have the authority of an electoral mandate, as politicians do, it can lay claim to cover a huge range of areas, interests and activities. This diversity is effectively a decentralization of power, Rob Reich argues. Philanthropy is a centrifugal force. At its best it throws power out to a wide range of groups – from charities to churches, voluntary groups to neighbourhood organizations, pressure groups to community development associations, and all the other 'little platoons' of civil society.

It is, of course, not representative. Some have argued that the causes sponsored by liberal philanthropists balance out those funded by conservative philanthropists, but this is a weak argument. Mega-rich philanthropists do not represent a cross section of the population in either their interests or their views. Their tastes can be culturally elitist and, as we have seen, their views tend to be more right-wing or conservative than those of most people. The views of the ultra-wealthy are even more skewed.

But the wide range of philanthropic preferences and idiosyncrasies means that, albeit in an unsystematic way, philanthropy also can give support to a rich tapestry of grassroots organizations through which, directly or indirectly, ordinary people hold the powerful to account. True, philanthropy can weaken elected governments, especially in the developing world, by bypassing national systems or declining to nurture them. And it can favour causes which only reflect the interests of the wealthy. But where philanthropists support community organizations, parent-teacher associations, co-operatives, faith groups, environmentalists or human rights activists, they can help empower ordinary people to challenge authoritarian or overweening governments. In those circumstances philanthropy may be said to strengthen rather than weaken democracy.

Over the centuries the history of philanthropy, as earlier chapters of this book have shown, contains a strong thread of philanthropists campaigning to take issues from the margins to the mainstream. Often they do so in the teeth of indifference or opposition from an existing democratic structure. 'The most important steps in human progress may be opposed to the prejudices, not only of the multitude, but even of the learned and leaders of thought in a particular epoch,' said the political reformer Thomas Hare in 1869.[177] The philanthropist can be an activist to challenge social orthodoxies. John Howard looked at the state of prisons in the eighteenth century, which were deemed acceptable by the authorities, and declared them to be a moral outrage. William Wilberforce did the same with slavery. Campaigners to end the practice of small boys being sent to climb up sooty chimneys were initially looked at askance by their nineteenth-century contemporaries. The campaign for women's and universal suffrage met stiff opposition at the start of the twentieth century, as did the campaign for gay rights many decades later. Philanthropy provides prophets with the space to run counter to prevailing public and political opinion. It is only with the benefit of hindsight that we can determine who is on the right side of history.

In any case, democracy too can have its shortcomings. Winston Churchill acknowledged that when he famously said 'democracy is the worst form of government, except for all those other forms that have been tried from time to time'.[178] After all, democracy is a means to an end, not an end in itself. The health of democracy relies upon the values which underpin it – values of freedom, tolerance, respect, fairness, honesty and compassion. A democracy in which the majority rides roughshod over the rights of minorities is not a true democracy but a majoritarian tyranny. An independent judiciary and a free press are key mechanisms to guard against that, but philanthropy can also help. It can create an alternative space in which minorities, and those with unorthodox views, can both create their own communities and feel some public support for their position or cause. Philanthropy can, in this way, provide a means to challenge a democracy which has become illiberal.

In the aftermath of the election of Donald Trump in 2016, the American historian of philanthropy Benjamin Soskis set out a manifesto in the *Chronicle of Philanthropy* which he entitled 'New Realities for Philanthropy in the Trump Era'. He began by lamenting the fact that the philanthropic elite – like the political elite – had clearly failed to understand the hopes, beliefs and frustrations of large swathes of the electorate, especially the white working class. Philanthropists had largely ignored those sections of society who suffered from the dislocations caused by global trade. They had neglected, in particular, the rural communities which became a bastion of Trumpism. The same was true of the 'left behind' regions in the UK which made their presence felt in 2016 by voting for Britain to leave the EU. Yet in light of such facts, 'philanthropy must serve not as an instrument of accommodation but as an agent of resistance,' Soskis wrote.[179] 'The fundamental liberal values, those of tolerance and respect for others, of decency, charity, and moderation, have been enfeebled in our public life . . . Philanthropy must be a place in which those values are preserved, defended, and championed.'

The problem comes, of course, in determining who should decide what those values should be. Rob Reich is clear that, while it is important to preserve the ways in which philanthropy serves liberty and pluralism, it must also be redirected to give more to organizations that promote equality by serving the poor. Philanthropy should domesticate plutocrats so that they 'serve, rather than subvert, democratic aims'.[180] Yet, as the political scientist Jacqueline Pfeffer Merrill points out, philanthropy has wider and more varied aims than equality or justice. Reich might prefer charities which support a soup kitchen rather than an elite art institution, but that surely does not invalidate the philanthropy of the art lover? 'Is not beauty worthy of charitable support alongside equality and justice?' Merrill asks.[181]

The truth is that philanthropy belongs not to the political realm but to civil society and a world of social institutions which mediate between individuals, the market and the state. In democratic politics justice and equality may be prime virtues. But in civil society we pursue wider virtues such as community, trust, honour, compassion and empathy. And there is something more. Rob Reich expresses disapproval of the fact that tax subsidies are paid out on charitable donations made by ordinary givers to churches, synagogues, mosques and other faith organizations. He argues that because much of this is spent on buildings, operating costs and clergy salaries, 'in this sense, religious groups look less like public charities and more like mutual benefit societies'.[182] They are, he suggests, therefore less worthy of tax relief from the public purse.

But Reich is open to challenge here. Again it is hard to determine by what calculus such a judgement can be made, other than the philosopher's personal preference. Those who value transcendence – in religion or art – can make a plausible case that the pursuit of metaphysical values is ultimately as desirable as the virtue of economic fairness. There are compelling arguments on both sides. But when the political realm is paralleled by both social and spiritual spheres of life, who is to arbitrate on the relative values of one over another? The pitfalls of leaving that to the state are clear, as Rowan Williams points out in his interview (see page 197). One of the virtues of philanthropy is that it keeps alternatives in the public debate.

Interview: Eliza Manningham-Buller on accountability

Lady Eliza Manningham-Buller is Chair of the Wellcome Trust, the fourth-biggest philanthropic foundation in the world. Set up in 1936 under the will of the pharmaceutical magnate Sir Henry Wellcome, it funds scientific and medical research all around the world. Before joining Wellcome, Baroness Manningham-Buller served for decades in the British security service, MI5, retiring as its Director General in 2007. She now supervises Wellcome's £26 billion investment portfolio, from which it spends approximately £1 billion a year – funding scientists and researchers in biomedical science, population health, medical innovation, humanities and social science, and public engagement.

You came to Wellcome after a long career in the intelligence service at MI5. They sound like very different worlds.

Well, they're not that far apart in the sense that in MI5 your overall objective was to try and save lives, usually from terrorism. And that's what the Wellcome Trust is trying to do in a different way and on a different scale. It's not as different as you might first think.

Wellcome is a much bigger organization than MI5 presumably?

No, it's much, much smaller. But it's much, much richer. The difference is that MI5 does its own work; its staff do the investigations and intelligence work. At Wellcome we fund other people to fulfil our mission. MI5 has about 5,000 people; here we're just 800. A fundamental difference is that in MI5 I was an executive – accountable to the law, the government, the Intelligence and Security Committee, the Treasury, the National Audit Office, etcetera. Here, I'm the non-executive chair – and accountable, we believe, to the public who are the focus of our mission. Working out to whom we're accountable is much more difficult here than it was in government.

Many philanthropists say they want to give away their fortunes in their lifetimes. But Wellcome is a permanent foundation.

We are, but we don't have to be. We could spend the money down. There's nothing to stop us doing so. But successive generations of governors at Wellcome have felt that they wished this to be a fund in perpetuity. Why would we not want to be going in 100 years if we continue to do good and address the challenges that arise? I think one should trust one's successors – because what we judge today to be a really overwhelming priority may, in 20 years, look completely different. If we spend all the money now we'd have denied our successors the opportunity to spend the money differently.

If we look back 10 years few were worrying about climate change. The fear of antibiotic resistance and drug-resistant infections wasn't as acute as it is now. Mental health was certainly not high on the agenda. Nor was Big Data. Obviously, cancer and a lot of other issues were. But some of the big issues that have arisen in the last 10 years wouldn't have been on the agenda. Equally, when we've gone the next generation will have a different set of priorities.

How do you strike the balance between honouring the vision of the founder and being flexible enough to change to respond to new circumstances?

We don't actually have to abide by the vision of the founder. It's not like the American system where a foundation can be quite constrained by the founder's wishes and you are required by law to spend 5 per cent of your capital every year. We don't have the constraints that come from a living donor. That said, Henry Wellcome's vision was incredibly broad and enabling. There's pretty well nothing we want to do that couldn't be covered by his will. At MI5 if you wanted to spend on something which was classed by the Treasury as what they called 'novel and contentious' you'd need special permission to do it. Here we determine our own direction, who we're accountable to, where we sit, what we do and what we don't do.

You have set up a new fund, the Leap Fund, to do that 'novel and contentious' work, I gather.

The Leap Fund is not yet properly launched, but the idea behind it is to fund ideas which require significant investment, which have a large-scale, potentially transformative effect for human health, but which would probably fall through the traditional routes of funding science.

It's to fund high-risk, high-return projects. It'll be semi-independent from us.

The way science generally is funded is that proposals come in, they're seen by panels and they are graded according to excellence, and a proportion of them are funded. The drawback of that is, if you've got a really off-the-wall idea that might work – and if it did, it'd be extraordinary – it's hard to get it through those panels. Recently in Munich I met a Nobel prize winner, Stefan Hell, who made a major breakthrough in microscopy. But throughout his career he'd been told it wouldn't work, he didn't get grants, and people rejected his ideas. Where people have such a radical idea, it's difficult for government to fund it – because it's hard with taxpayers' money to try something high-risk with the *Daily Mail* looking over your shoulder. A foundation can do things differently to government.

Leap is deliberately seeking to fund some science which is currently difficult to fund because it is so outside the box. Stefan Hill's microscopy completely transformed the definition in which you can see living tissue – yet throughout his career he'd met opposition and been repeatedly told he was on the wrong track.

Leap is a new initiative. But you've also recently divided your main pot of money into a primary and a reserve fund. What's that about?

The primary fund, which is topped up so that it's inflation-proof, and which is where the bulk of the resources lie, is the traditional way we fund science: a scientist comes in with a bid, applies for a grant for their team, and either gets the money or not. The reserve fund is targeted on what we call priority areas. In those, we fund science within them but we add to that, advocacy and politics. Take vaccines and pandemics, which is one of our priority areas: in addition to funding science in that area, we've sought to influence governments at the G7, the United Nations, and a range of other places. And we've leveraged support from others like the Gates Foundation.

Are there any downsides to making a philanthropic foundation permanent?

There could be. But if you are determined to go on experimenting, being ambitious – realizing that your independence doesn't just give you freedom, but responsibility to take the risks I've been talking about – I think those are very strong advantages. The downsides would be if a foundation became stale, always did the same thing, didn't change itself, just became self-perpetuating or self-satisfied. But I think a really important characteristic of Wellcome is that we challenge ourselves probably more than anybody outside challenges us. We've got to be sure that we're giving ourselves as hard a time as the voters might give government funding.

What mechanisms do you use to challenge yourselves?

We're much better at it than we used to be. At Executive Leadership Team meetings, and Board meetings, we're always looking at our ways of doing things. Could we do this better? Could we do it more efficiently?

Is it built into your templates and processes?

Yes. I think there is a danger with individual philanthropists, however wise and generous they are, that they have fixations which may cease to be valid, and quite often they want things to go on in perpetuity that shouldn't, whereas we are sufficiently flexible, that we can stop doing things and we don't have to do anything in perpetuity. It's always quite difficult when people found things with their name on. They want them to go on forever, but we're full of disruptive technologies and the world is changing very rapidly. We've got to be quick on our feet to make sure we're investing in things of the future, not things of the past. And we need a long-term horizon – both in terms of the science we fund but also in our investments.

In what sense?

I'll give you two little stories. When I was very early on here, I listened to a bid of a candidate who we'd been funding for 20 years. He was coming back for a further tranche of funding for another five or seven years. Being ignorant at that stage, I said, 'Goodness, why is he taking so long?' All the scientists rounded on me and said, 'Science, to get from A to B to C to D, via all sorts of circuitous routes and roadblocks and changes and diversions, often takes a long time and we have to be patient. Actually, he's going at a much greater speed than you might expect.' So long-term matters.

Secondly, we can invest in things that aren't actually going to give us a return for 30 years. That allows us to buy things at good value which nobody else wants to buy, because we don't have shareholders screaming at us. In 2018 we decided we'd try and raise £750 million by issuing a bond. The bidding started early in the morning and before long we were oversubscribed to the tune of three-point-something billion. Eventually investors bought their share of the bond at 2.4 per cent. The point of the story is, this was over 100 years. So we've borrowed 750 million over 100 years at around 2.5 per cent, which if you think what inflation will be in that century is very cheap money.

So being able to have that long-term time horizon is very helpful for both our investments and the science we fund. Many scientists can spend their life, literally, on one particular problem, and it won't be till their successor-but-three that we get the answer. But each scientist will be a key stage on the way.

Such a long-term perspective raises the question of accountability. A government is answerable to the electorate, a business to shareholders, a charity to the public who donate its funds. But who do you answer to – for the way you spend that money?

We did some work on this last year because we realized we were unclear about who we're accountable to. We thought long and hard about it and we had plenty of discussions. We concluded that we are really accountable to the society for whose health we're trying to find improvements. It's not just British society, it's the world. The difficulty is: how do they hold us accountable, because many of them have never heard of us? Many of them have no idea that we're behind the treatment they're receiving, particularly in the developing world. That's something that we have had difficulty resolving. What we have ended up with is this: we say to ourselves, whenever we're making decisions – on expenditure or direction of travel or priority areas – that we must at all times think first about the people who are going to be receiving it at the end. So that if one of them came in and said, 'Why have you spent this amount of money on X?' we could give an account of ourselves in describing what advance in human health we were hoping to have from that.

If they said to you, 'Well, that's not how we see it. We think this is a bigger problem than that', what's your response?

We haven't got to that stage yet. They can write to us at any time or email us. Next door in the Wellcome Collection* we quite often get comments or expressions of opinion. And obviously we get feedback from the people who we don't give grants to or the people we choose not to fund – though in a way they're not the people to whom we're accountable. We have a duty towards them. We have an obligation to treat them fairly and decently and judge fairly between them, but they don't have an entitlement to the money we're giving out. Our accountability to our mission has to override that. But we've spotted what's been happening with some American foundations where people like the Koch brothers are funding some terrific science but are very interfering politically. That reminds us that we couldn't and shouldn't do that.

Do you have an actual accountability process?

I wouldn't say there was a process. What we've done is given a lot of thought to it – and we believe that we can give an account for ourselves. But nobody is actually calling us to do so. We definitely have a policy that we fess up. If it's clear that we've messed up, which we sometimes do – or if we've got something rather wrong which we regret – we're open about it. But if you're a person who's had brain surgery as a result of research funded by us, you might not have a clue that we existed. That's slowly changing. When I joined the trust, which is now a dozen years ago, I said, 'Why do more people not know about us?' I was told that we don't blow our own trumpet. But that misses the point. We're not blowing our own trumpet. We're trying to blow trumpets for science and how to advance human health.

So accountability is about recognizing that everybody has a legitimate interest in what we do. We don't feel that questions to us, or challenges too, are somehow impertinent. Rather we feel we have a responsibility to listen to them. We try and answer them. We cannot be transparent about everything we do. (There are some issues of confidentiality.) But our aim is to be as open as we possibly can, and about as much as possible.

---

* The Wellcome Collection is a free museum and library at its London headquarters with exhibitions, lectures, broadcasts and digital publishing about the connections between science, medicine, life and art.

And, of course, as you've already implied, in philanthropy a lack of accountability can be a strength as well as a weakness. It allows you to take more risks.

That's a really important flip side. If we have the privilege of not having to account to the Treasury or to shareholders or to voters, that should allow us to do something which would be difficult for people who do have to answer to those groups. That brings us straight back to the Leap Fund.

How do you decide what is enough risk, too much risk, not enough risk?

We try and push ourselves to have a greater appetite for risk than we might first of all have. One of our principles is 'Be bold.' When we are deciding on things, we think about accountability, we think about our principles, and boldness in taking risks is one of them. There isn't a definitive answer to your question, because it moves. Obviously, there are whole lot of things on which we're totally risk-averse – health and safety, financial acuity and so on – but on some of the science we want to take risks. If we're not having failures, we're not taking enough risk . . .

People say that, but in practice how do you ensure that?

Well, science is unpredictable. I can remember a case of a person who spent ages doing a TB vaccine. When it went into clinical trials, it completely failed. Was that a waste of our money? No, because in the process, a lot was learned and next time we have a potential TB vaccine – which it looks as though we might have at the moment – we are building on the shoulders of what failed last time.

What we do have is a success framework to try and judge our own performance and our own success. It's not like the bottom line in a company, because if you go back to my TB story, the first scientist hadn't found a vaccine, but by some measures she'd been very successful.

Because she eliminated a lot of blind alleys?

Yes. It doesn't seem to me that this issue of accountability is static. As I said, it does have some weaknesses in how do 'the public' actually hold us to account. But I don't think we'll stop there. It's something we will come back to and think about ways we can improve.

Chapter 17

Effective Altruism – What Could be Wrong with That?

Hardly anyone noticed one crucial detail when Mark Zuckerberg and his wife Priscilla Chan announced one of the biggest acts of philanthropy ever. To mark the birth of their daughter in 2015, the founder of Facebook and his paediatrician wife wrote an open letter to the new baby. Posted, aptly enough, on his Facebook page, it announced that the couple had decided to give away 99 per cent of their shares in the company – valued at \$45 billion on the day of the announcement.[1] That sounded like the largest charitable gift in history – bigger than Warren Buffett's \$30 billion donation to the Gates Foundation in 2006. Indeed, it exceeded the assets of the entire Gates Foundation.[2] The money was to go towards tackling some of the biggest problems their daughter, Max, and her generation might face – heart disease, cancer, stroke, neuro-degenerative and infectious diseases. They pledged to begin the transfer of their fortune by giving \$1 billion a year for the next three years to 'have a real shot at preventing, curing or managing all or most' of these diseases. That was not all. They wanted to address the inequality of opportunity which faced the next generation by empowering people 'regardless of the nation, families or circumstances they are born into' – and lobbying to influence governments to do the same. 'We want you to grow up in a world better than ours today,' they wrote to their newborn baby. It was an extraordinarily ambitious agenda.

Their decision was widely applauded. The newspapers and television stations were filled with praise. Their fellow billionaire philanthropist

Warren Buffett congratulated Zuckerberg and Chan, proclaiming of the couple, who were in their early thirties, that when it comes to giving away your fortune, '30 is the new 70'.[3] The young couple had joined Buffett, Bill Gates and a number of other billionaires in a commitment to 'giving while living' rather than seeking to pass their fortunes down to their descendants. Having created a hugely successful company that has generated almost unimaginable wealth, Zuckerberg – on behalf of a new generation – was sending a powerful message to Wall Street hedge fund managers, Russian oligarchs, European industrialists, Arab oil sheiks, and anybody else who has accumulated a vast fortune: from those to whom much is given, much is expected.[4]

There were a few doubters. Zuckerberg's first big venture into philanthropy, five years earlier, had not been a great success. In 2010 he had given $100 million to a flagship project to reform schools in Newark, New Jersey, across the river from New York. His idea, he announced, was not simply to save education in one large city but rather to 'develop a model for saving it in all of urban America'. Yet much of the money was wasted, according to an investigation by Dale Russakoff for the *New Yorker*. She reported that $30 million went on a back-pay deal demanded by the teachers' union and $20 million went on consultants who were hired at $1,000 a day – but that top teachers did not see the additional merit pay they were promised and that parents were not consulted about the changes to the system which were introduced with precipitate speed.[5]

Zuckerberg later admitted that he knew little about urban education policy and had never even been to Newark. He had given the money, he said, because he had found the two local politicians behind the plan persuasive in their pitch. 'Newark is really just because I believe in these guys,' he told Russakoff with disarming candour.[6] The project was widely condemned as a failure.[7] One local resident protested, referring to one of the pupils who was supposed to be being helped: 'Everybody's getting paid, but Raheem still can't read.' Five years and a huge amount of money produced more rancour than reform, said the *Washington Post*.[8] Zuckerberg had shrugged that off. He suffered no ill effects beyond having to admit he'd made mistakes – which he did, five years later, on his Facebook page.[9] The sociologist Beth Breeze sardonically noted: 'A failed philanthropic experiment does not result in the donor losing his or her job or elected office. They are, perhaps uniquely, free to follow Samuel Beckett's advice to: "Try again. Fail again. Fail better.""[10]

And, indeed, Zuckerberg and Chan did try again. Four years later, in 2014, they donated \$120 million to improve schools in San Francisco's Bay Area – only this time the improved classroom technology and better teacher-training that they funded were introduced incrementally, and in consultation with families, teachers, elected officials and other experts in the local community.[11] 'It's a very, very different and much more humble approach to trying to change education,' Dale Russakoff now observed.[12] A year later Zuckerberg joined Bill Gates and other business leaders to launch a clean-energy research initiative, the Breakthrough Energy Coalition, after the 2015 United Nations Climate Change Conference.

Yet despite all that, for some, the shadow of Newark hung over the Zuckerbergs' big 2015 announcement. In that confession on Facebook, Zuckerberg had said by way of mitigation: 'Change in education takes time and requires a long-term focus. We are committed to working to improve public education for many years to come, and to improving our approach as we go.' Five years, one critic noted, is not a long time to fix a failing system, but it is a long time in the life of a child who is being failed. All of that was recalled by sceptics who spoke of hubris when the ambitious Chan Zuckerberg Initiative was announced in 2015.

Perhaps that was unfair. Mark Zuckerberg clearly had sought to learn the lessons of his early errors. But what it did mean was that his big \$45 billion announcement was subjected to closer scrutiny than might otherwise have been the case. Several diligent reporters contacted the US Securities and Exchange Commission to consult the papers which Facebook Inc had filed there about its boss's new charity. They discovered it was not a charity at all. Its title was the Chan Zuckerberg Initiative LLC. The three letters at the end of the name were significant. They stood for Limited Liability Company. Zuckerberg had decided to break from the example of his childhood hero Bill Gates. Instead of setting up a charitable foundation, he had opted for a structure which was a cross between a corporation and a business partnership. It was an altogether more flexible arrangement. A Gates-style not-for-profit foundation is required to give away 5 per cent of its money to charitable causes each year. It is also bound to publish tax returns which are open to scrutiny by the public. By contrast an LLC is not legally restricted to give only to charity. It can invest in commercial businesses and give funds to political parties, both of which are outlawed for charitable foundations. Moreover, it is not obliged to make its activities public. The documents lodged at the Securities and Exchange Commission showed that Mark Zuckerberg had complete control of 'the voting and disposition of any shares' in the Chan Zuckerberg Initiative. He intended to 'retain his majority voting position' in the organization 'for the foreseeable future'.[13]

Sceptics immediately responded by saying that the $45 billion gift was therefore some kind of tax-saving ploy. In many ways, said the *New York Times*, what the Zuckerbergs had devised was 'more like a private investment vehicle for the couple'.[14] The ProPublica investigative journalist Jesse Eisinger complained that Zuckerberg had simply 'moved money from one pocket to the other'. Although he had amassed one of the greatest fortunes in the world he was 'likely never to pay any taxes on it'.[15] The sociologist Linsey McGoey dismissed the Initiative as business rebranded as philanthropy; good deeds did not blend with good deals, she suggested. 'Philanthrocapitalism is what happens to charity after capitalists swallow it,' she added tartly.[16] Peter Bloom and Carl Rhodes, authors of *CEO Society: The Corporate Takeover of Everyday Life*, asserted there was an incompatibility between 'being generous, seeking to retain control over what is given, and the expectation of reaping benefits in return'. They called the Zuckerberg strategy a 'reformulation of generosity'.[17]

Mark Zuckerberg hit back at his critics on his Facebook page, insisting that the new structure was the opposite of a tax dodge. 'By using an LLC instead of a traditional foundation, we receive no tax benefit from transferring our shares to the Chan Zuckerberg Initiative, but we gain flexibility to execute our mission more effectively,' he wrote. 'Being structured as an LLC allows the Chan Zuckerberg Initiative to support any idea – whether it's from a non-profit or a for-profit organization working on issues we care about – that could make a real difference in people's lives.' It would, for example, allow CZI to invest in a clean energy company, which it hoped might make a profit but which was undoubtedly good for the environment. It was entirely wrong to suggest the structure conferred a tax advantage. 'In fact, if we transferred our shares to a traditional foundation, then we would have received an immediate tax benefit, but by using an LLC we do not.'

Indeed, an LLC might even generate additional tax liabilities as they could be taxed on any profits the LLC made and would have to pay capital gains tax if they sold Facebook shares through the new Initiative.

It was slightly more complicated than that, pointed out John Cassidy in the *New Yorker*. If the Chan Zuckerberg Initiative made grants to charities in the form of Facebook shares, rather than cash, that would generate tax credits for Zuckerberg and Chan, which 'seem likely to add up to very large sums'. By transferring almost all of their fortunes to philanthropic organizations, billionaires like Zuckerberg and Gates 'are placing some very large chunks of wealth permanently outside the reaches of the Internal Revenue Service. That means the country's tax base shrinks,' Cassidy noted.[18] The taxes the Zuckerbergs were avoiding could have been used by the government to fund public priorities. Instead, the money was allocated according to the personal preferences of two wealthy individuals, wrote Vassilisa Rubtsova in the *Berkeley Economic Review*, 'with very little accountability or transparency, and absolutely no democratic or political process that takes into account the will of the people'. The Chan Zuckerberg Initiative, she said, 'exemplifies the shift of philanthropy from charity to capitalism'.[19]

Mark Zuckerberg himself was anxious to make a slightly different distinction. One media company reported that it had been contacted by an ad agency employed by Facebook anxious to correct its reporting on the subject.[20] The Zuckerberg money would be invested in a number of projects where the recipient will not be a charity but the result will be of public benefit. The Chan Zuckerberg pledge, it insisted, was not charity; it was philanthropy. It is a distinction which is something new in the history of philanthropy.

THE GEEKS INHERIT THE EARTH

Mark Zuckerberg is far from alone in this shift to a wider definition of philanthropy as an expression of private wealth in pursuit of public good. Limited Liability Companies are becoming an increasingly popular financial vehicle in philanthropy, particularly among new technology donors.[21] Pierre Omidyar, co-founder of e-Bay, uses a hybrid structure which incorporates an LLC in his Omidyar Network to invest $900 million in companies and non-profit organizations dedicated to bringing economic, social and political change. Laurene Powell, widow of the Apple guru Steve Jobs, chose an LLC as the basis for her Emerson Collective, which focuses on social justice causes including activism over immigration reform.[22] Part of her armoury is investments in a range of media outlets, including *The Atlantic* magazine. The LLC enables all that, in the same way that a green campaigner can use an LLC to make investments in companies working on green energy, donate to charities fighting climate change and buy bonds in green investments, says Kimberly Dasher Tripp, a San Francisco philanthropy consultant.[23] For Laurene Powell Jobs it also helps guard her privacy.

This hybrid strategy is becoming more common, as people seek flexibility, freedom and anonymity in their investments, says Laura Arrillaga-Andreessen, who teaches philanthropy at Stanford University. 'We are now seeing a blurring of the lines between the sectors in a way that was not even discussed 10 years ago. The way that we are going to solve social problems is by working with multiple different types of investing.'[24] But it also means there is even less transparency than before about which organizations receive grants and the size of those grants.

But the LLC is not the only alternative vehicle to which younger philanthropists are turning. Many began giving on a large scale far younger than did the previous generation. The world's billionaires increasingly include individuals who started out as computer programmers with a free-thinking 'hacker mentality' that led them to innovations which earned them enormous fortunes. These internet innovators should now use the 'disrupter' talents that made them rich to transform the world of philanthropy, argues Sean Parker, the billionaire creator of the music file-sharing service Napster and founding president of Facebook. He has even coined a term for it: 'hacker philanthropy'. Setting out his ideas in a manifesto in the *Wall Street Journal* he wrote:

Hackers share certain values: an anti-establishment bias, a belief in radical transparency, a nose for sniffing out vulnerabilities in systems, a desire to 'hack' complex problems using elegant technological and social solutions, and an almost religious belief in the power of data . . .

This newly minted hacker elite is an aberration in the history of wealth creation. They achieved success at a young age . . . At the same time, they are intensely idealistic, so as they begin to confront the world's most pressing humanitarian problems, they are still young, naive and perhaps arrogant enough to believe that they can solve them . . .

This budding sense of purpose is now bringing the hacker elite into contact with traditional philanthropy – a strange and alien world made up of largely antiquated institutions . . . in which the primary currency of exchange is recognition and reputation, not effectiveness . . .

Hackers have shown themselves to be less interested in this conventional form of philanthropy. Instead . . . this new generation of philanthropists wants to believe there is a clever 'hack' for every problem, and they have launched a number of radical experiments.[25]

Parker has in mind initiatives like that of his co-Facebook founder Dustin Moskovitz who – hearing of the chequered history of a long list of failed projects attempting to transform one of the world's biggest slums, the shanty town of Kibera, in the Kenyan capital of Nairobi – decided to try sending cash directly to the mobile phones of Kibera's residents instead.

Hacker philanthropists, Parker says, are willing to make bold experiments and embrace failure as a learning experience. His own philanthropy offers another example. With a personal and family history of asthma and allergies he has long taken an interest in the human immune system. This led him to wonder whether the body's own immune system could be 'hacked' and used to fight tumours. He discovered that such work was considered too speculative to attract traditional sources of funding. So Parker pledged $250 million to reshape the field of cancer immunology. The result was a new Parker Institute for Cancer Immunotherapy, which funds the work of 300 scientists at 40 laboratories in six major universities and hospitals. The teams aim to pool their research to speed up the development of new drugs.[26] In such innovative work 'private philanthropists can step in and have a huge impact,' Parker told the *Financial Times*.[27] So engaged has he become that he now spends more time on his philanthropy projects than he does on his continuing high-tech business interests. 'This is both much more intellectually interesting and a lot more rewarding than building yet another product for teenage girls.'

These new younger philanthropists are turning to a variety of tools, according to Emmett D. Carson, the former chief executive of the Silicon Valley Community Foundation, a not-for-profit organization through which the new tech titans have channelled funds worth $13 billion over recent years.[28] Parker, in pursuit of his philanthropy, uses a conventional charitable foundation but also commercial companies. His Cancer Institute has an innovative structure which allows its academics to retain the intellectual property rights over their research, but the Institute takes the lead in licensing and negotiating with industry to bring any therapies to market.[29] Among the new structures used by the current generation of high-tech philanthropists are the controversial donor-advised funds.[30]

FLEXIBLE GIVING – OR TAX SCAM?

Donor-advised funds were pioneered by community foundations in the 1930s. They were designed to allow philanthropists to reap the tax advantages which they would have obtained if they had set up their own charitable foundation – but without the administrative cost and effort that would involve. More than that, they earned tax deductions for the donor as soon as the donations were made, and yet allowed the donor to postpone the decisions about what the money should be spent on until some time in the future. But it was only in the late 1990s that donor-advised funds (DAFs) began to grow in visibility and popularity after philanthropists realized that they had another key advantage. Contributions to these donor-directed foundations do not have to be made public, so individuals or corporations can hide their identity. They can also keep hidden the causes they choose to fund. Today, DAFs are philanthropy's fastest-growing vehicle in both Britain and America. In the United States there are now more than five times more DAFs than private foundations. In the US their assets exceeded $110 billion in 2018 – and now account for 3 per cent of all philanthropic grant-making. In the UK some £1.3 billion has been lodged in DAFs in concealed donations – and it is predicted to rise by £1 billion a year by 2025.[31]

Donor-advised funds gained in popularity thanks to the work of a right-wing fundraiser, Whitney Ball, who set out to find a funding mechanism by which ultra-conservative philanthropists could secretly give money to controversial causes. Efforts to limit voting rights, restrict abortion, promote Islamophobia, or discriminate against LGBT people have all been funded in this clandestine way. Ball had previously worked at the Cato Institute in the policy world funded by conservatives and libertarians like the Koch brothers. In 1999 she founded Donors Trust 'to help donors promote liberty' through 'limited government, personal responsibility, and free enterprise'.[32] A second DAF, Donors Capital Fund, was set up operating out of the same town house in Washington DC to handle larger donations, of $1 million or more.

The funds were designed to offer a counterweight to the more progressive agenda of most major philanthropic foundations. Ball assured wealthy donors that – whereas permanent foundations established by the philanthropists of the past might have their aims altered over the years by successions of trustees – Donors Trust funds would never be diverted to liberal causes. Nor, once money is locked up inside such DAFs, can it later be redirected by the donor's heirs who may differ in terms of their political philosophy. As we saw in Chapter 15, it was these funds which were used to funnel 'dark money' to fund think tanks and academics to create a 'climate change counter movement'.[*] They have also been used to promote the reform of trade unions, state education, and to press for the continuing deregulation of the economy. Their bias is quite open: 'Greenpeace won't get a dime from us,' Ball told the *National Review* in 2001.[33] But the confidentiality of DAFs was absolute, with the result that it is hard to identify who gives – or what causes they fund. DAFs are far more secretive even than foundations.

But it was not just conservative ideologues who recognized the advantages of the DAF system. They became more generally used, and on such a scale that a DAF managed by Goldman Sachs quietly gathered holdings of £3.2 billion. Secrecy ought to have protected the identities of the donors, but a slip-up by the US tax authorities in 2018 revealed that the former chief executive of Microsoft, Steve Ballmer, poured $1.9 billion into the fund. It also disclosed that Laurene Powell Jobs – whose Emerson Collective had chosen an LLC structure rather than that of a charitable foundation – had placed $526 million in the same DAF. And Jan Koum, who co-founded WhatsApp and then sold it to Facebook Inc in 2014, had contributed $114 million.[34] It also emerged that the Silicon Valley Community Foundation in the San Francisco Bay Area had become a similar vehicle for high-tech entrepreneurs who had just profited from a major windfall. In 2012, just months after Facebook went public, Mark Zuckerberg donated $500 million

---

[*] See page 584 above.

of Facebook shares to the foundation which, despite its low-key name, is a massive warehouse of donor-advised funds which make it America's third biggest philanthropy, with more money than the Ford Foundation. In 2014, soon after Facebook acquired WhatsApp for $19 billion, Jan Koum and his co-founder Brian Acton donated a combined $846 million to the foundation, reaping both men a significant tax advantage on their windfall. Other billionaire donors to the same foundation included Netflix's Reed Hastings, Twitter's Jack Dorsey, Google's Sergey Brin and Microsoft's Paul Allen.[35] The Zuckerbergs' total contribution to the fund in 2018 stood at $1.75 billion.[36]

That year the *New York Times* launched an investigation into the private workings of the Silicon Valley Community Foundation. It focused on a donation of $500 million worth of stock by Nicholas Woodman, founder of the video camera and software company GoPro. Woodman announced the gift just after taking his company public when it suddenly became worth $3 billion. The donation was made not in cash but in GoPro shares. He announced that he was forming the Jill and Nicholas Woodman Foundation whose assets would be housed in a DAF lodged in the Silicon Valley Community Foundation. Four years on, the *New York Times* was asking what had happened to the Woodman Foundation. 'The foundation has no website and has not listed its areas of focus, and it is not known what – if any – significant grants it has made,' the newspaper reported. 'An extensive search of public records turned up just one beneficiary: the Bonny Doon Art, Wine and Brew Festival, a benefit for an elementary school in California.' The Silicon Valley Community Foundation, it noted, 'is not required to disclose details about how, if at all, individual donors spend their charitable dollars'.[37]

But if the benefit to good causes was hard to see, the benefit to Nicholas Woodman was clear. GoPro's successful flotation had confronted him with an enormous tax bill that year. His donation of stock worth $500 million eased that tax burden in two ways. It meant he avoided paying capital gains taxes which would have run into tens of millions of dollars. And it made him eligible for a tax deduction which probably reduced his personal tax bill for years to come. The problem was that the share price of GoPro then dramatically fell – from $86 per share at the time of the gift to less than $6 per share by the middle of 2019.[38] The value of the shares held in the DAF plummeted over those four years – and yet Nicholas Woodman's tax savings were pegged to the shares' all-time high. 'Smart donors have been playing timing games with the charitable deduction for a long time,' the *New York Times* was told by Roger Colinvaux, a tax professor at the Catholic University of America's law school. 'In this case, he potentially gets a very large deduction and gives nothing away. That's a disturbing public policy issue.' Woodman defended himself in an online chatroom, insisting that his donated money was reaching charities: 'The Foundation has gone on to fund causes supporting women and children and will continue to do so!!!!'[39] But Woodman is not required to provide any evidence for that claim.

The overall system of DAFs was defended by Karey Dye, president of the Goldman Sachs Philanthropy Fund. 'People have irrevocably given money away to charity,' she said. But Ed Kleinbard, a tax professor at the University of Southern California, was unimpressed. DAFs are 'a fraud on the American taxpayer,' he said. 'They're a way for the affluent to have their cake and eat it, too.'[40] A number of law professors want to see the law changed to lessen the secrecy and the potential for abuse. There are no rules on how long donors can retain funds in their accounts without ever giving them to charity; they can even leave the decision to their heirs. Donors are even allowed to moved funds from one DAF to another. 'We've put this rule in place that says you get maximum tax benefits when you make a donation,' said Professor Ray Madoff of the Boston College Law School. 'But you don't have to do anything with it.' Colinvaux and Madoff, point out that DAFs have not increased the overall amounts given to charity; they have merely diverted giving away from traditional philanthropy. They want rules to oblige donors to spend their funds within a set time. To justify the tax advantages they are given DAFs should be seen to donate to charities which 'serve the neediest among us, strengthen civil society, promote pluralism, reduce the burdens on government, and fuel our economy,' Madoff and Colinvaux have told the US Senate.[41]

No one has questioned the good faith of Mark Zuckerberg and Priscilla Chan or accused them of engaging in dubious activity. But concerns are voiced as to the opacity of the Chan Zuckerberg Initiative. As a limited liability company, CZI is not required to list donations on its tax forms. For the first three years of its existence it announced a number of its grants on Facebook or in press releases, but the amounts and identities of the vast majority of its recipients were kept private. In 2018 the education website Chalkbeat pressed CZI to release more details about the millions it had given to 'personalize learning, reshape teacher training, and diversify the ranks of education leaders'. The Zuckerbergs revealed that, since it began operations in January 2016, the organization had given £308 million in education grants – via its donor-advised fund with the Silicon Valley Community Foundation. But the details of the 19 specific grants it provided only added up to a third of the total amount given.[42] The largest was $30 million for a Harvard/MIT project, Reach Every Reader, to develop a web-based screening tool to diagnose reading difficulties in pre-school children.[43]

The scale of the donations was such that only two philanthropic funders – the Gates and Walton Family foundations – have given more. This raised questions, Chalkbeat said, on 'the appropriate role for private dollars in education policy'. Chalkbeat suggested that, as CZI's billions continued to enter the education system, its influence on the US public education service would grow even more significantly. This was because Zuckerberg had said he would steadily sell Facebook stock as its price rose – and transfer more funds to the Chan Zuckerberg Initiative. The challenge, therefore, says Jeff Snyder, who works on education philanthropy at Cleveland State University, is this: can limited liability companies like the Zuckerbergs' fund 'evolve into institutions that democratically work with communities they seek to shape?'[44] The degree of secrecy built into LLCs – and even more so into DAFs – add an extra layer of impenetrability which make it harder for the public to know what is being done with donations to which the taxpayer has given a massive subsidy.

In answer to such questions the Chan Zuckerberg Initiative shifted its policy a year later. In March 2019 it published an interactive database of its grant-giving going back to 2018. It has promised to update the information every February.[45] The move brought CZI in line with the best practice of the Gates and Walton Family foundations, which have for some time now published searchable lists of their grants going back many years. But the Zuckerbergs have yet to do the same for their DAFs.

Overall, it is hard not to conclude that in recent years there has been a rapid growth in what David Callahan has called 'a shadow giving system that funnels billions of dollars in gifts in ways that leave no fingerprints'. Never before has so much giving occurred in secret. 'The world of philanthropy is becoming less transparent, and that's not a good thing.'[46]

TWO WAYS FORWARD FOR PHILANTHROPY

Mark Zuckerberg's new model has taken philanthrocapitalism a step further than that of the generation of Bill Gates. But it is a further step down the same road. The Zuckerberg generation, like that of Gates and Buffett, is excited by big new ideas. It is driven by the urge to find innovative technical solutions that focus philanthropy where it can have the greatest impact. It is concerned with efficiency and effectiveness and sees a knowledge-based approach as likely to produce the best results. It sees benevolence in terms of an investment targeted at a specific problem to which it can bring a specific solution. It is convinced that the techniques and approach which brought such success in business will do the same in philanthropy. Modern philanthrocapitalism is growing ever stronger.

But its strengths are also its weaknesses. It is driven by the hunches of the individual philanthropist. Areas of activity and approaches are determined top-down by the personal whim of the man or woman with the money. As in the days of Andrew Carnegie and his fellow philanthropists, this new generation of self-made men and women are convinced that they know best. The success of their entrepreneurial activity has persuaded them of the general superiority of their own judgement. As the course of this book has shown, that is a sense which the rich have embraced throughout history, whether they have earned their riches through special talent and application or simply fallen into them by good fortune. But the Chan Zuckerberg generation – with their LLCs and DAFs – have the tools and mechanisms to entrench that sense of superiority and entitlement to a new degree.

However, another thread has consistently run through the chapters of this book. It is that philanthropy is not simply something to be measured in material terms. Philanthropy may, as Professors Madoff and Colinvaux told the US Senate, serve the needy, strengthen civil society, promote pluralism, reduce the burden on government, and fuel our economy. But it does something more. At its best it creates a bond between those who give and those who receive. That bond is personal, communal and in some sense reciprocal because it acknowledges that philanthropy requires something of both the giver and the receiver. What I will call Reciprocal Philanthropy places both responsibilities and rights on each side. That has been clear since the Middle Ages when, for all the rigid economic and material inequalities of the medieval era, charity placed as much emphasis on the relationship between giver and receiver as on the value of the gift itself. This is summed up in the words of Thomas Aquinas, quoting St Paul: 'If I bestow all my goods to feed the poor but have not love, it profits me nothing.'[47] Philanthropy can create a relationship, not just between donor and recipient, but also with wider society. It is part of what binds a community together. Philanthropy should not just bring personal satisfaction but also social harmony.

Philanthrocapitalism has brought practical gains in the clarity of its focus, but it has also lost a sense of these deeper, almost spiritual dimensions. What philanthropy needs in the twenty-first century is to bring together the strengths of both these philanthropic traditions. In these final two chapters I want to look at the philosophies which underpin these two approaches in the hope of arriving at a synthesis to produce the best of both worlds.

THE MAN WHO GAVE HIS KIDNEY AWAY

Zell Kravinsky made his money buying and selling property. He started by renting out the other half of the house where he and his girlfriend lived and ended up with a $45 million property empire. But, though he was good at business, he was unsatisfied with life. He did not just one but two PhDs – the first in Rhetoric, the second on Milton's *Paradise Lost*. He wrote poetry. He taught literature at the University of Pennsylvania where the students loved his classes. It was not enough. As his property portfolio grew, so did the impulse to do something more. Just before 2000 he began to talk about giving away all his money. For years his friends tried to dissuade him. But in 2002 he gave away a large apartment building so it could become a school for the disabled and donated over $6 million to the US Center for Disease Control. It was still not enough. So, retaining only his modest family home and enough to meet his family's ordinary expenses, he gave everything else away. 'He gave away the money because he had it and there were people who needed it,' his friend Barry Katz said. 'But it changed his way of looking at himself. He decided the purpose of his life was to give away things.'[48]

Yet even that was not enough. He had read in the *Wall Street Journal* that thousands of people with failing kidneys die each year while waiting for a transplant because there was a shortage of organs available. He also discovered that donors had only a one-in-four-thousand chance of dying after giving away a kidney. Kravinsky resolved that, having given away almost all his money, he should give away one of his two kidneys too. 'I had a one-in-four-thousand chance of dying,' Kravinsky told Ian Parker of the *New Yorker.* 'But my recipient had a certain death facing her.' To Kravinsky the calculation was straightforward: 'I'd be valuing my life at four thousand times hers if I let consideration of mortality sway me.' This 4,000-to-one ratio was, he said, 'obscene'.[49]

He discussed with his family and friends the idea of donating one of his kidneys. 'I thought, at first, that people would understand. But they don't understand math,' he told Parker. 'I've had to repeat it over and over. Some people eventually got it. But many people felt the way my wife did: she said, "No matter how infinitesimal the risk to your family, we're your family, and the recipient doesn't count".' Kravinsky resolved to go ahead without his wife's consent. 'I can't allow her to take this person's life!' he told a friend, declaring that anybody who could donate a kidney, and does not, was by definition taking someone's life.

Kravinsky contacted a Philadelphia hospital and announced his intention to donate one of his kidneys to a complete stranger. They tried to dissuade him, but he was adamant. At 6 a.m. one morning Zell Kravinsky crept out of his house while his wife and children were still asleep. Emily Kravinsky learned that her husband had donated a kidney when she read about it that evening in a local newspaper.[50]

Some time later the moral philosopher Peter Singer read about what Kravinsky had done and invited him to Princeton to address the university's philosophy students. Kravinsky was the living embodiment of the ultra-utilitarian philosophy Singer had been developing called 'Effective Altruism'. It asserts that living a fully ethical life involves doing the most good we can and – since all human lives have equal value – we are all obliged to do as much to help others as we can. 'What marks Kravinsky from the rest of us,' wrote Singer afterwards, 'is that he takes the equal value of all human life as a guide to life, not just as a nice piece of rhetoric.' Rather he 'puts his altruism in mathematical terms'.

There was no moral justification for placing a greater value on our own lives than we do on the lives of strangers, Kravinsky told the students. He even went so far as to suggest that if a scientist was on the verge of curing cancer, but was about to die from kidney failure, Kravinsky would feel it morally incumbent upon himself to donate his second kidney to the scientist – if his kidney was the only correct match in the world – in order to save the lives of millions of cancer sufferers. Singer called Kravinsky 'a remarkable person who has taken very seriously questions of what are our moral obligations to assist people . . . I think it's very difficult for people to go as far as he has, and I don't think we should blame people who don't, but we should admire those who do.'

The case of Zell Kravinsky illustrates, in peculiarly stark form, the principles at work behind Effective Altruism – the philosophy which has found favour with many of today's philanthrocapitalists, most particularly among the tech titans of Silicon Valley. Indeed, Singer's Ethical Altruism slogan 'All Lives Have Equal Value' appears in large capital letters at the top of the website of the Bill & Melinda Gates Foundation. PayPal founder Peter Thiel, Skype developer Jaan Tallinn and Tesla CEO Elon Musk are all enthusiasts.

Ethical Altruism, abbreviated by its disciples to EA, has much in common with philanthrocapitalism. Both are enthusiasts for subjecting data to ruthless scrutiny to determine the most efficient way of operating. EA insists every life has equal value and the goal of philanthropy should be to save as many lives as possible. So resources should be used where they can save most lives. Donors should avoid falling into the trap of giving to what makes them feel good and instead choose what has the greatest impact. To do this EA enthusiasts, like philanthrocapitalists, deploy metrics to gauge effectiveness. But where mega-donors do that after their causes have been chosen, Effective Altruists use the same technique to choose the best cause in the first place.[51] Cash gifts save far more lives when they are spent in the developing world, Singer concludes. And the biggest life-savers are organizations which run health-based programmes in the poorest countries. That is where a philanthropist should spend 'to maximise the amount of good we can do'. It is a calculus that coincides almost completely with the spending strategy of the Gates Foundation.

Effective Altruism is rooted in a book entitled *Famine, Affluence and Morality*, which Peter Singer published in 1972 and which was republished in 2016 with a foreword by Bill and Melinda Gates.[52] It begins with a thought experiment which has become known as The Shallow Pond *versus* The Envelope. What would you do, he asks, if you were walking past a shallow pond in which a small child was drowning?

Most people would wade in to save the child, even if it meant ruining their $200 pair of shoes. 'Anything else would be callous, indecent, and, in a word, wrong,' he writes. But what would you then do if you opened an envelope containing an appeal from a charity to give $200 to save the lives of 200 children in a poor country? Many people, Singer laments, will ignore it, and not feel guilty about doing so. But, Singer then argues, there is no moral difference between letting a child drown in front of you and letting one die in a faraway country as a result of extreme poverty. There is a psychological and emotional difference, caused by the fact that you can see one child but not the others. But in moral terms the result is the same. Therefore, Singer insists, those who seek to do good ought to give a large proportion of their income to disaster relief funds.

Developing his argument over the years Singer addresses a number of emotive arguments against this. When someone dies of cancer surely it is moral for their relatives to fund cancer research at home rather than giving to causes overseas? And it must be good for someone in the UK to give to a collection for a child from the next street who has leukaemia and needs to raise £10,000 to fly elsewhere for specialized treatment. Or what about giving to a charity which trains guide dogs for the blind? No, says Singer, such responses are sentimental. The way to maximize 'the good you can do' is to look for more cost-effective ways to donate. The money donated to speculative cancer research would be guaranteed to save lives if it were spent on vitamin supplements in sub-Saharan Africa which have been proven to reduce child mortality. The £10,000 collected to treat one British child with leukaemia could save the lives of 10,000 African children if it was spent on buying insecticide-treated nets to protect their beds against malaria. And the cost of training one guide dog for a single blind person here is the same as saving 30,000 children from river blindness in Africa. 'Do the math,' Singer writes. Use your head as well as your heart.[53] Other Effective Altruists have made similar arguments suggesting that giving to the arts is morally flawed.[54] Singer's arguments have since inspired numerous philanthropic initiatives around the world.

But Effective Altruism applies its data-driven approach to more than our choice of charities. It has also been applied to choosing a career. Its votaries have set up organizations dedicated to assisting idealistic young graduates to find the job in which they can earn the most money – in order to be able to give more to the best charities. Some of those choices are highly counter-intuitive. The inspiration for this was one of Singer's most brilliant philosophy students at Princeton. Matt Wage won the prize for the best thesis in the department when he graduated. He was destined for postgraduate work at Oxford. But instead this young man, with a reputation for deep ethical thinking, took a job at an arbitrage trading firm on Wall Street. Far from disowning Wage as a sell-out, Singer holds his former student up as an exemplar of Effective Altruism. For within a year of graduating he had donated more than $100,000 – roughly half his pre-tax income – to the effective charities favoured by Singer. Matt Wage reckons he is on course to save many more lives than he might have done had he become an aid worker. 'If you somehow saved a dozen people from a burning building, then you might remember that as one of the greatest things you ever did,' Wage told the *New York Times*. 'But it turns out that saving this many lives is within the reach of ordinary people who simply donate a piece of their income.'[55]

'WHY A BANKER IS BETTER THAN AN AID WORKER'

Two of Peter Singer's other acolytes, the Oxford philosophers Toby Ord and William MacAskill, set up organizations to put the ideas into practice. Together in 2009 they started Giving What We Can which, acknowledging its debt to Peter Singer and the German philosopher Thomas Pogge, aims to build an EA community of people who give at least 10 per cent of their income on a regular basis to alleviate world poverty. In 2020 it had more than 4,500 members who had so far given away $126 million to their favoured charities.[56] It is linked to the US organization GiveWell, which was founded by two hedge fund managers at around the same time and is supported by Singer himself. The two groups recommend which charities save most lives with the same donations. Both argue that the impact that different charities have varies dramatically. They contend these differences can be measured by close scrutiny. Those they favour include charities to combat malaria and the parasitic bilharzia worm which swells the stomach of children throughout the developing world. Other preferred charities supply vitamins which make a direct reduction in child mortality. Others run low-cost sight-saving programmes. High on their list are de-worming programmes, which MacAskill claims improve schoolchildren's educational performance more than providing more textbooks or teachers. Both recommend a charity called GiveDirectly, which sends unconditional transfers of cash direct to the mobile phones of very poor individuals in Kenya, Rwanda and Uganda.[57] We shall consider this later.*

In 2011 MacAskill set up another organization named 80,000 Hours – taking the name from the number of hours he estimates people will spend working in their lifetime. It took as its model Matt Wage's example of 'earning to give'. The organization is a careers advice service for idealists. Its website proclaims that it reveals 'which global problems are most pressing, how you can best contribute to solving these problems, and how to plan your career based on your individual strengths and situation'[58]. Together the two organizations are part of the Centre for Effective Altruism headquartered in Oxford. Chapters of Effective Altruists have sprung up among intellectuals in Oxford, London, New York, Princeton, Harvard and Silicon Valley.

At the roots of the whole Effective Altruism movement is the philosophical tradition of utilitarianism. Its founder, the eighteenth-century philosopher Jeremy Bentham, asserted that whatever produces 'the greatest happiness of the greatest number' must be the measure by which society determines what is right and wrong. Utilitarian thinkers have never been able to agree on what exactly constitutes 'happiness', but they do agree that, whatever it is, we need more of it. Individuals should therefore be encouraged to generate as much of it as they can – by 'maximizing good'. Today's utilitarians have different opinions on what counts as 'the most good' and they also debate the extent to which individuals should be expected to make sacrifices to achieve this. Toby Ord fixed a maximum income on which he ought to live – starting at £20,000 a year but later lowered to £18,000.[59] William MacAskill and Peter Singer have pressed for giving to be a percentage of income; Giving What We Can recommends 10 per cent, but Singer has increased his personal giving to a quarter and then a third of his earnings.[60] But then, as Singer concedes, 'there is no logical stopping place' on how much to give away – until the point is reached where donations cause the giver more pain than the recipient is set to gain. Singer calls that 'the point of marginal utility'.[61]

---

* See page 721 below.

One thing is clear. What is 'good' can seem contrary to common sense. In William MacAskill's book *Doing Good Better: Effective Altruism and a Radical New Way to Make a Difference* he lists a number of examples which he describes as counter-intuitive but which others regard as contentious. If you want to improve animal welfare, it is better to stop eating eggs than beef, since caged hens live worse lives than farmed cows – and consumers eat eight times more eggs and chicken than they do beef. Buying locally is not as green as people suppose since only 10 per cent of the carbon footprint of food comes from transport costs; tomatoes grown in the UK can have five times the carbon footprint of tomatoes shipped from Spain because of the energy required to hothouse them. There isn't much point in unplugging your electrics, either: leaving your mobile phone charger plugged in for a whole year contributes less to your carbon footprint than one hot bath.[62] All these are contestable assertions, as is his insistence that fair trade does very little to help the poorest farmers, or that boycotting fashion companies which use sweatshops might make things worse for the global poor. His claim that de-worming contributes to better educational outcomes among schoolchildren in Kenyan than paying for more books or teachers has been challenged. So has his insistence that people who pursue high-income careers such as Wall Street bankers or plastic surgeons can do more good than an aid worker in a refugee camp. MacAskill insists his claims are based on empirical evidence, but they also rely on a raft of other assumptions. If you don't become an aid worker, he suggests, someone else will and they will probably do the job as well as you would. But if someone else takes the job in high finance they probably won't give away half their earnings to effective charities. So he is presupposing marginal benefits not absolute ones.

Moreover the 'empirical evidence' on which all this relies is questionable. For example, MacAskill proposes that doing 'good' can be measured using a unit devised by welfare economists to decide priorities in public spending. A Quality-Adjusted Life-Year (QALY) allows comparisons between needs which would be otherwise hard to compare. One QALY is a single year of life lived at 100 per cent health. According to a standardized scale, a year as an AIDS patient not on antiretrovirals is worth 0.5 QALYs; a year with AIDS lived on antiretrovirals is worth 0.9 QALYs. A year of life for a blind person is worth 0.4 QALYs.

These figures are supposedly derived from self-assessments by AIDS patients and blind people. This, says the philosopher Julian Baggini, is 'Jeremy Bentham's old utilitarian principle of the greatest happiness of the greatest number updated for the age of cost-benefit analysis'.[63] Thinking in terms of QALYs makes it possible to compare that which seemingly cannot be compared: blindness with AIDS; increases in life expectancy with increases in life quality. Or as another philosopher, Amia Srinivasan, sardonically puts it: 'Qalys free us from the specificity of people's lives, giving us a universal currency for misery.'[64] The system enables us to calculate that curing a 20-year-old blind man does more good than giving antiretrovirals to a 40-year-old woman with AIDS. Even if those figures were reliable, which many would challenge, there is something unpalatable about making such a choice. MacAskill then goes on to use QALYs to determine what are the most worthwhile occupations for individuals who want to commit themselves to making the world a better place. Since a doctor practising in a very poor country will save more lives (measured in QALYs) than a doctor practising in the rich world, the career path for an idealist is clear. A pound spent in a poor country, MacAskill asserts, can do one hundred times more good than it can in a rich one.

It's not hard to see why Effective Altruism so appeals to philanthrocapitalists. Both think like investors, looking for the maximum return on the money they lay out. Both understand the importance of selectivity and targeting. Both value critical thinking, using data, evidence and reasoning to determine what will produce the greatest positive impact. One Effective Altruist, Eric Friedman, even suggests donors should move from one cause to the other to create the most positive social change – an approach which would undermine the stability and sustainability of charities. But enthusiasts insist that Effective Altruism may be said to prioritize the poorest, serve redistributive justice, and encourage global empathy. It does all that by forcing donors to look beyond their old university, their local hospital or their favourite ballet company. Instead, EA asserts the value of every life regardless of nationality, creed, ancestry, religion, or proximity.

Most members of the general public today think that Effective Altruists are slightly odd, but then in the past most people thought it was acceptable to benefit from the slave trade, suggests Jeff McMahan, White's Professor of Moral Philosophy at the University of Oxford. In a broadside against critics of Effective Altruism, he writes: 'It is salutary to recall that the early efforts of those we now recognize as having been in the vanguard of moral progress – abolitionists, campaigners for women's rights and female suffrage, vegetarians and opponents of vivisection – have always been fiercely resisted and ridiculed by those to whom it was inconceivable that the common sense view at the time might be mistaken.'[65]

WHAT'S WRONG WITH EFFECTIVE ALTRUISM?

Yet those critics articulate some powerful reservations about Effective Altruism. The philosopher and priest Giles Fraser said of EA: 'There is a hard-headedness here that I find both attractive and disappointing at the same time: attractive because it cuts through the sentimentality that so often drives our charitable giving, making it more about the beneficiaries of our money than our own need for warm and fuzzy feelings; and yet also disappointing because it forces all human need to express itself on a single comparable scale because of the giver's rather nerdish requirement that the world possesses some sort of measurable order.'[66] A similar ambivalence is expressed by Phil Buchanan, chief executive of the Center for Effective Philanthropy, which conducts research and advises the world's largest foundations, including Ford, Hewlett Packard, MacArthur and Rockefeller. 'I do think that the Effective Altruist types have a sort of relentless rationality [which is] a helpful challenge,' he says. 'At the same time, I think it's too absolute. There is a natural human desire to give locally, for example, and to be connected to a community. I don't think we should necessarily tell all givers that they need to squelch that desire and give internationally because their dollars go further. And I also believe that there is a role for thriving arts and cultural organizations in our societies that it's harder to make the case for using Effective Altruists' methodology.'[67] It is worth unpacking some of these qualms as they have particular relevance to the influence of EA on contemporary philanthropy.

The most basic objection to Effective Altruism concerns its over-confidence in the reliability of its empirical evidence. Critics have raised doubts, for example, about the dependability of the study which purports to show the unexpected impact of de-worming on children's education. MacAskill has attempted to rebut their attacks. But the Nobel

prize-winning economist Angus Deaton raises a deeper concern about
the alleged effectiveness of the de-worming initiative which Effective
Altruists continue to place in their list of preferred charities. The
dispute about the trustworthiness of the figures, he says, suggests that
the effectiveness of de-worming varies from place to place depending,
among many other things, on climate and on local arrangements for
the disposal of human waste. He writes:

> More broadly, the evidence for development effectiveness, for
> 'what works', mostly comes from the recent wave of randomized
> experiments, usually done by rich people from the rich world on poor
> people in the poor world, from which the price lists for children's
> lives are constructed. How can those experiments be wrong? Because
> they consider only the immediate effects of the interventions, not the
> contexts in which they are set . . . However counterintuitive it may
> seem, children are not dying for the lack of a few thousand dollars
> to keep them alive. If it were so simple, the world would already be a
> much better place. Development is neither a financial nor a technical
> problem but a political problem.[68]

The real difficulty, Deaton argues, is the chronically disorganized and
underfunded healthcare systems about which most donors concern
themselves very little. They prefer instead to cast themselves as heroic
saviours of the helpless and see those in receipt of their largesse as passive
victims. But why, asks Deaton, 'do the world's poor have such a passive
role in all of this happiness creation?'[69]

An additional problem comes from what Caroline Fiennes calls
'the theory of change' which underpins the way that charities work.
Charities which work direct with a simple solution – distributing
mosquito nets in Africa or delivering wheelchairs to disabled children –
will inevitably score high on the Effective Altruist matrix. 'Their theory
of change . . . is simple,' writes Fiennes. 'The intervention is well
understood, the outcome is predictable, and most of the variables are
clear. From a funder's perspective, the risk is low. These interventions
are like machines, and advertise themselves as such: 'Three dollars in
= one bed net out.'[70] By contrast the theory of change is much more
complex for an international NGO such as Global Witness, which
works to hold oil, mining and logging multinationals to account by

exposing the economic links between conflict, corruption, human rights abuses, poverty and environmental destruction. Its work – to increase transparency, responsible management, and a fairer distribution of natural resources – involves a wide range of activities, from undercover investigations and painstaking financial research, to information-gathering on the ground and close co-operation with partners and activists all over the world.[71] A bald calculation of their work, in terms of lives saved or acres of rain forest protected, is impossible.

The danger with the EA model of effectiveness is that its reliance on quantitative analysis, which is helpful in understanding simpler charities, is not up to the task of evaluating charities with a broader and more complex vision of how to bring about change. What EA's critics call its 'metrics madness' – a charge also routinely levelled against the more over-zealous philanthrocapitalists – reduces a messy and complicated world to black and white. In this sense it turns its back on one of the great strengths of philanthropy – its ability to fund innovative projects which the public and private sectors, both inherently risk-averse in such matters, are less likely to support.

A more fundamental objection is articulated by critics on the left who see Effective Altruism as an essentially conservative movement. Whatever its rhetoric, its working assumption – that there is no incompatibility between making money and making change – in practice means ignoring the causes of poverty and merely addressing the symptoms. Effective Altruism attempts to game the system rather than challenge it. In doing that, it reinforces existing power structures rather than calling them into question. 'MacAskill does not address the deep sources of global misery – international trade and finance, debt, nationalism, imperialism, racial and gender-based subordination, war, environmental degradation, corruption, exploitation of labour – or the forces that ensure its reproduction,' argues the Oxford philosopher Amia Srinivasan.[72] 'Effective altruism doesn't try to understand how power works, except to better align itself with it. In this sense it leaves everything just as it is. This is no doubt comforting to those who enjoy the status quo – and may in part account for the movement's success.' Like philanthrocapitalism, these critics say, EA presses only for change which does not challenge the current neoliberal orthodoxy. Indeed Effective Altruists 'acknowledge how important it is that the wheels of the capitalist economy keep turning,' argues Julian Baggini.[73] EA is another example of capitalism's chameleon ability to produce enough of a superficial adjustment to maintain its control. It may even be said to weaken the forces working for systemic change by making a broken system look capable of improvement.

It is not only from the left that such criticism comes. The logic of Effective Altruism is 'superficially enticing' but ultimately leads to 'a moralistic, hyper-rationalistic, top-down approach to philanthropy that can kill the very altruistic spirit it claims to foster,' assert two philanthropy professionals, Ken Berger and Robert Penna of Charity Navigator, an organization which rates charities according to a wider set of criteria than EA does. They agree that philanthropists should become better informed and 'give with their heads as well as their hearts'. But the idea has been taken to such extremes by EA that it has been 'infused with logic so cold that even Mr Spock would cringe upon hearing it'. The result is not Effective Altruism but Defective Altruism.[74] Berger and Penna accuse EA of 'charitable imperialism' because it reinforces the principle beloved of philanthrocapitalists that successful business tycoons are, by virtue of their entrepreneurial skills, far better equipped to decide on how money should be spent than are the communities in receipt of their grants. Although this may have always been the case with philanthropy to some degree, since the idea was first articulated by Andrew Carnegie, the weakened power of cash-starved governments and the erosion of public institutions have made this power imbalance even greater. Angus Deaton is equally as impatient. When students anxious to relieve suffering in the world ask him if they should focus on mosquito bed nets or de-worming he replies tartly:

> I tell them to go to Washington or London and to work to stop the harm that rich countries do; to oppose the arms trade, the trade deals that benefit only the pharmaceutical companies, the protectionist tariffs that undermine the livelihoods of African farmers; and to support more funding to study tropical disease and health care. Or they could go to Africa, become citizens, and cast their lot with those they want to help. That is how they can save the lives of African kids.[75]

Some have suggested that Effective Altruism could reposition itself in this regard. 'There is no principled reason why Effective Altruists should endorse the worldview of the benevolent capitalist,' Amia Srinivasan has argued. 'Since Effective Altruism is committed to whatever would maximise the social good, it might for example turn out to support anti-capitalist revolution'. Although MacAskill chooses health as a proxy for goodness, there is no principled reason why Effective Altruism should not, instead, prefer values such as justice, dignity or self-determination and plug those into its algorithms. It could even adapt 'earning to give' to support more radical solutions, much as Friedrich Engels used the money from his uncle's Manchester factory to finance Karl Marx in his writing and publishing of the revolutionary masterwork *Das Kapital* – an act of greater integrity by Engels than would have been his high-minded refusal to work in the factory, which he hated.[76]

EFFECTIVE ALTRUISTS HAVE SECOND THOUGHTS

In fact the organizations which make up the Centre for Effective Altruism in Oxford have shown themselves capable of adapting in response to criticism of their 'earn to give' strategy and their initial unwillingness to address problems of structural injustice. MacAskill had begun in 2009 by giving young idealists the career advice that they should steer clear of charity work. Instead, they should get a job in high finance where they would earn large sums from which they could become generous givers to effective charities. 'If we take the salary earned by a fairly typical UK banker over their lifetimes, and assume they choose to give half of it away (leaving them still very well off) they end up able to distribute more than 600,000 malaria nets. That saves about 1,000 lives,' his website said, up until 2012.

But the page was updated in 2014 to say that this 'no longer fully reflects our views'.[77] By 2015 MacAskill was writing that his previous advice now applied only to a 'small proportion' of graduates. 'The proportion of people for whom we think earning to give is the best option has gone down over time,' he wrote. Now, he added, 'it seems unlikely to me that earning to give would ever be the best choice for the majority of people, just for the boring mathematical reason that there are many more non-earning-to-give paths than there are earning-to-give paths. Moreover, one successful person earning-to-give can support several people doing direct work.'[78]

It was not just the numbers which changed. At the outset MacAskill had argued that earning a high salary from which to give was the right choice even if the highly paid job was 'morally controversial'. He cited, as an example, Oskar Schindler, who provided munitions to the Nazis and thereby earned enough money to literally buy the lives of 1,200 Jews. 'A key aspect of the story is that he deliberately ran his factories less efficiently than whoever would have been in his place,' MacAskill argued in a philosophical paper *Replaceability, Career Choice, and Making a Difference*.[79] It stated: 'As regards career choice, we often think that working for an immoral organization is thereby immoral. The example of Schindler shows this not to be the case.'

By 2015, however, MacAskill had changed his tune. In a blog on the 80,000 Hours website he announced he wanted to clear up certain 'common misconceptions' about the Effective Altruism movement.[80] The problem with his original argument was that it set no boundaries which would create a moral limit on what could be justified. Would it really be OK to work as a drug dealer or a conman so long as generous charitable donations were made from the proceeds? Was it acceptable to work as a Wall Street broker who profited from dodgy sub-prime mortgages or set up tax avoidance schemes for the rich? Was it alright for a tax consultant to advise a mining company on how to dodge tens of billions of pounds in tax in Africa every year so long as they donate millions to combat malaria? This ethical incoherence led MacAskill to revise his argument. Now he distinguished between 'morally controversial' careers and 'reprehensible careers'. The merely controversial included – 'working for a petrochemical company, working for a company involved in the arms industry, and some careers within finance, such as those that involve speculating on wheat, thereby increasing price volatility and disrupting the livelihoods of the global poor'. But the reprehensible included 'working as a hit man, a concentration camp guard, a drug dealer or a child trafficker'.[81] Reprehensible jobs were, in the main, illegal; the morally controversial jobs were not. Even so, the 80,000 Hours approved list of 'earning to give' top jobs was now limited to morally neutral occupations such as computer science, quantitative hedge fund trading, high-end law, management consulting and technology start-ups.[82]

MacAskill has also amended his 'replaceability thesis'. This had argued that if an idealistic graduate called Sophie did not become an aid worker, then someone else would take the job. Even if they did not save as many lives as Sophie, the job would still get done by someone of similar competence and dedication. So Sophie's choice produced a marginal as well as an absolute difference. What MacAskill and his team came to realize was that it was harder to work out those marginal differences than they had supposed. There were, in the language of the philosophers, too many counterfactuals. Sophie might just increase the total number of bankers, economists told MacAskill's team, rather than changing which individuals got the job.[83-84]

Defenders of Effective Altruism, like Jeff McMahan, insisted that direct giving to save lives is not incompatible with lobbying against structural injustice. 'It is obviously better,' he wrote, 'if people do both.' Some people may prefer to take direct action to address the plight of the poorest people. Others may prefer to try to bring about institutional changes through political action. But 'to suppose that the only acceptable option is to work to reform global economic institutions, and that it is self-indulgent to make incremental contributions to the amelioration of poverty through individual action, is rather like condemning a doctor who treats the victims of a war for failing to devote his efforts instead to eliminating the root causes of war'.[85] This was a significant concession. It marked an important shift in the balance of argument and action. It is one which many traditional philanthropists understood some time ago. But it is one which many of the most zealous philanthrocapitalist admirers of Effective Altruism now need to take on board too.

THE FOLLIES OF PHILOSOPHY

But there is a more fundamental fear about Effective Altruism, and it is one which also applies to much contemporary philanthropy. What is the moral basis for its assertion that the goal of philanthropy should be to save as many lives as possible? There is no doubt that its major thinkers like Peter Singer and William MacAskill are driven by an ethical imperative. MacAskill ends one of his academic papers with a lament for the terrible waste of all the 'brilliant young people' who have gone into 'ethical' careers instead of getting a highly paid earning-to-give job. Each one of those well-meaning idealists had squandered the opportunity to 'do huge amounts of good in the world'. Instead, each one was allowing thousands of people to die whom they could have saved. 'We don't normally see this as a moral catastrophe,' he concludes. 'But we should.'[86]

This is flawed thinking. Effective Altruism sounds uncontroversial because it combines two terms generally viewed as incontrovertibly good – effective and altruism. The only limitation it acknowledges is, in Singer's words, that 'there is no logical stopping place' which tells the extreme altruist when he or she has given away enough. But the difficulty that causes some is clear. Zell Kravinsky, who gave away his fortune and his kidney – and then actually thought about the circumstances in which he should sacrifice his second kidney, and die – is an extreme example. But another Singer apostle, Julia Wise, feels guilty eating ice cream when there are unvaccinated children in the world.[87] And the philosopher Toby Ord is unusual with his radical resolve to give away everything above £18,000 from his income every year.

The real worry about Effective Altruism is not that it demands too much, but that it demands the wrong things. It begins by asserting that being moral requires achieving the greatest good for the greatest number of people. But even if we accept that as a starting point – and it is questionable – we might ask 'Is saving lives the only way of being good?' The political philosopher John Gray questions Peter Singer's insistence that there are objective answers to such questions. None of the classic utilitarian thinkers has ever been able to explain why anyone should devote their lives to maximizing good in the world. 'Neither Bentham nor Mill was able to provide a convincing justification for the utilitarian principles that, in different ways, they both held to be fundamental in moral reasoning,' writes Gray. Nor does Singer. The claim that living ethically means 'doing the most good' seems so obvious to Singer that 'nowhere . . . does he tell us why this should be so'. He merely leaves the claim 'hanging in mid-air'. The fact that his thinking runs counter to most ordinary people's intuitions is, in itself, he seems to feel, proof of its superior rationality.[88]

Other thinkers agree that there is more to philanthropy than maximizing utility. Being effective is not the only worthwhile yardstick. Other philosophers, such as Kwame Anthony Appiah, who teaches with Singer at Princeton, offer a different basis for our moral obligations. Appiah argues, for example, that we are not compelled to do the maximum good but are impelled only to carry 'our fair share of the burden of relieving global poverty'.[89]

Gray upbraids Singer for insisting, more generally, that there are objectively right answers. In his search for a calculus to adjudicate between every option in some hierarchy of ethical value, Singer considers the guards at Auschwitz. He asks whether they might be said to have acted morally if they believed that if they had refused to do the job they would have been replaced by someone who would have been even more brutal. Singer accepts that, on these grounds, 'at least some of the guards at Auschwitz were not acting wrongly'. But not everything can be judged only by its consequences – and whether, on balance, an act does more good than harm. Giles Fraser writes: 'A blinkered concern for the greatest happiness of the greatest number can always be used to justify moral outrages. What if an overall increase in the total sum of human happiness could be brought about by murdering an innocent man? Would his murder be justified? Obviously, not.'

The consequentialist idea that maximizing good can be measured by weighing good outcomes against bad ones belongs in economics, if it belongs anywhere, Gray suggests. It does not belong in ethics. He adds: 'Those who believe it would be wrong to serve as a guard in a Nazi death camp, even if doing so would prevent greater suffering, are not guilty of any flaw in reasoning. They are refusing to be complicit in practices they believe to be categorically and intrinsically wrong.' If utilitarian ethics requires such a choice, Gray concludes, 'so much the worse for utilitarianism'. This is a classic example of the follies of philosophy.'⁹⁰

Other traditions in philosophy see morality as most fundamentally about being a good person, rather than making the world better. That involves a whole nexus of considerations beyond maximizing good. It includes holding to wider precepts of right conduct; embracing social, familial and parental responsibilities; cultivating virtues and striving to avoid vices; and refusing to perform actions we believe are wrong in all circumstances. Where these duties conflict or create tensions, ethical living is about finding an apt balance. In some cases, notes John Gray, there may be no single right answer to the questions which this raises. Amia Srinivasan asks, how far should the adherent go with the logic of Effective Altruism? 'If you're faced with the choice between spending a few hours consoling a bereaved friend, or earning some money to donate to an effective charity, the utilitarian calculus will tell you to do the latter.' But perhaps you should stay and console your friend 'not because you've already met your do-gooding quota, but because it's *your* friend that is in distress'.[91] Effective Altruists, one wag asserted, know the price of everything and the value of nothing.

There is another dimension of human psychology which Effective Altruists – and the philanthropists influenced by their focused data-driven approach – should bring to mind. Effective Altruism encourages a way of life in which too many singular values are sacrificed to a generalized altruism. The conservative thinker David Brooks set out the difficulty when he read about a 25-year-old computer whizz, Jason Trigg, another Peter Singer disciple. Trigg's skills were such that he could equally have got a job writing software for the next tech giant or working to cure cancer. Instead, he decided to join a high-frequency trading hedge fund, to earn a fortune to give away to fight malaria. Trigg seems like an earnest morally serious man, Brooks noted, and if he lives out his plan, he could indeed help save many lives. But the brain is a malleable organ, Brooks warned:

> Every time you do an activity, or have a thought, you are changing a piece of yourself into something slightly different than it was before. Every hour you spend with others, you become more like the people around you . . . If there is a large gap between your daily conduct and your core commitment, you will become more like your daily activities and less attached to your original commitment. You will become more hedge fund, less malaria.[92]

More profoundly, he cautioned, the process might make you 'a person who values the far over the near' – someone who loves humanity in general but doesn't have much time for the real people around them. But a human life is not just a means to produce outcomes. It is an end in itself. And our daily activities eventually mould us into the person we become. 'If your profoundest interest is dying children in Africa or Bangladesh, it's probably best to go to Africa or Bangladesh, not to Wall Street.'[93]

There is something about empathy bound up in that. Empathy – a quality more than just feeling sorry for another person, but actually experiencing what they're experiencing, intellectually or imaginatively – is a quality which can immensely enhance philanthropy. But it is not a quality much valued by Effective Altruists. Peter Singer actually disparages it. In his 2015 book *The Most Good You Can Do* he has a chapter entitled 'Is Love All We Need?' Singer answers his own question by proclaiming that: 'Effective altruism does not require the kind of strong emotional empathy that people feel for identifiable individuals.'[94]

Indeed, empathy, he says, can be an obstacle to maximizing good. To support this Singer cites a study in which some people were shown a photograph of a girl and given her name and age. They were then told she needed a $300,000 drug to save her life. Another group were shown photographs of eight children, with their names and ages, and told that the same sum, $300,000, would buy drugs to save all their lives. Those who were shown the photo of the single child gave more. Singer is outraged by this and says: 'To Effective Altruists, this is an absurd outcome, and if emotional empathy is responsible for it, then so much the worse for that kind of empathy. Effective altruists are sensitive to numbers and to cost per life saved or year of suffering prevented.'[95]

Those who cannot buy into this utilitarian consequentialism are equally outraged, but in the opposite direction. 'Effective altruists treat people as units not persons. They turn philanthropy into a science and there is something dehumanising about that,' says Giles Fraser. 'If you're rushing from a burning building – and you can only save a screaming baby or a sack containing a million pounds with which you could save thousands of lives – do you grab the money? That would be a profoundly inhuman reaction.'[96]

Effective Altruists dismiss such a reaction as ignorant or irrational. But there could be another explanation. There may be a more profound good in human empathy, to which the cold logic of Effective Altruists are blind. There is a revealing example of this in William MacAskill's book *Doing Good Better*. In it he recounts his visit to the Hamlin Fistula Hospital in Ethiopia in 2009 while trying to work out how to turn Effective Altruism into a charity. A fistula, which the hospital's website defines as 'a hole between the birth canal and the bladder or rectum', is most common among poor and malnourished women. It can result in permanent incontinence, with many of the women 'abandoned by their husbands and ostracised by their communities because of the offensive smell'.[97] MacAskill was clearly moved by his visit and uneasy with his decision not to support the hospital (on the grounds that more lives could be saved per-pound elsewhere). He wrote:

> I'd hugged the women who suffered from this condition, and they'd thanked me for visiting them. It had been an important experience for me: a vivid first-hand demonstration of the severity of the problems in the world. This was a cause I had a personal connection with. Should I have donated to the Fistula Foundation, even knowing I could do more to help people if I donated elsewhere? I do not think so. If I were to give to the Fistula Foundation rather than to charities I thought were more effective, I would be privileging the needs of some people over others for emotional rather than moral reasons. That would be unfair to those I could have helped more. If I'd visited some other shelter in Ethiopia, or in any other country, I would have had a different set of personal connections. It was arbitrary that I'd seen this particular problem at close quarters.[98]

MacAskill's inability to locate the source of his own unease here is instructive. In reviewing his book another philosopher, Amia Srinivasan, when considering this passage picked out the word 'arbitrary' from his account. It was, indeed, arbitrary that MacAskill went to this hospital and not another, in Ethiopia and not some other country. But then it is equally as arbitrary that we have the family, friends, lovers and neighbours we do. As Srinivasan asks: 'Doesn't such arbitrariness come to mean something else, ethically speaking, when it is constitutive of our personal experience: when it becomes embedded in the complex structure of commitments, affinities and understandings that comprise social life? We might even think that the arbitrariness of time and place is transformed into something else, ethically speaking, through the exchange of a fleeting hug or thanks.'[99]

MacAskill's need to remind himself that there were worse-off people in the world must have been cold comfort to women who were victims of a humiliating condition he deemed too costly to be worth funding. Another reviewer had a similar reaction to the story: 'To most of us it seems neither reasonable nor desirable to expect people to remain untouched by the particular individuals they know and the particular causes that affect them. Should we suppress the urge to bring dinner to our elderly neighbour because we could use those hours more effectively by researching charities and sending a cheque to the best one?'[100] MacAskill's inability to comprehend this was 'chilling', the reviewer concluded.

In the end morality, and the kind of philanthropy which draws from it, does not see things from some cold universal perspective. It is tempered by the warmth of a personal response. Values such as empathy, compassion, responsibility and personal loyalty are key parts of that. They are essential to the business of living in a community. Such qualities might sometimes lead us to make decisions which seem poor on a material cost-benefit calculus but which are rich in the other dimensions of life. All this leads to the alternative of what the final chapter of this book calls Reciprocal Philanthropy.

'Poverty is not just a lack of money,' as Amartya Sen famously said. 'It is not having the capability to realise one's full potential as a human being.'[101] Personal relationships are intrinsic to that. So are many of the causes which philanthropy traditionally has favoured, such as academia, the arts, or religious faiths that contribute to the intellectual, aesthetic and spiritual dimension of those relationships. Effective altruism pays lip service to that. 'I would be delighted if there were a world in which everyone could have that rich kind of cultural life,' Peter Singer told his fellow philosopher Julian Baggini in an interview for the *New Statesman* in 2015.[102] 'But I think at the moment, when you have a billion people in extreme poverty, there is something indecent about saying that you think it is more important to renovate the concert hall at the Lincoln Centre than it is to help people get enough to eat or prevent people going blind.'

The problem with EA's relentless insistence on data, metrics and ranking everything in a hierarchy to maximize good is that it condemns philanthropy to a linear sense of progress. Life is not so black-and-white. Most people feel uncomfortable about the idea of choosing one cause and abandoning all others. The notion that everyone should forsake the higher things in life in pursuit of what John Gray calls 'a thin universal benevolence' is not attractive to most people. The idea that we should all give, and live, as though bare survival were the only goal worth pursuing is reductive and dull. Such a view, as we shall see in the interview below and in the final chapter, fails to touch the pulse of the general public's view of philanthropy.

Effective Altruism and philanthrocapitalism have brought practical gains in the clarity of their focus. But they threaten to rob us of some of these deeper dimensions. We cannot eschew all life-enriching activities, such as the arts, until the whole planet has been de-wormed. Our experiences are simultaneous, not sequential. Life is about quality not just quantity. Centuries of art, poetry, spiritual transcendence and valiant self-sacrifice – in everything from caring to the battlefield – demonstrate that. Fortunately, one of the threads which has repeatedly surfaced in our survey of the history of philanthropy is that there is another way. In the final chapter of this book I want to turn to how modern philanthropy can recover its lost soul.

Interview: Lenny Henry and Kevin Cahill on public philanthropy

Sir Lenny Henry and Kevin Cahill CBE are the two life-presidents of Comic Relief, the biennial BBC charity telethon which, with its sister charity Sport Relief that operates in the alternate years, has raised more than £1 billion for disadvantaged people across the developing world and also in Britain. Lenny Henry has presented the event over three decades, during which time he has also been a trustee of the organization. Kevin Cahill was, for a similar period, the chief executive of the charity. The TV event follows Red Nose Day, which encourages the public to engage in wacky fundraising activities.

Philanthropy has become the concern of ordinary people in recent years through initiatives like Comic Relief. What made you both get involved?

Lenny: Richard Curtis organized a night in the theatre in 1986, the year after Live Aid, to raise money for the famine in Ethiopia. I had my own television show on BBC1 at the time, so he asked me to join in with Rowan Atkinson, Billy Connolly, Stephen Fry, Kate Bush and Cliff Richard.* I did *Romeo and Juliet* with Frank Bruno.† Afterwards there was a do at my house. I think drink may have been involved. I'd seen TV shows in America where famous people come on and appeal for money, but they didn't really do sketches or characters or scenes or monologues. So I just said we could do comedy all night on TV and they'd give us loads of money, wouldn't they? Then the next thing we knew Richard had figured out a deal with the BBC and suddenly we were on telly. The first one raised £15 million.

---

* Richard Curtis is one of Britain's most successful comedy screenwriters. His films include *Four Weddings and a Funeral, Notting Hill, Bridget Jones's Diary* and *Love Actually*. His TV comedies include *Blackadder, Mr Bean* and *The Vicar of Dibley*.
† The former British heavyweight boxer.

Kevin: It was an amazing experience. The comedy was a reward for watching a series of short documentary films made by the BBC about Africa and the UK.

Lenny: I went to Ethiopia and did things like holding up a goat and saying '£3 will buy a goat for this family' and talking to a woman who walked 10 miles to get water. In one shot I wore local Ethiopian dress and I'm sitting there against the wall with these elders. The camera just panned along, and it came to me and I said, 'This could be somebody you know.' And, of course, it was, because it was me! [Laughs] It really struck a chord with people at home because they'd never thought about it like that before. And they gave the money.

Kevin: Live Aid had just happened and we'd all seen the footage of famine. Comic Relief was keen to move beyond the crisis and tell the story of sustainable development.

Lenny: When you look at the coverage now there can be a real sense of white saviour syndrome. A white man with a microphone saying: 'Look at that. Look at the skinny child with a distended stomach. Isn't it awful. We must do something.' But because we were all comedians it didn't really feel like that to us. Particularly for me being the only black person who went out for Comic Relief. I felt like I had a real connection. The minute I arrived in Ethiopia I went 'Whoa!!' It was like a massive energy wave right from my feet to the top of my head. I thought: This is somewhere I know. I had almost, like, a spiritual permission to be there to present these things.

Kevin: By the way, that goat that Lenny was holding up was a sheep.

Lenny: [Laughs] That's how much we knew at the beginning. I didn't even know the difference between the sheep and the goats.

Kevin: I was working at the National Theatre running the education department, which I'd founded for Peter Hall. One day Richard Curtis turned up and said he was looking for someone to help the Comic Relief audience understand why they were being asked to give money. I loved working at the National. If you work in the theatre there's no better place in my estimation. So I said: 'Well, that's brilliant, but I don't want to do it, because I love it here.' I gave him a few names of people to check out. Three months later he came back and made it sound so exciting I changed my mind.

When I got to Comic Relief I looked at all the films that had been made and cut them up into little packages for schools so teachers could do lessons around them, about malnutrition or women's education or whatever. We called it Teacher Relief. Lenny wrote and filmed little scripts to introduce these little films and they went into all the schools in the UK. Because they featured people the kids regarded as their heroes from television it was a great success.

It was quite a steep learning curve for you both but, from the way you talk, it was clearly energizing.

Lenny: Huge. It's been half of my life. It wasn't really my job but I decided to just go for it because I could see that it was a really good thing. It was just this bunch of young people thinking: 'Let's have a go at this.' There was a lot of passion, a lot of determination. I think that our youth had a lot to do with the energy of it. The objective was to try and balance things out and make the world a fairer place.

Kevin: Richard liked to quote the anthropologist Mary Mead who said: 'Never doubt that a small group of committed people can change the world. It's the only thing that ever has.' So it began with that steep learning curve and we probably made mistakes along the way, but the charity landscape didn't have anything like it going on – raising money by kids saying to their teachers: 'Shave your beard off' or 'Spray your hair red', and we'll collect money for you to do it. Comic Relief, as our slogan had it, 'put the fun into fund-raising'. It said: 'You don't have to be angst-y and guilt-ridden to give money and to try and help people change their lives. You can actually have a bit of fun at the same time. Then everybody gets something out of it.'

This Day of Misrule began, which was a bit like what April Fool's day could be if someone orchestrated it. Kids loved the fact that they could stay up a bit later and watch telly. Parents and teachers loved the fact they're able to open up conversations about complicated things. And because from the outset we funded work in the UK, as well as internationally, it opened up bits of the domestic agenda like street homelessness or domestic violence or disability.

Lenny: But to make films – short simple films – about complex projects can be quite challenging.

Kevin: If you make a film about Africa it's easier to see the universal truths. If a child is malnourished and they don't have the food they need to grow properly and fulfil their potential, that's a no-brainer. But in the UK, where we talk about the deserving and the undeserving poor, some issues are more complex. People think: 'Well, that homeless person shouldn't be homeless. He should get a job.' If you show a film about the street homeless to a family at home, there might be four different points of view on street homelessness in the room.

Lenny: We wanted people to learn why people are on the streets – whether it's Margaret Thatcher closing all the halfway houses, or mental health issues, or sexual abuse or whatever. People need to be informed. Then they can connect the dots. This idea of blind giving – where people are just shown a terrible image and give in an automatic way – had to be done away with. Informed giving is what we were trying to do and are still trying to do. Some people still say, 'Why can't we just have the jokes and we'll give the money?' But we strongly believe in informed giving.

Dawn* narrated a film for us about child sex abuse and it was very, very uncomfortable to watch. I went to a place in Cardiff for Somali refugee women who had been abused by their husbands. I thought: 'If people don't understand they'll just see a group of brown women with their hand out – and they'll never give any money.' But if they learned the stories behind the refuge, the British public would give you their heart.

Kevin: We made this film with Lenny looking over a whole year at homeless rough sleepers. You learn about yourself doing something like that. At first you see someone sleeping in a doorway and think if you get him help to get a flat or something then he'll be all right. But it's never that straightforward. In one scene Lenny got in a cardboard box in which this young couple were sleeping . . .

Lenny: Round the back of the London Palladium . . .

Kevin: They looked like ordinary young people who'd left home for whatever reason. But it turned out he'd been working as a rent boy. He'd smashed up the benefit office. She had been living in Barnet where her brother had raped her. She went to the police, told the police about the rape. Her brother's friends then turned on her and were threatening to beat her up if she stayed in Barnet so she went onto the street with her boyfriend. When you put the camera on them people say: 'Here's an ordinary young couple living on the

---

* The comedian Dawn French of the comedy duo French & Saunders. She and Lenny Henry were married for 25 years.

streets – let's help them get some accommodation.' But you find it's not like that; it's much more multi-layered. The boy, Jason . . .

Lenny: He was a heroin addict. We followed him for twelve months and sadly he died at the end of the year. Once you learn the stories behind why you're giving, they're complex, but they trigger a genuine empathy rather than a fake or superficial one. Over the years Comic Relief has changed. It has got more complex, the bigger we've got. But this idea of informing the public about things, so that they can give wisely – that grew too.

Doesn't it go beyond giving wisely, though? Doesn't it become political in a sense? So it's about changing public policy on such issues.

Kevin: You can't ever become party-political, because you need to work with whoever is in power if you are to try and create a better world for the people that you're there to support. But we used to talk about creating a climate of understanding. This is where the creative and the comedic community come together with the other side. I remember going to see Gordon Brown[*] with Richard. That week we had the No. 1 single in the charts, the No. 1 book on the best-seller list, and the No. 1 show on television. When you go and see a senior politician or the Prime Minister with that in your armoury, they take note, because they think: 'Well, this lot must represent a constituency that's big. Let's be nice to them rather than send them off with a flea in their ear.' David Cameron, I remember, once made a speech when he was putting British aid up to 0.7 per cent of Britain's national income.[†] In the speech he referenced Comic Relief, and we felt proud and thought, 'Well, that's great if we played a small part in making this happen.'

But the comedy prevented it from feeling nakedly political. I remember Frank Skinner, who was in Ghana with David Baddiel, going in to this hut and he bashed his head because the hut was kind of low. All the women he was talking to burst out laughing

---

[*] British prime minister from 2007 to 2010.
[†] British prime minister from 2010 to 2016. See Owen Bennett, 'David Cameron believes tackling world poverty will help Britain beat extremists', *Daily Express*, 8 June 2013.

because it was a piece of slapstick. He got a sore head and they were laughing at him, and it encapsulated the way that with Comic Relief the comedy cuts through, and sugars the pill of the serious messaging that comes along with it.

Lenny: As you get older, though, you do want politicians to understand about what this actually is. At the stroke of a pen, they could solve a lot of the things that are wrong. Our job, every two years, was to poke them with a stick and go: 'Have you seen this over here?' Often, they seem to be reacting to things like they've never seen them before, like they didn't know it was happening, though of course they knew it was happening.

But they can no longer ignore it, once you've drawn it to their attention.

Lenny: Our job is to be the Lords of Misrule, who come in and say: 'Here's some japes over here, and while you're looking at that, we want to tell you about this thing too.' Sometimes it can weigh heavy. But the fact that we're comics means that we can often tell stories about the things people otherwise don't want to hear. We did a thing about child grooming within the body of *EastEnders*, and at the end of it, there was a phone helpline and a donation-giving line. We did a programme called *Dad*, written by Lucy Gannon, a whole one-hour drama about elder abuse. And Richard Curtis has written two films about charity and giving in Africa, *Mary and Martha* and *The Girl in the Café*. I'm hoping that the newer generation of comedians, directors, writers, creatives, will come in now and apply their storytelling skills.

Are you aware of a younger generation going to come and pick up the torch from you? Or do you think it might end with you?

Kevin: One of the biggest existential challenges for Comic Relief is the changing media landscape. When Lenny and the others began it, there were only four terrestrial television stations, and so basically, if you had a Friday night on BBC One, and you could bring the star power to it, you'd get 15 million viewers. And the science of it is, of that 15 million a certain percentage, say 2 per cent, will give money. So 2 per cent of 15 million giving 35 quid each equals £10 million plus, which is a big sum. When the audience drops into five million or six million – or they watch a recorded version later online – that then challenges one of your central planks of being able to raise the money. When people watch two days later they fast-forward through the little documentary films. Then they don't give money in the way they do if they watch it live when there's the vibe going on that this is a big event, and we're all involved . . .

Lenny: We're thinking slowly about a new broadcast strategy, how to use online, how to use streaming, how to use social media – because we're in the twenty-first century now and people watch TV differently. So how can we get people to give? If you're on your phone on the train, and there's a brilliant sketch by Alan Partridge or Jennifer Aniston, how can we get people to give?

The time is coming where we might not be able to curate six hours live on a Friday night. It might be that there's a two-week window for Comic Relief-related activities, where we want people to donate whenever they watch a Comic Relief bit of content. But the technology is going to be tricky.

Kevin: It might be a subscription. You pay, say, £6 a month to get everything that Comic Relief produces. It needs to adapt to a world where there's a multitude of offerings and people are defining themselves more tribally and are being more niche. But we think there's an unchanging truth at the heart of what we're saying. It is that when people are poor or disadvantaged, and other people are in a position to help, they will – and I think that will go on for as long as human beings are on this planet.

Lenny: Once when I was in Somalia I made a little kind of speech to camera. I said: 'Imagine the world as a street. If those people over there were starving, or had just been kicked out of their house or something, you'd cross the street and help them, and give them a bit of money so they could survive. Well, the people in Africa are also your neighbours . . .'

The first time I went to Ethiopia I talked to this great-grandad in a village which had been very badly hit by the famine. He was 90-something but was a really vital old man. We'd funded something in the village and he was really grateful. Now, this guy had lost the middle generation of his family. Everybody dead. He was looking after his great-grandkids. Anyway, he said to me, through an interpreter: 'Thank you guys so much for coming here and helping us.' And then he says: 'And if ever you need us,' he said, 'just say the word and we'll come and help you sort things out at your end.' And I thought: 'That's amazing. We've been seeing you as a victim, but actually, you're just a bloke that this has happened to, and you're saying "When you need us, we're ready". It's a human thing – an instinctual thing to help. And we must, must, must, whatever happens hold on to that thing. Because if we lose that then we're lost.

Kevin: If you're a billionaire, you can afford to, say, give £100 million away. If you're a kid in a shop with your Mum you may buy three red noses for £3 for charity. But they're both philanthropic acts. And Comic Relief has enabled hundreds of thousands of those acts.

One of the things we always talked about is 'sweating people's assets'. You look at what someone can give. Someone like J. K. Rowling can say: 'Well, I've got this little story in my bottom drawer if you want it', and the book can go on to raise over £20 million for Comic Relief. A comedian can give comedy; they can't necessarily give loads of money, but their comedy can bring people to the show. And those people can make their small donations. It's a virtuous circle.

It's a kind of democratization of philanthropy. But it is more than that, because one of the things that is distinctive about Comic Relief is that you don't just ask people to dip into their pockets – you ask them to 'do something funny for money?' So they give their time too.

Kevin: You get more committed if you do something.

Lenny: It stimulates people's imagination more. I remember going to drop my daughter off at school one Comic Relief day. As we went to school we saw teachers wearing their clothes backwards, with bright red wigs on and their faces painted red. We saw children all walking backwards to school, or refusing to speak, or saying 'wibble' at the end of every sentence. The headteacher of the school looked at all this chaos and said: 'Thanks a lot, Len.' But if you tie giving with some activity, even if it's stupid, you'll remember for the rest of your life. My bank manager sat in a bath full of baked beans all day outside the bank and people gave money and put it into a bucket. He talked about it for months after. It brings people together, at school, at work. They have a good time and, oh my God, you've raised some money too.

How do you decide what to spend the money on?

Lenny: There's a load of trustees who decide, advised by an Africa grants committee and a UK grants committee, with experts on both.

Kevin: For the first couple of Red Nose Days, a third of the international money went to Oxfam and a third went to Save the Children, but then over the years we developed our own process so we can be fully accountable for the money the public have given us – and trust us to spend well.

So when people apply for grants Comic Relief has staff members who field the first inquiry. Then it goes to an issue-based expert. There'll be an expert on street homelessness and another on HIV-AIDS and so on. Then, if they like the look of it, the expert in conjunction with another staff member sends it to a grants committee who are another bunch of experts. They look at them, and then they decide which ones they want to back and which ones they don't. Sometimes the committee, before deciding, will send it back with additional questions to seek clarifications. Then once that committee's made its decisions, that goes to the Comic Relief Board of Trustees, who are the ultimate governance body. More often than not they ratify what's come to them because there has been such work done on it already by then. But they can say: 'We're not sure about this one. Could we send it back and find out about this or that aspect?'

It sounds complex, but it's developed as Comic Relief's become a more mature organization with greater public expectations and therefore a need for greater public accountability. What's also happened, apart from all this layering, is that Comic Relief has decided more what its attitude is to certain things. So instead of giving a thousand smaller grants it has begun to say: let's pick a couple of areas where we think over five years we might be able to make a strategic difference.

Lenny: Speaking as a Comic Relief trustee, it is complex if you're going to pick with intelligence and proper thought. But it means you give as wisely as you can, though you can still make mistakes.

You say Comic Relief has changed over the years. How?

Lenny: I think in the last few years we've started to question that white saviour syndrome, which is probably a holdover from Empire – the idea of the white guy in the pith helmet arriving somewhere in

Africa, pointing at a poor person and saying, 'I will help these poor people. I will give them the Bible.' Of course, when we first went to Africa we didn't have that saviour syndrome in our mind at all. But even with good intentions you can make mistakes. Until recently the majority of documentaries we've made have been done by white people and have been very mono-cultural. There'll be the odd black or Asian person, but not very many. Anyway, diversity is really about who makes the decisions behind the scenes. Most people at the BBC or ITV went to the same universities, Oxbridge, and basically go through life employing each other or taking each other's jobs. If you're going to shake that up, you've got to change the structure. Structural change is very, very difficult to effect.

There's got to be another way to tell our stories. What I've been saying in the last few years is that the continent of Africa is full of award-winning filmmakers, so why aren't we working with those guys? Diversity is about reflecting the demographics of where you are. London is 40 per cent BAME. If you don't have 40 per cent of BAME people around the table, you're operating a deficiency, you're missing a thought process. You have to have diversity of culture, diversity of thought, diversity of attitude if you are going to shake things up – and not just here but in Africa too.

When I used to film in Africa it was always with a white film crew, and I would carry the legs of the camera. The local kids would go along the line of white people saying: 'Hello, how are you? I am fine. Hello, how are you? I am fine.' Then they'd get to me and ignore me because they thought I was just the black bloke carrying the leg of the camera. Then when I started to speak to the camera the kids could be forgiven for thinking: 'Who is that man? Why is he talking to the camera? Why is a black guy talking to the camera?'

I went to Africa for the first time this year with an African-born director, a guy called Yemi. He made this film for Comic Relief about things that are happening in Cape Town. It was great. If we can change who makes the films you will see a big change.

Philanthropy at its best, this book has concluded, is not just about giving. It's also about developing a good two-way partnership which acknowledges the dignity of those who receive as well as those who give. It's something which has been lost with a lot of

top-down philanthropy over the years. But it sounds as though that's something which has been intuitively part of the Comic Relief approach.

Lenny: I think it is.

Kevin: Comic Relief has always been obsessed by projects that are user-led. Right from the outset, when we were funding work on disability, there was a requirement that the board of management of any disability charity should be 51 per cent-plus disabled people. That was radical, way back then, because it was saying that the people who know best what disabled people need are disabled people, not non-disabled people. In the early years we raised money and passed it on to Oxfam or Save the Children to spend. But over the years we've moved overwhelmingly towards funding African-led organizations. And, where there was a white person running the project, we needed to know that in three years' time it would evolve so there was a local person running the project.

Lenny: In the end it's all about love. Comic Relief is about being decent human beings in a world of xenophobia and weird 'isms' – racism, homophobia, sexism, *#MeToo*. Just trying to be a decent person can be very difficult, whoever you are, wherever you're from, whatever your job is. But, in the end, I think there's something about Comic Relief which celebrates human goodness.

Chapter 18

How Philanthropy Can Recover its Lost Soul

Patty Stonesifer looked out of the window and wondered. She had been a high-flyer all her life. Before the age of 40 she had risen to become the highest-ranking woman at Microsoft. Already she had run the software giant's entire operation in Canada. Then she had revamped the whole organization's product support and consumer products divisions before becoming vice-president of its $800 million interactive media division, where she oversaw its entertainment, news and information products. She had earned enough that she would never have to work for money again. So much so that she did not need to draw a salary when she became the first chief executive of the Bill & Melinda Gates Foundation as it set out to eradicate polio, combat malaria and treat AIDS. Stonesifer set its strategic priorities, monitored results, and managed relationships with key partners.[1] She helped build the foundation into the world's largest philanthropy with a budget bigger than the gross domestic product of 70 per cent of the world's nations.[2] But every night she would look out of the window of the Gates Foundation offices on McPherson Square in Washington DC and see a white van pull up by a nearby city park. Every night it gave out hot food to those who were homeless and hungry in the capital city of the world's richest nation.

The van arrived without fail, every day, 365 days a year. It came from an organization named Martha's Table.[3] Stonesifer understood the reference. In the Christian gospels Martha is the woman who remains in the kitchen preparing the food while her sister Mary sits at the feet of Jesus listening to him teach. Stonesifer had heard the story many times at the church she attended as a child in Indianapolis where she grew up in a big Catholic family. 'The No. 1 lesson you learn, being sixth out of nine children, is: It's not about you,' she told Maureen O'Dowd from the *New York Times*. 'Our family didn't talk about volunteerism. It was just baked in. We went down and put the new missals in the church pews, and we volunteered at the Sunday soup kitchen, and we went with my dad to pick up the deaf children for church. We had foster children a significant part of the time that I was growing up.'[4] The Stonesifer family set up a scheme to ensure every child in their locality went home from the maternity hospital with a cot in a move to reduce infant deaths.

Now, in Washington, Stonesifer and her husband began to make donations to Martha's Table to help support the work of its local volunteers. Then one day, in a newsletter the little charity sent out to its donors, she saw that the mobile food bank was advertising for a CEO. She applied and got the job. The world of philanthropy was stunned. 'Having Stonesifer come run a small local charity,' observed the *Washington Post*, was like having the head of General Electric 'showing up to manage the corner appliance store'.[5] But watching the van provide hot food to the homeless who congregated in that park had stirred memories for Stonesifer of the service she and her family had given 'close to the front lines'. She wanted, she told O'Dowd, 'to go beyond white papers and PowerPoint presentations and get my boots dirty'. She wanted 'to learn what it takes to change one child's experience from a child born in poverty to a child that's president of something'. Her move raises a far wider question. What was it that she found lacking in the model of Strategic Philanthropy? The answer, this final chapter suggests, is to be found in what I am calling Reciprocal Philanthropy.

ANOTHER WAY

We live in a culture that encourages us to think about the external side of our natures rather than our inner selves, declares the conservative intellectual David Brooks in his book *The Road to Character*. Brooks takes a variety of historical figures – from St Augustine, through Samuel Johnson and George Eliot, to Dwight Eisenhower. All of them, in very different ways, he argues, reconciled their external and internal natures. Brooks, who was raised in a secular Jewish family and describes himself

as an atheist,[6] goes on to draw a distinction between what he calls
résumé virtues and eulogy virtues. The former are the qualities you list
on your CV, the skills that you bring to the job market. Eulogy virtues,
by contrast, are the qualities you would hope people might mention
at your funeral – kindness, honesty, compassion, courage, loyalty,
integrity. They are the qualities we bring to the relationships we form
in life. True fulfilment, he concludes, is to be found in the counter-
intuitive truth that to fulfil ourselves we must learn to forget ourselves.

Philanthropy also has two sides to its personality. Strategic
Philanthropy is most embodied today in philanthrocapitalism. But over
the centuries it has had various other names: 5 per cent philanthropy,
scientific philanthropy, muscular philanthropy, judicious philanthropy,
systematic philanthropy, corporate philanthropy, entrepreneurial
philanthropy, smart philanthropy, venture philanthropy, hedge
fund philanthropy, managerial philanthropy, catalytic philanthropy,
hacker philanthropy and effective philanthropy. All of these essentially
believed in harnessing market forces toward philanthropic ends.
They are results-oriented. Their drive is undeniable. But their focus is
questionable. Mark Zuckerberg, Facebook's chief executive, once told
colleagues that 'a squirrel dying in your front yard may be more relevant
to your interests right now than people dying in Africa'. At Facebook,
'relevance' is virtually the sole criterion that determines what users see.
'Focusing on the most personally relevant news – the squirrel – is a
great business strategy,' Eli Pariser wrote in the *New York Times*. 'But
it leaves us staring at our front yard instead of reading about suffering,
genocide and revolution.'[7]

The other side of philanthropy is what this book calls Reciprocal
Philanthropy. It began in the time of Aristotle, when philanthropy was
seen primarily as a device to strengthen social relationships. But, as we
have seen, it was most decisively developed through the revolutionary
rise of religions which rejected many gods in favour of a single God.
That changed our understanding of human nature. A new philanthropy
flowed from that shift. Jewish, early Christian and Muslim teachings
all brought the understanding that the act of giving creates a three-way
relationship between the giver, the receiver, and the society in which they
both live. It was embodied in a millennium of Catholic Christendom.
After the Reformation it resurfaced repeatedly in various forms – in
Enlightenment activist philanthropy, feminine philanthropy, Utopian

socialist philanthropy, Quaker philanthropy, George Cadbury's seminal philanthropy and Bono's fusion philanthropy. All these are forms of Reciprocal Philanthropy. They all stand in opposition to what Jonathan Sacks calls 'our new secular mythology' – the fallacy 'that life is made of unfettered individual choices through which we negotiate our private paths to happiness'.[8] Instead, they all share the insight that philanthropy at its best is rooted in relationship, mutuality and partnership. Reciprocal Philanthropy is philanthropy with a human face. It is focused on people rather than product. It is process-driven rather than results-oriented. It comes from the heart as much as the head.

Given this tradition – which was seen by many to have ended when the Catholic worldview was challenged at the Reformation – it is perhaps unsurprising that some of the most prominent modern reaffirmations of the importance of mutuality in philanthropy have come from recent popes. Pope John Paul II's writings speak of mutuality as 'solidarity'. This, he insists, is 'not a feeling of vague compassion or shallow distress at the misfortunes' of others. Rather, as we saw in Chapter 10,[*] it is 'a firm and persevering determination to commit oneself to the common good . . . because we are all really responsible for all'.[9]

Pope Benedict XVI in a 2005 encyclical entitled *Deus caritas est* (God is love) reiterates that giving to the needy is an indispensable element of the Christian life. He rejects the leftist view that charity has been replaced by justice in the journey towards a fairer society. Almsgiving, Benedict concedes, can be just 'a way for the rich to shirk their obligation to work for justice and a means of soothing their consciences, while preserving their own status and robbing the poor of their rights'.[10] But it can be more than that. 'Love – *caritas* – will always prove necessary, even in the most just society,' Benedict writes. No society can be made so just that it eliminates the need for love. 'There will always be suffering which cries out for consolation and help. There will always be loneliness,' he writes, so there will always be situations where 'love of neighbour' is indispensable. The bureaucracy of the state is no substitute for 'loving personal concern'. The idea that justice will one day render charity superfluous is rooted in a false materialist view of what it is to be human.[11] Benedict then goes on specifically to praise

---

[*] See pages 402–3 above.

philanthropy but adds that the giver needs to be 'personally present' in their gift.[12] Only a gift endowed with love can cultivate humility in the giver and protect the dignity of the receiver.

Benedict's successor, Pope Francis, goes further. In his first major teaching document, *Evangelii Gaudium* (The Joy of the Gospel), he reasserts these long-standing principles of mutuality and partnership, writing: 'This is why I want a Church which is poor and for the poor. They have much to teach us.'[13] The poor know much better than outside experts how to improve their own condition. Charitable activity, Francis suggests, must assert human values in the face of a market economy which has become an 'economy of exclusion and inequality'.[14]

Philanthropy, for these popes, should be a humanizing force in which the giver acknowledges the full humanity of the recipient in a way that neither the impersonal bureaucracy of the state nor the unforgiving efficiency of the market can do. When giving to a beggar, says Pope Francis, 'it is not a good thing just to throw a few coins' without even looking at the person. 'Gesture is important . . . looking them in the eyes and touching their hands. Tossing the money without looking in the eyes, that is not the gesture of a Christian . . . Charity is not about offloading one's own sense of guilt, but it is touching, looking at our inner poverty . . .'[15] Central to all these expressions of Reciprocal Philanthropy is the understanding that every gift should bind the donor and recipient together in a relationship which also involves the whole of the community.

CROWDFUNDING AND THE DEMOCRATIZATION
OF PHILANTHROPY

Revealingly, the intuitions of most ordinary people are closer to the thinking of Reciprocal Philanthropists than they are to the approach of the Effective Altruists. This is of more consequence than might once have been the case, since philanthropy is becoming increasingly democratized, thanks in part to the growing influence of the internet and social media. The voices of ordinary givers are having greater influence. In the workplace in Britain, for example, in 2011 giving by employees overtook corporate donations. The result has been a shift in emphasis. Previously, senior managers were responsible for selecting charitable causes and partners. They often did so by focusing on how best to promote the company's brand to win new customers. By contrast, the charity choices of shop-floor staff are much more dictated by their personal emotions and experiences. They want to support causes that have most profoundly touched their lives. A survey conducted by Beth Breeze of the Centre for Giving and Philanthropy showed that favoured shop-floor causes included cancer research, local hospices and children's charities.[16]

Ordinary workers are inspired by the causes they choose. But workplace charity fundraising activities also provide an opportunity to relieve the monotony of low-paid work. More significantly, perhaps, they are perceived as something of a workplace leveller, offering the chance to challenge normally rigid corporate hierarchies and conventions. Making more powerful colleagues 'prove they are game' is a core attraction of much workplace fundraising, Breeze writes. It changes the dynamic of the workplace, like a medieval period of misrule – the same analogy used by the life-president of Comic Relief, Sir Lenny Henry, in his interview for this book.[*] 'I think morale would be really bad if we didn't let our hair down,' one supermarket worker told Breeze. The sense of fun this creates momentarily breaks down barriers between bosses, staff and customers. 'You go down the chilled meat, and there's some guy standing there in a blue wig and some Elton John blue sunglasses,' said one shopworker. 'It's just a bit of fun and the customers love it.'[17] This public philanthropy has raised significant sums. In the UK both the Comic Relief and BBC Children in Need telethons have raised more than £1 billion each.[18]

The democratization of philanthropy extends well beyond the workplace. Giving online has brought another transformation. The internet and social media have brought donors and recipients much closer together. The practice of crowdfunding has enabled significant sums to be raised from a large number of people each giving a relatively small amount. The phenomenon has been used to raise money for commercial investments, to make loans and to fund projects in the arts – movies, stage shows, classical compositions, video games, and recordings by new rock bands. The Kickstarter website has received nearly $5 billion in pledges from 17 million backers to fund 480,000 creative projects.[19] The same technique is also now being used to raise

---

[*] See interview on page 700.

sums for collective philanthropy through platforms such as JustGiving in the UK or Kiva, GlobalGiving and DonorsChoose in America. Crowdfunding has grown exponentially in recent years. In 2010 it raised $880 million worldwide; five years later that had mushroomed to $34 billion. Philanthropy is the second-biggest component of that crowdfunding.[20] What is innovative is that most donors have no previous acquaintance with the recipients but can form a strong relationship with them and their cause through their online connection. This new phenomenon, says Erik Stam, Professor of Strategy, Organization & Entrepreneurship at the University of Utrecht, taps into 'the wisdom of crowds'.[21-25]

What the democratization of philanthropy tells us is that many of the arguments of the Effective Altruists fail to chime with the public imagination. They are seen as reductive, cold-hearted and ultimately unpersuasive. Their rigid idea that the world's problems must be sorted out in strict order of effectiveness – meaning you cannot donate to the arts or other life-affirming activities, until malaria has been conquered – is alien on the public pulse. That emphasizes even more the necessity of finding some kind of middle way.

THE BEST OF BOTH WORLDS

Intriguingly, however, in recent times some advocates of Effective Altruism have come to recognize its limits. Sean Parker, in championing 'hacker philanthropy',* insists 'it's important for hackers to embrace the values that made them successful in the first place', but admits that means focusing on what he calls hackable problems. In his manifesto in the *Wall Street Journal* he advised his fellow tyro tech-philanthropists: 'Hack systems that can be hacked and ignore the rest. I care deeply, for example, about the plight of refugees and the peril of global warming, but I don't pretend to have some special insight into how to deal with them.'[26] Some other way than philanthrocapitalism needs to be found to address that kind of problem. Hacker insights might be useful but they are clearly no substitute for political action – nor, as Patty Stonesifer's move to Martha's Table suggested, for personal engagement.

---

* See pages 665–6 above.

The world's richest man, Jeff Bezos, founder of Amazon – whose fortune was estimated by the Bloomberg Billionaires Index in May 2020 at $139 billion[27] – has shown an intuitive prejudice in the same direction. In 2017 he announced on Twitter that he wanted to develop a philanthropy based on 'helping people in the here and now – short term – at the intersection of urgent need and lasting impact'.[28] He asked his million Twitter followers for ideas. He was not interested, he said, in Strategic Philanthropy.

The big question is: how can the effectiveness of Strategic Philanthropy be married to the empathy of Reciprocal Philanthropy? Some have suggested a return to the 'old philanthropy' practised by charitable foundations, which sought to address root causes but were, and are, bottom-up as well as top-down in their distribution of grants. Jeremy Beer, author of *The Philanthropic Revolution: An Alternative History of American Charity*, proposes something he calls 'philanthro-localism' in contrast to philanthrocapitalism.[29] Beer sums up what he calls the 'absurdities' of Strategic Philanthropy in a stark anecdote about how the Gates Foundation has homelessness as one of its strategic areas of concern yet will not provide direct assistance to any of the displaced people sleeping outside its $500 million Seattle headquarters. A foundation spokeswoman justified this paradox by explaining that Gates was 'trying to move upstream to a systems level' to prevent homelessness. Strategic philanthropy, Beer concludes, is about metrics, not mercy. Its focus is problem-solving, not helping people. Beer is equally scathing about an effective philanthropist who refused to help a woman with a sick child in an African village on the grounds that 'upon running the numbers it simply wouldn't have been strategic to pursue such a course'.[30] The philanthropist Howard Buffett, son of Warren, who runs his own charitable foundation, admitted: 'That was a hard lesson to learn.' Beer witheringly adds: 'No doubt the child's mother felt the same way.' Beer's alternative, philanthro-localism, is a philosophy of giving 'that prioritizes the use of resources to help one's own place, including one's neighbors, community members, churches, businesses, cultural institutions, civic associations, and ecology'.[31] This is a return to the Aristotelian view of philanthropy which sees human flourishing as embedded in local relationships. Beer's vision is perhaps too literal for our globalized world – though Richard Branson's philanthropic philosophy of Virgin Circles is an attempt to make this work for multinational companies.*

At the other end of the politico-philanthropic spectrum a solution more in line with social justice is offered by the political scientist Emily Clough, who thinks the answer is to redirect large amounts of philanthropic cash to fund advocacy organizations which hold politicians and government more to account.[32] Such a vision aims to give a voice to groups who are normally marginalized. It also wants structural change and the redistribution of social, political and economic power. Jamie Drummond's plan to create a global alliance of philanthropists is an attempt to make that real.† Both Clough's 'advocacy philanthropy' and Beer's 'philanthro-localism' offer challenges to the West's neoliberal philosophy which prioritizes individual self-interest and offers a purely materialist calculus in both economics and philanthropy.[33-36]

There is more to this than theory, according to the late Paul Connolly, who spent more than twenty years as a consultant in the philanthropy sector. Working directly with big donors he observed that the two separate approaches to philanthropy – which this book has traced throughout history – are both still very much alive today. Isolating the strengths and weaknesses of both approaches, he points to a number of examples where they are being helpfully fused – so that giving with the heart and giving with the head are not in tension but enrich one another.

Connolly examines the two methodologies in five specific areas.[37] The first is their overall philosophy. Those who give with their head see themselves as objective and dispassionate; they are data-driven and instrumentalist. Those who give with their heart, by contrast, are driven by value and passion; they are empathic and expressive. Connolly's second area is the giving of grants: here the first group are proactive, rationalistic and disciplined; the second are responsive, opportunistic and intuitive. His third area concerns the relationship between donors and their recipients; here Strategic Philanthropists are hands-on, top-down, and tend to treat recipients as contractors who are there to discharge the donor's wishes; Reciprocal Philanthropists,

---

* See interview with Richard Branson, pages 447–9.
† See pages 593–5.

by contrast, are hands-off, bottom-up and more flexible, being willing to accept innovative suggestions from the grassroots. Connolly's fourth area of analysis is an evaluation of the projects the two groups fund: here those who give with their head are more quantitative and focused on accountability; whereas those who give from the heart are more concerned with quality and willing to change as they learn from the results of the project. Finally, Strategic Philanthropists see what they are about as a science with disciplined frameworks and precise tools; by contrast, Reciprocal Philanthropists treat philanthropy more as an art which is difficult to codify.

The difference between the two approaches is stark. Paul Connolly then proceeds to make a judgement about their relative strengths and weaknesses. Strategic Philanthropists, who adopt what he calls a technocratic approach, have increasingly come to dominate philanthropy over the past two decades. This is because their approach brings many obvious benefits. Its application of business and social-science principles to philanthropy has helped donors devise focused goals and strategies, measure results rigorously, and work closely with grantees to improve performance. But it has also enabled funders to fool themselves into thinking that they are smarter than they are, or smarter than those who actually experience the problems they want to address. As a result, says Connolly, many funders 'care only *whether*, rather than *why*, a program works'. Their preoccupation with 'social return on investment' can create 'overly rigid strategies' which turn into 'obsessive measurement disorder'. They often overlook the wisdom of the recipient community and adopt an approach which is 'arrogant and unsuccessful, mostly creating solutions that were looking for problems'. They should remember that some outcomes are not measurable on a materialist abacus. But those who give only with their hearts throw up a different set of problems. Their far less critical altruism, intuitive approach to grant-giving and distaste for business metrics can lead to the squandering of money.

Yet the two approaches need not be contradictory. The head and the heart can, instead, complement one another. How? By changing the organizational culture in both types of philanthropy to champion moderation and balance. 'Foundation executives can achieve the right balance by hiring staff members who possess sound judgment and a blend of hard and soft skills,' says Paul Connolly. 'The best philanthropic leaders are not only analytical, objective, and expert, but also self-aware, respectful, and intuitive – and can adjust the mix when needed.'[38] Philanthropic programmes can be based on careful data analysis but can also be rooted in the deep experience and wisdom of those who work with groups at the grassroots. Those who give with the head cannot afford to leave their humanity outside the workplace; they should attend to relationships with authenticity and compassion. Those who give from the heart should seek to work with others who are skilled at strategy and performance measurement to complement their emotional intelligence. Both should look hard for the blind spots that cause over-confidence.[39] Values can be applied with rigour, data scrutinized with empathy, intuitions explored as part of strategic planning, top-down instincts wed to bottom-up intelligence. A hybrid model can incorporate the best of both the head and heart approaches.

Sometimes, to achieve this balance, it is not the project which needs changing but the donor's brief, as we saw with the case study of Teens and Toddlers, a British project designed to reduce teenage pregnancy but whose biggest impact was in improving educational outcomes for teenage girls at risk of low achievement or drop-out.* Heart and head brought a rebalancing there. Paul Connolly cites a US charity to illustrate heart and head working together in practice. The NoVo Foundation is run by Warren Buffett's youngest son, Peter, with his wife Jennifer. Endowed with $1 billion by Buffett Sr, it gives away around $55 million in grants each year, chiefly to empower girls and women.[40] Jennifer Buffett, the foundation's co-president, says that her father-in-law advised her and Peter to focus their funding, take risks, be patient, and assess their impact. That involves a blend of Strategic and Reciprocal Philanthropy. 'In a field that works to build and support human capacities and change entire systems, it is not a good idea to fall into the trap of relying exclusively on metrics or a technocratic approach,' she says. 'We work in a very thoughtful way to equalize power relationships, build expertise on the ground, and listen and nurture . . . balancing and considering the head and the heart. That doesn't mean we are not interested in sound structures, evaluation, and solid results. But, again, to us, solutions should always have a human being, a human

---

* See pages 456–8 above.

voice, at the centre.'[41] Connolly quotes Joshua L. Liebman, a rabbi who sought to reconcile religion with psychoanalytic theory, and concluded that 'maturity is achieved when a person accepts life as full of tension'.[42] Gillian Rose's philosophy of 'the broken middle' might lead us to call this 'good-enough philanthropy'.*

CAN PHILANTHROPY BE BOTH STRATEGIC AND RECIPROCAL?

Some mechanisms already exist which make this kind of synergy possible. Let us consider two examples – social impact investing and cash transfers. Impact investing is the modern equivalent of Octavia Hill's 5 per cent philanthropy. The idea is that philanthropists and charitable foundations can invest in a project which does good for society and also returns them a profit. The notion is growing in popularity. In 2018 some $228 billion were placed in social investments in the United States alone – around a third of the total sum given to charity, according to the Global Impact Investing Network.[43] In Britain an independent organization, Big Society Capital, was set up in 2012 by the Cameron/Clegg coalition government with the aim of growing the social investment market in the UK. Its founding chairman, Sir Ronald Cohen, a former venture capitalist, lamented the 'sorry state' of philanthropy: 'it has too great a focus on giving, rather than on achieving social outcomes; its timelines are too short; it is of too limited scale; and it pays inadequate attention to growth.'[44]

David Cameron's Big Society was short-lived, but Cohen's determination to foster social investing saw it pioneered in the UK and then spread beyond under the slogan 'How Capitalism Can Better Serve Society'. The first 'social impact bonds' involved private companies taking on a government project – and only being paid if it succeeded. The idea is to harness market disciplines and techniques with socially desirable outcomes. One of the first schemes was designed to cut the reoffending rate of prisoners coming out of Peterborough Prison. The private company which undertook the task was only to be paid if it succeeded in cutting the reoffending rate by 7.5 per cent over 12 months. It succeeded, reducing the rate by 9 per cent. As a result

---

* See pages 631–2 above.

the 17 investors in the Peterborough Social Impact Bond – including a variety of charitable trusts – were repaid their capital plus a return of just over 3 per cent per annum.[45] Had the company hit a 10 per cent target, the pay-out to investors would have been bigger. According to the Brookings Institute, in 2019 there were 192 of these impact bonds in 32 countries, in areas such as employment, social welfare, health, education, criminal justice, agriculture and the environment.[46] They raised over \$420 million.[47] The largest number are still focused in the UK, and most target social welfare and employment. Yet they are increasingly being applied internationally – from the US to Uganda.[48] Sir Ronald Cohen, now chairman of the Global Social Impact Investment Steering Group, has plans to sharply accelerate the trend. The venture capitalist's ambition is to raise \$300 billion in 19 countries to improve the lives of a billion poor people by the end of 2020. 'Impact investment does not have to involve delivering below-market returns,' he told investors in India. 'We can make more profits because of impact.'[49] It is possible, he insists, to do well and do good at the same time.

A more surprising, and revealing, advocate of the social impact model is Pope Francis, who has been a fierce critic of unfettered free-market capitalism. 'Such an economy kills,' he once memorably wrote.[50] But the Pope too has embraced social impact investing. In 2014 he called together a special conference to consider its applicability to the Church, to Catholic institutions and to Catholic philanthropists. The Gospel may admonish Christians, 'You cannot serve both God and money',[51] but Pope Francis is seeking a way to do both. Launching the conference, the pontiff said that the innovation of social investment 'acknowledges the ultimate connection between profit and solidarity, the virtuous circle existing between profit and gift'. And he went further: 'Christians are called to rediscover, experience and proclaim to all, this precious and primordial unity between profit and solidarity.'[52]

There are, of course, differences of nuance between the Effective Philanthropist and the empathetic pontiff. Where Ronald Cohen insists social impact investing can produce returns at the same rate as normal investments, the Pope would like the financial return for investors to be more modest than for other types of investment. And Pope Francis insists that impact investing is not suitable for all areas of social improvement. He has told Catholics it can help with promoting the economic and social development necessary to satisfy basic needs in agriculture, access to clean water, affordable housing, primary health care and educational services. But not all causes lend themselves to models that pay investors a financial return. Issues such as domestic violence or chronic homelessness cannot be addressed through impact investing, because there is no revenue model associated with them. It is also important to guard against the danger that financial return may elbow aside social concerns, says Jane Wales, chief executive of the Global Philanthropy Forum, a network of grant-makers and social investors. Others like Larry Kramer, president of the Hewlett Foundation, fear that impact investing could divert money from conventional philanthropy.[53]

The Pope, however, is prepared to take the risk. By 2017, three years after he launched the Vatican conference, social impact investments by Catholic institutions totalled around $1 billion. Several new Catholic impact funds have been formed. The Oblate International Pastoral Investment Trust, which handles the resources of more than 200 Catholic organizations from over 50 countries, pledged in 2019 to use its investments as part of a $34 trillion alliance for action on climate change.[54] Another major fund, the Catholic Impact Investing Collaborative, manages assets of $50 billion for 30 American Catholic institutions. Smaller 'retail' funds have also been set up to allow ordinary Catholics in the pew to pay as little as $30 a head to buy a share in social impact investing.[55] That is but a fraction of the Church's assets. If Catholics channel more of their investments through social impact funds, Rome has the potential to transform the size of the impact-investment market in what would be a major development in the marriage of Strategic and Reciprocal Philanthropy.

Cash transfers are another good example of how the gulf between Effective Altruism and Reciprocal Philanthropy can be bridged. The idea is best summed up in the title of the book which gave birth to the movement, *Just Give Money to the Poor*. Its three authors are academics who specialize in the economics of international development. In 2010 the researchers – Joseph Hanlon, Armando Barrientos and David Hulme of the Global Development Institute at Manchester University – set out a raft of evidence which proved that transferring cash to poor people in poor countries is a highly effective way of promoting economic development. Child benefit, family allowance, old age pensions and other guaranteed long-term payments do not just benefit the individuals who receive them. They also stimulate economic growth in the whole community. The evidence ran counter to the common supposition that the poor do not use money wisely but squander it on alcohol or other frivolities. On the contrary, a decade of research in Asia, Africa and Latin America, in a range of different economies, showed that the poor use cash gifts wisely. They are spent mainly on better food and school fees for children. But the whole family benefits. After five years, families given cash in this way have an income which is more than the value of the cash they were initially given. Cash transfers create a positive spiral. These results surprised even the researchers. The book demonstrated the political and economic feasibility of direct cash transfers as a form of aid for chronically poor people in sub-Saharan Africa and South Asia.

These findings were subsequently endorsed by other academics who exploded the prejudice that giving money to the poor would make them work less and have more children. Neither is true.[56] Rather cash transfers have a long-term beneficial impact. Greater school attendance is consistently accompanied by a reduction in child labour. Where there is an old age pension, parents do not feel the need to have a lot of children to support them in their old age.[57] Cash transfers 'provide the boots which allow people to pull themselves up by their own bootstraps,' says Joseph Hanlon.[58]

Projects like this can appeal in equal measure to Effective Altruists and Reciprocal Philanthropists. For those who are data-driven the evidence is there in research from middle-income countries and poor countries alike. The data sets out the precise conditions in which cash transfers work. They must be permanent programmes, and not a relief response to some particular crisis. The sums involved do not have to be large, but they have to be big enough to make a difference to the family budget. The practicalities will vary from country to country, but all the schemes need to be transparent so everyone can see that they are fair. The sums have to be delivered unconditionally, not as a charitable gift, but as a right, and to a sizeable proportion of the population – somewhere between 20 and 40 per cent – to make them politically popular so that they carry on despite changes of government.

But the scheme is also a classic example of the values of Reciprocal Philanthropy. The idea did not originate in the developed world, but came from poor countries themselves. That is a key element in successful Reciprocal Philanthropy. Poor recipients know far better than rich donors what works on the ground, says David Hulme. Poor and rich also need to work together on the practicalities of implementation.[59] Hulme worked with field staff from the grassroots development organization BRAC in Bangladesh on the idea of cash transfers. Groups on the ground had a better understanding of both local conditions and of the real lives of the poorest people. What is true in Bangladesh is true universally, according to Professor Ngaire Woods of the Blavatnik School of Government in Oxford. Projects which local people 'own' – and in which they invest their own time, sweat and money – are the projects that are by far the most likely to work, she says in her interview for this book.*

Cash transfers thus satisfy both the spiritual commitment of Reciprocal Philanthropy and the scientific and technical rigour demanded by Effective Altruism and Strategic Philanthropy. They validate Reciprocal Philanthropists' intuition that the poor often know much better than outside experts how to improve their own lives. But they are also deemed effective by utilitarians like Peter Singer, who includes the unconditional cash transfer programmes of the charity GiveDirectly on his list of EA recommendations.[60] It sends what it calls a Universal Basic Income to more than 20,000 of the poorest people in Kenya. It cuts out middleman organizations by sending the money directly to recipients through their mobile phones.[61] Cash transfers also appeal to mainstream philanthropic organizations such as the International Rescue Committee (IRC), one of the world's largest aid organizations, which is now committed to delivering 25 per cent of its humanitarian assistance in the form of cash relief by the end of 2020 – up from approximately 6 per cent in 2015.[62] Unconditional cash transfers have now taken off in 45 countries where they are assisting 110 million families.[63]

So how should philanthropists today seek out more of these mechanisms which combine the relative strengths of the Strategic and Reciprocal approaches? First they must learn the lesson of the PlayPump. This invention consists of a children's playground roundabout which, when pushed around, draws drinking water from deep below ground. The idea was widely applauded when it was first proposed for African villages; it would simultaneously provide children with recreation and

---

* See page 508 above.

families with water. 'Pumping water is child's play', read the laudatory newspaper headlines. In the first decade of this century 1,800 of these pumps were installed across Africa. Unfortunately, the roundabouts were too hard to push and a number of children were injured using them. William MacAskill cites PlayPumps as proof of what goes wrong when philanthropists do not follow the Effective Altruist paradigm of strict data analysis. PlayPumps were four times more expensive than the old hand pumps they replaced and were five times slower.[64] But Georgina White, in *The Ethics of Philanthropy*, borrows templates from Aristotle, Cicero and Seneca to lay over the problem.[65] 'In the majority of cases no-one had asked the recipients if they wanted a PlayPump prior to installation, and they were deeply unpopular among those who received them,' she writes. So the project did not simply fail from a lack of modern data analysis. It also fell short of the more ancient ideal that a gift must create a mutually satisfactory relationship between donor and recipient, in a way which creates both a personal bond and social harmony.

LEARNING TO LISTEN – AND LISTENING TO LEARN

Perhaps the greatest failing of the big philanthrocapitalists at the start of the twenty-first century has been their inability to listen. Like their robber baron predecessors at the turn of the previous century they have been seized by the certainty that the talents which brought them such success in business will automatically work in philanthropy. As the example of Bill Gates has shown, their drive and acumen has brought huge benefits for humankind. The eradication of polio and other great strides in global health have shown that. But their strengths have also been their blind spot, as the ill-fated adventures of both Gates and Mark Zuckerberg in education have shown. The waste of five years and several hundred million dollars might be of small consequence to a multi-billionaire. But five wasted years in the education of a child are another matter. If only these great innovators had first been great listeners. Listening is probably the key quality needed to bridge the gap between Strategic and Reciprocal Philanthropy.

After she quit her job at the head of the Gates Foundation in 2008, Patty Stonesifer decided that there was something she needed to do before she joined Martha's Table to work among the poor and homeless. Stonesifer decided that she needed to know what it was like to walk in the shoes of those she would be helping. So she resolved to live off the same budget as the people who lived off 'food stamps' – the US government's Supplemental Nutrition Assistance Program. It worked out at about $4 a day. 'If you're relying on food stamps to eat, you're in real trouble,' she said afterwards. 'Carbs are vastly cheaper than nutrients, so it was easy for me to see why hunger and obesity can coexist in the same household.'[66] She lasted one week. Families who have to live off food stamps for a whole month find that, by the third week, they have virtually run out of money. 'You don't even want to think about what happens when your dollars get down that low,' Stonesifer said.[67] The experience of even that one week gave 'feedback to the heart as well as the head,' she told another interviewer, bridging the gap between Strategic and Reciprocal Philanthropy in a single phrase.[68]

Listening makes you equal with the other person. It creates the partnership which is the essential ingredient in Reciprocal Philanthropy. Martha's Table, before Stonesifer arrived, 'always did a fantastic job with children and food programs', she told one interviewer.[69] But to go further meant listening more closely to those the charity set out to serve. Within six months of Stonesifer's arrival, her charity set up a youth council. It not only influenced the shape of the charity's services, it also empowered young people to speak out in the community. Listening has become deeply embedded, working across the generations. Martha's Table now hires individuals who have come up through the programmes it created. Stonesifer regularly conducts what she calls 'short and long surveying of our community'. She listens not simply by attending to what people say – though she does that – but by attending to what they do.

What Stonesifer strives for is a conversation of equals. 'At our Joyful Food Markets, we talk to folks about their cooking habits: what foods they want to have, and where the gaps are.' She encourages her staff to learn how their clients cook in their own homes, so Martha's Table can stock its free store with the right foods in the right season. 'We want our offerings to match what people want and need'.[70–72] Listening is the first step on the road to mutual respect and a partnership in which both sides treat one another as equals, learning in tandem and making changes together.

That is an understanding which experience has gradually taught to several Strategic Philanthropists. When Melinda Gates was asked in

2019 in an interview on BBC Radio what gave her the right to go into communities in the developing world and change their ways in accordance with Western ideals, she replied: 'We can only go into communities if they want us to be there. And we have to listen carefully to what they want and what their needs are.' That learning curve began with a programme the Gates Foundation launched to combat HIV/AIDS in India. The infection had not spread to the wider population but was largely contained among sex workers. Yet Melinda Gates knew that if it spread beyond sex workers and truckers there could be an explosion of AIDS in India:

> We went in to talk to the sex workers about what could be done, thinking that we could ask them to demand condoms of their clients, and to be HIV tested themselves. But what we learned from those sex workers was that we first had to help them with violence. They said, 'If you don't help us with the violence we have from our clients, we can't begin to demand a condom'. So we had to take an approach that was led by them and their community.

The people on the ground clearly knew more than the outside experts. Ultimately they kept AIDS from breaking out into the general population. This approach was so successful that the Indian government took the programme up over time. 'To us, that's what listening means, and that's what success looks like,' Melinda Gates concluded. 'You have a shared goal – let's not have HIV spread into the population of the whole country – but you listen and learn in a way that's culturally appropriate.'[73]

Bill Gates, having listened and learned from the grassroots experience of those he was funding to combat the 2014 Ebola crisis, changed – and did his best to make others also listen. In 2015 he had set out his strategic plan to tackle future global epidemics. It represented an about-turn on his previous dismissive attitudes to strengthening health infrastructure rather than simply focusing on individual diseases. In 2020, as the COVID-19 coronavirus pandemic took hold across the globe, writing in the *New England Journal of Medicine*, he now insisted: 'When you build a health clinic, you're also creating part of the infrastructure for fighting epidemics. Trained health care workers not only deliver vaccines; they can also monitor disease patterns, serving as part of the early warning systems that alert the world to potential outbreaks.'[74]

This was not a new message. In his 2015 campaign to persuade world leaders to prepare a co-ordinated international pandemic early warning system and rapid response programme he had warned: 'If anything kills over 10 million people in the next few decades, it's most likely to be a highly infectious virus rather than a war'.[75] A year later in a BBC interview he repeated the message that global systems for responding to emergencies were not strong enough and that the world was merely keeping its fingers-crossed against a fatal pandemic.[76] The world had been saved from the SARS, MERS and zika infections, which were deadlier but less infectious, more by good luck than good management. In 2017, speaking at the Munich Security Conference, Gates noted that epidemiologists had warned that a fast-moving airborne pathogen could kill more than 30 million people in less than a year – and it could occur in the next 10 to 15 years.[77] Giving the Massachusetts Medical Society's annual lecture in 2018 he admonished that 'the world wasn't making much progress' on pandemic preparedness: 'If history has taught us anything, it's that there will be another deadly global pandemic'.[78] 'The world needs to prepare for pandemics the way the military prepares for war', he said. 'Planners need to carry out Germ Games, as soldiers do war games, to discover the holes in our medical defences'.[79]

In March 2018 Bill Gates presented his concerns at a private meeting in the White House with President Donald Trump.[80] He urged Trump to build upon the work of presidents George W Bush, who had devoted $7 billion to preparing for an influenza epidemic, and Barack Obama who had launched a $1 billion Global Health Security Agenda after the Ebola outbreak. Trump asked Gates if he was interested in becoming his official scientific adviser – and then, two months later, dissolved the White House pandemic office having already declined to renew $600 million of funding to the Center for Disease Control, which had been approved under Obama.[81] When the COVID-19 pandemic hit the United States the Trump administration struggled.

Unable to persuade the world's governments to co-ordinated action, Gates had his Foundation act where it could, funding multiple grants and research programmes geared toward developing new vaccines to prevent pandemic influenza. He invested in the Coalition for Epidemic

Preparedness Innovations, an international alliance that launched at Davos in 2017. At the end of 2019, just weeks before the COVID-19 outbreak was identified in China, the Bill & Melinda Gates Foundation joined with the Johns Hopkins Center for Health Security to host 'a high-level simulation exercise for pandemic preparedness and response' – the global Germ Game that Gates had been requesting for four years. The exercise brought together business, government, security and public health leaders to address a hypothetical global pandemic scenario.[82] Asked what the exercise had revealed, the president of Davos, Børge Brende, said that it showed that 'the global community was woefully unprepared'. Two months later the coronavirus crisis began. Gates donated $100 million 'to help kickstart the global response' and then announced he was spending 'billions' to build seven factories to manufacture the seven most promising COVID-19 vaccines with the aim of finding two that worked. Other philanthropists made rapid contributions of over $10 billion.[83] But the interventions were too little too late. Global pandemic prevention is the business of governments co-operating at the highest international level, though philanthropists may well have an important role to play in the rebuilding of civil society in the post-coronavirus era.

Still philanthropists insisted that they were listening and learning.

The Zuckerbergs made similar missteps to Gates at first. Their early philanthropic foray into reforming education in the United States* was also less than satisfactory. But just two years after the Newark fiasco Priscilla Chan gave an interview to the *Chronicle of Philanthropy* in which she insisted that she and her husband were committed to listening, learning and improving. They were starting young 'so that we can get better over time'.[84] The seasoned British philanthropy observer Rhodri Davies, Head of Policy at the Charities Aid Foundation, is optimistic that Zuckerberg and Chan 'seem to have realised' fairly early on the importance of both 'learning from experts and engaging communities and individuals in finding the solutions to their own problems'.[85] One of the biggest philanthropy foundations to have taken on board this message most completely is Peter and Jennifer Buffett's NoVo Foundation. 'My wife and I know we don't have the answers, but

---

* See pages 661–2 above.

we do know how to listen,' Buffett wrote, setting out his philosophy of giving in the *New York Times*. 'As we learn, we will continue to support conditions for systemic change,' he said. The NoVo Foundation's website declares that the best solutions come from within communities, which is why 'we support social movements that build the power of people to create lasting change'.[86] But listening is not easy – as the Buffetts discovered when they faced a barrage of criticism after announcing big cuts in funding after their assets collapsed in the coronavirus stock market crash.[87] 'The more excluded people are,' says Darren Walker, president of the Ford Foundation, 'the harder it is truly to hear them'.[88]

Those who do listen may sometimes be told something they would rather not hear. 'There is a growing realisation that, in order for philanthropy to be a true force for progress, when it comes to dealing with inequality, it cannot simply be about transfers of money – it must involve a transfer of *power* as well,' writes Rhodri Davies of the Charities Aid Foundation. Many philanthrocapitalists are resistant to that. 'When you have put so much effort into gaining both wealth and power, the temptation is to hold on to them. And whilst philanthropy has long provided a template for disposing of wealth, that has not always been accompanied by a disposal of power.'[89] Yet if progress is not made on that there is a danger that philanthropy will continue to be dismissed as merely a vehicle for the wealthy to promote their pet projects and advance their own views and interests – missing the opportunity to bring real transformation.

HOW MUCH SHOULD YOU LEAVE TO YOUR CHILDREN?

There is one area in which philanthropy has made a big shift. The new generation of self-made mega-philanthropists embrace the idea of 'giving while living'. A number have pledged that they will dispose of their fortunes before they die rather than setting up permanent charitable foundations to outlive them. Many more are committed to the idea of 'leaving less to the kids' to force their children to make their own way in the world as their parents did. That is a significant departure. Traditionally, the wealthy left all their money to their children and grandchildren, but today's super-rich fear 'affluenza' – the dissatisfaction that comes from modern materialism. Excess wealth, they fear, may be a burden rather than a blessing to their children. 'The last thing you want is to ruin your kids,' says Richard Branson in his interview in this book.* Many of them have come to see philanthropy as an antidote to affluenza – and a mechanism for securing a selfless happiness for their offspring and a tool for teaching them ethics.

The idea is not new. In 1958 Garfield Weston, who built a huge British food-processing empire after starting as a baker in Canada, wrote to all his children saying, 'Great wealth has great responsibility. It can destroy all those who have it, or if they can wisely control it . . . it can bring great blessings in its distribution.' Setting up what is now one of the largest philanthropic charities in Britain, the Garfield Weston Foundation, he told them: 'We must seriously think about how we can do the most good with what we have to give away.' He persuaded his children to give their share of the business to the foundation. Today its nine trustees are all Garfield Weston's children or grandchildren. The innovative Weston model – where the charity holds the majority stake in the family business – has kept the family grounded. 'It has the remarkable effect of keeping the family together in pursuit of a common goal for good,' says Pippa Charles, the foundation's director. 'They are stewards of a significant sum of money and they take that responsibility extremely seriously.'[90]

Bill and Melinda Gates came to much the same conclusion. 'Creating our foundation and being in the philanthropy sector [has] helped us to live out our values as a couple, both in our work in the world and back at home because we talk about our values often with our kids now around the dinner table,' Melinda Gates told *Woman's Hour* on BBC Radio in 2019.[91] Asked how she kept her children's feet on the ground, when they know they are fabulously wealthy, she replied:

> Our children have been fortunate enough to travel . . . to many different countries in Africa and South-East. And while they get to go on a nice tourism-type trip, we almost always as a family try also to go and see the reality on the ground. So my children were very early in some townships in Africa, very early did some home stays in Africa. And what they know is that they are lucky. Any child who grows up in the UK or the US is lucky, and so we instilled those values early in

---

* See page 449 above.

our kids. We always talked [about how] their job in life was to figure
out their talents and their passions and how to eventually give those
back to the world. So I don't know what's right for all parents but I
know that's what's been right for us.

In the Gates household conversation round the dinner table is about
what Bill and Melinda are working on at the foundation, so their
children are deeply familiar with what their parents do. In fact,
Melinda told another interviewer: 'I sometimes wondered if I had gone
overboard. When my oldest daughter was three, she said to her doll,
"Lay down, you have AIDS! I'm gonna give you a shot!" I thought, "Oh
my God, what have I done?" Clearly we're talking about AIDS so much
my three-year-old knows what it is.'[92]

How much should you leave to your children? Warren Buffett, who in
2020 was the fourth-richest man in the world[93] – worth $90 billion – has
a well-rehearsed answer to that question: 'Enough money so that they
would feel they could do anything, but not so much that they could
do nothing.'[94] Buffett's three children each have a $2 billion charitable
foundation funded by their father. The rest of his money is pledged to
go to charity, and a lot of it has already gone. Bill and Melinda Gates
are said to be giving $10 million to each of their three children[95] – small
change out of the couple's estimated $114 billion fortune.[96] This shift is
not confined to the super-rich. A survey by Lloyds TSB of people with
liquid assets of more than £250,000 found that 54 per cent said they
would prefer to spend their money or give it to charity than pass it on to
their children.[97] One of Britain's most generous philanthropists, David
Sainsbury, has set up his personal charitable trust, the Gatsby Foundation,
as a 'spend-out' trust which will disburse all its funds within ten years
of his death.* But the family wealth has enabled his daughters, fifth-
generation Sainsburys, to become philanthropists in their own right. One
of them, Fran Perrin, said: 'Because I grew up in a family where there are
18 charitable trusts it never really occurred to me not to.' Her foundation,
the Indigo Trust, makes grants to help create a world of active informed
citizens and responsive accountable governments in sub-Saharan Africa.

---

* See page 236 above.

It donates around £750,000 a year and she too has said she plans to give the majority of her wealth away during her lifetime.[98]

WILL THE ZUCKERBERGS LEARN
THE LESSONS OF THE PAST?

So what are the implications of all this for the manifesto which Mark Zuckerberg and Priscilla Chan launched upon the world in their letter to their first newborn child? When in 2015 the Zuckerbergs announced that they would give away 99 per cent of their Facebook shares – then worth $45 billion – the news was widely applauded. 'Choosing philanthropy over personal luxury is admirable,' a *Financial Times* editorial proclaimed. 'It sets a powerful example for others to follow in donating money, expertise and time – from fellow billionaires [to] companies and individuals with far more modest means.'[99] What was unclear was whether the new limited liability company (LLC) they had chosen as the vehicle to do this was another step in the relentless march of philanthrocapitalism – or an expansive device to enable an approach more open to the insights of Reciprocal Philanthropy.

The *Financial Times* was prepared to give the move the benefit of the doubt with regard to the greater secrecy the LLC allowed the donors. It pointed out that the limited company structure will offer more scope for the Zuckerbergs to invest in commercial companies with social goals rather than just giving out grants to researchers. But Chan and Zuckerberg could silence those who were critical of this built-in opacity quite simply, the newspaper added. They could voluntarily commit their Initiative to be far more open about its activities than company law requires. 'They should set a good example with high levels of transparency and accountability for their donations and the results they generate,' the *FT* editorial suggested.[100] The Zuckerbergs made some concession to this in 2019 when, for the first time, they published an interactive database of their grant-giving for the previous twelve months. But there is more they could do. Fran Perrin, the Sainsbury with a reputation for innovative thinking, agreed: 'I'd love them to go beyond what's required on transparency and demonstrate what they're doing.'[101]

There was, likewise, an ambiguity about the fact that the LLC would allow the Zuckerbergs to be more overtly political in their philanthropy.

The analysis of Rhodri Davies of the Charities Aid Foundation is that the limited liability structure has been chosen to allow Chan and Zuckerberg to engage in significant efforts to influence public policy, more so perhaps than the law would permit for a charitable foundation. 'This is fascinating,' writes Davies. 'It's not often that you hear the complaint that the problem with charitable organisations is that they are *not political enough* – it tends very much to be the other way round'. And yet, he notes, 'to hear a philanthropist overtly state that they want even more freedom to influence policy than has traditionally been the case may well set alarm bells ringing for some'.[102] Indeed, as we have seen, one of the real worries about modern philanthrocapitalism is the distorting effect that it can have on democratic decision-making. That can be the unintended consequence of big philanthropy even when its intentions are benign. And some consequences are far from unintended, as we saw in the case of the climate change philanthropy of the Koch brothers and their libertarian peers.*

But business, politics and philanthropy have been mixed elsewhere with very different results. Victorian industrialists such as the chocolate manufacturer George Cadbury saw no real dividing lines between the commercial, charitable and political when it came to promoting the change that his Quaker worldview inspired.† Zuckerberg, whose Facebook empire is much criticized for its extensive tax avoidance, might do well to emulate Cadbury more closely. The Victorian industrialist did not just give large sums to charity, he also altered his business practices in the light of his philanthropic principles – not the other way around, as modern philanthrocapitalists so often do. Mark Zuckerberg seems to keep his business practices in a separate silo from his philanthropy. The consequence of this, as the *Financial Times* has noted, is that when companies like Facebook pursue aggressive tax avoidance strategies, they are depriving governments of the revenues needed to tackle the same health problems that Zuckerberg says he wants his philanthropy to address.[103] That paradox opens him and his fellows to the charge that their philanthropy is giving with one hand while their business takes away with the other hand. To avoid that charge Facebook – which paid only one per cent in tax on its £1.3 billion UK sales in 2017 – must begin to pay a fairer share of its

---

* See pages 576–587 above.
† See pages 317–326 above.

taxes.[104] Large companies have a responsibility to the society which enables them to flourish. Philanthropy, however generous, only partly discharges that moral duty. If Mark Zuckerberg wants to demonstrate the moral seriousness of his philanthropy, he should pay more tax.

Close scrutiny of the long and reflective letter which Mark Zuckerberg and Priscilla Chan wrote to their newborn baby suggests that they may be open to the combination of the Strategic and Reciprocal approaches to philanthropy which this book is advocating. The letter balances head and heart. It demonstrates the force of their personal conviction but acknowledges the need for listening and learning in respectful partnership with others. On the one hand, some of the shibboleths of Effective Altruism remain in evidence in the text. Chan and Zuckerberg have borrowed from Bill Gates his slogan 'All lives have equal value'. They talk of how accelerating technology will give them 'a real shot at preventing, curing or managing all or most' of the world's most serious diseases. They remain focused on other technical solutions such as personalized learning. They see universal internet access as the way to lift people out of poverty and create new jobs – which would clearly have beneficial side effects for Facebook's digital empire. But, on the other hand, they acknowledge that 'technology can't solve problems by itself' and admit that 'building a better world starts with building strong and healthy communities'.[105]

What follows in the rest of the letter is a mixture of the Strategic and the Reciprocal. Zuckerberg and Chan are strategic in wanting to make investments over 25, 50 or even 100 years – acknowledging that 'the greatest challenges . . . cannot be solved by short-term thinking'. But they are reciprocal when they concede: 'We must engage directly with the people we serve. We can't empower people if we don't understand the needs and desires of their communities.' Strategically they assert: 'We must build technology to make change', since most progress comes from productivity gains achieved through innovation. But reciprocally they add: 'We're early in our learning and many things we try won't work, but we'll listen and learn and keep improving.' And they add: 'Partnering with experts is more effective for the mission than trying to lead efforts ourselves.'[106]

But does all this go beyond rhetoric? Some remain sceptical. One leading figure with reservations is Michael Edwards, whose decades of experience in the philanthropy sector encompass working for Oxfam in Africa, with the Ford Foundation and the World Bank in the US, and then as an academic in the UK. He insists that the couple need to partner not just with experts but 'most particularly [with] those people at the grassroots who are the objects of their ministrations' – those 'who do the work' and 'suffer the consequences' and 'know what's happening on the ground'. Philanthropists need to shake off the idea that he who pays the piper calls the tune. They must be educated into partnership. 'Paradoxically, the more you try to control social change, the less you succeed and the more opposition you create along the way. So it's a self-defeating process,' Edwards writes. 'Far better to let go – and take advantage of the multiplier effects that come from liberating other people to get on with the work they want to do.'[107] But other seasoned commentators such as Rhodri Davies have been impressed: 'These are pretty positive statements to my mind, which encapsulate some key principles of how philanthropy should be done, so it is encouraging to see them set out up front,' he writes.[108] The letter does suggest that Zuckerberg and Chan have developed 'that most precious gift for philanthropists, humility, and taken on board the need to engage with those on the ground before deciding how best to help them'.

Who will prove to be right, the sceptics or the enthusiasts? So far the Chan Zuckerberg Initiative has committed only to detailed spending on a fraction of its founders' monumental $45 billion pledge – which, by now, will be worth much more since Mark Zuckerberg was valued at $83 billion at the start of 2020, according to the Bloomberg Billionaire Index.[109] The focus in this last chapter has been on the Zuckerbergs because they represent the future of philanthropy in the way that Bill and Melinda Gates exemplify its present. But the central dilemma which I have set out around them is one that applies to the whole new generation who will determine the future direction of twenty-first-century philanthropy.

It is possible that this new generation will default to the model of business-oriented philanthrocapitalism which has come to dominate the world of giving over the past half century. If that happens, philanthropists will persist in the century-long self-certainty they inherited from Andrew Carnegie that only the rich are capable of deciding how to spend money well – and that only the techniques the dot.com titans used to amass their fortunes can solve the problems of the world. Philanthropy should, and will, become ever more like business. If that happens each prodigious gift may serve to massage the ego of the individual philanthropist, but it will reinforce the inequality built into our current political economy. Philanthropists then will do no more than continue the attempt to remake the world in their own image.

Yet, on the other hand, it is possible, as the optimists hope, that the Zuckerbergs and others will begin to take on board the lessons of the tradition of Reciprocal Philanthropy. These have fallen from favour in recent times but they were integral to philanthropy for the first thousand years of its history and, as this book has shown, have repeatedly surfaced since in the philanthropy of Robert Owen, Titus Salt, Octavia Hill, George Cadbury, Joseph Rowntree and many others. Those pioneers brought something of philanthropy into business as well as making philanthropy more business-like. It is a tradition of philanthropy with a more human face, which focuses on people rather than results, which is two-way rather than top-down, which listens and involves itself in a conversation of equals, and which understands that a gift should create a bond between giver and receiver, which respects and benefits both – and also our wider society.

This book has told the story of how philanthropy has two sides to its personality. It has a heart as well as a head. The challenge for the new generation, of which the Zuckerbergs can be role models, is to marry the effective and empathetic strands of philanthropy. These pages have given examples of how that is possible. It is up to the new generation of philanthropists to discover imaginative ways to do that on a more ambitious global scale. But to do it they must listen more carefully, be more open and accountable in their donations, and be more transparent about the results their giving creates on the ground. To do so will benefit both those who give and those who receive. Above all, they must cease to view the world as a series of problems they can solve. Instead, they must begin to see it as a succession of people who can be their partners in leaving our children a better, safer and more sustainable world in which to live. If they do that, they will have gone some way to recovering the lost soul of philanthropy.

Epilogue

Philanthropy after the Pandemic

The post-pandemic world will be different from the world we knew before. So will its philanthropy. What has yet to emerge is whether fear or fellow-feeling will be the primary influence on the new world order. Both selfishness and self-sacrifice were widely on display as the COVID-19 virus swept the globe claiming lives and destroying livelihoods. As this book has shown, philanthropy can be an expression of anxiety as well as altruism, of control as well as compassion. If the coronavirus proves to be a turning point in history, then the big changes which are to come may be made worse or made better by big givers. Whichever, the questions raised by this history of philanthropy will still apply – and with more urgency. Philanthropy may become even more important in a world where only the super-rich could have enough spare cash to give.

The era of unimpeded globalization of the past half-century is almost certainly over. An economic system that increasingly relied on long supply chains stretching right across the world made products cheaper. But it also made societies more vulnerable to unexpected disruptions such as a global pandemic. The virus exposed the downside of globalization and the dangers of an interconnectedness dependent on just-in-time deliveries. The imprudence of nations relying on one single country, China, for the production of many of the world's essential medical supplies is now clear.[1] So is the folly of a nation like Britain – whose economy is driven by the engine of financial services – taking globalization as its cue to phase out farming and manufacturing and instead import its food and essential kit. Global trade will continue.

Consumers will still want low prices and high choice. And businesses will resist the dismantling of their established supply systems. But globalization may well have peaked. Now, for each nation, the resilience with which its economy can deal with unexpected events will henceforward be seen as important a virtue as efficiency. Security and stability will rise up the public policy ladder. All this is bound to impact upon philanthropy since the great boom in giving of recent decades was the by-product of rapidly accelerating globalization.

The check on globalization will come from the nation state which was already gaining in strength from the wave of populist nationalism sweeping the world. That trend may well be accelerated by the pandemic. The variety of international responses to COVID-19 – responses which were widely different in their degrees of success in staving off early deaths – gave a new legitimacy to national governments as the most powerful and effective forces to tackle such threats. International organizations like the European Union were slow in showing the solidarity which is supposed to be one of their core virtues. The richer member states were tardy in coming to the aid of Italy when its health service became the first in Europe to be overwhelmed by the pandemic. EU leaders showed a lack of initiative and their bureaucracy was sluggish.[2] Elsewhere world leaders starved international bodies like the United Nations and the World Health Organization of the political will to act effectively on a global level, with President Donald Trump even cutting the funding of the WHO[3] – much as he had slashed the funding of America's pandemic preparedness organizations in the years before the outbreak of COVID-19.* Trump's insistence on repeatedly abdicating America's role as a global leader, and deliberate undermining of a range of international organizations, has quickened the decline of the rules-based liberal international order – a phenomenon which Russia and China look set to continue to exploit. The nation state is fighting back against globalization.

FROM AMERICA FIRST TO CHINA FIRST

The impact of all this upon philanthropy will vary from one country to another. In China – where philanthropy had flourished for centuries,

---

* See pages 725–6 above.

taking inspiration from the values and beliefs of Confucianism, Taoism and Buddhism – it re-emerged with the growth of state capitalism. Charitable giving, which surged after the 2008 Sichuan earthquake, has since quadrupled. This is because China's rapid economic development has concentrated wealth in the hands of a small number of individuals – the country now has the second-highest number of millionaires in the world.[4]

The growing number of philanthropists among them have changed the nature of Chinese philanthropy, transforming it from being largely reactive and local to something more strategic along the model of Western philanthropy. Yet their activities are conducted in line with the priorities of the country's authoritarian government, which has enacted a Charity Law to improve tax incentives on giving and expand the range of state-approved charitable activities.[5] Chinese philanthropists are looking abroad to increase their reach – an approach encouraged by the Chinese government as it pushes for ever-greater global influence. Since the initial outbreak of COVID-19, in the Chinese province of Wuhan, the Communist Party has used the virus to expand its surveillance state and introduce even stronger political control.[6] That is bound to bring philanthropy into even closer alignment with China's attempts to increase its global political influence as it increasingly rivals the United States as the world's dominant economic power. Chinese philanthropists will enter into global philanthropy partnerships only where it suits the Chinese state. The same will be true of philanthropy in other states where authoritarian politics is on the rise, from Brazil and Bolivia to Poland and Hungary – where the populist nationalist leader, Viktor Orbán, forced the Central European University endowed by the billionaire philanthropist George Soros to leave the country.[7] Philanthropy's role as a promoter of alternative ways of thinking is likely to be diminished within illiberal regimes.

In the United States some kind of retreat from untrammelled globalization looks likely to continue. The global reach of America's digital industries will persist, as will the philanthropy of which they are so much the source. While the arrival of the virus wiped a third off the value of most shares, the fortune of the world's richest man, Jeff Bezos, had actually grown by $24 billion a month later because his online retail conglomerate, Amazon, continued to operate throughout the international lockdowns.[8] The model of big philanthropy established by the high-tech super-rich is also likely to endure – though probably at lesser levels than before. (In 2008 after the global financial crisis, giving by America's biggest 1,000 foundations fell by 5 per cent, and fell again by another 14 per cent in 2009, as falls in share prices reduced the value of philanthropic assets.[9]) The gap between the rich and the poor widened under Donald Trump thanks to his aggressive policies of tax cuts, tariff increases, deregulation and weakening of social safety nets which saw the number of Americans without health insurance rise.[10] Income inequality was wider under Trump in 2019 than in any year since records began.[11] But the growth of inequality has been a feature of US politics for more than five decades – and, as this book has shown, philanthropy has done little to rectify that.[12] Even with subsequent changes in political administration inequality is very likely to persist in the post-pandemic world.

The challenges for philanthropy in the US will, therefore, remain those of the past decade, but they too are likely to be magnified. Economic and social change will accelerate, producing further political and cultural polarization. Impatience will grow with tax avoidance by global corporations like Amazon, Facebook, Apple and Google. The public mood will become more volatile as tensions develop between populist politics and consumer economics. Confronted by these frictions the super-rich will feel even greater pressure to act philanthropically. That may come from a heightened sense of the need to 'give something back' out of the pot of what Richard Branson calls the 'extreme wealth' of the billionaire class[*] – a pressure Branson himself felt intensely during the economic crisis provoked by COVID-19 when the multi-billionaire was roundly criticised for having paid no personal tax in the UK for 14 years and then asking the British government for a £500 million loan to save his Virgin Atlantic airline.[13] Or it may come from the subconscious urge which critics have detected among philanthropists to promote the interests of the rich and simultaneously placate political murmurings about inequality. Fears would then grow among the rich that the further growth in inequality could lead to the kind of anti-capitalist unrest which might threaten the social order to such a degree that could render philanthropy quite irrelevant. The apocalyptic fears of those members of

----

[*] See pages 448–450 above.

the super-rich who, as we have seen, as an alternative to philanthropy built themselves remote hideaway bunkers, might then not seem so paranoid*.

Either way the questions about the nature and purpose of philanthropy discussed in the last three chapters of this book will then apply even more forcefully. How can we tell when philanthropy is a mere reputation-launderer or a tool of political manipulation – and when it is an act of genuine altruism and social good? Are the rich sufficiently accountable for the way they use their cash? Does philanthropy lessen or increase inequality? Is philanthropy bad for democracy? Do tax incentives for philanthropy need reform? The need for philanthrocapitalists to curb their top-down instincts, to listen more, and enter into genuine partnership with the grassroots, will increase rather than diminish. Without that, the criticisms of philanthropy this book has outlined will grow more vehement, vitriolic and persuasive.

THE ALTERNATIVE — RETHINKING A BETTER WORLD ORDER

But there is another possibility. The world did not simply respond to the coronavirus pandemic with an every-man-for-himself psychology. Signs of social solidarity were in evidence at all levels – local, national and international. Revealingly the most successful responses in early containment of the epidemic came in Asian countries like South Korea where cultural traditions prioritise collective well-being more than personal autonomy. Something similar was seen in Europe where the social democratic model of government which held sway in countries like Germany, Denmark, and Norway seemed better able to cope than countries like Italy, Spain, France and Britain whose governments had previously embraced a mission of austerity to shrink the state, cut taxes and borrowing, and dismantle public services. Those governments discovered that market forces are no protection against a virus. The example of Germany was a tribute to the Rhineland model of philanthropy and government, which we explored earlier.† This approach allowed a greater role for the state and a co-operative relationship between national and local government, business, trade unions, civil

---

* See pages 641–2 above.
† See pages 386–9 above.

society and Germany's philanthropy foundations which are some of the richest in Europe. Such a model may become increasingly attractive if the post-pandemic world revolts against structural short-termism, global monopolies and the dominance of the market. The approach reveals the advantage of 'just-in-case' caution over 'just-in-time' hyper-efficiency. The opposite of efficiency is not always inefficiency: it can be robustness and resilience.[14]

A general rise in a sense of solidarity could feed that. In Britain even Boris Johnson, ostentatiously abjuring the legacy of Margaret Thatcher, rediscovered the idea that 'there really is such a thing as society'.[15] The UK, in line with the great tradition of volunteering which, as we saw,* characterises Anglo-Saxon public philanthropy, saw more than half a million members of the general public step forward to volunteer to help the National Health Service, though the British government initially seemed uncertain how best to use them. What could occur, in societies which prefer solutions of social solidarity over those of authoritarian government or the untrammelled free market, is the growth of a permanently larger social safety net. There is precedent for that. Out of the Great Depression of the 1930s grew the idea of social security and the minimum wage, along with a widespread conviction that government should guarantee a minimum standard of living. Amid the 2020 pandemic the idea of a Universal Basic Income began to garner increased support. Backing came from public figures as diverse as Pope Francis and the chief economist of the United Nations Development Programme who warned that the alternative to the idea was 'social unrest, conflict, unmanageable mass migration and the proliferation of extremist groups that capitalize and ferment on social disappointment'.[16] Several major philanthropists, including Mark Zuckerberg, supported the idea – with the eBay founder Pierre Omidyar going so far as to fund a pilot scheme in Kenya.[17] Leading Democrat politicians called for a Universal Basic Income to be introduced in America during the pandemic and beyond.[18] More generally societies underwent what the historian Peter Hennessy called a "redistribution of esteem" with a re-evaluation of the importance of jobs traditionally seen as low-status, and therefore low-paid, but which

* See pages 382–6 above.

had proved vital during the pandemic – nurses, hospital porters, care workers, shop workers and refuse collectors.[19] If politics takes a turn in that direction, globally or within individual nations, philanthropists may find themselves compelled to pay more tax and to direct their giving towards ends determined by democratic priorities rather than their own interests, preferences, prejudices or whims.

One final development during the coronavirus pandemic may have a significant influence on the future of philanthropy. All across the globe – from Ukraine to the United States, France to the Philippines, India to Indonesia – grassroots organizations sprang up of ordinary people helping their neighbours. In the UK thousands of mutual aid groups sprang up all across the country – caring for elderly neighbours, shopping for the vulnerable, collecting and delivering medicines, installing digital equipment for old people and setting up telephone friendship teams.[20] This sense of community and connection illustrates the affinity which philanthropy and grassroots activism share in occupying the space which the state and the market leave vacant. The pandemic has given a new authority to the idea of ordinary people doing extraordinary things. As the latter chapters of this book have shown, an alliance between philanthropists and local communities can be extremely effective where philanthrocapitalists learn to listen and work in partnership with the grassroots instead of imposing top-down initiatives.

Partnerships need to be global as well as local. The coronavirus pandemic is a graphic example of a problem which cannot be solved by one country alone. Early attempts to do that simply resulted in countries trying to outbid one another for scarce resources – when they should have been adopting a global plan to increase capacity for testing kits, ventilators and protective equipment for doctors, nurses and care workers. 'Even the most isolationist nations must know that you cannot solve it simply in the US or Europe,' said Gordon Brown, the former British prime minister who masterminded the international co-operation which saved the global banking system from total collapse during the 2007-8 great financial crisis. To restore economic growth internationally once again requires 'a coordinated fiscal and monetary stimulus, and that will need countries to work together', he said. Likewise finding a COVID-19 vaccine demanded a global effort. 'Even if you find a vaccine that is available at a price in the richest countries, you're not going to be able to stop the disease unless you can make it available to the poorest'. It would take global levels of financing to mass-manufacture a vaccine for the whole world. Yet unless that is done the disease could flow back from the poor world into the West in a second and third round of infection.[21]

That global partnership must also involve philanthropists, insists Bill Gates, who pledged 'billions' to build factories to produce the seven best candidate vaccines.* Advances in the three key areas of scientific research – on vaccines, diagnostics and anti-viral drugs – could be partly financed by philanthropists but, he said, only governments could set up the organizations needed to head off the next pandemic. 'Our progress won't be in science alone,' Gates wrote. 'It will also be in our ability to make sure everyone benefits from that science.' After the Second World War, the world's leaders built international institutions like the UN and what became the World Trade Organization to prevent future conflict. Today's leaders need to create or strengthen national, regional and global organizations to prevent the next pandemic. Revealing how far he has travelled over the years Gates – the man who once[†] declared he was 'vehemently against health systems'– now called for 'more foreign aid' to be devoted to 'building up their primary health-care systems'.[22]

Philanthropists can have a key role in shaping the wider post-pandemic agenda. The world will require both new social and health safety nets and major scientific research – traditional areas for modern philanthropy. Big givers, both individuals and foundations, need to increase their overall donations to fund this, much as the Bill & Melinda Gates Foundation did after the 2007-8 financial crisis when it upped its giving from 5 per cent to 7 per cent of its total assets.[23] The virus has also brought into sharper focus some of the structural problems caused by long-term social and economic inequality. Philanthropists will need to work more with the poor people who were already at the sharp end of this inequality and who were then hardest hit by COVID-19.

But that is merely revitalising the old agenda. Making a new world will also need new economic investment in job-creating enterprises which must be ecologically sustainable to help combat climate change. This is an area which could play to the strengths of Limited

---

* See page 726 above.
† See page 494 above.

Liability Companies, the new alternatives to traditional charitable foundations which philanthropists like Mark Zuckerberg are pioneering.* Philanthropists could expand into social and economic investing to create the new jobs and even new industries we will need as part of a revitalized and reformulated eco-economy.

The question is whether the philanthropic community will grasp the opportunity to shape an intellectual and strategic agenda at the scale and level needed. In recent times philanthropy has focused largely on doing and not thinking. The post-coronavirus crisis could provide a rare opportunity for reshaping and recasting a new world order based upon new thinking and ideas. The Quaker industrialists did precisely that at the height of the Industrial Revolution when they allowed their philanthropy to reshape their business principles† –in contrast to the impulse of modern philanthrocapitalists who have tried to reshape philanthropy to fit to their business methods. Will the new generation of philanthropists step up to the intellectual plate rather than simply going for quick measurable results? Do philanthropists have the insight and courage to learn from this crisis?

To help save the world from an economic depression, as from some future pandemic or from climate change, will require philanthropists to abandon their pet projects and think afresh, along the lines set out in the final three chapters of this book. Above all they must forge partnerships with one another, with governments, with the business sector, and with communities at the grassroots. The MeFirst alternative is too grim to contemplate.

---

* See pages 662–5 and 730–1 above.

† See pages 317–326 above.

Sources and Further Reading

To keep this book to a manageable size for the general reader the extensive source notes – indicated by superscript numbers in the text – can be found online at *www.philanthropyatoz.com*. The notes are published online with weblinks to give direct one-click access to this book's sources. The website also includes full picture credits, more comprehensive acknowledgments and suggestions for further reading.

Acknowledgements

Some books start with an inspiration, others with a commission. After years of writing about public ethics, social justice and religion, I was approached by a British philanthropist, Trevor Pears, who was conscious that there had not been a major history of English philanthropy written for more than half a century. He offered me a generous research grant from the Pears Foundation to undertake the task. There were to be no restrictions on what I could write. It was, I only later came fully to realize, an object lesson in philanthropy.

I have many others to thank too, and I have done so at greater length online at *www.philanthropyatoz.com*. But I'd like to record their names here: Professor Ian DeWeese-Boyd at Gordon College in Massachusetts; the Dominican scholar, Richard Finn, OP, at Blackfriars in Oxford; Beth Breeze, Director of the Centre for Philanthropy and her University of Kent colleague Professor Hugh Cunningham. Reverend Reg Sweet, Catherine Secker and John Hodges at The Hospital of St Cross in Winchester; Joe Whiteman and Ian Hammond Brown at the Edinburgh Festival Fringe; Ronald Cohen, William Shawcross, Frank Prochaska, Theresa Lloyd, Cheryl Chapman, Justin Forsyth, Laurie Lee, Graham Young, Clifford Longley, Canon Giles Fraser and Jamie Drummond. Thanks for generous giving of their time to my interviewees: Rabbi Jonathan Sacks, Jonathan Ruffer, Naser Haghamed, John Studzinski, Archbishop Rowan Williams, David Sainsbury, Bob Geldof, Trevor Pears, Rajiv Shah, Ian Linden, Richard Branson, Chris Oechsli, Ngaire Woods, Patrick Gaspard, Eliza Manningham-Buller, Lenny Henry and Kevin Cahill. Thanks to professors Giuseppe Ceraudo, Danny Dorling, Eamon Duffy, Peter Hennessy, David Hulme, Katherine Ibbett, David McCoy, Jamie Woodward and particularly Brian Pullan who made perceptive suggestions on the early chapters; to charity professionals Jane Leek, Bernadette McClew, Joanne Hay, Carmel McConnell, and Martin Cottingham; to journalists Conor O'Clery and John Cassidy; to my brothers Martin and Tony Vallely and Martin Hall, and my student researchers Tom Vallely and Sam Woodward. Thanks to Henry Voigt for generously allowing me to reproduce his original menu for the 1882 Delmonico's dinner for Herbert Spencer.

Thanks to my ever-patient Bloomsbury editors Robin Baird-Smith and Jamie Birkett, and copy-editor Richard Mason. Special thanks to Paddy Coulter of the Oxford Poverty and Human Development Initiative, to Ian Johnson, formerly of the World Bank and the Club of Rome, and to Malcolm Raeburn, a perceptive sounding board since our days as philosophy undergraduates. They all offered invaluable insights throughout my drafts. Most of all to my wife, and primary editor, Christine Morgan without whom nothing would be possible.

Philanthropy is far more than the impulse of one driven individual. That is both the message of this book, and the story of its making.

Index